Japan
day BY day

1st Edition

by Matt Alt, Hiroko Yoda & Melinda Joe

WILEY

John Wiley and Sons, Inc.

PAGE 14

PAGE 23

PAGE 63

Contents

PAGE 314

PAGE 338

PAGE 392

PAGE 410

PAGE 466

PAGE 482

PUBLISHED BY

John Wiley & Sons, Inc.

111 River St., Hoboken, NJ 07030-5774

ISBN 978-0-470-90826-6

Frommer's®

Editorial by Frommer's

EDITOR
Emil J. Ross

PHOTO EDITOR
Cherie Cincilla

CARTOGRAPHER
Tim Lohnes

CAPTIONS
Matt Alt, Hiroko Yoda & Melinda Joe

COVER PHOTO EDITOR
Richard Fox

COVER DESIGN
Paul Dinovo

Produced by Sideshow Media

PUBLISHER
Dan Tucker

MANAGING EDITOR
Megan McFarland

PROJECT EDITOR
Carissa Bluestone

PHOTO EDITOR
John Martin

PHOTO RESEARCHERS
Shizuka Kikuchi and Tessa Perliss

DESIGN
Kevin Smith, And Smith LLC

SPOTLIGHT FEATURE DESIGN
Em Dash Design LLC

For information on our other products and services or to obtain technical support, please contact our Customer Care Department within the U.S. at 800/762-2974, outside the U.S. at 317/572-3993 or fax 317/572-4002.

Wiley also publishes its books in a variety of electronic formats. Some content that appears in print may not be available in electronic formats.

MANUFACTURED IN CHINA

5 4 3 2 1

How to Use This Guide

The Day by Day guides present a series of itineraries that take you from place to place. The itineraries are organized by time (The Best of Tokyo in 1 Day), by region (Okinawa Island), by town (Matsue), and by special interest (Japan for Nerds). You can follow these itineraries to the letter, or customize your own based on the information we provide. Within the tours, we suggest cafes, bars, or restaurants where you can take a break. Each of these stops is marked with a coffee-cup icon ☕. In each chapter, we provide detailed hotel and restaurant reviews so you can select the places that are right for you.

The hotels, restaurants, and attractions listed in this guide have been ranked for quality, value, service, amenities, and special features using a star-rating system. Hotels, restaurants, attractions, shopping, and nightlife are rated on a scale of zero stars (recommended) to three stars (exceptional). In addition to the star-rating system, we also use a kids icon kids to point out the best bets for families.

The following **abbreviations** are used for credit cards:

AE American Express	**MC** MasterCard
DC Diners Club	**V** Visa
DISC Discover	

A Note on Prices

Frommer's lists exact prices in local currency. However, the 2011 Tohoku earthquake and tsunami caused a great deal of turmoil not only in the Tohoku region, but throughout Japan as a whole; many regional attractions closed briefly for repairs during the preparation of this book. While the nation continues to recover, the ripple effect of the disaster has deeply affected Japan's tourist and hospitality industries, resulting in a more precarious situation for many establishments than normal. Although we double-checked our listings prior to publication, you should make sure to recheck the prices and availability of any establishments that you have your heart set on visiting before making the trip. In addition, dramatically fluctuating currency rates may result in different prices than those listed here. Before departing, and during your trip, consult a currency exchange website such as www.oanda. com/currency/converter for up-to-the-minute conversion rates.

How to Contact Us

In researching this book, we discovered many wonderful places—hotels, restaurants, shops, and more. We're sure you'll find others. Please tell us about them, so we can share the information with your fellow travelers in upcoming editions. If you were disappointed with a recommendation, we'd love to know that, too. Please email us at frommersfeedback@ wiley.com or write to:

Frommer's Japan Day by Day, 1st Edition
John Wiley & Sons, Inc.
111 River Street
Hoboken, NJ 07030-5774

Travel Resources at Frommers.com

Frommer's travel resources don't end with this guide. Frommers.com has travel information on more than 4,000 destinations. We update features regularly, giving you access to the most current trip-planning information and the best airfare, lodging, and car-rental bargains. You can also listen to podcasts, connect with other Frommers.com members through our active reader forums, share your travel photos, read blogs from guidebook editors and fellow travelers, and much more.

Advisory & Disclaimer

Travel information can change quickly and unexpectedly, and we strongly advise you to confirm important details locally before traveling, including information on visas, health and safety, traffic and transport, accommodation, shopping and eating out. We also encourage you to stay alert while traveling and to remain aware of your surroundings. Avoid civil disturbances, and keep a close eye on cameras, purses, wallets and other valuables.

While we have endeavored to ensure that the information contained within this guide is accurate and up-to-date at the time of publication, we make no representations or warranties with respect to the accuracy or completeness of the contents of this work and specifically disclaim all warranties, including without limitation warranties of fitness for a particular purpose. We accept no responsibility or liability for any inaccuracy or errors or omissions, or for any inconvenience, loss, damage, costs or expenses of any nature whatsoever incurred or suffered by anyone as a result of any advice or information contained in this guide.

The inclusion of a company, organization or Website in this guide as a service provider and/ or potential source of further information does not mean that we endorse them or the information they provide. Be aware that information provided through some websites may be unreliable and can change without notice. Neither the publisher or author shall be liable for any damages arising herefrom.

About the Authors

Matt Alt (born in Washington, D.C.) and **Hiroko Yoda** (born in Tokyo) are a husband-and-wife team (chapters 1–3 and 7–14) that co-founded AltJapan Co., Ltd., which specializes in producing the English-language versions of Japanese video games. Longtime fans of Japanese culture both traditional and "pop," they are the authors of numerous books about Japan, including *Yokai Attack! The Japanese Monster Survival Guide* and *Yurei Attack! The Japanese Ghost Survival Guide*. They live in Tokyo.

Originally from Louisiana, **Melinda Joe** (chapters 1–2, 4–6, and 15) planned to stay in Japan for a year, but fell in love with Japanese food and sake. The rest, as they say, is history. A freelance journalist specializing in food, drinks, and culture, she's the bar editor for the Tokyo Food Page of CNNGo.com. Her work has appeared in publications such as *The Guardian*, *The Japan Times*, and *Wine Enthusiast*. You can read about her adventures in gastronomy on the blog "Tokyo Through the Drinking Glass," voted one of the "Top 10 Blogs about Japan" by *The Guardian*.

About the Photographers

Twenty-nine-year-old **Romain Alary** is a French photographer and world traveler. For more information on him, visit www.alaryromain.com.

Marco Garcia was raised in San Antonio, Texas. He graduated from St. Mary's University with a Master's degree in International Relations, before moving to Honolulu in 2003, where he specializes in people and assignment photography. His photographs have appeared in magazines and newspapers, advertisements, and websites nationally and internationally.

Norihiro Haruta, born in Shizuoka, Japan, has traveled to Eastern European countries like Romania and Bosnia on his own photography project. He has had exhibitions in Bucharest and Sarajevo in Romania; Seoul in South Korea; and Tokyo.

Hiro Komae, born in Osaka, Japan, is a graduate of the University of North Texas with a degree in Photojournalism. He currently work for the Associated Press, Tokyo Bureau. A freelance photographer, his works have been published worldwide.

John Lander is a freelance photographer who has been based in Tokyo and Bangkok for 25 years. He has a passion for Japanese gardens, Thai cuisine, and local festivals.

Jérémie Souteyrat was born in Lyon, France, in 1979. He started taking photographs in 2002. After working as a mechanical engineer in France, he decided to focus on photography and escaped to Japan in 2009. Currently based in Tokyo, he receives assignments from *The Guardian*, *Le Monde*, and *Elle*, among others, in the fields of documentary, portraits, and architecture.

Japan native **Akihiko Takaba,** born in 1969, enjoys photographing surfing, skiing, and other outdoor sports. He especially likes shooting outdoors because he loves nature.

1
The Best
of Japan

Our Favorite Japanese Moments

> *PREVIOUS PAGE A contemplative snow monkey in the hot springs of Jigokudani Snow Monkey Park. THIS PAGE A pilgrim makes his way along Shikoku's 88 Temple Pilgrimage.*

Watching waves of humanity ebb and flow through Tokyo. On weekends, the six-way pedestrian crossing in front of Shibuya Station is a sight to behold. Take up a seat on the second floor of the Starbucks across the street and watch the hypnotic rhythms of crowds streaming through. See p. 52, ❸.

Seeing where your sushi comes from at Tsukiji Fish Market. Tokyo's famed wholesale fish market is a feast for the senses, and capping it off with a sushi breakfast will make it a feast for the palate as well. An early-morning visit is a tradition for first-time visitors to the city. See p. 56, ❶.

Knocking back a beer with salarymen in a Tokyo izakaya. There's no better way to get a sense of life in this city than by watching its inhabitants unwind. Watering holes abound, but we prefer the tiny *izakaya* (pubs) to the flashier clubs and restaurants. See p. 59, ❻.

Hiking the foothills of holy Mount Takao. Located about an hour west of downtown Tokyo, the quiet, easily hiked paths of this mountain are a classic way for urbanites to get back in touch with nature—and perhaps run into a *tengu,* a mountain goblin of Japanese legend. See p. 114.

Watching the sunrise from Mount Fuji, Japan's most famous peak. Revered since ancient times, this dormant volcano is one of Japan's most iconic sights. Climbing all night to catch the sunrise from the summit is something nearly every Japanese citizen aspires to do once in his or her lifetime. See p. 134.

Soaking with snow monkeys in Jigokudani's hot springs. This hidden valley's naturally heated waters are heaven on earth for both humans and Japanese macaques, who have bathed here—occasionally in the same tubs—since time immemorial. See p. 149, ❸.

Strolling the streets of Kyoto, Japan's most traditional city. Kiyomizu-dera temple. Sanjusangedo hall. The Zen gardens of Ryoan-ji temple. Kinkaku-ji temple. Fushimi Inari Shrine. This is what one might call a target-rich environment for getting in touch with your spiritual side. You won't regret making a visit to Kyoto one of your priorities. See p. 240.

Feeding the tame deer in Nara Park. Buying a bag of *shika-sembei* ("deer crackers") and making some furry new friends is as much a tradition as visiting nearby Todai-ji, the temple that is home to Japan's largest bronze Buddha effigy. See p. 200.

Munching on *takoyaki* in Osaka's Namba district. As far as we're concerned, the mayo-and-sauce-slathered fried octopus dumplings called *takoyaki* are Osaka's high-carb gift to the world. Pick up a six-pack (or more!) from one of the district's many vendors and munch as you take in the glittering nightscape of the city. See p. 219.

> *The "scramble" in front of Shibuya station is one of the world's most crowded pedestrian intersections.*

Sipping sake in Murakami. There is absolutely no better place to tipple Japan's national beverage than in the mountains of Niigata prefecture, famed for both its pure mountain waters and delicious rice, both key ingredients in making rice wine. See p. 170.

Savoring the greenery of Korakuen garden. Okayama's most-visited sight is considered one of the top three gardens in all of Japan. The combination of natural materials arranged according to samurai sensibilities is a sublime experience. It's also home to a *kyudo* (traditional archery) practice ground—if you get lucky, you might just see some young warriors in training. See p. 300, ❶.

Contemplating the Genbaku Dome in Hiroshima's Peace Memorial Park. Given how clean, quiet, and inviting Hiroshima is today, it's hard to believe that 80,000 people lost their lives in an instant here on a summer morning in 1945. The skeletal remains of the city's "A-Bomb Dome," which survived the blast, are a silent testament to the devastation wrought here. A visit to the Peace Park is sobering but not to be missed. See p. 309.

Imagining the sound of sword against sword at Ganryu-jima Island. Located right off the coast of Shimonoseki, this island was the site of a legendary duel between two of Japan's most famous swordsmen: Miyamoto Musashi and Sasaki Kojiro. Reflecting on the duel—in which Miyamoto got the drop on Sasaki using a hand-carved boat oar—will put you in touch with the rich samurai history of Japan. See p. 288.

Watching the pilgrims go by on Shikoku's 88 Temple Pilgrimage route. Pilgrims dressed in distinctive traditional white clothing are a common sight in Shikoku; they're on a journey around the island's 88 holy spots, such as Ishite-ji Temple. See p. 332, ❷.

Gazing into the whirlpools of Naruto from on high. The Seto Inland Sea is famed for riptides and turbulent waters. The largest and most famous of these is the Naruto, which can reach some 15m (49 ft.) wide and 2m (6½ ft.) deep. Hiking out onto the footpath of the Naruto suspension bridge to see it from above is a local tradition. See p. 342, ❶.

Our Favorite Neighborhoods

> *The neon glitz of Osaka's Dotonburi area.*

Kagurazaka (Tokyo). Tokyo's "little Kyoto," located right outside Iidabashi Station, has long benefitted from its prime location in the heart of the city. It teems with interesting boutiques and some of the city's best restaurants, such as **Kuroba-tei** (for *kaiseki*) and **Seigetsu** (an *izakaya* pub). See p. 90 and p. 108.

Dotonbori (Osaka). This glitzy, neon-festooned nightlife quarter is where Osakans go to *kuidaore*—eat till they drop. Its food stalls sell *takoyaki* (fried octopus) and other tasty morsels, while Ebisubashi footbridge offers unparalleled views of the Namba district's futuristic neon nightscapes. From tipsy college students to pink-wig-wearing transvestites, people from all walks of life congregate here. See p. 212, ❻.

Gion (Kyoto). The quintessential traditional neighborhood; you'll feel like you've wandered back through time here. Hanami-koji and Shimbashi are considered two of Japan's most picturesque streets; they're the best place to catch a glimpse of geisha and *maiko* (geisha in training) as they slip through the doors of the 17th-century wooden buildings. See p. 248, ❽.

Pontocho (Kyoto). Another Kyoto tradition. Pontocho is found alongside the Kamo River, and is filled with charming little restaurants that serve up some of the best food in the city with a waterfront view. It's a great place for a gourmet pub crawl. It's also a prime location for geisha- and *maiko*-spotting. See p. 248, ❾.

Kibiji (Okayama). This district's bike trails, snaking through Okayama's suburbs, take riders past scenery ranging from traditional and picturesque (such as rice paddies and farms) to the downright ancient (such as *kofun*, keyhole-shaped burial mounds dating back well over a thousand years). See p. 280, ❻.

Motomachi (Hakodate). A picturesque collection of turn-of-the-20th-century Western-style clapboard homes, consulates, churches, and other buildings perched along steep slopes makes this one of Hakodate's most charming neighborhoods. Filled with boutiques and tourist attractions, it's a wonderful way to get acquainted with the city's history. See p. 454, ❹.

Our Favorite Small Towns

Jigokudani (Central Honshu). One of Japan's most popular spa towns, Jigokudani's cobblestone main street looks unchanged from centuries past, dotted with rustic little baths for visitors who want to do a "hot spring hop." But it's most famous for its nonhuman residents: Japanese macaques, or snow monkeys as they're known abroad. Innkeepers know to keep their doors closed lest the furry guys sneak in for a dip. See p. 149, ③.

Murakami (Central Honshu). Home to some of Japan's top sake brewers, this idyllic seaside town is also known for its salmon, which is still hung out to dry and cure in the traditional way. Black-painted Edo-style buildings and fresh sea breezes make this a wonderful place to simply stroll away an afternoon—or more. See p. 170.

Matsue (Western Honshu). Okay, so it's on the large side for a "small town." But that doesn't change our minds: Matsue is one of Japan's most fun destinations. Beautiful scenery, historic temples and buildings, a castle with beautiful gardens—and ghosts. Did we mention ghosts? This is one of Japan's foremost towns for tales of terror; many folktales originated here. See p. 282, ①.

Kurashiki (Western Honshu). It's hard to get more picturesque than little Kurashiki, a suburb of Okayama that was a regional administrative center in times of old. Now its rice warehouses have been transformed into boutiques and museums, preserving the atmosphere while adding new value to this most traditional-seeming of Japanese towns. See p. 301, ④.

Tono (Tohoku). Northern Honshu (or Tohoku, as it's known in Japan) is dotted with tiny towns, but this cradle of folklore is one of our favorites. It's supposedly the home of the *kappa,* a mysterious cucumber-loving water creature that drags unwary swimmers down. If you're not looking for a brush with the supernatural, it's also filled with historic buildings and temples. An overnight in one of its traditional *magariya* (farmhouses) is like spending the night in a fairy tale. See p. 406, ③.

> *Kurashiki's architecture will make you think you've traveled back a few centuries.*

Taketomi Island (Okinawa). The red-tiled roofs, stuccoed walls, and *shisa* (gargoyles) of the dwellings in this tropical paradise are undoubtedly like nothing you've seen before; the whole island is a perfectly preserved bubble of traditional life in Okinawa. A lazy ox-drawn cart ride along dirt roads is a good primer to Taketomi, followed by a dip in the crystal blue waters just offshore. See p. 486, ①.

Our Favorite Hot Springs & Spa Towns

> The homey charm of a Hakone spa.

Hakone (Tokyo Area). Tokyo's favorite hot-spring hangout since before the city was even called Tokyo. Dotted with lakes, museums, and restaurants, Hakone is a traditional Japanese resort destination. The alpine retreat is crisscrossed with scenic train lines, cable cars, and smaller ropeways, making a visit here about something more than just soaking. (Not that there's anything wrong with just soaking!) And when it comes to the aforementioned soaking, there are few better places to do it here or anywhere than the 380-year-old **Ichinoyu** (p. 121) spa. See p. 118.

Kusatsu Onsen (Central Honshu). It's hard to pick a favorite hot spring from this region of Japan, which is dotted with wonderful spa resorts. But the village of Kusatsu is certainly a top contender. Fed by a massive natural *yubatake* ("hot water field") that powers the resorts here, Kusatsu is known for its distinctive style of entering the waters: *awase-yu*. It's

a bathing technique that involves soaking in a series of progressively warmer pools. Our favorite hot spring in town is **Netsunoyu** (p. 157, ❷), where traditionally dressed women sing while using large paddles to rhytmically churn the baths to their optimum temperatures. See p. 147, ❶.

Ikaho Onsen (Central Honshu). Although this hot-spring resort area often gets passed by for Kusatsu, we're fascinated by its waters—they're so sulfurous, they often turn towels red. You can't beat the town's atmosphere, either: A giant stone staircase runs through the center, acting as its main street. Lined with *ryokan* (traditional inns) and public baths, it also features a series of observation points to let spa fanatics see just where their waters are coming from. The **Ikaho Rotenburo** here is the "Goldilocks" of Japanese spas: It features baths divided by temperature, so you can always find one that's just right. See p. 159, ❻.

> *Inside Dogo Onsen.*

Dogo Onsen Honkan (Shikoku). This very well might be Japan's single most beloved *onsen* (traditional spa), the kind of place spa lovers wish they could be when they're in other spas. Its elegant, spectacularly appointed Honkan public bathhouse is fit for an emperor. It was even used as the inspiration for a hit movie: *Spirited Away,* Studio Ghibli's internationally renowned anime film. If you visit one hot spring in all of Japan, it should be this one—even if you're actually staying in one of the area's other highly worthy spa hotels. Yes, it's that good. See p. 332, ❸.

Unzen Spa (Kyushu). This tiny spa resort area, located an hour and a half from Nagasaki, is particularly popular in spring, when the local azaleas burst into color. It's right in the middle of Unzen-Amakusa Park, a geothermically active area dotted with steam vents and fumaroles. The Western-Japanese fusion **Kyushu Hotel** (p. 359) is a great place for day soakers and overnighters alike; in addition to great food, it boasts a family bath that you can reserve if you want some privacy, a rarity among Japanese hot springs. See p. 356, ❶.

Nyuto Onsen (Tohoku). Now this is getting away from it all. Only accessible via bus from a far-flung countryside train station, this is rural hot-spring bathing at its most traditional. Notice we didn't say "finest"—many of the baths in this village are housed in ramshackle buildings that look ready to fall down. But don't let that deter you. A visit to Nyuto Onsen today is much like it was in centuries past. The alpine scenery is incredible, and the naturally milk-colored waters renowned for their theraputic value have drawn bathers here since times of old. **Tsurunoyu Onsen** is our favorite hot spring in Nyuto. See p. 432.

Tsuta Onsen (Tohoku). Built in 1909, this inn is a downright young upstart compared to many of the nation's spa resorts. An architectural beauty in and of itself—details are hand-carved, with an ivy motif running throughout the structure—the bathouses feature aromatic cypress and vaulted ceilings. Hiking trails into the dense beech forest that surrounds the inn make it a great stop for those who love the outdoors. See p. 415.

Noboribetsu Onsen (Hokkaido). The first spa in this village opened in 1858. Today it is the largest spa resort town in Hokkaido, Japan's northernmost island. Located between the cities of Hakodate and Sapporo, the area boasts 11 types of hot water, each with its own mineral content and purported healing properties. The village also sits on the edge of Shikotsu-Toya National Park, making it a great destination for active types who want to soak away a day spent hiking. If you can afford it, splurge on the secluded **Oyado Kiyomizu-ya** hotel (p.459). See p. 456.

Our Favorite Museums

> *The Tokyo National Museum is a repository of holy treasures.*

Edo-Tokyo Museum (Tokyo). Ever wonder how a tiny fishing village transformed into one of the world's biggest cities? Here's your chance to find out. Housed in a high-tech modern building, this ambitious museum chronicles the fascinating and somewhat tumultuous history of Tokyo (known as Edo during the Feudal Era) with models, replicas, artifacts, and dioramas. Even better, it offers free guided tours in English. See p. 58, ❸.

Tokyo National Museum (Tokyo). Even professed museum-phobes should make a point of visiting the National Museum, the largest repository of Japanese arts in the world. The collections here boggle the mind, with lacquerware, china, kimonos, samurai armor, swords, woodblock prints, religious art, and more. If you have time to visit only one museum in Japan, this should be it. Regular special exhibitions are often very much worth paying extra to see as well. See p. 68, ❷.

Hiroshima Peace Memorial Museum (Hiroshima). While we can't exactly call a visit here pleasant, it is a powerful testament to the devastation wrought by the atomic bombing of the city. It was created with the express aim of contributing to the abolition of nuclear weapons, and after viewing its displays, it's hard to imagine anyone disagreeing with the sentiment. See p. 306, ❶.

Oyamazumi Shrine (Shikoku). It's undoubtedly difficult to get to, located as it is on the distant island of Omishima. But this shrine's treasure museum is really one of a kind. After achieving victories, Japanese warriors would return here with offerings such as helmets, armor, and swords. Today, the shrine's museum now houses some 80% of the country's designated national treasures. If you're into Japanese history, this is worth the trip. See p. 323, ❷.

Poroto Kotan (Hokkaido). The single most important facility dedicated to preserving the heritage of the Ainu, the aborignal inhabitants of Japan, is nestled on the shores of Lake Poroto in Shiraoi. The grounds feature a mock village of native houses made entirely from wood and reeds, a native plant garden, a dance area, a museum building filled with information about the Ainu people, and a research center dedicated to preserving Ainu culture. See p. 442, ❸.

Our Favorite Offbeat Museums

Meguro Parasitological Museum (Tokyo). This occasionally stomach-churning museum has inexplicably become one of Tokyo's top date spots. While it isn't large, what it lacks in size it makes up for in sheer impact: 300-plus pickled specimens of various critters extracted from unfortunate victims' bodies (often still attached to the organs they colonized). The gift shop (yes, there's a gift shop) is not to be missed. See p. 70, 7.

Iga-ryu Ninja Museum (Iga). Everything you've always wanted to know about Japan's black-clad assassins. Features include a "ninja house" laden with all sorts of traps and pitfalls (helpfully sprung by a lady ninja dressed in shocking pink). In addition to a display of weapons, there's a live show on the Ninja Experience Plaza where ninjas demonstrate their skills. Those who feel they have what it takes can try their hand at chucking *shuriken* (throwing stars), too. See p. 164, 5.

Kitahara Tin Toy Museum (Yokohama). Fans of Japanese toy robots will want to make a beeline for Kitahara-san's museums, which showcase his collection of thousands upon thousands of vintage Japanese tin toys. In addition to robots, the collection includes spaceships, ray guns, and other "retro-future" ephemera. The bright colors and pop designs are eye candy even for those normally not interested in playthings. See p. 110, 2.

Shin-Yokohama Raumen Museum (Yokohama). If you love ramen, those Chinese noodles made world-famous by Japanese instant noodle companies, make time to visit this museum. It chronicles the spread of ramen's popularity from the port city throughout the islands of Japan. The main attraction is a painstakingly executed replica of a Tokyo neighborhood from the 1950s, populated by ramen joints that serve up noodles and broth in a mind-boggling array of styles. Come hungry. See p. 71, 11.

Hakone Open-Air Museum (Hakone). At first glance, this doesn't seem particularly offbeat: Rolling, beautifully landscaped grounds with

> A veritable robot rampage awaits at the Kitahara Tin Toy Museum.

glens and meadows are used as a backdrop to showcase approximately 400 20th-century sculptures, from Giacomo and Rodin to Henry Moore. It's also home to the Picasso Pavilion, housing 200 of the artist's works. But what we love about it are the interactive sculptures, on which visitors can climb and play. See p. 118, 1.

Our Favorite Restaurants

> *Farmer's Kitchen is a haven for vegetarians and meat eaters alike.*

Dons de la Nature (Tokyo). The decor of this Ginza steakouse may be underwhelming, but the *wagyu* (Japanese beef) it serves up is anything but. It's a very different sort of experience from an American steakhouse; the steaks are marbled to an almost unimaginable degree and simply melt in the mouth. Pure luxury for meat lovers. See p. 87.

Farmer's Kitchen (Tokyo). This macrobiotic restaurant treats the farmers who supply it like superstars; the walls are even adorned with giant signed posters featuring their faces. Dedicated to the "farm-to-table" experience, it features fresh meats and vegetables. We are big fans of the all-you-can-eat raw bar, which features all sorts of interesting local veggies, some of which aren't often seen outside Japan. See p. 87.

Kyubei (Tokyo). Foodies love to argue over which Tokyo destination serves up the best sushi, and some claim this restaurant has slipped down the list of late. While the title of "greatest ever" is always up for grabs, Kyubei (also known as Kyubey) is a solid performer. But more to the point, its openness to foreign visitors makes it a great place to relax, eat, and even learn. See p. 90.

Ajiro (Kyoto). This is a real Kyoto experience: a Michelin-starred restaurant that serves some of the most refined *shojin-ryori* (Zen Buddhist cuisine) in the city. Set lunches are served in exquisite lacquered bento boxes, which you eat while sitting in a tatami-floored room. Don't worry, even devoted carnivores are guaranteed to come away satisfied by the presentation, flavors, and portions. See p. 263, **7**.

Mampei Hotel (Karuizawa). Although you've undoubtedly arrived in Japan to eat Japanese food, this French restaurant may well change your mind. A local institution—it's been in business since 1894—the Mampei Hotel has served up everyone from commoners to dignitaries and even rock stars over the years. The emphasis is on the classics such as foie gras and steaks; this is Western-style fine dining at its Japanese best. See p. 177.

Yabaton (Nagoya). Who says a favorite has to be a fine dining experience? This chain has been serving up *miso-katsu*, deep-fried pork cutlet with a sweet and tangy miso sauce (a twist on the more widely known *tonkatsu*, or fried pork cutlet), for more than a half century. It's a Nagoya specialty and it is done to exquisite and artery-clogging perfection here; we guarantee you'll be in hog heaven. See p. 187.

Kanga-an (Kyoto). This restaurant on the grounds of Kanga-an temple is more of a draw than the temple itself thanks to its lavish *fucha-ryori* meal. (*Fucha-ryori* is a Chinese-inflected variation of the more commonly known *shojin-ryori*, introduced to Japan by Zen Buddhists.) The meal consists of no fewer than 10 courses (with multiple cups of thick green tea), yet no two bites are the same. Munch on these delicate morsels amid a tranquil setting overlooking a beautifully sculpted moss and gravel garden. See p. 263, ❾.

Shunpanro Hotel (Shimonoseki). This hotel and its associated restaurant have stood at the crossroads of culture since the 19th century. It is famed for its fugu (poison pufferfish), which is actually pronounced "fuku" in this part of Japan. Don't let fugu's reputation for causing harm deter you: When prepared properly it is as harmless as it is delicious. Served as sashimi, deep-fried, grilled, and even in rice wine, it doesn't get any better than here. See p. 315.

Goshiki Honten (Matsuyama). The roots of this venerable establishment extend back some 375 years. It's the best place in Shikoku to experience regional delights such as *taimeshi* (rice casserole with red snapper). In addition to the five-colored *goshiki somen* noodles from which the restaurant takes its name, Goshiki also serves *shabu-shabu* (meat or vegetables cooked in a boiling pot at your table) and a wide variety of regional dishes including tempuras and grilled vegetables and meats. See p. 11.

Kameki (Sendai). While Tokyoites continue to battle over which of their restaurants represents the best sushi joint in the country, more than a few gourmets swear that the very best sushi can only be found in the chilly northern reaches of Tohoku. Kameki is certainly a contender for the crown. Its chefs pride themselves on using nothing but locally sourced ingredients to create *nigiri* (sushi with a clump of rice and usually a fish protein placed on top), *maki* (sushi roll), and sashimi that tastes like nothing you've had elsewhere. If you have time for a trip up north, make sure to drop by. See p. 421.

> *One of Tokyo's top sushi bars: Kyubei.*

Our Favorite Hotels & *Ryokan*

> *Ryokan Kurashiki offers Japanese-style accommodations at their finest.*

Claska (Tokyo). Quite possibly the city's hippest hotel, this tiny establishment (just nine rooms) combines cutting-edge design with high-tech service. It also has the plus of being located right in the heart of things downtown. See p. 98.

Park Hyatt Tokyo (Tokyo). A favorite of high-rolling Tokyo visitors ever since it opened, the Park Hyatt rose to new levels of fame after being showcased in the film *Lost in Translation*. First-class service and accommodations combined with first-class restaurants and bars make this a stay to remember—just don't forget to bring your credit card. See p. 100.

The Ritz-Carlton, Osaka (Osaka). With its Italian marble fireplaces, chandeliers, and tasteful antiques, the Ritz-Carlton wears an aura of sophisticated old-world charm. It's one of the city's finest luxury hotels, equipped with spacious and comfortable rooms, a fantastic health club, a swanky whiskey bar, and two Michelin-starred restaurants. Its convenient location in the Umeda district is also a plus. See p. 215.

The Screen (Kyoto). The stark concrete exterior of Kyoto's first boutique hotel belies the stylishly inviting atmosphere inside. The minimalist white lobby, accented with vibrantly colored paper umbrellas, welcomes guests into a world where sleek design meets traditional *ryokan* (Japanese-style inn) hospitality. Each of its 13 rooms, by 13 different designers, has its own style. In summer, relax with a glass of bubbly at the terraced rooftop bar. See p. 274.

Tawaraya (Kyoto). The grand-dame of Kyoto *ryokan*, this venerable inn has been owned and operated by the same family since the 1700s. Refined taste, simplicity, and tranquility are manifest in each of its exquisitely appointed rooms, some of which look out onto a lantern-lit moss garden. In the evenings, beautifully presented *kaiseki* meals are served by the demure, kimono-clad staff. See p. 274.

Hyatt Regency Kyoto (Kyoto). With a sumptuous interior designed by Takashi Sugimoto, the Hyatt marries high style with the friendly service of a boutique hotel. Occupying the former residence of Emperor Goshirakawa, it also has a beautiful 850-year-old garden, complete with a waterfall and pond. Pamper yourself with the range of Asian spa treatments such as acupuncture and shiatsu. See p. 272.

> *The triple towers of the Park Hyatt Tokyo.*

Minami-Kan (Matsue). Luxury, Japanese style. A beautifully renovated example of a traditional *ryokan*, it has stood on the shores of Lake Shinji since 1888. Renowned for its expertly balanced mix of tradition and modern convenience, this is a must-stay if you are in the area. See p. 298.

Ryokan Kurashiki (Kurashiki). Located in the midst of the Bikan Historic Quarter, this tiny little *ryokan* boasts buildings that date back some 250 years, renovated for modern comfort and convenience in true Japanese style. What better way to relax than by slipping back a few centuries? See p. 305.

Grand Hyatt Fukuoka (Fukuoka). While we generally prefer to stay in Japanese-style accommodations, we'll make an exception for this super-upscale hotel located in the heart of one of Kyushu's most livable cities. Easy access to sights and shopping combined with stylish rooms and lavish service make this a luxurious city retreat. See p. 383.

Minshuku Magariya (Tono). If you want a taste of the Japan of old, you can't beat this century-old *magariya,* or farmhouse turned inn. It is rustic to the extreme, heated by a hearth and stuffed to the gills with old antiques. An "only in Tohoku" sort of experience that you absolutely will not find anywhere else in Japan. See p. 425.

Shiretoko Grand Hotel Kitakobushi (Utoro). If your plans take you to the far northern reaches of Hokkaido, make a beeline for this hotel. It avoids the impersonality of other large-scale establishments with its amenities, from opulent nightly buffet dinners of local delicacies to beautiful rooftop baths to an iceberg display (!) in the lobby. See p. 475.

Busena Terrace Beach Resort (Okinawa). Looking to get away from it all? Surrounded by crystal blue waters and within walking distance of beaches and a marine park, this resort is a great choice whether you're solo, looking for a romantic retreat, or have kids in tow. See p. 495.

Our Favorite Temples & Shrines

> *A soaring* torii *gate marks the entrance to Meiji Jingu Shrine.*

Meiji Jingu Shrine (Tokyo). Soaring *torii* gates mark Tokyo's most venerable and refined Shinto shrine, which honors the Emperor Meiji and his empress. Simple yet dignified architecture surrounded by a dense forest will make you forget you're in the heart of the city. See p. 63, ❼.

Senso-ji Temple (Tokyo). The capital's oldest temple is also its liveliest. Throngs of visitors and stalls selling both traditional and kitschy items lend it a festival-like atmosphere. If you go to any one temple in Tokyo, make it this one. See p. 74, ❻.

Kotokuin Temple (Kamakura). This temple is home to the Great Buddha, Japan's second-largest bronze effigy. It sits outdoors against a magnificent wooded backdrop; the combination of man-made and natural, holy and corporeal, is a powerful one. See p. 124, ❷.

Toshogu Shrine (Nikko). Now a World Heritage Site, this shrine dedicated to the memory of Japan's most powerful shogun, Tokugawa Ieyasu, is the nation's most elaborate and opulent, covered in 2.4 million sheets of real gold leaf. It's gorgeous and almost gaudy. A must-see if you have time for a day trip outside of Tokyo. See p. 127, ❷.

Todai-ji Temple (Nara). In the midst of a park surrounded by tame deer sits an enormous building that is home to Japan's largest bronze Buddha. The temple building is actually the largest wooden structure in the world. If you've been to Kamakura, home to the second-largest bronze Buddha in Japan, go here to get a sense of contrast. See p. 223, ❹.

Kiyomizu-dera (Kyoto). Kyoto's most stunning—and possibly Japan's best-known—temple. Featuring an elaborate wooden veranda perched atop a hillside, Kiyomizu commands an exalted spot with a view over Kyoto. The pathway leading to the shrine is lined with pottery and souvenir shops, and the temple grounds have open-air pavilions, where you can drink beer or eat noodles. Couples in particular shouldn't miss a visit to Jishu-jinja shrine, right on the grounds—it's dedicated to the god of love. See p. 246, ❸.

Sanjusangendo (Kyoto). The display is stunning: an ancient wooden hall filled with more than 1,000 life-size wood-carved effigies of Kannon, the goddess of mercy. According to tradition, everyone who visits can always spot a statue with a face that resembles their own. See p. 244, ❶.

Kinkaku-ji (Kyoto). This gleaming, gilt structure is almost dazzling on a bright and sunny day. Constructed in the 14th century as a shogun's retirement villa, the three-story pavilion s topped with a bronze phoenix. Along with Kiyomizu-dera, this is one of Kyoto's signature sights and absolutely should not be missed. See p. 250, **③**.

tsukushima Shrine (Miyajima). You may well already be familiar with this shrine's iconic red *torii* gate, which rises from the waters of the Seto Inland Sea; it's one of the most photographed landmarks in Japan. Built over the tidal flats on a gem of an island called Miyajima, it's the most photographed for a reason: The scenic spot is beautiful by day and equally stunning by night, when it is illuminated. **See p. 287, ⑤**.

zumo Taisha (Izumo). Izumo is revered as the land of the gods in Shinto, and this is one of the most important Shinto shrines in all of Japan. First mentioned in historical records from 950, it's also one of the oldest. Originally taking the form of a 45m-high (148-ft.) tower accessed by a massive staircase, it was rebuilt into its current form over successive generations. See p. 298, **⑤**.

Akama Jingu (Shimonoseki). This small shrine overlooking the turbulent waters of

▸ *The beatific Great Buddha watches over Kotokuin Temple.*

Kanmon Strait is the final resting place of the Heike clan, who once ruled Japan but were wiped out in the epic Battle of Dan-no-Ura in 1185. Make sure to pay a visit to the statue of Hoichi the Earless, a blind monk whose ears were supposedly ripped off by furious spirits. See p. 312, **①**.

Chuson-ji Temple (Hiraizumi). Located in the midst of soaring cedar trees, this ancient temple complex dates back nearly a millennium. Simply strolling through its many paths and among its many smaller temples makes you feel as though you're among the gods. Don't miss Konjikido Pavilion, a glorious mausoleum containing the mummies of one of Japan's most famous warrior clans. See p. 405, **②**.

Seifa Utaki (Okinawa Island). For centuries, this holy ground was off-limits to males—even the king of the Ryukyu people had to dress in women's clothing to gain entrance. Now a designated UNESCO World Heritage Site, its massive stone altars make the place feel like the set of an adventure movie. If you're visiting Okinawa Island, make this one of your first stops. See p. 494, **③**.

Our Favorite Castles

Imperial Palace (Tokyo). Alas, there are no castles in Tokyo anymore, but this is the next best thing. Although currently the site of the emperor's residence, in times of old this was the center of the city, occupied by the formidable Edo Castle. While the castle itself is long since gone, many of its walls and other foundation structures remain. The massive stone fortifications are one reason we love Chidorigafuchi Moat. See p. 67, ❹.

Nagoyajo (Central Honshu). Once the center of one of Japan's most important "castle towns," and used as a POW camp during World War II, this castle burned to the ground in 1945. Reconstructed in 1959, it features air-conditioning and elevators—two luxuries that the original most certainly didn't. Wow your Japanese pals with some trivia: The castle met yet another (fictional) demise at the hands of Godzilla in the classic 1964 film *Mothra vs. Godzilla*. See p. 182, ❶.

Inuyama Castle (Central Honshu). While it may not be Japan's most famous, this 16th-century castle is Japan's oldest—a designated National Treasure. It miraculously survived centuries of earthquakes and other calamities, making it one of only 12 castles to survive into the modern era. Constructed atop a bluff (as most castles are), it offers beautiful views of the Kiso River. See p. 163, ❸.

Koga-ryu Ninjutsu Yashiki (Central Honshu). In contrast to the other castles of this region, this one is a decidedly different sort of fortress. At first glance, it's a seemingly innocuous 16th-century farmhouse, constructed in the traditional manner. But this farmhouse just happened to have been occupied by Mochizuki Izumonokami, the leader of the Koga ninja clan, who tricked it out with all sorts of hidden defenses worthy of a James Bond movie. See p. 165, ❼.

Osakajo (Kansai). The original version of this castle was constructed by *daimyo* (warlord) and "great unifier" Toyotomi Hideyoshi in 1583 as an emblem of his power and wealth. Although the current incarnation is a reconstruction, it is a faithful replica of how it once looked . . . externally, at least. The interior is now what one might call the world's most well-defended castle museum. See p. 209, ❸.

Matsue Castle (Western Honshu). Our favorite thing about this castle isn't actually the castle itself, but rather the flat-bottomed boat tour that tools around the moat. Trips las about an hour, threading under tiny bridges and offering great views of the imposing fortress. With sights like these, you won't even mind that the commentary is all in Japanese. See p. 282, ❶.

Okayama Castle (Western Honshu). Dubbed "Crow Castle" for its imposing (and quite uncommon) black exterior, we love this place because it looks like something the villain of a samurai movie would use as his headquarters Replica though it may be, the renovators used the original blueprints to make it as realistic as possible. See p. 300, ❸.

Himeji Castle (Western Honshu). Also known as White Heron Castle, this is widely believed to be the single most beautiful fortification of its type in Japan. One of the most advanced castles of the feudal period, it features defensive "loopholes" shaped to allow archers and riflemen to fire without exposing themselves. We're also fans of the drop chutes, used to give invaders a warm welcome with boiling oil. If you see any one castle in Japan, make this it. See p. 189.

Kumamoto Castle (Kyushu). This imposing structure, used as the setting for Akira Kurosawa's *Ran*, features an excellent example of castle design: steeply sloping ramparts with overhangs, designed to keep intruders at bay. They're called *musha-gaeshi*—"warrior-stoppers." How's that for a succinct description? We also like this castle because of its proximity to the Hosokawa Mansion, giving you a one-two introduction to how samurai lived. See p. 384, ❶.

> *The steep* musha-gaeshi *of Kumamoto Castle kept the hordes at bay.*

2
The Best
All-Japan
Itineraries

The Best of Japan in 1 Week

A week will fly by in the blink of an eye in a county as varied as Japan. This is particularly true in its fast-paced major cities, which often feel like life lived on fast forward. It's also true in its low-key, relaxed outlying regions. Still, 7 days is just barely enough time to hit Japan's most famous temples and sights, while still giving you enough flexibility to wander. And the best thing is, you won't need to rent a car (though a good pair of walking shoes is seriously recommended).

> PREVIOUS PAGE *The tranquil bamboo forest just outside Tenryu-ji Temple, Kyoto.*
THIS PAGE *Mount Fuji as seen from one of Tokyo's many observation decks.*

START **Fly into Tokyo's Narita Airport.**

1 Tokyo. If you arrive via Narita on an afternoon flight, as many international travelers do, you will probably find the majority of your first day taken up simply by getting to your hotel. There's no better way to confront your looming jet lag than with drinks and yakitori skewers in one of Tokyo's many *izakaya* (pubs). Depending on where you're staying, Asakusa's **Hoppy Street** (p. 59, **6**) or Shinjuku's

colorfully named **Piss Alley** (p. 63, **9**) are two good places to try.

On your first full day in the city, an early morning stop at **Tsukiji Fish Market** (p. 57, **1**) is de rigueur for any first-time visitor to the city. After browsing the wares and having a sushi breakfast at one of the market's many tiny restaurants, shoot over to the **Edo-Tokyo Museum** (p. 58, **3**), which explores how a tiny fishing village evolved into one of the

CHINA

RUSSIA

NORTH
KOREA

SOUTH
KOREA

Sea of
Japan

Korea Strait

East
China
Sea

PACIFIC
OCEAN

HOKKAIDO

Wakkanai

*Kuril Islands
(Russia)*

Abashiri

Shiretoko-
Shari

Asahigawa

*DAISETSUZAN
NAT'L
PARK*

*AKAN NAT'L
PARK*

Otaru

Kushiro

*SHIKOTSU-TOYA
NAT'L PARK*

Sapporo

Obihiro

Tomakomai

Uchiura-wan

Hakodate

Erimo saki

Tsugaru Strait

Mutsu Wan

Aomori

Hachinohe

Hirosaki

Lake Towada

*TOWADA-HACHIMANTEI
NAT'L PARK*

*RIKUCHU-KAIGAN
NAT'L PARK*

Akita

Morioka

HONSHU

Sakata

Yamagata

Sendai

*Sado
Island*

Niigata

Fukushima

*JOSHIN-ETSU
NAT'L PARK*

Nikko

Hitachi

Nagano

②

Mito

Toyama

Matsumoto

Tokyo

Kanazawa

★ ①

Oki Is.

Mt. Fuji ▲

Yokohama

③

Nagoya

Shizuoka

Matsue

Kyoto

Izu Peninsula

Osaka

Nara

Kobe

Okayama

④

⑥ ⑤

*ISE-SHIMA
NAT'L PARK*

Hiroshima

Takamatsu

Tsushima

Matsuyama

Tokushima

Shimonoseki

Kochi

Iki

Fukuoka

Sasebo

Oita

SHIKOKU

*ASO
NAT'L PARK*

Nagasaki

Kumamoto

KYUSHU

Miyazaki

Kagoshima

Oshima

Ibusuki

Tanega

Yaku

Ryukyu Islands

Okinawa

Naha

0		200 mi
0		200 km

①	Tokyo
②	Nikko
③	Kyoto
④	Nara
⑤	Osaka
⑥	Kobe

> *Nikko's Toshogu Shrine features a menagerie of imaginary creatures incorporated into its buildings.*

world's largest metropolises. Next up will be **Akihabara Electric Town** (p. 58, ❹), once famed as Tokyo's electronics district but now a haven for the city's geek subcultures. Even if you aren't a geek yourself, window-shopping on the neon-festooned Chuo Dori street is a feast for the eyes and ears. After all the bells and whistles of the electronics district, you'll

Travel Tip

You will definitely want to invest in a **Japan Rail Pass** before arriving, since you can't purchase them in Japan. These insanely handy tickets give you a free ride on the vast majority of Japan's public railways, including bullet trains. They come in 7-, 14-, and 21-day durations and are only available to tourists. (Japanese citizens and permanent residents aren't eligible.) They can be purchased through travel agencies and the airlines JAL and ANA. For more information, see p. 558.

undoubtedly be in the mood for something more serene. Try **Senso-ji Temple** (p. 74, ❻). Also popularly known as Asakusa Kannon, this is Tokyo's oldest and most popular temple, with a history dating from A.D. 628.

On your second day in Tokyo, make a bee-line for the **Tokyo National Museum** in Ueno (p. 68, ❷). If you visit any one museum in the city, this should be it. Divided into a variety of collections, it brims with Japanese antiquities such as swords, armor, lacquerware, woodblock prints, and pottery. Follow that up with a quick spin through **the Ginza** (p. 62, ❸). All of Japan's major department-store chains and many international luxury brands have flagship stores here. Once you've warmed up to Tokyo's glitzy side, there's no better place to see and be seen than the fashion district's main drag of **Omotesando** (p. 62, ❺), which is packed with boutiques, restaurants, and cafes ranging from holes in the wall to jaw-droppingly chic. Fashionistas could easily spend the day browsing. A stone's throw from Omotesando is **Meiji Jingu** (p. 63, ⑦), the largest and most opulent Shinto shrine in Tokyo. The towering *torii* gate at the entrance and long, cypress-tree-lined path approaching the inner precinct are classic examples of Japanese shrine design. Cap it all off with a nighttime view of the city from the 45th floor of the **Tokyo Metropolitan Government Building Observation Deck** (p. 63, ⑧). ⏱ 2½ days.

In the morning, from Asakusa Station, take the Tobu Nikko Line's Spacia train to Nikko Station (1½ hr.).

❷ **Nikko.** Since the publication of James Clavell's novel *Shogun,* many people are familiar with Tokugawa Ieyasu, the powerful real-life shogun of the 1600s on whom Clavell's fictional one was based. Quashing all rebellions and unifying Japan under his leadership, Tokugawa's heirs continued to rule Japan for 250 years without serious challenge. If you'd like to join the millions of Japanese who through the centuries have paid homage to the man, head north of Tokyo to Nikko, where **Toshogu Shrine** (p. 127, ❷) was constructed in his honor in the 17th century, and where he is entombed. As you make your way there from the station, you'll see the iconic, bright-red **Shinkyo (Sacred Bridge)** across the rushing Daiyagawa River and make a stop at **Rinno-ji Temple** (p. 126, ❶). Once you reach Toshogu, take time to ponder the fact that some 15,000 artists and craftspeople helped create it. They were brought to Nikko from all over Japan, and after 2 years' work, they erected a group of buildings more elaborate and gorgeous than any other Japanese temple or shrine, then or since. If you have time afterward, drop by nearby **Futarasan Shrine** (p. 128, ❸), dedicated to the god of fortune, god of happiness, god of trees, god of water, and god of good marriages. (Can't hurt to cover all your bases.) ⏱ 6 hr.

Return to Tokyo. In the morning take a bullet train from Tokyo Station to Kyoto Station (3 hr.). Then take bus 306 to Gojo-zaka.

❸ **Kyoto.** The heart and soul of the Kansai region, Kyoto is one of Japan's most beloved cities. Your first stop is the Higashiyama district, home to the UNESCO World Heritage

> *As darkness falls, the* maiko *appear in Kyoto's Gion quarter.*

site **Kiyomizu-dera** (p. 246, ❸). This "pure-water" temple's famously wide veranda is a quintessential Kyoto sight. From Kiyomizu-dera, take the winding narrow lane down to the neighborhoods of **Ninenzaka and Sanenzaka** (p. 247, ❹), where stone-paved roads and beautifully restored wooden buildings exude the romance of old Kyoto. As dusk creeps over the city, make your way to **Gion** (p. 248, ❽), Kyoto's famed geisha district. If luck is with you, you may well catch sight of a geisha or *maiko* (geisha in training) leaving her quarters for her parties that night. Cap off your evening with a walk down the lantern-lit street of **Pontocho** (p. 248, ❾), dropping by one of its many restaurants for a meal overlooking the Kamo River.

On your second day in Kyoto, pay a visit to **Kinkaku-ji** (p. 250, ❸), the iconic golden temple covered almost entirely in gleaming

> *Everything about Todai-ji is larger than life, including the main gate.*

gold leaf. Then compare and contrast it to **Ginkaku-ji** (p. 202, ❶), the Silver Pavilion, constructed as a rival and homage to Kinkaku-ji. When you're done admiring the pavilion, stroll the Philosopher's Path that leads from the temple to the neighborhood of Nanzen-ji. After enjoying the beautiful gardens and subtemples here, head back downtown to the **Nishiki Market** (p. 251, ❾) for some shopping or the **Kyoto International Manga Museum** (p. 203), which chronicles Japan's iconic comic-book culture. ⏲ 2 days.

In the morning take the Kintetsu Limited Express from Kyoto Station bound for Kintetsu Nara Station (30 min.).

❹ **Nara.** Head straight from the station down Nobori-Oji to **Nara Koen** (p. 200) and its adorable population of tame deer, who roam freely across the park's wooded lawns. After visiting **Kofuku-ji** (p. 220, ❶), cross under the main road and walk northeast to the beautiful garden of **Isuien** (p. 222, ❸). But the main reason you're here is **Todai-ji** (p. 223, ❹), the Buddhist temple that contains the world's largest wooden building, the massive **Daibut-suden,** which in turn houses famous **Daibutsu (Great Buddha)** statue. The Buddha is without

a doubt Nara's main attraction, for good reason: It's the world's largest bronze statue of the Buddha. Spend the rest of the day exploring the quaint streets and alleys of **Naramachi** (p. 224, ❻), a historic part of town full of well-preserved *machiya* (wooden town houses) and storehouses. ⏲ 1 day.

In the morning, take the Kintetsu Limited Express from Kintetsu Nara Station bound for Osaka, and get off at Osaka Namba Station. Transfer to Midosuji subway line and get off at Umeda Station (1 hr.).

❺ **Osaka.** Osaka is a city on the go, inhabited by no-nonsense, business-minded folk with a unique cultural identity. Out of Umeda Station, head to the **Umeda Sky Building** to take in the view at the **Floating Garden Observatory** (p. 208, ❶). Next, check out the Disney-esque Osaka **Museum of Housing and Living** (p. 209, ❷), a life-sized diorama of an Edo-period Osaka neighborhood. Then head for Osaka Castle, or **Osakajo** (see p. 209, ❸), considered one of the most magnificent fortresses in Japan. Although it's a reconstruction, it's still impressive. Round off your tour with a night of *kuidaore* (eating till you drop) amid the flashing lights and glowing neon along the **Dotonbori** "eating street" (p. 212, ➏) in the Namba area. 🕐 1 day.

In the morning, from Osaka Station, take a JR Kobe Line to Kobe Station (40 min.).

➏ **Kobe.** This historic port town is perhaps best known to foreigners for two things: being devastated in the 1995 Hanshin Earthquake, and for the quality of its beef, which has become a premium brand around the world. There are little signs of the former, but plenty of the latter, and lots of other sights making this a fun destination. A walk around the **Kitano district** (p. 230, ➊), with its Western-style houses, will make you feel as though you've stepped into a European village. The **Hyogo Prefectural Museum of Art** (p. 232, ➏), located on the Kobe waterfront in a building designed by architect Tadao Ando, showcases modern works domestic and foreign. Don't miss the night view from the **Nunobiki Herb Garden** (p. 230, ➋). Even more importantly, don't miss out on *wagyu* (Japanese beef) from one of the city's best restaurants, such as **Wakkoqu** or **Steakland Kobe** (p. 235). 🕐 1 day.

> *Kobe's Kitano district feels as much like Bavaria as Japan.*

> *Osaka's Dotonburi is a mechanized mix of light and sound.*

The 2011 Tohoku Earthquake & Tsunami

A DEVASTATING TRAGEDY WITH LONG-RANGING REPERCUSSIONS

by Matt Alt

In the early afternoon of March 11, 2011, an earthquake the likes of which few living residents of Japan can remember struck some 64km (40 miles) off of the coast of Tohoku (p. 400). It was an experience which I will never forget. The ground shook violently for close to 2 minutes. My wife and I were forced to our knees, crouching to avoid being knocked off our feet in our own home in the western suburbs of Tokyo.

> *The tsunami hits the sea wall of Miyako, washing away everything—including cars—in its path.*

But our experience was merely frightening. The light damage in Tokyo paled in comparison to the devastation unfolding up north in Tohoku, far closer to the epicenter. Within an hour, a shocked nation watched images of a massive tsunami tidal wave penetrating miles into the Tohoku coastline, causing far more damage and loss of life than the quake's tremors. The surging waters crested at well over 30m (100 ft.) in places, completely wiping entire towns and cities off the map.

Just as Japan was trying to come to terms with the fury wrought by the quake and tsunami, a new crisis reared its head: The tidal wave knocked out the cooling systems for the Fukushima Daiichi nuclear power plant. Within several days, the cores of two of the plant's four

> *Tokyo voluntarily dimmed its lights in the aftermath of the quake to conserve energy.*

reactors suffered partial meltdowns and a series of explosions wracked the facility. Although the blasts were not nuclear (they were caused by a buildup of hydrogen gas within the reactor buildings), they spread large amounts of radioactive material across the Japanese countryside. In response, the government evacuated a 20km (12.4-mile) radius around the reactors, displacing some 80,000 people who may never be able to return to their homes.

As of this writing, the toll stands at more than 20,000

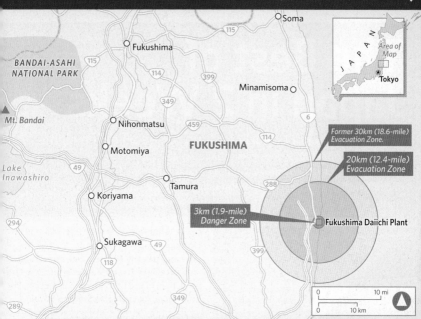

Soma

(115)

Fukushima

BANDAI-ASAHI
NATIONAL PARK

(115)

(114)   (399)

Minamisoma

(349)

▲ Mt. Bandai

Nihonmatsu   (459)

FUKUSHIMA

(114)

Motomiya

Lake
Inawashiro   (49)

Former 30km (18.6-mile)
Evacuation Zone.

20km (12.4-mile)
Evacuation Zone

Koriyama   Tamura   (288)

3km (1.9-mile)
Danger Zone

Fukushima Daiichi Plant

(294)

Sukagawa   (49)

(399)

(118)

(349)

(289)

JAPAN

Area of
Map

✳ Tokyo

0   10 mi
0   10 km

dead or missing from the tsunami, with some estimates of recovery costs reaching $300 billion USD, making it the most expensive disaster in history.

Nuclear Implications

Situations like this are understandably frightening. But it is important to note that there have been zero fatalities as a result of the nuclear crisis. That said, the immediate areas around the reactors will likely be uninhabitable, and contamination of food sources will be a major concern for decades to come. Background radiation levels have risen in many locations even quite far from the reactors, and the long-term implications of the cesium and other radioactive isotopes spread by the explosions will require constant monitoring and close study. While many

people feel the Japanese government needs to be more proactive, air- and food-safety monitoring efforts are under way. There are outliers on both sides of the debate, but **the scientific consensus as of this writing is that it is safe to travel to Japan.**

Deep Impact

At magnitude 9.0, the Tohoku earthquake is believed to be the largest ever to hit Japan, and one of the world's top five most powerful since modern record-keeping began in 1900. It unleashed almost unimaginable natural energies. In just 2 minutes, a 402km (250-mile) stretch of coastline dropped by 0.66m (2 ft.), and the entire main island of Honshu moved 2.4m (8 ft.) closer to the United States. And in an example of how disasters like this affect the entire world, the sheer force of the quake shifted the Earth's axis by 10

> *Radiation, measured by Geiger counter, will have long-lasting effects.*

to 25cm (4–10 in.), minutely shortening the length of a day for all of us.

How to Help

For information on how to volunteer, see p. 402.

The Best of Japan in 2 Weeks

Even 2 weeks isn't nearly enough to see all of the sights Japan has to offer, but it does give you the wiggle room to explore more of the countryside, particularly down south. This tour takes you from historic streets unchanged for centuries, to world-famous Hiroshima, and finally down to the southernmost islands for some hard-earned fun in the sun.

> Kurashiki's Bikan Historical Quarter is a great way to waltz back in time.

START After following "The Best of Japan in 1 Week," return to Osaka from Nara. In the morning, take the JR Kyoto Line from Osaka Station to Shin-Osaka Station. From Shin-Osaka Station, board the Sanyo shinkansen bullet train bound for Okayama Station (50 min.).

① Okayama. Okayama boasts what is considered to be one of Japan's most beautiful gardens: **Korakuen** (p. 300, **①**). Completed in 1700 after more than a decade of design and construction efforts, today it is the city's star attraction. A walk through its groves is a great way to relax during your travels. ⊕ 1 hr.

From Okayama Station, take the JR West Sanyo Main Line to Kurashiki Station (13 min.).

② Kurashiki. This is widely considered one of Japan's most picturesque suburbs and lies just outside Okayama. Its **Bikan Historical Quarter** is filled with warehouses that were used to store rice but have now been converted into shops and museums. It's a 10-minute walk from the south exit of Kurashiki Station and a major attraction for domestic and foreign tourists alike. While in the Quarter, don't miss the **Rural Toy Museum,** which is packed with traditional toys from all over Japan. Another must-see is the impressive **Ohara Museum of Art,** which contains a surprising number of international masterpieces for a countryside museum. ⊕ 1 day. See p. 301, **④**.

From Kurashiki Station, return via the Sanyo Main Line to Okayama Station to spend the night in Okayama. The next morning, from Okayama Station, board the bullet train for Hiroshima (about 1 hr.).

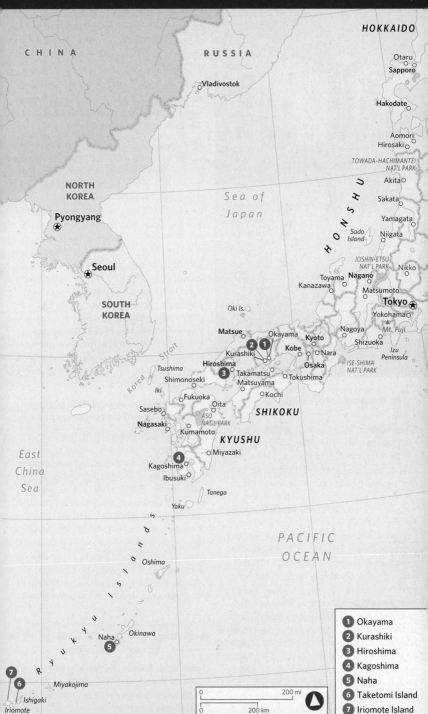

HOKKAIDO

CHINA

RUSSIA

Otaru
Sapporo

Vladivostok

Hakodate

Aomori
Hirosaki

NORTH
KOREA

TOWADA-HACHIMANTEI
NAT'L PARK

Akita

Sea of
Japan

Pyongyang

Sakata

Yamagata
Niigata

Sado
Island

Seoul

JOSHIN-ETSU
NAT'L PARK

Nikko

SOUTH
KOREA

Toyama
Kanazawa

Nagano

Matsumoto

Oki Is.

Tokyo

Yokohama

Matsue

Okayama

Kyoto

Nagoya

Mt. Fuji

Kurashiki

2 1

Kobe

Nara

Shizuoka

Izu
Peninsula

Strait

Hiroshima

3

Osaka

ISE-SHIMA
NAT'L PARK

Tsushima

Takamatsu

Matsuyama

Tokushima

Iki

Shimonoseki

Korea

Fukuoka

Kochi

SHIKOKU

Oita

Sasebo

Nagasaki

ASO
NAT'L PARK

Kumamoto

KYUSHU

East
China
Sea

Miyazaki

4

Kagoshima

Ibusuki

Tanega

Yaku

PACIFIC

OCEAN

Oshima

Ryukyu Islands

Naha

5

Okinawa

7

6

Miyakojima

Ishigaki

Iriomote

1 Okayama
2 Kurashiki
3 Hiroshima
4 Kagoshima
5 Naha
6 Taketomi Island
7 Iriomote Island

0   200 mi
0   200 km

> *Paper lanterns are set afloat during Hiroshima's annual Peace Memorial Ceremony.*

3 Hiroshima. This would undoubtedly be "just another city" were it not for its unfortunate historical distinction: On August 6, 1945, it became the site of the first atomic bomb ever dropped on human beings. Today, Hiroshima is a bustling and vibrant town, but a visit to the **Hiroshima Peace Memorial Park** (p. 309, **1**), which sits in the center of the city, is not to be missed. It is home to the **Genbaku Dome,** the skeletal remains of the city's former Industrial Promotion Hall and one of the few buildings that survived the atomic blast. But perhaps most moving is the **Hiroshima Peace Memorial Museum,** dedicated to chronicling the events leading up to and including that fateful August day in tactful but graphic detail. If your visit to the Memorial Park ends earlier than expected, head back to the station and board a train bound for **Miyajima,** home to one of Japan's most famous landmarks: **Itsukushima Shrine**'s huge red *torii* (shrine gate; p. 287, **5**) rising up out of

the sea. And no visit to Hiroshima would be complete without a taste of its signature dish, the savory pancakes called ***okonomiyaki*** (p. 311). ⏱ 1 day.

From Hiroshima Airport, fly to Kagoshima Airport (about 1½ hr.). From Kagoshima Airport, take a taxi or board a bus at stop no. 2 bound for Kagoshima City.

4 Kagoshima. Located on the southern end of Kyushu, this is a city of palm trees, flowering bushes, and wide avenues totally unlike those of northern Japan. It boasts one of the most unusual bay vistas in the world: **Mount Sakurajima** (p. 359, **3**), an active volcano whose last major eruption was in 1914. You can ferry over to see the volcano closer up, or stick downtown for attractions including the **Kagoshima City Aquarium** (p. 390, **1**), also known as Io World, which concentrates on sea life from waters surrounding Kagoshima Prefecture. And don't miss **Sengan-en** (p. 392, **4**), Kagoshima's most widely visited attraction. It's a garden laid out more than 300 years ago by the Shimadzu clan. While you're down south, enjoy southern comfort of a different sort by sampling the local liquor: ***shochu*** (p. 395), another Kagoshima claim to fame. ⏱ 1 day.

From Kagoshima Airport, fly to Ishigaki Island via Naha Airport in Okinawa (1½ hr.).

5 Naha. Having come all this way, chances are you won't want to stay in urban Naha, so rent a car at the airport and start driving north. Head straight for the **Ocean Expo Park** (p. 485, **2**). It's home to the amazing **Okinawa Churaumi Aquarium;** the **Native Okinawan Village,** which features more than a dozen sites modeled after a village from the Ryukyu Kingdom period; and perhaps most importantly, **Emerald Beach,** a large stretch of public shoreline where you can relax, swim, and catch some sun. Book accommodations in the **Nago area,** which has the best resort-style hotels. And if you happen to be a scuba diver, you're in luck, because some of Okinawa's **best diving** (p. 490) is to be found just off the coast of Okinawa Island. ⏱ 1 day.

From Naha Airport, fly to Ishigaki Airport (1 hr.). Take a taxi to Ishigaki Port (20 min.) and board a ferry bound for Taketomi Island (10–15 min.).

> *Visiting Kagoshima's Mount Sakurajima can be a blast.*

6 Taketomi Island. This gem of an island is a little time capsule of just 300 full-time residents who have dedicated themselves to preserving Okinawan architecture and culture. Simply exploring the streets of the village here is a fun way to while away an afternoon, admiring the distinctive red clay roofs and *shisa* gargoyles adorning the homes. **Nagomi-no-to Tower,** in the middle of the village, offers great views of the island and surrounding waters, and **water buffalo cart tours** are a somewhat authentic way to see the village. And since no visit to an island paradise would be complete without a trip to a pristine beach, budget plenty of time for loafing on and snorkeling near **Kaji Beach.** To maximize your time here, we recommend spending the night at one of the island's handful of **family-run hotels.** ⏱ 1½ days. See p. 500, **1** .

From Taketomi Island, board a ferry bound for Ishigaki Island. Switch ferries at the Ishigaki Ferry Terminal and ride to Iriomote Island (40 min.).

7 Iriomote Island. Since you've made it all the way out here, you might as well make a stop on this remote island that is sometimes called the Galapagos of Okinawa for its unique animal life. There are two main ways to enjoy the island: either with a guided tour that can be done as a day trip, or by renting a car and navigating the sights yourself. (If you navigate yourself, you'll want to stay over at least 1 night here.) First stop should be the semi-attached **Yubu Island** (p. 502, **3**), which is only accessible via ox-drawn cart. The **botanical garden** on Yubu is a great introduction to local flora and fauna. For those who want to chill out, **Hoshizuna no Hama (Star Sand Beach;** p. 502), back on Iriomote, is a great place to kick back and snorkel; more active travelers can aim for an **Urauchi or Nakama River kayak tours,** the only way to reach the interior of the island. (These are all-day affairs, so you'll need to make reservations in advance and plan on spending the night on the island.) ⏱ 1½ days. See p. 501, **2** .

Enter the Ninja

Is there anyone who isn't at least passingly familiar with the the ninja, those sneaky assassins of Japanese legend? Historically speaking, their heyday came in the 1500s: They played a key behind-the-scenes role during Japan's Era of Warring States, in which warlords clashed in a nearly century-long battle royal to take control of the country. Ninja worked for the warlords gathering intelligence and occasionally serving as mercenaries on the battlefield. Their true moment of glory was in 1582, when a team of ninja led by Hattori Hanzo spirited warlord Tokugawa Ieyasu to safety. When Tokugawa became shogun in 1601, he moved the nation's capital to Edo (now Tokyo), taking the ninja with him to use as the city's first police/defense force. Even today a surprising number of ninja-related attractions remain in Tokyo—including the Hanzomon subway line, named after Hanzo himself.

> *Ninja at play in the Iga-Ryu Ninja Museum.*

START Take the train to Tokyo's Hanzomon Station.

1 Tokyo. Although today one of the world's largest and most technologically advanced metropolises, Tokyo owes many of its most basic features to the ninja. Ninja were formerly garrisoned in and around **Harajuku** (p. 62, **5**); the mazelike warren of streets called **Ura-Harajuku,** now home to many of Japan's top fashion boutiques, was originally laid out in a complex pattern as a defensive measure, to delay invaders approaching from that side of the city.

①	Tokyo
②	Iga
③	Koga

Hanzomon Gate, on the west side of the Imperial Palace grounds, was the private entrance of Hattori Hanzo, who served the shogun as a strategic advisor. Truthfully there isn't much to see here—visitors are kept well away from the gate and wall by guards—but it is intriguing to think that the famed ninja once passed through this very gate, centuries ago.

Sainen-ji Temple, near Hanzomon Gate, is home to Hattori Hanzo's grave, located just to the right of the main temple building. Inside the main building, you'll find one of his spears—Hanzo was famed for his prowess with the weapon—on display.

The **inner Imperial Palace grounds** are home to the **Hyakunin Bansho Guardhouse** (p. 67, ④), which served as the base of operations for the Iga and Koga ninja who protected Edo in its earliest days.

And no ninja tour of Tokyo would be complete without a stop at the campy **Ninja Akasaka** restaurant (p. 92), which features gimmicked doors and hallways, with costumed waiters and waitresses who perform "ninja tricks" at your table. ⏱1 day. Sainen-ji: Wakaba 2–9, Shinkuku-ku. ☎03/3351-0662. Daily 9am–5pm. Free. Train: Yotsuya Station (Marunouchi Line).

In the morning, take the JR Shinkansen Nozomi bullet train to Kyoto. At Kyoto, switch to the Miyakoji Express bound for Nara (3¼ hr.). At Nara Station, take the Kansai Main Line to Kamo Station. At Kamo Station, switch to a Kameyama-bound train for Iga Ueno Station. At Iga Ueno Station, take the Iga Line to Uenoshi Station (total time 4½ hr.).

Myth of the Ninja

Stereotypes abound, but the ninja are one case where fact is even more interesting than fantasy. Most historians agree that the all-black outfits are largely fictional; the entire modus operandi of a ninja was to blend in, something difficult to do while prancing about in black pajamas. The vast majority came from isolated alpine villages in the Iga and Koga regions of Central Honshu, meaning that on any given day a ninja probably dressed more like a farmer than someone out of the film *Ninja Assassin*.

They also weren't actually called ninja back then, but rather a variety of regional terms including *shinobi*, *suppa*, and *rappa*.

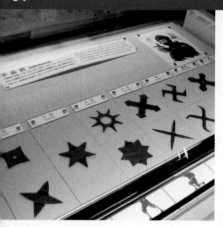

> Shuriken, *or throwing stars, are on display at the Iga-Ryu Ninja Museum.*

② **Iga.** The neighboring regions of Iga and Koga, located in the heart of Central Honshu, represent the birthplace of *ninjutsu* (ninja martial arts). In times of old, the alpine valleys here sheltered inhabitants from the prying eyes of the authorities, and allowed easy defense through homegrown guerilla tactics. The rivalry between Iga and Koga remains synonymous with the ninja even today. But this ninja homeland is decidedly off the beaten path. You wanted to meet the ninja—nobody said it would be easy.

Once you're here, the fascinating **Iga-ryu Ninja Museum** (p. 164, ⑤) will teach you everything you've always wanted to know about the ninja. The many tricks and traps found in the Iga-ryu Ninja House inside the museum are demonstrated by nimble-footed lady ninjas in bright pink outfits, and more than 400 types of weapons are on display.

Take the Iga Line from Uenoshi to Iga-Ueno Station, then switch to the Kansai Honsen Line bound for Kameyama. Disembark at Tsuge Station and switch to the JR West Kusatsu Line, then get off at Koga Station and take the shuttle bus to the village (1 hr.). (If the shuttle bus isn't there, you can call ☎ 0748/88-5000 from the station to request a pickup.)

③ **Koga.** The tiny **Koga Ninja Village** (p. 165, ⑥) in the woods outside Koga is dedicated to all things ninja. There's a ninja house—outfitted with hidden doors and escape hatches—you can explore, an area where you can improve your knife-throwing skills, and wall-scaling activities for aspiring young ninja.

From Koga Station, take the Kusatsu Line two stops to Konan Station, then take a taxi to the **Koga-ryu Ninjutsu Yashiki** (p. 165, ⑦). This former residence of Mochizuki Izumonokami, head of Koga's preeminent ninja clan, is filled with gimmicks, tricks, and booby traps. Like many ninja, Mochizuki was a farmer who grew herbs and devised medicinal potions—as well as poisons—that he administered to the 53 ninja families in the Koga region and regular folk looking for herbal cures.

The Ninja Experience

For those who want more of a hands-on experience, the **Jidai Academy Dojo** (http://ninjawarriors.ninja-web.net) offers several "ninja experience" courses. Held in Tokyo and conducted in Japanese with a running English interpretation, they're aimed at more active travelers who don't mind working up a little sweat.

The Basic Course teaches "ninja meditation" techniques followed by hands-on demonstrations of three classic ninja weapons, including throwing stars and blowgun darts. It ends with a photo session. The courses, which run an hour and a half, are held on both weeknights (8–9:30pm) and weekends (3–4:30pm). The cost is ¥12,000 for adults, and ¥9,000 for children between the ages of 5 and 11 (participating parental supervision required.)

There's also a Certificate Course that offers a slightly more expanded experience. Lasting 2 hours, this course teaches five different weapon techniques and goes a bit more in-depth into ninja philosophy and training practices.

Reservations are required and the course can be arranged for any weekday between the hours of 10am and 5pm. The cost is ¥15,000 for adults, and ¥12,000 for children between the ages of 5 and 11 (participating parental supervision required).

Reservations for both courses are required, and the Academy will send an "instructor ninja" to meet parties at the nearest station, which is JR Tabata Station on the Yamanote Line.

> Don't say we didn't warn you: beware of ninja.

Japan for Nerds

Once, not so long ago, things such as manga (comic books), *anime* (animation), and *tokusatsu* (special-effects-laden shows and films like *Ultraman* and *Godzilla*) were seen as pure kids' stuff. Not anymore. Today, Japanese pop culture, in the form of everything from Hello Kitty products to cutting-edge video games, represents one of the country's biggest exports. Japan is a veritable pop-cultural paradise, and the *otaku* (fanatical devotees) who love it see Tokyo as their motherland. That said, there's quite a few worthy destinations in Kyoto as well. The following is a quick tour through the best *otaku* sights each city has to offer.

> In Japan, manga (comic books) aren't just for kids.

START: **From Tokyo's Shinjuku Station, take the Chuo or Chuo-Sobu lines to Mitaka Station (30 min.).**

① **Tokyo.** Most of Tokyo's *otaku* destinations don't open until at least noon, so make your first stop the **Mitaka Ghibli Museum** (p. 70, ⑥). (*Note:* When you make your advance reservations—which are absolutely required for visiting the museum—make sure to specify that you want to enter right when the museum opens at 10am.) This place is a must-see for fans of the films of Studio Ghibli, Japan's premiere producer of animated fare; it looks like something right out of one of their movies. Exhibits include zoetropes and other early animation technologies, a mockup of Ghibli founder Hayao Miyazaki's personal studio festooned with original art and storyboards

Sea of Japan

HONSHU

Oki Is.

Fukushima

Nikko

Hitachi

Mito

Toyama **Nagano** *JOSHIN-ETSU NAT'L PARK*

Kanazawa

Matsumoto

Tokyo
① 1

Yokohama

Mt. Fuji ▲

Nagoya

Shizuoka

Izu Peninsula

Matsue

Takarazuka ❸ **Kyoto**
② 2

Okayama **Kobe**

Osaka **Nara**

Hiroshima

Takamatsu *ISE-SHIMA NAT'L PARK*

Shimonoseki

Matsuyama Tokushima

Kochi

SHIKOKU

PACIFIC OCEAN

Oita

ASO NAT'L PARK

KYUSHU

Miyazaki

| 0 | 100 mi |
| 0 | 100 km |

❶ Tokyo
❷ Kyoto
❸ Takarazuka

from his films, and a movie theater showing a variety of animated shorts that can only be seen at the museum. While the focus is on children, the charming little museum is absolutely appealing for visitors of all ages. There is a restaurant and snack bar serving up Ghibli-themed foods, and of course a gift shop as well.

If the weather is nice, walk from Ghibli Museum to Kichijoji Station (30 min.) and take the Chuo or Chuo-Sobu line to Nakano Station (15 min.). Here you'll find **Nakano Broadway** (p. 77, ❻), a shopping center brimming with all sorts of shops serving the subcultural demographic. Our personal favorite has to be the **Mandarake Complex** (p. 76, ❸), just down Chuo Dori; where else can you expect to see vintage '60s vinyl monster figures retailing for close to the cost of a new car? The Mandarake operates separate stores specializing in antique toys, comic books, costumes, and virtually any other form of pop-culture ephemera you can imagine. In addition to Mandarake's outlets, there are literally dozens upon dozens of independent specialty shops catering to *otaku* of every stripe here. Careful: In this windowless facility, it is all too easy to lose track of time—and the money you've spent.

> *One of Akihabara's ubiquitous maids.*

> *Astro Boy and Kimba the White Lion, smiling away at Osamu Tezuka World.*

From Nakano Station, and take the Chuo-Sobu Line to Akihabara Station (25 min.). Formerly the electronics district, **Akihabara** is now famed as the heart of the *"moe"* subculture-within-a-subculture, which focuses on perky *anime* girls. Maid Cafes like the @**Home Cafe** (p. 76, ④), in which costumed waitresses dote on *otaku* customers, and shops specializing in all sorts of *otaku* bric-a-brac abound here. ⏱ 6 hr.

In the morning, from Tokyo Station, take the Hikari or Shinkansen Nozomi bullet train to Kyoto Station (2½ hr.).

❷ **Kyoto.** While this city is famed throughout the world for its well-preserved temples and the Gion district, where geisha and *maiko* (geisha in training) go about their evenings, it's also home to several key spots for *otaku*. Make your first stop **Osamu Tezuka World,** a small gallery devoted to its namesake, Japan's "god of comics," the creator of Astro Boy and countless other hit characters. It's located in the Kyoto Station Building, just outside the JR central ticket gates. It features a small theater

screening Tezuka classics, a gift shop, and gallery area. (Admission is free, but tickets for the films are ¥200 for adults and ¥100 for kids.) Once you've whetted your appetite with a taste of the classics, head for the **Kyoto International Manga Museum.** Housed in a former elementary school building, this museum has a fine collection of manga-related items (around 300,000 pieces). In addition to comics and stills from local artists, comics from all over the world are on display. The museum also holds themed lectures and events such as *cosplay* (costume) shows.

Finish your stay in Kyoto with a visit to **Toei Kyoto Studio Park (Toei Eiga Mura).** Truth be told, this campy little theme park has seen better days, but it remains a fun way for buffs of Japanese films to spend a morning or afternoon. Used as an actual studio lot for decades, it was converted into a museum in the early '70s. The facility is tricked out to resemble a 19th-century Edo-period town, with costumed actors strolling the grounds wearing period clothing, swords, and sporting topknots. Live-action costume shows are held daily; fans of

All About *Otaku*

Today, the word *otaku* is used throughout the world to refer to what we in English call "geeks" or "nerds." Just as with those words, it's increasingly used as a badge of honor by foreign fans of manga (comic books) and *anime* (animation). But in Japan, the word has a darker history, giving it a nuance that takes many foreign fans by surprise.

Literally, *otaku* is a politer-than-polite way of saying "you." In 1983, however, a young subcultural writer by the name of Akio Nakamori used it to refer to young adults who remained fascinated with kids' pop culture—including idol singers, manga, *anime*, and more—well into adulthood. Nakamori's article painted a portrait of clueless "man-children" barely able to function in society, an image reinforced by the arrest in 1989 of a young serial killer whose home was discovered to contain vast quantities of manga and *anime*. For much of the '80s and '90s, *otaku* was a dirty word.

Today, things have changed. Japan has recognized its pop-cultural products as a unique and influential export, softening the social connotations of the word *otaku*. In fact, the government is even subsidizing what it calls a "Cool Japan" campaign to promote *anime*, video games, and manga around the world. The image of the *otaku* may certainly have been rehabilitated, but some baggage definitely remains. If you consider yourself an *otaku*, it's important to be careful when using the word to refer to yourself or other people—you might not get the reaction you're expecting.

ninja movies and *Power Rangers*–style shows will be in heaven here. There isn't much in the way of rides, but you will find carnival-style attractions such as a haunted house, ninja throwing star games, and dress-up souvenir photo stands. **Osamu Tezuka World:** ⏱ 30 min. Kyoto Station, 901 Higashishiokoji-cho, Shiokoji Sagaru, Karasuma Dori, Shimogyo-ku. ☎ 075/341-2376. Theater ¥200 adults, ¥100 kids. Daily 10am–7pm. Train: Kyoto Station. **Manga Museum:** ⏱ 2 hr. Karasuma-Oike, Nakagyo-ku.

☎ 075/254-7414. www.kyotomm.jp/english. ¥500 adults, ¥300 high-school and junior-high students, ¥100 elementary students, free for younger kids. Daily 10am–6pm. Train: Kyoto Station. **Studio Park:** ⏱ 2½ hr. 10 Uzumasa, Ukyo-ku. ☎ 075/864-7716. www.toei-eigamura.com. ¥2,200. Mar 1–Nov 30 daily 9am–5pm; Dec 1–Feb 28 daily 9am–6pm. Train: Hanazono Station.

From Kyoto Station, take the JR Tokaido Honsen Express to Amagazaki Station.

Switch to the JR West Fukuchiyama Line and ride to Takarazuka Station (60 min.).

3 Takarazuka. Osama Tezuka lived in this city until the age of 24, taking a great deal of inspiration from the local **Takarazuka Revue,** an all-female dramatic troupe that performs lavish Broadway-style musicals. (The theater, along with the museum below, is a 5-minute walk from Takarazuka Station; if you'd like to catch a show yourself, consult their website for the most up to date scheduling information.) If you're an *otaku,* you're here for the **Osamu Tezuka Manga Museum,** a small but charming gallery filled with life-sized replicas of his characters, original art, and a theater screening his works in high definition. This is a must-see for fans of Tezuka's characters, and also for the younger generation of *otaku* who can see the roots of some of their favorite characters. Revue: 1-1-57 Sakaemachi. ☎ 0570/00-5100. http://kageki.hankyu.co.jp/english/tt_stage.html. Ticket prices vary by show. Train: Takarazuka Station. Museum: ⏱ 2 hr. 7-65 Mukogawa-cho. ☎ 0797/81-2970. http://tezuka osamu.net/en/museum/index.html. ¥700 adults, ¥100 kids. Thurs–Tues 9:30am–5pm (closed irregularly; check website). Train: Takarazuka Station.

Otaku Festivals & Conventions

Tokyo is the epicenter of *otaku* culture, and many *otaku* time their visits to the city to coincide with one of the many *anime*- and manga-related conventions held there annually. Here's a list of some of the biggest. Even if you aren't a fan yourself, these are a great way to see what's hot in the world of pop culture—not to mention people-watch, as many attendees show up in elaborate costumes.

Held on the last weekend in March, the **Tokyo International Anime Fair (TAF;** www.tokyoanime.jp/en), in the Tokyo Big Sight International Exhibition Center, is a chance for Japan's many studios to showcase their upcoming products. It's actually 4 days long, but only the weekend days are open to the public. There isn't much in the way of shopping to do here, as the focus is on the studios themselves, but you'll get a sneak peak at upcoming films and shows. Check the official website for the most up-to-date information. Admission is ¥1,000.

Held twice annually in February and December, **Wonder Festival** (or "WonFes" as it's affectionately called by attendees; www.kaiyodo.co.jp/wf), in the Makuhari Messe exhibition hall, is a massive conglomeration of amateur craftsmen who sell limited-edition model kits, figurines, and toys based on popular characters. (Sellers get a special license to sell their products for the duration of the show only, making many of them instant collectibles.) A *cosplay* area on the roof allows costume-wearing fans to strut their stuff. Admission is ¥2,000.

Super Festival (http://artstorm.co.jp/sufes.html), a giant flea market of used and new toys and collectibles, is held three times a year (generally in Jan, Apr, and Sept) in the Science Hall museum on the Imperial Palace's inner palace grounds (p. 67, **4**), of all places. Fans begin lining up well before dawn to get their hands on limited-edition figures that go on sale when the show opens, but more casual visitors can drop by an hour after opening to avoid standing in line. In addition to the dealers' rooms, there are a variety of events such as signings and lectures by famous faces from the manga, *anime,* and TV worlds. Admission is ¥1,000.

Comic Market (Comiket; www.comiket.co.jp/index_e.html), held twice annually in late August and December in the Tokyo Big Sight International Exhibition Center, is a positively massive gathering of amateur and semipro comic book artists. First put on in 1975, it has bloomed into a giant event over the years; attendance now clocks in at half a million visitors over the duration of the convention. The focus here is on *dojinshi,* which are fan-created comic books based on original or popular characters. The mass of humanity is almost overwhelming, but it is a crystal-clear window into the *otaku* heart. Each of the 3 days features a different theme; if visiting with kids, check the website so as to avoid days focusing purely on adult-oriented works. Free admission.

> *"Whoa, no, there goes Tokyo!"*
> *Hibiya Park's Godzilla statue.*

Ghost & Monster Madness

Since times of old, Japanese mythology has described the nation as being home to a nearly uncountable number of gods, deities, spirits, monsters, and other creatures. In fact, the tongue-in-cheek tally is *yaoyorozu no kami*—"8 million gods." Even in today's modern era of cars, computers, and science, some believe these otherworldly creatures still inhabit the islands of Japan. While we can't promise any sightings, we can point you to next best thing: Unlike the monotheistic religions of the West, Japan's multifaceted approach to what's sacred means there are all sorts of holy—and unholy—places and things scattered throughout its cities and countryside.

> *A raven* tengu *stands guard over Mount Takao's Yakuoin Temple.*

START Take the train to Tokyo's Asakusa Station.

1 **Tokyo.** Tokyo is home to several key mythical sites, including **Senso-ji Temple** (p. 74, **6**), which is dedicated to Kannon, the bodhisattva of mercy. **Okadaya,** an umbrella shop located on the right side of Senso-ji's Nakamise shopping arcade, sells beautifully handmade paper renditions of the umbrella-shaped *yokai* (monster; p. 295) called *kara-kasa.* Further down,

Chingodo (p. 75, **8**) is a little-known subtemple located right behind the far more famous Senso-ji. It venerates the *tanuki* (raccoon-dog), a real-life animal that is portrayed as a trickster in Japanese folklore. Several giant statues and a garden filled with smaller portrayals of *tanuki* are visible as well. The quiet little space, off the beaten path, is a fun respite from the crowds outside.

Kappabashi (p. 64, **1**), Tokyo's famed kitchenware district, located just minutes from

1	Tokyo
2	Chofu
3	Mount Takao
4	Kyoto
5	Matsue
6	Shimonoseki

Senso-ji Temple, is best known for selling a mind-boggling variety of kitchen implements and machinery. But the area took its name from the *kappa* (p. 424). Legend has it that generations ago, a raincoat merchant enlisted the help of these aquatic creatures to build a bridge that funneled more pedestrian traffic to the area. The bridge itself is long gone, but a gleaming, golden, human-sized *kappa* statue stands on the right of Kappabashi's main drag. Even more fun for *kappa* fanatics, however, is nearby **Sogen-ji Temple,** otherwise known as Kappa-dera Temple, just a 10-minute walk from the statue. (It's tucked in a nondescript side street; look for a polished metal sign with a bilingual description of THE HISTORY OF KAP-PA-DERA TEMPLE.) Sogen-ji is home to a small repository of items relating to *kappa,* including what is purported to be the mummified hand of one of the creatures. While the building isn't open to the public, you can usually spot the shriveled paw through the glass on the left-hand shelf. ⊕ 3 hr. Okadaya: 1-37-1 Asaku-sa, Taito-ku. ☎ 03/3841-8566. www2.odn.ne.jp/okadaya. Train: Asakusa Station. Sogen-ji: 3-7-2 Matsugaya, Taito-ku. ☎ 03/3841-2035. Free. Daily dawn–dusk. Train: Tawaramachi Station.

From Tawaramachi Station, take the Ginza Line to Kanda Station. Switch to the Chuo Line and ride to Shinjuku Station. Switch to the Keio Line and ride to Chofu Station (1 hr.).

2 Chofu. This leafy suburb is home to Jindai-ji Temple and **Kitaro's Tea House,** a restaurant and gallery filled with characters from the hit animated series *Ge Ge Ge no Kitaro,* which centers on *yokai* monsters. Even if you aren't familiar with the show, poke through the weird souvenirs in the gift shop and take a look at the displays, which include miniature diora-mas of the *yokai* in their natural habitats. Even diehard fans probably won't spend more than an hour here, but the neighboring **Jindai-ji Temple** (深大寺), **Jindai Botanical Garden,** and **Jindai-ji shopping arcade** (all within walking distance) are a great way to while away an afternoon if the weather is nice. This area is known for the quality of its soba noodle shops, which are scattered throughout the shopping arcade. You can't go wrong in any one of them. Make sure to plan your visit for any day other than Monday, when the teahouse and many surrounding shops are closed. ⊕ 2½ hr. Tea Tea House: 5-12-8 Jindaiji Moto-Machi, Chofu-shi. ☎ 042/482-4059. www.youkai.co.jp/chaya.

html. Free. Tues–Sun 10am–5pm. Train: Chofu Station. Temple: 5-15-1 Jindaiji Motomachi. ☎ 0424/86-5511. Free. Daily dawn–dusk. Bus: 34 from Chofu Station. Botanical Garden: 5-31-10 Jindaiji Motomachi. ☎ 0424/83-2300. ¥500 adults, ¥250 seniors 65 and over, ¥200 junior-high students, free for younger kids. Daily 9:30am–4pm. Bus: 34 from Chofu Station.

Return to Shinjuku Station, and from there ride the Keio Line to Takao Station. Switch to the Keio Takao Line and disembark at Takaosanguchi Station (1 hr.).

3 Mount Takao. This easy-to-climb peak, located just an hour west of downtown Tokyo, is one of the most popular ways for Tokyoites to get a breath of fresh air. The mountain is also famed as one of the homes of the *tengu,* mythical long-nosed goblinlike creatures that dwell in alpine regions throughout Japan. *Tengu* come in two "species": the *karasu-tengu* look like bird-men with crow faces, while the *hanadaka-tengu* are red-faced, long-nosed humanoids with angel-like wings. (You may well be familiar with the latter, as masks of them are popular decorations in Japanese restaurants throughout the world.) **Yakuoin Temple** (p. 115, **2**), located roughly halfway up Mount Takao, features a variety of *tengu*-related art,

including giant statues, masks, and even a collection of the one-toothed *geta* sandals said to be the preferred footwear of the creatures. You'll need at least 2 hours to make it to the top, so factoring in travel time, plan on this being a day trip. ⏱ 5 hr. See p. 114.

Return to Tokyo Station and take the JR Shinkansen Nozomi bullet train to Kyoto Station. Switch to the Nara Line and disembark at JR Inari Station (3 hr.).

4 Kyoto. This city is one of Japan's holiest, and home to some of its most famous shrines and temples. Chief among them is **Fushimi Inari Shrine** (p. 256, **1**). Dating back to the 8th century and perched high in the Momoyama Hills, it venerates Inari, the god of rice and sake. Inari's name is virtually synonymous with his (or her—Inari is androgynous) messengers, the foxlike deities called *kitsune.* The 4km (2.5-mile) path that ascends to the main building is lined with 1,300 brilliant vermillion *torii* gates that appear to form a tunnel—a sight both stunning and surreal—and is dotted with bronze statues of the foxes.

Kyoto's Ichijo Dori street, otherwise known as **Yokai Street,** earned the nickname from an infamous incident that took place nearly a thousand years ago, when Kyoto (then known as Heian-kyo) was an oasis of culture surrounded by badlands. One night, hundreds of *yokai*, demons, and other creatures descended upon the city, parading down Ichijo Dori (then at the very edge of city limits) in a show of force against the humans who lived there. Although they were eventually driven back to their hiding places in the mountains, their appearance struck fear into the hearts of citizens, who immortalized it as the Hyakki Yagyo, or "demon's night parade." The image of strange creatures on parade remained a popular motif in Japanese folk art for generations thereafter, and today local merchants have unofficially renamed Ichijo Dori "Yokai Street" as an homage to the legendary incident. It's filled with statues, shops, and restaurants all featuring *yokai* themes, and hosts regular flea markets and other events.

Take the JR Shinkansen Nozomi bullet train to Okayama Station. Switch to the JR Express Yakumo and disembark at Matsue Station (3½ hr.).

Tracking the *Yokai*

Perhaps the most famous Japanese mythical creatures are the *yokai*, a word written with the Japanese characters for "otherworldly" and "weird." They are the monsters that have populated millennia of Japanese folk stories and fairy tales—essentially superstitions with personalities. Long ago in an era before science, they were blamed for all sorts of dangerous or inexplicable phenomena, from storms and plagues to the echoes that bounce back from canyon walls. The most famous is the *kappa*, a slimy froglike creature with a tortoiseshell back and a dish of water on its head that, when spilled, drains the monster's power like water from a bathtub. The *kappa* were once believed to inhabit lakes and streams throughout Japan, and their love for cucumbers is what gave the *kappa maki* (cucumber roll sushi) its name.

5 Matsue. This far-flung city in the countryside is the kind of place Japanese go to in order to get back to their cultural roots. It's also the adopted home of writer Lafcadio Hearn, who emigrated to Japan in the late 19th century and made a name for himself chronicling stories of Japanese ghosts, monsters, and gods. The **Lafcadio Hearn Residence** and **Lafcadio Hearn Memorial Museum** should be the first stop for any ghost lover. But ghost and monster fanatics simply can't miss the walking tour of the city's most famous temples. **Gessho-ji Temple** (p. 290, **1**) is decorated with the statue of an enormous tortoise that, according to legend, once came to life and devoured several residents of the city. **Seikoin Temple** (p. 292, **2**) is the site of an unfortunate incident involving a spurned lover cutting down a geisha on the steps of the temple. Her bloody footprints remain even to this day, and some say that ghostly singing can be heard issuing from the stairs at night. Meanwhile, **Yaegaki Shrine** (p. 292, **4**) doesn't boast any associated ghost or monster stories, but it is home to a pond with the mysterious power to predict one's future in love and marriage—a potentially scary prospect, depending on your personality. ⏲ 6 hr. See p. 296.

Take the JR Express Yakumo to Okayama Station. Switch to the JR Shinkansen Nozomi bullet train and disembark at Ogura Station. Switch to the JR Kagoshima Main Line and disembark at Shimonoseki Station.

6 Shimonoseki. You can clearly see Kyushu, right across Kanmon Strait, from this westernmost city at the tip of Honshu. The reason you're here is precisely because of that body of water: **Akama Jingu** is a shrine dedicated to the soul of child-emperor Antoku, who perished beneath the waves of Kanmon Strait during the epic Battle of Dan-no-Ura in 1185. Originally constructed just after the battle (in which the Genji clan wrested control of the country from the Heike clan) and rebuilt many times over the centuries (most recently in 1958), it houses the graves of the Heike clan, who were wiped out to a man in the confrontation. Note its staircase, which extends across the road and into the sea, the better for the souls of the Heike to make their way to the shrine from their watery graves. When

> *Beware of the . . . turtle? Meet the terror of Matsue's Gessho-ji Temple.*

you visit, make sure to drop by the **statue of Mimi-nashi Hoichi ("Hoichi the Earless")** just to the left of the shrine proper. He is the subject of a famous story by Lafcadio Hearn (p. 293): Hoichi, a blind lute player, was forced to play for the ghosts of the Heike clan night after night. Learning of Hoichi's plight, the abbot of the temple painted Hoichi's body with Buddhist sutras to render him invisible to the ghosts, but forgot poor Hoichi's ears, which were ripped off by the furious spirits as souvenirs.

And while you're here, don't miss a spine- (or at least tongue-) tingling encounter with a monster of a decidedly different variety: **fugu,** or poison pufferfish; most of the nation's catch comes from the waters around here. Although it has an overinflated reputation for causing bodily harm, fugu is an absolute delicacy when properly prepared. If you are going to sample it anywhere in Japan, do it here. ⏲ 2 hr. See p. 312.

Japan for Gourmands

Japan is a land of culinary delights. Some are familiar to foreigners, such as tempura. Others may be quite exotic even to locals, such as *barazushi* (see below). Whatever the case, while you're in Japan you owe it to yourself to experience as much of its unique culinary culture as possible. For natives, partaking of *meibutsu* (regional specialties) is a major part of the draw of traveling throughout the country; tasting trips to restaurants serving up seasonal local dishes should also be a part of any well-heeled explorer's tour.

> *No visit to Osaka would be complete without a serving or three of* okonomiyaki *pancakes.*

START Take the train to Tokyo's Asakusa Station.

1 Tokyo. This being the capital city, it is filled with restaurants catering to specialties from all over the country. (In fact, even if you never leave the city, you can sample excellent cooking from around Japan; this is a city of immigrants both domestic and foreign.) But Tokyo does have a few homegrown dishes of its own that foodies should make a definite point in trying. One of the most famous

is *monja yaki,* which is similar to the savory pancake called *okonomiyaki.* The big difference is in the batter, which is extremely thin and doesn't coalesce into an actual pancake; rather, you scoop up soft blobs of it from the hotplate with a scraper. The fillings differ from *okonomiyaki* as well, tending toward stronger-tasting fare such as *mentaiko* (roe), garlic, and cheese. **Matsuri Bayashi** in Asakusa is a great place to try the dish. And while you're in the area, drop by Asakusa's famed **Kamiya Bar** for

Legend:
1. Tokyo
2. Kyoto
3. Osaka
4. Kobe
5. Okayama
6. Takamatsu
7. Shimonoseki
8. Kagoshima

nother Tokyo classic: the "Den-Bran" cocktail
a concoction of gin, brandy, wine, vermouth,
uracao, and herbs). Matsuri Bayashi: 1-8-4
sakusa, Taito-ku. ☎ 03/3844-6363. www.
sakusa-monja.jp. All-you-can-eat ¥1,980. No
redit cards. Lunch & dinner daily. Train: Asaku-
a Station. Kamiya Bar: Kaminarimon Dori.
☎ 03/3841-5400. Entrees ¥610-¥1,500. MC,
, Lunch & dinner Wed-Mon. Train: Asakusa
ration.

rom Tokyo Station, take the JR Shinkansen
ozomi bullet train to Kyoto Station (2½ hr.).

❷ Kyoto. Japan's former and ancient capital is
med for its tempura, which really does seem
be better here than anywhere else, almost
ght in spite of being deep-fried. **Tempura
oshikawa** (p. 269) downtown is doubly fun if
ou get a counter seat, where you can watch
eals being prepared. But perhaps most ex-
tic to foreign visitors are Kyoto's *shojin-ryori*
(Buddhist vegetarian) and *kaiseki-ryori* (multi-
ourse) cuisines. For the former, head straight
r **Ajiro** (p. 263, ❼), a Michelin-starred
urveyor of vegetarian banquets. Meanwhile,
yotei (p. 265) is one of the city's best *kaiseki*
staurants. Founded 300 years ago as a
ahouse for devout travelers on pilgrimages

to Nanzen-ji Temple, it offers exquisite multicourse meals served by kimono-clad women
in tiny houses situated around a beautiful garden. You'll never feel more like you're in Japan
than when eating here. Of course, if you're just
looking for some of that traditional green tea,
you'll want to sit in on a highly ritualized tea
ceremony at Kodai-ji Temple (p. 262, ❺) for a
real taste of old Japan.

**From Kyoto Station, take the JR Shinkansen
Hikari bullet train to Shin-Osaka Station,
then switch to the Tokaido Main Line bound
for Osaka (30 min.).**

Sampling Japan

For those unfamiliar with Japanese cuisine,
we've provided a very basic overview of
some types of Japanese cuisine in the "History & Culture" chapter on p. 533. The following doesn't even come close to touching
on all of the regional specialties Japan has
to offer, but it is a good springboard to experiencing some of the best and most well
known. And the best part is, these stops
are close enough to Tokyo that at least a
few can be added to most itineraries.

> Sanuki udon *is the dish to have in Takamatsu.*

3 Osaka. The heart and soul of the Kansai region is known for a series of deliciously high-carb dishes that go great with alcohol: the savory pancakes known as *okonomiyaki,* and the deep-fried octopus dumplings called *takoyaki.* *Takoyaki* is quintessential street food, meaty pieces of *tako* (octopus), pickled ginger, and scallions folded into a gooey batter and grilled in special cast iron pans reminiscent of egg cartons. One of our favorite places to eat it is at **Takonotetsu,** which features tabletop grills that you use to cook the batter balls yourself. Meanwhile, fans of *okonomiyaki* won't want to miss out on **Chibo.** This five-story tower of pancake power cooks up some of the best stuff in the city. (The *negiyaki* mix, an Osaka specialty packed with scallions, is not to be missed.) And for those looking for something a bit lighter on the stomach, **Honfukuzushi** serves up another Osaka specialty: *oshizushi* (pressed sushi), where wooden blocks are used to compress the toppings against the rice (mackerel being a local favorite). See p. 216.

From Osaka Station, take the Tokaido Main Line to Kobe Station (40 min.).

4 Kobe. What gourmet tour of Japan would be complete without a taste of that quintessentially Japanese cut of meat, Kobe beef? Although a lot of the claims often made about Kobe beef cultivation abroad—such as that they are fed nothing but beer and massaged constantly—are more hyperbole than truth, Kobe cuts are still splendidly marbled pieces of beef. **Wakkoqu**—pronounced "wa-*ko*-ku"—is one of the city's premier purveyors of the to-die-for meat dish. ("We scrutinize our cows the way music composers labor over their favorite compositions," proclaims the website.) Cooked on large teppanyaki plates, this is *wagyu* (Japanese beef) at its absolute finest. See p. 235.

From Shin-Kobe Station, take the JR Shinkansen Nozomi bullet train to Okayama (40 min.).

5 Okayama. This city's claim to fame is one little known outside of Japan: *barazushi,* a casserole of sorts that consists of locally caught seafood (which varies by season) set atop a bed of rice mixed with wild mountain vegetables, shredded ginger, and cooked egg. It's a luxurious sort of affair that originated as a dish served to the samurai in Okayama Castle, according to legend. This is a real treat for seafood lovers, and something you'd be hard pressed to find anywhere outside of Okayama. (The closest analog would be the *chirashizushi,* sashimi atop a bed of vinegared rice, served throughout Japan.) The place to have it is **Shikisai,** conveniently located right outside of the famed Korakuen gardens. See p. 305.

From Okayama Station, take the JR Marine Liner Express to Takamatsu (1 hr.).

6 Takamatsu. Mention Takamatsu to a Japanese person and you'll undoubtedly hear "*Sanuki udon!*" in reply. Located on the island of Shikoku, Takamatsu claims to be the city that introduced Japan to the *udon* noodle around the 13th century. (The story goes that it was based on a recipe hand-carried from China by a Buddhist scholar; "*sanuki*" comes from the old name by which the Takamatsu area was once called.) Boiled and served in a simple broth with a variety of toppings, *sanuki*

Kagoshima's bars are all too happy to help you unwind with a little shochu liquor . . . or a lot.

don is virtually synonymous with the city. And the best thing about it is, budget prices and small portions mean you don't (and in fact shouldn't) restrict yourself to just one shop. Throw caution to the wind and make a day out of it! Each purveyor has their own distinctive take on the dish—it's one of those things that takes a moment to learn but a lifetime to master. Follow our "Takamatsu Noodle Hop" tour, which will take you to local institutions such as **Sakaeda, Matsushita Seimenjo,** and **Chikusei.** See p. 330.

From Takamatsu Station, take the JR Marine Liner Express to Okayama Station. Switch to the JR Shinkansen Hikari bullet train for Shinyamaguchi Station. Switch to the Sanyo Main Line for Shimonoseki Station (3½ hr.).

Shimonoseki. Fugu, the notorious poison pufferfish, is the claim to fame of this historic city. Located at the very southernmost tip of Japan's main island of Honshu, Shimonoseki's turbulent waters are the perfect breeding grounds for the strange-looking (and strangely delicious) fish. Don't sweat the stories about fatal mishaps involving fugu; while parts of it are undoubtedly venomous, all chefs are carefully licensed to prepare the fish, and incidents in restaurants are virtually unknown. Banned for generations, it became legal again in the late 19th century at the **Shunpanro Hotel,** which remains the single best place to try the dish. It's usually served in courses that consist of a sashimi plate, a marinated mix of meat and skin, and battered and fried chunks of fugu meat. In winter months, hotpots and *hire-zake*—hot rice wine with a dried fugu fin floating in it—are popular accompaniments. See p. 315.

From Shimonoseki Station, take the Sanyo Main Line to Ogura Station. Ride the JR Shinkansen Kodama bullet train to Hakata Station. Switch to the JR Express Relay Tsubame for Shinyatsushiro Station. Switch to the JR Shinkansen Tsubame bullet train and disembark at Kagoshima Chuo Station (3½ hr.).

8 Kagoshima. After all this travel, you're bound to have worked up a thirst. Fortunately, you're in just the right place to slake it . . . with some *shochu,* the distilled spirit that doesn't get any better than the stuff served here. Take a spin by **Galleria Hombo** to see how *shochu* is made, then make some friends in Kagoshima's watering holes, including the **Shochu-an Takezo** (one of the few with an English menu) and **Shochu Sasakura.** See p. 360.

Favorite Moments

Rebuilt from the ground up numerous times over the last century, Tokyo's towering skyscrapers, neon signs, and startlingly efficient train system can make time spent there seem like a visit to the future. Yet ancient charms still lurk beneath the city's high-tech facade, if you know where to look. Dotted with parks and museums, fascinating architecture traditional and modern, and retail establishments catering to every conceivable niche, there's something here for everyone.

> PREVIOUS PAGE *Don't let the long lens fool you: Mount Fuji is actually 100km (60 miles) from downtown Tokyo.* THIS PAGE *The gardens of the Imperial Palace are a great getaway from the city.*

❶ Tiptoeing through the Tokyo National Museum. Priceless antiquities such as samurai armor, swords, and traditional art are must-sees for anyone even remotely interested in Japanese culture. This is the museum to drop by if you only have time for one. See p. 68, ❷.

❷ Encountering real-life monsters in Ueno Park zoo. This excellent zoo is conveniently located right in the center of the city. The amazing endangered Japanese giant salamanders on display in the reptile house here can grow up to an alligator-sized 1.5m (5 ft.) in length. See p. 60, ❶.

❸ Navigating the throngs of pedestrians in Shibuya. The huge, six-way traffic crossing in front of Shibuya Station is legendarily crowded on weekends. The second floor of the Starbucks across the street offers an excellent view from above the fray.

❹ Meeting a maid in Akiba. Shop for electronics or action figures all you like, but you can't really say you've "done" Tokyo's geek-mecca neighborhood of Akihabara unless you take tea in one of its maid cafes, such as the storied **@Home Cafe.** See p. 76, ④.

Descending into gourmet paradise. Tokyo's *depa-chika,* literally "department store basements," are treasure troves of little culinary delicacies. They're packed with shops specializing in all sorts of raw ingredients and ready-to-eat foods, and also a great spot to pick up gourmet Japanese-style bento (boxed lunches). **Isetan** in Shinjuku has one of the city's best *depa-chika.* See p. 82.

Picnicking like an emperor in the Imperial Gardens. The Imperial Palace's surprisingly uncrowded East Garden is a tranquil place to stop and enjoy a boxed lunch purchased from a nearby vendor or convenience store. See p. 67, 4.

Browsing for books in Jimbocho. This street of used-book stores is paradise for bibliophiles. Only a few specialize in English texts, but even those that don't are fascinating to poke through. Try **Maruzen** for starters. See p. 82.

Soaking your troubles away in an urban hot spring. Oedo Onsen Monogatari might not be the nation's most traditional, but it's a great way for novices to get their feet wet in the world of *onsen* (traditional spas). See p. 109.

Getting lost in Meiji Jingu. Deep inside the cypress grove that lines the approach to Meiji Jingu, Tokyo's most storied Shinto shrine, you'll forget you're inside one of the world's largest cities. See p. 63, 7.

Finding your fashion on Takeshita Dori. For a quick taste of what's hip among Japanese kids at any given time, you could do worse than window-shopping on this legendary fashion street. While you browse, snack on a crepe from one of the street's many vendors. See p. 62, 5.

Searching for hidden treasure in a flea market. The monthly flea markets sponsored by certain temples, shrines, and community centers are a great way to find all sorts of stuff you never knew existed. The **Oedo Antique Market** is the city's largest. See p. 82.

Drinking in old-school glory on Hoppy Street. This legendary strip of watering holes behind Asakusa's Senso-ji Temple is a great way to end a day and meet some friendly locals. See p. 59, 6.

> *The Mode Gakuen Cocoon Tower is one of Shinjuku's more distinctive skyscrapers.*

⑬ Freaking out in one of the world's weirdest museums. The Meguro Parasitological Museum is tiny but stomach-churning. But strangely enough, rumor has it the bug museum also happens to be one of Tokyo's big date spots. See p. 70, 7.

⑭ Shopping till you drop on Omotesando. Stop by Harajuku Station on a weekend to take in the lavishly dressed "gothic Lolitas" parading in their finest, then stroll the Omotesando shopping boulevard for the latest fashions. See p. 62, 5.

⑮ Geeking out in Nakano Broadway. This shopping plaza is literally crammed with shops dedicated to every conceivable Japanese pop-cultural niche. If you're into Japanese *anime* (animation) or comic books, this is a can't-miss shopping opportunity. See p. 77, 6.

⑯ Getting your head in the clouds with a Shinjuku skyscraper. The 202m-high (663-ft.) observation deck of the Tokyo Metropolitan Government Building is an amazing vantage point for taking in the entire city at a glance— and it's free! See p. 63, 8.

⑰ Trekking up Mount Takao. Located about an hour west of downtown, the quiet, easily hiked footpaths of this mountain are a classic way to get away from the urban jungle. See p. 117.

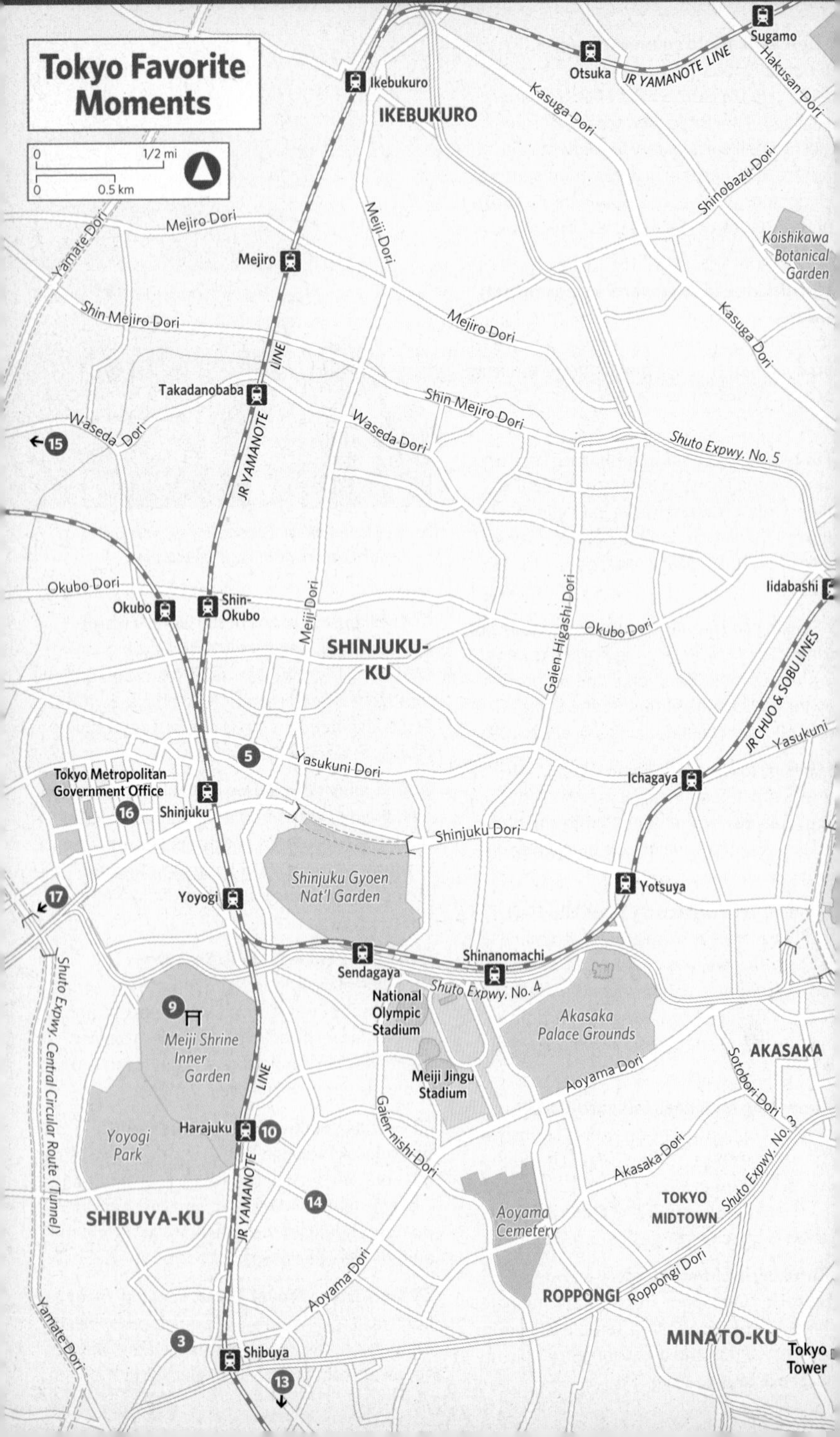

Tokyo Favorite Moments

```
0          1/2 mi
0      0.5 km
```

Sugamo

Otsuka

JR YAMANOTE LINE

Hakusan Dori

Ikebukuro

IKEBUKURO

Kasuga Dori

Shinobazu Dori

Koishikawa Botanical Garden

Mejiro Dori

Mejiro

Kasuga Dori

Meiji Dori

Mejiro Dori

Shin Mejiro Dori

Yamate Dori

JR YAMANOTE LINE

Takadanobaba

Shin Mejiro Dori

Waseda Dori

15

Waseda Dori

Shuto Expwy. No. 5

Iidabashi

Okubo Dori

Okubo

Shin-Okubo

Meiji Dori

Okubo Dori

Gaien Higashi Dori

JR CHUO & SOBU LINES

Yasukuni

SHINJUKU-KU

5

Yasukuni Dori

Ichagaya

Tokyo Metropolitan Government Office

16 Shinjuku

Shinjuku Dori

Yotsuya

17

Yoyogi

Shinjuku Gyoen Nat'l Garden

Shinanomachi

Sendagaya

Shuto Expwy. No. 4

Shuto Expwy. Central Circular Route (Tunnel)

9

Meiji Shrine Inner Garden

National Olympic Stadium

Meiji Jingu Stadium

Akasaka Palace Grounds

AKASAKA

Aoyama Dori

Sotobori Dori

Yoyogi Park

Harajuku **10**

14

Galen-nishi Dori

Akasaka Dori

Shuto Expwy. No. 3

TOKYO MIDTOWN

SHIBUYA-KU

JR YAMANOTE LINE

Aoyama Dori

Aoyama Cemetery

Roppongi Dori

ROPPONGI

Yamate Dori

3 Shibuya

13

MINATO-KU

Tokyo Tower

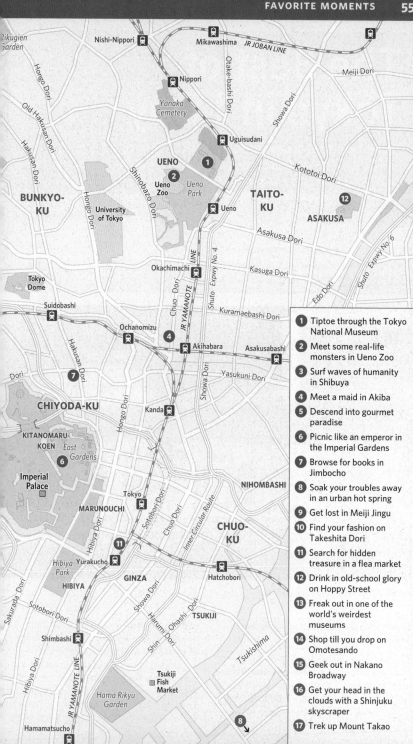

1. Tiptoe through the Tokyo National Museum

2. Meet some real-life monsters in Ueno Zoo

3. Surf waves of humanity in Shibuya

4. Meet a maid in Akiba

5. Descend into gourmet paradise

6. Picnic like an emperor in the Imperial Gardens

7. Browse for books in Jimbocho

8. Soak your troubles away in an urban hot spring

9. Get lost in Meiji Jingu

10. Find your fashion on Takeshita Dori

11. Search for hidden treasure in a flea market

12. Drink in old-school glory on Hoppy Street

13. Freak out in one of the world's weirdest museums

14. Shop till you drop on Omotesando

15. Geek out in Nakano Broadway

16. Get your head in the clouds with a Shinjuku skyscraper

17. Trek up Mount Takao

The Best of Tokyo in 1 Day

You'll find that 1 day goes by in the blink of an eye in a city as dynamic as Tokyo, whose metropolitan area is considered the world's largest. The trick is to hit the ground running and let the city's legendarily efficient public transit system make the most of your limited schedule. The sights on this whirlwind tour are some of the city's best known and most popular, even among jaded old hands. Although this tour begins super early—well before dawn if you want to catch the tuna auctions at the fish market—it's a great way to take advantage of your jetlagged condition. Just don't forget to bring a good pair of walking shoes—you'll need them.

> *Asakusa's homey, happy Hoppy Street.*

START Take the Toei Oedo subway line to Tsukijishijo Station.

① ★★★ **Tsukiji Fish Market** (築地市場). Officially known as the **Tokyo Metropolitan Wholesale Market,** an early-morning stop here is required for any first-time visitor to the city. This massive marketplace is where Tokyo's

eateries stock up on fresh seafood for the day. Although the marketplace itself is open all morning, you'll need to get here very early if you want to see one of the famed live auctions, where huge frozen tuna weighing hundreds of pounds are sold to the highest bidder. The Fish Information Center (at the Kachidoki entrance) issues 140 tickets on a first-come,

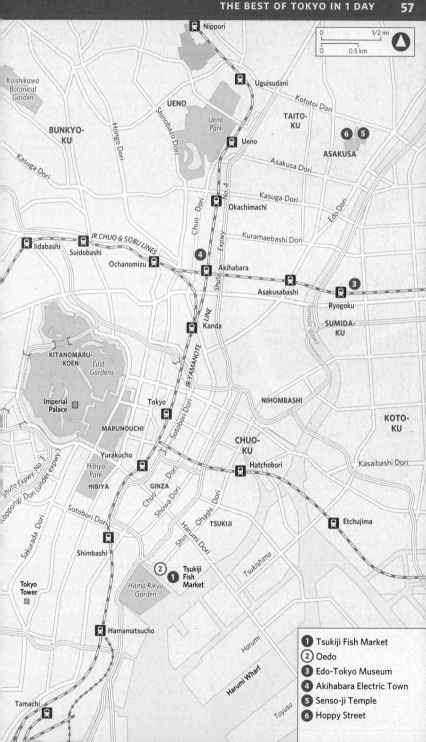

1 Tsukiji Fish Market
2 Oedo
3 Edo-Tokyo Museum
4 Akihabara Electric Town
5 Senso-ji Temple
6 Hoppy Street

Visiting the Fish Market

It's important to remember that the Tsukiji Wholesale Market is a workplace and not a tourist attraction. But the employees are used to tourists, so you shouldn't feel any hesitation at visiting—it's just important to remember common sense and courtesy when you do.

- Choose clothing and footwear accordingly. The floors can be slick, and employees frequently spray down their work areas with hoses.

- Take particular care if you are coming with small children. This is probably the least "child-proofed" place in the city.

- Refrain from touching any of the items on display, and in particular the giant (and expensive) frozen tuna, which are easily damaged by ungloved contact.

- Flash photography is prohibited in the auction area (it's fine in the marketplace itself). And tripods are a definite no-no.

first-serve basis starting at 4:30am. The first auction is at 5am, with a second at 5:40am. ⏱ 2–3 hr. 5-2-1 Tsukiji, Chuo-ku. No phone. www.tsukiji.or.jp/english. Free. Inner Market: Mon–Sat 5am–1pm; Wholesale Market: Mon–Sa 9am–1pm. Closed irregularly during the week. Subway: Tsukiji or Tsukijishijo stations.

② 🍴 ★★★ **Oedo** (大江戸). The Tsukiji Outer Market, a maze of tiny shops and restaurants crammed into several square blocks, is a great place to stop for a sush breakfast after checking out the wares ir the Tsukiji Fish Market. You really can't go wrong with any of the restaurants here, but those serving *donburi* (bowls o sushi rice piled with sashimi) are the bes choices—it doesn't get any fresher than this. We like Oedo in particular, which features large photo menus to help you order. Be prepared to line up, even if you're outside of what could be considered a normal mealtime. Trust us, it's worth the wait. 5-2-1 Tsukiji, Chuo-ku. ☎ 03/3547-6727. Donburi ¥1,000– ¥2,000. No credit cards. Breakfast, lunch & dinner daily. Subway: Tsukiji or Tsukijishijo stations.

③ ★★ **Edo-Tokyo Museum** (江戸東京博物館). Housed in a strikingly modern building, this museum explores how a tiny fishing village evolved into one of the world's largest metropolises. The scale models and life-size replicas of old buildings, fortifications, and even whole neighborhoods are a fascinating window into Tokyo over the years. The museum also happens to be located right next to the **Kokugi-kan,** 1-3-28 Yokoami, Sumida-ku (☎ 03/3623-5111; www.sumo.or.jp), where sumo tournaments are held seasonally. ⏱ 2 hr. 1-4-1 Yokozuna, Sumida-ku. ☎ 03/3626-9974. www.edo-tokyo-museum.or.jp/english. ¥600 adults, ¥300 students and seniors 65 and over. Tues–Sun 9:30am–5pm. Subway: Ryogoku Station.

④ ★ **Akihabara Electric Town** (秋葉原電気街). Once famed as Tokyo's electronics district, Akihabara has evolved over the last decade into a haven for *otaku,* Japanese slang for "geeks." Devotees of Japanese pop culture could easily spend an entire day hitting the many niche shops clustered in this area (and

> A sightseeing stop for centuries: Senso-ji.

n fact it's an integral part of the itinerary on . 76). For a quick taste of it all, take a stroll lown **Chuo Dori,** the neon-festooned "main lrag," which features model, doll, toy, and electronics shops. A word to the wise: Even n the duty-free shops, electronics aren't significantly cheaper here than abroad, so unless you find something you absolutely can't live without, you're probably better off buying at lome. ⏱ 1½–2 hr. Subway: Akihabara Station.

5 ★★★ **Senso-ji Temple** (浅草寺). With a history lating back well over a millennium, this iconic Buddhist temple is an absolute must-see for my Tokyo visitor. The imposing **Kaminarimon** "Thunder Gate"; p. 72, **2**), festooned with a giant-sized paper lantern, is a popular meeting spot, and the **Nakamise Dori** shopping arcade p. 73, **3**) leading to the temple proper is a great place to stock up on souvenirs ranging rom the tasty and tasteful to the utterly kitschy. The inner gate and five-story pagoda are beautiful examples of Japanese temple architecture, and Senso-ji Temple itself was extensively renovated in 2009 and 2010. Nearby **Demboin Garden** is a great place to sit down for a respite

from the crowds. If you have time, don't be afraid to wander the side streets and back alleys of this area—they are filled with all sorts of fun little restaurants and shops. See p. 74, **6**.

6 ★ **Hoppy Street** (ホッピー通り). This charming little boulevard is a great way to end the day. Its *izakaya* (Japanese-style pub) eateries specialize in tapas-style plates of traditional bar foods such as *motsu* (an aromatic stew of organ meats), yakitori chicken skewers, and perhaps most importantly, "Hoppy," a concoction of a nonalcoholic brew mixed with *shochu* (a distilled liquor) in a cheap simulacrum of beer. Surprisingly drinkable and worth a try even if you're a beer snob, this de-facto workingman's drink of the early postwar era has made a big comeback in recent years. It is the quintessential Tokyo cocktail. *Tip:* Although a Hoppy resembles a frosty beer, the *shochu* it contains is a distilled spirit and packs a wallop. Be sure to pace yourself and drink responsibly. Any of Hoppy Street's bright and boisterous establishments are a great place to spend an evening, but we like **Izakaya Koji** (p. 108). Asakusa, Taito-ku. Subway: Asakusa Station.

The Best of Tokyo in 2 Days

Two days gives you the freedom to hit more of Tokyo's quintessential sites, particularly those on the west side of town. The city's single best museum, its most storied Shinto shrine, and some breathtaking views await. Once you've had your fill of high culture, you'll also have a chance to take a plunge into Tokyo's seamy red-light district. Just remember: Look but don't touch.

> *The Ginza: a purr-fect place for boutique shopping.*

START Take the Ginza or Hibiya subway lines to Ueno Station.

1 ★ **Ueno Park** (上野公園). By far Tokyo's largest park, spacious Ueno is brimming with attractions, including several museums, gardens, a temple, and a world-class zoo (which you might prefer over the Tokyo National Museum, below, if you're with kids). None of them are open until 9:30 in the morning; if the weather is nice, wander the grounds and look at some of the outdoor displays until things open up. **Shinobazu Pond** is particularly scenic in summer, covered almost entirely with blossoming lotus plants. This park also happens to be one of the city's most popular spots for cherry-blossom-viewing parties at the end of March or early April. ⏱ 30 min. Subway: Ueno Station.

2 ★★★ **Tokyo National Museum** (東京国立博物館). If you visit any one museum in the city, this should be it. Hosting a variety of collections, it brims with Japanese antiquities such as swords, armor, lacquerware, woodblock prints, and pottery. The basic entrance fee covers admission to the regular galleries; separate entrance fees are charged for special exhibitions. See p. 68, **2**.

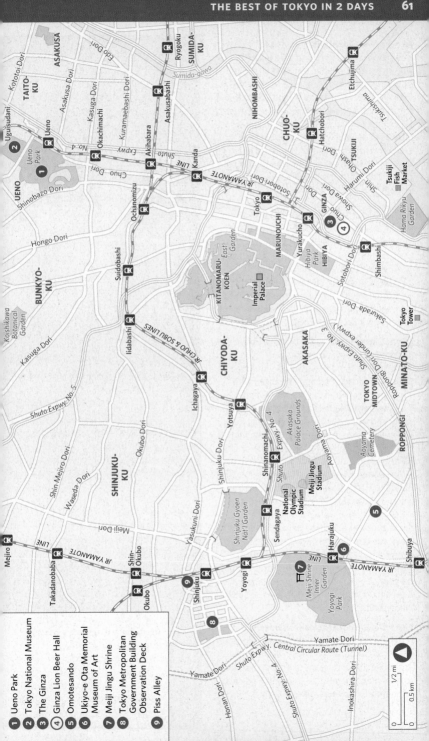

1 Ueno Park
2 Tokyo National Museum
3 The Ginza
4 Ginza Lion Beer Hall
5 Omotesando
6 Ukiyo-e Ota Memorial
   Museum of Art
7 Meiji Jingu Shrine
8 Tokyo Metropolitan
   Government Building
   Observation Deck
9 Piss Alley

③ ★★★ **The Ginza** (銀座). No visit to Tokyo would be complete without at least a cursory stop in the Ginza, Japan's storied shopping district that is often compared to New York's Fifth Avenue. All of Japan's major department store chains, such as Mitsukoshi (p. 83) and Takashimaya (p. 83), have flagship stores in the Ginza, making window-shopping a blast even if you don't have a lot of cash to spare. Start at the Chuo-Harumi intersection for the classic view of the area. ⏱ 1 hr. Subway: Ginza Station.

④ 🍺 **Ginza Lion Beer Hall.** This Tokyo mainstay features a striking Art Deco interior with beautiful mosaic tile work. Built in 1934, it is one of the city's few remaining prewar buildings. It goes without saying that the beer is great, but the menu (think European-style dishes such as sausages) is filling even for nondrinkers. See p. 106.

⑤ ★★ **Omotesando** (表参道). One of Tokyo's trendiest shopping areas, this wide, tree-lined boulevard is far more evocative of European cities than those of Japan. It's packed with boutiques, restaurants, and cafes ranging from low key to haute. Fashionistas could easily spend the day window-shopping here: The twisty maze of back streets branching off the main drag, known locally as Ura-Harajuku, is the epicenter of the Tokyo fashion scene.

As you ramble down the boulevard toward Harajuku station, you might want to take a detour to **Takeshita Dori** (竹下通り) street, which is closed to traffic and filled with shops aimed at a teenage demographic. It is epically crowded on Saturday and Sunday afternoons, but picking your way through the shoulder-to-shoulder crowd is part of the experience—as is the people-watching, which is second to none in this area. ⏱ 1½ hr. Subway: Omotesando Station.

⑥ ★★ **Ukiyo-e Ota Memorial Museum of Art.** The charming private museum located just off of Omotesando boasts a stunningly large collection of vintage *ukiyo-e* (woodblock prints), which are rotated through the display in monthly exhibitions. See p. 71, ⑨.

Meet the "Sky Tree"

The Tokyo Sky Tree (www.tokyo-skytree. jp/english) is the latest addition to the city's skyline. It's designed to house digital TV antennas too large to fit in the rapidly aging Tokyo Tower. At 634m (2,080 ft.), it's actually the tallest tower in the world as of this writing.

It's also set to be the world's most expensive tower to climb. Due to open to the public in May 2012, a ride up the elevator to the observation deck will cost a cool ¥3,000—close to $40 USD.

The fact that there are plenty of cheap or free observation decks throughout the city (such as the Tokyo Metropolitan Government Building, p. 63, ⑧) has led many locals to deride the Sky Tree project as an overpriced tourist boondoggle. But for those who want to make the climb, the Sky Tree is just a 20-minute walk from Asakusa. The nearest station is Oshiage, which is accessible via the Hanzomon Line or Toei Asakusa Line.

7 ★★★ **Meiji Jingu Shrine** (明治神宮). Meiji Jingu is the largest, most opulent, and most frequently visited Shinto shrine in Tokyo. The towering *torii* (gate) at the entrance and long, cypress-tree-lined path approaching the inner precinct are classic examples of Japanese shrine design. Although the shrine is impressive enough in and of itself, the dense forest surrounding it is enough to make you forget you're strolling through downtown Tokyo. The shrine's iris flower garden is a popular attraction during the summer months. ⏱ 1 hr. 1-1 Kamizonocho Yoyogi, Shinjuku-ku. ☎ 03/3379-5511. www.meijijingu.or.jp/english. Free. Daily sunrise–sunset. Subway: Meiji-Jingumae Station.

8 ★★ **Tokyo Metropolitan Government Building Observation Deck** (都庁の展望室). Also known as City Hall, the completion of this iconic, 248m-tall (814-ft.) building in 1991 knocked the Tokyo Tower out of its former spot as the best perch to get a bird's-eye view of the entire city. It's especially fun at dusk, when the lights give the Tokyo sprawl even more of a sci-fi feel than usual. There are two observation decks on the 45th floor, south and north, each offering different views of the city. Wintertime offers a better chance of spotting Mount Fuji in the distance. ⏱ 45 min. 8-1-2 Nishi-Shinjuku, Shinjuku-ku. No phone. www.metro.tokyo.jp/ENGLISH/TMG/observat.htm. Free. Daily 9:30am–11pm. Subway: Shinjuku or Tochomae stations.

9 ★ **Piss Alley** (思い出横町). Even if you choose not to partake of any of the establishments here, this densely clustered warren of tiny watering holes is worth a quick walk-through. The shantytown feel is a stark counterpoint to the towering office buildings that surround it. It's officially known as Memory Lane, but most refer to it by the earthier sobriquet it earned years ago for its onetime lack of plumbing facilities. Extensively renovated after a 1999 fire, this Tokyo landmark still feels like a window into a far less affluent era. The best strategy for picking a restaurant? Follow the crowds. Any place with a line is probably worth lining up for. We recommend **Kabuto**, 1-2-11 Shinjuku, Shinjuku-ku (☎ 03/3342-7671). ⏱ 2 hr. Subway: Shinjuku Station.

Kabukicho (歌舞伎町)

More adventurous visitors may enjoy a nighttime stroll through the sleazy glitz of Tokyo's red-light district. The wall of neon signs running along Yasukuni Dori is a ubiquitous backdrop for films set in Tokyo, and the signboards advertising the latest wildly coiffed arrivals at the area's host and hostess clubs are the sort of thing you'd be hard pressed to find anywhere else in the world.

While Kabukicho isn't exactly dangerous, it plays according to a different set of rules than the rest of the city, and you need to act accordingly. This is not a tourist area. It's best to keep your camera zipped away in this section of town, as some of its dicier elements don't like having their pictures taken. Young males in particular should be prepared for an unceasing barrage of come-hithers from touts, who will often follow you down the street. Aggressively ignore them. Never accept solicitations to enter establishments here. Unlike the rest of the city, Kabukicho is rife with con artists that target tourists domestic and foreign.

The Best of Tokyo in 3 Days

On day 3, you'll take a scenic cruise, drop by a beautiful garden or two, and work in some window-shopping in two of Tokyo's signature neighborhoods. Alternatively, many visitors elect to spend their third day outside of the city. Those looking for more traditionally Japanese architecture and sights would enjoy scenic Kamakura (p. 122), while those seeking a natural respite will want to try hiking up sylvan Mount Takao (p. 114).

> Relaxing in royal style on the Imperial Palace grounds.

START Take the Ginza subway line to Tawaramachi Station.

❶ Kappabashi (かっぱ橋道具街). A giant statue of a chef marks the entrance to Tokyo's kitchenware district, which pretty much single-handedly supplies Tokyo restaurants with the equipment they need. The neighborhood is named after the *kappa* water sprite, the folktale creature that gives *kappa maki* cucumber-roll sushi its name. Cute (and not-so-cute) representations of the creature abound here.

Dozens of wholesale shops, many specializing in arcane gear of one kind or another, are fascinating to window-shop in their own right. But the "fake food" stores, which provide the delicious-looking faux plates on display in many restaurant windows, are absolute must-sees. And if you're looking for a high-quality kitchen knife or Japanese tableware, Kappabashi is heaven on earth. The shops generally open between 9 and 10am. ⏱ 1 hr. Subway: Tawaramachi Station.

❷ Sumida River Tour (隅田川クルーズ). In times of old, citizens traveled through the city via a network of interconnected waterways, and a Sumida River cruise is a relaxing way to get a taste of what things were like back then. This short ride in a traditional Japanese barge runs

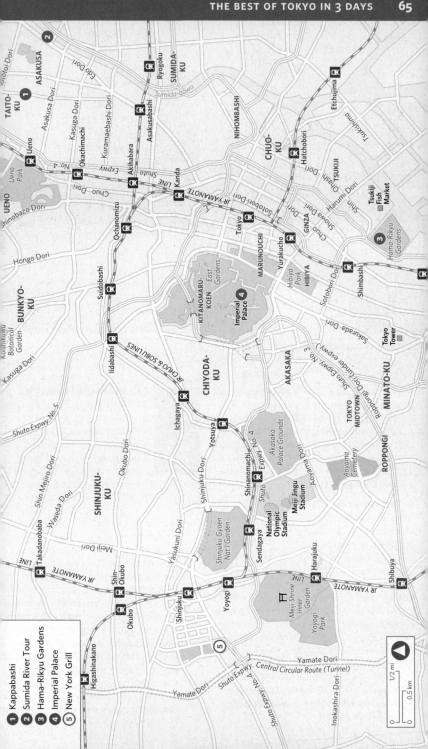

1 Kappabashi
2 Sumida River Tour
3 Hama-Rikyu Gardens
4 Imperial Palace
5 New York Grill

> *The Hama Rikyu Gardens in bloom.*

between Asakusa and the Hama Rikyu Garden. Featuring commentary in Japanese and English, it's a great way to get a view of the city you otherwise would never get to see, including a variety of famous bridges. ⊙ 45 min. 1-1-1 Hankawado, Taito-ku. ☎ 0120/977-311. ¥720 one-way. First cruise 10:35am; last cruise 6:30pm. Subway: Asakusa Station.

❸ **Hama Rikyu Gardens** (浜離宮恩賜庭園)**.** This little oasis at the end of the Sumida River boat tour is a classic example of a feudal lord's personal garden. Perhaps its most interesting feature is the tidal pond, which connects to the bay via a system of locks and is filled with seawater rather than the traditional freshwater. A beautiful traditional teahouse sits on an island in the middle of the pond. Depending on the season, a variety of specialty flower gardens showcasing summer irises, azaleas, and winter apricots may be in bloom. When you're done, head for the Tsukijishijo train station. ⊙ 1 hr. 1-1 Hama Rikyu Teien, Chuo-ku. ☎ 03/3541-0200. ¥300 adults, ¥150 seniors, free for elementary students and younger. Daily 9am–4:30pm. Subway: Shiodome or Tsukijishijo stations.

SITE GUIDE PAGE 67

❹ ★★★ **Imperial Palace** (皇居)**.** Home to the royal family of Japan, the palace and its grounds sit atop the site once occupied by Edo Castle. Although the castle itself is long gone, much of its moat and imposing stone fortifications remain, and its gardens are among the best in the city. See p. 67.

⑤ 🍴 **New York Grill.** If your budget accommodates it, there are few better places to have a last meal in Tokyo than at the ritzy, glitzy New York Grill. Perched atop the Park Hyatt Tokyo in Shinjuku (p. 100), this restaurant offers spectacular views and fusion Western-Asian cuisine all rolled into one—with prices to match. If you can afford it, splurge on the *wagyu* (Japanese beef). Even if you're on a budget, the attached **New York Bar** is a great way to taste the atmosphere without spending a fortune. Tip for frugal drinkers: Drop by early and make sure to leave before 8pm, when a ¥2,000 table charge kicks in. See p. 92.

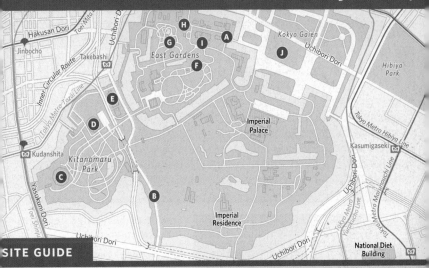

SITE GUIDE

④ Imperial Palace

In centuries past, this palace was the center of the city. It originally took the form of a castle that was occupied by a series of warlords and eventually the shogun Tokugawa Ieyasu himself in the late 1500s. Then, in 1888, it became the emperor's residence. Destroyed during World War II, it was rebuilt into its current form.

The 75-minute tours of the Ⓐ **inner palace grounds** are free and cover the Imperial Palace (pictured at right) and surrounding area, highlighting various buildings, bridges, and fortifications using English audio guides. Use the website to reserve a spot at least 1 week in advance.

A famed cherry-blossom viewing spot in season, the path along Ⓑ **Chidorigafuchi** moat offers excellent views into the former castle's first line of defense. The loop is almost exactly 5km (3 miles) if you want to jog it.

Kitanomaru Garden is home of the Ⓒ **Budokan Stadium**—formerly the city's largest stadium and famed abroad for hosting numerous rock bands in the 1970s—as well as several museums. The Ⓓ **Kids Science Museum** is a kid-friendly, hands-on science center, while the Ⓔ **Tokyo Museum of Modern Art** has the biggest collection of modern Japanese art under one roof in the city.

Continue on to the **East Gardens (Higashi Gyoen)**, a beautiful respite in the middle of the crowded city. The highlights here include the Ⓕ **Honmaru,** the remnants of where Edo

Castle once stood, and Ⓖ **Ninomaru,** a beautiful Japanese garden. Just beyond Ninomaru you'll find the Ⓗ **Sannomaru Shozokan,** a free museum with rotating exhibits of imperial treasures. Don't miss the Ⓘ **Hyakunin Bansho Guardhouse,** which once housed the ninja who kept (martial) law and order in old Edo.

The outer palace grounds, or Ⓙ **Kokyo Gaien,** are the best vantage point from which to view Nijubashi ("Double Bridge"), a popular photo op for visitors to the city. Trivia: The name comes from the fact that it was once a two-story wooden structure, not from the double arches. ⏱ 2 hr. Chiyoda 1-1, Chiyoda-ku. ☎ 03/3213-1111. http://sankan.kunaicho.go.jp/english/guide/koukyo.html. Free. Tues–Thurs and Sat–Sun 9am–5pm (to 4:30pm Mar to mid-Apr and Sept–Oct; to 4pm Nov–Feb). Closed Dec 23 and Dec 28–Jan 3. Subway: Otemachi, Takebashi, or Nijubashimae stations.

Tokyo's Top Museums

Tokyo boasts more museums than any other city in Japan.
Some are large and elaborate facilities of the sort seen in major cities all over the world. Others are smaller affairs. And more than a few were created by individuals in service of some quirky passion or interest. The following represents some of the city's best . . . and a few of its weirdest. You'll need to get an early start for this 3-day itinerary, so make sure you get to the first stop as soon as the museum opens.

> A display at the Edo-Tokyo Museum.

START Take the Toei Oedo subway line to Ryogoku Station.

① ★ **Edo-Tokyo Museum.** Perfect for architecture and history buffs, this is a one-stop shop for information about the founding and development of the city of Tokyo. It's also one of the few Tokyo museums that offers free English-language tours. (You need to place a request no later than 2 weeks ahead of time.) See p. 58, **③**.

② ★★★ **Tokyo National Museum.** *The* museum to see in Tokyo—it's both the largest and oldest museum in Japan and boasts the largest collection of Japanese art in the world. It consists of five buildings: The **Japanese Gallery (Honkan),** arguably the best, contains all manner of Japanese art from ceramics to samurai armor to calligraphy; the **Asian Gallery (Toyokan)** displays art and archaeological artifacts from everywhere else in Asia (closed for renovation until 2012); the **Heiseikan** gallery of archaeological relics from ancient Japan includes pottery and Haniwa clay burial figurines; the **Gallery of Horyu-ji Treasures** houses priceless Buddhist statues, ceremonial masks, lacquerware, and paintings from the temple of the same name in Nara; and the **Hyokeikan** is used for special exhibitions that usually have a separate entrance fee (it now holds some items from the closed-for-renovation Toyokan). The museum complex is a literal treasure trove of relics from Japan's past—items are shown on a rotating basis with about

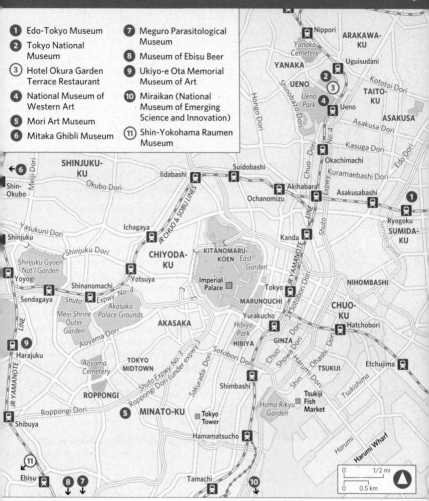

1. Edo-Tokyo Museum
2. Tokyo National Museum
3. Hotel Okura Garden Terrace Restaurant
4. National Museum of Western Art
5. Mori Art Museum
6. Mitaka Ghibli Museum
7. Meguro Parasitological Museum
8. Museum of Ebisu Beer
9. Ukiyo-e Ota Memorial Museum of Art
10. Miraikan (National Museum of Emerging Science and Innovation)
11. Shin-Yokohama Raumen Museum

3,000 on display at any one time, so no matter how many times you visit the museum, you'll always see something new. The special exhibitions also change frequently, and are very much worth paying extra to see. Devotees of antiques could easily spend a whole day here. ⏲ 2 hr. 13-9 Ueno Park, Taito-ku. ☎ 03/5405-8686 or 03/3822-1111. www.tnm.jp/en. ¥600 adults, ¥400 college students, free for seniors 70 and over (except during special exhibitions)

Travel Tip

Note that many museums are closed on Mondays.

and kids 18 and under. Tues-Sun 9:30am-5pm (Fri to 8pm; weekends and holidays Apr-Sept to 6pm). Subway: Ueno Station.

---

③ 🍽 **Hotel Okura Garden Terrace Restaurant.** Located inside the Tokyo National Museum's Gallery of Horyu-ji Treasures, this is an elegant (if slightly expensive) spot to stop for a bite to eat on museum grounds. The bilingual menu focuses on Western-style dishes such as smoked salmon and beef stroganoff. 13-9 Ueno Park, Taito-ku. ☎ 03/3827-7600. Lunch entrees from ¥1,300. MC, V. Lunch & dinner Tues-Sun. Subway: Ueno Station.

> *An ancient "Dogu" statue in the Tokyo National Museum.*

4 National Museum of Western Art. An interesting counterpoint to the Japanese artworks on display in the nearby Tokyo National Museum (see above), this museum explores Western art chronologically, beginning with old masters and working its way up to abstract expressionists like Pollock. Its collection of Rodin sculptures is one of the world's largest and includes renowned masterpieces such as *The Thinker*. ⏱ 2 hr. Ueno Park, Taito-ku. ☎ 03/3828-5131. www.nmwa.go.jp. ¥420 adults, ¥130 college students, free for kids 17 and under and seniors; special exhibits require separate admission fee. Free admission to permanent collection on the 2nd and 4th Sat of every month. Tues–Sun 9:30am–5pm (Fri to 8pm). Subway: Ueno Station.

5 Mori Art Museum. This state-of-the-art gallery perched on the 53rd floor of the Roppongi Hills Mori Tower features innovative exhibitions of contemporary art from around the world and hosts regular lectures from visiting artists. On clear days, the view from the museum's included Tokyo City View observatory is worth the price of admission in and of itself. ⏱ 90 min. 6-10-1 Roppongi, Minato-ku. ☎ 03/5777-8600. www.mori.art.museum. ¥1,500 adults, ¥1,000 college and high-school students, ¥500 kids. Wed–Mon 10am–10pm, Tues 10am–5pm. Subway: Roppongi Station.

6 ★ kids Mitaka Ghibli Museum. Dedicated to the films of Studio Ghibli, this is a must-see for fans of *anime* and manga. Located just outside of relaxing Inokashira Park, it is designed with children in mind but is absolutely appealing for visitors of all ages. The one catch is that you can't just drop by. Be aware that visits need to be arranged in advance, either through a foreign travel agency before you make your trip (highly recommended) or via a Lawson convenience store in Japan (a complicated process that requires some knowledge of Japanese). ⏱ 2 hr. 1-1-83 Shimorenjaku, Mitaka-shi. ☎ 0570/055-777. www.ghibli-museum.jp. ¥1,000 adults, ¥700 kids ages 13–18, ¥400 kids ages 7–12, ¥100 kids ages 4–6. Wed–Mon 10am–6pm. Train: Mitaka Station.

7 Meguro Parasitological Museum. Billed as the "world's only parasitological museum," this offbeat attraction isn't for the squeamish. Its small two floors are packed with replicas and more than 300 actual pickled specimens of various critters extracted from unfortunate victims' bodies. The gift shop, which sells stomach-churning photo books, T-shirts, tote bags, and key chains adorned with parasite motifs, is not to be missed. ⏱ 1 hr. 4-1-1 Shimo-meguro, Meguro-ku. ☎ 03/3716-1264. www.kiseichu.org. Free. Tues–Sun 10am–5pm. Subway: Meguro Station.

8 ★★ Museum of Ebisu Beer. After all those parasites, you're going to need a stiff drink. This museum is dedicated to Japan's oldest brand of premium beer. Although it doesn't offer free samples, the "Tasting Salon" at the end of the tour offers very reasonably priced flights of seasonal and limited-edition Yebisu beers, along with finger foods. ⏱ 1 hr. 4-20-1

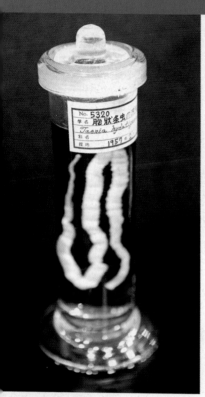

A resident of the Meguro Parasitological Museum.

...bisu (Ebisu Garden Place building), Shibuya-ku. ☎ 03/5423-7255. www.sapporobeer.jp/english/guide/yebisu. Free. Tues–Sun 11am–7pm (last entry to museum 5:10pm; last tasting salon order 6:30pm). Subway: Ebisu Station.

9 ★ **Ukiyo-e Ota Memorial Museum of Art** (太田記念美術館). This small, homey museum [i]s dedicated solely to the art of the Japanese *ukiyo-e* (woodblock print). A must for fans of the medium, it is also highly recommended for those into *anime* and manga, as *ukiyo-e* represent a fascinating bridge between traditional and modern illustrative styles. Only a fraction of the museum's 12,000-plus print collection is on display at any time, rotated through themed exhibitions that change on a monthly basis. ⏱ 1 hr. 1-10-10 Jingumae, Shibuya-ku. ☎ 03/3403-0880. www.ukiyoe-ota-muse.jp. Admission fee varies by exhibition. Tues–Sun 10:30am–5:30pm. Closed the last week of many months. Subway: Meiji-Jingumae Station.

10 ★ kids **Miraikan (National Museum of Emerging Science and Innovation).** Literally meaning "Hall of the Future," this museum of science and technology is housed in a strikingly modern building. With its many interactive exhibits, friendly staff, and exhibitions of cutting-edge technology such as Honda's "Asimo" humanoid robot, this is a great place for families to spend a morning or afternoon. This also means it is packed to the gills on weekends and holidays, so plan accordingly. ⏱ 2½ hr. 2-41 Aomi, Koto-ku. ☎ 03/3570-9151. www.miraikan.jst.go.jp. ¥600 adults, ¥200 kids. Wed–Mon 10am–5pm. Train: Telecom Center or Fune no Kagakukan stations.

11 🍜 **Shin-Yokohama Raumen Museum.** A must-visit for connoisseurs of the iconic ramen noodle dish, this Yokohama-based museum chronicles the spread of ramen's popularity from the port city throughout the islands of Japan. Its centerpiece is a detailed, life-sized re-creation of a 1950s Tokyo *shitamachi* (downtown) street scene, complete with nine different ramen shops selling unique variations on the dish. ⏱ 90 min. 2-14-21 Shin-Yokohama, Kohoku-ku, Yokohama. ☎ 045/471-0503. www.raumen.co.jp/ramen. ¥300 adults, ¥100 kids 12 and under and seniors. Mon–Fri 11am–9:45pm, Sat–Sun 10:30am–9:45pm. Train: Shin-Yokohama Station.

> *The '60s survive in the Shin-Yokohama Raumen Museum.*

A Walk Through Asakusa

You could easily spend an afternoon or an entire day exploring the nooks and crannies of this historic neighborhood. In centuries past, up until World War II, this was the center of the city's nightlife. Today it is far better known as a tourist attraction for visitors domestic and foreign. The relaxed—one might even say rundown—working-class atmosphere plays an appealing counterpoint to the polished skyscrapers of Shinjuku and Shibuya. Asakusa remains a bastion of "old Tokyo" charm.

> Senso-ji's distinctive temple architecture.

START Take the Ginza or Toei Asakusa subway line to Asakusa Station.

❶ Asahi Beer Tower. This distinctive office complex became a modern-day icon of the Asakusa area when it was unveiled in 1989. The white cap on the golden tower evokes foam atop a glass of beer. The mysterious blob on the lower structure, designed by Philippe Starck, is supposed to symbolize the brewer's "dynamic heart," though locals and visitors frequently compare it to other, less palatable things. You don't really need to get up close and personal to appreciate it, but should you feel like wandering across the river, the building complex houses a series of brewpubs, bars, and restaurants. 1-25-1 Azumabashi, Sumida-ku. Subway: Asakusa Station.

❷ Kaminarimon. The unmistakable symbol of Asakusa. This imposing gate and its massive paper lantern is the classic photo op in the area and a popular meeting spot for locals and visitors alike. In keeping with its name, which

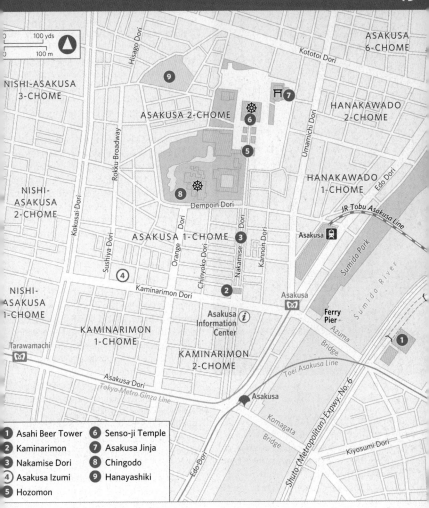

1 Asahi Beer Tower
2 Kaminarimon
3 Nakamise Dori
4 Asakusa Izumi
5 Hozomon
6 Senso-ji Temple
7 Asakusa Jinja
8 Chingodo
9 Hanayashiki

translates into "Thunder Gate," it is flanked by equally massive wooden statues of the god of wind and the god of thunder. **Senso-ji Temple,** 2-3-1 Asakusa, Taito-ku. Subway: Asakusa Station.

3 **Nakamise Dori.** Where else but Tokyo would shopping lead directly to spiritual enlightenment? Although it gets almost unbearably crowded on weekends, the Nakamise shopping arcade is a must-visit because it's both fun and historic: Its roots extend back to the 17th century, making it one of the oldest shopping centers in Japan. Dozens of vendors

of souvenirs and traditional foods line the street for a good quarter of a kilometer (more than 800 ft.). You'll want to take plenty of time so that you can browse and sample the treats—everything from fresh-made *senbei* (rice crackers) to Godzilla toys are on sale here. While the snacks are great and it's a quick fix for fun gifts, the quality of souvenir items is very much tourist-grade; you'll probably want to spend your money elsewhere if you're searching for fine art or collectible antiques. But Nakamise is far from the only game

> A popular meeting spot: Kaminarimon Gate.

❺ Hozomon. The "Treasure-House Gate" at the end of Nakamise Dori leads directly into Senso-ji Temple (see below). The very first gate on this spot was built well over a thousand years ago; over the centuries it has been rebuilt many times into its present form. The name isn't for show; this modern incarnation of the gate was constructed from flame-resistant materials and serves as the repository for the temple's priceless sutras and scriptures. It is flanked by a pair of statues of guardian deities called Nio. Don't miss the giant 400kg (882-lb.) straw sandals displayed on the back of the gate—they're a symbol of the size and power of the guardians protecting the temple. Senso-ji Temple, 1-3-1 Asakusa, Taito-ku. Subway: Asakusa Station.

❻ ★★★ Senso-ji Temple. A fixture in the area centuries before Tokyo was the capital city, or even known as Tokyo, Senso-ji Temple is Tokyo's oldest. It is also known as **Asakusa Kannon Temple,** as it venerates Kannon, the bodhisattva of mercy. According to a legend that is portrayed in a series of paintings displayed at the end of Nakamise Dori, the temple was founded in A.D. 628 by a pair of brothers who netted a golden statue of Kannon while fishing in nearby Sumida River. The statue actually exists—in fact, it's specifically to the statue that pilgrims are paying their respects—but don't expect to catch a glimpse, as it is not on display to the public.

Features within the temple complex include a beautiful example of a traditional five-story pagoda, all the more striking for being silhouetted against a backdrop of modern skyscrapers. A counter selling fortunes extends on the right side of the approach to the temple. Just before hitting the stairs to ascend to the worshipping area, you will encounter a large pot filled with sticks of burning incense. Visitors traditionally "bathe" themselves in the smoke from the incense, cupping it and waving it over their bodies, before approaching the temple. Even if you aren't religious yourself, don't hesitate to peek inside the temple itself, which features a resplendent dais and altar. ⏱ 2 hr. 1-3-1 Asakusa, Taito-ku. Free. Daily 6:30am–5pm. Subway: Asakusa Station.

in town when it comes to shopping in Asakusa. Not only are the streets parallel to Nakamise filled with **covered shopping arcades,** so too are the ones that branch off to the left and right from the main drag. This arrangement is typical of shopping centers in Japan, which tend to take the form of long covered passages rather than malls. The stores and restaurants on these side streets tend to be just the tiniest bit less touristy than those of Nakamise, so if you don't find what you're looking for there, feel free to peel off in search of adventure. Subway: Asakusa Station.

④ 🍴 ★★ **Asakusa Izumi.** This teahouse and confectionery specializes in traditional Japanese sweets, including *kaki-gori* (shaved ice) and *anmitsu* (sweet adzuki beans and cubes of agar jelly). 1-8-6 Asakusa, Taito-ku. ☎ 03/5806-1620. www.asakusa-izumi.co.jp. Desserts from ¥740. No credit cards. Lunch & dinner daily. Subway: Asakusa Station.

7 ★ **Asakusa Jinja.** Senso-ji is a Buddhist temple. Asakusa Jinja is a shrine of the native Japanese religion of Shinto. Actually a complex of smaller shrines, it was built far more recently than the temple—in 1649, to be exact. It deifies the two brothers who found the Kannon statue housed in Senso-ji. Worth a visit in its own right, it also happens to be an excellent vantage point for photographing the temple. **2-26-1 Asakusa, Taito-ku. Subway: Asakusa Station.**

8 **Chingodo.** This little-known side-temple of the Senso-ji complex venerates the *tanuki* (raccoon dog), a real-life animal that is portrayed as a trickster in Japanese folklore. (Statues of the rotund and well-endowed creatures are common good-luck charms throughout Japan, and a mascot of this neighborhood in particular.) You won't spend more than a few minutes here, but the quiet garden filled with *tanuki* statues is a lighthearted respite from the crowds outside. **2-3-1 Asakusa, Taito-ku. Subway: Asakusa Station.**

9 kids **Hanayashiki.** A pocket-sized urban amusement park that has, truthfully, seen better days, Hanayashiki (which means "Flower Mansion") is a local institution. Built in 1853 as a garden for aristocrats, over the years it has continually re-invented itself in an often-losing struggle to keep up with the times. In addition to a series of small-scale rides of the sort you might find at a fairground, it hosts regular live ninja and *anime*-character shows that are popular with the little ones. ⏱ 1 hr. **2-28-1 Asakusa, Taito-ku. ☎ 043/3842-8780. www.hanayashiki.net/e/index.html. ¥900 adults, ¥400 kids 5-12 and seniors, free for kids 4 and under. Wed–Mon 10am–6pm (to 5pm in winter). Subway: Asakusa Station.**

> The incense brazier at Senso-ji Temple.

Pop Culture Tokyo

In recent years, youth of the world have flocked to Tokyo for a taste of the fictional wonderlands portrayed in the nation's epic manga (comic book) and *anime* (animated) creations. Although stores and sites dedicated to these subcultures abound throughout the city, several neighborhoods in particular boast particularly deep associations to them: Akihabara, Nakano, and Ikebukuro. Here's a (very) brief tour of must-hit places for any dyed-in-the-wool fan of Japanese pop culture. A word of warning: The vast majority of shops catering to *otaku* (fans of *anime* and manga) open late, so you may want to time your visits for the afternoon.

> Akihabara is a tech and otaku wonderland.

START Take the Hibiya subway line to Akihabara Station.

❶ Yodobashi-Akiba. The flagship store of the Yodobashi electronics chain opens at 9:30am, making it a convenient first stop for early birds. (The majority of shops in Akihabara don't open until 11am.) The top floors boast an incredible selection of video games, action figures, toys, and model kits. 1-1 Kanda Hanaoka-Cho, Chiyoda-ku. ☎ 03/5309-1010. www.yodobashi-akiba.com. Daily 9:30am–10pm. Subway: Akihabara Station.

❷ UDX Anime Center. A tiny museum that offers a multilingual history about the *anime* industry. It includes a 3-D theater, a gift shop, and a recording studio that is used to demonstrate how *anime* shows are dubbed. 4-14-1 Sotokanda, Chiyoda-ku. ☎ 03/5298-1188. www.animecenter.jp/eng. Free. Tues–Sun 11am–7pm. Subway: Akihabara Station.

❸ Mandarake Complex. If you have time to visit only one *otaku* shop in the city, this should be it. The largest store in the Mandarake chain, it offers an astounding variety of "gently used" *anime* and manga paraphernalia, including books, DVDs, and toys from recent to antique. See p. 79.

④ 🍺@Home Cafe. A classic Akihabara-style maid cafe: Costumed waitresses flatter, pirouette, and play little games with the customers. Check the website for information about English-speaking maids. 1-11-4 Sotokanda, Chiyoda-ku. ☎ 03/3255-2808. www.cafe-athome.com. Entrees ¥450–¥1,200. No credit cards. Lunch & dinner daily. Subway: Akihabara Station.

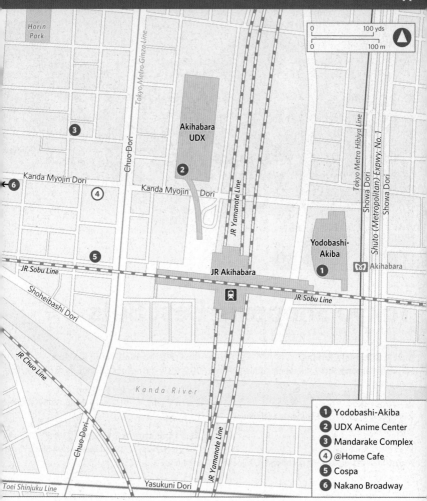

1 Yodobashi-Akiba
2 UDX Anime Center
3 Mandarake Complex
4 @Home Cafe
5 Cospa
6 Nakano Broadway

5 **Cospa.** Even if you aren't into this shop's specialty of "cosplay," the subculture of dressing up like an *anime* character, it also happens to be a great place to pick up *anime*-themed T-shirts and other gear. 1–10–11 Sotokanda, Chiyoda-ku. ☎ 03/5207-6842. www.cospa.com. Daily 11am–8pm. Subway: Akihabara Station.

6 **Nakano Broadway.** A guidebook could easily be written on this shopping complex alone. The building is located at the end of an otherwise normal-seeming shopping street just outside the north exit of Nakano Station. It is a multi-floor extravaganza of shops devoted to *otaku* themes, from comic books to toys and models and cosplay gear. 5–52–15 Nakano, Nakano-ku. ☎ 03/3388-7004. www.bwy.jp. Subway: Nakano Station.

Guided Walking Tours

As an alternative to this self-guided tour, the **Akihabara Tourism Promotion Association,** 3-13-12 Soto-Kanda, Chiyoda-ku (☎ 03/3253-9193; http://akihabara-tour.com), open 11am to 6pm daily, offers free, guided English-language walking tours of Akihabara. The schedule is irregular, so check the website for the most up-to-date information about activities in the area.

Tokyo Shopping Best Bets

Best Traditional Clothing
Hayashi Kimono, 2-1-1 Yurakucho, Chiyoda-ku (see p. 84)

Best Bookshop
Kinokuniya, 5-24-2 Sendagaya, Shinjuku-ku (see p. 82)

Best Antique Furniture
Kurofune Antiques, 7-7-4 Roppongi, Minato-ku (see p. 79)

Best All-in-One *Anime* **& Manga Shop**
Mandarake Complex, 3-11-12 Sotokanda, Chiyoda-ku (see p. 79)

Best Flea Market
Oedo Antique Market, 3-5-1 Marunouchi, Chiyoda-ku (see p. 82)

Best Off-the-Wall Youth Fashion
109, 2-29-1 Dogenzaka, Shibuya-ku (see p. 82)

Best Contemporary Fashion
Parco Part 1, 15-1 Udagawa-cho, Shibuya-ku (see p. 82)

Best Housewares & Hobbies Store
Tokyu Hands, 12-18 Udagawa-cho, Shibuya-ku (see p. 82)

Best All-Around Electronics Shop
Yodobashi-Akiba, 1-1 Kanda Hanaoka-Cho, Chiyoda-ku (see p. 76)

> *Bric-a-brac on display at Tokyu Hands.*

Tokyo Shopping A to Z

Anime & Manga

★ Mandarake Complex AKIHABARA

The secondhand *anime*- and manga-related ephemera, from comic books and DVDs to dolls, figures, monsters, and robot toys, fills up an entire building here. **Note:** Take care if visiting with small children, as the fourth and fifth floors contain a lot of adult material. 3-11-12 Sotokanda, Chiyoda-ku. ☎ 03/3252-7007. www.mandarake.co.jp/shop/index_cmp.html. AE, MC. Subway: Akihabara Station.

Antiques & Art

Antique Mall Ginza GINZA

As the name implies, rather than a single store this is actually a collection of individual specialty dealers under one roof. Although most focus on Japanese antiquities and folk art, some dealers carry a selection of American and European items as well. 1-13-1 Ginza, Chuo-ku. ☎ 03/3535-2115. www.antiques-jp.com/e-shop.html. Credit card acceptance varies by dealer. Subway: Ginza Station.

Japan Traditional Craft Center IKEBUKURO

A combination museum and boutique, this center showcases traditional ceramic, fabric, woodwork, and metalwork products. A fun visit even if you are only window-shopping. Metropolitan Plaza, 1-11-1 Nishi Ikebukuro, Toshima-ku. ☎ 03/5954-6066. www.kougei.or.jp/english/center.html. MC, V. Subway: Ikebukuro Station.

Kurofune Antiques ROPPONGI

Founded by an American, this is a great place for those seeking English-language antiquing advice. It carries a wide variety of furniture and ephemera. 7-7-4 Roppongi, Minato-ku. ☎ 03/3479-1552. www.kurofuneantiques.com. No credit cards. Subway: Roppongi Station.

Yamada Shoten JIMBOCHO

Founded in 1938, this is the spot to shop for *ukiyo-e* (woodblock prints). The drawers here overflow with specimens ranging from the tattered and cheap to mind-boggling rarities. 1-8 Jimbocho, Chiyoda-ku. ☎ 03/3295-0252. www.yamada-shoten.com. No credit cards. Subway: Jimbocho Station.

> *Kinokuniya is a one-stop shop for English-language books about Japan.*

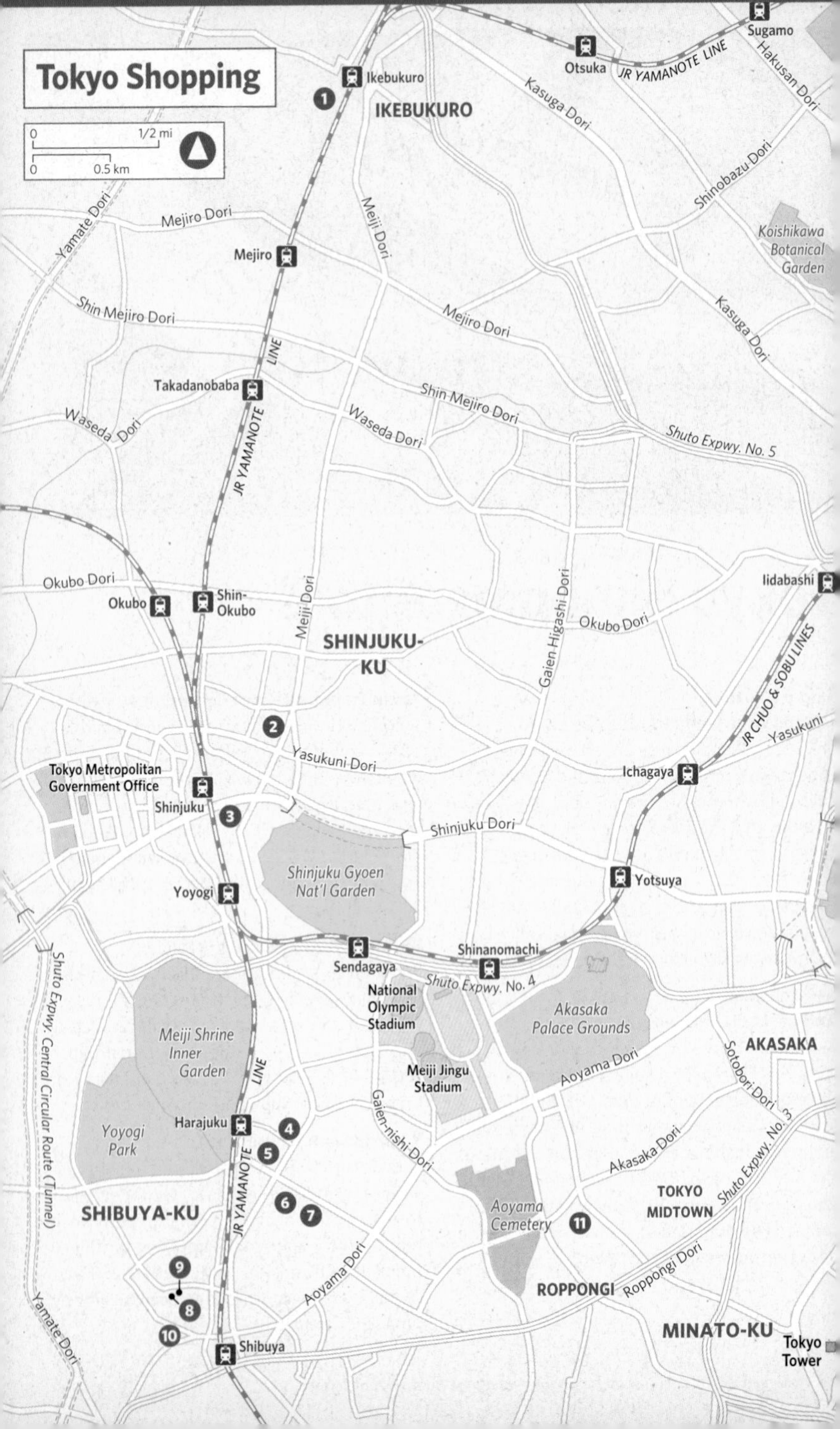

Tokyo Shopping

0 —— 1/2 mi
0 —— 0.5 km

1 Ikebukuro

IKEBUKURO

Sugamo
Hakusan Dori
Otsuka   JR YAMANOTE LINE

Kasuga Dori

Shinobazu Dori

Koishikawa Botanical Garden

Mejiro Dori

Mejiro

Mejiro Dori

Meiji Dori

Kasuga Dori

Shin Mejiro Dori

Takadanobaba

Shin Mejiro Dori

Waseda Dori

Waseda Dori

Shuto Expwy. No. 5

JR YAMANOTE LINE

Okubo Dori

Okubo   Shin-Okubo

Okubo Dori

Iidabashi

Meiji Dori

SHINJUKU-KU

Galen Higashi Dori

JR CHUO & SOBU LINES

2

Yasukuni Dori

Ichagaya

Yasukuni

Tokyo Metropolitan Government Office

Shinjuku

3

Shinjuku Dori

Shinjuku Dori

Yoyogi

Shinjuku Gyoen Nat'l Garden

Yotsuya

Shinanomachi

Sendagaya   Shuto Expwy. No. 4

National Olympic Stadium

Akasaka Palace Grounds

AKASAKA

Meiji Shrine Inner Garden

Meiji Jingu Stadium

Aoyama Dori

Sotobori Dori

Shuto Expwy. Central Circular Route (Tunnel)

Harajuku   **4**

Galen-nishi Dori

Akasaka Dori

Akasaka Dori

TOKYO MIDTOWN

Shuto Expwy. No. 3

5

Yoyogi Park

JR YAMANOTE LINE

6 **7**

Aoyama Cemetery

11

Roppongi Dori

ROPPONGI

SHIBUYA-KU

9

8

Aoyama Dori

10

Shibuya

Yamate Dori

MINATO-KU   Tokyo Tower

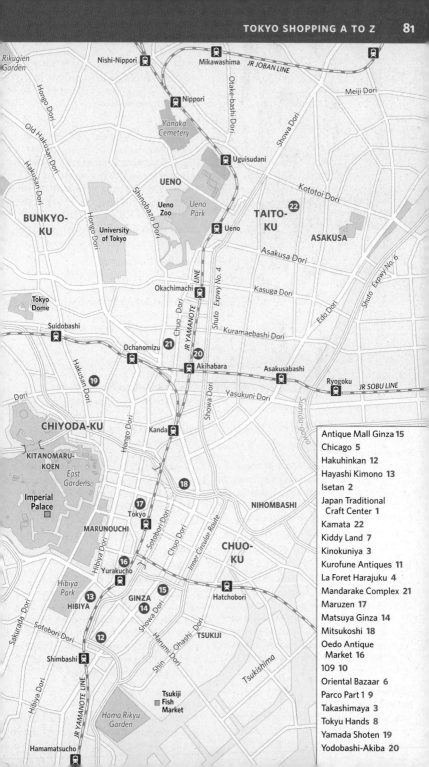

Antique Mall Ginza 15

Chicago 5

Hakuhinkan 12

Hayashi Kimono 13

Isetan 2

Japan Traditional
  Craft Center 1

Kamata 22

Kiddy Land 7

Kinokuniya 3

Kurofune Antiques 11

La Foret Harajuku 4

Mandarake Complex 21

Maruzen 17

Matsuya Ginza 14

Mitsukoshi 18

Oedo Antique
  Market 16

109 10

Oriental Bazaar 6

Parco Part 1 9

Takashimaya 3

Tokyu Hands 8

Yamada Shoten 19

Yodobashi-Akiba 20

> *Shibuya's youth fashion mecca: 109.*

Books
Kinokuniya SHINJUKU
There are many outlets of this well-known international chain of bookstores in Tokyo, but the biggest can be found in the Times Square building on the south side of Shinjuku station. 5-24-2 Sendagaya. ☎ 03/5361-3301. www.kinokuniya.co.jp. AE, MC, V. Subway: Shinjuku Station.

Maruzen TOKYO
Founded in 1870, this shop carries a large selection of English as well as Japanese books. Its English-language section, on the fourth floor, is huge and well laid out, with everything from dictionaries to travel guides to special-interest books on Japan. 1-6-4 Marunouchi, Chiyoda-ku. ☎ 03/5288-8881. www.maruzen.co.jp. MC, V. Subway: Tokyo Station.

Contemporary Fashion
La Foret Harajuku HARAJUKU
A combination museum space and department store located in the heart of Japan's fashion district. Particularly popular with trendy young women, it is home to many of Japan's top brands. 1-11-6 Jingumae, Shibuya-ku. ☎ 03/3475-0411. www.laforet.ne.jp. AE, MC V. Train: Harajuku Station.

109 SHIBUYA
This trend-setting tower/department store divided into boutiques is a mecca for the *gyaru* ("gal") subculture of young women who obsess over the season's newest styles and fashions. A companion store down the street, **109-2,** targets their boyfriends. 2-29-1 Dogenzaka, Shibuya-ku. ☎ 03/3477-5160. www.shibuya109.jp. Credit card acceptance varies by boutique. Subway: Shibuya Station.

Parco Part 1 SHIBUYA
This hip shopping complex focuses on the latest fashions for men and women. Nearby **Parco Part 3** features fashions for kids plus a selection of interior and lifestyle items. 15-1 Udagawa-cho, Shibuya-ku. ☎ 03/3464-5111. www.parco.co.jp. AE, MC, V. Subway: Shibuya Station.

Flea Market
★★★ Oedo Antique Market GINZA
Held on the first and third Sunday of every month from 9am to 4pm, this is your opportunity to purchase all sorts of antiques direct from the sellers, from kimono and pottery to woodblock prints and dolls. If there's any downside, it is that the prime location (right next to the Ginza) comes with prices to match—but there are bargains to be found. 3-5-1 Marunouchi (Tokyo International Forum Square), Chiyoda-ku. ☎ 03/6407-6011. www.antique-market.jp/eng. No credit cards. Subway Yurakucho Station.

Housewares & Hobbies
★★★ Tokyu Hands SHIBUYA
A trendy "general store" of housewares, gadgets, and gizmos beloved by locals and tourists alike, Tokyu Hands is also a repository of materials for hobbyists, craft lovers, and do-it-yourselfers. 12-18 Udagawa-cho, Shibuya-ku. ☎ 03/5361-3111. www.tokyu-hands.co.jp. AE, MC, V. Subway: Shibuya Station.

Department Stores
★ Isetan SHINJUKU
A Tokyo favorite for 120 years, Isetan features a broad selection of fashions from major designers. Its basement floor, filled with gourmet foods

Isetan's basement floor is filled with gourmet goodies.

nd confectioneries, is legendary. 3-14-1 Shin-
uku, Shinjuku-ku. ☎ 03/3352-1111. www.isetan.
o.jp. AE, MC, V. Subway: Shinjuku Station.

Matsuya Ginza GINZA
Matsuya is a particularly design-focused department store with a wide selection of Japanese folk items, household goods, and kitchenware in addition to the usual fashions. 3-6-1
Ginza, Chuo-ku. ☎ 03/3567-1211. www.matsuya.
om. AE, MC, V. Subway: Ginza Station.

Mitsukoshi NIHONBASHI
Although there are other branches of Japan's
oldest and best-known department store in
the city, this one is the most distinguished.
Look for kimono, perfumes, and name-brand
items here. 1-4-1 Nihombashi Muromachi,
Chuo-ku. ☎ 03/3241-3311. www.mitsukoshi.
co.jp/nihombashi. AE, MC, V. Subway: Mitsukoshimae Station.

★ **Takashimaya** SHINJUKU
The longtime rival of Mitsukoshi specializes
in tony fashion brands. Its latest branch, in the
Times Square building in Shinjuku, offers 10
solid floors of shopping. 5-24-2 Sendagaya, Shinjuku-ku. ☎ 03/5361-1111. www.takashimaya.co.jp/
shinjuku. AE, MC, V. Subway: Shinjuku Station.

> *Yodobashi is a great place to shop for electronics.*

Electronics & Hobbies
★★ **Yodobashi-Akiba** AKIHABARA
A tower of electronics power right outside of
Akihabara Station. Divided into nine floors by
type of equipment, this is a one-stop shop for
any kind of toys, video games, and consumer
electronics. (Make sure they work in your
home country, though!) See p. 76, ❶.

> Dolls on parade at Hakuhinkan Toy Park.

Kimono & Traditional Clothing

★ Chicago HARAJUKU
Chicago specializes in secondhand clothing of all sorts, but is famed for its selection of gently used kimono at very reasonable prices. 6–31–21 Jingumae, Shibuya-ku. ☎ 03/3409-5017. www.chicago.co.jp. No credit cards. Train: Harajuku Station.

Hayashi Kimono YURAKUCHO
This Tokyo institution is popular for its selection—it sells everything from traditional wedding attire to *yukata* (cotton kimono) to *tanzen* (heavy winter overcoats that go over the *yukata*)—and its reasonable prices. Located conveniently near the Ginza. 2–1–1 Yurakucho, Chiyoda-ku. ☎ 03/3501-4012. AE, MC, V. Subway: Yurakucho Station.

Oriental Bazaar HARAJUKU
This venerable destination has been a favorite of tourists for decades. It is a one-stop shop for general souvenirs ranging from the whimsical to the exquisite. 9–13–5 Jingumae, Shibuya-ku. ☎ 03/3400-3933. www.oriental bazaar.co.jp. AE, MC, V. Train: Harajuku Station.

Kitchenware

Kamata KAPPABASHI
With an astounding selection of the highest quality Japanese cutlery, this should be the first place you go if you're looking for any kind of kitchen knife. 2–12–6 Matsugatani, Taito-ku. ☎ 03/3841-4205. www.hocho.org/english. MC, V. Subway: Asakusa Station.

Toys

Hakuhinkan GINZA
The nine floors of wall-to-wall toys here range from the usual dolls, puzzles, and games to an assortment of gag gifts. It is especially well known for its selection of Licca dolls, Japan's answer to Barbie. There's also an arcade. 8–8–11 Ginza, Chuo-ku. ☎ 03/3571-8008. www.hakuhinkan.co.jp/eng/info.htm. AE, MC, V. Subway: Shimbashi Station.

Geta sandals for sale at Oriental Bazaar.

Destination Shopping

Tokyo is famed for its "themed" shopping districts. Here's where you should go when you want to scratch an itch of a particular type.

Kappabashi: This neighborhood is the spot for all things kitchen-oriented. Everything from industrial refrigerators and uniforms to chopsticks and even those fake-food samples are on sale here.

Jimbocho: The "book district." Stores specialize in Japanese-language texts, of course, but this is a fascinating section of town to wander for bibliophiles. *Note:* It all but shuts down on Sundays and Mondays.

Akihabara: Traditionally known for electronics, it also serves as the center of the *anime* and manga scene.

Harajuku: The mazelike back alleys of Harajuku are riddled with tiny fashion boutiques, while the "main drag" of Omotesando is populated with stores carrying major designer brands.

Ginza: Often compared to New York City's Fifth Avenue, the Ginza has been Tokyo's luxury shopping destination for well over a century. All of the major department stores are anchored here.

Ochanomizu: Mecca for musicians. This section of town is home to many shops specializing in musical instruments, mainly guitars, drums, and synthesizers.

Kiddy Land HARAJUKU

Located in the center of Japan's fashion district, Kiddy Land has been an institution for more than 60 years. Its Hello Kitty and other "cute character" goods selection is second to none. The main shop is undergoing renovations and will reopen in summer of 2012; in the meantime, there is a temporary shop 2 blocks behind the main location. 6–1–9 Jingumae, Shibuya-ku. ☎ 03/3409-3431. www.kiddyland. co.jp/en. MC, V. Train: Harajuku Station.

Tokyo Restaurant Best Bets

Best Asian-French Fusion
La Bombance, 2-25-24 Nishi Azabu, Minato-ku (see p. 90)

Best *Tonkatsu*
Butagumi, 2-24-9 Nishi Azabu, Minato-ku (see p. 87)

Best *Wagyu* Steak
Dons de la Nature, 1-7-6 Ginza, Chuo-ku (see p. 87)

Best Organic/Vegetarian Food
Farmer's Kitchen, 3-5-3 Shinjuku, Shinjuku-ku (see p. 87)

Best Sushi
Kyubei, 8-7-6 Ginza, Chuo-ku (see p. 90)

Best Conveyor-Belt Sushi
Magurobito, 1-5-9 Asakusa, Taito-ku (see p. 90)

Best Ramen
Menya Musashi, 7-2-6 Nishi-Shinjuku, Shinjuku-ku (see p. 91)

Best *Shabu-Shabu*
Shabusen, 5-8-20 Ginza, Chuo-ku (see p. 92)

Best Tempura
Tsunahachi, 3-31-8 Shinjuku, Shinjuku-ku (see p. 93)

Best Place to Catch Your Own Seafood
Zauo, 3-2-9 Nishi-Shinjuku, Shinjuku-ku (see p. 93)

> *Fishing for dinner at Zauo.*

Tokyo Restaurants A to Z

Alcatraz ER (アルカトラズ) SHIBUYA *JAPANESE*
Customers are handcuffed and led to their tables, and drinks are served in test tubes and flasks at this offbeat novelty restaurant with a goth/prison-hospital theme. Meals are periodically interrupted by "prison breaks" portrayed by staff members in hockey masks. -13-5 Dogenzaka, Shibuya-ku. ☎ 03/3770-100. http://alcatraz.hy-system.com. Entrees 700–¥900. AE, DC, MC, V. Dinner daily. Subway: Shibuya Station.

Brown Rice Café (ブラウンライス・カフェ)
MOTESANDO *VEGETARIAN/VEGAN* A rare aven for vegans and vegetarians in a posi-vely meat-obsessed city, this cafe serves up rganic and locally sourced dishes along with you guessed it) brown rice. 5-1-17 Jingumae, hibuya-ku. ☎ 03/5778-5416. www.brown.co.jp. et menu ¥1,680–¥2,100. No credit cards. Lunch dinner daily. Subway: Omotesando Station.

★ **Butagumi** (豚組) NOGIZAKA *TONKATSU*
onkatsu (fried pork cutlet) shops abound in e city. But for a place that's a cut above the

rest (pun intended), try here. Using a special blend of oils to fry a dozen varieties of pork, this is the place to go for lovers of the dish. Lunch is a great way to fill up without spending full dinner prices. 2-24-9 Nishi Azabu, Minato-ku. ☎ 03/5466-6775. www.butagumi.com/nishiazabu. Entrees from ¥1,950. MC, V. Lunch & dinner daily. Subway: Nogizaka Station.

★★★ **Dons de la Nature** GINZA *STEAKHOUSE*
Pricey but well worth every penny, this is one of the few Tokyo steakhouses that serves up prime A5-grade *wagyu* steaks. No smoking. 1-7-6 Ginza, Chuo-ku. ☎ 03/3563-4129. www.dons-nature.jp. Entrees (for two) ¥25,000–¥30,000. AE, DC, MC, V. Dinner Mon–Sat. Subway: Ginza-itchome Station.

★★ **Farmer's Kitchen** (農家の台所) SHINJUKU
MACROBIOTIC This organic, macrobiotic restaurant is dedicated to the locally grown, "farm-to-table" experience. But it caters to vegan and carnivore alike. It's worth paying extra for the all-you-can-eat raw bar, which features all sorts of interesting local veggies.

Brown Rice Cafe.

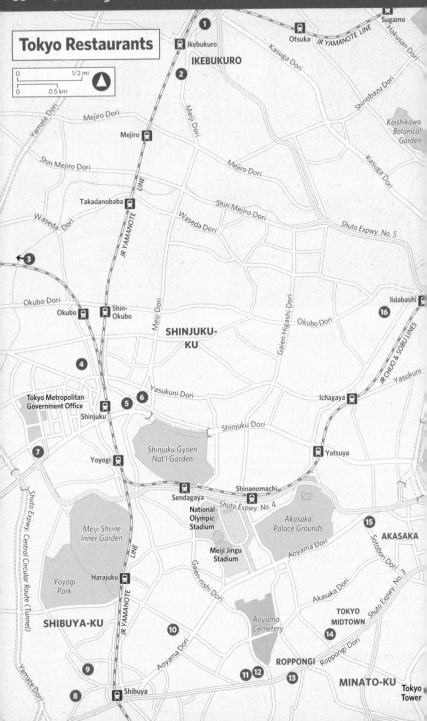

Tokyo Restaurants

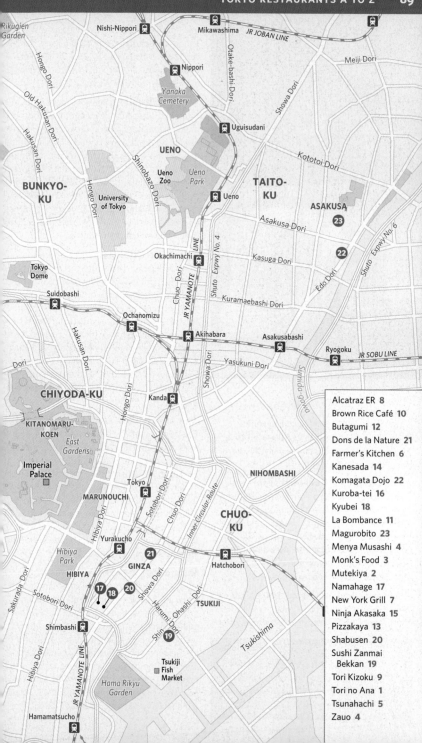

Rikugien Garden
Nishi-Nippori
Mikawashima   JR JOBAN LINE
Meiji Dori
Nippori
Hongo Dori
Old Hakusan Dori
Hakusan Dori
Yanaka Cemetery
Otake-bashi Dori
Showa Dori
Uguisudani
Kototoi Dori
UENO
Ueno Zoo
Ueno Park
TAITO-KU
ASAKUSA
23
BUNKYO-KU
University of Tokyo
Shinobazu Dori
Hongo Dori
University Dori
Asakusa Dori
22
Shuto Expwy No. 6
Okachimachi
Kasuga Dori
Edo Dori
Tokyo Dome
JR YAMANOTE LINE
Chuo Dori
Shuto Expwy No. 4
Kuramaebashi Dori
Suidobashi
Ochanomizu
Akihabara
Asakusabashi
Ryogoku   JR SOBU LINE
Hakusan Dori
Dori
Yasukuni Dori
Showa Dori
Sumida-gawa
CHIYODA-KU
Kanda
Hongo Dori
KITANOMARU-KOEN
East Gardens
NIHOMBASHI
Imperial Palace
Tokyo
MARUNOUCHI
Sotobori Dori
Chuo Dori
CHUO-KU
Inner Circular Route
Hibiya Dori
Yurakucho
Hibiya Park
21
Hatchobori
HIBIYA
GINZA
Showa Dori
Sakurada Dori
17 18 20
Harumi Ohashi Dori
TSUKIJI
Sotobori Dori
Shin
19
Shimbashi
Shuto
JR YAMANOTE LINE
Hibiya Dori
Tsukishima
Tsukiji Fish Market
Hama Rikyu Garden
Hamamatsucho

> Hog heaven: Butagumi.

No smoking. 3-5-3 Shinjuku, Shinjuku-ku. ☎ 03/3226-4831. Entrees ¥1,400–¥2,100. AE, DC, MC, V. Lunch & dinner daily. Subway: Shinjuku-sanchome Station.

★★ Kanesada (兼定) ROPPONGI *SUSHI*
This tiny and somewhat hard to find shop has been a favorite of sushi aficionados ever since the owner, Mr. Nakamura, went independent from Kyubei (see below) years back. 4-4-6 Roppongi, Minato-ku. ☎ 03/3403-3648. Entrees from ¥10,000. No credit cards. Dinner Mon–Sat. Subway: Roppongi Station.

★ Komagata Dojo (駒形どぜう) ASAKUSA *SEAFOOD* Here *dojo* refers to a small, eel-like fish of the loach family that is served whole, often

in a hotpot-style dish. A very traditional, old-school sort of place. 1-7-12 Komagata, Taito-ku ☎ 03/3842-4001. *Dojo* ¥1,250–¥1,650; set menu ¥2,300–¥7,100. AE, DC, MC, V. Lunch & dinner daily. Subway: Asakusa Station.

★★★ Kuroba-tei (久露葉亭) KAGURAZAKA *KAISEKI* Located in the elegant neighborhood of Kagurazaka, Kuroba-tei specializes in *kyo-kaiseki*: Kyoto-style, set-course cuisine. Situated in an old house, the atmosphere is romantic and relaxed. This is slow food at its finest, with multiple handmade courses served over the evening. Reservations required. 3-6-53 Kagurazaka, Shinjuku-ku. ☎ 03/5206-6997. Entrees ¥5,000–¥8,000. AE, DC, MC, V. Lunch & dinner daily. Subway: Iidabashi Station.

★★★ Kyubei (銀座 久兵衛) GINZA *SUSHI*
A Tokyo legend. This is the sort of sushi place Tokyoites bring people they want to impress. Everything from the decor to the food is absolutely picture-perfect. The set *kaiseki* (multicourse) meal in particular is to die for, but you will most definitely pay for the privilege. Reservations highly recommended. No smoking. 8-7-6 Ginza, Chuo-ku. ☎ 03/3571-6523. www.kyubey.jp/index_e.html. Entrees ¥10,000–¥30,000. MC, V. Lunch & dinner Mon–Sat. Subway: Shimbashi Station.

★★★ La Bombance ROPPONGI *ASIAN FUSION*
This award-winning bistro is one of the city's most talked-about eateries. Tucked away in the basement of a nondescript building, it serves up Japanese dishes prepared in a European style from an ever-changing *omakase* (chef's choice) menu. Reservations required. 2-25-24 Nishi-Azabu, Minato-ku. ☎ 03-5778-6511. www.bombance.com. *Omakase* from 10,000 per person. MC, V. Dinner Mon–Sat. Subway: Roppongi Station.

Magurobito (まぐろ人) ASAKUSA *SUSHI*
With a name that means "Tuna Man," you know you're in for a tuna treat. This restaurant is widely considered one of Tokyo's best gourmet *kaiten-zushi* (conveyor-belt sushi) restaurants. Everything is served a la carte off the constantly refreshed conveyor belt, making it the perfect stop for a snack or a full meal. 1-5-9 Asakusa. ☎ 03/3844-8736. www.maguro-bito.jp. Small plates from ¥140. V. Lunch & dinner daily. Subway: Asakusa Station.

Travel Tip

The Tokyo culinary scene is dynamic and constantly changing. If you have your heart set on visiting a particular restaurant or bar, definitely call ahead to make sure it's open.

Menya Musashi, masters of ramen.

Menya Musashi (麺屋武蔵) SHINJUKU *NOODLES* In a city as devoted to ramen as Tokyo, openly declaring a "best" can be a provocative statement. When pressed, though, you'll often hear locals name this ramen shop, whose hearty bowls of noodles and pork exemplify the Tokyo style. 7-2-6 Nishi-Shinjuku, Shinjuku-ku. ☎ 03/3363-4634. www.m634.com/honten.html. Ramen ¥800–¥1,000. No credit cards. Lunch & dinner daily. Subway: Shinjuku Station.

★ **Monk's Foods** KICHIJOJI *MACROBIOTIC* This quiet and relaxing "slow food" restaurant offers just three choices from the macrobiotic set menu: a chicken-based meal, a fish-based meal, or a vegan meal. The "Monk" refers to Thelonious, whose music often fills the air. No smoking. 1-2-4 Komagata, Taito-ku. ☎ 0422/83-3977. Set menus from ¥1,080. No credit cards. Lunch & dinner Thurs–Tues. Subway: Kichijoji Station.

Mutekiya (無敵屋) IKEBUKURO *NOODLES* The tonkotsu (pork-bone broth) at this ramen shop, painstakingly prepared for 20 hours a batch, is considered some of the best in the city. Long lines begin forming far ahead of mealtimes. No smoking. 1-17-1 Minami-Ikebukuro, Toshima-ku. ☎ 03/3982 7656. www.mutekiya.

> *Kyubei's chefs serve up some of the city's best sushi.*

com/world/index.html. Entrees ¥780–¥1,200. No credit cards. Breakfast, lunch, dinner & late-night daily. Subway: Ikebukuro Station.

★ **kids Namahage** (なまはげ) SHIMBASHI *NORTHERN JAPANESE* Named after a ferocious yokai (monster) from far-northern folklore, this

---

Sampling the Sushi

Tokyo's sushi is some of the country's freshest, thanks in large part to the incredible Tsukiji Fish Market (which is worth a visit in and of itself; see p. 56, ❶). There are hundreds upon hundreds of sushi restaurants in the city, which can make picking one a daunting task. You can't miss with our favorites, though, which are sprinkled throughout this section: **Kanesada, Kyubei, Magurobito,** and **Sushi Zanmai Bekkan.**

> *Meet the monsters at Namahage.*

restaurant specializes in cuisine from the Akita region of Japan. Every night at 7:15 and 10, staff dressed as *namahage* (bogeymen) stomp through the restaurant. Reservations recommended. 8-5-6 Ginza, Chuo-ku. ☎ 03/3571-3799. Entrees ¥1,480–¥1,850. Lunch & dinner daily. AE, DC, MC, V. Subway: Shimbashi Station.

★★ New York Grill SHINJUKU *STEAKHOUSE*
One of the city's ritziest restaurants, this institution is located on the 52nd floor of the Park Hyatt Tokyo hotel. With glorious views, live jazz most evenings, and a 1,600-bottle wine cellar, this is luxurious dining to rival any American steakhouse. Weekend brunches are a lot of fun as well. Reservations required. 3-7-1-2 Nishi-Shinjuku, Shinjuku-ku. ☎ 03/5322-1234. Entrees ¥4,800–¥9,000. AE, DC, MC, V. Lunch & dinner daily. Subway: Shinjuku Station.

★ kids Ninja Akasaka AKASAKA *JAPANESE*
Hugely popular with tourists, this gimmicky restaurant is stuffed with little tricks and staffed entirely by costumed "ninja" who perform while they serve. The food is actually above average for an establishment of this sort, but the experience is more about the atmosphere than the cuisine. 2-14-3 Nagatacho, Chiyoda-ku. ☎ 03/5157-3936. www.ninjaakasaka.com. Entrees ¥7,777–¥17,000. AE, DC, MC, V. Dinner daily. Subway: Akasaka-mitsuke Station.

★ kids Pizzakaya ROPPONGI *PIZZA*
The place Tokyoites head to when they simply *must* have an American (California-style) pizza. The menu also includes salads and bar appetizers like chicken wings. 3-1-19 Nishi Azabu, Minato-ku. ☎ 03/3479-8383. www.pizzakaya.com. Pizzas ¥2,240–¥3,530. AE, MC, V. Dinner daily. Subway: Roppongi Station.

★ kids Shabusen (しゃぶせん) GINZA *SHABU-SHABU* Shabusen is heaven for fans of *shabu-shabu*, that iconic Japanese dish in which customers cook paper-thin slices of pork in a fragrant hot pot at their table. The set dinner is enough to satisfy even the heartiest appetites. 5-8-20 Ginza (basement of Ginza Core building), Chuo-ku. ☎ 03/3572-3806. Entrees ¥2,310–¥5,880. AE, DC, MC, V. Lunch & dinner daily. Subway: Ginza Station.

★ Sushi Zanmai Bekkan (すしざんまい別館) TSUKIJI *SUSHI* Right in the heart of Tsukiji. It's worth waiting for a seat at the counter to watch the action. Every so often the chefs ring a bell to announce an "auction" of sushi prepared from a fish removed from the restaurant's central aquarium. (It's the same price as the already fresh sushi prepared from the bar, so feel free to speak up if you like what you see.) 4-10-6 Tsukiji, Chuo-ku. ☎ 03/5148-3737. www.kiyomura.co.jp/sushi-e. Entrees from ¥3,000. No credit cards. Breakfast, lunch & dinner daily. Subway: Tsukiji-shijo Station.

Tori Kizoku (鳥貴族) SHIBUYA YAKITORI
The recently opened branch of Osaka's most popular *yakitori* (grilled chicken skewer) chain. The big draw is the price: Every item on the menu is just ¥280—and it's excellent quality for the money. Open all night. 31-3 Udagawa-cho, 2d floor, Shibuya-ku. ☎ 03/6416-3328. www. torikizoku.co.jp/shops/detail/181. Yakitori ¥280. E, MC, V. Dinner daily. Subway: Shibuya Station.

Tori no Ana (鶏の穴) IKEBUKURO NOODLES
This relative newcomer to the ramen wars (see below) has been wowing customers with its signature dish, a sort of hybrid between ramen and chicken noodle soup. 1-39-20 Higashi-Ikebukuro, Toshima-ku. ☎ 03/3986-8311. Entrees from ¥999. No credit cards. Lunch & dinner daily. Subway: Ikebukuro Station.

Tsunahachi (つな八) SHINJUKU TEMPURA
In Japan, Kyoto is famed as the place to go for the nation's best tempura. But this venerable chain (founded in 1924) gives Kyoto tempura houses a run for their money. Order a la carte or try the reasonably priced seasonal menu to take the guesswork out of ordering. Reservations recommended. 3-31-8 Shinjuku, Shinjuku-ku. ☎ 03/3352-1012. www.tunahachi.co.jp. Entrees from ¥1,995. AE, DC, V. Lunch & dinner daily. Subway: Shinjuku or Shinjuku-sanchome stations.

★★ kids **Zauo** (ざうお新宿) SHINJUKU SEAFOOD
An "only in Japan" sort of restaurant: The interior is situated over a large pool of water that is stocked daily with live seafood from the Tsukiji Fish Market. Customers are provided with nets and fishing rods to hook their meals, which are then prepared to order (grilled, fried, or served as sashimi). It doesn't get any fresher. 3-2-9 Nishi-Shinjuku, Shinjuku-ku. ☎ 03/3343-6622. www.zauo.com/contents/zauo_shinjuku.html. Entrees ¥580–¥9,800. AE, MC, V. Lunch & dinner daily. Subway: Shinjuku Station.

> *Shabusen, Ginza's premier* shabu-shabu *spot.*

The Ramen Wars

Ask a dozen Tokyoites what their favorite ramen joint is and you'll get a dozen different answers. Tokyo's innumerable ramen shops have transformed this humble noodle dish of Chinese origins into a local culinary star. You'll find ramen shops all over the city, occupying roughly the same culinary niche that pizzerias do in America. (In particular, it's a late snack for drinkers after a night on the town.)

In certain downtown areas, multiple competing establishments have sprung up in close proximity to one another in a phenomenon Tokyoites call "ramen *gekisen-ku*"—ramen war zones. One of the most famous is in Ikebukuro, where two of our favorites, **Mutekiya** (p. 91) and **Tori no Ana** (p. 93), battle it out along with dozens more. It's fun to walk through and pick a shop on a whim—with all the competition, it's hard to go wrong.

Many ramen restaurants require customers to purchase tickets from vending machines placed at the front of the shop rather than ordering over the counter. If you're having trouble, just ask a clerk for help.

Tokyo Hotel Best Bets

Best City Views
Cerulean Tower Tokyu Hotel, 26-1 Sakuragao-ka-cho, Shibuya-ku (see p. 95)

Best Boutique Hotel
Claska, 1-3-18 Chuocho, Meguro-ku (see p. 98)

Best Capsule Hotel
Hotel Siesta, 1-8-1 Ebisu, Shibuya-ku (see p. 99)

Best Mid-Priced Hotel
Hotel Gracery Ginza, 7-10-1, Ginza, Chuo-ku (see p. 98)

Best Hotel Garden
Hotel New Otani, 4-1 Kioi-cho, Chiyoda-ku (see p. 98)

Absolute Cheapest Hotel
New Koyo, 2-26-13 Nihonzutsumi, Taito-ku (see p. 100)

Best Love Hotel
P&A Plaza, 1-17-9 Dogenzaka, Shibuya-ku (see p. 100)

Best Luxury Hotel
Park Hyatt Tokyo, 3-7-1-2 Nishi-Shinjuku, Shinkuku-ku (see p. 100)

Best Taste of Japan
Ryokan Shigetsu, 1-31-11 Asakusa, Taito-ku (see p. 100)

Most Intellectual Hotel
Yama no Ue Hotel, 1-1 Surugadai Kanda, Chiyodo-ku (see p. 101)

> *Elegant shared baths at Ryokan Shigetsu.*

Tokyo Hotels A to Z

Asakusa View Hotel ASAKUSA
Towering over the Asakusa skyline, this elegantly modern hotel is the only one of its class in the neighborhood. It's perfect for those who want to experience the old-school charm of Tokyo's Shitamachi (downtown) area without roughing it. And it's just a stone's throw from historic spots like Senso-ji Temple (p. 74, **6**). 3-17-1 Nishi-Asakusa, Taito-ku. ☎ 03/3847-1111. www.viewhotels.co.jp/asakusa. 332 units. Doubles ¥29,400–¥32,555. AE, DC, MC, V. Subway: Asakusa Station.

Asia Center of Japan (Asia Kaikan; アジア会館**)**
AOYAMA It may lack the frills of other hotels, but reasonable prices combined with a central downtown location make the Asia Center a favorite of budget travelers. It has a cafeteria with a breakfast buffet (separate charge) and free in-room Internet access. 8-10-32 Akasaka, Minato-ku. ☎ 03/3402-6111. www.asiacenter.or.jp. 173 units. Doubles ¥8,820–¥11,130. AE, MC, V. Subway: Aoyama-Itchome Station.

Capsule Hotel Asakusa River Side ASAKUSA
One of a handful of capsule hotels (p. 98) that offer accommodations for women as well as men, Asakusa River Side is separated by floor, college-dorm style. A separate fee is charged for storing luggage. Guests can't stay in their capsules during the day—there is a mandatory checkout at 10am. 2-20-4 Kaminarimon, Taito-ku. ☎ 03/3844-5117. www.asakusa-capsule.jp/english. 140 units. Capsules ¥3,000. AE, DC, MC, V. Subway: Asakusa Station.

★★ Cerulean Tower Tokyu Hotel SHIBUYA
This relative newcomer to the Tokyo luxury hotel scene is in the heart of Shibuya. If you want a room with a view (such as Mount Fuji, the skyscrapers of Shinjuku, or the Tokyo Tower) make sure to request it when you book. 26-1 Sakuragaoka-cho, Shibuya-ku. ☎ 03/3476-3000. www.ceruleantower-hotel.com. 411 units. Doubles ¥43,500–¥78,000. AE, DC, MC, V. Subway: Shinjuku Station.

The views from the Cerulean Tower Tokyu Hotel are some of the best in the city.

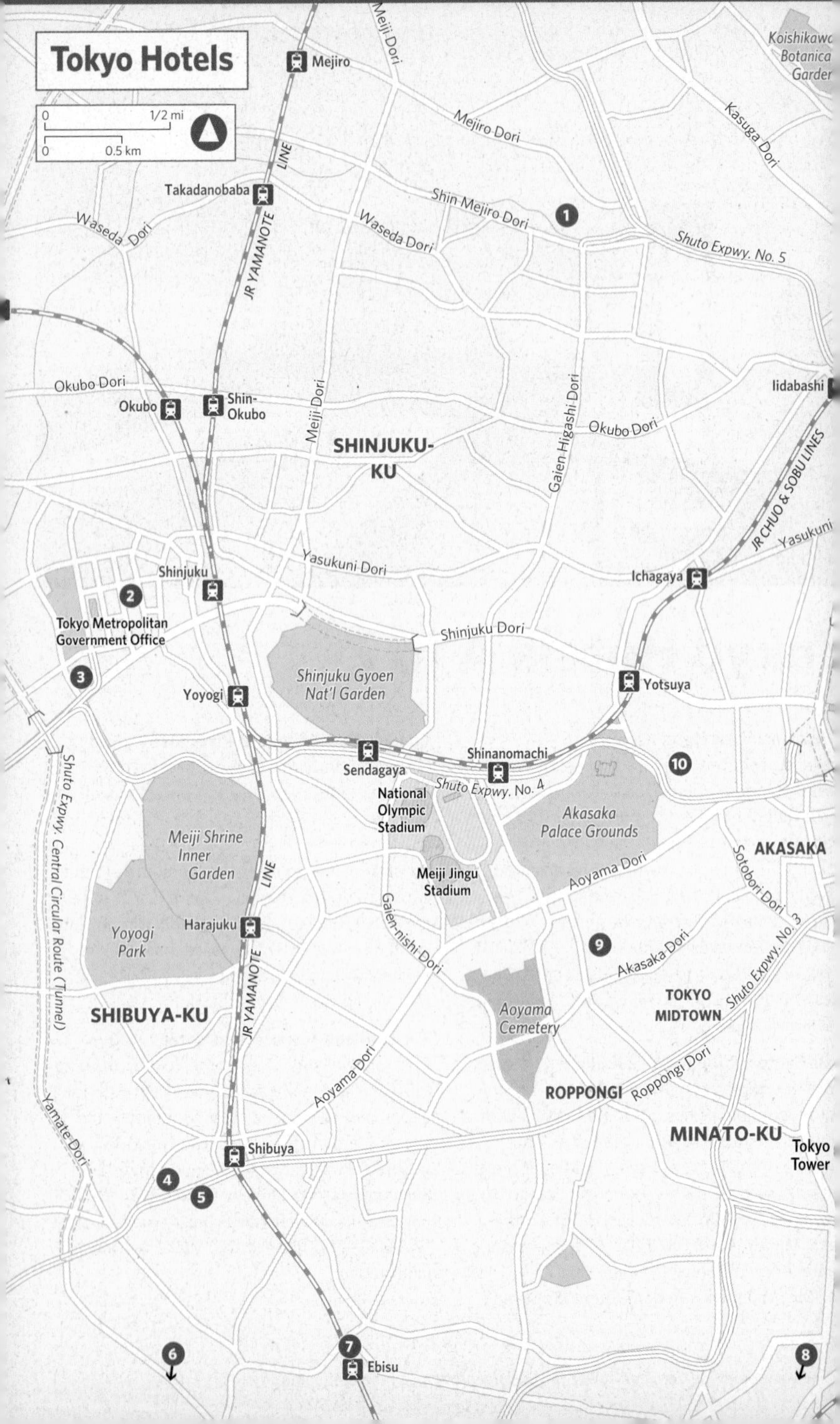

Tokyo Hotels

| 0 | | 1/2 mi |
| 0 | 0.5 km | |

Mejiro

Koishikawa Botanical Garden

Meiji Dori

Mejiro Dori

Takadanobaba

JR YAMANOTE LINE

Shin Mejiro Dori

1

Waseda Dori

Waseda Dori

Shuto Expwy. No. 5

Iidabashi

Okubo Dori

Okubo

Shin-Okubo

Meiji Dori

Gaien Higashi Dori

Okubo Dori

JR CHUO & SOBU LINES

Yasukuni Dori

SHINJUKU-KU

Yasukuni Dori

Ichagaya

JR CHUO & SOBU LINES

Yasukuni

Shinjuku

2

Tokyo Metropolitan Government Office

Shinjuku Dori

Shinjuku Dori

Yotsuya

3

Yoyogi

Shinjuku Gyoen Nat'l Garden

Shinanomachi

10

Shuto Expwy. No. 4

Sendagaya

National Olympic Stadium

Akasaka Palace Grounds

AKASAKA

Aoyama Dori

Meiji Shrine Inner Garden

Meiji Jingu Stadium

Aoyama Dori

Sotobori Dori

Shuto Expwy. No. 3

Shuto Expwy. Central Circular Route (Tunnel)

Harajuku

JR YAMANOTE LINE

Yoyogi Park

Galen-nishi Dori

9

Akasaka Dori

TOKYO MIDTOWN

SHIBUYA-KU

Aoyama Cemetery

Aoyama Dori

Roppongi Dori

ROPPONGI

Yamate Dori

MINATO-KU

Tokyo Tower

Shibuya

4

5

6

7 Ebisu

8

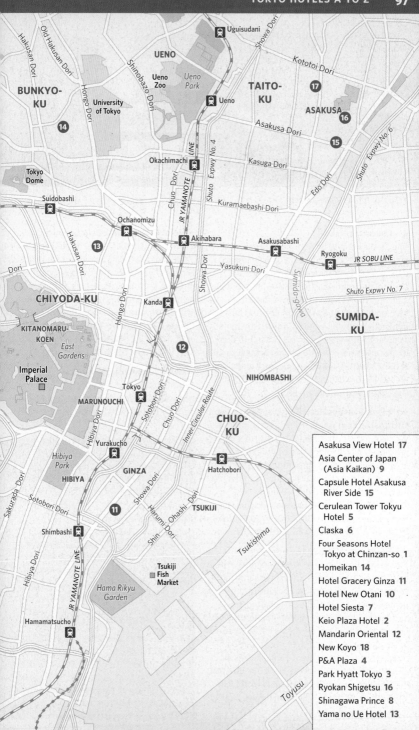

> *Claska: Tokyo's hippest hotel?*

★★ **Claska** MEGURO

The Claska is a hip, tiny boutique hotel with just nine rooms, each having its own unique design. The central location, personalized service, and high-tech feel make this a popular choice with the art and design crowds—in fact, on at least one occasion an artist has booked a room for a gallery show. Due to its popularity and size, it can be difficult to book longer stays here. 1-3-18 Chuocho, Meguro-ku. ☎ 03/3719-8121. www.claska.com. 9 units. Doubles ¥19,950–¥89,250. AE, DC, MC, V. Train: Gakugei-daigaku Station.

★★★ **Four Seasons Hotel Tokyo at Chinzan-so**

EDOGAWABASHI Aside from its rather unfortunate location off the beaten path, this is an absolutely classy place to stay. It features a beautiful garden and a traditional Japanese *onsen* spa fed with mineral water from the Izu Peninsula. 2-10-8 Sekiguchi, Bunkyo-ku. ☎ 03/3943-2222. www.fourseasons.com/tokyo. 259 units. Doubles ¥43,000–¥76,000. AE, DC, MC, V. Subway: Edogawabashi Station.

★★ **Homeikan** (鳳明館) OCHANOMIZU

The best place to experience a traditional *ryokan* (Japanese inn) in Tokyo. Run by the same family for three generations, Homeikan is off the beaten path but offers the sort of atmosphere and tranquility you can't find in Western-style hotels: As with all *ryokan,* rooms have sinks and toilets but no bath or shower; guests use communal (gender-segregated) bath facilities instead. 5-10-5 Hongo, Bunkyo-ku. ☎ 03/3811-1181. www.homeikan.com. 89 units. Doubles ¥11,550–¥12,600. AE, DC, MC, V. Subway: Kasuga Station.

★ **Hotel Gracery Ginza** GINZA

The rooms are on the small side here, but you can't beat the location, right in the heart of the Ginza. Bright rooms with ample windows and modern amenities make this a hit with business travelers as well as tourists. The hotel offers an entire ladies-only floor. 7-10-1 Ginza, Chuo-ku. ☎ 03/6686-1000. www.gracery-ginza.com. 270 units. Doubles from ¥21,200. AE, DC, MC, V. Subway: Ginza Station.

★★ **Hotel New Otani** AKASAKA

Although on the older side, this Tokyo institution is quiet, centrally located, and has wonderful views of both the city and the hotel's

Capsule Hotels

A Tokyo institution, these unique accommodations aren't as strange as they might at first sound. Capsule hotels are essentially hotel rooms in a tube, intended for hardworking "salarymen" who miss their last train home and need a cheap place to sleep. They are basically dormitories with shared bathing/toilet facilities, and the vast majority do not accommodate women at all. While they can be fun to stay in for a night or two, bear in mind that even the ones that do have facilities for both genders segregate them by floor—sharing of capsules is strictly forbidden. They also aren't well suited for travelers with large (or even moderate) amounts of luggage. Good options for capsule hotels include the **Capsule Hotel Asakusa River Side** (p. 95) and **Hotel Siesta** (p. 99).

> *The elegant Hotel Gracery Ginza.*

garden. (Rooms in the main building are best; make sure to request one overlooking the garden when booking.) It also offers Japanese-style tatami rooms with futons instead of beds. 4-1 Kioi-cho, Chiyoda-ku. ☎ 03/3221-2619. www.newotani.co.jp/en. 1,533 units. Double or twin ¥37,800–¥63,000. AE, DC, MC, V. Subway: Akasaka-mitsuke Station.

Hotel Siesta EBISU

Offering both tiny single rooms and capsule rooms allows this hotel to accommodate couples, a rarity for capsule hotels. It's also used to foreign guests. One catch: Capsule rooms are limited to male guests; females must stay in the single rooms. 1-8-1 Ebisu, Shibuya-ku. ☎ 03/3449-5255. www.siesta-en.com. 157 units. Capsules ¥3,300; singles ¥6,600. AE, DC, MC, V. Subway: Ebisu Station.

★ Keio Plaza Hotel SHINJUKU

This more reasonably priced alternative to luxury hotels is popular with business travelers because of its central location, but the huge size of the complex may be off-putting to those looking for a more personal touch. Still, it's a first-class place to stay. 2-2-1 Nishi-Shinjuku, Shinjuku-ku. ☎ 03/3345-8269. www.keioplaza.com. 1,441 units. Doubles

> *Sophisticated relaxation: the Mandarin Oriental.*

¥27,300–¥49,350; suites from ¥84,000. AE, DC, MC, V. Subway: Tochomae Station.

★★★ Mandarin Oriental TOKYO

A sophisticated, modern hotel decorated to the nines with crafts from Japanese artisans. The service is top-notch and the rooms are

> *The Park Hyatt's New York Bar, setting for* Lost in Translation.

some of the most technologically tricked-out in the city, including high-definition TVs and iPod docks. The concierge arranges hands-on cultural excursions such as tea ceremonies, *ikebana* (flower arranging), and guided tours of the city. 2-1-1 Nihombashi Marumachi, Chuo-ku. ☎ 03/3270-8800. www.mandarinoriental.com/tokyo. 179 units. Doubles ¥39,000–¥79,000. AE, DC, MC, V. Subway: Mitsukoshimae Station.

New Koyo (ニュー紅葉) MINAMI SENJU

This is Tokyo's absolute cheapest accommodation as of this writing. This hostel is a favorite of students and backpackers. The rooms are worn and small and lack amenities such as phones, but are clean. Unlike many hostels, it doesn't have a curfew. Book early, as it can fill up very quickly. 2-26-13 Nihonzutsumi, Taito-ku. ☎ 03/3873-0343. www.newkoyo.com. 76 units. Doubles from ¥4,800. AE, DC, MC, V. Subway: Minowa Station.

P&A Plaza SHIBUYA

P&A is located on Shibuya's Dogenzaka Street, colloquially known as "love hotel hill." It is most famed for rooms 901 and 902, which feature an in-room, glass-walled swimming pool and a faux rock-cave grotto bathtub,

respectively. Prices vary widely depending on the room. 1-17-9 Dogenzaka, Shibuya-ku. ☎ 03/3780-5211. www.paplaza.com. 29 units. Doubles ¥5,600–¥16,000 (rest); ¥9,800–¥29,600 (stay). AE, MC, V. Subway: Shibuya Station.

★★★ Park Hyatt Tokyo SHINJUKU

Featured in the film *Lost in Translation,* this hotel is one of the glitziest in the city. The rooms are spacious by Tokyo standards, while the staff seems to have an almost telepathic ability to discern your needs before you ask. And even if you aren't staying here, the weekend brunches at the **New York Grill** (p. 92) are highly recommended. 3-7-1-2 Nishi-Shinjuku, Shinjuku-ku. ☎ 03/5322-1288. www.tokyo.park.hyatt.com. 177 units. Doubles ¥62,370–¥80,850. AE, DC, MC, V. Subway: Shinjuku Station.

Ryokan Shigetsu ASAKUSA

This is a great choice for a taste of a real *ryokan* (traditional inn) on a budget. It's located right in Asakusa, making it the perfect springboard for strolling the Senso-ji area. The shared baths offer views of the temple's pagoda. For the true *ryokan* feel, make sure to book one of

> *Homeikan is a secluded getaway in the heart of the city.*

the tatami rooms. 1-31-11 Asakusa, Taito-ku. ☎ 03/3843-2345. www.shigetsu.com. 23 rooms. Doubles ¥14,700–¥16,800. AE, DC, MC, V. Subway: Asakusa Station.

★★★ kids **Shinagawa Prince** SHINAGAWA Tokyo's largest hotel complex is a virtual city unto itself. It is packed with sports and entertainment facilities, some of which wouldn't seem out of place in a Vegas resort, such as the aquarium and dolphin show. The rooftop restaurant offers expansive views of the city and bay. 4-10-30 Takanawa, Minato-ku. ☎ 03/3440-1111. www.princehotels.com/en/shinagawa. 3,679 units. Doubles ¥16,300–¥36,000. AE, DC, MC, V. Subway: Shinagawa Station.

★★ **Yama no Ue Hotel** (山の上ホテル) OCHANO-MIZU Built in 1937, this charming little hotel was once famed as a retreat for Japanese writers, novelists, and journalists. Now it's a unique boutique-style hotel with a variety of offbeat amenities, such as circulating oxygen in rooms to refresh guests. 1-1 Suru-gadai Kanda, Chiyoda-ku. ☎ 03/3293-2311. www.yamanoue-hotel.co.jp. 74 units. Doubles ¥23,100–¥29,400. AE, DC, MC, V. Subway: Ochanomizu Station.

Love Hotels

Love hotels may sound seedy, but they're the perfect privacy solution for couples who still live with their parents or other family, as is common in Japan. They allow guests to book rooms for a "rest," usually 2 to 3 hours, or a "stay," which means all night. Most are quite tidy and many feature themed rooms and other racy accoutrements. (**P&A Plaza** has an in-room rock grotto; see p. 100.) No reservations required: Just show up and pick a room from the menu. A caveat: The majority will only rent to male-female couples; solo travelers and same-sex couples may be turned away.

Tokyo Nightlife & Entertainment Best Bets

Best Bar for Game Geeks
8 Bit Cafe, 3-8-9 Shinjuku, Shinjuku-ku (see p. 103)

Best Jazz Club
Body and Soul, 6-3-19 Aoyama, Minato-ku (see p. 109)

Best Craft Beer Bar
Craftheads, 1-13-10 Jinnan, Shibuya-ku (see p. 106)

Best Old-School Tokyo Drinking Experience
Hoppy Street, Asakusa, Taito-ku (see p. 59, **6**)

Best Sake Bar
Kuri, 6-4-15 Ginza, Chuo-ku (see p. 106)

Best Place to Soak Your Hangover Away
Oedo Onsen Monogatari, 2-57 Omi, Koto-ku (see p. 109)

Best Cocktails
Tender Bar, 6-5-15 Ginza, Chuo-ku (see p. 107)

Best Dance Club
Womb, 2-16 Maruyama-cho, Shibuya-ku (see p. 108)

Best Whiskey Bar
Zoetrope, 7-10-4 Nishi-Shinjuku, Shinjuku-ku (see p. 107)

> *Belting it out at Body and Soul.*

Tokyo Nightlife & Entertainment A to Z

Bars

★ BYG SHIBUYA

This longtime college hangout worships at the altar of classic rock and roll. Dark, smoky, and covered with decades of graffiti, this is the kind of place to drop by when you're in the mood for some Zeppelin and whiskey. 2–19–14 Dougenzaka, Shibuya-ku. ☎ 03/3461-8574. www.byg.co.jp. Subway: Shibuya Station.

★ 8 Bit Cafe (エイトビットカフェ) SHINJUKU

Sort of like your parents' basement circa 1988, only with a bartender. Dedicated to "retro gaming," this bar is packed to the gills with old videogame technology from a bygone era—all of which can be played by the customers. It can be tough to find; it's on the fifth floor of a nondescript building. 3-8-9 Shinjuku, Shinjuku-ku. ☎ 03/2258-0407. http://8bitcafe.net. Closed Tues. Subway: Shinjuku-sanchome Station.

Gas Panic ROPPONGI

The sign over the bar in this legendarily sleazy dance/pick-up joint reads EVERYBODY MUST BE DRINKING TO STAY INSIDE, and they aren't joking around: If you're spotted with an empty cup in your hand you will be pressured to buy another. Weekends are packed shoulder to shoulder with bodies gyrating on every available surface, including tabletops. 3-15-25 Roppongi, Minato-ku. ☎ 03/3405-0633. www.gaspanic.co.jp. Subway: Roppongi Station.

Geronimo ROPPONGI

This Roppongi institution has been serving up the shots for generations of expats—this is where foreign party animals come to tie one on. It is packed and boisterous on the weekends. 7-14-10 Roppongi, Minato-ku. ☎ 03/3478-7449. www.geronimoshotbar.com. No cover charge. Train: Roppongi Station.

★ Kinsmen (キンズメン) SHINJUKU

A cozy, friendly place open to people of all persuasions, Kinsmen is located in the heart of Shinjuku's Ni-chome (pronounced "nee-cho-may"), Tokyo's gay and lesbian quarter. The playlist tends toward jazz and R&B. 2-18-5 Shinjuku, Shinjuku-ku. ☎ 03/3354-4949. Closed Mon. Subway: Shinjuku-sanchome Station.

> *A classic "hard shake" by Kazuo Ueda at Tender Bar.*

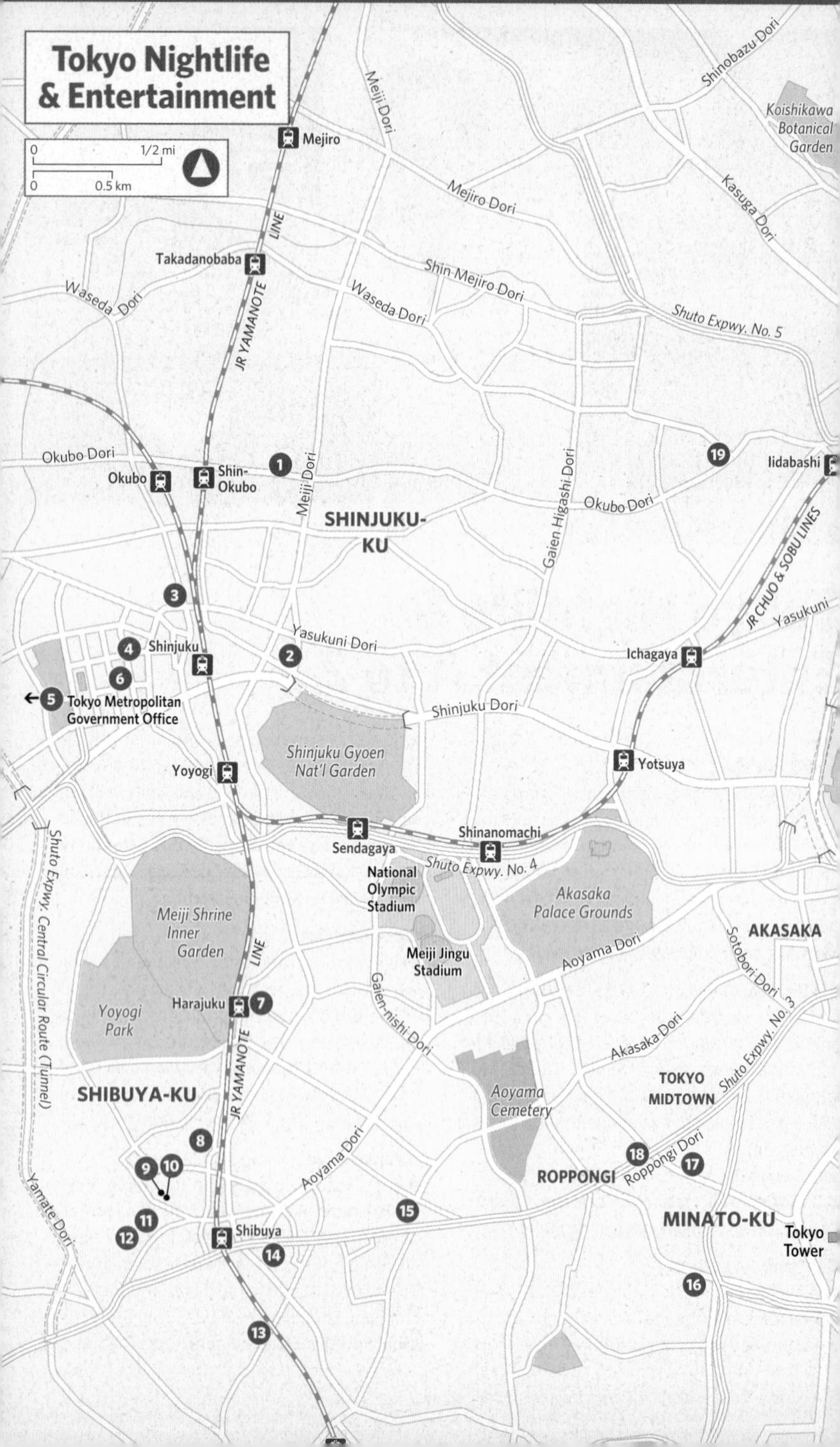

Tokyo Nightlife & Entertainment

0 ⸻ 1/2 mi
0 ⸻ 0.5 km

Mejiro

Meiji Dori

Shinobazu Dori

Koishikawa Botanical Garden

Mejiro Dori

Kasuga Dori

Shin Mejiro Dori

Takadanobaba

Waseda Dori

Waseda Dori

Shuto Expwy. No. 5

JR YAMANOTE LINE

Okubo Dori

Shin-Okubo

1

Okubo

Iidabashi

19

Okubo Dori

SHINJUKU-KU

Meiji Dori

Gaien Higashi Dori

JR CHUO & SOBU LINES

Yasukuni

3

Yasukuni Dori

2

Shinjuku

Ichagaya

4

6

Shinjuku Dori

5 ← Tokyo Metropolitan Government Office

Yotsuya

Yoyogi

Shinjuku Gyoen Nat'l Garden

Sendagaya

Shinanomachi

Shuto Expwy. No. 4

National Olympic Stadium

Akasaka Palace Grounds

AKASAKA

Shuto Expwy. Central Circular Route (Tunnel)

Meiji Shrine Inner Garden

Meiji Jingu Stadium

Aoyama Dori

Sotobori Dori, No. 3

Shuto Expwy. No. 3

Harajuku

7

Yoyogi Park

Galen-nishi Dori

TOKYO MIDTOWN

SHIBUYA-KU

Akasaka Dori

JR YAMANOTE LINE

Aoyama Cemetery

8

Aoyama Dori

18

17

Roppongi Dori

ROPPONGI

9 10

Yamate Dori

11

15

MINATO-KU

Tokyo Tower

12

Shibuya

14

16

13

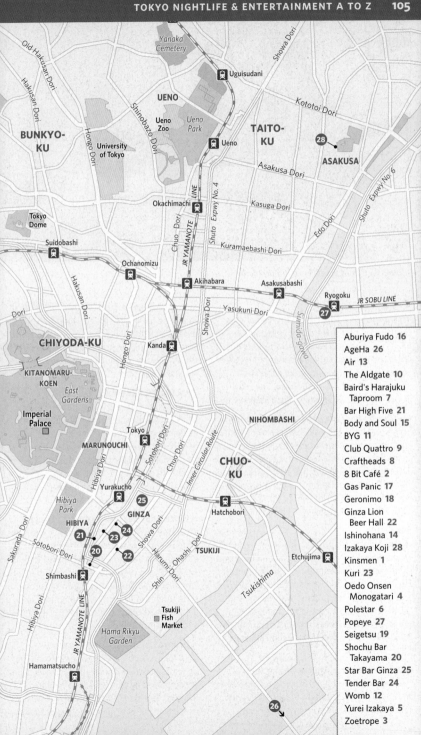

> *The 8 Bit Cafe, a haven for retro video gamers.*

★★ Kuri (庫裏) GINZA
This is the place to go if you're a fan of sake: Over 100 varieties from across Japan are available, with new seasonal variations debuting weekly. It also serves a variety of regional savory finger foods and small dishes as accompaniments. 6-4-15 Ginza, Chuo-ku. ☎ 03/3573-8033. Subway: Ginza Station.

★★ Shochu Bar Takayama (高山) SHIMBASHI
This is just what the name says: a bar specializing in the local firewater known as *shochu*, a powerful beverage brewed from rice or barley. The selection is excellent and this is a classy way to experience Japan's favorite distilled spirit. 1-11-5 Shinbashi, Minato-ku. ☎ 03/3569-0502. Closed Sun. Subway: Ginza Station.

Beer Bars
★ The Aldgate SHIBUYA
A traditional British pub with a solid food and drink menu, this is a popular stop for fans of European beers and whiskeys. It's the perfect place to go when you don't want to miss the latest televised soccer—oops, football!—game. 30-4 Udagawa-cho, Shibuya-ku. ☎ 03/3462-2983. www.the-aldgate.com. Subway: Shibuya Station.

★ Baird's Harajuku Taproom HARAJUKU
Nestled in the middle of Tokyo's fashion district, this is a cozy *izakaya* (Japanese-style pub) with a twist: It's run by a Japanese microbrewer who carefully pairs traditional Japanese bar foods served tapas-style with exceptional, locally brewed beers. No smoking. 1-20-13 Jingumae, Shibuya-ku. ☎ 03/6438-0450. www.bairdbeer.com/en/taproom. Train: Harajuku Station.

★★★ Craftheads SHIBUYA
This outstanding craft-beer bar serves up an ever-changing variety of American and Japanese microbrews, many of which are hard to find even in their home countries. Don't miss the handmade pizzas and finger foods. No smoking. 1-13-10 Jinnan, Shibuya-ku. ☎ 03/6416-9474. www.craftheads.jp. Closed Wed. Subway: Shibuya Station.

★ Ginza Lion Beer Hall (銀座ライオン) GINZA
Operated by Sapporo Brewery, this German-style beer hall features a striking Art Deco interior with beautiful mosaic tilework. Built in 1934, it is one of the city's few remaining pre-war buildings. The hearty menu of European-style food is fit for drinker and nondrinker alike. 7-9-20 Ginza, Chuo-ku. ☎ 03/3571-2590. Subway: Ginza Station.

★ Popeye (麦酒倶楽部 ポパイ) RYOGUKU
This Tokyo institution is dedicated to serving up drafts of regional brews from all over Japan, accompanied by very well done bar fare. 2-18-7 Ryogoku, Sumida-ku. ☎ 03/3633-2120. www.lares.dti.ne.jp/~ppy. Subway: Ryogoku Station.

Cocktail Bars

★★ Bar High Five GINZA

A cozy, atmospheric bar showcasing some of the city's finest cocktails. Try a "Bamboo" (sherry, vermouth, and orange bitters). 7-2-14 Ginza, Chuo-ku. ☎ 03/3571-5815. Cover charge ¥1,500. Subway: Ginza Station.

★★ Ishinohana (石の華) SHIBUYA

This formerly obscure bar got a big boost when Anthony Bourdain visited it as part of his televison show *No Reservations*. It's a classy little cocktail bar in a section of Tokyo that isn't necessarily home to many classy little cocktail bars. And although it's off the beaten path, it's highly recommended. 3-6-2 Shibuya, Shibuya-ku. ☎ 03/5485-8405. Subway: Shibuya Station.

★ Polestar SHINJUKU

Almost defiantly old-school, this clubby little cocktail bar perched atop the Keio Plaza Hotel features expert mix-masters and is an easy-to-find introduction to the Japanese-style cocktail bar scene. It also has great views of the city. 2-2-1 Nishi-Shinjuku, Shinjuku-ku. ☎ 03/3344-0111. Subway: Shinjuku Station.

★★ Star Bar Ginza GINZA

Run by the technical director of the Nippon Bartenders Association, Star Bar offers a picture-perfect portrait of meticulous Japanese cocktail-making, from bow-tied bartenders to spectacular shakes to perfectly spherical ice-cubes. 1-5-13 Ginza, Chuo-ku. ☎ 03/3535-8005. www.starbar.jp. Cover charge ¥2,000. Subway: Ginza Station.

★★★ Tender Bar GINZA

If you only have time to hit one cocktail bar in Tokyo, make it this one. It's home to dapper mixologist Kazuo Ueda, inventor of the famed "hard shake" method of mixing drinks. This is a bartender's speakeasy with some of the best recipes Tokyo has to offer. 6-5-15 Ginza, Chuo-ku. ☎ 03/3571-8343. Cover charge ¥1,500. Subway: Ginza Station.

★★ Zoetrope (ゾートロープ) SHIBUYA

A must-visit for whiskey lovers, this bar features some 250 varieties of single-malt Scotch and whiskey, including a large selection of hard-to-find Japanese varieties. The sign is in Japanese; look for the English words SHOT BAR

> On tap at Baird's Harajuku Taproom.

with a distinctive eyeball design. 7-10-4 Nishi-Shinjuku, Shinjuku-ku. ☎ 03/3363-0162. http://homepage2.nifty.com/zoetrope. Cover charge ¥600. Subway: Shinjuku Station.

Dance Clubs

★★ AgeHa SHIN-KIBA

This hip dance club is one of the city's biggest, with four floors, multiple VIP rooms, and some of the city's best DJs. It runs free shuttle buses to Shibuya at regular intervals throughout the night. 2-2-10 Shin-Kiba, Koto-ku. ☎ 03/5534-2525. www.ageha.com. Cover charge ¥3,500 and up, depending on event. Subway: Shin-kiba Station.

> *Zoetrope's whiskey selection is second to none in the city.*

★ **Air** SHIBUYA
Featured in the movie *Lost in Translation,* this hip house/progressive club is tucked away in a basement location beneath a restaurant. 2–11 Sarugaku, Shibuya-ku. ☎ 03/6145-6231. www. air-tokyo.com. Cover charge ¥3,500 and up, depending on event. Subway: Shibuya Station.

★★★ **Womb** SHIBUYA
Situated right in the middle of Shibuya, this is one of the city's most glamorous clubs; it was featured in the 2006 movie *Babel.* It's renowned for the quality of its sound (which tends toward house, techno, and trance) and for its legendary light show. 2–16 Maruyama-cho, Shibuya-ku. ☎ 03/5459-0039. www.womb. co.jp. Cover charge ¥2,500 and up, depending on event. Subway: Shibuya Station.

Izakaya **Pubs**

★ **Aburiya Fudo** (炙屋 風土) AZABU JUBAN
Aburiya specializes in local and regional cuisine, along with a superb selection of sake and *shochu.* 1–8–6 Azabu Juban, Minato-ku. ☎ 03/ 3568-6224. www.wid.co.jp/tenpo/fudo-azabu/ shop.html. Subway: Azabu-juban Station.

★★ **Izakaya Koji** (居酒屋浩司) ASAKUSA
This archetypical Tokyo *izakaya* is located smack-dab in the middle of Asakusa's famed Hoppy Street (p. 59, ➏), a boulevard lined with tiny mom-and-pop places for snacking and drinking. Make sure to try a "Hoppy cocktail," a local tradition that's a mix of low-alcohol beer and *shochu* liquor. The surrounding *izakaya* are all a lot of fun, too, making this a great place to start a bar hop. 2–3–19 Asakusa, Taito-ku. ☎ 03/3844-0612. Subway: Asakusa Station.

★★ **Seigetsu** (てしごとや 霽月) IIDABASHI
You would be hard-pressed to find a better introduction to the world of Japanese-style pubs than here. The grilled chicken dishes are particularly well done and the sake selection is stellar. 6–77–1 Kagurazaka, Shinjuku-ku. ☎ 03/ 3269-4320. Service charge 5%. Subway: Iida-bashi Station.

★ **Yurei Izakaya** (遊麗居酒屋) KICHIJOJI
Gimmicky fun on the west side of town. While the food isn't anything to write home about, the ambiance is pure, unadulterated haunted

house. (*Yurei* means "ghost" in Japanese.) Even the bathroom is finished in an unsettling faux-flesh motif. 1–18–11 Minami-Cho, Musashino. ☎ 0422/2241-0194. www.yurei.jp. Subway: Kichjioji Station.

Live Music

★★ Body and Soul OMOTESANDO

In a city filled with jazz clubs, Body and Soul offers some of the best musicians, ambience, and food of any jazz bistro in town. It's a bit of a hike from the nearest station, but aficionados hail it as a lower-priced, more laid-back alternative to the nearby Blue Note Tokyo. 6–3–19 Aoyama, Minato-ku. ☎ 03/5466-3348. www.bodyandsoul.co.jp. Cover ¥3,500 for most performances. Subway: Omotesando Station.

★ Club Quattro SHIBUYA

A "live house" located right in the middle of Shibuya, this club plays host to the concerts of an ever-changing array of rock musicians. Check the website for the most up-to-date schedule. 32–13 Udagawa-cho, Shibuya-ku. ☎ 03/3477-8750. www.club-quattro.com. Subway: Shibuya Station.

Spas

★★ Oedo Onsen Monogatari (大江戸温泉物語)

ODAIBA One of a very few true *onsen* (hot spring) experiences in the city, this is a popular day visit for families—and a late-night stop for those wanting to soak their upcoming hangovers away. There are no rooms, but customers are allowed to spend the night in a communal rest area. Make sure to follow proper *onsen* etiquette (p. 539) when visiting. 2–57 Omi, Koto-ku. ☎ 03/5500-1126. www.ooedoonsen.jp/higaeri/english/index.html. ¥2,900 (¥4,600 after 2am). AE, DC, V. Daily 11am–8am following morning. Train: Telecom Center Station.

Tips for Barhoppers

- Rather than at bars, many Tokyoites spend their evenings at *izakaya*, Japanese-style pubs that are a hybrid between bar and restaurant. Serving local beer and liquor (such as sake and *shochu*) along with tapas-style finger foods, they are a great way to get a taste of local cuisine while you drink.

- Most bars and *izakaya* have a per-person "table charge" or cover charge (also known as *otoshi-dai* in Japanese). This can range from ¥500 to ¥1,500 and more at fancier places. The fee usually includes a tiny appetizer of some kind. It is often not disclosed ahead of time, so if this is important to you, make sure to ask before ordering.

- Unless explicitly describing themselves as being of the British or Irish variety, establishments marked "pub" in English generally aren't bars but rather hostess clubs or other forms of adult entertainment.

- There is often a time limit (usually 2 hours) on seating on weekends at more popular establishments.

- Most establishments post maps on their websites. This is the best way to locate them.

> *Party all night long at Womb.*

Yokohama

A century ago, Yokohama was a tiny fishing village. In the mid-19th century, it grew into a bustling harbor and, as one of the few ports officially open to foreign vessels, the outside world's portal to Japan. In fact, it could be argued that Yokohama more than Tokyo represented the epicenter of Japanese culture at the time: Japan's first Western-style bakery, brewery, photo studio, daily newspaper, public restroom, and cinema, among many other things, all debuted here. Today, Yokohama ranks as Japan's second-largest city. Being part of the Greater Tokyo Area—it's only a half-hour ride at most from downtown Tokyo by train, connected by seemingly endless sprawl—it's a fun diversion for those who want to experience a city with a slightly different feel from the capital.

> *Yokohama retains a distinctive port-city charm.*

START From Tokyo's Shibuya Station, take the Tokyu Toyoko Line to Minato Mirai Station (32 min.).

❶ ★ **Chinatown.** For many Tokyo residents, this is Yokohama's star attraction—and the largest Chinatown in Japan. Packed with boutiques and restaurants, it's a great way to spend an afternoon or evening. Like the Chinatowns of most major cities, it leans toward the touristy, but there is still a lot of authentic eating to be found here. It's tough to go wrong with any of the stalls or restaurants, but one of our favorites is **Yokohama Daihanten** (p. 113). Train: Motomachi-Chukagai Station.

❷ ★★ kids **Kitahara Tin Toy Museum.** Featuring more than 3,000 toys from the collection of Teruhisa Kitahara, this museum focuses on tin toys from the late 18th century through the early 1970s, with a particular emphasis on robots and spaceships. It is fun for everyone

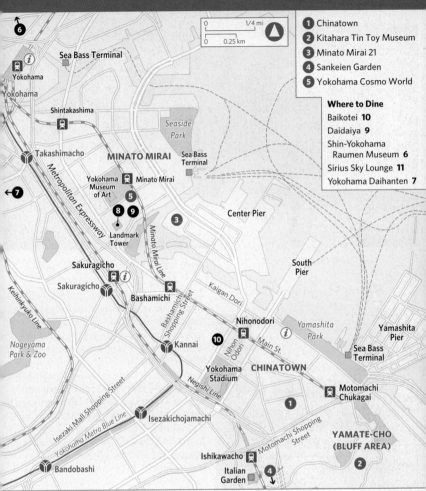

① Chinatown
② Kitahara Tin Toy Museum
③ Minato Mirai 21
④ Sankeien Garden
⑤ Yokohama Cosmo World

Where to Dine
Baikotei **10**
Daidaiya **9**
Shin-Yokohama
 Raumen Museum **6**
Sirius Sky Lounge **11**
Yokohama Daihanten **7**

but an absolute must-see if you have any interest in antique Japanese toys. ⏲ 1 hr. 239 Yamate-cho, Naka-ku. ☎ 045/621-8710. www. toysclub.co.jp/muse/tintoy.html. ¥200 adults, ¥100 high-school students and younger. Daily 9:30am–6pm (to 7pm Sat–Sun). Train: Motomachi-Chukagai Station.

③ ★★ **Minato Mirai 21.** This massive harbor complex consists of a state-of-the-art convention facility, three first-class hotels, Japan's largest building, many offices, two great museums, several shopping malls, and an amusement park. The most conspicuous of the bunch is the **Landmark Tower,** Japan's tallest building, which also features Japan's highest observatory in a building. Best to skip the observatory and experience the view through the **Sirius Sky Lounge** (p. 113) instead. Also recommended is the ★★ kids **Yokohama Port Museum,** which concentrates on Yokohama's history as a port, beginning with the arrival of Commodore Matthew Perry's "Black Ships." Other displays chart the evolution of ships from Japan and around the world from the 19th century to the present, with lots of models of everything from passenger ships to oil tankers. There's even a full-scale simulator that lets you bring a cruise ship into Yokohama's port. ⏲ 2 hr. 2-1-1 Minato Mirai. Museum: ☎ 045/221-0280. www.nippon-maru. or.jp. ¥600 adults, ¥ 300 kids. Tues–Sun 10am–5pm. Train: Minato-Mirai Station.

> *The Kitahara Tin Toy Museum.*

> *The opulent gate to Yokohama's Chinatown.*

Travel Tip

Because of its proximity to Tokyo, Yokohama is a very easy day trip and there's no need to book special accommodations. For hotels in Tokyo, see p. 94.

❹ ★★★ **Sankeien Garden.** This lovely park contains more than a dozen historic buildings that were brought here from other parts of Japan, including Kyoto and Nara, all situated around streams and ponds and surrounded by Japanese-style landscape gardens. The park, divided into an Inner Garden and Outer Garden, was laid out in 1906 by Tomitaro Hara, a local millionaire who made his fortune exporting silk. As you wander along the gently winding pathways, you'll see a villa built in 1649 by the Tokugawa shogunate, a 500-year-old pagoda, and a farmhouse built in 1750 without the use of nails. ⏱ 1 hr. 58-1 Sanmotani, Honmoku. ☎ 045/621-0634. www.sankeien.or.jp. 9am–4pm daily. ¥500 adults, ¥300 seniors, ¥200 kids. Bus: 8 or 125 from Yokohama Station to Honmoku Sankeien-mae.

❺ ★ **kids** **Yokohama Cosmo World.** This amusement park is an offshoot of the Minato Mirai 21 complex. Its towering Ferris wheel is an instantly recognizable part of the Yokohama skyline. Other diversions include a roller coaster that looks like it dives right into a pond (but vanishes instead into a tunnel), a haunted house, a simulation theater with seats that move with the action, kiddie rides, a games arcade, and much more. Admission is free but rides cost ¥300 to ¥700 apiece. ⏱ 2 hr. 2-8-1 Shin-Minato. ☎ 045/641-6591. www.senyo.co.jp/cosmo. Summer daily 11am–10pm; winter Fri–Wed 11am–8pm. Train: Minato-Mirai Station.

Where to Dine in Yokohama

★★ **Baikotei** (梅香亭) *JAPANESE*
A Yokohama legend, this restaurant boasts more than 75 years of history and specializes in the peculiarly Japanese dish known as "*hayashi* rice." It's sweet meat sauce, something like a pork version of beef stroganoff, served over rice. They serve a variety of other dishes as well, including *omuraisu* (an omelet atop rice) and pork cutlets. 1–1 Aoicho, Naka-ku. ☎ 045/681-4870. Entrees from ¥850. No credit cards. Lunch & dinner Tues–Sat. Train: Kannai Station.

★★ **Daidaiya** (橙家) *ASIAN*
One of Yokohama's hippest restaurant chains. This popular Asian-fusion restaurant has innovative takes on sushi, tempura, *udon* (thick buckwheat noodles), and other classic dishes. The lighting and interior decoration is as stylish as the cooking. 2–3–8 Minato Mirai, Nishi-ku. ☎ 045/228-5035. Set menus from ¥2,500. AE, DC, MC, V. Lunch & dinner daily. Train: Minato-Mirai Station.

★ **Shin-Yokohama Raumen Museum** *NOODLES*
Fans of the instant ramen most widely available in the United States and elsewhere will have their minds blown by the variety and richness of the real deal served in Japan, and there is no better way to sample it than in the food court of this very fun museum. See p. 71, ⑪.

★ **Sirius Sky Lounge** *CONTINENTAL*
Perched on the 70th floor of the Landmark Tower (p. 111, ③), the Royal Park Hotel's Sirius Sky Lounge offers spectacular seaside views. Their daily buffet focuses on a variety of ethnic and non-Japanese foods, including salmon, lamb, pizza, and such; in the evenings it turns into a cocktail lounge and restaurant. 2–2–1–3 Minato-Mirai, Nishi-ku. ☎ 045/221-1111. www.yrph.com/en. Lunch buffet ¥3,500, set dinners from ¥6,300. Cover charge ¥1,050 5pm–7pm, ¥2,100 7pm–11pm (includes live music), ¥1,050 11pm–1am. AE, DC, MC, V. Lunch & dinner daily. Train: Sakuragicho Station.

★★★ **Yokohama Daihanten** (横浜大飯店) *CHINESE*
Yokohama Daihanten is mainly Cantonese but serves up a variety of Chinese cuisine, including Shanghai-, Sichuan-, and Beijing-style

> Try one of the dozens of noodle vendors at the Shin-Yokohama Raumen Museum.

dishes. They also offer an all-you-can-eat dim sum (served off of menus rather than carts, alas, but fun nonetheless). 154 Yamashita-cho, Naka-ku. ☎ 0120/35-4893. www.yokohama daihanten.com. Set menus from ¥3,150. AE, DC, MC, V. Lunch & dinner daily. Train: Ishikawacho or Motomachi-Chukagai stations.

Mount Takao

This easy-to-climb peak, located just an hour west of down-
town Tokyo, is a great way to get a taste of the countryside on a tight schedule.
Treated as holy ground by generations of Buddhist monks, dotted with temples
and teahouses and even a monkey park (see below), it is a local, homey sort of
place. That said, some 2.6 million people visit the 559m (1,834-ft.) mountain
every year. (For this reason alone, we highly recommend climbing on a weekday
if at all possible.) And like so many mountaintops in Japan, Takao is marred
by vending machines and souvenir stands, but the view more than makes up
for it: On a clear day, you can see Mount Fuji, the skyscrapers of Tokyo, and
occasionally even as far as Yokohama.

> *A view from the top of Mount Takao.*

START From Tokyo's Shinjuku Station,
take the Keio Line Semi Special Express to
Takaosanguchi Station (47 min.).

1 ★ kids **Takao Monkey Park & Botanical
Garden** (高尾山さる園)**.** Its location 2 minutes
from the top of the funicular railway or chairlift makes this little park easy to visit, even
with kids in tow. It's a small but entertaining
zoo dedicated to Japanese macaques, aka
"snow monkeys." Unlike many Western zoos,
they encourage visitors to feed the monkeys
(chow is sold for ¥100 a pop). The attached

botanical garden isn't the world's most thrilling, but does a decent job showcasing local
alpine flora and fauna. ⊕ 1 hr. 2179 Takaomachi,
Hachioji. ☎ 042/661-2381. www.takaotozan.
co.jp/takaotozan_eng1. ¥400 adults, ¥200

Travel Tip

Because of its proximity to Tokyo, Mount
Takao is a very easy day trip and there's no
need to book special accommodations. For
hotels in Tokyo, see p. 94.

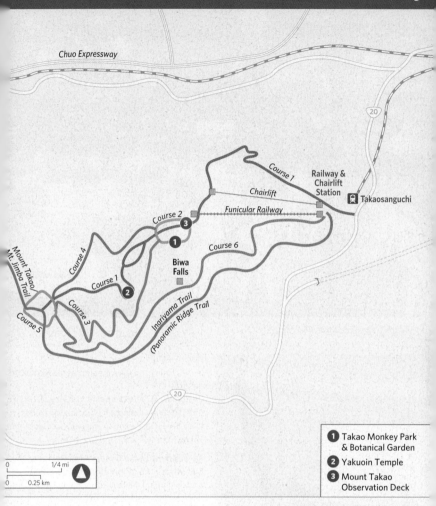

Chuo Expressway

20

Course 1

Railway &
Chairlift
Station   🚉 Takaosanguchi

Chairlift

Course 2   Funicular Railway

3

1   Course 6

Mount Takao/
Mt. Jimba Trail   Course 4

Course 1   Biwa
Falls

2

Course 3   Inariyama Trail
(Panoramic Ridge Trail)

Course 5

20

0   1/4 mi

0   0.25 km

1 Takao Monkey Park
   & Botanical Garden

2 Yakuoin Temple

3 Mount Takao
   Observation Deck

elementary students and younger. Daily Dec–
Feb 9:30am–4pm; Mar–Apr 10am–4:30pm;
May–Nov 9:30am–4:30pm. Access: Mount
Takao Course 1 or 2.

2 ★★★ **Yakuoin Temple** (薬王院). Even if you
skip past this temple by taking one of the
side trails, it's worth a visit on the way back
down. Believed to have been built in the 8th
century, it is a magnificent structure in which
Buddhist services are still conducted today.
In addition to wonderful architecture, the
temple complex features beautiful statuary
as well. Take particular note of the pair of
tengu, winged humanoid creatures traditionally believed to dwell in mountains throughout

Time Your Climb

You can climb Mount Takao at any time of
year, but each season has its own charms.
The crisp air of the **winter** months offers
the best views from the peak. **Spring** is fun
for watching the green of budding trees
spreading across the mountains. **Summer**
offers the best chances for seeing birds
and other wildlife. And **fall**—particularly
around mid-November—offers spectacular
views of the changing foliage. (Be forewarned that this is by far the most popular
and crowded time of year to climb.)

> *Bottoms up on the Takao Beer Mount!*

> *Flying squirrels, called* musasabi *in Japanese, are residents of the forest on Mount Takao.*

Japan, including Mount Takao. Feared in times of old, today they are treated as local mascots of sorts.
🕐 30 min. 2177 Takaomachi, Hachioji. ☎ 042/661-1115. www.takaosan.or.jp/english/index.html. Free. Daily sunrise–sunset. Access: Mount Takao Course 1 or 2.

❸ ★ **Mount Takao Observation Deck.** Located halfway up the mountain, near the chairlift and funicular railway stops, the observation-deck building offers not only excellent views but several sit-down restaurants and cafes. **Kitchen Musasabi,** an Italian restaurant, is touted as the highest-altitude eatery in Tokyo; it offers all-you-can-eat-and-drink buffet meals on weekends. The only catch is the irregular operating schedule. From July through September, Kitchen Musasabi shuts down and the **Takao Beer Mount** opens, serving similar fare but remaining open later into the evening. 2205 Takaomachi, Hachioji. Musasabi/Beer Mount: ☎ 042/665-9943. www.takaotozan.co.jp/takaotozan_eng1. Buffet ¥3,300 for men, ¥3,000 for women, ¥1,500 for kids. No credit cards. Oct–Jun daily 11am–5pm (last order 4pm); July–Sept daily 2:30pm–9:30pm. Access: Mount Takao Course 1 or 2.

Hiking Mount Takao

The great thing about Mount Takao is that it's geared towards any level of climber, with eight separate hiking "courses." We've listed them below. Those in the mood for a little exercise and a taste of nature can take one of the narrow river trails extending from the base; those who want to take it easy can hop on the funicular railway or chairlift, which takes you halfway up the peak for easy access to the main tourist spots. Even without the assist, it only takes a few hours to climb on foot, with the vast majority of paths being paved and inset with staircases. There are also numerous restaurants, teahouses, and soft-drink machines for those who need a little rest and refreshment along the way. Untamed wilderness this isn't, but make sure to wear proper footwear and take the usual precautions (sunblock, extra water, and so on) that you would for any mountain hike.

COURSE 1
A broad, paved trail offering easy access to the peak (3.8km/2.4 miles; 1½ hr.).

COURSE 2
A loop trail midway up the peak that offers access to the peak's monkey park, arboretum, and observatory building (1km/.6 miles; 30 min.).

COURSE 3
A side trail extending from Course 1, leading through a more wooded trail (1km/.6 miles; 30 min.).

COURSE 4
A side trail that detours over a suspension bridge before heading to the peak (1.5km/.9 miles; 45 min.).

COURSE 5
Peak loop trail; circles the peak of Mount Takao for 360-degree views (1km/.6 miles; 30 min.).

COURSE 6
Biwa Falls trail. Our personal favorite path up the peak, this trail follows a meandering stream up the side of the mountain. More rugged than the other courses, with no refreshment along the way. Biwa Falls is still used as a training ground by monks, so you can't go in the water, but you can see the area from behind a gate (3.3km/2 miles; 1½ hr.).

COURSE 7
Similar to Course 6, but passes through groves of Japanese maples along the way (3.1km/1.9 miles; 1½ hr.).

COURSE 8
Takao-Jinba link trail. This path links Mount Takao to its sister peak of Mount Jinba; it's recommended only for experienced hikers. That said, it is definitely possible to do it in a day if you ascend Takao early enough. Transportation back to Tokyo is available from the base of Mount Jinba (15km/9.3 miles; 6 hr.).

Hakone

Hakone has been a resort destination for centuries, and it remains one of the closest and most popular day trips from Tokyo. Located high in the mountains, it is crisscrossed with scenic alpine train lines, cable cars, and ropeways. It has about everything a vacationer could wish for: hot-spring resorts, mountains, lakes, breathtaking views of Mount Fuji, and interesting historical sites. You can tour Hakone as a day trip if you leave early in the morning and limit your sightseeing to a few key attractions (such as the first three on the list below), but adding an overnight stay—complete with a soak in a hot-spring tub—is the traditional way to visit.

> *Unleash your inner pirate on a Lake Ashi cruise.*

START If you have a Japan Rail Pass (p. 558), take the Tokaido Shinkansen bullet train from Tokyo to Odawara Station (40 min.). At Odawara Station, purchase an Odakyu Railways Hakone Free Pass ticket (p. 121). Take the Hakone-Tozan Line from Odawara to Hakone-Yumoto Station (15 min.). Transfer to Hakone Tozan Railway and ride to Chokoku-no-mori Station (30 min.). If you do not have a Japan Rail Pass, buy a Hakone Free Pass in Tokyo's Shinjuku Station and take the Hakone Limited Express to Hakone-Yumoto Station (85 min.), and continue as above.

1 ★★★ kids **Hakone Open-Air Museum** (箱根彫刻の森美術館). One of Hakone's top attractions, this very fun museum uses nature as a backdrop for a wide variety of 20th-century sculpture. Works by major names such as Joan Miró and Willem de Kooning are silhouetted against glens, formal gardens, ponds, and meadows. Meanwhile, the Picasso Pavilion displays one of the world's largest collections of his works, including a photo history covering the last 17 years of his life. The museum also offers several installations that invite children to climb and play upon them.

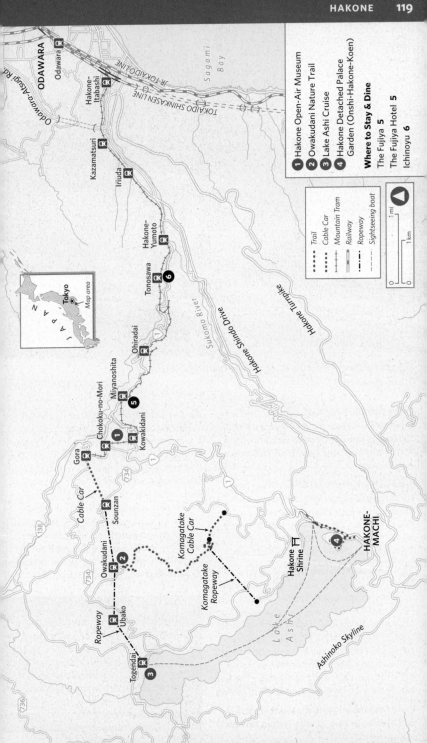

ODAWARA

Odawara

Odawara-Atsugi Rd.

Hakone-Itabashi

JR TOKAIDO LINE

TOKAIDO SHINKANSEN LINE

Sagami Bay

Kazamatsuri

Iriuda

Hakone-Yumoto

6

Tonosawa

Ohiradai

Sukumo River

Hakone Shindo Drive

Hakone Turnpike

Miyanoshita

5

Chokoku-no-Mori

1

Kowakidani

Gora

Cable Car

Sounzan

Owakudani

2

Ropeway

Ubako

Togendai

3

Komagatake Cable Car

Komagatake Ropeway

Hakone Shrine

4

HAKONE-MACHI

Lake Ashi

Ashinoko Skyline

JAPAN

Tokyo

Map area

Where to Stay & Dine

The Fujiya **5**
The Fujiya Hotel **5**
Ichinoyu **6**

1 Hakone Open-Air Museum
2 Owakudani Nature Trail
3 Lake Ashi Cruise
4 Hakone Detached Palace Garden (Onshi-Hakone-Koen)

Trail
Cable Car
Mountain Tram
Railway
Ropeway
Sightseeing boat

0 ___ 1 mi
0 ___ 1 km

> *Fun for the young—and young at heart—at the Open-Air Museum.*

🕐 1 hr. 1121 Ninotaira, Hakone. ☎ 0460/82-1161. www.hakone-oam.or.jp. ¥1,600 adults, ¥1,100 college and high-school students and seniors, ¥800 kids. Daily 9am–5pm. Train: Chokoku-no-mori Station.

From Chokoku-no-mori Station, take the Hakone-Tozan Line to its last stop, Gora Station. At Gora, switch to the cable car bound for Sounanzan (9 min.). At Sounanzan, switch to the ropeway bound for Togendai. Disembark at Owakudani Station (15 min.).

❷ ★ **Owakudani Nature Trail.** *Owakudani* means "Great Boiling Valley," and you'll soon understand how it got its name when you see (and smell) the sulfurous steam escaping from fissures in the rock, testimony to the volcanic activity still present here. Most Japanese commemorate their trip by buying boiled eggs cooked here in the boiling waters, available at the small hut midway along the trail. (The trail takes about a half-hour to traverse.) 🕐 30 min.

From Owakudani Station, take the ropeway to its terminus at Togendai Station (15 min.).

❸ ★★★ **Lake Ashi Cruise.** From Togendai you can take a pleasure boat across Lake Ashi. It takes about half an hour to cross to Hako-nemachi (also called simply Hakone), on the southern edge of the lake. (This end of the lake affords the beautiful view of Mount Fuji most often depicted in tourist publications.) Boats are in operation year-round (though they run less frequently in winter and not at all in stormy weather). Several operators run boats across the lake; the Hakone Free Pass (p. 121) only works on the ones run by **Hakone Sightseeing,** which are incongruously shaped ke pirate frigates. The boats operated by their competitor **Izu-Hakone** cost ¥970 one-way. ⏱ 30 min. Hakone Sightseeing: Hakonema-chi Port, Moto-Hakone Port, or Togendai Port. ☎ 0460/83-6325. www.hakone-kankosen.co.jp/gaikoku.hp/index.htm. ¥1,780 adults round-trip, ¥890 kids round-trip. Mar–Nov cruises leave every 40 min.; Dec–Feb cruises leave every 50 min. Bus: Onshi-Koen Mae.

❹ ★ **Hakone Detached Palace Garden (Onshi-Hakone-Koen;** 県立恩賜箱根公園**).** Located on a small promontory on Lake Ashi minutes from the pier, this garden offers spectacular views of the lake and, in clear weather, Mount Fuji. Originally part of an imperial summer villa built in 1886, the garden is open to the public 24 hours and admission is free. It's a great place for wandering. The lakeside observation building (which is open daily 9am–4:30pm) offers views from a slightly higher vantage. ⏱ 1 hr. Motohakone, Hakonemachi. ☎ 0460/83-7484. Free. 24 hr. Bus: Onshi-Koen Mae.

Travel Tip

Part of the fun of visiting Hakone is simply getting around. An easy loop tour through Hakone includes various forms of unique transportation: Starting out by train from Tokyo, you switch to the Hakone Tozan Railway (a three-car tram that zigzags up the mountain), then change to a cable car, then to a smaller ropeway, and end your trip with a boat ride across Lake Ashi, stopping to see major attractions along the way.

The **Hakone Free Pass** (¥5,000 adults, ¥1,500 kids for 2 days) is by far the simplest way to explore Hakone, as it covers all modes of public transportation within the city (including not only trains but buses, ropeways, cable cars, and even boats). It also gives small discounts on entry to most attractions. That said, it only really pays for itself on overnight stays; if you're whisking in and out on a day trip, paying as you go might make more sense.

Where to Stay & Dine in Hakone

★★ **The Fujiya** (ザ・フジヤ) *CONTINENTAL*
Wonderful little mom-and-pop places abound in Hakone, but this is a good bet for when you want something a little fancier. Located in the Fujiya Hotel, Hakone's grandest and oldest, this restaurant offers a memorable place for a good Western meal. (Think staples such as trout, prawns, lamb, and steak.) Reservations are required for dinner. 359 Miyanoshita. ☎ 0460/82-2211. Set lunches from ¥5,000; dinner entrees from ¥2,200; set dinners from ¥11,500. AE, DC, MC, V. Lunch & dinner daily. Train: Miyanoshita Station.

★★★ **The Fujiya Hotel** (富士屋ホテル)
The Fujiya, established in 1878, is quite simply the grandest, most majestic old hotel in Hakone; indeed, it might be the loveliest historic hotel in Japan. A landscaped garden out back, with a waterfall, pond, greenhouse, outdoor pool, and stunning views over the valley, is great for strolls and meditation. There's also a small hotel museum and an indoor thermal pool and public hot-spring baths (hot-spring water is also piped in to each guest's bathroom). Even if you don't stay here, come for a meal or tea. 359 Miyanoshita. ☎ 0460/82-2211. www.fujiyahotel.jp/english.146 units. Doubles from ¥20,040. AE, DC, MC, V. Train: Miyanoshita Station.

★★ **Ichinoyu** (一の湯)
Located next to a roaring river, this delightful, rambling wooden building stands on a tree-shaded winding road that follows the track of the old Tokaido Highway. Opened more than 380 years ago, Ichinoyu is now in its 15th generation of owners. Old artwork, wall hangings, and paintings decorate the place, and the rooms are all Japanese-style. The one catch is that they cannot accommodate single travelers. 90 Tonosawa. ☎ 0460/85-5331. http://english.ichinoyu.co.jp/honkan. 24 units. Doubles ¥8,400–¥15,225 per person. Rates include 2 meals. AE, DC, MC, V. Train: Tonosawa Station.

Kamakura

If you take only one day trip outside Tokyo, it should be to Kamakura, especially if you're unable to include the ancient capitals of Kyoto and Nara in your travels. It is a delightful hamlet with no fewer than 65 Buddhist temples and 19 Shinto shrines spread throughout the town and surrounding wooded hills. Kamakura played a central role in Japanese history: In 1192, a warrior named Minamoto Yoritomo seized political power in a coup d'état, establishing Kamakura as the military and political center of the nation for the next 141 years. (The fun ended in 1333, when the emperor crushed the upstart government by sending in troops from Kyoto.) Although the city's influence in politics waned in the intervening centuries, Kamakura has lost none of its charms. Today it is a thriving seaside resort, and a trendy suburb for those who want to live close to the capital, with a traditionally Japanese aesthetic of old wooden homes, temples, shrines, and deep forests.

> A komainu *(moondog)* statue guards the entrance to Hachimangu Shrine.

START From Tokyo's Shinjuku Station, take the JR Shonan Shinjuku Line to Kamakura Station. (1 hr.).

❶ ★★ Tsurugaoka Hachimangu Shrine (鶴岡八幡宮)**.** Located a 10- to 15-minute walk from Kamakura Station, this is the spiritual heart of Kamakura and one of its most popular attractions. It was built by Yoritomo and dedicated to Hachiman, the Shinto god of war who served as the clan deity of his family line. The pathway to the shrine is along Wakamiya Oji, a cherry-tree-lined pedestrian lane that was also constructed by Yoritomo in the 1190s so that his oldest son's first visit to the family

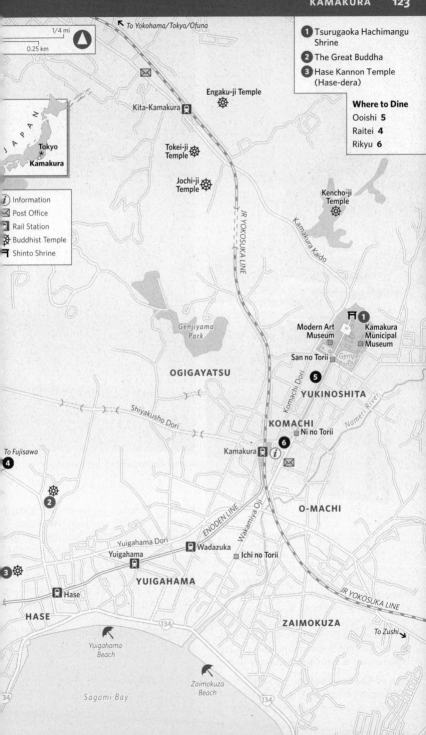

1/4 mi
0.25 km

To Yokohama/Tokyo/Ofuna

1 **Tsurugaoka Hachimangu Shrine**

2 **The Great Buddha**

3 **Hase Kannon Temple (Hase-dera)**

Where to Dine

Ooishi 5

Raitei 4

Rikyu 6

JAPAN

Tokyo

Kamakura

ⓘ Information

✉ Post Office

🚉 Rail Station

卍 Buddhist Temple

⛩ Shinto Shrine

Engaku-ji Temple

Kita-Kamakura

Tokei-ji Temple

Jochi-ji Temple

Kencho-ji Temple

JR YOKOSUKA LINE

Kamakura Kaido

Genjiyama Park

Modern Art Museum

Kamakura Municipal Museum

San no Torii

Gempei Pond

OGIGAYATSU

5

YUKINOSHITA

Shiyakusho Dori

Nameri River

KOMACHI

Komachi Dori

Ni no Torii

6

Kamakura

ⓘ

To Fujisawa

4

2

O-MACHI

Wakamiya Oji

ENODEN LINE

Yuigahama Dori

Yuigahama

Wadazuka

Ichi no Torii

3

Hase

YUIGAHAMA

JR YOKOSUKA LINE

HASE

134

ZAIMOKUZA

To Zushi

Yuigahama Beach

34

Zaimokuza Beach

Sagami Bay

134

> *The Great Buddha of Kotokuin Temple.*

> *Hase Kannon Temple's gilt goddess.*

shrine could be accomplished in style with an elaborate procession. An added bonus: On clear days, the panoramic view of the sea from the top of the shrine's enormous staircase is a sight to behold. ⏱ 45 min. 2-1-31 Yukinoshita. ☎ 0467/22-0315. www.hachimangu.or.jp. Free. Daily sunrise–sunset. Train: Kamakura Station.

❷ ★★★ **The Great Buddha** (大仏). Called the Daibutsu in Japanese, this is by far Kamakura's most famous attraction. Located in

Kotokuin Temple, it stands 11m (36 ft.) high and weighs 93 tons, making it the second-largest bronze image in Japan. The massive Buddha of Nara may outrank it in size, but Kamakura's Buddha has the better backdrop, outside amid beautiful buildings and wooded hills. Cast in 1252, the Kamakura Buddha was indeed once housed in a temple like the Nara

Travel Tip

Kamakura is a very easy commute from downtown Tokyo and the majority of its sights can be covered in a day, so there's no need to book special accommodations. For hotels in Tokyo, see p. 94.

uddha, but a huge tidal wave destroyed the ooden structure—and the statue has sat nder sun, snow, and stars ever since. For an dditional ¥20, you can even take a look inde. ⏱ 1 hr. Temple: 2-28-4 Hase. ☎ 0467/22-703. ¥200. Daily Apr–Sept 7am–6pm; Oct–Mar am–5:30pm. Train: Kamakura Station.

⦁ ★★★ Hase Kannon Temple (Hase-dera; 谷寺). This is the home of an 11-headed gilt :atue of Kannon, the goddess of mercy, oused in the Kannon-do (Kannon Hall). More an 9m (30 ft.) high and the tallest wooden nage in Japan, it was made in the 8th century om a single piece of camphor wood. Note ow each face has a different expression, epresenting the Kannon's compassion for arious kinds of human suffering. The temple

has a museum with religious treasures from the Kamakura, Heian, Muromachi, and Edo periods. Also on the grounds is **Benten-kutsu Cave,** which contains many stone images, including one of Benzaiten (seated, with a lute and a money box in front). A sea goddess and patroness of music, art, and good fortune, she is the only female of Japan's Seven Deities of Fortune (also called the Seven Lucky Gods). The whole complex is located on a hill with a sweeping view of the sea; the 10-minute **Prospect Road** hiking path features flowers in bloom and panoramic views. ⏱ 1 hr. 3-11-2 Hase. ☎ 0467/22-6300. ¥300 adults, ¥100 kids. Mar–Sept daily 8am–5pm; Oct–Feb 8am–4:30pm. Train: Kamakura Station.

Where to Dine in Kamakura

★ Ooishi (おおいし) *TEMPURA*
amakura devotees revere this tiny restaurant r its magical touch with tempura—its batter-ied shrimp, fish, and vegetables are always relatively) light and fluffy, never oily. The nenu consists of four options: three courses f ascending cost (*hana, tsuki,* and *yuki*) and *tendon* (tempura atop a bowl of rice). In the venings, more expensive set meals replace ne lunch courses. It's all *omakase* style—the igredients depend on what is fresh that day. lo smoking. 1-9-24 Yukinoshita. ☎ 0467/23-500. Set lunches from ¥3,800, set dinners om ¥5,500. V. Lunch & dinner Thurs–Tues. rain: Kamakura Station.

★★ Raitei (らい亭) *JAPANESE*
hough it's a bit inconveniently located, this is ne absolute winner for a meal in Kamakura. 'isiting Raitei is as much fun as visiting the ity's temples and shrines. The restaurant is ituated in the hills on the edge of Kamakura, urrounded by verdant countryside, and the vonder is that it serves inexpensive *soba* buckwheat noodles) and lunchboxes, as well s priestly *kaiseki* feasts. Take the stone steps n the right to the back entry, where you'll be

given an English-language menu with such offerings as noodles with chicken, various bento, and *kaiseki*. If you make a reservation in advance for *kaiseki*, you'll dine upstairs in your own private room in a refined traditional setting with great views. 3-1-1 Kamakurayama. ☎ 0467/32-5656. Entry fee ¥500, which counts toward the price of your meal; noodles from ¥900; bento from ¥3,675; entrees from ¥2,625; kaiseki from ¥6,300. AE, DC. Daily 11am–sundown (about 7pm in summer). Bus: 4 from platform 6 at Kamakura Station.

★★ Rikyu (利休) *CURRY*
Japanese-style fast food! This hole-in-the-wall restaurant specializes in curried rice, that ubiquitous dish consisting of a thick and sweet meat-based sauce ladled over rice. It also serves up deep-fried pork and chicken cutlets. Showcased on Japanese TV for its amazing flavors at such reasonable prices, Rikyu can get quite harried at peak times; you might want to aim for a little earlier or later for a more relaxed experience (it opens at 10:30am). 2-10-1 Komachi. ☎ 0467/23-0317. Entrees from ¥500. No credit cards. Lunch & dinner daily. Train: Kamakura Station.

Nikko

There is an old Japanese saying that goes, "You can't say '*kekko*' ['perfect'] until you've seen Nikko"—a reputation largely driven by Toshogu, the final resting place of legendary shogun Tokugawa Ieyasu and hands down the most opulent shrine in all of Japan. In addition to the shrine, there are more than enough worthy sights to keep a visitor occupied for several days here. But that said, the launch of Tobu Railway's direct Nikko Kegon Line makes it easier than ever to see Nikko in a single (very full) day trip from Tokyo. Plan on 4 to 5 hours for round-trip transportation.

> *Crossing the Sacred Bridge.*

START From Tokyo's Asakusa Station, take Tobu Railway's Nikko Line to Nikko Station (2 hr.).

1 ★★ **Rinno-ji Temple** (日光山 輪王寺)**.** Located just beyond the iconic, bright-red Shinkyo (Sacred Bridge) across the rushing Daiyagawa River, this temple was founded by the priest Shodo in the 8th century, long before the Toshogu (**2**) was built. The temple's **Sanbutsudo Hall** enshrines three 8.4m-high (28-ft.) gold-plated wooden images of Buddha. The

Shoyo-en Garden, opposite Sanbutsudo Hall, was completed in 1815. Typical of Japanese landscaped gardens of the Edo period, this small strolling garden provides a different vista with each turn of the path, making it seem much larger than it is. There is also a small **"treasure house,"** where relics are displayed on a rotating basis. Rinno-ji is undergoing renovations until 2017, and may be inaccessible at times, but the grounds will remain open. ⊙ 1 hr. 2300 Sannai. ☎ 0288/54-0531. ¥400 for Sanbutsudo, ¥300 for treasure house

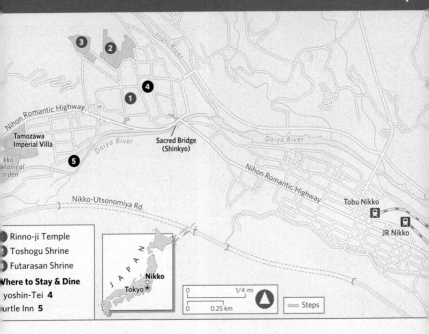

- Rinno-ji Temple
- Toshogu Shrine
- Futarasan Shrine
- **Where to Stay & Dine**
- yoshin-Tei **4**
- urtle Inn **5**

nd garden. Daily Apr–Oct 8am–5pm; Nov–Mar
am–4pm. Train: Nikko Station.

★★★ Toshogu Shrine (日光 東照宮). The most
nportant and famous structure in Nikko was
riginally built by second Tokugawa shogun
okugawa Hidetada and greatly expanded by
te third shogun, his son Tokugawa Iemitsu,
s an act of devotion to the first shogun,
okugawa Ieyasu. No expense was too great in
reating the monument: Some 15,000 artists
nd craftspeople were brought to Nikko from
ll over Japan, and after 2 years' work, they

erected a group of buildings more elaborate
and gorgeous than any other Japanese temple
or shrine, then or since. Rich in colors and
carvings, Toshogu Shrine is gilded with over
2 million sheets of gold leaf (they could cover
an area of almost 2.4 hectares/6 acres). The
mausoleum was completed in 1636, almost 20
years after Ieyasu's death, and houses his remains; it was most certainly meant to impress
anyone who saw it as a demonstration of the
Tokugawa shogunate's wealth and power. The
densely layered architectural detail rewards
time spent contemplating it, revealing new

Travel Tip

JR rail passes won't work on the private Tobu
Railway lines, but Tobu offers several passes
of its own for foreign visitors to Nikko. The
All Nikko Pass (¥4,400 adults, ¥2,210 kids)
gives unlimited access to all public transportation associated with Nikko, including the
ride there from Tokyo, local buses, and local
train lines, for 4 days. Meanwhile, the World
Heritage Pass (¥3,600 adults, ¥1,700 kids)
covers the train ride from Tokyo, local buses,
and basic admission to Toshogu Shrine,
Futarasan Shrine, and Rinno-ji Temple.

They're available at the **Tobu Sightseeing
Service Center** or the Tobu travel agency in
Asakusa Station (☎ 03/3841-2871; www.
tobu.co.jp.).

Some caveats: The passes are limited to
foreign visitors (Japanese citizens can't purchase them), they are limited to local or rapid
trains (which are slower than the limited express or express; you can ride those by paying
an additional ¥1000 each way), and you can't
get off at any stations outside of the free zone
specified by the passes.

> A statue of shogun Tokugawa Ieyasu.

Spending the Night in Nikko

The excellent, nonsmoking ★ **Turtle Inn** (タートルイン) pension, 8–28 Takumi-cho (☎ 0288/53-3663; www.turtle-nikko. com), is located within walking distance of Toshogu Shrine in a newer two-story house on a quiet side street beside the Daiyagawa River. The friendly owner, Mr. Fukuda, speaks English and is very helpful in planning sightseeing itineraries. Rooms are bright and cheerful in both Japanese and Western styles; the five tatami rooms are without bathrooms. Excellent Japanese dinners (served on local Mashiko pottery) are available for ¥2,100, as are Western breakfasts for ¥1,050. Dinner must be ordered the day before; note that it's not available on Sundays, Tuesdays, or Thursdays. Doubles are ¥12,400; ¥300 extra per person in peak season.

Besides eating at the Turtle Inn, another option is **Gyoshin-Tei** (尭心亭), 2339–1 Sannai (☎ 0288/53-3751), a lovely Japanese restaurant with a simple tatami room and a view of pines, moss, and bonsai. It serves two kinds of set meals—*kaiseki* and Buddhist vegetarian cuisine—both of which change monthly and include the local specialty, *yuba*, a paper-thin tofu dish produced only in Kyoto and Nikko. Even if you're a devoted carnivore, the Buddhist vegetarian course is a real treat, offering a wide variety of tiny dishes ranging from sweet to savory, and all so good you won't even miss the beef. The one drawback is the restaurant's hard-to-find location, but it's only a 4-minute walk northeast of Rinno-ji Temple (p. 126, ❶). Reservations recommended. Vegetarian/*kaiseki* set menus are ¥3,990 to ¥5,775; a set lunch menu is ¥3,150.

animals and creatures every time you look. The shrine is a 30-minute walk or a 10-minute bus ride (to Shinkyo or Nishi Sando) from Nikko Station. Like Rinno-ji, Toshogu is being extensively renovated until 2017. While some of it may be covered or inaccessible at any given time, the grounds will be open to the public all the while. ⏲ 2 hr. 2301 Sannai. ☎ 0288/54-0560. ¥1,300. Daily Apr–Oct 8am–5pm; Nov–Mar 8am–4pm. Train: Nikko Station.

❸ ★★ **Futarasan Shrine** (日光二荒山神社). Directly to the west of Toshogu Shrine is the oldest building in the district (from 1617), which has a pleasant garden and is dedicated to the gods of mountains surrounding Nikko. You'll find miniature shrines dedicated to the god of fortune, god of happiness, god of trees, god of water, and god of good marriages. On the shrine's grounds is the so-called "ghost lantern," enclosed in a small vermilion-colored wooden structure. According to legend, it used to come alive at night and sweep around Nikko in the form of a ghost. It apparently scared one guard so much that he struck it with his sword 70 times; the marks are still visible on the lamp's rim. Entrance to the miniature shrines and ghost lantern is ¥200 extra. 2307 Sannai. ☎ 0288/54-0535. Free. Daily sunrise–sunset. Train: Nikko Station.

> *The beautiful garden at Futarasan Shrine.*

Shimoda

The Izu Peninsula is virtually synonymous with summertime beachside fun for Tokyoites. Jutting into the Pacific Ocean southwest of Tokyo, Izu boasts some fine beaches and a dramatic coastline marked in spots by high cliffs and tumbling surf. It also has a verdant, mountainous interior with quaint hot-spring resorts, and a series of ferry-accessible islands hopscotch out into the Pacific. For those who want to explore Izu's beaches, Shimoda retains a relatively small-town feel and is easy to explore on foot, though you may want to use local buses to get to the beaches. In the summer months, the white sands and sparkling blue waters give the city an almost tropical feel. Given that it takes close to 3 hours to get here from Tokyo, you will most likely want to spend at least 1 night, though it is possible for very focused travelers to make it to the beach and back in a day trip.

> *Shirahama Beach at sunset.*

START From Tokyo Station, take JR Tokaido Line Odoriko Express to Izukyu-Shimoda Station (2¾ hr.).

① ★★ kids **Shimoda Floating Aquarium** (下田水中水族館). As the name says, this facility's main claim to fame is a large domed aquarium built atop a lagoon. The focus is on sea life in the Izu area, but like most Japanese aquariums it has dolphin and seal shows as well. ⏱ 2 hr. 3-22-31 Shimoda. ☎ 0558/22-3567. www.shimoda-aquarium.com. ¥1,700 adults, ¥900 kids 12 and under. Daily 9am–4pm. Train: Izukyu-Shimoda Station.

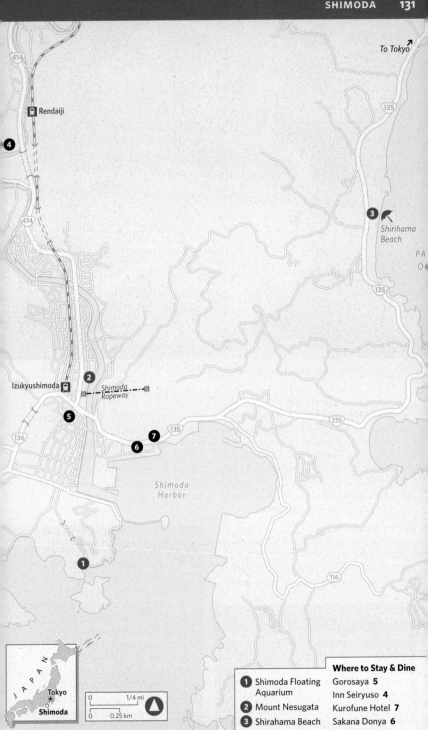

414

Rendaiji

4

414

135

3 Shirihama
Beach

PA
O

135

Izkyushimoda

2 Shimoda
Ropeway

5

136

7

6

135

135

Shimoda
Harbor

116

1

J A P A N

Tokyo

Shimoda

0   1/4 mi
0   0.25 km

Where to Stay & Dine

1 Shimoda Floating   Gorosaya **5**
    Aquarium
                        Inn Seiryuso **4**
2 Mount Nesugata
                        Kurofune Hotel **7**
3 Shirahama Beach
                        Sakana Donya **6**

> *Inhabitants of the Shimoda Floating Aquarium.*

2 ★ **Mount Nesugata** (下田ロープウェイ 寝姿山). The Shimoda Ropeway shuttles tourists to the top of Mount Nesugata for beautiful views of the surrounding area and ocean. There is also a small park and temple on the peak. ⏱ 2 hr. 1-3-2 Higashi Hongo. ☎ 0558/22-1211. www.ropeway.co.jp. ¥1,000 adults, ¥500 kids. Daily 9am–5pm. Train: Izukyu-Shimoda Station.

3 ★★★ **Shirahama Beach** (白浜ビーチ). This beautiful white-sand beach is the main reason most people come to Shimoda. Officially, beach season kicks off in mid-July and lasts until the end of August, but the conditions are usually pleasant well into September. Stands on the beach rent umbrellas (¥1,000) for sunbathers and body boards (¥500) for those who want to ride the waves. ⏱ 3 hr. 2745-1 Shirahama. ☎ 0558/22-5240. www.izu-shirahama.jp. Free. Daily sunrise–sunset. Bus: 9 from Izykyu-Shimoda Station.

Travel Tip

Keep in mind that all of Izu's beach resorts can get terribly crowded during the summer vacation period from mid-July to the end of August. If you do travel during the peak summer season, try to make your reservations for accommodations at least several months in advance.

Commemorating the Commodore

Shimoda is perhaps best known as the place where American commodore Matthew Perry arrived with his fleet of heavily armed steam-powered frigates in 1853, successfully opening Japan to the outside world after more than 2 centuries of isolation. Japanese nicknamed his (then) cutting-edge warships the *Kurofune*—"Black Ships." Today, they're treated as local mascots of sorts. In fact, on the third weekend of every May, the city throws a festival to commemorate the event, including a parade and fireworks.

Where to Stay & Dine in Shimoda

> Poolside at the Inn Seiryuso.

★★★ Gorosaya (旬の味 ごろさや) *SEAFOOD*

An elegant little restaurant located just a stone's throw from the train station, Gorosaya is the place to go for a taste of local seafood, whether steamed, fried, in soups, or as sashimi. It also has an English menu, a helpful touch for foreign travelers. You can order à la carte, of course, but we recommend trying one of the 10 different courses for more variety—even the lower-priced ones are a lot of fun. 1644-1 Shirahama. www.gorosaya.com. Lunch entrees from ¥1,575, dinner entrees from ¥3,150. No credit cards. Lunch & dinner Fri–Wed. Train: Izukyu-Shimoda Station.

★★★ Inn Seiryuso (清流荘)

While unquestionably on the expensive side, this luxurious rural retreat offers a surprising array of amenities normally not found in *ryokan,* including a swimming pool, a beauty spa, a bar with bartender, and even a little movie theater. The top class of rooms have their own private *rotenburo*—outdoor baths. (Those without share a common outdoor bath with other guests.) Seiryuso is also known for its *kaiseki* course meals, which are served right in your room. With only 15 rooms, Seiryuso can fill up quickly, particularly in the summer months, so book ahead. 2-2 Kochi. www.seiryuso.co.jp. 15 units. Doubles from ¥37,800 per person. Rates include breakfast and dinner. AE, DC, MC, V. Train: Ren-daiji Station.

★ Kurofune Hotel (黒船ホテル)

Named for the "Black Ships" (p. 132) that steamed their way through Shimoda's harbor in the 19th century, the Kurofune Hotel offers spacious Japanese-style rooms with beautiful ocean views. It is a large, resort-style hotel with amenities including an indoor pool. Built in 1963, its least expensive rooms are clean but definitely showing their age; meanwhile, the more expensive are quite nice, with their own private *onsen* baths for a touch of luxury. 3-8 Kakisaki. ☎ 0558/22-1234. www.kurofune-hotel.com. 73 units. Doubles from ¥11,800. AE, DC, MC, V. Train: Izukyu-Shimoda Station.

★ kids Sakana Donya (魚どんや) *SUSHI*

This fun and funky little restaurant right across the street from the Kurofune Hotel feels like the Japanese equivalent of an American boardwalk joint. Its whiteboards feature an ever-changing array of locally caught seafood that is prepared by hand on the premises and served on conveyor belts. You can either wait for your favorite to swing around, or ask the chef to make up a plate for you on the spot. 1-1 Sotogaoka. www10.ocn.ne.jp/~donya/index.html. Small plates from ¥180. No credit cards. Lunch & dinner daily; may close irregularly, check website for updates. Train: Izukyu-Shimoda Station.

Mount Fuji

Mount Fuji, affectionately called "Fuji-san" by Japanese, has been revered since ancient times. Throughout the centuries, Japanese poets have written about it, painters have painted it, pilgrims have flocked to it, and more than a few people have died on it. There is no question that it is a stunningly impressive sight. At 3,766m (12,356 ft.), it's the tallest mountain in Japan, towering far above anything else around it, a cone of almost perfectly symmetrical proportions. To Japanese, it symbolizes the very spirit of their country. Though it's visible on clear days (mostly in winter) from as far as 150km (99 miles) away—even from Tokyo itself—Fuji-san is far more often cloaked in clouds. If you catch a glimpse of this elusive mountain, consider yourself extremely lucky. And for those who want a closer look without having to strap on the climbing gear, some of the best spots for views of Mount Fuji are Hakone (p. 118) and Izu (p. 130).

> *Fuji is a constant presence, visible from many places in Japan—even Tokyo.*

START From Tokyo's Shinjuku Station, take a Fujikyu or Keio bus to Kawaguchiko Fifth Station (2½ hr.).

❶ Getting to Fuji-san. In July and August there are six buses daily that travel directly from Tokyo's Shinjuku Station to Kawaguchiko Trail's Fifth Station, costing ¥2,600 one way and taking roughly 2½ hours. Buses, which depart a 2-minute walk from the west side of Shinjuku Station in front of the Yasuda Seimi No. 2 Building, require reservations, which you can make at the **Keio Shinjuku Highway Bus Terminal** (☎ 03/5376-2222) or a local travel agency such as JTB.

If you want to use your Japan Rail Pass to get to Mount Fuji, you can leave from Tokyo's

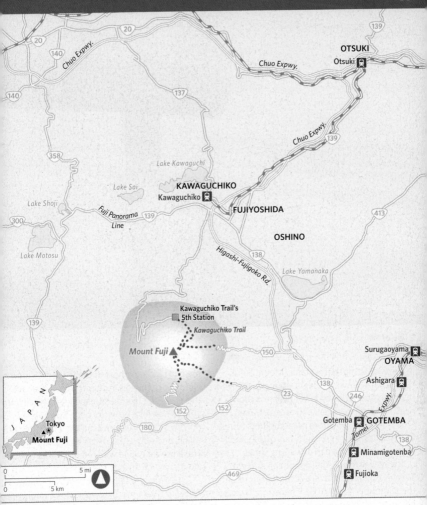

Shinjuku Station via the **JR Chuo Line** to Otsuki, where you change to the **Fuji Kyuko Line** for Kawaguchiko Station. The entire trip takes about 3 hours. Note, however, that you must pay an extra ¥1,110 for the last leg of the journey, and from Kawaguchiko Station you must still take a 45-minute bus ride onward to the Fifth Station.

2 **When to Climb.** There are four ascents to the summit of Mount Fuji (and four descents), each divided into 10 stations of unequal length, with most climbs starting at the Go-go-me, or the Fifth Station, about 1,400m to 2,400m (4,600–7,900 ft.) above sea level.

The "official" climbing season is very short, only from July 1 to August 31. Climbers are discouraged from climbing outside the season, due to low temperatures, super-strong winds, and no emergency services. To beat the crowds, try to schedule your climb on a weekday during the first 2 weeks of July, before the start of Japan's school vacation (around July 20). Thereafter, you will likely find yourself in a massive line of fellow climbers queuing their way to the peak; some 400,000 make the climb every year. (The crowds are considered part of the experience, and if you're hungering to commune with nature in solitude, you would be better off picking another peak.)

> *Top of the world, on Mount Fuji.*

In contrast to most mountains, Mount Fuji is traditionally climbed at night—the idea being to catch the sunrise from the peak. You don't need climbing experience to ascend Mount Fuji (you'll see everyone from grandmothers to children making the pilgrimage), but you do need stamina and a good pair of walking shoes.

It gets very chilly on Mount Fuji at night. Even in August, the average temperature on the summit is 43°F (6°C). There are places to eat and rest on the way to the top, but prices are high, so carry as many snacks and liquids with you as you can.

❸ **Climbing the Kawaguchiko-Yoshidaguchi Trail.** Mount Fuji is part of a larger national park called Fuji-Hakone-Izu National Park. Of the handful of trails leading to the top, most popular for Tokyoites is this trail, which is divided into 10 different stages. **Kawaguchiko Fifth Station,** located about 2,475m (8,120 ft.) up and served by bus (see above), is the usual starting point. From here it takes about 6 hours to reach the summit and 3 hours for the descent.

Don't be disappointed by the souvenir shops, restaurants, and busloads of tourists at the Fifth Station; most of these tourists aren't climbing to the top. As soon as you get past them and the blaring loudspeakers, you'll find yourself on a steep rocky path, surrounded only by scrub brush and the hikers on the path below and above you. After a couple of hours, you'll probably find yourself above the roily clouds, which stretch in all directions.

The usual procedure for climbing Mount Fuji is to take a morning bus, start climbing in early afternoon, spend the night in a hut near the summit (p. 137), get up early in the morning to climb the rest of the way to the top, and then watch the sun rise (at about 4:30am) from atop Mount Fuji. (You can, of course, also wake up in time to see the sun rise and then continue climbing.) At the summit is a 1-hour hiking trail that circles the crater. Hikers then begin the descent, reaching the Fifth Station before noon.

Hardier climbers can do the trip in one shot, arriving at the Fifth Station late in the evening, climbing to the top during the night with the aid of flashlights, watching the sunrise, and making your descent. That way, you don't have to spend the night in one of the huts.

Spending the Night on Mount Fuji

There are about 16 **mountain huts** along the Kawaguchiko Trail above the Fifth Station. They're very primitive, providing only futons and toilet facilities. Some have the capacity to house 500 hikers. Note that meals are always Japanese-style: generally dried fish, rice, miso soup, and pickled vegetables; if you aren't a fan, you'll have to pack meals yourself—but they will have to be instant foods as there is no cooking allowed. (Drinking is prohibited in many huts, so leave the beer behind.) Book as early as you can to ensure a place. Some recommendations are below; call the **Japanese Inn Union of Mount Fuji** at ☎ 0555/22-1944 for more information.

Seikanso Hut. Offers flush toilets. Sixth stage. ☎ 0555/24-6090. www.seikanso.jp. ¥5,250 per person without meals, ¥7,350 per person with 2 meals. July to mid-Oct.

Toyokan Hut. Seventh stage. ☎ 0555/22-1040. www.fuji-toyokan.jp/english/index. htm. ¥8,000 per person with 2 meals in large shared room, ¥9,000 per person with 2 meals in small shared room; ¥500 extra per person Fri, Sun, and holidays; ¥1,500 extra per person on Sat and days preceding holidays. June–Sept.

Taishikan Hut. Eighth stage. ☎ 0555/22-1947. www.mfi.or.jp/w3/home0/taisikan. ¥8,000 per person with 2 meals; ¥1,000 extra Fri; ¥1,600 extra Sat.

MASTER OF THE "FLOATING WORLD"

Hokusai was Japan's undisputed champion of the art of the woodblock print BY MATT ALT & HIROKO YODA

VISIONARY KATSUSHIKA HOKUSAI (1760–1849) has been synonymous with Japanese art for close to 2 centuries. Even if you don't know his name or aren't particularly familiar with Japanese design, chances are you know his masterpiece *The Great Wave Off Kanagawa*, an iconic print of a huge wave breaking off the coastline.

Woodblock Print Culture

The era of relative peace beginning in 1600 led to the rise of a consumer class in Japan and, by the mid-17th century, a thriving marketplace for books and periodicals. However, the sheer quantity of *kanji* (Japanese characters) needed to write sentences precluded the widespread adoption of moveable type. Instead, Japanese relied on hand-carved woodblock prints for reading material.

At the age of 18, Hokusai began studying the *ukiyo-e*—"pictures of the floating world," a term used for the elaborate woodblock print illustrations of historical figures, geisha, and actors that dominated Japanese art from the mid-18th to early 19th centuries. Starting in the 1790s, Hokusai turned from these "highfalutin" subjects to focus instead on

everyday landscapes, animals and insects, scenes of daily life, and episodes from folk stories—revolutionizing the *ukiyo-e* world, and giving future generations a rare glimpse into the past.

Hokusai's Masterworks

◀ THE GREAT WAVE OFF KANAGAWA
This print, produced in the 1830s, is undoubtedly Hokusai's most famed woodblock.

▲ RED FUJI
A print from the *Thirty-Six Views of Mount Fuji* series showcases Japan's iconic mountain at sunset.

HOKUSAI *MANGA*
Hokusai was an inveterate doodler, and many of his sketches were collected together under the title of *manga*, or "playful pictures." Today, the word is used to refer to comic books, and Hokusai is considered a pioneering cartoonist.

Woodblock Printing

Although the end result is beautiful, the process of making woodblock prints is a laborious one. It requires drawing a master illustration on thin paper, attaching it to a block of wood, carving away all of the negative space to create an outline master block, and then creating multiple filler blocks to achieve the full range of colors. Every color pass requires its own individual block. Typically, artists such as Hokusai worked with teams of assistants who performed much of the manual labor of printing.

Tokyo Fast Facts

Arriving & Getting Around

BY PLANE **Narita International Airport** (☎ 0476/34-8000; www.narita-airport.jp) is the main international hub in Tokyo. Domestic flights usually land at **Haneda Airport,** also called Tokyo International Airport (☎ 03/5757-8111). The **Airport Limousine Bus** (☎ 03/3665-7220; www.limousinebus.co.jp) picks up passengers and their luggage from just outside both airports and delivers them to downtown hotels. BY TRAIN If you're traveling to Tokyo from elsewhere in Japan, you'll most likely arrive via **Shinkansen bullet train** at Tokyo, Ueno, or Shinagawa stations (avoid Tokyo Station if you can; it's very big and confusing). All are well served by trains (including the useful JR Yamanote Line), subways, and taxis. BY BUS Long-distance bus service from Hiroshima, Nagoya, Osaka, Kyoto, and other major cities delivers passengers to Tokyo and Shinjuku stations, both of which are connected to the rest of the city via subway and commuter train, including the JR Yamanote Line, which loops around the city. BY FERRY There are no international ferry services to Tokyo, but domestic long-distance ferries arrive at Ariake Ferry Terminal, located on an artificial island adjacent to Odaiba in Tokyo Bay; the nearest station is Kokusai-Tenjijo-Seimon. Cruise lines usually dock at Harumi Terminal.

ATMs

In contrast to those abroad, many ATMs only operate during banking hours. ATMs are also very hard to find outside of major cities, so plan accordingly. Most post offices (see below) have ATM facilities, although hours are limited. For 24-hour access, your best bets are the ATMs in **7-Eleven** convenience stores, which accept Visa, Plus, American Express, JCB, Union Pay, or Diner's Club International cards for cash withdrawals. (They recently stopped accepting MasterCard, Maestro, and Cirrus cards.) **Citibank** and **Shinsei Bank** ATMs accept foreign bank cards as well.

Doctors & Hospitals

Large hospitals in Japan are open only a limited number of hours (designated hospitals remain open for emergencies, however, and an ambulance will automatically take you there). However the **Tokyo Midtown Medical Center** has some English-speaking staff and is popular with foreigners living in Tokyo; it is an affiliate of Johns Hopkins and located on the sixth floor of Midtown Tower, 9-7-1 Akasaka, Minato-ku, near Roppongi Station (☎ 03/5413-7911; www.tokyomidtown-mc.jp; open Mon–Fri 10:30am–1pm; accepts walk-ins, appointments, and emergencies).

Emergencies

The national emergency numbers are ☎ **110** for police and ☎ **119** for ambulance and fire.

Internet Access

Tokyo has very little free Internet access. Some hotels have it, others charge extra for it, and a great many don't offer it at all. However, there are many Internet cafes to be found throughout the city. Rates vary but are about ¥300 per hour of use, with free beverages thrown in. The **Manboo!** (www.manboo.co.jp) chain is one of the largest, with outlets all over the city. Look for the English language logo with the big yellow fish. The **Bagus Gran Cyber Cafe** (www.bagus-99.com/netcafe) is another option, with many outlets downtown. Don't expect much in the way of English hand-holding at Internet cafes, but the registration process is simple enough to make it through without knowing Japanese. An increasing number of cafes are offering free Wi-Fi access. One of our favorites is the **Wired Cafe** (www.cafecompany.co.jp/brands/wired/index.html) chain, which has outlets near many major stations, including Shibuya, Ueno, Shinjuku, Kichijoji, and Roppongi.

Pharmacies

Drugstores, called *yakkyoku* (薬局) are ubiquitous in Japan, but they are not 24-hour operations. Your best bet is to ask your hotel concierge for the closest location. If you're looking for specific pharmaceuticals, a good bet is the **American Pharmacy,** in the basement of the Marunouchi Building, 2-4-1 Marunouchi, Chiyoda-ku (☎ 03/5220-7716; Mon–Fri 9am–9pm, Sat 10am–9pm, Sun and holidays 10am–8pm), which has many of the

> *Another quiet afternoon on the Imperial Palace grounds.*

same over-the-counter drugs you can find at home (many of them imported from the United States) and can fill American prescriptions—but note that you must first visit a doctor in Japan before foreign prescriptions can be filled, so it's best to bring an ample supply of any prescription medication with you.

Police
The national emergency telephone number is ☎ 110. The Metropolitan Police Department also maintains a telephone counseling service for foreigners at ☎ 03/3501-0110 (Mon–Fri 8:30am–5:15pm).

Post Office
The **Shibuya Central Post Office,** 1-12-13 Shibuya (☎ 03/5469-9907), has longer business hours than most post offices in Tokyo (Mon–Fri 9am–9pm; Sat–Sun and holidays 9am–7pm). An after-hours counter remains open throughout the night for mail and packages, making it the only 24-hour post office in town.

Safety
Tokyo is one of the safest cities in the world. However, crime is on the increase, and there are precautions you should always take when traveling: Stay alert and be aware of your immediate surroundings. Be especially careful with cameras, purses, and wallets, particularly in crowded subways, department stores, or tourist attractions (such as the retail district around Tsukiji Fish Market), especially because pickpocketing has been on the rise. Some Japanese also caution women against walking through parks alone at night.

Visitor Information
The excellent **Tourist Information Center (TIC)** run by the **Japan National Tourist Organization (JNTO)** is in downtown Tokyo, 2-10-1 Yurakucho (☎ 03/3201-3331). Another source of information is the **Tokyo Tourist Information Center** in the Tokyo Metropolitan Government Building (p. 63, ❽), 2-8-1 Nishi-Shinjuku (☎ 03/5321-3077).

Favorite Moments

The natural terrain of Central Honshu, which stretches across Japan's main island from Aichi in the southwest to Niigata in the northeast, is as varied as it is wide, and much of it is distractingly beautiful. One of the country's most stunning waterfalls, Japan's oldest wooden castle, and Olympic skiing can all be reached in just over an hour outside of Tokyo. If you make the effort to go farther afield, however, you'll catch glimpses of Japan as it was in ancient times and experience the kind of warm hospitality that has all but disappeared from today's modern cities.

> PREVIOUS PAGE *The works of artist Yayoi Kusama on display at the Matsumoto Museum of Art.* THIS PAGE *Strolling the leafy grounds of Matsumoto Castle.*

1 Staring down into the caldera lake Yugama. This 32,00-wide (985-ft.) body of water at the bottom of a crater sparkles like a giant jewel in the dry, volcanic terrain. In the summer, the trail leading to the lookout point on Mount Shirane blooms with flowers. See p. 159.

2 Bathing in Sainokawara Rotenburo. Tucked into the woods of Sainokawara Park, this open-air bath is the largest in Kusatsu, with room for more than 100 bathers at a time. It's particularly atmospheric in the winter, when the steam that rises from the hot water shrouds the bath in mist. See p. 158, 4.

3 Going on an art scavenger hunt in Tokamachi. The rural city of Tokamachi has become the unlikely setting for over 100 large-scale contemporary artworks, scattered around the countryside like brilliant—and sometimes bewildering—Easter eggs. See p. 154.

4 Visiting a 200-year-old brewery in Shibata. The original buildings of the Ichishima Brewery, founded in 1790, now house displays of early sake-brewing equipment, drinking vessels, and a collection of beautiful kimono. Best of all, the tour includes a tasting of Ichishima's award-winning brews. A visit could (and should) be combined with a trip to the neighboring town of Murakami, famous for sake and salmon. See p. 171, 5.

5 Learning the tricks of the ninja trade at Iga-ryu Ninja Museum. You'll see firsthand how the ninja used the many traps and gimmicks built into their houses, and watch dazzling demonstrations of their fighting prowess. See p. 164, 5.

1 Staring down into the caldera lake Yugama
2 Bathing in Sainokawara Rotenburo
3 Going on an art scavenger hunt in Tokamachi
4 Visiting a 200-year-old brewery in Shibata
5 Learning the tricks of the ninja trade at Iga-ryu Ninja Museum
6 Admiring the treasures in the Tokugawa Art Museum
7 Discovering Shiraito Falls
8 Climbing the *donjon* at Matsumotojo
9 Descending the depths of Sado Kinzan Mine

6 Admiring the treasures in the Tokugawa Art Museum. The Tokugawas had a taste for the finer things, and they proved to be great collectors. This museum houses nine National Treasures and thousands of documents, samurai armor, swords, and objects d'art that once belonged to the family. See p. 162, **2**.

7 Discovering Shiraito Falls. After a walk through fragrant white birch and larch you'll emerge to one of Karuizawa's most breathtaking sights. Around 70m (230 ft.) wide, this magnificent waterfall resembles a giant curtain of fine silk threads. See p. 176, **8**.

8 Climbing the *donjon* at Matsumotojo. The steep steps of the *donjon* (keep) of the famous black-and-white-walled castle lead up six flights to the top level, where you'll have a commanding view of the city. If you can, visit the grounds during the autumn moon-viewing festival. The illuminated castle is striking against the romantic backdrop of the starry night sky. See p. 178, **1**.

9 Descending the depths of Sado Kinzan Mine. This gold mine on Sado Island was once Japan's most productive, yielding 400kg (882 lb.) of precious metal per year at its peak. These days, it's a museum with fascinating displays depicting the working conditions and extraction techniques used in the mine. See p. 190, **9**.

The Best of Central Honshu in 3 Days

Nature is the star in Central Honshu, where you'll find quiet spa towns nestled among green hills, lush forests, and active volcanoes. If you're looking for 3 days of superb hiking, off-the-beaten-track cycling, and hard-core relaxing, you've come to the right place.

> *Majestic Mount Asama, seen from Karuizawa.*

START From Ueno Station in Tokyo, board the Toki Shinkansen to Naganohara-Kusatsuguchi Station (150 min.). Then ride the JR bus line for 30 minutes and get off at Kusatsu Onsen.

1 Kusatsu Onsen. Bathers have been soaking in the therapeutic waters of Kusatsu Onsen, in Gunma prefecture, since at least the 12th century, but the town only became popular as a spa resort after German doctor Erwin von Baelz wrote about the water's curative powers in the 1800s.

The town boasts the largest output of water in Japan. Kusatsu's hot springs are fed by nearby volcano **Mount Shirane** (p. 159) at an astounding rate of 32,000L (8,500 gal.) per minute. The town has 18 public baths, most of which are open 24 hours a day. A 10-minute walk from the station, the steaming, gurgling **Yubatake fountainhead** (p. 156, **1**) forms an arresting sight—particularly at night, when the bubbling pool is illuminated—in the middle of the city.

The Yubatake serves as the town's physical as well as symbolic center, with most of the

1	Kusatsu Onsen
2	Karuizawa
3	Shibu Onsen

ops, restaurants, and public baths concen-
ated around the giant, gourd-shaped "water
ld." Along the shopping street that leads
Sainokawara Park you'll find stores selling
sen-manju, sweet buns filled with red bean
ste, and stalls grilling skewered river fish
nong the souvenir shops. A walk through the
rk will bring you to the **Sainokawara Roten-
uro** (p. 154, **8**), where you can take a dip au
turel in one of Japan's largest outdoor baths.
In the spring, summer, and fall, allow time
r a hiking trip around the volcano Mount
irane (p. 159) to see the marvelous **Yugama caldera
ke** (p. 159). ⏱ **1 day.**

Board the Kusakaru bus from Kusatsu Onsen
bus stop and get off at **Karuizawa Station (75
min.).**

2 Karuizawa. Located at the base of Mount
Asama in southeastern Nagano, Karuizawa
sits on a verdant plateau 1,000m (3,280 ft.)
above sea level. Thanks to its alpine elevation,
the town has become a favorite summer retreat for Tokyoites looking to escape the heat.
Karuizawa was first established as a resort
town in 1886 by Canadian missionary Alex-
ander Croft Shaw, who spread the word of the
area's natural beauty to wealthy westerners
living in Japan. Western influence on architecture and culture remains to this day.

> *Bubble, bubble: At night, the Yubatake in Kusatsu Onsen gurgles and steams like a giant cauldron.*

The town is easily navigated on foot, but bicycles are available for rent at several shops in front of the station. (A bike costs about ¥500 per hour or ¥1,800 for the day.) The main road, called **Karuizawa Ginza,** is an 800m (½-mile) stretch lined with shops and eateries. It's a pleasant walk in the cooler months, but the road is packed with tourists during the summer peak.

Northwest of the station, just beyond a cemetery for Karuizawa's former foreign residents, lies tranquil **Kumoba-ike Pond.** From the pond, continue north through the **Kajima no Mori Forest** to the city's most famous landmark, **Saint Paul's Catholic Church.** The **A. C. Shaw Memorial Chapel** is tucked deep in the woods beyond.

A 20-minute bus ride from Karuizawa Station, **Shiraito Falls** is one of the area's most stunning sights. Although the falls are only 3m (10 ft.) high, they stretch out in a 70m (230-ft.) curtain of fine, silky-white water threads. Hence, the name Shiraito, which means "white threads." If you have time, you can take the 3-hour hike past Ryugaeshi Falls to the **Former Mikasa Hotel.** ⏱1 day. See p. 175, **7**.

Monkey Business

The monkeys of Nagano have gotten some bad press recently for their mischievous behavior. Having grown accustomed to the attention of humans, the monkeys no longer fear them and have few moral qualms about popping into shops and residences to steal food. Stories have even been told of monkeys running off with bags and wallets left unattended near outdoor hot springs. It's a rare occurrence, but it's always a good idea to keep your belongings safely stowed in a locker while bathing.

Although the monkeys in Jigokudani Snow Monkey Park seem cute and cuddly, remember that they are still wild animals. Observe the monkeys from a distance and do not try to touch them, or stare them in the eyes. Naturally, you should refrain from feeding them. And hard as it may be, try not to smile—bared teeth are a sign of aggression in the monkey world, and your mirth may be misinterpreted.

Dip your toes into the relaxing ashi-yu *footbaths scattered throughout Shibu Onsen.*

rom Karuizawa Station, board the Asama
ain to Nagano. Change to the Nagano Den-
etsu Limited Express and get off at Yudanaka
108 min.). From Yudanaka Station, get on the
anbayashi or Shiga Kogen Line bus and get
ff at Shibu Onsen (5 min.).

Shibu Onsen. With its scenic, stone-paved
aths and buildings that date back over 400
ears, the quiet spa town of Shibu Onsen has
etained much of its historic beauty. Even
oday, people can be seen wandering in and
ut of the city's nine **public baths** wearing
ukata (summer kimono) and geta (traditional
ooden clogs). This custom, which visitors are
ecommended to observe, is one of the most
elightful aspects of a trip to Shibu Onsen.

In Shibu, you may encounter a few furry tour-
ts from the famed **Jigokudani Snow Monkey**
ark. Don't worry, they won't climb into the
ot springs with you: They have their own bath.
visit to the Snow Monkey Park is a relatively
asy trip—and well worth it. Since check-in time
t most ryokan (traditional inns) isn't until 3pm,
e recommend sticking your bags in a locker
nd heading to the park as soon as you arrive.

The park is about a 30-minute walk through
the forest from Kanbayashi Onsen-guchi stop
(5 min. by bus from Shibu Onsen). The main
attraction centers on the manmade baths in
the middle of the park, where the monkeys
gather to bathe. It's a small park, basically
consisting of one main and two sub-baths
built into a river valley. Nothing separates the
people and monkeys, and the monkeys can
come and go as they please. They "commute"
from the mountains every morning because
they know the park rangers will leave food for
them. The monkeys need little encouragement to hop in the tub during the cold winter
months, but even in the summer, they can be
bribed into bathing with treats from the park
rangers. The path to the park is clearly marked
with signs in Japanese and English. ⊙ 1 day.
Monkey Park: 6845 Yamanouchimachi Shimo-
takai-gun, Nagano. ☎ 026/933-8521. www.
jigokudani-yaenkoen.co.jp. ¥500 adults, ¥250
kids. Daily Apr–Oct 8:30am–5pm; Nov–Mar
9am–4pm. Bus: Kanbayashi or Shiga Kogen lines
to Kanbayashi Onsen or Kanbayashi Onsen-
guchi. Some hotels and ryokan operate shuttles
that will take you close to the park.

The Best of Central Honshu in 1 Week

If you can spend a week in Central Honshu, use part of it to explore some of the lesser-known areas, in addition to the famous spots. The island of Sado is a favorite among tourists but the fact that relatively few take time to visit the snowy, mountainous region of Tokamachi is one of the best reasons to go. After Shibu Onsen, we recommend stopping for a night in the attractive town of Matsumoto.

> Artist James Turrell's meditative House of Light.

START From Shibu Onsen, take the bus back to Yudanaka Station and get on the Nagano-Dentetsu train to Nagano Station. At Nagano, change to the Shinano Wide View Limited Express and get off at Matsumoto Station (130 min.).

① **Matsumoto.** The history of Matsumoto goes back as far as 12,000 years, but the town really came into its own after the construction of the **Matsumotojo** castle in 1504. Surrounded by a placid moat filled with ducks and white swans, the castle cuts an imposing figure. Because of it black roof and the black-painted walls of its six-story *donjon* (keep), the castle is often referred to as Karasujo, or "Crow Castle." The country's oldest wooden castle, it's one of only four castle in Japan to be designated as National Treasures (along with Hikone, Himeji, and Inuyama).

Anticipating gun warfare, the Ishikawa clan rebuilt the castle in 1593 and reinforced it with arrow and gun slots and walls thick enough to

1 Matsumoto
2 Tokamachi
3 Sado

withstand bullets, but the castle never came under attack. No longer under constant threat of civil war, the samurai finally had time to contemplate the stars and write poetry, and a moon-viewing pavilion was added in 1635. Every autumn, a **moon-viewing festival** takes place on the castle grounds.

While Mastmotojo is the city's main attraction, you should also take time to walk around the **Nakamachi** area, a former merchant district whose stately old wooden buildings are now filled with cute shops and cafes. Continue on to the **Japan Ukiyo-e Museum,** a stylish contemporary building that houses one of the largest

and impressive collections of woodblock paintings in the world. ⏱1 day. See p. 180, **3**.

From Matsumoto Station, take the Shinonoi Line to Nagano, then the Asama Line to Takasaki, followed by the Max Tanigawa Line to Echigo-Yuzawa Station (3½ hr.).

SITE GUIDE
PAGE 154

2 Tokamachi. The winding roads of Tokamachi curve around beautifully sculpted rice fields and patches of forest silhouetted against a backdrop of snow-capped mountains. The splendid natural landscapes in this part

> *Dramatic seascapes greet you on Sado Island, off the coast of Niigata.*

of Niigata are interrupted here and there by strange and wonderful sights—a giant "stage" made of recycled metal scraps, a house covered in a cobweb-veil hewn from thick cords, a garden of golden pebbles and mirrors. Over 100 large-scale installation artworks, created by world-famous artists from over 38 countries, are nestled around the countryside like Easter eggs.

Once a center of rice production, the region has suffered greatly from the effects of depopulation, as members of the younger generation have resettled in the cities. In 1996, local governments launched the **Echigo-Tsumari Art Necklace** program in an attempt to give an economic boost to the area by transforming the agricultural area into a vast field of contemporary art.

Rent a car from an outlet near Echigo-Yuzawa Station, and take to the open road. There's a lot to discover, but if you only have time to visit a few places (the artworks are rather spread apart), start with the futuristic **Noubutai** visitor center and then *Last Class,* a chilling reflection on the Holocaust and depopulation created by French multimedia artist Christian Boltanski and lighting director Jean Kalman. Then, soldier on through the hills to the *House*

of Light, a mesmerizing light installation and meditation room designed by California artist James Turrell. The work was inspired by Junichiro Tanizaki's 1933 treatise on aesthetics, *In Praise of Shadows.*

If you reserve in advance, you can stay overnight at one of the installations in one of Tokamachi's converted houses. Otherwise, spend the night in Echigo-Yuzawa. ⏲ 1 day. See p. 154.

From Echigo-Yuzawa Station, take the Max Toki Limited Express to Niigata Station (46 min.). From Niigata, Sado Kisen runs up to si: ferries (2½ hr.) and several jetfoils (1 hr.) to the port of Ryotsu on Sado Island.

❸ **Sado.** A remote island off the coast of Niigata, Sado was once a place of ill repute. Political dissidents, controversial artists, and rulers who fell out of power were banished to this island between the 8th and 18th centuries Among the most famous of Sado's exiles are the monk Nichiren, who founded the Nichiren school of Buddhism, the former emperor Juntoku, and the artist Zeami Motokiyo, one of the originators of Noh drama.

Thanks to the large number of artists, poets, and free thinkers sent to Sado, high ulture flourished on the island, and Sado is till a center for traditional arts such as classial musical drama, or Noh. A visit to the **Sado ogakunosato,** near the island's main port of yotsu, will teach you everything you've ever vanted to know about this esoteric art form. Masks, costumes, and props used in performances are on display, and visitors can also vatch a drama enacted by high-tech robots. It's surprisingly absorbing.)

After the show, pay your respects to Nichi-en at **Konpon-ji,** a temple built on the site vhere the unfortunate monk was first brought fter his exile to Sado in 1271, and then hike up o Sado's oldest temple, **Kokubun-ji.**

In 1601, a gold mine was built on Sado sland, in Aikawa, near the minor port of Ogi. eemingly overnight, the tiny town became he hub of an economic boom fueled by the iscovery of gold and the shipping industry. n the early days of the gold rush, the mines were worked by exiles; later, criminals and the homeless were shipped out of urban areas to toil under near-slavery conditions. At its peak, **Sado Kinzan Mine** produced a staggering 400kg (882 lb.) of gold annually, most of which was used to finance the Tokugawa government. Situated halfway up a steep mountain, it's been turned into a fascinating museum that traces the history of the mine, with guided tours that lead you through the defunct mining tunnels.

On the way down back to the bus stop, check out the **Aikawa Folk Museum.** Exhibits at this museum provide insight onto the living conditions and customs of the people in the town.

Despite its sad history, Sado is an island of warm, welcoming people with a vibrant culture, and it's one of the few places in Japan to retain so much of its unspoiled natural beauty. 🕐 2 days. See p. 186.

Operating the taraibune *tub boats from Ogi harbor is exclusively the domain of Sado's little old ladies.*

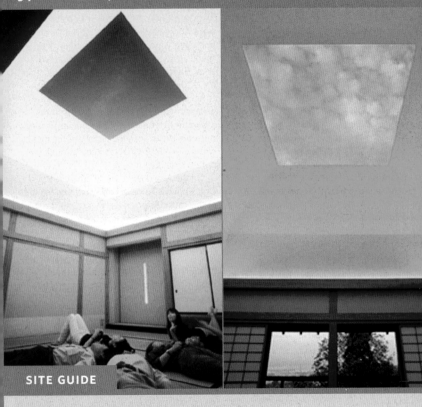

SITE GUIDE

2 Tokamachi

The rural towns of Tokamachi and nearby Matsudai have become the unlikely setting for over 100 large-scale contemporary installation artworks. The pieces, mostly contained within old wooden houses and former school buildings, pepper the spectacular natural landscape with sparks of human inspiration. The 1924 Ⓐ ★ **Ubusuna House (うぶすなの家)** has become the site of a gallery dedicated to pottery. The sunken hearth, fire-burning stove, sink, and bath are all works of modern art, and the gallery holds seasonal exhibitions of local crafts.

California artist James Turrell has created a meditative space, Ⓑ ★★★ *House of Light* (光の館**),** that melds traditional and modern Japanese architecture and showcases one of his most stunning light installations. The centerpiece of the house is the remote-controlled sliding panel that can be opened to reveal a perception-bending, picture-perfect

frame of the sky (pictured above). Guests can opt to spend the night here in order to watch the colors of the sky change at sunset and sunrise.

Designed by Netherlands-based architectural firm MVRDV, the wide, flat structure of the Ⓒ ★★ **Matsudai Yukiguni Agricultural Culture Village (Noubutai;** まつだい農舞台**)** appears to hover like a spaceship over the outdoor event space below. Inside, there's a gallery, a cafe, and a shop selling local products and artsy souvenirs. The interior is thoroughly modern, divided into areas for different functions by the dramatic use of color. Exhibitions vary, but among the highlights of the permanent collection are outdoor installations by contemporary artists Yayoi Kusama and the Russian duo Ilya and Emilia Kabakov, on display in the beautifully sculpted rice terraces that surround the building.

In conjunction with a team of sculpture

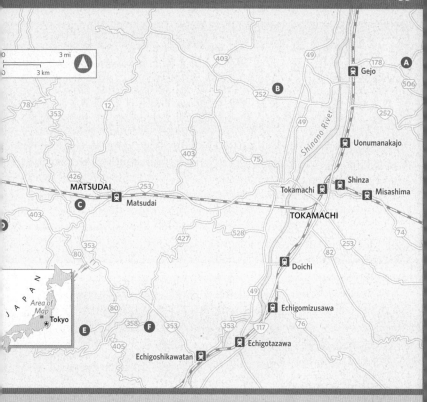

tudents from the Nihon University College f Art, Japanese artist Junichi Kurakake gave ew life to one of the area's empty houses by arving curves and swirls into every surface of s wooden interior. D ★★ *Shedding House* 脱皮する家) took over 2 years to complete, and he obsessive quality of the etched surfaces is esmerizing, as well as tactilely pleasing.

Renowned Serbian performance artist arina Abramović chose as the site of er 2009 E ★★★ *Dream House* (夢の家) a ormer wooden residence that overlooks a ce field and leans, Tower of Pisa–like, to ne side. In the *Dream House,* Abramović as created a minimal space intended to timulate the subconscious. On one floor, the valls are covered with cryptic incantations crawled in red ink ("In times of doubt, keep small meteorite stone in your mouth"), nd the "dream rooms" are furnished with offin-shaped boxes to sleep in. Visitors are

instructed to don, prior to bedtime, different colored sleeping suits (they all look vaguely like Teletubby outfits). In the morning, guests record their dreams in a book.

French multimedia artist Christian Boltanski and lighting director Jean Kalman teamed up to create F ★★★ *Last Class* (最後の教室), a haunting reflection on depopulation. The installation encompasses a former school. On the first floor, the gymnasium has been transformed into a barren field of ankle-deep straw. The floors above are equally menacing: Inside classrooms shrouded in swathes of white satin sit coffinlike glass boxes filled with fluorescent lights. As you walk the dark, empty halls, the sound of amplified heartbeats (recorded from previous visitors) thunders down the corridors. ⊕ 2 days. Tourist Information Center: ☎ 0255/95-6688. www. echigo-tsumari.jp. Admission and hours vary. Train: Tokamachi Station.

The Hot Springs of Central Honshu

While frequent earthquakes are the negative result of Japan's location in the middle of an active volcanic belt, there is a positive side: namely, the more than 3,000 natural hot springs scattered around the country. The tiny *onsen* (spa town) of Kusatsu Onsen, nestled in the northwest corner of Gunma prefecture, is considered one of the finest. Although less famous, its neighbor Ikaho Onsen is another fantastic place to have a traditional Japanese *onsen* experience. We recommend 2 days for this tour, but if you have time for only 1, use it to relax in Kusatsu Onsen.

> *Water, water, everywhere, flowing in and out of Kusatsu Onsen's Yubatake.*

START From Ueno Station in Tokyo, board the Toki Shinkansen bullet train to Naganohara-Kusatsuguchi Station (150 min.). Then ride the JR bus line for 30 minutes and get off at Kusatsu Onsen.

1 ★★ **Yubatake** (湯畑)**.** This impressive natural "hot water field" supplies Kusatsu with boiling water all year round. Seven wooden aqueducts channel and simultaneously cool the water en route to the town's many public baths, *ryokan,* and homes. The fountainhead gushes up to 4,000L (1,000 gal.) of piping-hot geothermal water per minute and creates a particularly memorable sight in winter, when the steam rising from the surface resembles that of a giar

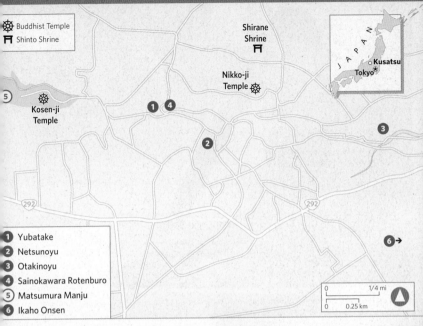

✿ Buddhist Temple
⛩ Shinto Shrine

Shirane
Shrine ⛩

Nikko-ji
Temple ✿

Kosen-ji
Temple

JAPAN ● Kusatsu
Tokyo ⊛

1 Yubatake
2 Netsunoyu
3 Otakinoyu
4 Sainokawara Rotenburo
5 Matsumura Manju
6 Ikaho Onsen

cauldron. The gourd-shaped pool was designed by artist Taro Okamoto. The Yubatake is a 5-minute walk from the bus terminal. ⏱ **10 min.** Bus: JR Line to Kusatsu Onsen.

2 ★★ **Netsunoyu** (熱の湯). Next to the Yubatake, this facility features shows demonstrating *yumomi,* a traditional method of cooling the springs' boiling-hot waters. During these unusual performances, two rows of women use long, thin paddles to churn the water in rhythm, while singing "Kusatsu Bushi," a folk song. Tourists are invited to join in and help with the stirring, but the songs are best left to the ladies. ⏱ 30 min. 414 Kusatsu. ☎ 027/988-3613. ¥500. Shows daily at 10am, 10:30am, 11am, 3:30pm, and 4pm. Bus: JR Line to Kusatsu Onsen.

3 ★★ **Otakinoyu** (大滝乃湯). The traditional style of bathing in the Kusatsu Onsen area is called *awase-yu,* and involves acclimating yourself to the heat by soaking in a series of progressively warmer pools. This popular public bathhouse (the name means "Great Waterfall Hot Spring") features various hot tubs, each filled with water of different temperatures, accented with miniature waterfalls that reflect the bathhouse's namesake. ***Tip:*** There are special hours for ladies in the lower baths, so check

> *Ikaho Onsen's 300m (985 ft.) answer to the StairMaster.*

> *Sing and stir: The* yumomi *demonstrations at Kusatsu Onsen's Netsunoyu are perennially popular.*

Onsen Dos and Donts

Although in everyday life, the Japanese tend to be reserved and quite shy, the *onsen* (traditional spa) is one place where they really let their hair down. Japanese people have no problem stripping down and settling into a tub of hot water with perfect strangers. With the exception of very few mixed bathing areas, bathing suits are not only unnecessary, they're prohibited. While this may take some getting used to at first, your self-consciousness will soon melt away in the soothing hot water.

First things first: Before even going near the baths, be sure to soap up and rinse off thoroughly in the shower rooms that precede the bathing areas. Baths in *ryokan* will provide you with soap, shampoo, and an array of other fun beauty products, but public baths frequently do not. The pools are very hot (usually above 108°F/42°C), so before taking the plunge, splash yourself with water from the tubs to warm up.

Do smile and be friendly, but don't bring your towel into the bath with you. After soaking, don't rinse off: You'll wash away all of the beneficial minerals.

in advance. It's a 15-minute walk from the Yubatake. ⏱ 30 min. 596–13 Kusatsu. ☎ 0279/88-2600. www.kusatsu.ne.jp/otaki/otaki. ¥800 adults, ¥400 kids. Daily 9am–9pm (last entry 8pm). Bus: JR Line to Kusatsu Onsen.

❹ ★★★ **Sainokawara Rotenburo** (西の河原露天風呂)**.** Tucked into the woods of Sainokawara Park, this expansive outdoor bath affords fabulous views of the tree-covered mountains (especially pretty in the fall and winter, when the hills are blanketed in snow). Measuring a formidable 435 sq. m (4,700 sq. ft.), it's the largest open-air bath in Kusatsu, with room for more than 100 bathers at a time. There are separate baths for men and women, but

A Splash of Art

The ★★ **Hara Museum ARC,** 2855-1 Kanai, Shibukawa-shi, Gunma (☎ 0279/24-6585; www.haramuseum.or.jp), an annex to the Hara Contemporary Art Museum in Tokyo located in Ikaho, is a small but excellent museum that's definitely worth a visit between hot tub soaks. Opened in 2008, the Kankai Pavilion showcases paintings, calligraphy, and ceramic ware from the Hara Rokuro Collection of East Asian art.

...hanks to the *onsen*'s location halfway up a ...ill, it's possible for hikers to peer into the ...en's side (sorry, guys). The bath's milky-...hite waters are extremely popular, so be ...repared to encounter crowds at peak times. ...'s a 5-minute walk from the Yubatake along ...n old-fashioned shopping street lined with ...hops and food stalls. ⏲ 45 min. 521-3 Oaza ...usatsu. ¥500. Daily Apr-Nov 1am-8pm; Dec-...Mar 9am-8pm (last entry 7:30pm). Bus: JR Line ...o Kusatsu Onsen.

⑤   🍡 ★★ **Matsumura Manju** (松むら饅頭). Some locals claim that the *onsen manju*—flat, circular buns filled with sticky-sweet *anko* (adzuki-bean paste)—at this shop west of the Yubatake are the best in the city. They're haltingly sweet, but just short of cloying. 389 Kusatsu. ☎ 0279/88-2042. Buns ¥80. Wed-Mon 7am-6pm. Bus: JR Line to Kusatsu Onsen.

...rom Kusatsu Onsen, take the JR bus to ...Naganohara-Kusatsuguchi Station. Get on ...he JR Agatsuma train to Shibukawa (45 ...min.). From there, take the Gunma bus and ...et off at Ikaho Onsen (30 min.).

⑥ **Ikaho Onsen.** At the northeastern foot of Mount Haruna-san, Ikaho Onsen is a hot spring ...esort located on a highland rising approxi-...nately 800m (2,625 ft.) above sea level, in the ...entral part of Gunma. The level of sulfate and ...arbonic acid in its water is so high that it some-...imes dyes towels red. The ★ **Ikaho stone steps** (伊香保石段街), a 300m (985-ft.) stone staircase, ...orm the main street running through the center ...f the town. The street is lined with shops and ...raditional *ryokan*, and four observation points ...along the way allow you to follow the flow ...of the hot water underground as it makes its ...way to each inn. At the top you'll find the dark, ...wooden **Ikaho Shrine,** where the Ikaho Matsuri ...estival is held every September. A short walk (250m/820 ft.) along a road to the right of the ...staircase will lead you to **Kajika Bridge,** a gently ...curved, red bridge straight out of a picture book ...n Japan. Ikaho Onsen's distinctive iron-rich ...water flows beneath this bridge en route to ...he town's many onsen spas and can be tasted ...rom a water fountain on the side of the road. ...The steps are a 10-minute walk from the bus ...erminal.

Mount Shirane

If you visit Kusatsu Onsen between April and November, a side trip to nearby Mount Shirane (白根火山) is a must. Located a mere 35-minute bus ride from Kusatsu Onsen, this cluster of volcanoes offers excellent opportunities for hiking. The most popular route leads from the Shirane Rest House around **Yugama,** the area's famous turquoise crater lake. The 300m-wide (985-ft.) body of water sparkles like a giant jewel in the middle of the dry, volcanic terrain.

The lookout point can be reached after an easy 15-minute walk, but visitors are not allowed to venture down to the lake's shore. The trails are only open from June to mid-October; buses do not operate in the winter. The buses run infrequently and stop early, so be sure to check the schedule carefully. The JR bus line from Kusatsu Onsen to Shirane-Kazan costs ¥1,100.

When you're all finished walking, make your way to the large outdoor bath of ★★ **Ikaho Rotenburo** (伊香保露天風呂), divided in half by temperature: One side is piping hot, and the other pleasantly tepid. ⏲ 1½ hr. Rotenburo: 581 Ikaho-yumoto. ☎ 0279/72-2488. ¥450. Daily Oct-Mar 9am-6pm; Apr-Sept 9am-7pm. Closed 1st and 3rd Thurs of each month. Bus: Gunma Line to Ikaho Onsen.

Winter Sports in Honshu

The only Asian country to have hosted the winter Olympics (in 1972 and 1998), Japan offers plenty of opportunities for fans of winter sports. Thanks to Japan's unique geography and climactic conditions, it enjoys first-rate powder and a skiing season that lasts from December until April. The skiing and snowboarding in Central Honshu is second only to Hokkaido. This tour should keep you busy for 3 or more days, but you could focus on only one area in Hakuba or Naeba.

> Riding high at Naeba Ski Resort, Niigata.

START From Nagano Station, take the Nagano Hakuba bus and disembark at Happo. Nagano is 233km (145 miles) northwest of Tokyo.

❶ ★★★ Happo-one (白馬八方尾根). Made famous as the site of the men's and women's downhill races at the 1998 Winter Olympics, this ski resort in northwestern Nagano boasts some of the most amazing panoramic views of the Hakuba mountain range. Some of the highest snowfall and the longest vertical pitches in Japan make Happo-one particularly popular for seasoned powder hounds. The 13 courses range in difficulty from beginner to advanced, with both smooth and bump runs. (Night skiing courses are also open until 9pm later in the season.) There's a kid's park for aspiring snow demons, as well as several restaurants and cafes where snow bunnies can keep warm. For a mid-run break, the stylish ★ **Virgin Cafe Hakuba,** located 1,680m (5,500 ft.) up the mountain (immediately at the top of the Alpen Quad Lift), is one of the best choices for lunch or a warming cup of cappuccino. ⊙1 day. 5734-1 Happo Hokujo, Hakuba-mura (Happo Information Center). ☎ 0261/72-3066. www.hakuba-happo. or.jp/en. Ticket prices and times of operation vary, so check in advance. Virgin Cafe: ☎ 0261/72-7573. Entrees from ¥800. AE, MC, V. Breakfast & lunch daily. Bus: Hakuba Line to Happo.

Resort- and hotel-run shuttle buses, as well as a public bus, operate between Happo-one and Hakuba and throughout the Hakuba Valley.

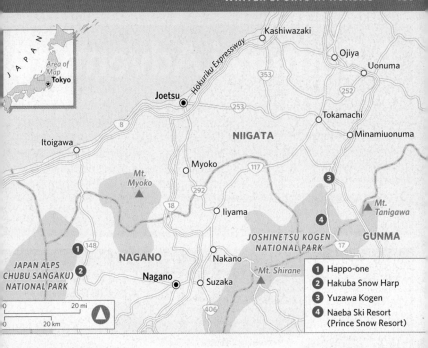

Area of Map
Tokyo

JAPAN

Kashiwazaki

Hokuriku Expressway

Ojiya

Uonuma

353

Joetsu

252

253

Tokamachi

NIIGATA

Minamiuonuma

Itoigawa

8

Myoko

117

Mt. Myoko

292

3

Mt. Tanigawa

18

Iiyama

JOSHINETSU KOGEN NATIONAL PARK

4

GUNMA

148

1

NAGANO

Nakano

17

2

JAPAN ALPS (CHUBU SANGAKU) NATIONAL PARK

Nagano

Mt. Shirane

406

Suzaka

20 mi

20 km

1 Happo-one
2 Hakuba Snow Harp
3 Yuzawa Kogen
4 Naeba Ski Resort (Prince Snow Resort)

2 ★★ **Hakuba Snow Harp** (白馬スノーハープ). The venue for cross-country events at the 1998 Nagano Winter Olympics, this difficult 6km (3.7-mile) course is recommended for advanced skiers. Less experienced skiers can try the two other courses for free. ◷ Half day. 3003 Kamishiro, Hakuba-mura. ☎ 0261/72-5000 (Hakuba Village Office). ¥200. Winter Tues–Sun 9:30am–4pm; summer Tues–Sun 9am–5pm. Bus: Hakuba Line to Hakuba.

From Hakuba, board the JR Oito Line to Itoigawa. Change to the Hokuriku Line and, at Naoetsu, board the Hakutaka 21 train (you must buy a reserved seat) to Echigo-Yuzawa (190 min.).

3 ★ **Yuzawa Kogen** (湯沢高原スキー場). This scenic resort, perched high on a plateau, is great for families. Roughly half of the slopes are for beginners, and if you're not up for skiing or snowboarding, you can rent an inflatable snow tube and toboggan down the hills. The Yuzawa Kogen Ropeway, which features the largest gondola car in the world, will whisk you to a spectacular viewing platform 1,000m (3,280 ft.) above the ground. Once you come down from the mountain, relax in one of the

town's numerous hot springs. ◷ 1 day. 490 Yuzawa, Yuzawamachi. ☎ 0257/784-3326. www.yuzawakogen.com. Ticket prices and times of operation vary, so check in advance. Train: Echigo-Yuzawa Station.

From Echigo-Yuzawa, take the local bus (40 min.) to the Naeba Prince Hotel at the Naeba Ski Resort.

4 ★★★ **Naeba Ski Resort** (**Prince Snow Resort**; 苗場スキー場). Japan's largest ski resort has slopes for skiers and boarders of all levels. The 20 *pistes* are covered with fine powder from mid-November to early May. The resort is connected to nearby **Tashiro Kogen** (かぐらスキー場) ski resort (part of Kagura Kogen; www.princehotels.co.jp/ski/kagura/index.html) by the 5.5km-long (3.4-mile) **Dragondola** (ドラゴンドラ)**,** the longest ski gondola in the world. In the summer, the resort explodes with the music and mayhem of the Fuji Rock Festival, a 3-day outdoor party featuring musical artists from around the globe. ◷ 1 day. Mikuni, Yuzawa. ☎ 0257/89-2211. www.princehotels.co.jp/ski/naeba. Ticket prices and times of operation vary, so check in advance. Bus: Naeba Prince Hotel Express from Echigo-Yuzawa Station.

A Samurai Adventure

Japan's history is a long and complicated tale of civil wars, riddled with intrigue and starring a cast of samurai (military nobility) heroes and villains. While most of the action focused on the capital cities of Kyoto and Edo, Central Honshu played an important part, too. Three of the country's greatest rulers—generals Oda Nobunaga and Toyotomi Hideyoshi, as well as shogun Tokugawa Ieyasu—hail from Nagoya. The vast majority of ninja, covert agents skilled in espionage and assassination techniques, also came from isolated alpine villages in the Iga and Koga regions of Central Honshu. This tour covers the best spots to seek out those places central to samurai and ninja history.

> *Samurai fashion at the Tokugawa Art Museum.*

START From Shiyakusho Station, walk to Nagoyajo castle. Nagoya is 131km (81 miles) northeast of Kyoto.

1 ★ **Nagoyajo.** Nagoyajo castle was completed in 1612 and served as a strategic stronghold for the Owari branch of the Tokugawa family for nearly 250 years, until the Meiji ended their rule in 1868. Although all but three turrets and three gates were destroyed in a fire during World War II, faithful concrete replicas of its main structures were constructed in 1959. See p. 182, **1**.

Walk east to Higashiote Station, then take the Meitetsu Seto Line to Morishita (30 min.).

2 ★★★ **Tokugawa Art Museum** (徳川美術館). Located on the grounds of a former mansion owned by the Owari branch of the Tokugawa family, this museum houses thousands of documents, samurai armor, swords, pottery, lacquerware, Noh costumes and masks, and paintings that once belonged to the Tokugawa family. There are also replicas of structures and items that once adorned Nagoya Castle, including decorative alcoves, a teahouse, and a Noh

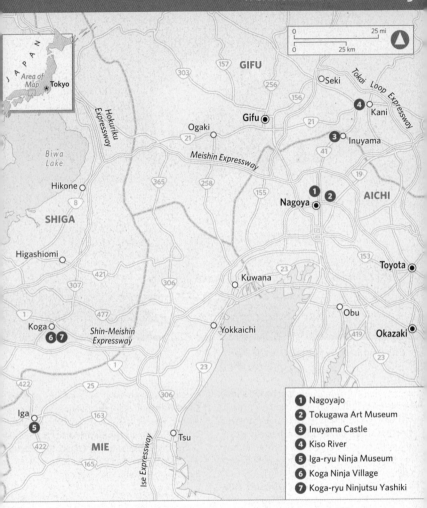

1 Nagoyajo
2 Tokugawa Art Museum
3 Inuyama Castle
4 Kiso River
5 Iga-ryu Ninja Museum
6 Koga Ninja Village
7 Koga-ryu Ninjutsu Yashiki

tage. Of the museum's nine National Treasures, most famous is the 12th-century picture scrolls of *The Tale of Genji,* but they're displayed only 1 week a year at the end of November (check with the tourist office); otherwise, replicas are on display. Don't miss the museum's garden, the **Tokugawaen,** with its calm pond, whispering waterfalls, and strolling paths. ⏱ 45 min. 1017 Tokugawa-cho, Higashi-ku, Nagoya. ☎ 52/935-6262. www.tokugawa-art-museum.jp. ¥1,200 adults, ¥1,000 seniors, ¥700 college and high-school students, ¥500 kids. Tues–Sun 10am–5pm. Train: Nagoya Station.

Walk north to Ozone Station, and take the train to Heiandori Station. From Heiandori, the Kamiiida Line to Inuyama Station (75 min.). The castle is a 15-min. walk northwest.

❸ ★ **Inuyama Castle** (国宝犬山城)**.** Constructed in 1537 atop a bluff overlooking the Kiso River, this four-story *donjon* (keep) is Japan's oldest and a designated National Treasure. It miraculously survived centuries of earthquakes (part of it was damaged by an 1891 earthquake but was then repaired) and wars, including in 1584 when Toyotomi Hideyoshi and his 120,000 retainers used it to stage war against Tokugawa Ieyasu, whose forces were spread

> *Cormorant fishing by firelight in the Kiso River.*

over Komaki Mountain. Owned by the same family from 1618 to 2004, it displays a few samurai outfits and offers a nice, expansive view over the river, which is especially worth a look if you intend to do any cormorant fishing (see below). It's a 15-minute walk from the station. ⏱ 45 min. 65-2 Kitakoken, Inuyama. ☎ 0568/61-1711. ¥500 adults, ¥100 kids. Daily 9am–5pm. Train: Inuyama Yuen Station.

The castle overlooks the Kiso River.

④ ★ Kiso River. Cormorant fishing takes place on the Kiso River from June to mid-October. Spectators can board wooden boats departing from 6 to 8pm June to August, or 5:30 to 7:45pm September and October to observe the spectacle firsthand. While waiting for the full darkness that must descend before the fishing takes place, you can dine on bento box meals for ¥2,500 or ¥3,500, which you must order at least 2 days in advance, or you can bring your own food and drink onboard with you. (Beer and soft drinks are also sold before boarding.) In any case, the actual fishing itself occupies only 20 minutes, so board one of the earlier boats to make it worthwhile. Call **Kiso Gawa Kanko** to make reservations and then pick up your tickets at its ticket office near the bridge. ⏱ 20 min. Kiso Gawa Kanko: ☎ 0568/61-0057. June and Sept to mid-Oct ¥2,500 adults, ¥1,250 kids; July–Aug ¥2,800 adults, ¥1,400 kids. Train: Inuyama Yuen Station.

Return to Nagoya; then take the JR Kansai Line and change at Kameyama to Iga-Ueno Station; from Iga Ueno, take the Kintetsu Iga Line to Uenoshi Station (2½ hr.).

⑤ ★★★ Iga-ryu Ninja Museum (伊賀流忍者博物館) This fascinating museum will teach you everything you've always wanted to know about Japan's famous medieval assassins. The many tricks and traps found in the Iga-ryu Ninja House are demonstrated by nimble-footed lady ninjas in bright pink outfits. Over 400 ninja weapons are exhibited in the Ninja Experience Hall, and you can watch how they were used on the video screens in the minitheater. For an extra ¥200, you can try your hand at throwing *shuriken* stars, those deadly little disc-shaped knives. Best of all, the Ninja Expeience Plaza features a live show demonstrating ninja skills (complete with real weapons!). Explanations are in Japanese, with an English-language pamphlet. Plus, if you've always dreamed of being a ninja (or just looking like one), here's your chance: There are numerous shops near the museum where you can rent a ninja costume for ¥500 per person. ⏱ 1½ hr. 117-13-1 Ueno Marunouchi, Iga. ☎ 0595/23-0314. www.iganinja.jp/en/index.html. ¥700 adults, ¥400 kids, ¥200 extra for the live show. Daily 9am–5pm (last entry 4:30pm). Train: Ue-noshi Station.

Take the Kintetsu Iga Line to Iga-Ueno Station, then take the Kansai Line on to Tsuge Station and finally on to Koga Station (50 min.).

⑥ ★★ Koga Ninja Village (甲賀の里). This tiny village in the woods is dedicated to all things ninja. There's a ninja house—outfitted with hidden doors and escape hatches—you can explore, an area where you can improve your knife-throwing skills, and wall-scaling activities for aspiring young ninjas. Ladders and throwing knives were indispensible to the ninja's art, and you'll see plenty of them on display, along with their trademark black outfits (it turns out that the ninjas rarely wore them). A free shuttle bus is available from Koga Station. If there's no bus waiting, call to schedule a pickup. ⏱ 45 min. 394 Chuo-Oki, Kogamachi. ☎ 0748/88-5000. http://koka.ninpou.jp/index.html. ¥1,000 adults, ¥800 junior-high and high-school students, ¥700 elementary students, ¥300 kids 4 and over. Tues–Sun 10am–4:30pm. Train: Koga Station.

From Koga Station, take the Kusatsu Line two stops to Konan Station, then take a taxi.

⑦ ★ Koga-ryu Ninjutsu Yashiki (甲賀流忍術屋敷). This is the former residence of Mochizuki Izumonokami, head of Koga's preeminent ninja clan. Like many ninja, Mochizuki was a farmer who grew herbs and brewed medicinal potions—as well as poisons. He administered them to the 53 ninja families in the Koga region and to regular folk looking for herbal cures. The Mochizuki family still deals in medicine (they own a pharmaceutical company), but they retired from the ninja business long ago.

> What, no black pajamas? Ninja gear on display at the Koga Ninja Village.

The Edo-era farmhouse, still in its original location, features all of the sneaky revolving doors, hidden passageways, and secret rooms you'd expect in a ninja house. Although no records exist of an attack on the house, the Mochizuki family would have been well prepared. Costumes and tools of the trade are displayed in glass cases (including the collapsible wooden flotation rings the ninjas used to stealthily wade through water). Unfortunately, most of the explanations are in Japanese. ⏱ 30 min. 2331 Ryuboshi, Konanmachi. ☎ 0748/86-2179. ¥600 adults, ¥300 elementary students. Daily 9am–5pm. Train: Konan Station.

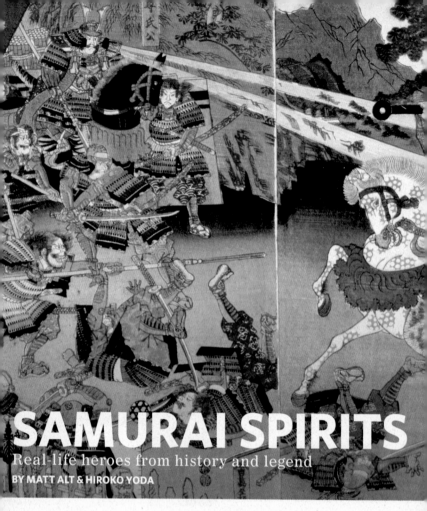

SAMURAI SPIRITS

Real-life heroes from history and legend

BY MATT ALT & HIROKO YODA

THE IMAGE OF THE STOIC SAMURAI WARRIOR, clad in elaborate armor and equipped with trademark twin swords, is almost inseparable from Japan as a whole. So too are those black-clad assassins, the ninja, who have become virtually synonymous with the concept of stealth tactics. Neither samurai nor ninja have stalked the islands of Japan for centuries, so it's telling that they have left such an indelible impression on the hearts and minds of people abroad. We love a good samurai or ninja movie as much as the next person, but when it comes to these warriors of legend, fact is often more fascinating than fiction.

Tool of the Trade: The *Katana*

At the peak of samurai culture's influence, every samurai carried a pair of swords with him at all times as a symbol of his rank. The longer of the two, called a *katana*, was used in sword-fighting. The smaller, known as the *wakizashi*, was typically only used for the purpose of ritual suicide, though in the 17th century, an enterprising swordsman by the name of Miyamoto Musashi (p. 288) developed a technique for using it in battle as

well. Renowned for their craftsmanship, *katana* and *wakizashi* are common sights in Japanese museums. (A note for would-be modern-day samurai: They are still treated as deadly weapons in Japan even today, and it is illegal to purchase or even possess them without a special permit.)

The Era of Warring States

Officially stretching from 1493 to 1573, but generally encompassing the whole of the 16th century, the Era of Warring States represents the heyday of both the samurai and the ninja. It was a dog-eat-dog time in which warlords competed for power—by any means necessary. These warlords, called "daimyo," used armies of samurai to conquer or threaten neighboring territories into submission. And behind the scenes, clans of ninja, either allied with certain daimyo or operating independently, served their masters by reporting troop movements, acting as freelance mercenaries, and conducting the odd assassination or two.

THE BATTLE OF MAGARI (1487)
This is celebrated as the first "official" participation of ninja in a major battle. Ninja under the command of Mochizuki Izumonokami invaded the Shogun Ashikaga's stronghold, sowing chaos with smoke bombs and mortally wounding the shogun. Ninja would go on to play a key behind-the-scenes role in the coming century of civil war.

THE BATTLE OF OKEHAZAMA (1560)
When an upstart named Oda Nobunaga managed to get the drop on the far better equipped Imagawa Yoshimoto with a daring night-raid during a raging storm, Japanese history would never be the same. Over the next 2 decades, Oda would manage to consolidate nearly all of Japan under his iron fist.

THE IGA-NO-RAN CONFLICT (1581)
Oda flooded the mountainous Iga region with tens of thousands of troops in an effort to crush the Iga ninja clan that lived there. Razing an indiscriminate swath of destruction through the area, he forced the Iga clan into an Alamo-esque last stand from which they never recovered.

Samurai History

Japan has boasted warriors since time immemorial. But the term "samurai" appeared around the 10th century; it only became associated with the warrior class around the 12th century. Both in Japan and abroad, the word is also almost synonymous with Bushido, the philosophy translated as the "Way of the Warrior."

But it's important to note that samurai is only the term for a male member of the aristocratic class of pre-modern Japan. While samurai were encouraged to study the martial arts, and came to carry a pair of swords as a symbol of their elite status, not all were master swordsmen or even particularly good fighters. In other words, samurai essentially refers to a caste, not a warrior per se.

▲ **THE BATTLE OF SEKIGAHARA (1600)**
Tokugawa Ieyasu's victory in this epic conflict allowed him to unify all of Japan, becoming the first shogun of the Tokugawa era, which lasted for some 2 centuries. It was Tokugawa's decision to move the capital to Edo, now Tokyo, where it remains today. The grounds of his former castle in the center of the city are now occupied by the royal family.

Niigata for Sake Lovers

Niigata is one of Japan's preeminent sake-making regions, and its crisp, delicate brews have garnered fans around the world. Niigata's producers tend to be rather spread out, and many aren't open to the public, but a bit of perseverance (and some Japanese ability) will get you through the doors, cup in hand. We recommend 2 or so days for this tour, but if you have only a little time, focus on the northern towns of Murakami and Shibata.

> *Niigata is one of the best places to experience Japan's national tipple.*

START Take the train to Echigo-Yuzawa Station. Echigo-Yuzawa is 188km (117 miles) northwest of Tokyo.

① ★★ **Ponshukan** (ぽんしゅ館). Even if you have only a passing interest in sake, a visit to the Ponshukan museum is recommended. Its convenient location inside Echigo-Yuzawa Station (a useful hub for those headed to Tokamachi or Naeba) means that you can start tasting almost as soon as you walk through the ticket gates. Over 100 Niigata varieties, lined up along one wall in cool metal dispensers, are available for sampling. ⏱ 30 min. Echigo-Yuzawa Station, Yuzawamachi. ☎ 025/784-3758. www.ponshukan. com. ¥500 for 5 samples. Daily 9:30am–8pm. Train: Echigo-Yuzawa Station.

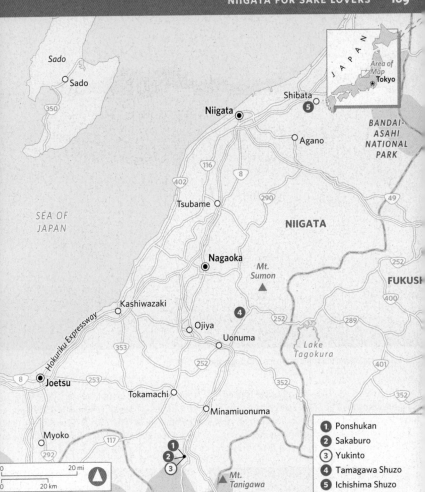

1 Ponshukan
2 Sakaburo
3 Yukinto
4 Tamagawa Shuzo
5 Ichishima Shuzo

2 ★ **Sakaburo** (酒風呂). After you've had your [fi]ll at the Ponshukan, head next door for a [f]ull-body sake experience. The *sakaburo* is a [n]atural hot spring bath that contains, along with a host of beneficial acids and minerals, a [s]mall addition of sake. Not merely delicious, [t]he drink is supposedly good for the skin—but [d]on't drink the bath water! ☉ 30 min. Echigo-[Y]uzawa Station, Yuzawamachi. ☎ 025/784-[3]758. www.ponshukan.com. ¥800. Daily [1]0:30am–7:30pm. Train: Echigo-Yuzawa Station.

3 🍱 ★ **Yukinto** (雪ん洞). The biggest rice balls you've ever seen—much less eaten—await you at Yukinto, a small stand in the shopping plaza opposite

the Ponshukan. They're called *bakudan onigiri* (rice ball bombs), and you'll need a doggie bag. Echigo-Yuzawa Station, Yuzawamachi. ☎ 025/784-3758. Rice balls ¥400. No credit cards. Lunch & dinner daily. Train: Echigo-Yuzawa Station.

Take the Joetsu Sinkansen to Urasa and change to the Joetsu Line. Get off at Oide and take a bus to Suhara (1½ hr.).

4 ★★ **Tamagawa Shuzo** (玉川酒造). The history of this brewery stretches back to the 17th century, when the chief of the local village decided to start making sake. The beautifully preserved 300-year-old building is worth a visit, especially in the snowy months, when

> *Sake's myriad flavors come from rice and rice alone.*

the brewery's *yukikura* (storehouse) is piled high with snow. The snow serves as a natural refrigerator and keeps the brew fresh all year round. In winter, walking into the *yukikura* is like stepping into an igloo. The short brewery tour ends with a complimentary tasting of 10 varieties of sake. ⏱ 40 min. 1643 Suhara, Uonuma-shi. ☎ 025/797-2777. www.yukikura. com. Free. Daily 9am–4pm. Bus: Tadami Line to Suhara.

Sake no Jin

Niigata city's ★★★ **Sake no Jin festival** （酒の陣）, in Toki Messe, the Niigata Convention Center, 6–1 Bandaijima (☎ 025/246-8400; www.niigata-sake.or.jp/torikumi/sakenojin), is an absolute must for any sake lover. Around 100 of Niigata's producers exhibit their sake here over one weekend in mid-March, and in 2010, nearly 800,000 guests attended. One of Japan's largest and most accessible sake fetes, it's a terrific opportunity to sample a wide variety of brews in one location. It doesn't quite match the mayhem of other sake festivals, but that's not exactly a bad thing. Make sure to stay hydrated and pace yourself, though: There are no spittoons. Admission is ¥2,000.

Sake and *Sake* in Murakami

Home to the venerable brewers Taiyo Shuzo (Taiyozakari) and Miyao Shuzo (Shimeharizuru), the idyllic seaside town of Murakami （村上） is known for its delicious sake. But it's also famous for its *sake,* or salmon. *Shiobiki-zake,* salted and dried salmon, is the local specialty. The people of Murakami have a special technique for cutting and drying their fish, and it's still common to see salmon hanging in the windows and doorways of shops. The town itself, with its black-painted Edo-style buildings, is lovely to walk around, and there are many places to taste Murakami's other famous product, succulent Murakami *wagyu* (Japanese beef). From Niigata Station, take the Inaho Limited Express to Murakami (¥2,720; 50 min.).

Sip, don't chug, your sake from traditional o-chokko cups.

Take the train to Shibata Station (3 hr.). Ichishima Shuzo is a short walk west of the station.

5 ★★ **Ichishima Shuzo** (市島酒造)**.** Helmed by 5th-generation owner Kenji Ichishima, this brewery's history dates back over 200 years. Ichishima Shuzo was one of the first breweries to open its doors to the public nearly 30 years ago, and its original buildings now house displays of early sake-brewing equipment (including wooden tanks once used for fermentation, and an impressive old *fune,* a wooden sake-pressing machine), drinking vessels, and a collection of beautiful kimono that have been in the Ichishima family for years. The self-guided tour ends with a tasting of Ichishima's elegantly understated brews, including selections of their award-winning Omon label. ⏱ 40 min. 3–1–17 Suwacho, Shibatashi. ☎ 025/422-5150. www.ichishima.jp. Free. Daily 9am–4pm. Train: Shibata Station.

Sake Fundamentals

Although we often refer to sake as "rice wine" in English, it is not technically wine. It is a brewed beverage, like beer, but is consumed and appreciated much like wine. (See p. 258 for a description of the brewing process.) While its alcohol content may be as high as 21%, it is not a distilled beverage. It is made of only rice, despite the fact that it may demonstrate a range of flavors from fruity to earthy. The quickest way to start appreciating the brew is to learn the grades of sake.

The classifications for premium sake are established by the government based on *seimai buai* (milling rates) and ingredients. Most of the sake on the market, however, is called *futsuu-shu* ("normal," or "ordinary"). In this case, any milling rate is allowed, and there may be additives and distilled alcohol in the drink.

HONJOZO

Milled to at least 70%, made with rice, water, *koji* (the catalyst that converts starch to sugar), and a small amount of distilled alcohol to enhance flavor and aroma. This kind of sake is generally light, nicely balanced, with a quiet nose and a quick finish.

GINJO

A minimum polishing rate of 60%, made from rice, water, *koji*, and brewer's alcohol. This style of sake is generally light, fragrant, complex, and refined, often fruity.

DAIGINJO

Milled to at least 50%, made from rice, water, *koji,* and brewer's alcohol. It is the most fragrant of all the premium sake, lightest in body, and typically the hardest to pair. Daiginjo tends to be floral, fruity, and very delicate, often with noticeable sweetness.

JUNMAI-SHU

Any milling rate is permissible, provided that it is listed on the label. The ingredients are rice, water, and *koji*. No extra alcohol is added. It generally displays prominent acidity, fuller body, and flavors of rice rather than fruit. Junmai pure-rice versions of ginjo and daiginjo also exist. They tend to have a slightly fuller flavor profile.

Karuizawa

More often considered a destination for Japanese tourists, the quiet town of Karuizawa has a lot to offer nature lovers. Its sylvan slopes and fresh alpine air have made it an attractive option for Tokyoites looking to purchase summer homes for well over a century. The area is blessed with abundant nature and excellent hiking opportunities. Whiskey fans, too, will find much of interest at the Mercian Musee d'Art.

> *Kumoba-ike Pond shows its glorious autumn colors.*

START Take the train to Karuizawa Station (68 min.). Karuizawa is 159km (99 miles) northwest of Tokyo.

1 ★ **Karuizawa Ginza.** Cafes, restaurants, and souvenir shops have taken the place of the traditional inns that once lined Karuizawa Ginza, the main street that leads north from the station. It's at its busiest at the height of summer, when flocks of tourists from Tokyo descend upon Karuizawa. Still, it's fun for a stroll, and fans of animation artist Hayao Miyazaki (*My Neighbor Totoro, Spirited Away*) won't want to miss the **Donguri Kyouwa Koku** shop, devoted to the films of production company Studio

Ghibli, along the road. Just look for the adorable Totoro sign (the company's mascot). ⏲ 20 min. Donguri Kyouwa Koku: 611 Kyu-Karuizawa, Karuizawamachi. ☎ 026/742-4336. Free. Train: Karuizawa Station.

2 ★★★ **Kumoba-ike Pond** (雲場池). Legend has it that this pond, commonly referred to as "Swan Lake," was formed when the footprint of a giant who lived in nearby Mount Asama filled with rain. The area is spectacular in the autumn when the water mirrors the vibrant leaves of the surrounding trees, and you can walk around the entire pond in about 20 minutes. ⏲ 20 min. Bus: Seibu Kogen Line to Roppon-tsuji.

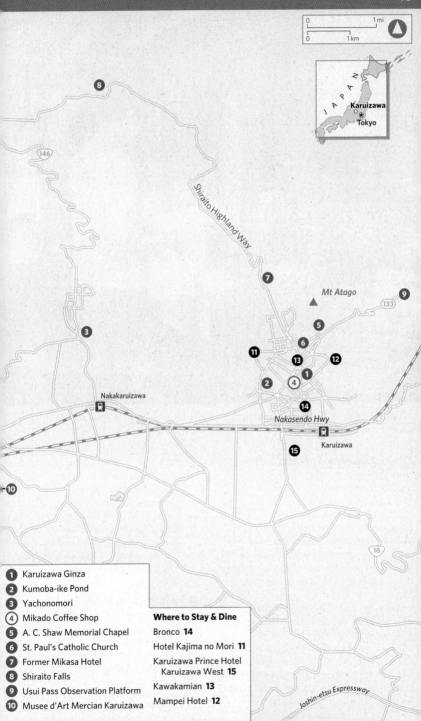

1 Karuizawa Ginza
2 Kumoba-ike Pond
3 Yachonomori
4 Mikado Coffee Shop
5 A. C. Shaw Memorial Chapel
6 St. Paul's Catholic Church
7 Former Mikasa Hotel
8 Shiraito Falls
9 Usui Pass Observation Platform
10 Musee d'Art Mercian Karuizawa

Where to Stay & Dine

Bronco **14**

Hotel Kajima no Mori **11**

Karuizawa Prince Hotel
Karuizawa West **15**

Kawakamian **13**

Mampei Hotel **12**

> *Snacking is easy on Karuizawa Ginza street.*

③ ★★★ **Yachonomori**（野鳥の森）**.** With its cool, mossy slopes and fragrant groves of white birch and larch trees, Karuizawa offers a sanctuary for an abundance of wildlife. This 100-hectare wild bird sanctuary was established by one of the founders of the Japan Wild Bird Protection Society. Up to 130 species of birds inhabit the woods; bird-watchers might see fine specimens of owl, great spotted woodpecker, and Siberian blue robins. Inquire at the Tourist Information Center for a map of the 2.4km (1.5-mile) bird-watching trail. A healthy population of red fox, *tanuki* (raccoon dogs), and rare giant flying squirrel also live among the white birch and larch. ⏱ 2 hr. ☎ 0267/45-7777 (visitor center in the park). http://picchio.co.jp/sp. Apr–Oct Mon–Fri 9:30am–6pm, Sat–Sun 8:30am–6pm. Bus: Nishi-ku Iriguchi Line from Karuizawa Station.

④ 🍴 ★ **Mikado Coffee Shop** （ミカドコーヒー）**.** In summer, fans line up for mocha soft ice cream at this shop conveniently located along Karuizawa Ginza. Or stop in for a cup of bittersweet café mocha. 786-2 Kyu-dou, Karuizawa-cho. ☎ 0267/42-2453. http://mikado-coffee.com. Ice cream ¥300–¥600. No credit cards. Daily 10am–7pm. Bus: Sogen Line to Kyu-Karuizawa.

⑤ ★ **A. C. Shaw Memorial Chapel.** Tucked deep into the woods, this modest wooden chapel was the first church for Westerners in Karuizawa, where the "father of Karuizawa," missionary A. C. Shaw, held his sermons. ⏱ 15 min. 57-1 Karuizawa. ☎ 0267/42-4740 Free. Daily Oct–Jun 9am–5pm; Jul–Sept 9am–4pm. Bus: Kusakaru Line to Kyu-Karuizawa.

East meets West, architecturally, at the former Misaka Hotel.

St. Paul's Catholic Church. Often described as the symbol of Karuizawa, this wooden church was founded in 1935 and designed by American architect Antonin Raymond. The church was mentioned in writer Tatsuo Hori's novella *Ki no Jujika* (*The Wooden Cross*). The interior, with its natural wooden beams, wooden pews, and simple furnishings, resembles a rustic log cabin. ⏱ 15 min. 179 Karuizawa. ☎ 0267/42-2429. www.karuizawa-stpaul.org. Free. Daily 7am–6pm. Bus: Kusakaru or Seibu lines to Kyu-Karuizawa.

Former Mikasa Hotel (旧三笠ホテル)**.** The old Mikasa Hotel once served as a meeting place for both Japanese and Western intellectuals, aristocrats, and politicians. One of the oldest Western-style hotels in Japan, this East-meets-West fusion of architectural styles was designed about 60 years ago by a Japanese architect who was influenced by the aesthetics of the alpine houses he had seen while studying in Germany. ⏱ 20 min. 1339-342 Karuizawa. ☎ 0267/42-7072. ¥400 adults, ¥200 kids. Daily 9am–5pm (last entry 4:30pm). Bus: Kusakaru Line to Mikasa.

Take a Hike

The popular **Shinoji hiking route,** which leads 10km (6.2 miles) through the Asama Highlands, takes approximately 4 hours to complete. It begins at the Minenochaya teahouse and winds along the Yukawa River through fragrant white birch forests, terminating at the Mikasa Hotel. On the way, you'll pass Shiraito Falls and Ryugaeshi Falls, and you can take a dip at Kose Onsen (highly recommended). Take the Kusakaru bus from Nakakaruizawa Station and get off at Mine-no-chaya (28 min.). Maps are available at the Tourist Office.

> *Delight in the calm of Shiraito Falls.*

8 Shiraito Falls (白糸の滝)**.** One of Karuizawa's most breathtaking sights, this magnificent waterfall resembles a giant curtain of fine silk threads—hence the name, which translates as "White Thread Falls." Although only 3m (10 ft.) high, the crystal-clear waters of the Yu River tumble over a broad rock ledge, creating waterfalls that are about 70m (230 ft.) wide. Situated amid a dense white birch forest, the falls are glorious at all times of the year. ⏱ 30 min. Bus: Kusakaru Line to Shiraitonotaki.

9 Usui Pass Observation Platform. From the Nitebashi Bridge at the end of Kauizawa Ginza, follow the path 80 minutes uphill to the peak. It's not a difficult hike by any means, and you'll be rewarded with commanding views of Karuizawa's surrounding mountains: Mount Asama, Mount Myogi, and the Yatsugatake mountain range. It's especially pretty during October, when the fall colors are at their fiery best. It's a 30-minute walk from Shaw Chapel. ⏱ 2 hr. Bus: Kusakaru Line to Kyu-Karuizawa.

10 Musee d'Art Mercian Karuizawa (メルシャン 軽井沢美術館)**.** Run by beverage giant Mercian, this museum park contains an art gallery, a restaurant, and a fine wine and whiskey shop on its lovely green grounds. The buildings are the former whiskey warehouses of the Mercian Karuizawa Distillery, and the complex was designed by renowned French architect Jean-Michel Wilmotte. Exhibitions change seasonally and cost extra, but visitors can take a guided tour of the ivy-covered distilling facility and even sample some of the fine single malts, along with a selection of Mercian's wines, for free. ⏱ 30 min. 1799-1 Maseguchi, Miyota-cho, Kitasaku-gun. ☎ 0267/32-0288. www.mercian.co.jp/musee. Grounds free; fees for exhibitions vary. Wed-Mon 9:30am-5pm. Train: Miyota Station.

Where to Stay & Dine in Karuizawa

Bronco (ブロンコ) *CREPES*

The rustic wooden interior of this charming creperie in Kyu-Karuizawa looks a bit like the inside of a log cabin. Homemade crepes stuffed with savory fillings like ham and cheese, or sweets treats such as blueberry jam and whipped cream, are the specialty here. 23–12 Karuizawa Higashi. ☎ 0267/42-3226. Crepes from ¥700. No credit cards. Lunch & dinner Thurs–Tues. Bus: Kusakaru or Seibu lines to Kyu-Karuizawa.

Hotel Kajima no Mori

All of the rooms at this hotel in the middle of Karuizawa look out onto the vast garden, where cute woodland animals such as squirrels are wont to roam. Rooms are quiet and comfortable, if a tad dated in decor. It's a 5-minute taxi ride from the station. 1373–6 Ohaza-karuizawa, Karuizawamachi. ☎ 0267/42-3535. www.okura.com/hotels/kajimanomori/index.html. 50 units. Doubles ¥25,000–¥42,000. AE, DC, MC, V. Train: Karuizawa Station.

Karuizawa Prince Hotel Karuizawa West

With easy access to ski slopes, this hotel is ideal for those interested in winter sports. Surrounded by pine forests, the extensive grounds also feature golf courses, tennis courts, cycling opportunities, and *onsen*—as well as a spa just for pets. Rooms are clean and spacious, with windows overlooking the trees and free Internet access. It's a bit of a trek from public transportation, but hourly shuttles are available between Karuizawa Station and the hotel. Call to arrange a pickup. 1016–75 Karuizawa. ☎ 0267/42-1111. www.princehotels.com/en/karuizawa-west. 180 units. Doubles from ¥20,000. AE, DC, MC, V. Train: Karuizawa Station.

★ Kawakamian (川上庵) *NOODLES*

This soba shop is popular for its heaping portions of tasty tempura, as well as the *kamo-seiro*, cold buckwheat noodles served with a hot dipping sauce flavored with Japanese leeks and slices of duck. The airy main

> Refined French fare at the Mampei Hotel.

dining area is stylishly appointed with smooth wooden surfaces and Japanese shoji screens, and pets are allowed on the relaxing outdoor terrace. It's a 25-minute walk from the station, or a 10-minute cab ride. 6–10 Karuizawa, Karuizawamachi. ☎ 0267/42-0009. www.kawakamian.com/ka/index.html. Entrees from ¥1,200. No credit cards. Lunch & dinner daily. Train: Karuizawa Station.

★★★ Mampei Hotel (万平ホテル) *FRENCH*

The Mampei Hotel has been in business since 1894 and its long history has seen a number of famous guests, most notably John Lennon. The real reason to visit is for the food, though; its French restaurant serves well-prepared classic dishes such as sautéed foie gras and grilled steaks with Madeira. The spacious dining room is outfitted with all of the accoutrements of a traditional fine dining establishment—white tablecloths, candles during dinner service, and a grand piano in the lobby. It's a 4-minute taxi ride from the station. 925 Karuizawa. ☎ 0267/42-1234. www.mampei.co.jp. Set lunches from ¥4,620, set dinners from ¥7,300. AE, DC, MC, V. Lunch & dinner daily. Train: Karuizawa Station.

Matsumoto

The second-largest city in Nagano, Matsumoto is a convenient stopping point for travelers journeying to the Japan Alps. Originally known as Fukashi, the town developed during the 14th and 15th centuries, when the Ogasawara clan constructed a fortress that would later become the famed Matsumotojo castle. Today, the town's atmosphere blends tradition and modernity; among the streets lined with stately white-and-black-walled *kura* (Japanese warehouses) are some striking examples of contemporary architecture.

> *Follow those hats: Discover Matsumoto's local talent at the Museum of Art.*

START Take the Town Sneaker bus to the Matsumotojo Kuromon stop. Matsumoto is 220km (137 miles) northwest of Tokyo.

1 ★★ **Matsumotojo.** Undoubtedly the symbol of the city, Matsumotojo castle sits proudly in the center of town, surrounded by a calm, carp-filled moat. The country's oldest wooden castle, it's one of only four castles in Japan to be designated as National Treasures (along with Hikone, Himeji, and Inuyama).

The castle's most impressive structure is its imposing **donjon,** or keep. Built in 1595 by the Ishikawa clan, the black-and-white-walled *donjon* is the oldest existing one in Japan. The building rises six sneaky stories above the water (there's a low-ceilinged, secret third floor, so the tower looks like it's only five stories high), with nice views on every level. Take your shoes off at the entrance and walk across the worn, wooden floors and climb the steep steps to the top floor, which would have served as the feudal lord's headquarters in the case of an attack. The fifth floor, where the generals would have convened during the war, affords panoramic views of the city.

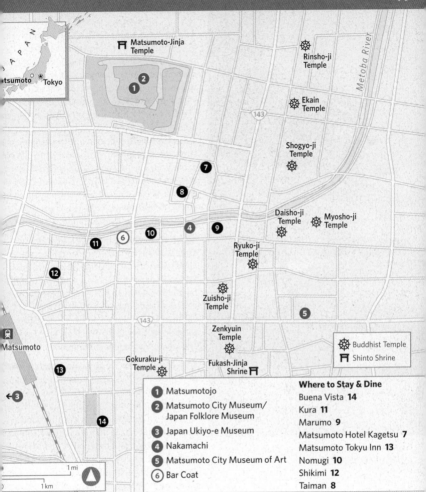

	Where to Stay & Dine
1 Matsumotojo	Buena Vista **14**
2 Matsumoto City Museum/ Japan Folklore Museum	Kura **11**
3 Japan Ukiyo-e Museum	Marumo **9**
4 Nakamachi	Matsumoto Hotel Kagetsu **7**
5 Matsumoto City Museum of Art	Matsumoto Tokyu Inn **13**
6 Bar Coat	Nomugi **10**
	Shikimi **12**
	Taiman **8**

✿ Buddhist Temple
🗼 Shinto Shrine

Although the Ishikawa clan rebuilt the castle in anticipation of gun warfare (guns were introduced to Japan in 1543) with many arrow and gun slots and walls thick enough to withstand bullets, Matsumotojo was never attacked because Japan's numerous civil wars ended with the coming of the Edo Period (1603–1867). Nevertheless, guns were manufactured in Japan throughout the Edo Period, and on display inside the castle are approximately 370 matchlocks, armor, and guns made in Japan from 1543 to the late Edo Era, for those with an interest in mechanisms of ancient warfare. The peaceful Tsukimi Yagura moon-viewing room was added in 1635, after the threat of war had

passed. English-speaking Goodwill Guides provide free, 1-hour tours daily outlining the castle's history and architectural features. ⏱ 45 min. 4-1 Marunouchi. ☎ 0263/32-2902 or 0263/32-7140 to reserve English-speaking Goodwill Guides in advance. ¥600 adults, ¥300 kids (includes admission to Matsumoto City Museum/Japan Folklore Museum, below). Daily 8:30am–5pm (mid-Jul–Sept until 6pm). Bus: Town Sneaker to Matsumotojo Kuromon.

2 Matsumoto City Museum/Japan Folklore Museum. Your ticket to Matsumotojo also includes admission to this museum next to the castle. Inside, you'll find various displays relating to Matsumoto's history, culture, and

> *Shh—Matsumoto Castle's keep is really six, not five, stories high.*

its kind in the world—and it's quite simply one of the best museums of woodblock prints in Japan. The collection includes representative masterpieces of all known *ukiyo-e* artists, with works by masters such as Hokusai (p. 138), Hiroshige, and Utamaro, exhibited in rotation every 3 months. Signs are mostly in Japanese but an English-language pamphlet is available and a 15-minute slide show with English-language explanations introduces the current exhibition. The museum shop contains reproduction and original prints. ⏲ 45 min. 2206-1 Koshiba. ☎ 0263/47-4440. www.ukiyo-e.co.jp. jum-e. ¥1,050 adults, ¥530 kids. Tues–Sun 10am–5pm. Train: Oniwa Station.

❹ ★★ **Nakamachi** (中町)**.** The atmospheric streets of this former merchant district are lined with *kura* (warehouses) from the Edo Period. Most of these black-and-white-walled buildings have been turned into trendy cafes, galleries, and boutiques. Walk 10 minutes south of Matsumotojo down Daimyo Dori to Metoba River. ⏲ 30 min. Free. Bus: Town Sneaker to Matsumotojo Kuromon.

❺ ★ **Matsumoto City Museum of Art** (松本市美術館)**.** Opened in 2002, this museum showcases the talent of artists who have connections to Matsumoto. Among the highlights are works by avant-garde artist Yayoi Kusama, landscape painter Kazuo Tamura; Yayoi Kusama, known for her exuberant colors and polka-dot modern art; and calligrapher Shinzan Kamijo, who elevated calligraphy to an art. The contemporary building incorporates design elements from Matsumotojo into its striking facade. ⏲ 30 min. 4-2-22 Chuo. ☎ 0263/39-7400. www.city.matsumoto.nagano.jp/artmuse. ¥400 adults, ¥200 high school students, free for elementary and junior-high students. Tues–Sun 9am–5pm. Bus: Town Sneaker to Matsumoto-shi Bijutsukan.

numerous festivals (including the Tanabata Star Festival, held in summer, and the Dosojin Matsuri Fertility Festival, held in the fall). And if you've always wanted to see a collection of wooden phalluses, this is your chance. ⏲ 30 min. 4-1 Marunouchi. ☎ 0263/32-2902 or 0263/32-0133. ¥600 adults, ¥300 kids (includes admission to Matsumotojo, above). Daily 8:30am–4:30pm. Bus: Town Sneaker to Matsumotojo Kuromon.

❸ ★★★ **Japan Ukiyo-e Museum** (日本浮世絵博物館)**.** This impressive museum, housed in a stylish contemporary building, contains the collection of the Sakai family. Over five generations, the family collected more than 100,000 *ukiyo-e* (woodblock prints), paintings, screens, and books into the largest private collection of

⑥ 🍸 ★★ **Bar Coat** (バーコート)**.** This cozy, dimly lit bar is just the place to end the evening with a cocktail. The owner has mixed award-winning cocktails at contests both in Japan and abroad. Miwa Building 2F, 2-3-5 Chuo. ☎ 0263/34-7133. Drinks from ¥800. No credit cards. Dinner & late night daily. Train: Matsumoto Station.

Where to Stay & Dine in Matsumoto

Buena Vista

Matsumoto's biggest hotel is gleaming white, and a round fireplace welcomes arriving guests to the attractive lobby. Rooms range from small, spartan singles to swanky executive-floor digs. 1-2-1 Honjo. ☎ 0263/37-0111. www.buena-vista. co.jp. 200 units. Doubles ¥19,635–¥24,255. AE, DC, MC, V. Train: Matsumoto Station.

Kura (蔵) *TEMPURA*

This restaurant occupies Matsumoto's largest *kura* (warehouse). Enter through the thick, vaultlike door and sit at the dark wood counter. Kura is known for its delicious tempura, though it also offers sushi and *zaru* soba (cold buckwheat noodles). Try to avoid peak meal times, when the service can be brusque. 1-10-22 Chuo. ☎ 0263/33-6444. Lunch entrees ¥1,000–¥2,100, dinner entrees ¥945–¥4,000. AE, MC, V. Lunch & dinner daily. Train: Matsumoto Station.

★ Marumo

This wooden *ryokan* may lack the luxury of a more modern hotel, but it makes up for it in charm. The bamboo garden and coffee shop are delightful. If you're searching for "traditional Japan," this is it. 3-3-10 Chuo. ☎ 0263/32-0115. 8 units, none with bathroom. Rooms from ¥5,250 per person. Japanese breakfast ¥1,050 extra. No credit cards. Bus: Town Sneaker to Nakamachi.

★ Matsumoto Hotel Kagetsu

This *ryokan* is constructed in the style of a Japanese *kura*. Japanese- and Western-style rooms are comfortably large for the price. For the best views, ask for a Western room facing the castle. 4-8-9 Ote. ☎ 0263/32-0114. www.hotel-kagetsu.jp/englishtop.html. 85 units. Rooms ¥7,350–¥10,500 per person. Breakfast ¥1,200 extra. AE, MC, V. Bus: Town Sneaker to Agetsumachi.

Matsumoto Tokyu Inn

Visible from the station, this clean, functional business hotel's main selling point is its convenient location. The majority of the rooms are singles and twins, all with semi-double beds and feather quilts. On clear days, rooms facing west

> Tempura, fried food of the gods.

have views of the Japan Alps. 1-3-21 Fukashi. ☎ 0263/36-0109. www.tokyuhotelsjapan.com. 160 units. Doubles ¥15,750–¥19,110. AE, DC, MC, V. Train: Matsumoto Station.

★ Nomugi (野麦) *NOODLES*

There are only three tables at this popular local eatery, which means you may have to wait for a seat. The restaurant serves only one dish: *zaru* soba—cold buckwheat noodles. In winter, the soba is served with boiled toppings. 2-9-11 Chuo. ☎ 0263/36-3753. Soba from ¥1,100. No credit cards. Lunch Thurs–Mon. Train: Matsumoto Station.

★ Shikimi *SUSHI*

This restaurant specializes in eel and sushi. The *unagi donburi* (grilled strips of eel over rice) comes with soup and pickles. *Moriawase* (assorted sushi platters) are also a good bet. 1-5-5 Chuo. ☎ 0263/36-7716. Entrees ¥1,680–¥3,150. No credit cards. Lunch & dinner daily. Train: Matsumoto Station.

★★★ Taiman (鯛萬) *FRENCH*

Ivy-covered Taiman is rustic yet elegant, with a view of a garden. In business for nearly 60 years, it offers wonderful French cuisine from a seasonal menu. 4-2-4 Ote. ☎ 0263/32-0882. Set lunches ¥5,250–¥9,450; set dinners ¥12,000–¥18,900. AE, DC, MC, V. Lunch & dinner Thurs–Tues. Train: Matsumoto Station.

Nagoya

Nagoya has the reputation of being Japan's hardest-working city, and we can certainly see why: Home to the automobile giant Toyota, as well as many of Japan's major manufacturing companies, Nagoya is the industrial heart of the country. While rarely regarded as a sightseeing destination, the city has some interesting attractions and is famous for its unique, robustly flavored cuisine.

> Nagoyajo, one of Central Honshu's strongest fortresses for 250 years.

START Nagoyajo is a short walk from Shin-yakusho Station, off the Meijo Line train. Nagoya is 131km (81 miles) northeast of Kyoto.

❶ ★ **Nagoyajo** (名古屋城). Built by shogun Tokugawa Ieyasu for his ninth son, Yoshinao, Nagoyajo was completed in 1612 and served as a strategic stronghold for the Owari branch of the Tokugawa family for nearly 250 years. Although it was destroyed in a fire during World War II, faithful concrete replicas of its main structures were constructed in 1959. The museum inside the castle houses a fine collection of treasures that survived the bombing during the war. You can take the elevator up.

Don't miss the replicas of the two golden dolphins that adorn the roof of the *donjon*

(keep). Each of these gilded creatures is 3m (10 ft.) long and weighs 1,193kg (2,630 lb.).

East of the castle is **Ninomaru Garden,** which is most beautiful during the cherry blossom season. Stop by the **Ninomaru Tea House,** where you can sip tea brewed in a golden kettle—it's rumored to add 5 years to your life. ⏱ 1 hr. 1-1 Honmaru. ☎ 052/231-1700. www.nagoyajo.city.nagoya.jp/13_english. ¥500 adults, free for junior-high students and younger. Daily 9am–4:30pm (last entry to donjon 4pm). Closed Dec 29–Jan 1. Train: Shinyakusho Station.

❷ ★★★ **Tokugawa Art Museum.** Thousands of artifacts that once belonged to the Tokugawa family are on display at this fascinating museum. See p. 162, ❷.

Bus route
Railway
Subway
Tourist Info

1 Nagoyajo
2 Tokugawa Art Museum
3 Noritake Garden
4 Osso Brasil
5 Port of Nagoya
  Public Aquarium
6 Atsuta Jingu

Where to Stay & Dine
Eikokuya 13
Nagoya Marriott Associa
  Hotel 8
Petit Ryokan Ichifuji 14
Sofitel The Cypress
  Nagoya 7
Tokyo Dai-Ichi Hotel
  Nishiki 10
Torigin Honten 11
Yabaton 12
Yamamoto-ya Honten 9

To Inuyama City

Shindeki
Yamaguchi-cho
Akatsuke Shirakabe
Shirakabe
Shimizuguchi
Dekimachi Dori
Ote

Nagoya Castle

Shiyakusho
Airport Bus Stop
Otsu Dori
Isemachi Dori
Gofukucho
Shichikencho
Hommachi
Chojamachi
Nagashimacho
Kuwanamachi

Sakura Dori
Hommachi
Marunouchi
Dori
Dori
Dori
Dori
Dori

Sakura Dori
Misono Dori
Fushimi
Marunouchi
Solobori Dori
Kikunoo Dori
Sengen-cho

MEITETSU SETO LINE
SAKURA-DORI LINE

Takaoka
Hisaya-odori
Toyota Motor Corporation
Nagoya TV Tower
Sakaemachi
Sakae

Hisaya Odori
Hisaya
Odori
Park
Sakae

HIGASHIYAMA LINE
Shinsakae-machi

Sakae Bus Terminal
Otsu Dori
MEIJO LINE
Yabacho

TSURUMAI LINE (SUBWAY)
Hirokoji Dori
Iriecho Dori
Mitsukura Dori
Shirakawa Dori
SHIRAKAWA PARK

Fushimi Dori
Fushimi
Osu Kannon
Osu Dori

Yaba-cho
KEY BUS ROUTE
Maruta-machi

Sapporo Beer
JR CHUO LINE

Horikawa River
Nagoya Expressway

Kokusai Center
Hijie-cho
City Bus Terminal
Nagoya Sta.
Airport Bus Stop

Nagoya Central Post Office
Airport Bus Stop
Nakamura Police Station
Taiko Dori
Komeno

JR TOKAIDO SHINKANSEN
JR KANSAI LINE
KINTETSU LINE
KINTETSU LINE

Nagoya
Tokyo

JAPAN

1/4 mi
0.25 km

> *Serious samurai armor on display at the Tokugawa Art Museum.*

> *Say a prayer at Atsuta Jingu, one of Japan's most sacred spots.*

③ ★★ Noritake Garden (ノリタケの森). This museum, dedicated to Japan's largest porcelain producer, is situated among pleasant, tree-lined gardens, on the grounds where the first factory was built in 1904. At the Craft Center, you can see displays explaining the manufacturing and decorating processes involved in making porcelain, as well as watch artisans at work. Other highlights include a display of the company's fabulous Art Deco collection. ⏱ 45 min. 3-1-36 Noritake Shinmachi. ☎ 052/561-7290. www.noritake.co.jp/mori. ¥500 adults, ¥300 high-school students, free for kids and seniors. Tues–Sun 10am–5pm (last entry 4pm). Train: Kamejima Station.

④ 🍴 ★★ Osso Brasil (オッソブラジル). This authentic Brazilian restaurant serves succulent grilled meats at lunchtime (you can't miss the huge rotisserie filled with rows of whole chickens), and Brazilian snacks like *empadinhas* (meat pies) all day. 3-41-13 Osu. ☎ 052/238-5151. Entrees from ¥700. No credit cards. Lunch & dinner Tues–Sun. Train: Kamimaezu Station.

⑤ ★★★ Port of Nagoya Public Aquarium. One of Japan's largest aquariums, the Port of Nagoya's Public Aquarium is also one of the most enjoyable. It features educational displays that concentrate on marine life from the seas around Japan. There's a 15-minute hologram show that transports you to the deep sea in a "submarine"; a touch tank with sea urchins, starfish, and other animals; and an IMAX theater. The Beluga whales are a perennial favorite, as are the turtles and penguins, housed in a tank that copies the frigid environment of the Antarctic. ⏱ 2½ hr. 1-3 Minatomachi. ☎ 052-654-7000. www.nagoyaaqua.jp. ¥2,000 adults, ¥1,000 kids. Jul 21–Aug Tues–Sun 9:30am–8pm; Apr–Jul 20 and Sept–Nov Tues–Sun 9:30am–5:30pm; Dec–Mar Tues–Sun 9:30am–5pm. Subway: Nagoya-ko Station.

⑥ Atsuta Jingu (熱田神宮). If, like many Japanese, you have a special place in your heart for Amaterasu-Omikami (the sun goddess who gave birth to the Japanese people), you won't want to miss the legendary Kusanagai-no-Tsurugi sword housed in this 1,900-year-old shrine. It's one of the three regalia that were bequeathed to the Imperial family by Amaterasu herself. The only problem is that you can't see it: It can only be viewed by the emperor and a handful of Shinto priests. Still, Atsuta Jingu is one of Nagoya's top tourist attractions, and the grounds, surrounded by ancient cypress trees, make for a peaceful stroll. ⏱ 15 min. 1-1-1 Jingu. ☎ 052/671-4151. Free. Daily noon–midnight. Train: Jingu-mae Station.

Where to Stay & Dine in Nagoya

★ **Eikokuya** (えいこく屋) EASTERN NAGOYA
INDIAN Tasty chai tea and curry are the spe-
ialty of this old-school Indian place on the
nain street of Kakuozan. 2-58 Kakuozan.
☎ 052/763-2788. Entrees ¥950–¥1,600. No
redit cards. Lunch & dinner daily. Subway:
Kakuozan Station.

★ **Nagoya Marriott Associa Hotel** NAGOYA
STATION Occupying the 15th to the 52nd
floors of the city's tallest building, this offers
great views (ask for a room facing the castle
and downtown). Rooms are up-to-date and
spacious. There's also a swanky sky lounge
called Zenith on the 52nd floor. 1-1-4 Meieki.
☎ 052/584-1113. www.associa.com/nma. 774
units. Doubles ¥30,000–¥42,000. AE, DC, MC,
V. Train: Nagoya Station.

★ **Petit Ryokan Ichifuji** NORTHERN NAGOYA
This family-run *ryokan* is a 20-minute ride
from Nagoya Station. Ishida Tomiyasu, who
speaks a little English, has created a restful
Japanese interior with wood floors, designer
basins, and a cypress public bath. All rooms
except one are tatami. 1-7 Saikobashi-dori,
Kita-ku. ☎ 052/914-2867. www.ichifuji-nagoya.
com. 10 units, none with bathroom. Doubles
¥11,600–¥30,000. Rates include breakfast. AE,
MC, V. Subway: Heiandori Station.

★ **Sofitel The Cypress Nagoya** NAGOYA
STATION The Sofitel has contemporary furnishings, a European atmosphere, and friendly
multilingual service. Standard rooms are fairly
small; ask for a room on a higher floor, where
you might have an urban view. 2-43-6 Meieki.
☎ 052/571-0111. www.sofitelthecypress.com.
115 units. Doubles ¥27,200–¥32,000. AE, DC,
MC, V. Train: Nagoya Station.

★ **Tokyo Dai-Ichi Hotel Nishiki** CENTRAL
NAGOYA The Dai-Ichi has prices comparable
to those of a business hotel but with a much
classier atmosphere and decor. Rooms facing
another building have tinted windows, so if
seeing out is important to you, be sure to let the
staff know. 3-18-21 Nishiki. ☎ 052/955-1001.
www.tdh-nishiki.co.jp. 233 units. Doubles from
¥15,015. AE, DC, MC, V. Train: Sakae Station.

> Enjoy the view from the Nagoya Marriott Associa
Hotel. (Yes, there's a sky lounge!)

★★ **Torigin Honten** (鳥銀本店) CENTRAL NAGOYA
JAPANESE This casual restaurant is known for
its *Nagoya cochin* (free-range chicken), which
is served in various styles: grilled as yakitori,
simmered as *miso-nabe* (with rice cake, tofu,
and vegetable stew), or steamed in *kamameshi*
(rice casseroles). 3-14-22 Nishiki. ☎ 052/973-
3000. Set dinners ¥3,000–¥5,000. AE, DC,
MC, V. Dinner daily. Train: Sakae Station.

★★ **Yabaton** (矢場とん) CENTRAL NAGOYA
TONKATSU This Nagoya institution is famous
for *miso-katsu*, a deep-fried pork cutlet bathed
in a sweet and tangy miso-based sauce. 3-6-18
Osu. ☎ 052/252-8810. www.yabaton.com. Set
dinners ¥1,000–¥1,700. No credit cards. Lunch &
dinner Tues–Sun. Train: Yaba-cho Station.

★★ **Yamamoto-ya Honten** NAGOYA STATION
NOODLES This chain noodle shop specializes
in *miso nikomi udon*—its handmade noodles
are thick, hard, and chewy and are served in
a type of bean paste that's special to Nagoya.
25-9 Meieki. ☎ 052/565-0278. www.yama
motoyahonten.co.jp. Entrees ¥1,000–¥1,600.
Lunch & dinner daily. Train: Nagoya Station.

Sado

The island of Sado (called Sadogashima in Japanese), off the coast of Niigata, is a postcard-perfect landscape of green-carpeted mountains in the south, craggy rocks jutting up from tempestuous ocean waves in the north, and crystal-clear blue waters hugging the gravelly shore. With its extensively varied terrain, Sado is like a miniature version of Japan before the age of modernization. The island's combination of untouched natural beauty and rich cultural heritage make it a truly unique destination. We recommend at least 2 days for this tour, starting at Sado's main port of Ryotsu.

> *The turtle-shaped Ono-game rock formation, on the northern tip of Sado Island.*

START Ferries from Niigata run to the Port of Ryotsu. Sado is 405km (252 miles) north of Tokyo.

① 🍽 ★★ **Tenkuni** (天國). A favorite among locals, this simple Japanese restaurant specializes in fresh seafood served in a variety of ways—sliced raw as sashimi, deep-fried as tempura, and simmered in comforting *nabe* (hot pots). **Tip:** Ask for specials that aren't listed on the menu. 206 Ryotsu-Minato. ☎ 0259/23-2714. Entrees from ¥1,000. No credit cards. Lunch & dinner daily. Bus: Ryotsu Port.

❷ ★ **Sado Nogakunosato** (佐渡能楽の里). Sado Island contains a third of all of the Noh stages in Japan. Most Noh, or classical Japanese musical dramas, are performed as rituals, on stages outside of shrines, but the Sado Nogakunosato is the first facility built expressly for tourists. This small museum exhibits masks and costumes used in traditional Noh theater performances. Visitors can also watch a play enacted by high-tech robots (though there are other performances starring humans as well). Look for the tower with two large Noh masks. 🕐 30 min. 1839 Agata. ☎ 0259/23-5000. ¥500. Daily 8:30am–5pm. Bus: Minamisen Line to Sado Nogakunosato.

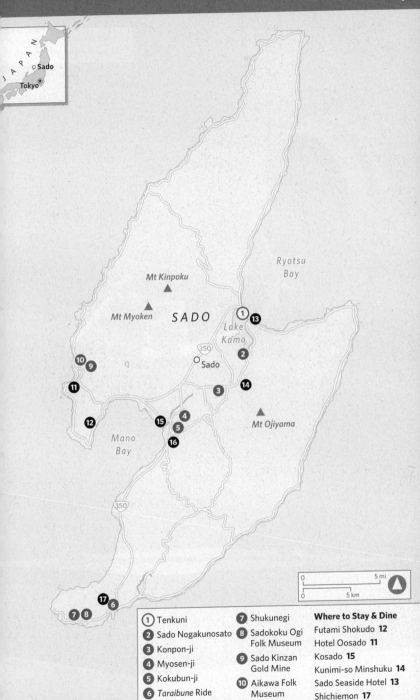

Mt Kinpoku

Mt Myoken

SADO

Ryotsu Bay

Lake Kamo

Sado

Mt Ojiyama

Mano Bay

350

350

①	Tenkuni
②	Sado Nogakunosato
③	Konpon-ji
④	Myosen-ji
⑤	Kokubun-ji
⑥	*Taraibune* Ride
⑦	Shukunegi
⑧	Sadokoku Ogi Folk Museum
⑨	Sado Kinzan Gold Mine
⑩	Aikawa Folk Museum

Where to Stay & Dine

Futami Shokudo **12**
Hotel Oosado **11**
Kosado **15**
Kunimi-so Minshuku **14**
Sado Seaside Hotel **13**
Shichiemon **17**
Yuzuru **16**

> Taiko-tastic: A world-famous Kodo drummer in Kodo Village.

★★ **Konpon-ji** (根本寺). Located in the town Mano, this temple is the site where the onk Nichiren was taken after his exile to ado Island in 1271. Its thatch-roofed buildings urround a peaceful green garden. ⏱ 30 min. 337 Niiboono. ☎ 0259/22-3751. ¥300. Daily am–4pm. Bus: Minamisen Line to onpon-ji-mae.

★ **Myosen-ji** (妙宣寺). Founded by the monk ichiren and his first disciple, Nittoku Abut- bo, this shrine dates back to 1221 and boasts fine, five-story pagoda measuring 24m (79 .). Myosen-ji is a 5-minute walk west of onpon-ji. ⏱ 30 min. 29 Abutsubo. ☎ 0259/55- 061. Free. Bus: Minamisen Line to Takedabashi.

★ **Kokubun-ji** (国分寺). Founded in 741 by mperor Shomu and completed in 764, this illside temple is Sado's oldest. The original uilding was destroyed in a fire in the 1500s nd the present structure dates back to 1679. ⏱ 20 min. Kokubun-ji, Manomachi. ☎ 0259/55- 059. http://sadokokubunji.com. Free. Bus: Minamisen Line to Takedabashi.

★ *Taraibune* **Ride** (たらい船). Back in the day, raibune (tub boats) were used by women nd fishermen to harvest *wakame* (a dark- reen seaweed) and tasty, snail-like sea mol- usks called *sazae*. These days, they're a popu- r tourist attraction in Ogi Harbor, operated y older ladies in traditional costumes. The val-shaped boats are made of *sugi* wood (a ype of Japanese cedar) and built in the same ay as barrels. To steer one, you have to use

> *Steering a* taraibune *tub boat is best left to the professionals.*

a long, skinny paddle. The dock is a 4-min- ute walk from Ogi ferry terminal. ⏱ **2 hr. 184 Ogimachi.** ☎ **0259/86-3153. ¥450. Daily Mar 22–July 31 8:20am–5pm; Aug 1–Aug 16 8am– 5pm; Aug 17–Nov 30 8:30am–5pm; Dec 1–Mar 21 9am–4pm. Bus: Mano Line to Ogi-ko.**

❼ ★★ **Shukunegi** (宿根木). This sleepy fish- ing village on the southern coast began as a port town in the 13th century and prospered from the 17th to 19th centuries, thanks to its location along a major shipping route. The traditional wooden houses built over a century ago here retain an Edo-era atmosphere today. Some of these former homes of wealthy ship owners are open to the public. A visit to the town makes for a pleasant afternoon stroll. Buses are very infrequent, especially during winter months, so check bus schedules. ⏱ **2½ hr. Bus: Shukunegi Line to Shukunegi.**

The Earth Celebration Festival

The Earth Celebration Festival (www.kodo. or.jp/ec) is the biggest event on Sado Is- land. The music and dance extravaganza turns the ordinarily drowsy port of Ogi into party central for 3 days during the 3rd week in August. Most of the buzz hovers around the famous Kodo drummers, a troupe of celebrated *taiko* (Japanese drum) percussionists who live in a remote village north of Ogi. The group spends most of their time traveling around the world, but they come home every year to give an elec- trifying performance at the Earth Celebra- tion Festival.

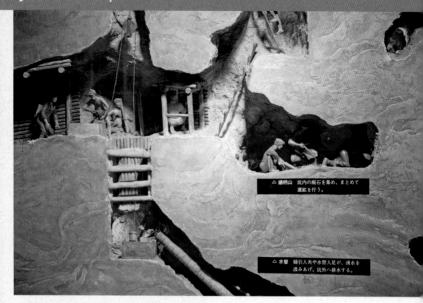

△ 搦柄山 坑内の鍰石を集め、まとめて 選鉱を行う。

△ 水替 樋引人夫や水替人足が、湧水を 汲みあげ、坑外へ排水する。

> *Meander through the tunnels and the dark history of Sado's gold mines.*

8 ★ **Sadokoku Ogi Folk Museum** (佐渡国小木民俗博物館). A mishmash of quotidian items from old and not-so-old times on the island can be viewed at this small but interesting museum, housed in a former school from the 1920s. One of the highlights is the full-scale replica of a 19th-century freight vessel. Buses here are very infrequent, especially during winter months, so check bus schedules. ⏱ 30 min. 270-2 Shukunegi. ☎ 0259/86-2604. ¥500. Daily 8:30am–5pm. Closed late-Dec–Feb. Bus: Shukunegi Line to Hakubutsukan-mae.

9 ★★★ **Sado Kinzan Gold Mine** (佐渡金山). This fascinating museum inside the Sado Kinzan Gold Mine traces the history of Japan's most productive mining operation—which produced nearly 400kg (882 lb.) of gold annually—from 1601 until 1989. The two walking trails lead through the former mining tunnels, past displays featuring animatronic figures demonstrating the harsh conditions of the Edo Period. The exhibits in the Meiji-era tunnels focus on more modern mining techniques and machinery. From the bus stop, the museum is a 40m (131-ft.) walk uphill, but buses run directly to the entrance in the summertime. Buses are very infrequent, especially during winter months, so check bus schedules. ⏱ 2 hr. 1305 Shimoaikawa. ☎ 0259/74-2389. ¥800 for tour of 1 trail, ¥1,200 for 2 trails. Daily Apr–Oct 8am–5pm; Nov–Mar 8:30am–4:30pm. Bus: Nanaura-Kaigan Line to Sadokinzan.

10 ★ **Aikawa Folk Museum** (相川郷土博物館). The photographs, textiles, and objects—such as snow shoes woven from straw—on display at this museum shed light on everyday life of the inhabitants of Aikawa, the mining town of Sado Kinzan Gold Mine. Buses are very infrequent, especially during winter months, so check bus schedules. ⏱ 30 min. 2 Sakashitamachi. ☎ 0259/74-4312. ¥300. Daily 8:30am–5pm. Closed year-end holidays and weekends and holidays in Jan and Feb. Bus: Nanaura-Kaigan Line to Aikawahakubutsukan-mae.

The Seasons of Sado

There are various festivals all year round, but the best time to visit Sado is mid-spring to mid-fall. Although the snowy winter-scapes are not without their charms, lodging options are minimal and public transportation is virtually nonexistent.

Where to Stay & Dine on Sado

★ **Futami Shokudo** (二見食堂) AIKAWA *NOODLES*
This modest ramen shop always seems to be packed, despite the daunting 40-minute drive from the harbor. (It's not accessible by public transportation.) Fans praise the lightly flavored soup and slick, firm noodles. 137-2 Futami. ☎ 0259/76-2754. Ramen from ¥800. No credit cards. Lunch Fri–Tues. Car: From Aikawa, drive south on Rte. 31; take a right on Rte. 45. Futami is a 5-minute walk from Futami Post Office.

★ **Hotel Oosado** AIKAWA
Located on Kasugazaki Point, this large hotel provides lovely sunrise and sunset views of the Sea of Japan. Some of the Japanese-style rooms are nicely appointed with scroll paintings, and some of the rooms are Western-style. There's also a large *o-furu* (communal bath) and a relaxing *rotenburo* (open-air *onsen*) overlooking the water. The English-speaking hotel staff operates a shuttle service from Aikawa; call to arrange a pickup. 288-2 Aikawabuse. ☎ 0259/74-3300. www.oosado.com. 130 units. Rooms from ¥9,450 per person. Rates include 2 meals. AE, MC, V. Bus: Kanaura Kaigan Line to Sadokaikan-mae.

★ **Kosado** MANO *YOSHOKU*
This friendly restaurant serves a variety of *yoshoku* (Western-inspired Japanese cooking) standards, from steak and fries to *omuraisu* (rice omelets topped with a thick demi-glace) to hefty portions of *tonkatsu* (deep-fried pork cutlets) with a sesame-miso sauce. The barista takes particular delight in adorning your café au lait with cute characters drawn in the foam. 275-2 Mano-Shinmachi. ☎ 0259/55-5004. www.kosado.com. Lunch & dinner Thurs–Tues. Entrees ¥930–¥11,600. No credit cards. Bus: Niigata Kotsu Sado Line to Mano-Shinmachi.

Kunimi-so Minshuku RYOTSU
This popular *minshuku* (budget *ryokan*) guesthouse has a history going back 400 years. The owner has an interesting collection of *bunya ningyo* (storytelling puppets) that he will be happy to demonstrate to guests. 734 Niibo Uryuya. ☎ 0259/22-2316. 11 units. Rooms from ¥7,000 per person. Rates include 2 meals. No credit cards. Bus: Niigata Kotsu Sado Line to Uryuya.

> The seafood on Sado is first rate—grilled, fried, or served raw over rice in *kaisendonburi.*

★ **Sado Seaside Hotel** RYOTSU
This conveniently located hotel near the beach has simple, Japanese-style rooms and a communal bath. Japanese and Western breakfasts are available and English-speaking staff is a plus. 80 Sumiyoshi. ☎ 0259/27-7211. www2u.biglobe.ne.jp/~sado/englishpage.htm. 13 units, 5 with bath. Doubles from ¥10,800. Breakfast ¥840 extra, dinner ¥1,575 extra. AE, DC, MC, V. Bus: Ryotsu Port (shuttle service available from port; call for pickup).

★★ **Shichiemon** (七石衛門そば) OGI *NOODLES*
Its convenient location near Ogi Harbor makes this soba shop a popular lunch destination. The restaurant's hand-cut buckwheat noodles, which you're to dip in a small bowl of sauce, are flavorful and firm to the bite. 643-1 Ogimachi. ☎ 0259/86-2046. Soba from ¥500. No credit cards. Lunch daily. Closed the 1st and 15th every month. Bus: Ogi-ko.

★ **Yuzuru** (夕鶴) MANO *JAPANESE*
This Japanese restaurant inside the Sado Rekishi-Densetsukan museum serves nicely prepared (and extremely reasonable) multi-course lunches. Each set lunch comes with homemade *shio-kara,* a pungent snack of fermented fish innards, and *fuki-miso,* a savory paste made from mildly bitter butterbur. Reservations are required 3 days in advance. 655 Mano. ☎ 0259/55-2525. Set lunches from ¥1,050. No credit cards. Lunch daily. Bus: From Ogi, Ogi Line to Manogoryo-iriguchi.

Central Honshu Fast Facts

Arriving & Getting Around

BY TRAIN By far the easiest way to get to Central Honshu is by train. There are convenient trains to the hubs of Karuizawa, Matsumoto, Nagoya, Echigo-Yuzawa, and Niigata that operate daily, with frequent departures. Other areas in Central Honshu can be accessed via these cities. To reach **Karuizawa,** Asama trains on the Nagano Shinkansen Line run from Tokyo Station to Karuizawa (67 min.) daily. To reach **Matsumoto,** the limited express Azusa, on the Chuo Honsen Line, has daily departures from Shinjuku Station in Tokyo (2½ hr. or 3½ hr.). To reach **Nagoya,** the Shinkansen bullet train from Tokyo Station is the fastest way to get to Nagoya Station (2 hr.). To reach **Echigo-Yuzawa,** TOKI Max trains run along the Joetsu Shinkansen Line and connect Echigo-Yuzawa with Tokyo (84 min.). To reach **Niigata,** the TOKI Max also provides service to Niigata Station (134 min.). BY BUS Buses also run from Shinjuku Station in Tokyo to **Matsumoto** (3¼ hr.).

ATMs

In contrast to those abroad, many ATMs only operate during banking hours. ATMs are also very hard to find outside of major cities, so plan accordingly. Most post offices (see below) have ATM facilities, although hours are limited. For 24-hour access, your best bets are the ATMs in **7-Eleven** convenience stores, which accept Visa, Plus, American Express, JCB, Union Pay, or Diner's Club International cards for cash withdrawals. (They recently stopped accepting MasterCard, Maestro, and Cirrus cards.) **Citibank** and **Shinsei Bank** ATMs accept foreign bank cards as well.

Doctors & Hospitals

The general level of healthcare availability in Japan is high. If you need to consult a physician, you should always first ask your hotel concierge for a nearby recommendation, as the facilities below may only have limited English capabilities and are generally only open during business hours. The U.S. Embassy's website carries an up-to-date list of foreign-friendly doctors throughout Japan (http://tokyo.usembassy.gov/e/acs/tacs-7119.html). KARUIZAWA **Karuizawa Hospital** is at 2375-1 Nagakura (☎ 0267/45-5111). MATSUMOTO **Shinshu University Hospital** is at 3-1-1 Asahi (☎ 0263/35-4600; wwwhp.md.shinshu-u.ac.jp/english/). NAGOYA **Nagoya University Hospital** is at 65 Tsuruma-cho, Showa-ku (☎ 052/741-2111; www.med.nagoya-u.ac.jp/english02). SADO **Ryotsu Hospital** is at 1771 Hamada, Sado-shi (☎ 0259/23-5111; www.city.sado.niigata.jp/hp/ryotsu).

Emergencies

Dial ☎ **119** for ambulance and fire. Dial ☎ **110** for police and other emergencies.

Internet Access

Most hotels (but not all *ryokan*) are equipped with Internet access, but Wi-Fi is still uncommon. Even if Wi-Fi is available, it still may be necessary to use a LAN cable at certain times of the year. Your concierge can also direct you to the nearest Internet cafe.

Pharmacies

Drugstores, called *yakkyoku* (薬局) are ubiquitous in Japan, but they are not 24-hour operations. Your best bet is to ask your hotel concierge for the closest location. Note that you must first visit a doctor in Japan before foreign prescriptions can be filled, so it's also best to bring an ample supply of any prescription medication with you.

Police

Dial ☎ **110** for police.

Post Offices

Central post offices are generally open Monday to Friday 9am to 7pm, Saturday 9am to 5pm, and Sunday 9am to 12:30pm. Their ATMs are generally available Monday to Friday 7am to 11pm, Saturday 9am to 9pm, and Sunday 9am to 7pm. Branches will have shorter hours, as specified below. KARUIZAWA **Karuizawa Post Office** is at 767-3 Karuizawa (☎ 0267/42-2076). MATSUMOTO **Matsumoto Post Office** is at 2-7-5 Chuo (Mon–Fri 9am–4pm; ATM open Mon–Fri 8:45am–9pm; Sat-Sun 9am–7pm). NAGOYA **Nagoya Central Post Office** is at 1-1-1 Meieki, just north of

The Shinkansen bullet train is the fastest, easiest way to travel to Central Honshu.

agoya Station (☎ 052/564-2106; Mon–Fri am–7pm, Sat 9am–5pm, Sun 9am–12:30pm). **NIIGATA Niigata Central Post Office** is at 2-6– 5 Higashi Dori, just north of Niigata Station ☎ 025/244-3429).

afety
ke the rest of Japan, Central Honshu is ex- emely safe, but take common-sense precau- ons for personal safety and valuables that u would anywhere else in the world.

isitor Information
ARUIZAWA Karuizawa Tourist Information ffice is in Karuizawa Station (☎ 0267/42- 191; www.town.karuizawa.nagano.jp/html/ glish; daily 9am–5:30pm, until 6pm in

summer). **MATSUMOTO Matsumoto Tourist Information Center** is in Matsumoto Station, directly in front of the ticket gate on the sec- ond floor (☎ 0263/32-2814; http://welcome. city.matsumoto.nagano.jp; daily 9am–5:45pm. **NAGOYA Nagoya Tourist Information Center** is in Nagoya Station, central concourse, out- side of the Central exit ticket gates (☎ 052/ 541-4301; www.ncub.or.jp; daily 9am–7pm. **SADO Sado Tourism Association Tourist Desk,** Ryotsu Port, is in the Ryotsu Port Termi- nal Building, second floor (☎ 0259/23-3300; www.visitsado.com/en; daily Sept–June 8:30am–5pm, July–Aug 8:30am–6:50pm).

5
Kansai

Favorite Moments

The people of Kansai are proud, and rightfully so. Japanese culture as we know it was born here and continues to flourish. Ancient cities like Kyoto and Nara are windows into Japan's rich historical past, while Osaka and Kobe are kaleidoscopes looking into the future. Thanks to convenient train lines connecting Kansai's major cities, you can move around with ease.

> PREVIOUS PAGE Osaka at night is an electric playground. THIS PAGE Don't mess with Nara's Big Buddha.

1 Confronting Todai-ji. As you approach the monolithic Daibutsu, the iconic Buddha statue within Todai-ji temple's gates, you'll recognize the feeling of awe that comes from being in the presence of a truly huge structure. Amazingly, the massive reconstruction is only two-thirds the original size. See p. 223, **4**.

2 Exploring the ocean depths at Osaka Aquarium. A moon-faced giant sunfish, graceful manta rays, and dozens of species of sharks: What more can you ask for in an aquarium? Osaka's aquarium, or Kaiyukan, ups the ante with spindly legged giant spider crabs that walk up to the glass like robots and luminous jellyfish that float like iridescent flowers. See p. 213, **8**.

3 Taking in the night view over Kobe. Those who left their hearts in San Francisco will likely feel a tug of nostalgia as they take in the view of Kobe Harbor, with its terrestrial firmament of twinkling lights hugging the bay. See p. 230, **2**.

4 Walking the scenic streets of Kyoto. Much is made of its temples and gardens, but one of the great pleasures of a visit to Kyoto is a stroll through its scenic old neighborhoods—like stepping back in time. See p. 247, **8**.

5 Feeding the deer in Nara. Even if you're not an animal lover, it's hard not to be charmed by the friendly deer in Nara Koen. If you buy a bag of *shika-sembei*, "deer crackers," for ¥150 from one of the many vendors, they'll eat right out of your hand. See p. 200.

6 Finding yourself at Sanjusangendo. Legend has it that among the 1,001 statues of Kannon lined up inside of this long, narrow building you can find the faces of yourself and your family members. Guess what? It's true. See p. 244, **1**.

7 Eating *takoyaki* in Namba. Osaka's most famous street food, a sort of octopus dumpling is also the best thing to munch on as you take in the glittering nightscape from Ebisubashi. Join the throngs of snackers and get an order to go from one of the countless stalls. See p. 216.

8 Drinking in sake history at Hakutsuru Sake Brewery Museum. The fascinating displays at Hakutsuru Sake Brewery Museum shed real light on the labor-intensive process that goes into the making of Japan's national drink. The free tasting at the end of the tour is equally enlightening. See p. 233, **8**.

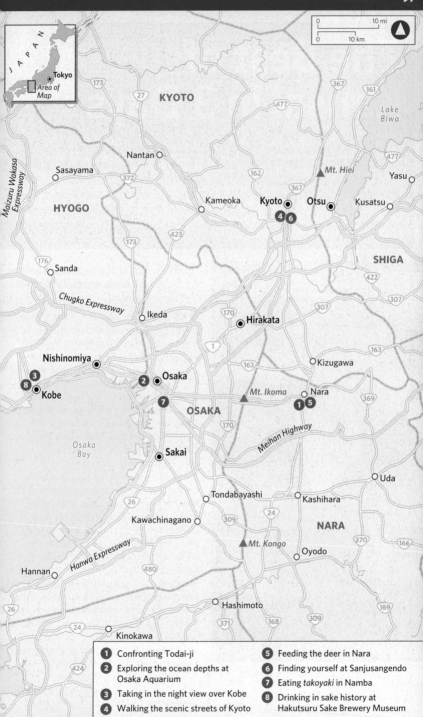

0   10 mi
0   10 km

KYOTO

HYOGO

SHIGA

OSAKA

NARA

Lake Biwa

Maizuru Wakasa Expressway

Chugko Expressway

Hanwa Expressway

Meihan Highway

Osaka Bay

Sasayama
Nantan
Mt. Hiei
Yasu
Kameoka
Kyoto
Otsu
Kusatsu
Sanda
Ikeda
Hirakata
Nishinomiya
Kizugawa
Osaka
Mt. Ikoma
Nara
Kobe
Sakai
Uda
Tondabayashi
Kashihara
Kawachinagano
Mt. Kongo
Oyodo
Hannan
Hashimoto
Kinokawa

1 Confronting Todai-ji

2 Exploring the ocean depths at Osaka Aquarium

3 Taking in the night view over Kobe

4 Walking the scenic streets of Kyoto

5 Feeding the deer in Nara

6 Finding yourself at Sanjusangendo

7 Eating *takoyaki* in Namba

8 Drinking in sake history at Hakutsuru Sake Brewery Museum

The Best of Kansai in 3 Days

Between the historical wonders of Kyoto and Nara, the cosmopolitan atmosphere of Kobe, and the urban intensity of Osaka, you'll find no shortage of exciting things to do in Kansai. Most of the iconic images of Japan—the fiery red gates of Fushimi Inari Shrine, the mammoth Great Buddha, the giant neon tarot card of the Glico Running Man—can be found here. The Kansai region is the cradle of Japanese culture, where the traditional and ultramodern nestle side by side.

> A maiko *flutters by in Kyoto's Gion district.*

START From Kyoto Station, take bus no. 206 to Gojo-zaka. Kyoto is 463km (288 miles) southwest of Tokyo.

1 Kyoto. If you have only one day to spend in the scenic city of Kyoto, set your sights on Higashiyama. Several of Kyoto's many attractions are concentrated in the southern Higashiyama district, and touring the area on foot is easy as well as extremely enjoyable. The grande dame of Higashiyama's temples is the UNESCO World Heritage site **Kiyomizu-dera,** the "pure water" temple, whose famously wide veranda (referred to locally as the "Kiyomizu stage") attracts thousands of visitors each year.

From Kiyomizu-dera, take the winding narrow lane down to the neighborhoods of **Ninenzaka** and **Sanenzaka,** where stone-paved roads and beautifully restored wooden buildings exude the romance of old Kyoto. Like Gion, Ninenzaka is an architecturally protected "preservation zone" filled with historic sites. Walking north from the end of Ninenzaka, follow in the footsteps of Kita-no-Mandokoro (widely known as "Nene"), the wife of Toyotomi Hideyoshi, to the entrance of the temple she built in his memory, **Kodai-ji.**

As dusk creeps over the city, make your way to **Gion,** Kyoto's famed geisha district. The geisha are still there, although their numbers have declined significantly over the years—down to around 200, less than a fifth of the numbers during their peak at

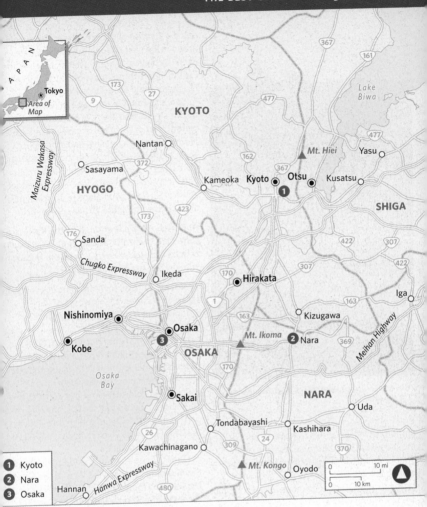

1 Kyoto
2 Nara
3 Osaka

the beginning of the 20th century. You may encounter geisha or *maiko* (geisha in training) along the cobbled streets of Gion, but even if you don't, this lovely stretch of Kyoto is well worth a stroll at night, when the tastefully illuminated black-painted facades of the wooden buildings recall descriptions from Junichiro Tanizaki's *In Praise of Shadows*. Cap off your evening with a walk down the lantern-lit street of **Pontocho**. ⏱1 day. See p. 238.

Return to Kyoto Station and board the Kintetsu Tokkyu Limited Express train (35 min.), and get off at Kintetsu Nara Station.

2 **Nara.** In keeping with Shinto tradition, Japan's capital moved with each new emperor until the 7th century. This practice ended with the rise of Buddhism and, in 710, Nara, which was then called Heijokyo, became the first established capital of the country. Although its time as the capital was short—lasting only 75 years, compared to Kyoto's 1,000-year tenure—those years saw the birth of Japan's arts, crafts, and literature, thanks to the avid importation of influences from China.

One of the city's best attributes is its manageable scale: Most of the sights can be covered on foot in a day. Head straight from the

> Serene Sarusawa Pond, beside Kofuku-ji temple in Nara.

station down Nobori-Oji to **Nara Koen.** The most unusual (and adorable) feature of the park is the thriving population of **tame deer,** who roam freely across the park's wooded lawns. The 1,200 deer are considered National Treasures and were revered as messengers of the gods in Buddhist times. In fact, killing one of these sweet-faced Bambis was a capital crime until 1637.

After visiting the temple of **Kofuku-ji,** cross under the main road and walk northeast to the beautiful garden of **Isuien.** If you're there at the end of October, be sure to check out the *Jugatsu-zakura,* an early blooming variety of cherry blossom tree. From Isuien, follow the signs to **Todai-ji,** the Buddhist temple that contains the world's largest wooden building, the massive **Daibutsuden,** which houses the famous **Daibutsu (Great Buddha).** The Buddha is without a doubt Nara's main attraction, and hoards of tourists flock to Todai-ji daily to

catch a glimpse of it. Fortunately, the temple grounds are vast enough to accommodate even the biggest groups. The approach to the Daibutsuden, through a wide, open courtyard is a memorable experience in itself.

Spend the rest of the day exploring the quaint streets and alleys of **Naramachi,** a historic part of town full of well-preserved *machiya* (wooden houses) and storehouses. Most of these former merchants' residences have been converted into shops and small galleries, and there are a few nice restaurants in the area. It's a good place to drop in a meal after hitting the sights. ⏲ 1 day. See p. 220.

At Kintetsu Nara Station, take the Kintetsu Nara Line toward Osaka and get off at Osaka Namba Station (40 min.). Take the Midosuji subway line to Umeda (9 min.).

❸ **Osaka.** With its towering blocks of neon-lit skyscrapers, teeming networks of underground arcades, and subway cars packed tightly with commuters, Osaka may seem like a den of mayhem after placid Nara. Osaka is a city on the go, inhabited by no-nonsense, business-minded folk with a unique cultural identity. Known for their sense of humor (as well as their colorful *Kansai-ben* dialect), the people of Osaka are outspoken, and they take particular pride in their food culture. The expression *"kuidaore,"* which means "eat till you drop," originated here.

Out of Umeda Station, head to the **Umeda Sky Building** to take in the view at the **Floating Garden Observatory.** Next, check out the Disney-esque **Osaka Museum of Housing and Living.** This life-sized diorama of an Edo-Period Osaka neighborhood is complete with the sounds of merchants doing business in their shops and townspeople gossiping at the well, and lights that change the skies from day to night.

Although its history spans over 1,500 years, Osaka first came to power with the building of **Osakajo castle** in 1583. At the time, it was considered the most magnificent in Japan. The present structure, a reconstruction from 1931, is smaller but nonetheless impressive. Round off your tour with a night of *kuidaore* along the **Dotonbori** "eating street" in the Namba area, and take a dip at **Spa World** before hitting the sack. ⏲ 1 day. See p. 206.

> Going up: Take the super-express escalator to Osaka's Floating Garden Observatory.

The Best of Kansai in 1 Week

If you can spend a week here, take a few extra days to explore Kyoto and try to split your time between temples and city sights to avoid temple fatigue. We also recommend taking a side trip to Kobe for a change of scenery and finishing your tour with some spiritual enlightenment in Koya-san.

> *Looking for enlightenment at Ryoan-ji.*

START **From Osaka Station, board the JR Shinkaisoku train to Kyoto Station (29 min.). Then take bus no. 205 to Kinkaku-ji-mae.**

❶ Kyoto. No trip to Kyoto is complete without a visit to **Kinkaku-ji** (p. 250, ❸), the golden temple built by Ashikaga Yoshimitsu, who lived in luxury while his people suffered from famine and plague. (The temple also became a symbol of erotic obsession for the main character in Mishima Yukio's novel *The Temple of the Golden Pavilion*.) Although the profligate shogun had planned to cover the entire structure in gold, he had only succeeded in gilding the third floor by the time of his death. Gold leaf now covers the top two floors of the reconstruction and on sunny days you need sunglasses to view the coruscating structure.

Kinkaku-ji was the inspiration behind the 15th-century **Ginkaku-ji,** the Silver Pavilion. Ginkaku-ji was commissioned by Ashikaga's son, Yoshimasa, who used it as a villa retreat during times of civil war. Like his father, Yoshimasa intended to cover the building with precious metals (in this case, silver) but his wish never materialized.

1 Kyoto
2 Kobe
3 Koya-san

Almost as famous as Ginkaku-ji is the **Philosopher's Path** that leads from the temple to the neighborhood of Nanzen-ji. The eminent philosopher Nishida Kitaro practiced meditation as he walked this road to Kyoto University. The path, which winds along the canal in southern Higashiyama, is lined with restaurants, cafes, and—best of all—cherry trees, making it an ideal spot during cherry blossom season.

While you're around there, stop in at **Ryoan-ji** temple to admire the beautiful Zen rock garden, and then head back downtown to browse the bounty of **Nishiki Market** (p. 251, 9).

If you're up for more temples but want a change of atmosphere, head for the mossy hills of Arashiyama to find pockets of calm in the gardens of **Tenryu-ji** (p. 252, 1) and the eerily beautiful **Adashino Nembutsu-ji** (p. 255, 6).

If, however, the idea of more temples—and the hour-long trip out to Kyoto's western mountains—tires you out just thinking about it, check out some contemporary culture at the **Kyoto International Manga Museum.** Housed in a former elementary school building, this museum has a fine collection—around 300,000 pieces—of items related to manga (Japanese comics and print cartoons). In addition to manga and stills from local artists, comics from all over the world are on display. The museum also holds interesting lectures and events such as cosplay shows (short for "costume play," in which actors dress up as characters from manga or pop fiction), as well as illustration demonstrations on weekends. Check the website for details in English. ⏱ 2 days. **Ginkaku-ji:** ⏱ 1 hr. 2 Ginkaku-ji-cho, Sakyo-ku. ☎ 075/771-5725. ¥500. Daily Mar–Nov 8:30am–5pm; Dec–Feb 9am–4:30pm. Bus: 5 to Ginkaku-ji-michi. **Nanzen-ji:** ⏱ 30 min. Fukuchi-cho, Nanzen-ji, Sakyo-ku. ☎ 075/771-0365. Free to enter grounds; ¥500 for garden. Daily Mar–Nov 8:40am–5pm; Dec–Feb 8:40am–4:30pm. Bus: 5 to Nanzen-ji Eikando-michi. **Manga Museum:** ⏱ 1½ hr. Karasuma Dori, Oike-agaru, Nakagyo-ku. ☎ 075/254-7414. www.kyotomm.jp/english. ¥500 adults, ¥100 kids. Thurs–Tues 10am–6pm. Subway: Karasuma-Oike Station.

From Karasuma Station, take the Hankyu line to Umeda (41 min.) and transfer to the Tokkyu Limited Express bound for Hankyu-Sannomiya (27 min.).

② **Kobe.** Long before Tokyo became an international capital, Kobe had trade links with China (the relationship dates back around a thousand years) and was one of the first Japanese cities to open up to the Western world in the 19th century. Thanks to its substantial foreign population and its embrace of Western culture, this small port town has a distinctively cosmopolitan feel. A walk around the **Kitano district,** with its Western-style houses, will make you feel as though you've stepped into a European village, while a visit to **Chinatown** feels like, well, the global phenomenon that is Chinatown, but it's fun at night.

Kobe was devastated in 1995 by an earthquake measuring 7.2 on the Richter scale. Over 6,400 people lost their lives, countless others were wounded, and the area sustained damages of over $100 billion. The city was rebuilt, however, and today Kobe is a vibrant town with fine examples of contemporary architecture such as the **Hyogo Prefectural Museum of Art** and the superb **Disaster Reduction Museum.**

Don't miss the night view from the **Nunobiki Herb Garden** and the many opportunities to dine on Kobe's famously luxurious *wagyu* (Japanese beef). You may consider heading back to Osaka for the night. ⏱ 1 day. See p. 230.

Hop on the Hankyu Line from Hankyu-Sannomiya to Osaka (27 min.). Change to

the Midosuji Line and go to Namba before boarding the Nankai-Koya Line to Gokurakubashi (90 min.). At Gokurakubashi, take the cable car to Koyasan (5 min.) and catch a bus from there to Senjuinbashi.

③ **Koya-san.** If you're on a quest to find monks meditating in wooden temples nestled among trees, the sacred mountain of **Mount Koya** is the place to go. The top of the mountain, called Koya-san by Japanese, is home to more than 115 temples scattered through the mountain forests. Some 50 of these offer accommodations, making this one of the best places in Japan to observe temple life firsthand. Founded in 812 by the monk Kukai (known posthumously as Kobo Daishi), it's one of Japan's most sacred places and the mecca of the Shingon Esoteric sect of Buddhism.

The most awe-inspiring of Koya-san's temples, **Okunoin** contains the mausoleum of Kobo Daishi, as well as the tombs of roughly 200,000 of his disciples over the centuries. The most dramatic way to approach Okunoin is from the Okunoin-guchi bus stop, where a pathway leads 1.5km (1 mile) to the mausoleum. And be sure to return to the mausoleum at night; the stone lanterns (now lit electrically) create a mysterious and powerful effect. Before heading there, though, stop at the **Koya-san Tourist Association** in the center of town to purchase tickets to sights, rent English-language audio guides, and book accommodations in temples or hotels, if you wish.

Another important site is the **Garan,** a temple complex that's considered the center of religious life in the community. It's an impressive sight with a huge *kondo* (main hall), first built in 819 by Kobo Daishi, and a large vermilion-colored *daito* (pagoda), which contains an image of the Dainichi-nyorai (Cosmic Buddha). ⏱ 1 day. **Okunoin:** ⏱ 1½ hr. 550 Koyasan, Koya-cho. ☎ 0736/56-2002. Free. Open 24 hr. Bus: Okunoin Line to Okunoin-guchi or Ichinohashi-mae. **Koyasan Tourist Association:** 600 Koyasan, Koya-cho. ☎ 0736/56-2616. www.shukubo.jp/eng. Daily July–Aug 8:30am–5:30pm; Sept–June 8:30am–4:30pm. Bus: Senjuinbashi. **Garan:** ⏱ 1 hr. 152 Koyasan, Koya-cho. ☎ 0736/56-3215. ¥200 each for the kondo and daito. Garan complex open 24 hr.; kondo and daito daily 8:30am–5pm. Bus: Okunoin Line to Senjuinbashi.

> *Kobe tower illuminated at night.*

An Osaka Subculture Safari

Osaka is known throughout Japan as an international and progressive business center. As the capital of Osaka Prefecture, and with a population of about 2.6 million (the third-most-populated city in Japan after Tokyo and Yokohama), it's the mover and shaker of the Kansai region. But despite outward appearances, Osaka—like many Japanese cities—is also home to a thriving subculture, which has spawned trends ranging from mildly wacky to downright strange. This tour will give you a taste of them.

> Get a taste of otaku culture at one of Osaka's many maid cafes.

START Take the subway to Umeda Station. Osaka is 55km (34 miles) southwest of Kyoto.

1 ★★ Sega Amusement Theme Park. Game fans, you've found your spiritual home. This amusement park overwhelms the senses with seizure-inducing flashing lights, bells, and hoards of screaming teens and "tweens." Arcade games, virtual-reality games that simulate flight or white-water rafting, and the largest collection of Purikura photo booths in Kansai. Who even needs the Ferris wheel on the roof? ⏱ 30 min. HEP FIVE 8F/9F, 5-15 Kakuda-cho, Kita-ku. ☎ 06/6366-3647. Free, attractions from ¥400. Daily 11am–11pm (last entry 10:15pm; children 15 & under not admitted after 7pm; children 17 & under not admitted after 10pm). Subway: Umeda Station.

2 ★★ Hozen-ji (法善寺). This small, lantern-lit temple is accessed via a charming alley that cuts through a neighborhood filled with hostess bars (where female staff sit at your table, talk to you, pour your drinks, listen to your problems, and boost your ego). Rumor has it that those working in Osaka's infamous *mizu-shobai* (literally "water trade"—the hostess or cabaret entertainment industry) stop here on their way to work to pay their respects to the goddess Mizukake Fudo, whose moss-covered image is enshrined in the temple. We're not sure where they're employed, but there are always people in line to throw water on the statue. ⏱ 10 min. 1 Namba, Chuo-ku. No phone. Free. Open 24 hr. Subway: Namba Station.

3 ★★ Amerikamura (アメリカ村). A short walk from the Dotonbori covered shopping arcade, Amerikamura is a mecca of youth culture. Used-clothing shops, music stores, and boutiques selling the latest in goth fashion fill the streets, along with cafes and karaoke bars. At the heart of Amerikamura is **Sankaku Koen** park, where teenagers in Harajuku-style Lolita outfits and punk gear turn out in droves on the weekends. Just look for the replica Statue of

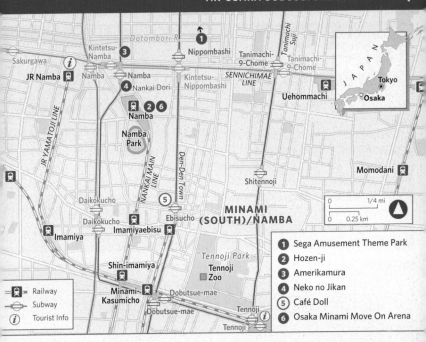

1. Sega Amusement Theme Park
2. Hozen-ji
3. Amerikamura
4. Neko no Jikan
5. Café Doll
6. Osaka Minami Move On Arena

Railway
Subway
Tourist Info

iberty planted on top of one of the buildings. rom Midosuji, walk west one or two blocks. ⏱ 20 min. 2 Nishi-Shinsaibashi, Chuo-ku. Free. ubway: Midosuji Shinsaibashi Station.

④ ★★★ Neko no Jikan. The cat cafe boom, where patrons pay a fee to watch and play with cats at local cafes, started in Osaka and, after nearly a decade, it's still going strong. This cat cafe in Amerikamura is a relaxing haven of wooden surfaces and muted earth tones, where ¥1,050 will buy you one drink and 1 hour of playtime with the cafe's 22 cuddly felines. ⏱ 1 hr. Villa Ijo 2FA, 2-17-10 Nishi-hinsaibashi, Chuo-ku. ☎ 06/6214-2020. www. ekonojikan.com/amemura/top.htm. ¥840 for hr., ¥420 each additional 30 min. until 6pm, ¥1,050 after 6pm until closing. Mon and Wed- at 11am–10pm; Tues 11am–7pm; Sun 11am–9pm. ubway: Midosuji Shinsaibashi Station.

⑤ ★ Café Doll. Like Tokyo, Osaka has its fair share of *otaku* (*anime,* or Japanese animation, and manga fanatics), and there are plenty of places that cater to their peculiar tastes. At this maid cafe in Nipponbashi, cheerfully smiling waitresses in French maid outfits greet patrons with a warm, "Welcome home, Master." In addition to sweet coffee drinks, there are *otaku* favorites such as *omuraisu* (rice omelet). 5-4-20 Nipponbashi 3F, Naniwa-ku. ☎ 06/6631-8829. www.cafedoll.com. Entrees ¥750–¥1,000. No credit cards. Lunch & dinner weekends and holidays. Subway: Midosuji Ebisucho Station.

⑥ ★ Osaka Minami Move On Arena. Although Japan is best known for its heavyweight sumo champions, American-style pro wrestling enjoys a degree of popularity among a certain crowd. Run by Osaka Pro Wrestling, an organization promoting WWE-style wrestling in Japan, this wrestling arena in Dotonbori has an eye-searing yellow-and-red facade decorated with posters and images of muscular fighters in colorful masks. ⏱ 1 hr. 1-8-21 Sennichimae, Chuo-ku. ☎ 06/4708-1141. www.osaka-prowres. com. Sat-Sun ¥3,000 adults, ¥2,000 students, ¥500 kids. Mon–Fri ¥2,000 men, ¥1,000 women and students, ¥300 kids. Match times vary, so check website for details. Subway: Nipponbashi Station.

Osaka

If, in the family of Japan, Kyoto is like the impeccably dressed, demure aunt and Tokyo like the trend-savvy younger sister, then Osaka is the convivial, down-to-earth cousin. Osakans are known for two things: their business acumen and love of food. A visit to Osaka is less about seeing the sights and more about soaking up the fun-loving vibe of the city. That said, Osaka's history stretches back almost 1,500 years; it first gained prominence when *daimyo* Toyotomi Hideyoshi built Japan's most magnificent castle here in the 16th century. To develop resources for his castle town, he persuaded merchants to resettle here, and the city became an important distribution center.

> *The imposing figure of Osaka Castle stands firm in the midst of the city's relentless modernity.*

START Take the subway to Umeda Station. Osaka is 55km (34167 miles) southwest of Kyoto.

1 ★ **Floating Garden Observatory** (空中庭園の展望台)**.** This floating observatory, 167m (548 ft.) above the ground, connects the two

towers of the futuristic **Umeda Sky Building.** Views from the observation deck on the 39th floor are impressive, particularly at night (you won't fail to notice the couples on dates), but the best part is the ride to the roof. Take the super-fast elevator from the third floor before getting on a glass-enclosed escalator that will

> *Make a date with the Glico Running Man on Ebisubashi.*

take you up five more floors to the top. Brace yourself for the serious case of butterflies in the stomach you're likely to experience on your way up. ⏱ 20 min. Umeda Sky Building, 1-1-88 Oyodo-naka, Kita-ku. ☎ 06/6440-3901. www.kuchu-teien.com. ¥700 adults, ¥500 junior-high and high-school students, ¥300 kids. Daily 10am-10:30pm. Subway: Umeda Station.

② ★★ **Osaka Museum of Housing and Living** (大阪くらしの今昔館). Step back in time as you walk through this life-sized reproduction of an Osaka neighborhood from the 1830s. The street contains re-creations of a public bath (you can borrow a *yukata,* or cotton kimono, to wear as you stroll around), as well as various shops and merchants' living quarters. There's also a section displaying detailed dioramas of Osaka after the Meiji Period. English-language audio guides are available. ⏱ 40 min. Housing Information Center, 8th floor, 6-4-20 Tenjinbashi, Kita-ku. ☎ 06/6242-1170. http://house.sumai.city.osaka.jp/museum/frame/0_frame.html. ¥600 adults, free for junior-high students, kids, and seniors. Wed–Mon 10am–5pm. Subway: Tenjinbashisuji 6-chome Station.

③ ★ **Osakajo** (大阪城天守閣). Toyotomi Hideyoshi ordered the construction of this massive castle in 1583 as an emblem of his power and wealth. Over the next decade, Toyotomi used Osakajo as a military stronghold, and by the time of his death in 1598, he had achieved his goal of unifying Japan. Seventeen years later, this seemingly impregnable fortress was destroyed at the hands of Tokugawa Ieyasu. The Tokugawas rebuilt the castle in 1629, but their progeny burned it to the ground in 1868 prior to the Meiji Restoration in order to prevent the Imperial forces from taking control of the castle.

The present concrete structure dates from 1931 and was extensively renovated in 1997. The eight-story *donjon* (keep) houses a museum that uses videos, holograms, models, and artifacts to describe the life and times of Toyotomi Hideyoshi and history of the castle. Unfortunately,

Osaka

KITA-KU (NORTH WARD)

HIGASHI (EAST)

1 Floating Garden Observatory
2 Osaka Museum of Housing and Living
3 Osakajo
4 Osaka Museum of History
5 Museum of Oriental Ceramics
6 Dotonbori
7 Spa World
8 Osaka Aquarium
9 Universal Studios Japan

Where to Stay

Family Inn Fifty's Edobori 25
Hearton Hotel Nishi Umeda 19
Hotel Dormy-Inn 28
Hotel Granvia Osaka 17
Hotel Il Monte 14
Hotel Nikko Osaka 26
Imperial Hotel Osaka (Teikoku Hotel) 15
New Otani Osaka 23
Righa Royal Hotel 24
The Ritz-Carlton, Osaka 20
Sheraton Miyako Hotel 35
Swiss Hotel Nankai Osaka 33

Where to Dine

Bubutei 13
Chibo 31
Enoteca 18
Gyoza Stadium 16
Honfukuzushi 27
Kani Doraku 30
Maimon 21
Mitsutomi 32

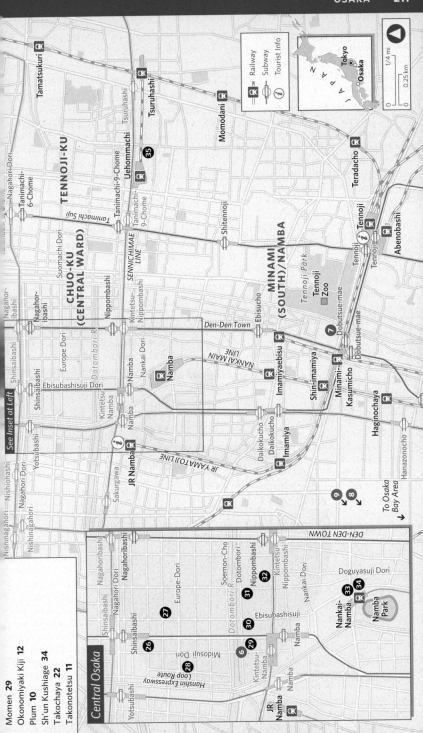

Railway
Subway
Tourist Info

1/4 mi
0.25 km

JAPAN

Tokyo
Osaka

Tamatsukuri

Tsuruhashi

Tsuruhashi

Momodani

Nagahori-Dori

Uehommachi

Tanimachi-6-Chome

Tanimachi-9-Chome

TENNOJI-KU

Tanimachi Suji

Tanimachi-9-Chome

Teradacho

Suomachi Dori

SENNICHIMAE LINE

Shitennoji

Tennoji

Tennoji

CHUO-KU
(CENTRAL WARD)

Nippombashi

Kintetsu-Nippombashi

Nagahor-Ibashi

Nagahor-ibashi

Den-Den Town

Ebisucho

MINAMI
(SOUTH)/NAMBA

Tennoji Park

Tennoji Zoo

Abenobashi

Dobutsue-mae

See Inset at Left

Europe Dori

Dotombori-R

Shinsaibashi

Shinsaibashi

Nankai-Dori

Namba

Namba

NANKAI MAIN LINE

Imamiyaebisu

Shin-imamiya

Minami-Kasumicho

Dobutsue-mae

Ebisubashisuji Dori

Kintetsu-Namba

Namba

Daikokucho

Daikokucho

Imamiya

Haginochaya

Nishinaganori

Nagahori-bashi

Nagahori-bashi

Yotsubashi

JR Namba

JR YAMATOJI LINE

Imamiya

Hanazonocho

Sakurgawa

To Osaka Bay Area →

Central Osaka

DEN-DEN TOWN

Nagahoriborashi

Nagahori-Dori

Nagahoribashi

Soemon-Cho

Nippombashi

Nippombashi

Kintetsu-Nippombashi

Nankai Dori

Doguyasuji Dori

Shinsaibashi

Shinsaibashi

Europe-Dori

Dotombori

Dotombori-R

Ebisubashisuji

Nankai-Namba

Namba Park

Yotsubashi

Midosuji Dori

Kintetsu-Namba

Namba

Namba

Namba

JR Namba

Hanshin Expressway Loop Route

27

26

28

6

30

29

31

32

33

34

7

9

8

35

Momen **29**
Okonomiyaki Kiji **12**
Plum **10**
Sh'un Kushiage **34**
Takochaya **22**
Takonotetsu **11**

most explanations are in Japanese only. ⏱45 min. 1–1 Osakajo, Chuo-ku. ☎06/6941-3044. www.osakacastle.net. ¥600 adults, free for kids 15 and under. Daily 9am–5pm. Train: Osakajo-Koen Station.

④ ★ kids **Osaka Museum of History** (大阪歴史博物館). Indulge your inner amateur archeologist at this museum occupying the top three floors of an ultramodern building south of Osakajo. Your journey through time begins on the 10th floor, with a life-size re-creation of Osakajo castle, and follows Osaka's history as you make your way down to the 7th floor. With the help of volunteer guides and printed information, you can dig for artifacts and piece them together, or become a banker, weighing and exchanging Osaka money for currency from other areas of Japan. ⏱1 hr. 4-1-32 Otemae, Chuo-ku. ☎06/6946-5728. www.mus-his.city.osaka.jp. ¥600 adults, ¥360 college and high-school students, free for junior-high school students and kids. Wed–Mon 9:30am–5pm, Fri 9:30am–8pm. Subway: Tanimachi 4-chome Station.

⑤ ★★★ **Museum of Oriental Ceramics.** This stylish museum houses one of the world's most impressive collections of rare ceramics from China, Korea, and Japan. The permanent collection comprises over 2,700 pieces, and at any one time, 300 are displayed on a rotating basis. Built specifically for the collection, the museum does a superb job showcasing the exquisite pieces as the masterpieces they truly are, in darkened rooms that utilize natural light and computerized natural-light simulation. The stunning Song-dynasty Chinese celadon ranks among the collection's

> One of more than 2,700 treasures at the Museum of Oriental Ceramics.

highlights. ⏱30 min. 1-1-26 Nakanoshima, Kita-ku. ☎06/6223-0055. ¥500 adults, ¥300 students, free for kids. Tues–Sun 9:30am–5pm. Subway: Keihan Naniwabashi Station.

⑥ ★★★ **Dotonbori** (道頓堀). Osaka's teeming nightlife district is a jumble of flashing lights, animatronic signs, and food stalls selling *takoyaki* (octopus dumplings) and other tasty morsels along its famous "eating street." The **Ebisubashi** (戎橋) footbridge offers unparalleled views of Namba's futuristic neon nightscapes—and fantastic people-watching opportunities. People from all walks of life congregate here to be photographed in front of the **Glico Running Man** billboard, which beams brightly over the bridge. Ebisubashi is between Shinsaibashi-suji and Dotonbori-suji. Subway: Namba Station.

⑦ ★★ kids **Spa World** (スパワールド). With two floors of baths and a rooftop water park complete with pools, water slides, Jacuzzis, and restaurants, this sprawling bath complex is the largest in the world. The floors are segregated by gender, and each bath has a different theme—Finnish sauna, Roman bath, Balinese spa, even a Disney-like fantasy of Atlantis. Swim suits are required in the water park (you can rent one for ¥300) but are prohibited in the baths. Be forewarned that those with tattoos are not allowed to enter, suit or no suit. ⏱1 hr. 3-4-24 Ebisu-higashi, Naniwa-ku. ☎06/6631-0001. www.spa-world.co.jp/english. Weekdays ¥2,400 adults, ¥1,300 kids for 3 hr.; ¥2,700 adults, ¥1,500 kids for all day. Weekends ¥2,700 adults, ¥1,500 kids for 3 hr.; ¥3,000 adults, ¥1,700 kids for all day. Daily 24 hr. (maintenance takes place in some areas 8:45–10am). Subway: Sakai-suji Dobutsuenmae Station.

Mesmerizing jellyfish dreamily adrift at the Osaka Aquarium.

★★★ kids **Osaka Aquarium (Kaiyukan;** 海遊). Encompassing 26,500 sq. m (286,000 sq.) and containing 11 million liters (2.9 million allons) of water, this spectacular aquarium one of the world's biggest. Tours begin rough a tunnel filled with reef fish, followed y an escalator ride to the 8th floor; from ere, you'll pass through 15 different habitats anging from arctic to tropical as you follow spiraling corridor back to the ground floor. ver 580 species are represented, including hale sharks, rays, jellyfish, and penguins. nglish audio guides are available for ¥300. If ossible, avoid weekends and holidays. ⏱ 1½ r. 1-1-10 Kaigan Dori, Minato-ku. ☎ 06/6576- 501. www.kaiyukan.com. ¥2,000 adults, ¥900 ds ages 7-15, ¥400 kids ages 4-6, kids 5 and nder free. Daily 10am-8pm. Closed 7 days a ear (in June and in winter). Subway: Osakako tation.

⑨ ★★★ kids **Universal Studios Japan.** Following the tradition of Universal's Hollywood and Orlando theme parks, this park takes guests on a fantasy trip through the world of American blockbuster movies, with thrill rides, live entertainment, back-lot streets, restaurants, and shops. Unfortunately, most of the attractions based on actual movies have been dubbed into Japanese. Plan for an entire day here, but note that it is immensely popular: Avoid weekends, arrive early, and buy a Universal Express Pass Booklet, which allows priority entry into designated rides. Check the website for a current list of prices for individual rides. ⏱ 4 hr. 2-1-33 Sakurajima, Konohana. ☎ 06/6465-3000. www. usj.co.jp. Studio Pass to all attractions ¥5,800 adults, ¥5,100 seniors, ¥3,900 kids ages 4-11. Hours vary according to the season; generally daily 10am-5pm in winter, 9am-8:30 or 9pm in summer, and 9 or 10am-7pm the rest of the year. Subway: Universal City Station.

Where to Stay in Osaka

★ Family Inn Fifty's Edobori KITA
This motel-like facility, south of Nakanoshima Island, offers low prices and no-nonsense small but clean rooms, outfitted with double beds and sofa beds. The catch is that the place is a bit far from Osaka Station. (Some travelers have been known to use the Rihga Hotel's shuttle bus across the bridge.) 2–6–18 Edobori, Nishi-ku. ☎ 06/6225-2636. www.fiftys.com. 80 units. Doubles from ¥8,400. Rates include breakfast. AE, MC, V. Train: Nakanoshima Station.

★★ Hearton Hotel Nishi Umeda KITA
Three minutes from Osaka Station, this hotel is convenient to shops, restaurants, clubs, and transportation. It offers simple, spotless rooms facing the railroad tracks but with double-paned windows that block out noise. 3–3–55 Umeda, Kita-ku. ☎ 06/6342-1111. www.hearton.co.jp. 471 units. Doubles ¥17,000–¥18,500. AE, DC, MC, V. Train: Osaka Station.

Hotel Dormy-Inn MINAMI
This chain in Amerikamura offers standard business-type rooms, spotlessly clean with sliding window panels to cut out light and highway noises, as well as 10 rooms with tatami areas and twin beds. Public baths made of cedar are a plus, but little English is spoken. 2–17–3 Nishishinsaibashi, Chuo-ku. ☎ 06/6211-5767. www.hotelspa.net. Doubles ¥11,000–¥18,000. Rates include breakfast. AE, DC, MC, V. Subway: Nipponbashi Station.

kids Hotel Granvia Osaka KITA
You can't get any closer to Osaka Station than this hotel, with discounts for holders of Japan Rail Passes making it especially attractive. Parents might also rejoice at discounts offered for Universal Studios. The tradeoff is a ground-floor lobby that's hard to find inside Osaka Station, crowded elevators, and cramped rooms on floors 22 to 26. Discounts are available for holders of a Japan Rail Pass. 3–1–1 Umeda, Kita-ku. ☎ 06/6344-1235. www.granvia-osaka.jp. 650 units. Doubles ¥24,255–¥48,510. AE, DC, MC, V. Subway: Osaka Station.

★ Hotel Il Monte KITA
With its helpful staff and a convenient location, this smart-looking hotel has is our top choice for budget lodging near the station. In the lobby there's free coffee and tea and computers with Internet connections. 7–13 Doyama-cho, Kita-ku. ☎ 06/6361-2828. www.ilmonte.co.jp. 122 units. Doubles ¥15,000–¥20,000. AE, DC, MC, V. Subway: Osaka or Umeda stations.

★ Hotel Nikko Osaka MINAMI
The Nikko has a great location above a subway station right on Midosuji Dori. Rooms have a pleasing, modern design, and because there are no high buildings to obstruct views, city panoramas are a plus from most floors. But you'll pay more for rooms on higher floors and for more space. 1–3–3 Nishi-Shinsaibashi, Chuo-ku. ☎ 06/6244-1111. www.hno.co.jp. Doubles ¥32,917–¥43,890. Subway: Shinsaibashi Station.

★★★ Imperial Hotel Osaka (Teikoku Hotel) CENTRAL OSAKA The Imperial is situated north of Osaka Castle on the cherry tree–lined Okawa River. It provides free shuttle ride service to Osaka Station and complimentary bikes to explore the area. The high-ceilinged, spacious rooms offer large windows with great views (request rooms facing the river). 1–8–50 Temmabashi, Kita-ku. ☎ 06/6881-1111. www.imperialhotel.co.jp. 390 units. Doubles ¥34,650–¥54,600. AE, DC, MC, V. Train: Sakuranomiya Station.

★ New Otani Osaka CENTRAL OSAKA
Everything about the public spaces at this hotel near Osaka Castle Park is visually appealing, from the airy, four-story atrium lobby to the indoor pool with its glass-vaulted ceiling. Rooms, however, are rather standard. The best provide dramatic views of Osakajo, which is lit at night—but at fairly hefty prices. 1–4–1 Shiromi, Chuo-ku, Osaka 540-8578. ☎ 06/6941-1111. www.osaka.newotani.co.jp. 525 units. Doubles ¥39,900–¥45,150. AE, DC, MC, V. Train: Osakajo-Koen Station.

Stay in the lap of Western luxury at the Ritz-Carlton.

Rihga Royal Hotel KITA

Located on Nakanoshima, Osaka's oldest and largest hotel offers comfortable rooms ranging in style from modern to classical drawing room. The lobby lounge is a restful oasis where you can sip your drink and watch a cascading waterfall against a backdrop of cliffs and foliage. 5-3-68 Nakanoshima, Kita-ku. ☎ 06/6448-1121. www.rihga.com. 974 units. Doubles ¥32,340–¥56,595. AE, DC, MC, V. Train: Nakanoshima Station.

★★★ The Ritz-Carlton, Osaka KITA

This luxury hotel features an old-world–style lobby with overstuffed sofas, 100-year-old Persian carpets, and Italian marble fireplaces. Standouts include **The Bar,** with its 110 kinds of whiskey, and two Michelin-starred restaurants, **La Baie** and **Xiang Tao.** Stylish rooms offer panoramic views, especially from deluxe corner rooms. 2-5-25 Umeda, Kita-ku. ☎ 800/241-3333 in the U.S. and Canada, or 06/6343-7000. www.ritzcarlton.com. 292 units. Doubles ¥58,138–¥75,564. AE, DC, MC, V. Subway: Osaka or Umeda stations.

★★ Sheraton Miyako Hotel CENTRAL OSAKA

This hotel features a multilingual staff providing excellent service, easy access to both Itami and Kansai airports, and good dining choices. It's also well located for sightseeing: The Osaka Museum of History, Osakajo, and Namba, with its many bars and restaurants, are all 1.5km (1 mile) away. Spacious and comfortable rooms offer city views. 6-1-55 Uehonmachi, Tenoji-ku. ☎ 06/6773-1111. www.miyakohotels.ne.jp/osaka. 575 units. Doubles ¥27,720–¥39,270. AE, DC, MC, V. Subway: Uehonmachi Station.

★★★ Swiss Hotel Nankai Osaka MINAMI

This 36-story hotel in the Namba area exudes luxury, from its sophisticated, four-story lobby to its spacious, well-appointed rooms. The rooms have nice city views. 5-1-60 Namba, Chuo-ku. ☎ 06/6646-1111. www.swissotel.com. 548 units. Doubles ¥40,425–¥84,315. AE, DC, MC, V. Subway: Nankai Namba Station.

Where to Dine in Osaka

> Gooey, oozy takoyaki octopus dumplings are a local obsession.

★ Bubutei (ぶぶ亭) KITA *TAKOYAKI/AKASHIYAKI*
This tiny shop in the basement of the Hankyu Station building serves *takoyaki* (octopus dumplings) and *akashiyaki,* the lightly flavored version that originated in Kobe. The *akashiyaki* come with a dish of clear *dashi* (broth) for dipping. While not the best we've ever had, they're quite good. And if you've just traveled 45 minutes from Kyoto, they make the perfect snack. Hankyu Sanbankai Minamikan B2, 1-1-3 Shibata. ☎ 06/6373-3563. Entrees from ¥480. No credit cards. Lunch & dinner daily. Subway: Higashi-Umeda Station.

★ Chibo (千房) MINAMI *OKONOMIYAKI*
This five-story restaurant in the heart of Dotonbori specializes in *okonomiyaki*—thick, savory pancakes stuffed with cabbage, pork, seafood, or all three (some varieties come layered with fried noodles). These pancakes are cooked on a hot iron griddle and then slathered with a sweet and tangy brown sauce and finished with a drizzle of mayonnaise and a sprinkling of dried *nori* seaweed. The top floor is the curiously named President Chibo *teppanyaki* steakhouse. 1-5-5 Dotonbori. ☎ 06, 6212-2211. www.chibo.com. Entrees from ¥1,18(AE, DC, MC, V. Lunch & dinner daily. Subway: Nipponbashi Station.

★ Enoteca KITA *ITALIAN*
Shelves filled with wine bottles line the walls of this upscale shop, which houses a casual restaurant offering reasonably priced, wine-friendly meals and a relaxed ambience in the back. Herbis Plaza, 2nd floor, 2-5-25 Umeda. ☎ 06/6343-7175. Entrees ¥1,000–¥1,800. AE, DC, MC, V. Lunch & dinner daily. Subway: Nishi-Umeda Station.

★★ Gyoza Stadium KITA *DUMPLINGS*
Located above the Namco Game Center, this food theme park features, as the name suggests, *gyoza* (dumplings). Dumplings from all over the country are represented in this indoo recreation of a Showa-Era townscape. Portions are perfectly sized for (lots of) snacking OS Bldg. 3F, 3-3 Komatsubaracho, Kita-ku. ☎ 06/6313-0765. Plates of 6 gyoza from ¥360. No credit cards. Lunch & dinner daily. Train: Osaka Station.

★★ Honfukuzushi (本福寿司) MINAMI *SUSHI*
More than just a place to dine, this sushi shop, in operation for more than 180 years, is part of the Osaka experience. Back in the old days, sushi shops were strictly take-away operations, with customers bringing in their own dishes, making their orders, and then returning home to wait for *geta*-clad deliverers. Best are the counter seats, where you can watch sushi being pressed in wooden molds, Osaka-style. 1-4-19 Nishi Shinsaibashi-suji.

06/6271-3344. Set meals ¥1,200–¥3,300.
E, MC, V. Lunch & dinner daily. Subway: Shin-
aibashi Station.

ani Doraku MINAMI SEAFOOD

hough perhaps not the best restaurant in
otonbori, this crab specialist is certainly the
ost conspicuous: It has a huge model crab
n its facade, with moving legs and claws.
art of a chain originating in Osaka a couple
f decades ago, this is the main shop of more
han 50 locations throughout Japan, including
nother one just down the street. Sample *kani*
crab) in various guises—roasted with salt,
oiled and served with citrusy *ponzu* dipping
auce, or deep-fried in creamy croquettes.
-6-18 Dotonbori, Chuo-ku. ☎ 06/6211-8975.
et lunches from ¥1,900, set dinners from
4,400. Lunch & dinner daily. Subway: Namba
tation.

★ Maimon KITA PUB

uxurious, contemporary decor, consistently
ood fresh oysters, and a convenient location
nake this spacious modern *izakaya* (Japanese
ub) a popular choice for dinner parties. The
nternational menu may include *wagyu* beef
heeks stewed in beer, or a lineup of bril-
antly presented oyster shooters, served in
ndividual glasses on ice. Herbis Plaza ENT 5F,
-2-22 Umeda, Kita-ku. ☎ 06/6456-2144. Set
unches from ¥1,800, set dinners from ¥5,800.
E, DC, MC, V. Lunch & dinner daily. Subway:
Jmeda Station.

★ Mitsutomi (美津富) MINAMI SEAFOOD

ocated in the Namba area, this traditional
apanese restaurant offers the chance to try
wo of Kansai's regional specialties—*hamo*
ike eel, and the potentially deadly delicacy
ugu, or blowfish. Here it's served in a variety
f ways: raw as sashimi, deep-fried as fugu
arage, and simmered in a *nabe* hot pot. Seat-
ng is Japanese-style, in *tatami* rooms (a tradi-
ional Japanese room with straw mats on the
oor). Reservations required. 1-4-22 Senichi-
nae, Chuo-ku. ☎ 06/6211-3038. Set dinners
rom ¥10,500. AE, DC, MC, V. Dinner Mon–Sat.
ubway: Sakaisuji Nipponbashi Station.

> More crab than you can shake a stick at, at Kani Doraku.

★★★ Momen MINAMI KAISEKI

A favorite with local foodies, this counter-only
kaiseki (multicourse set menu) restaurant
serves elegant Japanese dishes in an intimate
but unpretentious setting. The chef utilizes
top-quality fresh ingredients to create seasonal menus that may include *matsutake* (mushrooms) in autumn, or tender young bamboo
shoots in a light broth with shrimp dumplings
in spring. The reasonable prices and relaxed,
friendly clientele are a pleasant surprise. Reservations are required and should be made
well in advance. 2-1-3 Shinsaibashisuji,
Chuo-ku. ☎ 06/6211-2793. Set dinners from
¥10,000. No credit cards. Dinner Mon–Sat.
Subway: Shinsaibashi Station.

★ Okonomiyaki Kiji KITA OKONOMIYAKI

Some Osakans swear that this restaurant,
located in the Takimikoji Alley restaurant floor
in the basement of the Umeda Sky Building,

> *Half restaurant, half boutique wine shop: Enoteca.*

makes the best *okonomiyaki* in town. (In truth, it's hard to tell.) Queues of people waiting to get in are common, but when you finally sit down your order arrives quickly. Umeda Sky Bldg., 1–1–90 Oyodo-naka. ☎ 06/6440-5970. Okonomiyaki ¥600–¥900. No credit cards. Lunch & dinner Fri-Wed. Subway: Umeda Station.

★ **Plum** KITA *PUB*
Though the food is nothing to write home about, this stylish modern *izakaya* is one of the best places to drink *umeshu* (plum wine): There are over 100 varieties on the menu. Takamura Bldg. 3F, 4–6 Chayamachi, Kita-ku. ☎ 06/6377-0701. Dinner entrees from ¥2,500. Dinner daily. Subway: Umeda Station.

★★ **Sh'un Kushiage** MINAMI *FRENCH FUSION*
Osakans claim southern Osaka as the birth-place of *kushiage* (breaded and deep-fried meat, seafood, and vegetables), but this restaurant offers its own sophisticated version by combining *kushiage* and French cuisine and utilizing organic and seasonal vegetables. In addition, some 500 international wines are on offer to complement the *kushiage.* Swissôtel, 5–1–60 Namba, Chuo-ku. ☎ 06/6646-1111. Set dinners from ¥9,124. AE, DC, MC, V. Dinner

Wed–Sun. Subway: Nankai Namba Station.

★★ **Takochaya** (たこ茶屋) KITA *SEAFOOD*
Octopus sashimi is the star of the menu at th small, brightly lit restaurant in Umeda. In fact the octopus here is so fresh that you may find yourself in a chopstick tug-of-war with the tentacles of your still-squirming dinner. (The octopus is no longer alive; it just looks that way.) Choose a glass or two from the excelle selection of sake while you work up the cour-age to face it. Kitashinchi Star Bldg. 6F, 1–11–19 Sonezakishinchi. ☎ 06/6341-6300. www. takochaya.com. Set dinners from ¥5,000. No credit cards. Dinner Mon–Sat. Subway: Kitash-inchi Station.

★ **Takonotetsu** KITA *TAKOYAKI/OKONOMIYAK*
The grills at this old-school *takoyaki* special-ist are built into the tables, so you can try your hand at turning each blob of batter into a perfect ball. (Don't worry, the staff will help.) Maru Bldg., B2F, 1–9–20 Umeda, Kita-ku. ☎ 06/6345-0301. www.takonotetsu.com. Takoyaki from ¥580. No credit cards. Lunch & dinner daily; closed 3rd Mon each month. Sub-way: Umeda Station.

Specialty Foods of Osaka

TAKOYAKI

Osaka's signature street food consists of meaty pieces of *tako* (octopus), pickled ginger, and scallions folded into a gooey batter and grilled in special cast-iron pans reminiscent of egg cartons. The piping hot balls are then brushed with *okonomiyaki* sauce and sprinkled with bonito fish flakes and dried seaweed.

OKONOMIYAKI

These thick, savory pancakes (pictured above, on the griddle) can be stuffed with any number of ingredients. Indeed, the name translates literally to "as you like it." The most common fillings are cabbage, pork belly, and/or seafood. Like *takoyaki*, *okonomiyaki* are covered in a sweet, tangy sauce and drizzled with mayonnaise, served with a sprinkle of bonito fish flakes and dried seaweed. In Osaka, you can often cook your own, on a sizzling-hot griddle at the table.

HAKOZUSHI

Traditional Osaka-style sushi is made with vinegared pieces of fish or other seafood, pressed onto rectangles of rice using a special box press. It is usually more strongly flavored than Kanto-style *nigiri-zushi*.

KITSUNE UDON

This simple dish is made with thick *udon* (buckwheat noodles) and pieces of fried *udon* in a clear broth.

TESSA

This beautifully presented sashimi dish consists of layers of sliced raw blowfish, cut so thinly that you can see the pattern of the dish underneath it.

Nara

Established in 710 as the first permanent capital of Japan,
the lovely town of Nara is the historical jewel in the cultural crown of Kansai. It's
home to eight UNESCO World Heritage sites (second in number only to Kyoto),
including the magnificent Daibutsu, a giant statue of the Great Buddha. Most of
Nara's treasures are enclosed in a peaceful, tree-lined park, where 1,200 tame deer
roam in search of treats from tourists. The best way to see the sights is to arrive
early in the morning, walk through the park, and then stroll through Naramachi, a
historic area filled with well-preserved traditional *machiya* (wooden houses).

> *Thousands pass though Todai-ji's immense main gate daily.*

START Take the train to Kintetsu Nara Station.
Nara is 42km (26 miles) south of Kyoto.

❶ ★ Kofuku-ji (興福寺). Kofuku-ji was established in 710 as the temple of the powerful
Fujiwara family. At one time as many as 175
buildings were erected on the Kofuku-ji temple grounds; however, most of the structures
were destroyed in fires and as a result of centuries of civil war. Only a handful of buildings
remain, but even these were rebuilt after the
13th century.

The five-story **pagoda,** first erected in
730, was burned down five times. The present pagoda dates from 1426 and is an exact
replica of the original. At 50m (164 ft.) tall,
it's the second-tallest pagoda in Japan (the
tallest is at Toji Temple in Kyoto). Also of
historical importance is the **Eastern Golden
Hall (Tokondo),** originally constructed in 726
by Emperor Shomu to speed the recovery of
the ailing Empress Gensho. Rebuilt in 1415,
it houses several priceless images, including

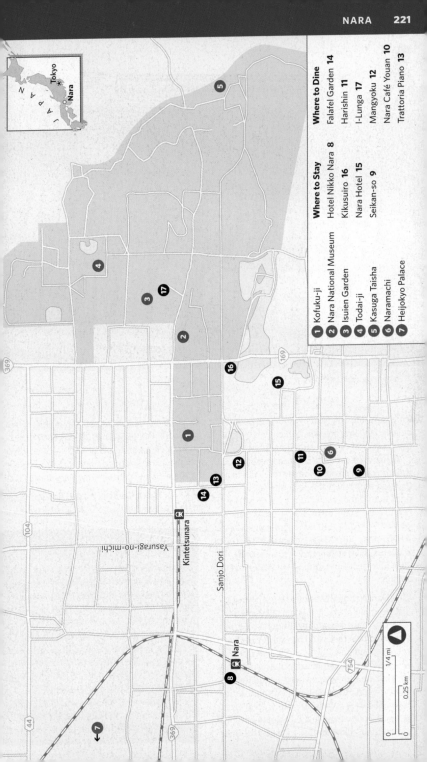

Where to Dine

Falafel Garden **14**
Harishin **11**
I-Lunga **17**
Mangyoku **12**
Nara Café Youan **10**
Trattoria Piano **13**

Where to Stay

Hotel Nikko Nara **8**
Kikusuiro **16**
Nara Hotel **15**
Seikan-so **9**

1 Kofuku-ji
2 Nara National Museum
3 Isuien Garden
4 Todai-ji
5 Kasuga Taisha
6 Naramachi
7 Heijokyo Palace

Yasuragi-no-michi

Kintetsunara

Sanjo Dori

Nara

0   1/4 mi
0 0.25 km

> *Lanterns outside of Kofuku-ji.*

a bronze statue of Yakushi Nyorai, a Buddha believed to cure illnesses, which was installed by Emperor Shomu on behalf of his sick wife.

Also on the grounds is the impressive **Kokuhokan Treasure House.** You have to pay to enter, but it's worth a look to see the wooden statues dating back to as early as the 8th century. ⏱ 15 min. 48 Noborioji-cho, Kokuhokan. ☎ 0742/22-7755. www.nara-kofukuji.net. ¥500 adults, ¥400 high-school and junior-high students, ¥150 elementary students. Daily 9am–5pm (last entry 4pm). Train: Kintetsu Nara Station.

② ★ **Nara National Museum** (奈良国立博物館). Just beyond Kofuku-ji, this museum opened in 1895 to house invaluable Buddhist art and archaeological relics and has since expanded into a second building, used for special exhibits. Many masterpieces formerly in Nara's temples are now housed here, including Buddhist sculptures from various periods in Japan's history, paintings, masks, scrolls, calligraphy, and archaeological objects obtained from temple ruins, tombs, and sutra mounds

(a small dirt pile under which Buddhist scriptures are buried). ⏱ 20 min. ☎ 0742/22-7771. www.narahaku.go.jp. ¥500 adults, ¥250 students, free for kids and seniors. Tues–Sun 9:30am–5pm. Train: Kintetsu Nara Station.

③ ★★★ **Isuien Garden** (依水園). Across the main road on the way to Todai-ji, stop off at

Volunteer Tour Guides

Although Nara is a small city, and most of the sights can be easily navigated on your own, the **Nara YMCA Goodwill Guides** (☎ 0742/45-5920) and **Nara Student Guides** (☎ 0742/26-4753; www.narastudentguide.org) offer tours in English conducted by volunteers. There's no charge for the tour, but you will be asked to pay for the cost of your guide's transportation. While not mandatory, it's good karma to pay for your guide's lunch as well. This service is a great option for solo travelers, or non-Japanese speakers with burning questions about the sights. Reserve at least 1 day in advance.

A peaceful Buddha inside the Nara Museum.

his immaculately maintained garden complex, which contains two beautiful gardens, tea-ceremony houses, and a delightful pottery museum. The front garden, which dates back to the Edo Period, features moss-covered slopes and lush greenery surrounding a carp-filled pond. Through a narrow lane, past two small tea-ceremony houses, is the splendid back garden, laid out in the Meiji Era. The garden ingeniously incorporates Nara's mountainous natural landscape into its design. Adjacent to the garden is the **Neiraku Museum,** which exhibits pottery and bronze artifacts from China and Korea. Admission to the museum is included in your ticket. ⏱ 30 min. 74 Suimon-cho. ☎ 0742/25-0781. www.isuien.or.jp. ¥650 adults, ¥400 junior-high students, ¥250 elementary students. Wed–Mon 9:30am–4:30pm (last entry 4pm). Train: Kintetsu Nara Station.

> Savor green tea and quiet contemplation in the lovely Isuien garden.

④ ★★★ **Todai-ji** (東大寺). Nara's premier attraction is Todai-ji Temple and its **Daibutsu (Great Buddha),** Japan's largest bronze Buddha. The Daibutsu is housed in the tremendous **Daibutsuden** (大仏殿)**,** the world's largest wooden structure. Reconstructed in 1709, the present building is 48m (157 ft.) high and measures a whopping 57m x 50m (187 ft. x 164 ft.)—but it's only two-thirds of its original size!

Emperor Shomu commissioned work for both the Daibutsuden and the Daibutsu in 743. At a height of more than 15m (49 ft.), the Daibutsu is made of 437 tons of bronze, 130kg (287 lb.) of pure gold, 75kg (168 lb.) of mercury, and 7 tons (over 15,000 lb.) of vegetable wax. Thanks to Japan's frequent natural calamities, however, the Buddha of today isn't quite what it used to be. In 855, the statue lost its head in an earthquake. It was repaired in 861, but the huge wooden building housing the Buddha was burned twice during wars, melting the Buddha's head. The present head dates from 1692.

Behind the Great Buddha stands a model of Todai-ji's original layout, and on either side are two imposing guardian statues carved from wood. On the right is a huge wooden column with a hole through its base. According to popular belief, if you manage to crawl through this opening (which is the same size as one of the Great Buddha's giant nostrils), you'll be sure to reach enlightenment. This feat is a snap for children, but less so for adults. If you're determined to give it a try, go through with your arms outstretched and make sure there's someone around to pull you out in case you get stuck. ⏱ 30 min. 406–1 Zoshi-cho. ☎ 0742/22-5511. ¥500 adults, ¥300 kids. Daily Nov–Feb 8am–4:30pm, Mar and Oct 8am–5pm, Apr–Sept 7:30am–5:30pm. Train: Kintetsu Nara Station.

⑤ ★ Kasuga Taisha (春日大社社務所)**.** Founded in 768 to house the guardian deities meant to protect the powerful Fujiwara clan, this Shinto shrine was torn down and reconstructed every 20 years (in accordance with Shinto concepts of purity) until 1863. Nestled in the midst of verdant woods, the shrine features vermilion-colored pillars and an astounding 3,000 stone and bronze lanterns. The most spectacular time to visit is mid-August or the beginning of February, during the **Mantoro festivals,** when all 3,000 lanterns are lit. At other times we recommend visiting the shrine well before dusk, especially in winter—the path through the woods back to the main roads is not particularly well lit.

Although admission to the grounds is free, you must pay to enter the garden of Kasuga Grand Shrine, **Shin-en,** a botanical garden preserving about 300 varieties of native Japanese plants and famous for its wisteria. (It's located to the left on the approach to the shrine.) Fork out the extra yen only if you have time and the interest. ⏱ 20 min. 160 Kasugano-cho, Nara. ☎ 0742/22-7788. Grounds free, Shin-en ¥525, Homotsuden Hall ¥420. Daily 9am–4:30pm; to 4pm in winter. Shin-en and Homotsuden closed Mon. Bus: 70 to Kasuga Taisha Honden.

⑥ ★★ Naramachi. After taking in the sights of **Nara Koen park,** home to Kofuku-ji, the Nara National Museum, Isuien, Todai-ji, and Kasuga Taisha, wander south of Sanjo Dori and Sarusawa-ike pond into Naramachi. This area, with its beautifully preserved *machiya*

> *Eerily glowing lanterns line the path to Kasuga Taisha.*

> This adorable Bambi in Nara Koen park will be your best friend . . . for a cracker.

> Reconstructed buildings on the site of the former Heijokyo imperial palace.

wooden houses) and *kura* (traditional store-houses), exudes an atmosphere of old Japan. Most of these buildings have been converted into charming shops, restaurants, and galleries. Note, though, that nearly all of these places close early—you'll be hard-pressed to find something open past 6pm.

The **Naramachi Koshi-no-ie** (奈良町こしの家) is a reconstruction of a typical *machiya* that you can walk through and look around. The **Naramachi Shiryokan** exhibits an interesting hodgepodge of objects, including old coins and bills, ceramics, and prints. Koshi-no-ie: ⏱ 10 min. 44 Gango-ji-cho. ☎ 0742/23-4820. Free. Tues–Sun 9am–5pm. Shiryokan: ⏱ 15 min. 14 Nishishinya-cho. ☎ 0742/22-5509. Free. Tues–Sun 10am–4pm. Train: Kintetsu Nara Station.

⑦ ★ **Heijokyo Palace** (平城宮跡). The former Imperial Palace takes its name from the historical name for Nara (Heijokyo). Originally, the complex covered a vast stretch of land measuring 129 hectares (320 acres), with the palace situated at the northern end of Suzaku Dori, and most of the official buildings surrounding Suzaku-mon gate. None of the original buildings remain, but the site was declared a UNESCO World Heritage site in 1998, and some of the structures—including the red-and-white Suzaku-mon and the Daigoku-den imperial audience hall—were reconstructed in preparation for the city's 1,300th anniversary celebration in 2010. ⏱ 30 min. Free. Tues–Sun 9am–4pm. Train: Kintetsu Saidaiji Station.

Where to Stay in Nara

> The Nara Hotel's original rooms are steeped in old-world charm.

★ Hotel Nikko Nara

This hotel next to the west exit of the Nara Station is one of Nara's most convenient: Drop off your bags, hop on a rental bicycle to see the sights, and then soak away all cares in the hotel's large public baths. Rooms are comfortable, with fluffy, quilted spreads and plenty of desk space. The best rooms are on the 9th and 10th floors with great views toward distant mountains and Nara's temples, especially beautiful when lit at night in summer. 8–1 Sanjo-honmachi. ☎ 0742/35-8831. www.nikkonara. jp. 330 units. Doubles ¥20,000–¥30,000. AE, DC, MC, V. Train: Nara Station.

★★★ Kikusuiro (菊水楼)

You can't find a more beautiful example of a ryokan (traditional inn) than this lovely 120-year-old one, an imposing structure with an ornate Japanese-style roof, surrounded by a white wall. Rooms, some of which face Ara-ike Pond, are outfitted with scrolls and antiques and are connected to one another with rambling wooden corridors. There's also a beautiful garden. 1130 Takahata-cho Bodaimachi. ☎ 0742/23-2001. 14 units, 8 with bathroom. Rooms from ¥30,000–¥40,000 per person. Rates include 2 meals. AE, DC, MC, V. Train: Kintetsu Nara Station.

★★★ Nara Hotel

One of the most famous places to stay in Nara, the Nara Hotel sits like a palace atop a hill on the south edge of Nara Koen park. Built in 1909 in the Momoyama Period style of architecture and similar to Japan's other hotels built to accommodate foreigners who poured into the country following the Meiji Restoration, it's constructed as a Western-style hotel but has many Japanese features. You have your choice of accommodations in the old section of the hotel, with its wide corridors, high ceilings, antique light fixtures, fireplaces (no longer in use), and comfortable old-fashioned decor, or in the newer addition, which offers modern rooms and verandas overlooking woods or the old town. Though the rooms in the new wing are larger, the older rooms in the main building have much more atmosphere. Nara Koen-nai, 1096 Takabatake-cho. ☎ 0742/26-3300. www.narahotel. co.jp. 129 units. Doubles ¥28,875–¥57,750. AE, DC, MC, V. Train: Kintetsu Nara Station.

★ Seikan-so (静観荘)

This is a lovely choice in inexpensive Japanese-style accommodations. It boasts a beautiful garden, complete with azalea bushes and manicured trees—the kind of garden usually found only at ryokan costing twice as much. Located in quaint Naramachi, a historic neighborhood about a 10-minute walk south of Nara Koen park, the traditional Japanese building dates from 1916 and wraps around the inner garden. Unfortunately, the rooms are beginning to show their age, but all is forgiven if you can get one of the four facing the garden—be sure to request one when making your reservation. The friendly owners speak English, and a Japanese (¥735 extra) or Western (¥473 extra) breakfast is available. 29 Higashikitsuji-cho. ☎ 0742/22-2670. 9 units, none with bathroom. Rooms from ¥4,200 per person. AE, MC, V. Train: Kintetsu Nara Station.

Where to Dine in Nara

Falafel Garden *ISRAELI*

This is a good choice for quick and inexpensive vegetarian food near Kintetsu Nara Station. Pita sandwiches come stuffed with hummus, baba ghanoush, and, of course, falafel. There are also spicy chicken kebabs and fried schnitzel plates for carnivores. 13–2 Minamimachi. ☎ 0742/24-2722. www.falafelgarden.com/english. Sandwiches from ¥380. No credit cards. Lunch & dinner daily; closes at 8:30pm. Train: Kintetsu Nara Station.

★★★ Harishin (はり新) *BENTO/KAISEKI*

Located in Naramachi, near Gango-ji Temple, this highly recommended restaurant is housed in a 200-year-old home of ochre-colored walls and a wood-slat facade. Dining is on tatami with a view of a garden. The only thing on the menu is a seasonal bento, although a mini-*kaiseki* meal at dinnertime can be arranged 2 days in advance. 15 Nakashinya-cho. ☎ 0742/22-2669. Bento ¥2,900. AE, DC, MC, V. Lunch & dinner Tues–Sun; closed Tues if Mon falls on a national holiday. Train: Kintetsu Nara Station.

★★★ I-Lunga *ITALIAN*

Chef Junichiro Horie serves expertly prepared, refined Italian cuisine at this intimate restaurant in the middle of tranquil Nara Koen. Homemade pastas, like the pappardelle with fresh porcini in Bolognese sauce, are delicious, but the meat dishes (in particular, the game meats) are outstanding. The elegantly appointed dining room overlooks a pleasant garden, so ask for a table near the window at lunchtime. The well-chosen wine list offers mostly bottles from Italy. 16 Kasugano-cho. ☎ 0742/93-8300. www.i-lunga.jp. Set lunches from ¥3,400, set dinners from ¥6,400. AE, DC, MC, V. Lunch & dinner daily. Train: Kintetsu Nara Station.

★★ Mangyoku (まんぎょく) *JAPANESE*

Housed in a former *okiya,* a boardinghouse for geishas, this attractively decorated restaurant in Naramachi specializes in traditional Japanese dishes. Especially popular are the tofu topped with sea urchin and the steamed white fish wrapped in silky *yuba* (tofu skin), as well as home-style classics like *niku-jaga* (beef and potato stew). The wooden building dates back

> Firing up the grill at a local yakitori-ya.

to 1742 and features antique furniture from its days as an *okiya.* 9 Ganriin-cho. ☎ 0742/22-2265. Entrees from ¥1,000. No credit cards. Dinner Tues–Sun. Train: Kintetsu Nara Station.

★★ Nara Café Youan *JAPANESE/CAFE*

This charming cafe serves basic but tasty vegetarian set lunches, as well as grilled fish and meat dishes such as teriyaki chicken over rice. For those with a sweet tooth, there's green-tea cheesecake and persimmon cake in the fall and winter. Seating is mostly on raised tatami platforms, but there are a few wooden tables with cushion-covered stools. 13–1 Takamikado. ☎ 0742/26-4455. www.naracafe-youan.com. Set lunches from ¥900. No credit cards. Lunch Wed–Mon. Train: Nara Station.

Trattoria Piano *ITALIAN*

If you find yourself hungry near the station, try this restaurant in downtown Nara. Located on the second floor above a bar, it offers pastas, pizzas (both Napoli-style and those with Japanese ingredients), as well as main dishes like veal scaloppini or grilled pork with lemon sauce, along with a fish of the day. 15–1 Hashimoto-cho. ☎ 0742/26-1837. www.syncronicity.co.jp. Entrees from ¥1,480. AE, DC, MC, V. Lunch & dinner daily. Train: Kintetsu Nara Station.

MEET THE MASCOTS

Japan is a veritable paradise of cute character culture

BY MATT ALT & HIROKO YODA

SUPER-CUTE MASCOTS SEEM TO BE EVERYWHERE IN JAPAN. Just as in the West, every school and sport has its cast of cuddly cheerleading characters. But unlike the West, so too do national monuments like Mount Fuji; entire towns, cities, and prefectures; police and fire departments; even the Japan Self-Defense Forces; and they may pop up to educate about earthquake and tsunami evacuation systems. Unlike their commercial character cousins (like Hello Kitty), these are Japan's "working characters." They aren't designed to be money-making superstars, but rather to enhance communication.

A (Very) Brief Who's Who

HIKONYAN
Currently Japan's single most popular local character, Hikonyan is the mascot of Hikone Castle. A rotund house-cat sporting a samurai helmet, his name is a contraction of "Hikone" and the sound of a cat's meow in Japanese, "nyan."

KUU-TAN
This plump little fly-boy is one of the first working characters you'll encounter in Japan: He's the official mascot of Narita Airport. You can spot him on vending machines and signs throughout the concourses.

SENTO-KUN
Created to com-memorate the 1,300th anniversary of the city of Nara (p. 220) as the ancient capital of Japan, Sento-kun debuted in 2010 to great controversy. Tak-ing the form of a round boy with antlers, he's meant to synthesize the city's famed giant Buddha statue and the sacred deer that roam its grounds.

PEPO-KUN
This elfin creature with an antenna on his head is the mascot of the Tokyo Metropolitan Police Department. He can be found on *koban* (police boxes), where he serves to soften the formidable presence of police officers. His name sounds like the Japa-nese onomatopoeia for a police siren.

THE TOKYO CATFISH
A constant presence on Tokyo's roadways, he marks highways that are used as escape routes after earthquakes or other natural disasters. (In Japan, legend has it catfish can sense earthquakes before they occur.)

PRINCE PICKLES
Perhaps most shock-ing to non-Japanese, Prince Pickles is the mascot of the Japan Self-Defense Forces. Yes, even Japan's military has its own cuddly character. Visi-tors to Okinawa should keep an eye open for a large painting of him on a military hangar alongside the runway of Naha Airport.

Working Characters

Having been designed for public outreach rather than to make money, "working characters" tend to lack the polish of their commercial cousins. That said, in recent years these sorts of characters have enjoyed a surge of popularity. Today, having a wacky fur-suited mascot is a status symbol for many municipalities and organizations.

Cult of Cute

So why is Japan so obsessed with mascots? There is a centuries-old tradition of cute illustrations in the form of doodles and woodblock prints, and folk tales featuring weird characters have an even longer his-tory. The country's postwar tradition of producing manga (comic books) and *anime* (animated films) undoubtedly fans the flames as well.

Where to See Them

You can spot working characters in all sorts of places. Some of the most "target-rich" environments include:

CONSTRUCTION SITES
Even the smallest construction zone inevita-bly features signs with cute characters guid-ing pedestrians safely through the area.

INSTRUCTION MANUALS
The pages of electronics manuals often feature anthropomorphic versions of the product leading the consumer through how to use their new purchase.

DRUGSTORES
Cute characters appear on all sorts of pack-ages, but especially on signs advertising remedies for embarrassing maladies such as constipation. When it comes to that, who can you trust more than "Mr. Poop?"

Kobe

Although Kobe is considered more of a destination for
Japanese rather than international tourists, the port town has a lot to offer. It's
an attractive city to walk around, and the picture-perfect views of the bay are
thoroughly romantic. There are also several tantalizing options for gourmets:
Kobe is, after all, Japan's largest sake-producing region and home to the
deliciously marbled Kobe beef.

> *Summer fun on the boardwalk at
> Kobe Harborland.*

START Take the train to Sannomiya or Shin-
Kobe Station. Kobe is 75km (47 miles)
southwest of Kyoto.

❶ ★ Kitano (北野). In this former European
settlement, approximately 20 Victorian- and
Gothic-style homes are open to the public,
many with lovely views of the sea from

verandas and bay windows. Although you may
not be interested in visiting most of these *ijink
an* (literally, "foreigners' houses"), Kitano is
very pleasant for an hour's stroll. It's located
about a 15-minute walk north of Sannomiya
Station (via Kitano-zaka) or a 10-minute walk
west of Shin-Kobe Station. Or take the City
Loop bus to Kitano Ijinkan.

   Moegi no Yakata is a pale-green, 107-year-
old home built for a former American consul
general, Hunter Sharp, filled with antiques.
Across the street, **Kasamidori-no-Yakata** is
commonly referred to as the Weathercock
House because of its rooster weathervane.
This 1909 brick residence was built by a German merchant and is probably Kobe's most
famous home, if not its most elaborate.
🕐 1 hr. Moegi no Yakata: 3-10-11 Kitano-cho.
☎ 078/222-3310. Kasamidori-no-Yakata: 3-13-3
Kitano-cho. ☎ 078/242-3223. Moegi or Kasamidori ¥300, combination tickets for both houses
¥500; free for kids. Daily Apr–Nov 9am–6pm;
Dec–Mar 9am–5pm. Kasamidori closed the first
Tues in June and Feb. Train: Sannomiya or Shin-
Kobe stations.

❷ ★ Nunobiki Herb Garden (布引ハーブ園). Take
the Shin-Kobe Ropeway, a 3-minute walk from
Shin-Kobe Station, up to this green retreat
with remarkable views of the city (especially
dazzling at night). The walk downhill, past
fragrant gardens blooming with roses and
lavender, mint and sage, is almost as nice as
the ride up. 🕐 45 min. 1-4-3 Kitanocho, Chuo-
ku. ☎ 078/271-1160. www.kobeherb.com. ¥200,
ropeway ticket ¥1,000. Sept to mid-July Mon–Fri
10am–5pm, Sat–Sun 10am–8:30pm; holidays
and mid-July to Aug daily 10am–8:30pm. Train:
Shin-Kobe Station.

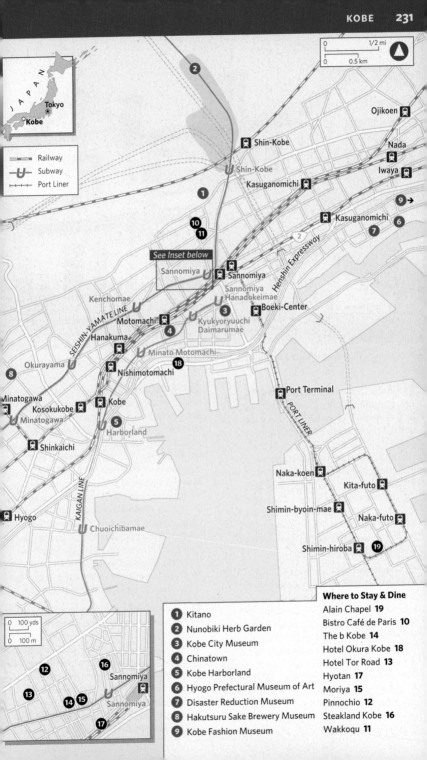

Railway
Subhway
Port Liner

2 Shin-Kobe

Shin-Kobe

Ojikoen

Nada

Iwaya

9 →

1

Kasuganomichi

Kasuganomichi   **6**

10   **7**

11

See Inset below

Sannomiya   **Sannomiya**

Sannomiya Hanadokeimae

Kenchomae   Boeki-Center

SEISHIN-YAMATE LINE   Motomachi

Hanakuma   Kyukyoryuuchi Daimarumae

4

Minato Motomachi

Okurayama   **18**

8   Nishimotomachi

Minatogawa   Port Terminal

Kosokukobe   **Kobe**

Minatogawa   **5**

Harborland   PORT LINER

Shinkaichi

KAIGAN LINE   Naka-koen

Kita-futo

Shimin-byoin-mae

Hyogo   Naka-futo

Chuoichibamae   Shimin-hiroba   **19**

Where to Stay & Dine

1 Kitano
2 Nunobiki Herb Garden
3 Kobe City Museum
4 Chinatown
5 Kobe Harborland
6 Hyogo Prefectural Museum of Art
7 Disaster Reduction Museum
8 Hakutsuru Sake Brewery Museum
9 Kobe Fashion Museum

Alain Chapel **19**
Bistro Café de Paris **10**
The b Kobe **14**
Hotel Okura Kobe **18**
Hotel Tor Road **13**
Hyotan **17**
Moriya **15**
Pinnochio **12**
Steakland Kobe **16**
Wakkoqu **11**

0   100 yds
0   100 m

12   **16**

Sannomiya

13

14 **15**   Sannomiya

17

> *Charming Western-style houses are the legacy of Kobe's international heritage.*

❸ ★ Kobe City Museum (神戸市立美術館)**.** Among the highlights of this museum, inside a former bank from the 1930s, is a collection of East-meets-West "Nanban" paintings, on screens and scrolls dating back to the 1500s and 1600s. *Nanban* translates literally as "Southern Barbarians," and the painters in this school were greatly influenced by European artists from the Renaissance. ⏱ 45 min. 24 Kyomachi, Chuo-ku. ☎ 078/391-0035. www. city.kobe.lg.jp/culture/culture/institution/ museum/main.html. ¥200. Tues–Sun 10am– 5pm. Train: Sannomiya Station.

❹ Chinatown (南京町)**.** Streets crammed with the red-and-gold signs of restaurants serving Peking duck and dumplings, shops selling souvenirs, and chaos all around—this is Kobe's own Chinatown. Chinatown here is no different from its counterpart in any other city, except for its size—this one is made up of only a few busy streets. As is the case with some Chinatowns, you're better off going elsewhere if you're looking for great Chinese food, but it's still fun to walk around, particularly in the evening when the storefronts are illuminated. ⏱ 30 min. Train: Motomachi Station.

❺ Kobe Harborland (神戸ハーバーランド)**.** Kobe Harborland is a leisure center that's fun to stroll and browse. It's a few minutes' walk from either Kobe Station or Meriken Park, or you can take the City Loop bus to Harborland. For shopping, stop by Kobe Hankyu department store or Promena Kobe mall, but best is **Mosaic,** a restaurant and shopping complex designed to resemble a Mediterranean village. Beside it is **Mosaic Garden,** a small amusement park for younger children complete with kiddie rides, a carousel, a roller coaster, an enclosed Ferris wheel, and a games arcade. ⏱ 20 min. Mosaic: Shops open daily 11am–8pm. Mosaic Garden: Rides ¥300–¥600. Daily 11am– 10pm. Train: Kobe or Meriken Park stations.

❻ ★ Hyogo Prefectural Museum of Art (兵庫県 立美術館)**.** Designed by contemporary architect Tadao Ando, this museum shows modern works by Japanese and international artists. Located on Kobe's waterfront, the impressive glass-and-concrete building was part of the reconstruction scheme after the devastating Hanshin Earthquake of 1995. ⏱ 30 min. 1-1-1 Wakihama Kaigan Dori, Chuo-ku. ☎ 078/262- 0901. www.artm.pref.hyogo.jp. ¥500 adults,

Take a crash course in sake history at the Hakutsuru Sake Brewery Museum.

¥400 college students, ¥250 high-school students and seniors, free for junior-high students and younger. Tues–Fri 10am–6pm; Sat–Sun 10am–8pm (last entry 30 min. before closing). Train: Hanshin Iwaya Station.

7 ★★★ **Disaster Reduction Museum** (人と防災未来センター). Despite this museum's rather dull, pragmatic-sounding name, its exhibits, which describe the magnitude of the Great Hanshin earthquake of 1995, are extremely affecting. After a powerful 7-minute film re-creating the exact moment that the earthquake struck, visitors emerge into a life-size diorama of a Kobe neighborhood destroyed by the quake. Some scenes may not be suitable for children. 1-5-2 Wakinohama Kaigan Dori, Chuo-ku. ☎ 078/262-5050. www.dri.ne.jp/english. ¥500 adults, ¥400 college and high-school students, ¥250 kids. Tues–Sun 9:30am–5:30pm, Fri–Sat 9:30am–7pm (July–Sept until 6pm); last entry 1 hr. before closing. Train: Nada Station.

8 ★★ **Hakutsuru Sake Brewery Museum** (白鶴酒造資料館). Everything you ever wanted to know about sake production is available at this museum, housed in the former Hakutsuru Brewery building. English-language videos and

pamphlets describe the various painstaking steps and compare the old techniques to those used today. The Nada region of Kobe is Japan's largest producer of sake, and Hakutsuru, established in 1743, is one of the largest breweries in Japan. The interesting self-guided tour concludes, naturally, with a free tasting. ⏱ 30 min. 4-5-5 Sumiyoshi-minamimachi, Higashinada-ku. ☎ 078/822-8907. www.hakutsuru-sake.com. Free. Tues–Sun 9:30am–4:30pm. Train: Hanshin Sumiyoshi Station.

9 ★ **Kobe Fashion Museum** (神戸ファッション美術館). Located on artificial Rokko Island, this is Japan's first museum devoted to fashion, housed in a futuristic building with a sophisticated, contemporary interior that does justice to the highbrow costumes on display. Exhibits change four or five times a year, rotating the many costumes owned by the museum. Fashionistas will swoon over the collection of colorful rare kimono and fabulous designs by the likes of Dior and Yves St. Laurent. ⏱ 30 min. 2-9 Koyocho-naka, Rokko Island. ☎ 078/858-0050. ¥500 adults, ¥250 kids and seniors. Thurs–Tues 10am–6pm. Monorail: Rokkoliner Monorail to Island Center Station.

Where to Stay & Dine in Kobe

> Dinner at Alain Chapel is a splurge, but you're worth it.

★★★ Alain Chapel FRENCH

For elegant dining and contemporary French cuisine, Alain Chapel is one of the city's top choices. In a stately drawing room setting with great panoramic views of either Kobe city or the sea, this Kobe institution is good for a romantic splurge. Reservations recommended. Kobe Portopia Hotel, 31st floor, 6–10–1 Minatojima, Port Island. ☎ 078/303-5201. www.portopia.co.jp. Entrees ¥3,696–¥10,395. AE, DC, MC, V. Lunch & dinner daily. Monorail: Portliner Monorail to Shimin Hiroba Station.

★ Bistro Café de Paris FRENCH

With its sidewalk seating and chansons (French songs) in the background, this lively bistro is a little slice of Paris. Dinner offers substantial fare, with main dishes ranging from roast lamb with mustard to beef bourguignon. 1–7–21 Yamamoto Dori. ☎ 078/241-9448. Set lunches from ¥1,050, set dinners from ¥2,940. AE, MC, V. Lunch & dinner daily. Train: Sannomiya Station.

★ The b Kobe

Located just minutes from Sannomiya Station, this hotel wins hands down as Kobe's most chic moderately priced hotel, offering mostly twin rooms smartly but sparingly done up in brown and red tones. Reception is on the second floor, where you'll also find a machine dispensing free coffee and a computer you can

use gratis. 2–11–5 Shimoyamate Dori, Chuo-ku. ☎ 078/333-4880. www.ishinhotels.com. 158 units. Doubles ¥13,650–¥19,950. AE, DC, MC, V Train: Sannomiya Station.

★★ kids Hotel Okura Kobe

This majestic 35-story hotel has the prestige of the Okura name, as well as a grand location right beside Meriken Park, within easy walking distance of the Motomachi covered shopping arcade and Chinatown. Each elegantly appointed room has all the comforts you'd expect plus the bonus of great views from its more expensive rooms. (Standard rooms provide only city views.) Ask for immediate free membership in the Okura Club International, which allows late checkout, discounts to its health club, free use of the outdoor pool, and other privileges. 2–Hatoba-cho, Chuo-ku. ☎ 078/333-0111. Doubles ¥22,050–¥47,250. AE, DC, MC, V. Bus: City Loop Bus to Meriken Park.

★ kids Hotel Tor Road

The decent-size rooms at this tourist hotel are clean and tastefully decorated with double-size beds (except in the singles) and larger-than-usual bathrooms. Each of the so-called Concept Rooms on the ninth floor is designed around a different theme. Images of cats are repeated everywhere—on the drapes, pillows, sheets—in the Cat Room. Fun for kids, but not exactly conducive to a romantic evening à deux. 3–1–19 Nakayamate Dori, Chuo-ku. ☎ 078/391-6691. 76 units. Doubles ¥13,000–¥18,000. AE, DC, MC, V. Train: Sannomiya or Motomachi stations.

Hyotan (瓢たん) DUMPLINGS

Roll up your sleeves and join the working class at this greasy hole-in-the-wall eatery underneath the tracks of Hanshin Sannomiya Station It must be doing something right, as it's been selling nothing but gyoza—dumplings favored for the light texture of their skin and stuffed with minced pork, leek, and cabbage—for more than 40 years. Avoid the noontime rush, when this tiny place is like an assembly line for speed eating. 1–31–37 Kitanagasa Dori. ☎ 078/331-1354 Plate of 7 gyoza ¥370. No credit cards. Lunch &

dinner Mon–Fri; closed 2nd and 4th Mon of each month. Train: Sannomiya Station.

★ Moriya (モーリヤ) *STEAKHOUSE*

This casual steak specialist in the heart of downtown grills up a pretty mean sirloin. Moriya has been in the beef business since 1885 and the main branch has an old-school, dinerlike atmosphere. 2–1–17 Shimoyamate Dori, Chuo-ku. ☎ 078/391-4603. www.mouriya.co.jp/en. Set lunches from ¥4,000, set dinners from ¥7,500. AE, DC, MC, V. Lunch & dinner daily. Train: Sannomiya Station.

Pinnochio *PIZZA/PASTA*

This small and cozy corner establishment opened in 1962 is still producing the same handmade pizza. You can order from the menu or create one yourself by ordering the basic pizza for ¥945 and adding ingredients such as garlic, asparagus, mushroom, chicken, or bacon, all priced at ¥105 each. 2–3–13 Nakayamate Dori. ☎ 078/331-3330. Pizza and pasta from ¥1,260. AE, DC, MC, V. Lunch & dinner daily. Train: Sannomiya Station.

Steakland Kobe (ステーキランド) *STEAKHOUSE*

If you want to eat *teppanyaki* steak (cooked at the table on a griddle) but can't afford the high prices of Kobe beef, one of the cheapest places to go is Steakland Kobe, which is used to tourists and offers an English-language menu. More expensive Kobe beef is also available. 1–8–2 Kitanagasa Dori. ☎ 078/332-1653. Set lunches from ¥980, set steak dinners ¥2,680. AE, DC, MC, V. Lunch & dinner daily. Train: Sannomiya Station.

★ Wakkoqu (和黒) *STEAKHOUSE*

This tiny, second-floor restaurant has room for only 30 diners at two counters, where expert chefs cook sirloin, tenderloin, or other cuts of tender Kobe beef on the grill in front of them. Fixed-course meals come with such side dishes as soup and fried vegetables. This is a good place to try Kobe's most famous product. Reservations recommended. Hillside Terrace, 1–22–13 Nakayamate Dori. ☎ 078/222-0678. Set lunches from ¥2,940, set dinners from ¥7,500. AE, DC, MC, V. Lunch & dinner daily. Train: Sannomiya Station.

→ *Kobe's famously decadent marbled beef is best served well done and hot off the grill.*

Kansai Fast Facts

> *We love the old-school design of Osaka's Hankyu Line (the seats are more comfy, too). 324D*

Arriving & Getting Around

BY PLANE Most overseas travelers will arrive at Osaka's **Kansai International Airport** (KIX; ☎ 072/455-2500; www.kansai-airport.or.jp). The two major domestic airlines that fly into KIX are Japan Airlines (JAL; www.jal.com) and All Nippon Airways (ANA; www.ana. co.jp). Most domestic flights, however, arrive at **Itami Airport** (ITM; ☎ 06/6856-6781), north of the city. From KIX, the **Kansai Airport Transportation Enterprise** (☎ 072/461-1374; www.kate.co.jp) provides bus service to major stations in Osaka and Kyoto, Nara, and Kobe Sannomiya. Fares start at ¥1,500, and tickets can be purchased at counters in the arrival lobby. The **OCAT Shuttle** (☎ 06/6635-3000; www.ocat.co.jp) travels from KIX to the Osaka City Air Terminal downtown (¥1,000; 48 min.). The **JR Airport Express Haruka** travels to Tennoji (¥2,070; 35 min.) and Shin-Osaka

(¥2,470, 50 min.). The **JR Rapid Service** (JR Kanku Kaisoku) also travels from KIX to Tennoji (¥1,030; 50 min.) and Osaka stations (¥1,160). *Tip:* When returning to the airport from Osaka, make sure you're in a compartment that goes all the way to KIX; not all of them do. If you have a Japan Rail Pass, you can ride these trains for free. The private **Nankai Line "rapi:t a"** travels from KIX to Namba (¥1,390; 35 min.). From ITA, buses connect to Osaka Station (25 min.). **Limousine buses** travel from ITM to Nara (☎ 074/22-5110; www.narakotsu.co.jp). **BY TRAIN** The **Shinkansen bullet train** offers service from Tokyo to Shin-Osaka (¥13,240; 160 min.), Shin-Kobe (¥21,520; 52 min.), and Kyoto (¥12,710; 140 min.). The **Kintetsu Line** and **JR Kansai Line** both connect Nara with Osaka. The **Hankyu Line** and **Hanshin Line** connect Kobe with Osaka. **BY BUS** **JR "Dream" night buses** depart from both Tokyo Station's Yaesu exit and Shinjuku Station's New South exit several times nightly (¥5,000; 9 hr.). There are also many **JR day buses** from Tokyo Station to Osaka Station (¥6,000; www.jrbuskanto. co.jp).

ATMs

In contrast to those abroad, many ATMs only operate during banking hours. ATMs are also very hard to find outside of major cities, so plan accordingly. Most post offices (see below) have ATM facilities, although hours are limited. For 24-hour access, your best bets are the ATMs in **7-Eleven** convenience stores, which accept Visa, Plus, American Express, JCB, Union Pay, or Diner's Club International cards for cash withdrawals. (They recently stopped accepting MasterCard, Maestro, and Cirrus cards.) **Citibank** and **Shinsei Bank** ATMs accept foreign bank cards as well. Citibank has branches in Kyoto, Osaka, and Kobe, but not Nara (www.citibank.co.jp/en/ bankingservice/branch_atm).

Doctors & Hospitals

OSAKA For emergency care in Osaka, call the **Osaka Municipal Emergency Information Service** (☎ 06/6582-7119). **KOBE** In Kobe, onsult the **Community House & Information Center** (☎ 078/857-6540; www.chickobe.om/CHIC_KOBE/Home.html). **NARA** In Nara, contact the **Nara International Foundation** (☎ 0742/27-2436; www.nifs.or.jp/en).

Emergencies

Dial ☎ **119** for ambulance and fire. Dial ☎ **110** or police and other emergencies.

Internet Access

Most hotels are equipped with Internet access, but Wi-Fi is still uncommon. **OSAKA** Near the Midosuji exit of Osaka Station is an area called Float Court, where you'll find **New Square** (☎ 06/6341-7870; daily 8am–10pm), an Internet cafe. **Media Café Popeye** ☎ 06/6292-3800; www.media-cafe.ne.jp) is near Umeda. **KOBE** In Kobe, **Litz Comic Café,** Tatsumi Bldg. 6F, 5-3-2 Asahi Dori ☎ 078/231-2217) is open 24 hours.

Pharmacies

Drugstores, called *yakkyoku* (薬局) are ubiquitous in Japan, but they are not 24-hour operations. Your best bet is to ask your hotel concierge for the closest location. Note that you must first visit a doctor in Japan before foreign prescriptions can be filled, so it's also best to bring an ample supply of any prescription medication with you.

Police

Dial ☎ **110** for police.

Post Offices

OSAKA The **Osaka Central Post Office,** in the Osaka Ekimae No. 1 Bldg., 1-3-1 Umeda, Kita-u, (☎ 06/6347-8112), is open 9am to 6pm, Monday to Friday. **NARA** **Nara Central Post Office,** 5-3-3 Omiya-cho (☎ 0742/35-1611), is open 9am to 9pm daily. **KOBE** The **Kobe Central Post Office,** 6-2-1 Sakaemachi Dori, Chuo-ku (☎ 078/360-9546; http://map.japanpost.jp/pc/syousai.php?id=300143001000), is open 9am to 8pm Monday to Friday; 9am to 5pm weekends and holidays.

Safety

Like the rest of Japan, Kansai is extremely safe, but take common-sense precautions for personal safety and valuables that you would anywhere else in the world.

Visitor Information

Kansei Scene (www.kansaiscene.com) is a free bilingual monthly magazine and website with articles, reviews, listings, and information on the Kansai area. More information on Osaka city is available on the Web at **www.osaka-info.jp**, and **www.kansai.gr.jp** gives information on the Kansai region. The **Nara Prefecture website** provides information in several languages (www.pref.nara.jp/nara_e). Kobe tourist information is available at **www.feel-kobe.jp/_en**. **OSAKA** **Visitors Information Center Umeda,** at the east (Midosuji) exit of Osaka Station in a kiosk (☎ 06/6345-2189; daily 8am–8pm), has good English-speaking staff that give out maps of the city and can assist in securing a hotel room. Other offices are the **Visitors Information Office Shin-Osaka** (☎ 06/6305-3311; daily 9am–6pm), **Visitors Information Center Namba** (☎ 06/6631-9100; daily 9am–8pm), and **Visitors Information Office Tennoji** (☎ 06/6774-3077; daily 9am–6pm). **KOBE** The **Shin-Kobe Tourist Information Office** (☎ 078/241-9550; daily 9am–6pm) and **Sannomiya Station Tourist Information Office** on Flower Road in the Kotsu Center Building (☎ 078/322-0220; daily 9am–7pm) can provide maps and sightseeing information and make hotel reservations. **NARA** There are tourist information offices at both **Nara Station** (☎ 0742/22-9821; daily 9am–5pm) and **Kintetsu Nara Station** (☎ 0742/24-4858; daily 9am–5pm). Both have good brochures and maps with useful information on how to get around Nara by foot and bus. For more detailed information on Nara, visit the **Nara City Tourist Center,** 23–4 Kami-sanjo-cho (☎ 0742/22-3900; daily 9am–9pm), located in the heart of the city on Sanjo Dori between both stations and about a 5-minute walk from each. Finally, there's **Sarusawa Information Center** (☎ 0742/26-1991; daily 9am-5pm), located at Sarusawa-ike Pond.

6
Kyoto

Favorite Moments

Welcome to Kyoto, the cultural heart of Japan. Heian-kyo, as the city was once called, remained the country's capital for over a millennium—from 794 until 1868, when the Meiji Restoration moved the imperial court to Edo. During the Heian Period (794-1185), Buddhism was at the height of influence, and the arts, poetry, and literature flourished under the auspices of the imperial family. The city suffered major damage in the Onin War (1467-77) but was restored to magnificence in the 16th century. With 17 UNESCO World Heritage sites, 20% of the country's National Treasures, and warrens of charming, narrow alleys, the city will beguile you with beauty and history.

> PREVIOUS PAGE *Take your place on the "Kiyomizu stage," the grand wooden veranda that hangs, literally over a cliff in eastern Kyoto.* THIS PAGE *The shops of Nishi Market are filled with barrels of colorful pickle fresh seafood, and delicacies you've never imagined.*

❶ **Making a wish at Kiyomizu-dera.** After taking in the views from the huge veranda of the main hall, sip the waters from the streams of Otowa-no-taki Falls and join pilgrims praying for wisdom, health, or longevity. Then, discover if you'll find true love by making your way blindfolded between the love stones at Jishu Jinja. See p. 246, ❸.

❷ **Finding Zen at Ryoan-ji.** The 15 stones in Ryoan-ji's serene rock garden inspire contemplation. According to Buddhist teachings,

the number 15 signifies completeness, but the garden is arranged so that only 14 of the stones can be seen at once. After 20 minutes by the garden, John Cage's experimental composition *Ryoan-ji* starts to make sense. See p. 250, ❹.

❸ **Having a sensory feast at Nishiki Market.** Take in the sights, sounds, and flavors of the "kitchen of Kyoto," a covered arcade full of shops that have been supplying the city's best restaurants for 400 years. The shopkeepers

1 Making a wish at Kiyomizu-dera

2 Finding Zen at Ryoan-ji

3 Having a sensory feast at Nishiki Market

4 Going geisha-watching in Gion

5 Feeding your soul at Tenryu-ji

6 Sipping sake at the source in Fushimi

7 Strolling through the bamboo grove in Arashiyama

8 Getting lost in the temple complex of Daitoku-ji

9 Making a pilgrimage to Fushimi Inari Shrine

> *A walk through Gion is where the past meets the present.*

greet you with cries of *"Irasshaimase!"* (Welcome!) and offer samples of pungent *nukazuke* pickles and tiny dried fish flavored with piquant *sansho* Japanese pepper. There's even a fish shop where you can eat your purchase at the adjacent standing bar. See p. 251, **9**.

4 Going geisha-watching in Gion. Wander through Hanami-koji and Shimbashi, two of Japan's most picturesque streets, and try to catch a glimpse of geisha and *maiko* (geisha in training) as they slip through the doors of the 17th-century buildings. See p. 247, **8**.

5 Feeding your soul at Tenryu-ji. With its room overlooking a carp-filled pond and beautiful gardens on the grounds of Tenryu-ji temple, Shigetsu is a great restaurant to experience the subtle vegetarian delicacies of *shojin-ryori* (Buddhist cuisine). It may be your most virtuous meal ever. See p. 252, **1**.

6 Sipping sake at the source in Fushimi. Fushimi is virtually synonymous with sake, Japan's national tipple. Experience the extremes of scale and sample fresh brews from one of Kyoto's largest breweries, the industrial giant Gekkeikan, and those of the tiny, artisanal producer Fujioka Shuzo. See p. 256.

8 Strolling through Kitasaga Bamboo Grove in Arashiyama. Walking through this silent grove of bamboo is an otherworldly experience. The towering trees are thick with mystery. It's possibly the most peaceful 10 minutes you'll spend in Kyoto. See p. 254, **2**.

9 Getting lost in the temple complex of Daitoku-ji. The vast, mazelike complex houses 24 subtemples and some extremely pretty gardens, including Japan's tiniest *karesansui* (dry landscape rock garden). Don't forget to pay your respects to the image of tea master Sen no Rikyu above the Sanmon Gate. See p. 251, **7**.

10 Making a pilgrimage to Fushimi Inari Shrine. The 4km (2.5-mile) hike up to the shrine dedicated to the god of rice and sake is lined with hundreds of brilliant red gates. Early in the morning, the gates blaze with color; in late afternoon, they take on a shadowy, mysterious beauty. Don't forget your camera: This is one of Kyoto's most iconic sights. See p. 256, **1**.

> Rain or shine, the hundreds of vermillion torii gates of Fushimi Inari Shrine will dazzle you.

The Best of Kyoto in 1 Day

If you have only 1 day to experience Kyoto, spend most of it exploring the historic Higashiyama ward, where many of the city's most beloved sites can be found. During the 15th century, the "Eastern Mountain District" was the center for Japanese arts based on Zen aesthetics—*chado* (tea ceremony), *ikebana* (flower arrangement), Noh drama, and *sumi-e* ink painting. This tour will lead you from the soaring heights of Kiyomizu-dera, down wandering lanes to the atmospheric pleasure quarters of Gion, and into the lantern-lit nightlife streets of Pontocho.

> *A bird's-eye view from Kiyomizu-dera on Mount Otowa.*

START Take bus no. 206 or 208 to the Sanjusangendo-mae stop.

1 ★★★ **Sanjusangendo.** Originally built in 1164 and reconstructed in 1266, the long, narrow hall of this Buddhist temple houses one of Kyoto's most arresting sights: 1,001 wooden statues of the thousand-armed deity Kannon. Five hundred life-sized figures flank the largest image of the seated goddess, carved from Japanese cypress in 1254 by the Kamakura-era

sculptor Tankei, on either side. Technically, the statues are short of a few limbs (each Kannon has 40 arms), but bear in mind that one hand has the power to save 25 worlds. Twenty-eight guardian figures stand watch in front.

Stretching an impressive 120m (395 ft.), Sanjusangendo is the longest wooden building in Japan. The Toshiya Matsuri competition, during which archers try to shoot as many arrows as they can from one end of the hall to the other, has been held every year since the

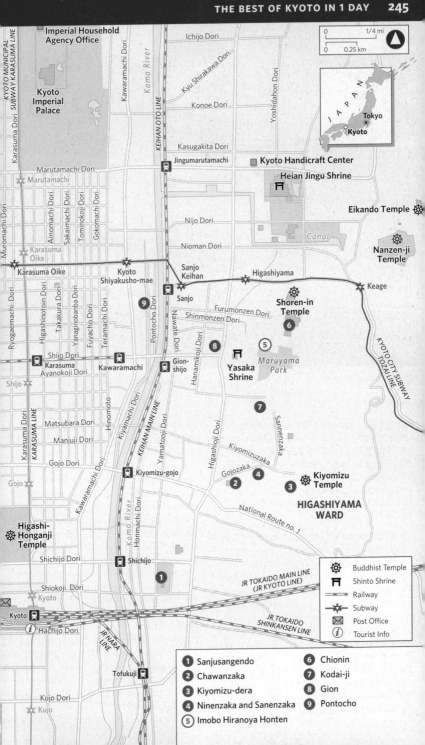

Imperial Household Agency Office

Kyoto Imperial Palace

Kyoto Handicraft Center

Heian Jingu Shrine

Eikando Temple

Nanzen-ji Temple

Shoren-in Temple ⑥

Kyoto Shiyakusho-mae

Sanjo Keihan

Higashiyama

Keage

Sanjo ⑨

Yasaka Shrine ⑧

Maruyama Park ⑤

Karasuma Kawaramachi

Gion-shijo

⑦

Kiyomizu-gojo

Kiyomizuzaka

Gojozaka ② ④

Kiyomizu Temple ③

HIGASHIYAMA WARD

National Route no. 1

Higashi-Honganji Temple

Shichijo ①

Kyoto

Kyoto

Tofukuji

JR TOKAIDO MAIN LINE (JR KYOTO LINE)

JR TOKAIDO SHINKANSEN LINE

✿	Buddhist Temple
🏮	Shinto Shrine
▬	Railway
✦	Subway
✉	Post Office
ⓘ	Tourist Info

① Sanjusangendo
② Chawanzaka
③ Kiyomizu-dera
④ Ninenzaka and Sanenzaka
⑤ Imobo Hiranoya Honten
⑥ Chionin
⑦ Kodai-ji
⑧ Gion
⑨ Pontocho

> *The tranquil gardens of Kodai-ji temple, built in honor of Toyotomi Hideyoshi by his widow, Nene.*

Edo Period, but no one has yet been able to break the all-time record of 8,000 arrows set in 1686. ⏱ 20 min. 657 Sanjujsangendomawari–cho, Higashiyama-ku. ☎ 075/525-0033. www.sanjusangendo.jp. ¥600 adults, ¥400 students, ¥300 kids. Daily Apr–mid-Nov 8am–5pm; mid-Nov–Mar 9am–4pm. Bus: 206 or 208 to Sanjusangendo-mae.

② ★ **Chawanzaka.** Charmingly named "Teapot Lane," this slope leading to Kiyomizu-dera is lined with shops selling *kyoyaki,* Kyoto's traditional pottery. Snack on *sembei* rice crackers or sugary, bean-paste-filled *wagashi* sweets as you browse the ceramic cups and decorative plates used for Japanese tea ceremony. Like all of the roads to Kiyomizu-dera, this narrow lane gets congested with tourists, so get there as early as possible to avoid foot-traffic bottlenecks. ⏱ 10 min. Chawanzaka. www.chawanzaka.com. Free. Bus: 18, 100, 206, or 207 to Gojozaka (walk up Gojozaka slope and head right at the fork in the road).

③ ★★★ **Kiyomizu-dera.** One of the city's mos famous landmarks, Kiyomizu-dera was built in 798 and reconstructed in 1633 by the third Tokunaga shogun, Iemitsu. Perched high on Mount Otowa, the temple's main hall features a vast wooden veranda supported by 139 pillars that extends over a cliff. Amazingly, no nails were used in the construction of the building. The grounds are especially beautiful during the spring and autumn months, though the temple gets very crowded.

Directly below is Otowa-no-taki waterfall, where pilgrims imbibe the waters of three streams, which are said to confer the gifts of wisdom, health, and longevity onto believers. Drink from one or two—but not all three—or you may invoke the fury of the gods. Behind Kiyomizu-dera's main hall is the Shinto shrine **Jishu Jinja,** dedicated to Okuninushi, the god of love and matchmaking. Try walking the 9m (30 ft.) between the shrine's "love stones" with your eyes closed: If you make it, your wish for true love will be granted. ⏱ 1 hr. 1-294

Kiyomizu, Higashiyama-ku. ☎ 075/551-1234 or 075/541-2097 (Jishu Jinja). www.kiyomizudera.or.jp. ¥300 adults, ¥200 kids ages 7–15, free for kids 6 and under. Daily 6am–6pm (until 6:30pm in summer). Jishu Jinja closes at 5pm. Bus: 100, 206, or 207 to Gojozaka.

④ ★★ **Ninenzaka and Sanenzaka.** Leaving Kiyomizu-dera, wander down the hill to the quaint neighborhoods of Ninenzaka and Sanenzaka. These two streets, whose names mean "Two-Year Hill" and "Three-Year Hill," respectively, are lined with wooden buildings and traditional shops and tearooms that evoke the atmosphere of old Kyoto. Free. Bus: 100 to Gojozaka.

③ 🍴 ★★ **Imobo Hiranoya Honten** (いもぼ平野家本店). *Imobo,* the signature dish of this traditional eatery in Maruyama Park, consists of taro root stewed with dried cod and has a history that dates back 300 years. The restaurant is located inside the Maruyama Park grounds, near the south gate. Maruyamacho, Higashiyama-ku. ☎ 075/561-1603. www.imobou.net. Set meals from ¥2,520. No credit cards. Lunch & dinner daily. Bus: 100 to Gojozaka.

⑥ ★★★ **Chionin.** This temple, first erected in 1234 on the site where the Buddhist priest Honen fasted to death in 1212, is the headquarters of the Jodo school of Buddhism. Chionin is perhaps most notable for the mammoth scale of its structures, which appeared in the film *The Last Samurai.* Its Sanmon entrance gate stands 24m (79 ft.) high and is the largest temple gate in Japan. The main hall, which can accommodate 3,000 guests, is fittingly proportioned. The corridor connecting the main hall and the Dai-Hojo abbots' quarters features a "nightingale" floor, which squeaks with every step; this crafty design was created to warn the monks of intruders. Most of the present buildings date from the 17th century.

Weighing 74 tons, Chionin's massive temple bell is the biggest in Japan. No fewer than 17 monks are needed to ring it at the temple's New Year ceremony. Thankfully, for the monks, this happens only once a year. ⏱ 20 min. 400 Rinka-cho, Higashiyama-ku. ☎ 075/531-2111. www.chion-in.or.jp. Free. Gardens ¥500 adults, ¥250 for kids. Daily 9am–4pm. Bus: 206 to Chionin-mae.

> *Pontocho, Kyoto's legendary nightlife district, is alive and well.*

⑦ ★★★ **Kodai-ji.** See p. 262, ⑥.

⑧ ★★★ **Gion.** Kyoto's legendary entertainment district was once home to thousands of geisha. Although modern life has encroached upon the nostalgic beauty of the area, you can get a flavor of the old city by wandering through some of Gion's picturesque roads. Among the streets lined with 17th-century restaurants and teahouses, it's still possible to spot brilliantly attired geisha and *maiko* (geisha in training). Note, though, that many of these places do not welcome casual visitors; most require a formal introduction from a regular patron.

The cobbled street of **Shimbashi,** just north of the intersection of Shijo Dori and Hanami-koji, is one of Kyoto's most beautifully preserved lanes. ⏱ 30 min. Gion is bounded by Sanjo Dori, Gojo Dori, Higashiyama Dori, and Kawabata Dori. Free. Train: Gion Shijo Station.

⑨ ★★★ **Pontocho.** An evening walk down this iconic alleyway, in Kyoto's famous nightlife district, is like stepping back in time. As night falls and the lanterns illuminating the traditional wooden buildings blaze to life, it's easy to imagine the city in its heyday. ⏱ 15 min. Pontocho is between Sanjo Dori and Shijo Dori. Free. Train: Kawaramachi Station.

The Best of Kyoto in 2 Days

The vast stretch of northwestern Kyoto is a predominantly residential area dotted with splendid sights. In fact, some of the city's most famous attractions—the coruscating Kinkaku-ji Golden Pavilion, the ornate Nijo Castle, and the minimalist Ryoan-ji temple—can be found here. Although all of the sights are easily accessible via public transportation, you should allow plenty of time to get around. After a full day of temple hopping, this tour finishes in central Kyoto at Nishiki Market, a feast for the senses.

> *Don't forget your sunglasses: The reflection of Kinkaku-ji temple beams brightly from the pond below.*

START Take the subway to Karasuma-Oike Station.

1 ★★ **Miyawaki Baisen-an** (宮脇賣扇庵). Miyawaki Baisen-an has been the premier place for wooden fans since 1823. Dozens of beautifully crafted painted and lacquered fans are on display in the elegant shop. ⏱ 15 min. Tomino-koji Nishi-iru Rokkaku Dori, Nakagyo-ku. ☎ 075/221-0181. www.baisenan.co.jp. Free. Daily 9am–6pm. Subway: Karasuma-Oike Station.

2 ★★★ **Nijojo.** Built in 1603 as the official residence of the first Tokugawa shogun, Ieyasu, Nijo Castle is an outstanding example of Momoyama architecture, with elaborate woodcarvings, gold-leaf-covered ceilings, and Kano-school paintings on the sliding doors. Nijojo is also known for its high-security nightingale floors, which creak with every move, and secret chambers where bodyguards could hide. Ironically, Ieyasu used the palace only three times.

Kyoto
Prefectual
Botanical
Garden

Kitayama Dori

KITA
WARD

Kamo River

Kitaoji

Kitaoji Dori

Shimei Dori

Kuramaguchi Dori

Kiuramaguchi

KYOTO MUNICIPAL
SUBWAY KARASUMA LINE

Kinkaku-ji
Temple

Nishioji Dori

Senbon Dori

Ryoan-ji
Temple

Ninna-ji
Temple

KAMIGYO
WARD

Shokoku-ji
Temple

Imadegawa

Imadegawa Dori

Ryanji   Tojiin

Myoshinju

Kitano-
Hakubaicho

Ichijo Dori

Imperial Household
Agency Office

Omuro-
Ninnaji

Horikawa Dori

Aburanokoji Dori

Ogawa Dori

Karasuma Dori

Kyoto
Imperial
Palace

Shimodachiuri Dori

Marutamachi Dori

Hanazono

Harimaya Station
Free Cafe

Marutamachi Dori

Emmachi

Marutamachi

Ainomachi Dori

Senbon Dori

Ebisugawa Dori

Nijo Dori

Shinmachi Dori

Karasuma
Oike

Kaikonoyashiro

Uzumasa-
tenjingawa

Nijo
Castle

Oike Dori   Nishioji-oike   TOZAI LINE

Nijo

Oshikoji Dori

Nijojo-mae

Oike Dori

Randentenjingawa

KEIFUKU
ARASHIYAMA LINE

Yamanouchi

Nishioji-sanjo

Aneyakoji Dori   Karasuma Oike

NAKAGYO
WARD

Takoyakushi Dori
Nishikikoji Dori

Nishinotoin Dori

Ryogaemachi Dori

Higashinotoin Dori

Miyawaki Baisen-an

JR SAN-IN MAIN LINE
(JR SAGANO LINE)

UKYO
WARD

Shijo Dori   Saiin

Sai

Nishioji Dori

Shijo Dori   Karasuma

Shijo

Omiya

Ayanokoji Dori

Karasuma Dori

KARASUMA LINE

Takakura Dori

Bukkoji Dori

Takatsuji Dori

Matsubara Dori

Manjuji Dori

HANKYU KYOTO LINE

Gojo Dori

Gojo

Buddhist Temple
Railway
Subway
Post Office
Tourist Info

Tambaguchi

SHIMOGYO
WARD

Higashi-Hongan-ji
Temple

Omiya Dori

Horikawa Dori

Shichijo Dori   Shichijo Dori

Kyoto

Kyoto

Hachijo Dori

1 Miyawaki Baisen-an
2 Nijojo
3 Kinkaku-ji
4 Ryoan-ji
5 Ninna-ji
6 Sakon
7 Daitoku-ji
8 Matsuno Shoyu Shop
9 Nishiki Market

1/2 mi
0.5 km

JAPAN
Tokyo
Kyoto

> *Intricate wood carvings on the walls of Nijojo castle.*

> *One of Kyoto's greatest cultural legacies is its impeccably presented, refined cuisine.*

Ninomaru Palace is divided into five buildings with 33 chambers. Be sure to walk through the lovely Ninomaru Palace Garden, designed by landscape artist Korobi Enshu. Audio guides are available for ¥500. ⏱ 1 hr. 541 Nijojo-cho, Horikawa Nishi-iru, Nijo Dori, Nakagyo-ku. ☎ 075/841-0096. ¥600 adults, ¥350 students, ¥200 kids. Daily 8:45am–5pm (last entry 4pm); closed Tues in Dec, Jan, July, and Aug; closed Dec 26–Jan 4. Bus: 9 to Nijojo-mae.

❸ ★★★ Kinkaku-ji. One of Japan's (and possibly the world's) most widely photographed tourist attractions, Kinkaku-ji is a monument to the lavish lifestyle of Shogun Ashikaga Yoshimitsu. The Golden Pavilion was built in 1397 as Ashikaga's retirement villa and converted into a Zen temple after his death in 1408.

The temple, whose top floors are covered in gold leaf, is an impressive sight, particularly on sunny days when its image is mirrored in the lake below. In 1950, a fanatical monk burned the original building to the ground (the story of the monk's obsession is recounted by Mishima Yukio in his novel *The Temple of the Golden Pavilion*), and the temple was reconstructed in 1955.

The surrounding park, with its moss gardens and teahouses, is also worth checking out. Arrive as early, or as late in the day, as possible. ⏱ 30 min. 1 Kinkakuji-cho, Kita-ku. ☎ 075/461-0013. www.shokoku-ji.or.jp. ¥400 adults, ¥350 kids. Daily 9am–5pm. Bus: 205 to Kinkakuji-michi.

❹ ★★★ Ryoan-ji. Founded in 1450, this Rinzai Zen temple is best known for its austerely beautiful *karesansui* (dry landscape) rock garden. The garden, which features 15 stones amid a swirling sea of white sand, is the quintessence of minimalism. The designer remains unknown to this day. Stroll through the temple grounds and take in the calm of the mossy gardens and Kyoyochi pond, which is especially pretty in the fall. Plan to arrive as early as possible, or just before closing. ⏱ 30 min. 13 Goryonoshitamachi, Ryoan-ji, Ukyo-ku. ☎ 075/463-2216. www.Ryoan-ji.jp. ¥500 adults, ¥300 kids under 15. Daily Mar–Nov 8am–5pm; Dec–Feb 8:30am–4:30pm. Subway:

ifuku Kitano Ryoan-jimichi Station.

★★ **Ninna-ji.** Completed in 888, Ninna-ji now the head temple of the Shingon school Buddhism. Many of the buildings were estroyed in the 15th century, and most of the esent structures date from the 17th century. e sprawling grounds feature several build- gs, including a 33m-tall (108-ft.) pagoda, d a profusion of rare Omuro cherry trees, hose fluffy pink blossoms attract a number visitors during the springtime. ⏱ 30 min. 33 muroouchi, Ukyo-ku. ☎ 075/461-1155. www. nnaji.or.jp. Grounds free, ¥500 for the temple uildings. Bus: 59 to Omuro-Ninnaji.

🍴 ★★ **Sakon** (左近)**.** Conveniently lo- cated a stone's throw from Ninna-ji, this cozy restaurant specializes in both tra- ditional Kyoto cuisine and French food. 25–37 Omurokomatsunocho, Ukyo-ku. ☎ 075/463-5582. www.sakon-kyoto. com/index.htm. Set meals from ¥4,600. No credit cards. Lunch & dinner daily. Bus: 59 to Omuro-Ninnaji.

★★★ **Daitoku-ji.** This sprawling, mazelike nzai Zen temple complex spans 23 hectares 57 acres) and encloses 24 subtemples. The ame refers to both the main temple and the omplex itself. Daitoku-ji is renowned for s peaceful gardens and the two venerable ojin-ryori restaurants, Izusen (p. 261, ❸) and kyu (p. 261, ❹) on the grounds. Some of the ubtemples also offer Zen meditation classes.

Originally founded as a monastery in 1319, e eponymous Daitoku-ji main temple was estroyed by a fire in 1474 and rebuilt in the 6th century. The Sanmon gate features a tatue of the eminent tea master Sen no Rikyu.

Not all of the subtemples are open to the ublic all year, but there's plenty to see. It's asy to get lost among the lanes of the temple omplex, so be sure to pick up a map at the en- rance. One of the largest and most interesting ubtemples is Daisenin, famous for its two love- y gardens. Kotoin is notable for its moss garden nd its maple trees, which are beautiful in the all. Ryogenin's claim to fame is its Totekiko rock arden, rumored to be the smallest rock garden Japan. ⏱ 1½ hr. Daitoku-ji: 53 Daitokuji-cho, Murasakino, Kita-ku. ☎ 075/491-0019. Free. Daily 9am–5pm. Daisenin: 54-1 Daitokuji-cho,

> *Soy sauce, made the old-fashioned way, at Matsuno Shoyu Shop.*

Murasakino, Kita-ku. ☎ 075/491-8346. ¥400. Daily Mar–Nov 9am–5pm; Dec–Feb 9am–4:30pm. Kotoin: 73–1 Daitokuji-cho, Murasakino, Kita-ku. ☎ 075/492-0068. ¥400. Daily 9am–4pm. Ryo- genin: 82–1 Daitokuji-cho, Murasakino, Kita-ku. ☎ 075/491-7635. ¥350. Daily 9am–4:30pm. Bus: 205 to Daitokuji-mae.

❽ ★★ **Matsuno Shoyu Shop** (松野醤油)**.** Pur- chase seven varieties of artisanal soy sauce at the shop in front of this traditional soy sauce factory. Denkichi Matsuno's family has been making the savory black liquid since 1805. ⏱ 15 min. 21 Takagamine Dotenjocho, Kita-ku. ☎ 075/492-2984. www.matsunoshouyu.co.jp. Free. Daily 9am–6pm; closed Dec 30–Jan 5. Bus: 1 to Dotenjocho.

❾ ★★★ **Nishiki Market.** Popularly known as the "kitchen of Kyoto," this covered market has a history of over 400 years and supplies most of the city's best restaurants with their produce. You'll find everything from *tsuke- mono* pickles to tofu doughnuts. It's a must- see for food lovers. ⏱ 30 min. Nishikikoji Dori, btw. Teramachi and Takakura. ☎ 075/211-3882. www.kyoto-nishiki.or.jp. Free. Daily 9am–5pm; some shops closed Wed. Subway: Hankyu Kawaramachi Station.

The Best of Kyoto in 3 Days

Once you've explored the sights of central Kyoto, take some time to discover the serene beauty of the temples in the western districts on the outskirts of the city. Arashiyama was a favorite spot among nobles during the Heian period (794–1185) and remains Kyoto's second most popular tourist destination to this day. Its lush, rolling landscape is spectacular in the spring and fall, when the hills explode with color. South of Arashiyama lies Saiho-ji, famous for the meditative atmosphere of the temple grounds and its magnificent moss-covered garden.

> *The melancholy stone Buddhas of Adashino Nembutsu-ji.*

START Take the Keifuku-Arashiyama train line to Arashiyama Station.

1 ★★★ **Tenryu-ji.** This Rinzai Zen Buddhist temple was built in 1339 on the site of the former villa of Emperor Go-Daigo, who had been overthrown by Ashikaga Takauji. Tenryu-ji takes its name—"Heavenly Dragon"—from the vision of a golden dragon seen by eminent priest Mus Soseki after Go-Daigo's death. Soseki interpreted the dream as a sign that the emperor's spirit was restless, and Ashikaga, disturbed by the ill omen, commissioned the construction of the temple complex. The original temple was destroyed by fire, and the current buildings date

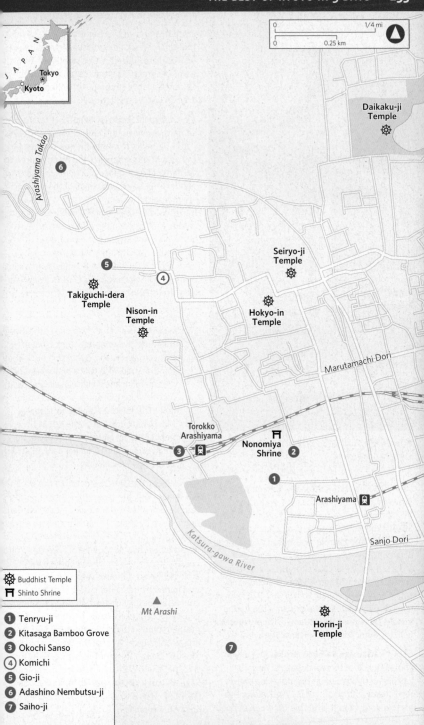

JAPAN

Tokyo

Kyoto

0 / 1/4 mi
0 / 0.25 km

Arashiyama Takao

6

Daikaku-ji Temple

5

④

Takiguchi-dera Temple

Seiryo-ji Temple

Nison-in Temple

Hokyo-in Temple

Marutamachi Dori

Torokko Arashiyama

3

Nonomiya Shrine

1

2

Arashiyama

Sanjo Dori

Katsura-gawa River

✿ Buddhist Temple
🎐 Shinto Shrine

▲ Mt Arashi

7

✿ **Horin-ji Temple**

1 Tenryu-ji
2 Kitasaga Bamboo Grove
3 Okochi Sanso
④ Komichi
5 Gio-ji
6 Adashino Nembutsu-ji
7 Saiho-ji

> *Tenryu-ji's beautiful Sogenchi garden is worth the trip to Arashiyama.*

stretches of towering bamboo trees, so thick that only the sound of rustling leaves can be heard. From Tenryu-ji, exit through the north gate; the grove is on the trail that leads to the Okochi Sanso villa complex. ⏱10 min. Free. Train: Arashiyama Station.

❸ ★★ **Okochi Sanso** (大河内山荘). It took silent samurai movie actor Denjiro Okochi (1898–1962) 30 years to complete this serene villa (no admittance allowed) and its surrounding gardens. The gardens, which are open to the public, offer sweeping views of the city and are marvelous in autumn, when the maple leaves display their vivid fall colors. Tea and cake are included in the admission price, so be sure to hold on to your tea voucher. It's a 10-minute walk through the bamboo grove from Tenryu-ji. ⏱30 min. 8 Tabuchiyama-cho, Ogurayama, Saga, Ukyo-ki. ¥1,000. Daily 9am–5pm. Train: Arashiyama Station.

④ 🍵 ★ **Komichi** (こみち). On the way to nearby Gio-ji, refuel with one of the sweet milky *matcha* green-tea drinks that are this cafe's specialty. Soba (thin buckwheat noodles) and *udon* (thick buckwheat noodles) set lunches are also available. Look for the white wall and green-and-white lantern outside. 23 Ojoin-cho, Nison-in Monzen, Ukyo-ku. ☎ 075/872-5313. Drinks from ¥600, set lunches from ¥1,300. No credit cards. Lunch & dinner daily. Bus: 62 or 72 to Saga-Shakadomae.

❺ ★★ **Gio-ji** (祇王寺). Dedicated to the Heian-era dancer Gio, this peaceful Shingon Buddhist temple is nestled among quiet mossy gardens and hidden by trees. The history of Gio-ji was made famous by the epic *Tale of Heike*. Gio was the beautiful concubine of Kiyomori Taira, head of the Taira clan. She became a nun after her failed romance with Kiyomori and was joined by her sister Ginyo and the young courtesan Hotoke Gozen. Wooden statues of Gio, Ginyo, Hotoke Gozen, Kiyomori, and Gio's mother stand in the nunnery, along with an image of Dainichi Nyorai, the Buddha of Light. The temple is a 15-minute walk north from Okochi Sanso. ⏱20 min. 32 Kozaka, Toriimoto, Saga, Ukyo-ku. ☎ 075/861-3574. ¥300. Daily 9am–5pm (last entry 4:30pm). Bus: 62 or 72 to Saga-Shakadomae.

from 1900. Tenryu-ji's tranquil Sogenchi garden, however, dates back to the 14th century and is the site's primary attraction. Designed by Muso Soseki (the very same priest of golden dragon fame), the stone garden was based on paintings of Mount Horai in China and incorporates elements of Arashiyama's natural scenery into its composition. ⏱20 min. 68 Susukinobaba-cho, Saga-Tenryu-ji, Ukyo-ku. ☎ 075/882-9725. www.tenryuji.com. ¥500 for the garden, ¥100 for the temple. Daily Apr–Oct 8:30am–5:30pm; Nov–Mar 8:30am–5pm. Train: Arashiyama Station.

❷ ★★★ **Kitasaga Bamboo Grove.** Just a few steps outside of the north gate of Tenryu-ji lies one of Kyoto's most breathtaking sights: the Kitasaga bamboo grove. Walk along the narrow path from the temple between dense

A hidden treasure in the woods, Gio-ji is the place for poets and students of literature.

★★ Adashino Nembutsu-ji (化野念仏寺).
Upon entering the cemetery grounds of this
temple, you'll discover the remarkable field of
8,000 stone Buddhas, which commemorate
the passing of paupers whose families could
not afford a proper burial. The diminutive statues have a weathered, solemn beauty. (Arrive
in the late afternoon to view the statues at
their eerie best.) On the evenings of August 23
and 24, at the Sento Kuyo ceremony, 1,000
candles are lit in honor of these anonymous
souls. The main temple hall was erected in
1712 and houses a Kamakura-era figure of
Amida Buddha, carved by the sculptor Tankei.
The temple is a 15-minute walk from Gio-ji.
⏱ 20 min. 17 Adashino-cho, Toriimoto, Ukyo-ku,
Kyoto. ☎ 075/861-2221. ¥500. Daily Mar–Nov
9am–4:30pm; Dec–Feb 9am–4pm. Bus: 72 to
Toriimoto.

★★★ Saiho-ji. Saiho-ji was converted to a
Rinzai Zen Buddhist temple in 1339 and made
a UNESCO World Heritage site in 1994. One
of Kyoto's most picturesque spots, Saiho-ji is
commonly referred to as Koke-dera, "Moss
Temple," thanks to the 120 varieties of moss
that cover the grounds in a lush, velvety carpet
of green. The gardens are particularly lovely
after the rain, when the moss shimmers with
an otherworldly, iridescent light.

Before entering the garden, you'll be asked
to listen to a lecture in Japanese while you

copy a sutra using a traditional Japanese
brush. Copying the sutra is the easy part: You
can trace the characters on the page, and
you don't have to finish. More difficult is the
reservation process you must complete before
you arrive (see below)—you must reserve via
post well in advance and then participate in
the tour to enter the garden—but it's worth
the effort. ⏱ 1½ hr. 56 Jingatani-cho, Matsuo,
Nishikyo-ku. ☎ 075/391-3631. ¥3,000. Daily
9am–5pm. Bus: 72 from Adashino Nembutsu-ji
to Hankyu Arashiyama Station. Buses are infrequent; check schedule. Train: Matsuo Station.

Making a Reservation at Saiho-ji

In order to preserve both the moss and the
tranquil atmosphere, admission to the temple is limited; you must get permission to
visit. Send a note to the temple at least 10
days in advance. Write to Saiho-ji Temple,
56 Matsuo Kamigatani-cho, Nishikyo-ku,
Kyoto 615-8286 (☎ 075/391-3631), and
give your name, your address in Japan,
your age, your occupation, and the date
you'd like to visit (plus alternative dates).
Include a self-addressed return envelope
and International Reply Coupons for return
postage. (If you're in Japan, you should
send a double postcard, or *ofuku hagaki*.)
Alternatively, contact the Kyoto Tourist
Information Center (p. 277) for assistance.

Fushimi Sake

Home to over 30 sake breweries, the Fushimi district in
southern Kyoto is Japan's second-largest sake-producing region after Nada, in Kobe. This tour for sake lovers takes you from the Fushimi Inari Shrine, through the quiet streets lined with Meiji Era buildings along the Uji Canal. While most breweries are closed to the public, there are a few places where you can pop in to sip sake at the source.

> Kanpai! *The secret to Fushimi's delectable sake is the clear, soft water.*

START Take the JR Nara train line to Inari Station.

1 ★★★ **Fushimi Inari Shrine.** Pay your respects to Inari, the god of rice and sake, at this remarkable Shinto shrine, dating back to the 8th century and perched high in the Momoyama hills. The 4km (2.5-mile) path that leads to the main building is lined with 1,300 brilliant vermillion *torii* gates and dotted with bronze statues of foxes, the messengers of Inari. As you ascend, the gates appear to form a tunnel—a sight both stunning and surreal. It takes about 2 hours to climb to the apex, but you'll be rewarded with beautiful views of Kyoto. ⏱ 3 hr. 68 Fukakusa Yabunouchi-cho. ☎ 075/641-7331. www.inari.jp. Free. Daily dawn–dusk. Train: Inari Station.

2 ★ **Gekkeikan Okura Museum.** One of Japan's largest and most famous sake producers, Gekkeikan also has a small museum dedicated to the craft of brewing. The short, self-guided tour (with explanations in English) finishes with a complimentary sake tasting. ⏱ 30 min. 247 Minamihama-cho, Fushimi-ku. ☎ 075/623-2056. www.gekkeikan.co.jp. ¥300 adults, ¥100 kids ages 12–17, free for kids 11 and under. Daily 9:30am–4:30pm. Train: Chushojima Station.

3 🍜 ★★ **Genya Ramen** (玄屋ラーメン). The specialty at this friendly shop is *sake-kas* ramen, flavored with the sake lees left over after pressing. It's a unique dish, but the only problem is the lack of sake on the menu. 698 Higashikumi-cho, Fushimi-ku. ☎ 075/602-1492. www5b.biglobe.ne.jp/~genya-/. Ramen from ¥630. No credit cards. Lunch & dinner daily. Train: Fushimi-Momoyama Station.

4 ★★★ **Fujioka Shuzo Sakagura Bar En** (藤岡酒造). This tiny brewpub offers a striking contrast to sake giant Gekkeikan. Owner and

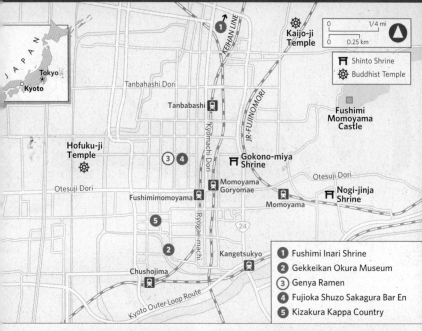

Map legend:

- 1 Fushimi Inari Shrine
- 2 Gekkeikan Okura Museum
- 3 Genya Ramen
- 4 Fujioka Shuzo Sakagura Bar En
- 5 Kizakura Kappa Country

The best time to view the red gates at Fushimi Inari Shrine is dusk, but watch out for the fox spirits that come out at night.

Fushimi Mizu

Fushimi rose to prominence as a sake-brewing capital during the Edo period (1603–1868), thanks to a fortuitous combination of high-quality rice, ease of transportation via the Uji Canal, and, above all, an abundant supply of soft natural spring water. In ancient times, the region was literally synonymous with this precious liquid: Both were referred to as "Fushimi *mizu*" (the "water of Fushimi").

Fushimi's water has long been prized for its low mineral content, which produces delicate sake. You can sample the water at the numerous free-flowing springs outside of sake breweries—just be sure to bring your own cup or water bottle.

master brewer Masaaki Fujioka ferments his excellent Soukuu sake in just four small tanks, visible through the glass window of the stylish tasting bar. Fujioka specializes in full-flavored, pure-rice *junmai* brews. The *nama-zake* (un-pasteurized sake) is a lovely green-tinged amber hue. ⏱ 30 min. 672-1 Imamachi, Fushimi-ku. ☎ 075/611-4666. www.sookuu.net. Free admission, sake from ¥420. Thurs–Tues 11:30am–5:30pm. Train: Fushimi-Momoyama Station.

5 ★ **Kizakura Kappa Country.** This brewing complex has both sake- and beer-making facilities, as well as a restaurant, nice gardens, and a small gallery dedicated to the mischievous, sake-related water sprite, the *kappa*. ⏱ 20 min. 228 Shioya-cho, Fushimi-ku. ☎ 075/611-9921. Free. Daily 11:30am–9:30pm (Sat–Sun until 10pm). Train: Chushojima Station.

BREW OF THE GODS

Making—and consuming—sake is part of
Japanese culture **BY MELINDA JOE**

SAKE, THE DELECTABLY INTOXICATING DRINK MADE FROM RICE AND WATER,
is Japan's national tipple. The roots of sake—or *nihonshu*, as it's called in Japan—go
back over 2,000 years, and the alcoholic concoction is produced in every prefecture
except Kagoshima. Once revered as the drink of the gods, sake is still offered at Shin
to shrines, drunk at weddings, and used for religious ceremonies. Although recently
the beverage has declined in popularity at home, it's been gaining new fans across
the globe. Today's consumers are spoiled for choice: Varieties abound and, thanks to
advances in technology, the quality of sake has never been better.

How to Enjoy Sake

ON ITS OWN
Highly aromatic, often sweet (and expensive) *daiginjos* (premium sakes) are great drunk solo as aperitifs.

AT DIFFERENT TEMPERATURES
Match the temperature of the sake to the temperature of the dish.

WITH DESSERT
Dark, earthy *koshu* (aged sake) is lovely at the end of the meal. Try it with chocolate or cheese.

TAKE BABY SIPS
Many department stores and some specialty shops offer sake tasting for free or a small fee.

Myths About Sake

SAKE IS ALWAYS DRUNK HOT
While some brews are intended to be served warm, many premium sakes are best served chilled. The plonk you first tried in the '80s was probably heated to make it go down easier.

SAKE CAUSES HANGOVERS
Don't blame the sake! Any alcohol, when drunk to excess, will cause a hangover. Sake's alcohol content is usually between 14% and 18%, which is closer to wine than whiskey.

SAKE ONLY GOES WITH SUSHI
Sake is an infinitely food-friendly drink. With its slight sweetness and high *umami* (savoriness) content, it pairs well with any cuisine.

The Brewing Process

1. POLISHING
Sake is the world's most labor-intensive brewed beverage. The process begins by milling the rice to remove part of the outer grain, which contains undesirable fats and proteins. The polishing rate determines the grades of sake (p. 171): The lower the rate, the higher the grade.

2. STEEPING AND STEAMING
The polished rice is rinsed and then soaked briefly to absorb water before steaming, which is done in a large vessel called a *koshiki.*

3. *KOJI* MAKING
Koji is steamed rice onto which a mold called *Aspergillus oryzae,* or *koji-kin,* has been individually propagated in order to break the starch molecules into sugars. Most brewers agree that this is the most important step in the sake-making process.

It takes about 2 days and is done in a special room with higher-than-average temperature and humidity.

4. YEAST STARTER
Rice, water, and *koji* are combined with yeast in a small tank, and a high concentration of yeast cells develops over the course of about 2 weeks.

5. FERMENTATION
The yeast starter is transferred to a larger tank and rice, water, and *koji* are added three more times. Fermentation takes 18 to 32 days. During this period for super-premium *ginjo-* and *daiginjo*-grade sake, the *toji* (master brewer) may actually stay at the brewery and sacrifice sleep.

6. PRESSING
This step may be done with a large steel machine or a wooden press; in some cases, the sake is allowed to drip out of cotton bags into jugs. The sake is left to age, and then may be pasteurized, microfiltered, diluted, and/or fortified before bottling.

Zen Palate

Kyoto is the spiritual home of *shojin-ryori,* Zen Buddhist monk cuisine. This elaborate style of vegetarian cooking originated in China but flourished here, and there are several places on (or near) temple grounds where you can dine overlooking peaceful gardens. Here are the best places to eat, pray, and meditate.

> *Feed your body and soul with Kyoto's famous* shojin-ryori, *traditional monk food. Who knew virtue could be this delicious?*

START Take the train to Arashiyama Station.

① ★★★ **Shigetsu.** Contemplate Zen as you dine on an array of subtle dishes based on tofu, *yuba* (creamy tofu skin), and vegetables. Situated by the carp-filled garden pond on the grounds of Tenryu-ji (p. 252, **①**), Shigetsu offers satisfying set lunches served on red lacquer trays. 68 Susukinobaba-cho, Saga Tenryu-ji, inside Tenryu-ji complex. ☎ 075/882-9725. Set lunches from ¥3,000. AE, DC, MC, V. Daily 11am–2pm. Train: Arashiyama Station.

② ★★ **Seigenin.** The specialty at this restaurant, located on the grounds of Ryoan-ji (p. 250, **④**), is *yudofu,* boiled tofu and vegetables topped with seven herbs. You can order it alone or as part of a set meal with several small side dishes. It's not the fancy, multi-course gastronomic experience you can find at other *shojin-ryori* restaurants, but Seigenin affords lovely views (especially in the fall) of the maple and pine groves from its tatami-mat dining room. Ryoan-ji Goronoshitacho 13,

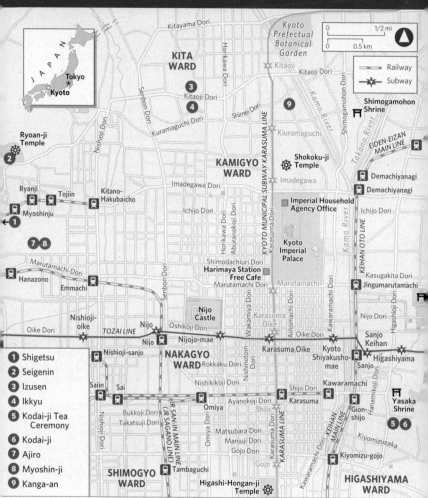

1 Shigetsu
2 Seigenin
3 Izusen
4 Ikkyu
5 Kodai-ji Tea Ceremony
6 Kodai-ji
7 Ajiro
8 Myoshin-ji
9 Kanga-an

inside Ryoan-ji complex, near Kyoyoike pond. ☎ 075/462-4742. Set lunches from ¥1,500. No credit cards. Daily 10am–5pm. Bus: 59 to Ryoan-ji-mae.

3 ★★ **Izusen** (泉仙). The dishes at this famous *shojin-ryori* restaurant in Daitoku-ji (p. 251, **7**) are delicately flavored and tastefully presented in a long series of small lacquered bowls. The meal begins with a sip of sweet *umeshu* (plum liqueur), served in a dainty glass cup. Although the interior is far from luxurious, the tatami-mat dining area looks out onto Daiji-in garden. Murasakino Daitokujicho 4, inside

Daitoku-ji complex, by Daiji-in. ☎ 075/491-6665. www.kyoto-izusen.com. Set lunches from ¥3,000. No credit cards. Daily 11am–4pm. Bus: 205 to Daitokuji-mae.

4 ★★ **Ikkyu.** Just outside of the gate of Daitoku-ji (p. 251, **7**), Ikkyu has been serving expertly prepared *shojin-ryori* lunches and early dinners since it opened in the 15th century. Murasakino Daitokuji-mae 20. ☎ 075/493-0019. www.daitokuji-ikkyu.jp. Set lunch from ¥4,000, set dinners from ¥8,000. No credit cards. Daily noon–6pm. Bus: 205 to Daitokuji-mae.

> Early morning at Kodai-ji temple.

⑤ ★★ Kodai-ji Tea Ceremony. *Chado* or *cha-no-yu*, Japanese tea ceremony, is highly ritualized and carefully choreographed; it is a meditation on harmony with nature and self-cultivation. The tea itself is thick, frothy, and alarmingly bitter, but that's not the point. Kodai-ji regularly offers *chado* in a tatami-mat-covered tearoom on the temple grounds. Special events, which may include several rounds of tea and *tenshin* (traditional snacks), are held monthly. Reservations are required for all *chado*; call the temple for more information. Kodai-ji Temple, Yasakatorii-mae Sagaru, Shimo-kawaramachi, Higashiyama-ku. ☎ 075/561-9966. Basic ceremony ¥2,000 per person. Bus: 206 to Higashiyama Yasui.

⑥ ★★★ Kodai-ji (高台寺). In 1605, Kita-no-Mandokoro (also known as Nene), the widow of Toyotomi Hideyoshi, built this temple to pacify the spirit of her late husband. The grounds feature beautifully landscaped gardens laid out by Kobori Enshu and teahouses designed by tea master Sen no Rikyu. Wooden images of the couple stand in the memorial hall. In the evenings, special illuminations are scheduled on the grounds during the spring, summer, and fall. Check the website (in Japanese only), or the

Buddhist Soul Food

Shojin-ryori arrived in Japan along with Zen Buddhism in the 13th century. Often called the "food of devotion," this labor-intensive style of cooking eschews meat and fish and relies heavily on seasonal vegetables, wheat gluten, and soy products. Tofu appears in various forms—*koyadofu* (freeze-dried), *abura-age* (deep-fried), and as thin sheets of *yuba* (tofu skin).

Buddhist temple food is about more than avoiding animal products. The hard-core *shojin-ryori* chefs chant sutras while they cook: It's as much about nourishing the soul as it is about nourishing the body.

When preparing these elaborate feasts, they take pains to incorporate the five tastes (sweet, bitter, salty, sour, and a more abstract idea that translates loosely as "delicate"), five colors (red, yellow, green, black, and white), and five cooking methods (steaming, frying, boiling, grilling, and serving raw). The limited range of ingredients forces chefs to be as creative as possible.

For a taste, the *fucha-ryori* at ★★ **Kanga-an,** on the grounds of Kanga-an temple (see below), may be more of a draw than the temple itself. The lavish meal costs ¥15,000 and consists of no fewer than 10 courses (with multiple cups of thick green tea)—yet no two bites are the same. Munch on these delicate morsels amid a tranquil setting overlooking a beautifully sculpted moss and gravel garden. Hidden beyond the main hall is a sweet little bar, formerly reserved as a private salon for guests of the priestess. Reservations required.

Azaleas in bloom at Myoshin-ji.

yoto Tourist Information Center (p. 277) or exact times. ⏱ 30 min. Yasakatorii-mae agaru, Shimo-kawaramachi, Higashiyama-u. ☎ 075/561-9966. www.kodaiji.com. ¥600 dults, ¥250 kids. Daily 9am–5pm. Bus: 206 to Higashiyama Yasui.

⑦ ★★★ **Ajiro** (あじろ). This Michelin-starred estaurant serves some of the most refined *hojin-ryori* in Kyoto. The owners of Ajiro had een catering the vegetarian banquets at earby Myoshin-ji for years before they decid-d to open a restaurant for the general public. et lunches are served in elegant lacquered ento boxes, set before you on low individual ables. 7 Hananozono-teranomae-cho, Hana-ono. ☎ 075/463-0221. www.ajiro-s.co.jp. Set unches from ¥3,000, set dinners from ¥10,000. hurs–Tues 11am–7pm. Train: Hanazono Station.

③ ★★ **Myoshin-ji** (妙心寺). Founded in 1338 y Kanzan Egen, this vast Rinzai Zen Bud-hist temple complex boasts a splendid arden, designed by landscape master Kano Motonobu. Don't miss the impressive *sumi-e*

charcoal paintings in the Hatto Dharma hall, where you stroll under the watchful eyes of a dragon painted on the ceiling. The impressive wooden Yokushitsu, a bathhouse complete with a steam room dating from the 17th cen-tury, may put you in the mood for a soak. The temple also offers Zen meditation lessons on Saturdays and Sundays (check website for times) for ¥2,000. 64 Myoshinjicho, Hanazono, Ukyo-ku. ☎ 075/463-3121. www.myoshinji.or.jp. Grounds free, ¥500 for entrance to subtemples. Daily 9am–5pm. Bus: 10 to Myoshinji-mae.

⑨ ★★ **Kanga-an** (閑臥庵). Built in the 17th century at the request of retired emperor Go Mizuno, this small temple in southern Kyoto is dedicated to Chintakurefushin, the Holy Spirit of Residental Protection. Kanga-an houses royal artifacts belonging to Go Mizuno, such as the former emperor's crown and cushion seat. ⏱ 20 min. 278 Karasuma Dori, Kuruma-guchi Higashi Iru. ☎ 075/256-2480. www.kangaan.jp. ¥500. Daily 3pm–10pm. Subway: Karasuma Kuramaguchi Station.

Kyoto Restaurant Best Bets

Best Upscale Bento
Hyotei, 35 Kusakawa-cho, Nanzen-ji (see p. 265)

Best Chicken Sashimi
Inaseya, 93 Aburayacho, Sanjo-sagaru (see p. 265)

Best Kyoto-Style Sushi
Izuju, 292-1 Kitagawa, Gionmachi (see p. 265)

Best Expense-Account *Kaiseki* Splurge
Kitcho Arashiyama, 55 Susukinobaba-cho, Tenryu-ji (see p. 266)

Best Budget French
Le Bouchon, 71-1 Enoki-cho, Nijo-sagaru, Tera-machi Dori (see p. 266)

Best Quick Noodle Lunch
Omen, Gokomachi Dori, Shijo-agaru (see p. 268)

Best Sake Bar
Sake Bar Asakura, Daikyu Bldg. 2F, 518-2 Kamiosaka-cho (see p. 269)

Best Kyoto-Style Ramen
Takaraya Ramen, 122-5 Ishiyacho, Nakagyo-k (see p. 269)

Best French *Kaiseki*
Takumi Okumura, 570-6 Gion-cho, Minami-Gawa (see p. 269)

Best Tempura
Tempura Yoshikawa, Tominoko-ji Dori, Oike-sagaru (see p. 269)

Best *Teppanyaki*
Teppan Kappo Sou, Onishi Bldg. II 1F, Nishino-cho 216-2, Nawate Dori (see p. 269)

Best *Sumibiyaki* Charcoal Grill
Touzan, 644-2 Sanjusangendo-mawari, Higashiyama-ku (see p. 269)

> Have a sublime bento at Hyotei—a far cry from the box lunches typically found at convenience stores.

Kyoto Restaurants A to Z

Ashoka CENTRAL KYOTO *INDIAN*
One of Kyoto's most popular and longest-running Indian restaurants, in business more than 20 years, serves vegetarian and meat curries prepared by Indian chefs, including mutton, chicken, fish, vegetable, and shrimp selections, as well as tandoori. Kikusui Bldg. 3F, 559 Teramachi Dori, Shijo-agaru. ☎ 075/241-1318. Entrees from ¥1,500. AE, DC, MC, V. Lunch & dinner daily. Bus: 4 or 205 to Shijo Kawaramchi.

★★ Hyotei (瓢亭) EASTERN KYOTO *KAISEKI/ BENTO* This 300-year-old restaurant first opened its doors as a teahouse to serve pilgrims and visitors on their way to Nanzen-ji Temple. Today it consists of two parts: one that offers expensive, exquisite *kaiseki,* which originated with the tea ceremony but is now associated with Kyoto cooking, and an annex offering seasonal bento lunch boxes. The *kaiseki* meals are served by kimono-clad women in tiny houses situated around a beautiful garden with a pond, maple trees, and bushes. Reservations are required for *kaiseki.* 35 Kusakawa-cho, Nanzen-ji. ☎ 075/771-4116. www.hyotei.co.jp. Kaiseki lunches from ¥23,000, kaiseki dinners from ¥27,000,

bento from ¥5,000. AE, DC, MC, V. Kaiseki daily 11am–7:30pm; bento boxes Fri–Wed noon–4pm; closed 2nd and 4th Tues of every month. Subway: Keage Station.

★★ Inaseya (いなせや) CENTRAL KYOTO *IZAKAYA* This hidden *izakaya* (brewpub) uses only the choicest free-range chickens for their house specialties, chicken sukiyaki (simmered in a hot pot), and sashimi. The menu also features dishes made with fresh, seasonal vegetables, and sake fans will be spoiled for choice. Japanese-style seating in the front room overlooks a lovely traditional garden. 93 Aburayacho, Sanjo-sagaru. ☎ 075/255-7250. Set meals from ¥4,200. AE, DC, MC, V. Lunch & dinner daily. Subway: Karasuma-Oike Station.

★★★ Izuju (いず重) CENTRAL KYOTO *SUSHI* This charming, century-old sushi shop specializes in Kyoto-style pressed sushi. Their most famous dish is *sabazushi,* mackerel pressed onto rice and covered with a thin layer of seaweed. 292–1 Kitagawa, Gionmachi. ☎ 075/561-0019. Entrees from ¥1,320. AE, DC, MC, V. Lunch & dinner Thurs–Tues. Subway: Gion Shijo Station.

Soak in the romance of Kyoto at one of Pontocho's many restaurants along the river.

> In Kyoto, the concept of omotenashi, or true hospitality, is about more than good service.

★★★ Kitcho Arashiyama (吉兆嵐山) NORTHERN KYOTO KAISEKI

Regarded as Kyoto's most venerable kaiseki restaurant, Kitcho is the pinnacle of refinement. Three-Michelin-starred chef Kunio Tokuoka uses only the freshest premium ingredients to prepare artful kaiseki-ryori, served on antique ceramic dishes, in elegantly appointed rooms overlooking idyllic gardens. It is, however, devastatingly expensive, and you'll need to reserve well in advance. 58 Susukinobaba-cho, Tenryu-ji. ☎ 075/881-1101. www.kitcho.com/kyoto/shoplist_en/arashiyama. Set lunches from ¥36,750, set dinners from ¥42,000. AE, DC, DISC, MC, V. Lunch & dinner daily. Train: Arashiyama Station.

★ Kushi Kura (串くら) CENTRAL KYOTO YAKITORI

Housed in a 100-year-old warehouse with heavy-beamed, dark-polished wood and whitewashed walls, this refined yakitori restaurant serves specially raised chicken grilled over top-grade charcoal, with an English-language menu offering various set meals and a la carte selections. Takakura Dori, Oike-agaru. ☎ 075/213-2211. Set lunches from ¥1,800, set dinners from ¥1,600. AE, DC, MC, V. Lunch & dinner daily. Subway: Karasuma-Oike Station.

★ Le Bouchon CENTRAL KYOTO FRENCH

This casual French bistro is a good choice for uncomplicated, rustic French fare at budget prices. Popular items include standards like the garlicky escargots, pâté, and a substantial dish of steak frites, topped with a disc of herbed butter. The wine list also offers some great bargains. 71-1 Enoki-cho, Nijo-sagaru, Teramachi Dori. ☎ 075/211-5220. www.bellecour.co.jp/bouchon file/bouchon.htm. Set lunches from ¥1,000, set dinners from ¥2,500. No credit cards. Lunch & dinner Fri–Wed. Subway: Sanjo Station.

★ Mikaku (みかく) EASTERN KYOTO TEPPANYAKI

Established almost a century ago, this restaurant on the second floor (with counter seating) and third floor (tatami rooms) of a modern building offers sukiyaki, shabu-shabu (sliced meat or vegetables cooked in a hot pot), oil-yaki (sliced beef cooked on an iron griddle and flavored with soy sauce, lemon, and Japanese radish), and teppanyaki, all made with high-grade Kobe beef. Nawate Dori, Shijo-agaru, Gion. ☎ 075/525-1129. Set meals from ¥10,000. AE, DC, MC, V. Lunch & dinner Mon–Sat. Bus: 100 or 206 to Gion.

★★ Minoko EASTERN KYOTO KAISEKI/BENTO

This former villa is an enclave of traditional Japan with a simple, austere exterior and an interior of winding wooden corridors, tatami rooms, and a garden. Opened nearly 100 years ago by the present owner's father, Minoko does its best to retain the spirit of the tea ceremony, specializing in an elaborate kind of kaiseki dinner called cha-kaiseki, usually served at tea-ceremony gatherings and utilizing seasonal ingredients. Lunch, which is served communally in a large tatami room with a view of a beautiful garden, is more economical and less formal than dinner but still draws on the tea ceremony for inspiration. 480 Kiyoi-cho, Shimogawara Dori, Gion. ☎ 075/561-0328.

Kyoto Restaurants

Ashoka 11
Hyotei 19
Inaseya 7
Izuju 14
Kitcho Arashiyama 2
Kushi Kura 3
Le Bouchon 4
Mikaku 13
Minoko 16
Misoguigawa 9
Okutan 10
Omen 10
Sake Bar Asakura 5
Takaraya Ramen 8
Takumi Okumura 15
Tempura Yoshikawa 6
Teppan Kappo Sou 12
Touzan 17
Yoramu 1

Buddhist Temple
Shinto Shrine
Railway
Subway
Post Office
Tourist Info

Eikando Temple
Nanzen-ji Temple
Shirakawa Dori
Heian Jingu Shrine
Kyoto Handicraft Center
Okazakimichi
Kazahidori Dori
Jingumarutamachi
Kasugakita Dori
Konoe Dori
Higashioji Dori
Ichijo Dori
Kyu Shirakawa Dori
Shoren-in Temple
Yasaka Shrine
Furumonzen Dori
Shinmonzen D.
Maruyama Park
Kiyomizu Temple
Kiyomizuzaka
Sannenzaka
Higashiyama
Canal
Sanjo Keihan
Sanjo
Gion-shijo
Pontocho
Hanamikoji Dori
Kiyomizu-gojo
National Route no. 1
Nioman Dori
Nijo Dori
Kyoto Shiyakusho-mae
Kawaramachi Dori
Kamo River
KEIHAN OTO LINE
Imperial Household Agency Office
Kyoto Imperial Palace
Marutamachi Dori
Tominokoji Dori
Ainomachi Dori
Takakura Dori
Fuyacho Dori
Hinomoto
Kawaramachi
Yamatooji Dori
Honmachi Dori
Shichijo
JR TOKAIDO MAIN LINE (JR KYOTO LINE)
KEIHAN MAIN LINE
Kamo River
Kawaramachi Dori
Oike Dori
Karasuma Oike
KARASUMA LINE
Gojo
Shijo
Karasuma Dori
Kyoto
Shiokoji Dori
Higashi-Honganji Temple
Horikawa Dori
KYOTO MUNICIPAL SUBWAY KARASUMA LINE
Shimodachiuri Dori
Ogawa Dori
Abura nokoji Dori
Horikawa Dori
Ichijo Dori
Harimaya Station Free Cafe
Takeyamachi Dori
Ebisugawa Dori
Wakamiya Dori
Nijo Dori
Nishinotoin Dori
Ryogaemachi Dori
Matsubara Dori
Manjuji Dori
Omiya Dori
Nijo Castle
Nijojo-mae
Sanjo Dori
Rokkaku Dori
Takoyakushi Dori
Nishikikoji Dori
Shijo
Bukkoji Dori
Takatsuji Dori
Gojo Dori
SHIMOGYO WARD
Tambaguchi
NAKAGYO WARD
Aneyakoji Dori
Nijo
Oshikoji Dori
Sai
Senbon Dori
Kitano-Hakubaicho
Nishioji Dori
Ichijo Dori
Marutamachi Dori
Hanazono
Emmachi
Nishiojo-oike
Nishioji-sanjo
Saiin
Nishioji Dori
TOZAI LINE
JR SAN-IN MAIN LINE (JR SAGANO LINE)
UKYO WARD
Oike Dori

0 1/2 mi
0 0.5 km

JAPAN
Tokyo
Kyoto
KYOTO CITY SUBWAY TOZAI LINE
Keage

> Udon *noodles with all the fixin's are on the menu at Omen.*

Mini-kaiseki lunches from ¥10,444, kaiseki dinners from ¥15,697, bento from ¥4,000. AE, DC, MC, V. Lunch & dinner daily; closed irregularly 3 days a month. Bus: 100 or 206 to Gion.

★★ **Misoguigawa** (禊川) CENTRAL KYOTO *FRENCH/KAISEKI* For more than 30 years—long before fusion cuisine burst onto the scene—this lovely restaurant has been serving nouvelle French cuisine that utilizes the best of Japanese style and ingredients. Owner-chef Teruo Inoue trained with a three-star Michelin chef and successfully blends the two cuisines into dishes that are arranged like works of art on Japanese tableware. The chef inquires about allergies and preferences to create your meal. Reservations required. Sanjo-sagaru, Pontocho. ☎ 075/221-2270. www.misogui.jp. Set lunches from ¥4,725, set dinners from ¥12,600. AE, DC, MC, V. Lunch & dinner Tues-Sun. Bus: 5 or 205 to Kawaramachi Sanjo.

★★★ **Okutan** (奥丹) EASTERN KYOTO *TOFU/VEGETARIAN* Founded about 350 years ago as a vegetarian restaurant serving Buddhist monks, this thatched-roof wooden retreat in a peaceful setting with pond and garden serves just two things: *yudofu* (a tofu set meal) and a more traditional tofu meal originally from China. Reservations are recommended (but not accepted in peak season). 86-30 Fukuchi-cho, Nanzen-ji. ☎ 075/771-8709. Yudofu set meal ¥3,150, traditional tofu meal ¥4,200. No credit cards. Lunch daily. Bus: 5 to Nanzen-ji-Eikando-michi.

★ **Omen** (おめん) CENTRAL KYOTO *NOODLES* A casual atmosphere and reasonably priced food make this tiny place popular. *Omen* (vegetable *udon*) is the specialty, and the house's traditional style is to serve the buckwheat noodles in a flat wooden bowl, the sauce in a pottery bowl, the vegetables delicately rranged on a handmade platter with a bowl f sesame seeds alongside. Gokomachi Dori, hijo-agaru. ☎ 075/255-2125. Set meals from ¥1,650. MC, V. Lunch & dinner Fri–Wed. Subway: hijo Station.

★★ **Sake Bar Asakura** (日本酒バーあさくら) CEN-RAL KYOTO PUB This hidden sake specialist erves fresh, premium brews, hand-picked by nowledgeable (and English-speaking) owner Yoshihito Asakura, in a casual, relaxed set-ing. The menu features light bar snacks (but no large plates); try some of the eye-opening ake and cheese pairings. Daikyu Bldg. 2F, 518-Kamiosaka-cho. ☎ 075/212-4417. Sake from ¥700. No credit cards. Dinner & late night Wed–Mon. Subway: Karasuma-Oike Station.

★★ **Takaraya Ramen** (宝屋ラーメン) CENTRAL KYOTO NOODLES This bustling ramen-ya noodle shop) on picturesque Pontocho serves teaming bowls of Kyoto-style ramen that re subtle in style but satisfyingly complex in lavor. The house specialty is sumashi ramen, oodles topped with deep-fried burdock root nd tiny cubes of mozzarella cheese. 122-5 shiyacho, Nakagyo-ku. ☎ 075/222-2778. www. akaraya.info. Ramen from ¥680. No credit ards. Dinner daily; lunch & dinner Sat–Sun. ubway: Sanjo Station.

★★ **Takumi Okumura** (匠奥村) CENTRAL KYOTO FRENCH/KAISEKI Nestled amid the postcard-perfect backstreets of Gion, this ophisticated eatery fuses modern French nd Japanese kaiseki cuisines together el-gantly. Chef Naoki Okumura uses Japanese produce to create inventive dishes that are rtfully presented on lovely dishes adorned vith delicate plant motifs. The space is a tran-quil haven of clean lines, wood, and polished urfaces that blend tradition and contem-porary design. Reservations recommended. 70-6 Gion-cho, Minami-Gawa. ☎ 075/541-2205. www.restaurant-okumura.com/takumi/nglish. Set lunches from ¥6,500, set dinners rom ¥15,000. AE, DC, MC, V. Lunch & dinner Ved–Mon. Subway: Shijo Station.

★★ **Tempura Yoshikawa** CENTRAL KYOTO EMPURA If you're hungering for tempura, his restaurant has a sign in English and is easy o find. The tempura counter, where you can vatch the chefs prepare delicate deep-fried

morsels, seats only 12. Meals served in tatami rooms, with views of an expansive garden (lit at night), are more expensive. Reserva-tions required. Tominokoji Dori, Oike-sagaru. ☎ 075/221-5544. Set lunches from ¥3,000, set dinners from ¥6,000. AE, DC, MC, V. Lunch & dinner Mon–Sat. Subway: Karasuma Oike Station.

★★ **Teppan Kappo Sou** (鉄板割烹爽) EASTERN KYOTO TEPPANYAKI Located in the heart of the Gion district, this intimate, counter-only restaurant specializes in teppanyaki—various ingredients (especially beef) grilled on a wide, hot iron griddle right before your eyes. The thickly marbled wagyu (Kobe) beef at Sou is top quality, and the English-speaking owner/chef is friendly and accommodating. Their meibutsu katsu sandwiches, deep-fried wagyu cutlets brushed with tangy sauce between white bread, are a local favorite. Onishi Bldg. II 1F, Nishino-cho 216-2, Nawate Dori Shinbashi-agaru. ☎ 075/551-4515. Set lunches from ¥2,500, set dinners from ¥8,400. AE, MC, V. Lunch & dinner Mon–Sat. Subway: Sanjo Station.

★★★ **Touzan** EASTERN KYOTO JAPANESE Modeled after a traditional Kyoto home but with innovative interior designs, Touzan offers views of a traditional rock garden and special-izes in expertly prepared sumibiyaki (meat or vegetables cooked on a charcoal grill). It also serves kaiseki and sushi. Hyatt Regency Kyoto, 644-2 Sanjusangendo-mawari, Higashiyama-ku. ☎ 075/541-1234. Set lunches from ¥2,000, set dinners from ¥6,000. AE, DC, MC, V. Lunch & dinner Tues–Sun. Bus: 100 or 206 to Hakubutsu-kan Sanjusangendo.

★★ **Yoramu** CENTRAL KYOTO PUB Israeli owner Yoram Ofer serves an impressive selection of limited-edition brews and aged sake at this sophisticated and intimate sake pub. If you're unsure of what to order, don't worry: Yoram is always happy to make recom-mendations. The food menu features a small but nicely prepared selection of light dishes, such as fried lotus root chips, halloumi cheese, and Yoram's homemade soba noodles. Nijodo-ri Higashinotoin Higashi-iru. ☎ 075/213-1512. www.sakebar-yoramu.com/about_eng.html. Sake from ¥1,000. No credit cards. Dinner Wed–Sat. Subway: Karasuma-Oike Station.

Kyoto Hotel Best Bets

Best City-View Public Bathing
Aranvert Hotel Kyoto, 179 Higashi Kazatiya-cho, Gojo Dori (see p. 271)

Most Romantic
Hiiragiya Ryokan, Nakahakusancho, Fuyacho Anekoji-agaru (see p. 271)

Most Convenient Location
Hotel Granvia Kyoto, JR Kyoto Station, central exit (see p. 272)

Best Boutique Hotel
Hotel Mume, 261 Shinmonzen Dori, Umemoto-cho (see p. 272)

Best Contemporary Luxury
Hyatt Regency Kyoto, 644-2 Sanjusangendo-mawari (see p. 272)

Most Affordable Old-World Charm
Iori *machiya*, various locations (see p. 275)

Best Room with a View
Kyoto Hotel Okura, Kawaramachi Dori, Oike (see p. 272)

Best Budget *Ryokan*
Matsubaya Ryokan, Higashinotoin Nishi, Kamijuzuyamachi Dori (see p. 272)

Warmest Welcome
Naoshiki Inn, Agaru Imadegawa Nashinoki Dor (see p. 274)

Best Designer Capsule Hotel
9H Nine Hours, 588 Teianmaeno-cho, Shijo (see p. 274)

Best Contemporary Cool
The Screen, 640-1 Shimogoryomae-cho (see p. 274)

Best Traditional Luxury
Tawaraya, 278 Nakahakusan-cho (see p. 274)

Best for Families
Westin Miyako, Keago, Sanjo (see p. 275)

> *Rest easy on the "Heavenly Beds" at the Westin Miyako.*

Kyoto Hotels A to Z

★★ ANA Hotel Kyoto CENTRAL KYOTO
Across the street from Nijojo (p. 248, ❷),
this hotel has small but attractive rooms with
castle views, and one of the flashiest lobby
lounges in town. Note that none of the singles
face the castle. Nijojo-mae, Horikawa Dori.
☎ 075/231-1155. www.ana-hkyoto.com. 298
units. Doubles ¥24,255–¥34,650. AE, DC, MC,
V. Subway: Nijojo-mae Station.

★ Aranvert Hotel Kyoto CENTRAL KYOTO
Halfway between Kyoto Station and central
downtown, this hotel offers functional, spotless rooms. There's a public bath on the 13th
floor with fantastic panoramic views, great for
relaxing at the end of a long day. 179 Higashi
Azariya-cho, Gojo Dori. ☎ 075/365-511. www.
aranvert.co.jp. 183 units. Doubles ¥15,015–
¥34,650. AE, DC, MC, V. Subway: Gojo Station.

★ Budget Inn KYOTO STATION
This comfortable, family-run *ryokan* (traditional inn) offers six tatami rooms and two
spacious dorm rooms with beds that sleep up
to five guests (good for families). All of the
rooms come with private bathrooms, and the
friendly, English-speaking staff is extremely

accommodating. Great choice in this price
range. 295 Aburano-koji. ☎ 075/344-1510.
www.budgetinnjp.com. 8 units. Dorm rooms
¥2,500 per person, triples ¥10,980. No credit
cards. Train: Kyoto Station.

★★★ Hiiragiya Ryokan CENTRAL KYOTO
This venerable *ryokan* in the heart of old Kyoto
offers the ultimate in Japanese-style living,
with a kind staff and beautifully decorated
traditional rooms. Built in 1818, Hiiragiya is a
haven of simple design that makes artful use
of wood, bamboo, and stone. Each room is
unique, outfitted with art and antiques, and
most also come with lovely cypress baths.
Dinners are delicious, multicourse *kaiseki*
feasts. Nakahakusancho, Fuyacho Anekoji-
agaru. ☎ 075/221-1136. www.hiiragiya.co.jp. 28
units. Doubles ¥30,000–¥90,000 per person.
Rates include 2 meals. AE, DC, MC, V. Subway:
Kyoto Shiyakusho-mae Station.

★ Hiraiwa Ryokan KYOTO STATION
This friendly, family-run inn has been welcoming guests from around the world since 1973.
The tatami rooms are modest but spotlessly
maintained. Shower and bathing facilities are

Check out Nijojo castle from the ANA Hotel Kyoto.

> *You're guaranteed a warm welcome at Hiraiwa Ryokan near Kyoto Station.*

limited and toilet stalls are unisex, affording little privacy for the shy. 314 Hayao-cho, Kaminoguchi-agaru, Ninomiyacho Dori. ☎ 075/351-6748. www.kyoto-ryokanhiraiwa.com/en/index.html. 18 units, none with bathroom. Doubles ¥8,400–¥9,450. AE, MC, V. Bus: 17 or 205 to Kawaramachi-Shomen.

★★ Hotel Granvia Kyoto KYOTO STATION
Kyoto's most conveniently located hotel is atop the futuristic-looking Kyoto Station. Rooms are large and well appointed, and a guest-relations desk helps with everything from sightseeing to restaurant reservations. The least expensive rooms have limited views, so opt for the rooms on higher floors. JR Kyoto Station, Central exit, Karasuma Dori Shiokoji-sagaru. ☎ 075/344-8888. www.granviakyoto.com. 535 units. Doubles ¥23,100–¥34,650. AE, DC, MC, V. Train: Kyoto Station.

★★★ Hotel Mume EASTERN KYOTO
The bright red door of this otherwise unassuming building opens onto Kyoto's best boutique hotel. Located on a quiet street in Gion, the stylishly appointed Hotel Mume blends luxurious textiles and antiques from all over the world into its modern design. The helpful, English-speaking staff is happy to recommend restaurants and assist with reservations. 261 Shinmonzen Dori, Umemoto-cho. ☎ 075/525-8787. www.hotelmume.com. 7 units. Doubles ¥23,100–¥47,250. AE, DC, MC, V. Bus: 206 to Chionin-mae.

★★★ Hyatt Regency Kyoto EASTERN KYOTO
This sumptuous designer gem in Higashiyama combines traditional materials and contemporary style. Occupying the former residence of Emperor Goshirakawa, it also has a beautiful 850-year-old garden, complete with waterfall and pond, visible from the restaurants and some of its rooms. Eight stunningly appointed deluxe rooms have Japanese bathtubs next to the balconies, with beautiful views. Its spa offers more Asian treatments than any other in Japan. 644–2 Sanjusangendo-mawari. ☎ 075/541-1234. www.hyattregencykyoto.com. 189 units. Doubles ¥22,000–¥43,000. AE, DC, MC, V. Bus: 206 to Hakubutsukan Sanjusanendo.

★★★ Kyoto Hotel Okura CENTRAL KYOTO
First built in 1888, one of Kyoto's oldest hotels underwent a complete metamorphosis in 1994 and is now the city's tallest building, with 17 floors. The lobby exudes an elegant 1920s ambiance, while rooms are spacious and tastefully appointed. The best views are of the Kamo River, especially from the most expensive rooms on upper floors that also take in the hills of Higashiyama-ku beyond the city. Kawaramachi Dori, Oike. ☎ 075/211-5111. www.kyotohotel.co.jp. 322 units. Doubles ¥31,185–¥56,595. AE, DC, MC, V. Subway: Kyoto Shiyakusho-mae Station.

★★★ Matsubaya Ryokan (松葉屋旅館) KYOTO STATION
First opened in 1885 and completely rebuilt in 2008, this inn is a star in its category. Fourteen rooms are Japanese-style, with the best rooms overlooking a garden, while six Western-style rooms, all on the fifth floor, are actually apartments complete with kitchenettes, miniature balconies, free Internet, and

Kyoto Hotels

Legend

- Buddhist Temple
- Shinto Shrine
- Railway
- Subway
- Post Office
- Tourist Info

Map labels

JAPAN

Tokyo
Kyoto

Kiuramaguchi

Shokoku-ji Temple

KAMIGYO WARD

Imadegawa

Demachiyanagi
Demachiyanagi

Imadegawa Dori

Imperial Household Agency Office

Ichijo Dori

Ichijo Dori

Kyu Shirakawa Dori

Konoe Dori

Yoshidadhon Dori

Okazakimichi

Kyoto Imperial Palace

Kamo River

Takano River

KYOTO MUNICIPAL SUBWAY KARASUMA LINE

KEIHAN OTO LINE

Kasugakita Dori

Kyoto Handicraft Center

Heian Jingu Shrine

Jingumarutamachi

Harimaya Station Free Cafe

Horikawa Dori
Aburanokoji Dori
Ogawa Dori

Shimodachiuri Dori

Marutamachi Dori

Marutamachi
Takeyamachi Dori

Karasuma-Dori

Marutamachi Dori

Nijo Dori

Ebisugawa Dori

Nijo Castle

Nijo Dori

Karasuma Oike

Nioman Dori

Sanjo Keihan

Higashiyama

Canal

ishikoji Dori

AKAGYO WARD

Oike Dori

Nijojo-mae

Karasuma Oike

Aneyakoji Dori

Sanjo Dori

Rokkaku Dori

Wakamiya

Muromachi Dori

Ainomachi Dori
Sakaimachi Dori
Tominokoji Dori
Gokomachi Dori

Kyoto Shiyakusho-mae

Sanjo

Keage

Shoren-in Temple

Furumonzen Dori

Shinmonzen Dori

Takoyakushi Dori

Nishikikoji Dori

Nishinotoin Dori
Koromonodana Dori
Ryogaemachi Dori

Higashinotoin Dori
Takakura Dori
Yanaginobanba Dori
Fuyacho Dori
Teramachi Dori

Pontocho Dori

Nawate Dori

Hanamikoji Dori

Yasaka Shrine

Maruyama Park

Omiya

Shijo Dori

Ayanokoji Dori

Karasuma

Shijo

Kawaramachi

Gion-shijo

Sannenzaka

Bukkoji Dori

Takatsuji Dori

Matsubara Dori

Manjuji Dori

KARASUMA LINE

Hinomoto Dori

KEIHAN MAIN LINE

Higashiyama Dori

Kiyomizuzaka

Kiyomizu Temple

Gojo Dori

Gojo

Kyoto Dori

Kiyomizu-gojo

Yamatooji Dori

Gojozaka

HIGASHIYAMA WARD

Higashi-Hongan-ji Temple

Omiya Dori

Horikawa Dori

Karasuma Dori

Kawaramachi Dori

Kamo River

Honnachi Dori

National Route no. 1

Shichijo Dori

Shichijo

Sanjusangendo Hall

JR TOKAIDO MAIN LINE (JR KYOTO LINE)

Shiokoji Dori

Kyoto

Kyoto

Hachijo Dori

JR NARA LINE

0   1/2 mi
0   0.5 km

> Tea for two at the elegant Sumiya Ryokan.

free use of the laundry facilities. It's owned and operated by the delightful Hiyashi family. Higashinotoin Nishi, Kamijuzuyamachi Dori. ☎ 075/351-3727. www.matsubayainn.com. 20 units, 18 with bathroom. Doubles ¥12,180–¥15,120. AE, MC, V. Subway: Kyoto Station.

★ Nashinoki Inn NORTHERN KYOTO
In a quiet, peaceful neighborhood north of the Kyoto Imperial Palace, this *ryokan* has been run since 1970 by a warm and friendly elderly couple that speaks some English. It's like living with a Japanese family, as the home looks very lived-in and is filled with the personal belongings of a lifetime. Bathrooms are communal and breakfast is served in your room. Agaru Imadegawa Nashinoki Dori. ☎ 075/241-1543. www.nande.com/nashinoki. 6 units, none with bathroom. Doubles from ¥10,100. Breakfast ¥945–¥1,050 extra. No credit cards. Subway: Imadegawa Station.

★★ 9H Nine Hours CENTRAL KYOTO
Opened in 2009, Nine Hours is the world's first designer capsule hotel. After checking in and showering in the gender-segregated bathrooms, guests climb into sleek, molded plastic pods equipped with hotel-quality beds and an ingenious computer-controlled lighting system invented by Panasonic. With its clean lines and überminimalist interior, the hotel has proven to be a hit with adventure-seeking, jet-set hipsters, but give it a pass if you're claustrophobic. 588 Teianmaeno-cho, Shijo. ☎ 075/353-9005. www.9hours.jp. 125 capsules. Single from ¥4,900 per person. AE, DC, MC, V. Subway: Hankyu Kawaramachi.

★★ The Screen CENTRAL KYOTO
Each of the cool, contemporary interiors of this stylish boutique hotel's 13 rooms was done by a different designer. Two Japanese-style rooms, for example, have futons on raised platforms along with black lacquered furniture, while another has a playful forest motif and yet another is lined with sheer white curtains. Unique and artistic. 640–1 Shimogoryomae-cho. ☎ 075/252-1113. 13 units. Doubles ¥27,000–¥45,000. AE, DC, MC, V. Subway: Karasuma Marutamachi Station.

★★★ Sumiya CENTRAL KYOTO
This centrally located *ryokan* is known for its attentive service, elegant surroundings, and fabulous *kaiseki* meals. (The unique wine list features exclusively Austrian wines.) A tea ceremony is performed after dinner twice a month. Sanjo-sagaru, Fuyacho. ☎ 075/221-2188. www.sumiya.ne.jp. 23 units, 17 with bathroom. Doubles ¥35,000–¥65,000 per person. Rates include 2 meals. AE, DC, MC, V. Subway: Kyoto Shiyakusho-mae Station.

★★★ Tawaraya CENTRAL KYOTO
Across the street from the Hiiragiya (see above) is another distinguished inn. This one's been owned and operated by the same family since it opened in the first decade of the 1700s. The impeccably appointed rooms all come with private bathrooms, and everything, from the gardens to the exquisite Japanese and Scandinavian furnishings, is perfect. Extremely expensive but worth it. 278 Nakahakusan-cho. ☎ 075/211-5566. 18 units. ¥42,263–¥84,525 per person. Rates include 2 meals. AE, DC, MC, V. Subway: Karasuma-Oike Station.

★ Toyoko Inn Kyoto Shijo-Karasuma CENTRAL KYOTO This popular budget chain in the heart of downtown offers tiny but functional rooms.

The Westin Miyako Hotel has hosted scores of foreign celebrities, from movie stars to royalty.

ere are free domestic phone calls and use of e computers in the lobby. **28 Naginataboko-** o, Shijo Dori, Karasuma-higashi-iru. ☎ 075/ 2-1045. www.toyoko-inn.com. 223 units. Dou- es from ¥8,820. Rates include breakfast. AE, C, MC, V. Subway: Shijo-Karasuma Station.

he Old-World Charm f Iori Machiya

 you're looking for unique Kyoto experi- nce, try staying in a refurbished tradi- onal *machiya* (p. 426). These wooden wn houses, originally used as both com- ercial and residential spaces, have been pidly disappearing due to development. unded in 2004, the **Iori group** (www. yoto-machiya.com/eng) gives visitors e chance to stay in a beautifully restored *achiya*, complete with all the amenities of modern hotel. The company has 10 prop- ties around the city. Check website for etails. Doubles start at ¥27,000.

★★★ 🔲 **Westin Miyako** EASTERN KYOTO
Built in 1890, this vast luxury hotel has hosted celebs from Queen Elizabeth II to Ted Kenne- dy. Rooms are tastefully appointed, and those on the fifth floor have great views overlooking the valley. There's a Japanese garden, and families will appreciate the indoor and outdoor pools and the small playroom equipped with billiards, video games, and an activity corner just for toddlers. **Keage, Sanjo.** ☎ 075/771-7111. www.westinmiyako-kyoto.com. 501 units. Dou- bles ¥33,500–¥59,000. AE, DC, MC, V. Subway: Keage Station.

★ **Yoshikawa Inn** CENTRAL KYOTO
Known for its tempura, this inn has quaint tatami rooms, some of which look out on a lovely garden. **Tominokoji Dori Oike-sagaru.** ☎ 075/211-5544. 8 units. Doubles from ¥32,400–¥66,000 per person. Rates include 2 meals. AE, DC, MC, V. Subway: Karasuma Oike.

Kyoto Fast Facts

Arriving & Getting Around

BY PLANE From **Kansai International Airport** (KIX) outside of Osaka, the **JR Super Express Haruka** train has direct service every 30 minutes to Kyoto station. The trip takes approximately 75 minutes (¥3,490 for a reserved seat, recommended during busy departure times or peak season; ¥2,980 for an unreserved seat; free with your JR Rail Pass). A cheaper, though slower and less convenient, alternative is the **JR Kanku Kaisoku,** which departs every 30 minutes or so from Kansai Airport and arrives in Kyoto 100 minutes later, with a change at Osaka Station (¥1,830). If you have lots of luggage, consider taking the **Kansai Airport Limousine Bus** (☎ 075/682-4400; www.kate.co.jp) from Kansai Airport; buses depart every hour (¥2,300). More convenient but costlier is **Yasaka Kansai Airport Shuttle** (☎ 075/803-4800; www.yasaka.jp/english), which provides transportation from the Kansai airport to any hotel or home in Kyoto (¥3,500, including one suitcase); reservations for this are required two days in advance. From **Itami Airport,** the airport has a bus that runs approximately every 20 minutes (¥1,280). **BY TRAIN** Kyoto is a major stop on the **Tokaido and San-yo Shinkansen bullet train** lines; trip time from **Tokyo** is 2½ hours, with the fare for an unreserved seat ¥12,710 one-way if you don't have a rail pass. Kyoto is only 20 minutes from Shin-Osaka Station in **Osaka,** but you may find it more convenient to take one of the local commuter lines that connect Kyoto directly with Osaka Station. From **Kobe,** you can reach Kyoto from Sannomiya and Motomachi stations on local JR trains. **Kyoto Station** is connected to the rest of the city by subway and bus. **BY BUS** Lots of buses travel between Tokyo and Kyoto; reservations are necessary. **JR Highway buses** (☎ 03/3516-1950; www.jrbuskanto.co.jp) depart from Tokyo Station's Yaesu south exit four times daily (with a stop at Shinjuku Station), arriving at Kyoto Station approximately 8 hours later (¥6,000). There are also three JR Dream Highway night buses (including one only for women) that depart Tokyo Station between 10 and 11:10pm, arriving in Kyoto early the next morning (¥8,180). Cheaper still are JR's Seishun Dream buses that depar Tokyo Station at 10pm and Shinjuku Station at 11:10pm, arriving at Kyoto at 5:41am and 7:21am respectively (¥5,000). Tickets can be purchased at any major JR station or a tra el agency like JTB. In addition, **Willer Expres** (☎ 050/5805-0383; www.willerexpress.co buses depart Tokyo and Shinjuku stations several times nightly, arriving at Kyoto Statio the next morning (¥4,200–¥8,600, depending on the date and type of seat selected); only online reservations are accepted.

ATMs

In contrast to those abroad, many ATMs only operate during banking hours. Most post offices (see below) have ATM facilities although hours are limited. For 24-hour access, your best bets are the ATMs in **7-Eleve** convenience stores, which accept Visa, Plus, American Express, JCB, Union Pay, or Diner' Club International cards for cash withdrawa (They recently stopped accepting MasterCard, Maestro, and Cirrus cards.) **Citibank** (Shijo Dori, between Karasuma and Maruma chi; www.citibank.co.jp/en/bankingservice/ branch_atm/kansai/br_kyoto.html) and **Shinsei Bank** ATMs accept foreign bank car as well.

Doctors & Hospitals

Kyoto University Hospital, Shogoinkawara-cho, Sakyo-ku (☎ 075/751-3111; www.kuhp. kyoto-u.ac.jp), offers consultations weekday 8:30am to 11am. **The International Community House,** 2-1 Torri-cho, Awataguchi, Saky ku (☎ 075/752-3010) can provide referrals English-speaking doctors.

Emergencies

Dial ☎ 119 for ambulance and fire. Dial ☎ 110 for police and other emergencies.

Internet Access

Most hotels are equipped with Internet capabilities, but Wi-Fi is still uncommon. **Tops Café,** Kyoto-eki, Hachijo-guchi (☎ 075/681-9270; www.topsnet.co.jp; 24 hours), is the

...using is a breeze with the detailed Bus Navi maps available at the Tourist Information Center.

...sest Internet cafe to Kyoto Station. **Media ...fé Popeye,** Kawaramachi Dori, Sanjo-...garu, Nakagyo-ku (☎ 075/253-5000; 24 ...urs), is conveniently located downtown. ...ere's also an Internet corner in the **HUKU ...fé** inside the Kyoto Handicraft Center, 21 ...ougoin Entomi-cho, Sakyo-ku (☎ 075/761-...42; www.kyotohandicraftcenter.com/en-.../index.html; daily 10am–7pm).

...armacies

...ugstores, called *yakkyoku* (薬局) are ubiq-...ous in Japan, but they are not 24-hour ...erations. Your best bet is to ask your hotel ...ncierge for the closest location. Note that ...u must first visit a doctor in Japan before ...eign prescriptions can be filled, so it's also ...st to bring an ample supply of any prescrip-...n medication with you.

...lice

...l ☎ **110** for police.

...st Offices

...e main **post office,** at 843–12 Higashishio-...i-cho, Shimogyo-ku (☎ 075/365-2471), is ...en Mon–Fri 9am–9pm; to 7pm Sat, Sun, and ...idays.

Safety

Kyoto is an extremely safe city. However, you should always take the same common-sense precautions you would when traveling elsewhere.

Visitor Information

Kyoto Visitor's Guide (www.kyotoguide.com) and **Kansai Scene** (www.kansaiscene.com) give up-to-date information on upcoming events, restaurants, nightlife, and articles on life and style. The new **Kyoto Tourist Information Center,** located on the north-south walkway of the 2nd floor of the Kyoto Station Building (☎ 075/343-0548; www.pref.kyoto.jp/koku-sai/10100035.html; daily 8:30am–7pm), offers assistance in Japanese, English, Chinese, and Korean. They dispense pamphlets and maps, sell tickets for public transportation and events, and help make arrangements for accommoda-tion within the city of Kyoto. The **Welcome Inn Reservation Center,** on the ninth floor of Kyoto Station in front of the south elevator of Isetan department store (☎ 075/343-4887; www.itcj. jp; daily 10am–6pm, closed second and fourth Tues of each month and Dec 29–Jan 3), can assist in finding and reserving accommodation in Kyoto and other areas.

Favorite Moments

The vast majority of visitors to this corner of Japan content themselves with a stop in Hiroshima, but that historic city is only one of many sights this region has to offer. Extending from the Kansai region (p. 194) to the island of Kyushu (p. 348), Western Honshu has been an inspiration to warriors and storytellers alike for generations. It is the site of epic samurai battles, the setting of terrifying ghost stories, and the origin of the country's most famous fairy tale. If you want to experience "real" Japan away from major cities, this is a great place to do it.

> PREVIOUS PAGE Sunset from Shimonoseki's Kaikyo Yume Tower. THIS PAGE Itsukushima shrine's torii gate rises from the waters.

❶ **Storming a castle moat.** The Horikawa Boat Tour through the moat of Matsue Castle is a great way to see some imposing fortifications and the city at the same time. See p. 284.

❷ **Meeting a truly terrifying turtle.** At night, the giant stone tortoise atop the tomb of a fearsome warlord in the graveyard Gessho-ji Temple comes to life and eats residents of Matsue . . . or so the legend goes. See p. 290, ❶.

❸ **Getting in touch with your inner child in Kurashiki.** Spin traditional tops and mess about with other playthings in this historic quarter's Rural Toy Museum. See p. 301, ❹.

❹ **Finding that special someone at Yaegaki Shrine.** Looking for love in all the wrong places? Float a coin atop a sheet of special paper on the pond in this Shinto shrine to reveal your fate in love and romance. See p. 292, ❹.

❺ **Relaxing in a traditional garden.** Okayama's Korakuen is considered one of the three best gardens in all of Japan; a walk through its groves is a great way to relax during your travels. See p. 300, ❶.

❻ **Biking through history.** The Kibiji District bike trail, which runs through a suburb of Okayama, is an amazing way to get a feel for rural Japanese life. See p. 284.

❼ **Loading up on carbohydrates in Hiroshima.** This city's iconic dish is not to be missed. Hiroshima-style *okonomiyaki* pancakes set atop fried soba noodles and drenched in a sweet sauce is the Japanese equivalent of diner food. See p. 311.

❽ **Gazing upon one of Japan's most iconic views at Itsukushima Shrine.** The enormous *torii* gate rising from the waters off the coast of Miyajima island is an instantly recognizable Japanese landmark across the world. See p. 287, ❺.

❾ **Taking a spin underwater at Kaiyokan.** Shimonoseki's aquarium is world-class, with numerous transparent tubes that allow visitors to experience its numerous tanks from the inside out. See your seafood in its native habitat! See p. 313, ❸.

❿ **Dining on a potentially deadly delicacy.** Japan's world-famous fugu (poison pufferfish) cuisine originated in Shimonoseki. Don't worry: The toxins are all carefully removed before it's served. See p. 315.

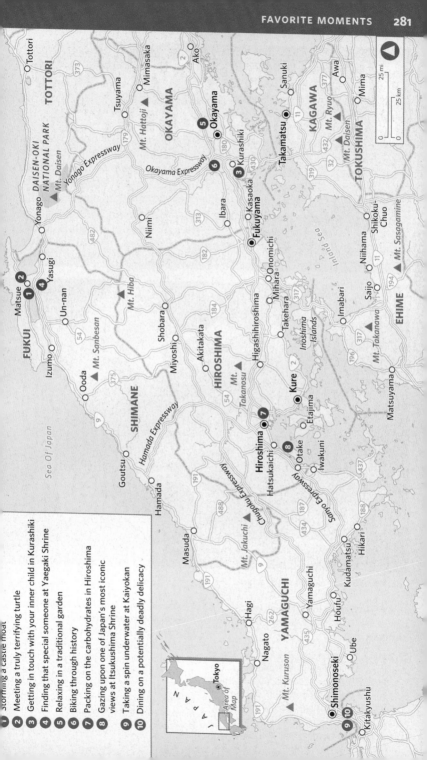

1 Storming a castle moat
2 Meeting a truly terrifying turtle
3 Getting in touch with your inner child in Kurashiki
4 Finding that special someone at Yaegaki Shrine
5 Relaxing in a traditional garden
6 Biking through history
7 Packing on the carbohydrates in Hiroshima
8 Gazing upon one of Japan's most iconic views at Itsukushima Shrine
9 Taking a spin underwater at Kaiyokan
10 Dining on a potentially deadly delicacy

The Best of Western Honshu in 4 Days

This particular tour starts in Matsue, a far-flung destination by most standards. Yet it is precisely this out-of-the-way location that makes it an amazing "time capsule" of traditions both architectural and cultural—and a place the vast majority of tourists generally never make time to see. While you can get there by rail, it isn't serviced by the bullet train, so the quickest way to get there is by plane. If your plans can't accommodate the flight there, you can just as easily begin this tour on Day 2, in Okayama.

> The Lafcadio Hearn manor's stately garden.

START Take the Matsue Lake Line bus to stop no. 6 or 8. Matsue is 313km (194 miles) northwest of Kyoto.

① Matsue. Japanese are quite fond of Matsue, and a fair number of them choose to vacation around here. It's the adopted home of writer Lafcadio Hearn (p. 293), who emigrated to Japan in the late 19th century and made a name for himself chronicling stories of Japanese ghosts, monsters, and gods.

This is why a visit to the ★ **Lafcadio Hearn Memorial Museum and Residence** (p. 296, **①**) is an absolute must for any visitor to the city. Hearn's perfectly preserved countryside manor is a wonderful view into how well-to-do Japanese lived at the turn of the 20th century; the museum houses more than 200 artifacts of Hearn's stay in the city. You'll get all the more out of it if you read one of Hearn's many books first.

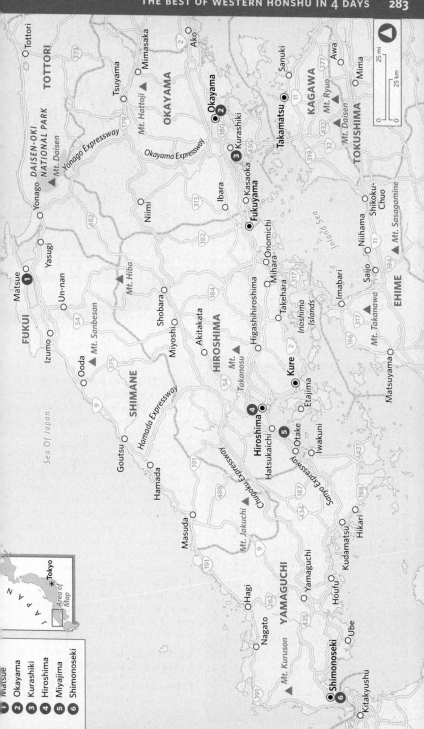

1 Matsue
2 Okayama
3 Kurashiki
4 Hiroshima
5 Miyajima
6 Shimonoseki

> *Korakuen garden was once home to high-ranking officials.*

Okayama by Bicycle

If the weather's nice and you don't mind a little exercise with your sightseeing, we heartily recommend renting bicycles and riding the **Kibiji District bike trail** (吉備路サイクリングロード), located in a western suburb of Okayama. Interesting sights abound on the well-marked path, particularly distinctive "keyhole" burial mounds called *kofun*—relics of a premodern Japanese civilization from well over a thousand years ago. But perhaps the best part is watching the traditional scenery slide by; in fact quite a bit of the trail leads directly through rice fields.

The best place to begin the trip is Soja Station, a half-hour train ride from Okayama Station (¥400). Bike rental fees are ¥400 for 2 hours, with ¥200 for each additional hour. You can pedal out and backtrack whenever you feel like turning around, but heartier souls can take the path to its end at Ichinomiya Station, 15km (9.3 miles) or 4 hours (at a slow pace) away. At Ichinomiya you pay a ¥600 drop-off fee and would have to take the train back to Okayama Station (11 min.).

The ★ kids **Horikawa Boat Tour of Matsue Castle** is a great way to see the city's castle, one of the few in Japan that is original, rather than a modern concrete reconstruction. Trips around the castle last about an hour, threading under tiny bridges in traditional flat-bottomed boats covered in tatami mats (don't forget to take off your shoes before boarding!). The tours run year-round, with heated *kotatsu* (tables with blankets) keeping riders warm in the winter months. The commentary is Japanese only, but anyone can appreciate the picturesque sights. Foreigners can get a ¥400 discount by showing their passports. ◷ 1 day. Boat Tour: ◷ 1 hr. Board at Karakoro Hiroba near the Kyobashi Bridge or Otemae near Matsue Castle. ☎ 0852/27-0417. www.matsue-horikawa meguri.jp. ¥1,200 adults, ¥600 kids. Tours run every 15 min. Daily Mar–Oct 9am–5pm; Nov–Feb 9am–4pm. Bus: Lake Line bus stop no. 6 or 8.

Take the JR Express Yakumo from Matsue Station to Okayama Station (2½ hr.).

❷ Okayama. Okayama is often described as the "gateway to Shikoku," as the nearby Seto Ohashi bridge now whisks cars and trains

Feeding a swan on the canals of Kurashiki.

ross the Inland Sea in a matter of minutes, mpared to the hour-long ferry ride it once ok. But you'll be focusing on the city itself re—it boasts what is considered to be one Japan's three most beautiful gardens, ★ **Korakuen** (p. 301, ❶). Completed in 00 after more than a decade of design and nstruction efforts, Korakuen was mainly ed as a retreat for high-ranking aristocrats. wnership transferred to Okayama Prefecture

Kurashiki Without the Crowds

A word of warning: The Bikan Quarter in Kurashiki can get extremely crowded on weekends. For those who are more interested in architecture and ambience than shopping or gallery-hopping, we recommend stopping by on a Monday, when the area's establishments close for the week and the number of visitors drops accordingly. It's particularly atmospheric very early in the morning and also in the evenings, when many of the historic structures along the canal are illuminated. Whenever you choose to visit, don't be afraid to explore; the side streets here are a lot of fun.

in 1884, however, and now the park is open to everyone. In fact, it is the city of Okayama's star attraction. Featuring broad expanses of grass, the feel is quite different from that of other Japanese gardens, which tend to cluster their attractions together; the grounds feature plum and cherry trees, a cypress grove teeming with wild birds, a stream, a pond, a teahouse, and beautiful views of the surrounding mountains. There is also an archery range; if you get lucky, you might spot sportsmen and -women practicing the art of *kyudo*—the way of the bow. ⏲ Half-day. See p. 300.

From Okayama Station, take the Sanyo Line to Kurashiki Station (13 min.).

❸ **Kurashiki.** This town, a suburb of Okayama, is widely considered one of Japan's most picturesque. Once an administrative center of the region, it is filled with warehouses that were used to store rice (which was used as a currency in times of old). Centuries later, many of these warehouses remain standing, clustered in a area called the ★★ **Bikan Historical Quarter** (倉敷美観地区), a 10-minute walk from the south exit of Kurashiki Station and a major attraction for domestic and foreign tourists alike. In fact, some 4 million visit every year. But don't let that number fool you: While it may be "touristy" in the literal sense of the word, the area has an unpretentious charm borne of the fact that its history is quite real. The streets along its willow-lined canals are home to dozens of traditionally designed warehouses that have been renovated into a variety of stores, restaurants, and galleries.

One of our favorites is the ★ kids **Rural Toy Museum** (日本郷土玩具館)**.** It's packed with traditional toys from all over Japan ("Hokkaido to Okinawa!" boasts the brochure), including a display dedicated to that great-grandfather of Japanese dolls, the iconic red Daruma.

Another must-see is the impressive ★★ **Ohara Museum of Art,** which packs a surprising number of masterpieces for a countryside museum. Works from the likes of Monet and Manet, Picasso and Matisse, and even pop artists like De Kooning and Warhol, line its walls. It also features regular displays of work from local and regional artists. ○ Half-day. Toy Museum: ○ 45 min. 1-4-16 Chuo. ☎ 086/422-8058. www.gangukan.jp. ¥400 adults, ¥300 junior-high and high-school

students, ¥200 kids. Daily 9am–5pm. Train: Kurashiki Station.Ohara Museum: ○ 1½ hr. 1-1-15 Chuo. ☎ 086/422-0005. www.ohara.or.jp. ¥1,000 adults, ¥600 college and high-school students, ¥500 kids. Tues–Sun 9am–5pm. Trai Kurashiki Station.

From Kurashiki Station, return to Okayama Station. Then take the Shinkansen Nozomi bullet train to Hiroshima Station (35–40 min

❹ **Hiroshima.** Hiroshima would undoubtedly be "just another city" were it not for its unfortunate historical distinction: On August 6, 1945, it became the site of the first atomic bomb ever dropped on human beings. Of the population of 350,000, more than 80,000 lost their lives instantly; the number would double over the coming weeks and months as radiation-related illnesses set in. Quickly rebuilt in the years following World War II, Hiroshima is now a bright and bustling city, with little indication that the city was quite literally wiped off the map just a half-century before.

Whatever your feelings about the ethics behind the decision to drop the bomb, it is a fact that the vast majority of victims were civilians

> Origami cranes at the Hiroshima Peace Memorial Park.

The striking sea-bound torii *of Itsukushima Shrine.*

...any of whom were children. The ★★★ **Hiro-shima Peace Memorial Park** (p. 309, **1**) sits ...the center of the city, showcasing the **Gen-baku Dome**—the skeletal remains of the city's ...rmer Industrial Promotion Hall and one of ...e few buildings that survived the atomic ...ast. The park is home to a variety of **memo-al cenotaphs,** including one for children and ...nother for Korean forced laborers who died ...the aftermath of the bombing. But perhaps ...ost moving is the **Hiroshima Peace Memo-al Museum,** dedicated to chronicling the ...vents leading up to and including that fateful ...ugust day in tactful but graphic detail. While ...may be a sobering experience, a visit here is ...ot to be missed. ⏱ 4 hr. See p. 306.

...rom Hiroshima or Nishi-Hiroshima stations, ...ake a JR train to Miyajimaguchi ferry terminal ...26 min.). The ferry ride takes 10 min. and ...osts ¥170. An alternate approach is via ...oat from downtown Hiroshima; Aqua Net ...iroshima dispatches ferries from Motoyasu-...ashi Bridge, near the Genbaku Dome, 11 to 12 ...mes daily (¥1,900 one-way).

5 Miyajima. Hiroshima happens to be within striking distance of Miyajima, a tiny island that is home to one of Japan's most famous land-marks: ★★★ **Itsukushima Shrine** (厳島神社)**.** Its huge red *torii* (shrine gate) rises straight up out of the sea. This massive structure—at 16m (52 ft.) tall, one of the largest of its type—was designated a UNESCO World Heritage Site in 1996. The island is home to many other sights as well; Miyajima's Tourist Information Office (in the ferry terminal) gives out free flyers with points of interest marked in English. ⏱ 2 hr. Itsukushima Shrine: 1–1 Miyajima-cho. ☎ 0829/44-2020. www.miyajima.or.jp. Free. Daily sunrise–sunset.

After returning to Hiroshima Station, take the Shinkansen Nozomi or Hikari bullet trains to Okura Station. Then switch to the Kagoshima Honsen line to Shimonseki Station (1½ hr.).

6 Shimonoseki. This is the westernmost city at the tip of Honshu, the main island of Japan; you can clearly see Kyushu right across the strait. Perhaps because of this prime location,

> *Eternal rivals Musashi and Kojiro face off on Ganryu-jima Island.*

Shimonoseki has found itself at the crossroads of Japanese history many times over the years. But to modern Japanese, Shimonoseki is virtually synonymous with a specific type of cuisine: fugu, or poison pufferfish (p. 315). Most of the nation's catch comes from the waters around here. This tiny fish with an (pardon the pun) inflated reputation for causing bodily harm is an absolute delicacy when properly prepared. If you are going to sample it anywhere in Japan, this is the place.

Even if you decide not to try fugu, you can experience the fish visually in the absolutely not-to-be-missed ★★★ kids **Kaiyokan Aquarium** (p. 313, ❸). In an "only in Shimonoseki" twist, the facility features nearly an entire floor dedicated to pufferfish. The other exhibits are world-class as well: a large reef tank showing life in the Setō Inland Sea, dolphins and porpoises, and an amazing penguin enclosure featuring a giant transparent tube visitors can walk through while observing the birds swimming underwater.

Shimonoseki also happens to be the site of one of the single most famous duels in Japanese history. On nearby ★ **Ganryu-jima Island** (p. 313) in 1612, wandering swordsman Miyamoto Musashi faced off against Sasaki Kojiro in a battle that would make his reputation. In order to counter Kojiro's unusually long sword, Musashi fashioned a makeshift weapon from an oar as he was rowed to the island. Arriving late—the better to throw his opponent off balance—Musashi leapt from the rowboat and straight into combat, successfully felling Kojiro with a series of powerful blows from the oar. Today, the site of their duel is commemorated with a pair of statues and a reproduction rowboat sitting on the beach. Reflecting on the duel is a fun way to spend an hour here, but the boat ride through the harbor is equally if not more fun. Several ferry operators offer trips to Ganryu-jima from Kanmon Wharf, right next to Kaiyokan Aquarium; the trip takes about 10 minutes and costs ¥800 for adults, ¥400 for kids. ⏲ 1 day. See p. 312.

A Side Trip to Himeji

The city of Himeji is a 30-minute hop by bullet train from Okayama, making it an ideal day or even half-day trip. One of the best aspects of visiting Himeji is that you can walk to all of its major attractions. **Otemae Dori boulevard** leads right to Himeji Castle; it's a 15-minute walk. A pair of shopping arcade streets called Miyuki Dori and Omizusuji are along the way. If you don't feel like walking, a **Himeji Castle Loop Bus** makes runs daily from 9am to 5pm (only on weekends and holidays Dec–Feb) every half-hour or so from Himeji Station to the castle and beyond. It costs ¥100 per ride or ¥300 all day.

Also known as "White Heron Castle," ★★★ **Himeji Castle,** 68 Honmachi (☎ 079/285-1146; www.himeji-castle.gr.jp), is widely regarded as the most beautiful in all of Japan. Established as a fort in 1333, it was rebuilt into a castle in 1618 and has stood in its present form for nearly 400 years, surviving everything from natural disasters to domestic strife and world wars. From 1956 to 1964, the castle underwent massive restoration, during which parts were totally disassembled and then rebuilt using traditional methods. In 1993, the castle, along with Horyu-ji Temple in Nara, became Japan's first UNESCO World Heritage Site.

It's definitely worth a trip; the huge size, startlingly bright white walls, and gabled rooftops are the embodiment of Japanese military architecture. Bilingual volunteers are often on hand to give free tours, but even if you go on your own, you'll find excellent English-language explanations throughout the castle grounds. Admission to the castle is ¥600 adults, ¥200 children. It's open June to August, daily 9am to 6pm, and closes an hour earlier September to April. Himeji is under renovation until 2014, so parts of the castle may be closed temporarily.

Most visitors to Himeji are content with a visit to the castle, but ★★★ **Kokoen Garden,** 68 Honmachi (☎ 079/289-4120; www.city. himeji.lg.jp/koukoen/english.html), is a wonderful diversion as well. Only laid out in 1992, it sits at the base of Himeji Castle, about a 5-minute walk away. It is composed of nine separate small gardens, each one different and enclosed by traditional walls, with lots of rest areas at which to soak in the views. Admission is ¥300 adults, ¥150 children; a combination ticket to both Himeji Castle and Kokoen is ¥720 adults, ¥280 children. There is a restaurant, **Kassui-ken,** on site as well. Kokoen is open daily 9am to 5pm (until 6pm May to August).

Matsue's Spookiest Temples & Shrines

As a friend of ours who was born there jokes, "Throw a rock and you'll hit a god in Matsue." For many Japanese, this city—and indeed, this section of Japan—has deep associations with the supernatural. Bear in mind that these stops are subtle charms, not haunted-house attractions; the fun comes from knowing the background story and getting a chill from imagining what happened on the very spot you're standing.

> Cowabunga, dude: the terrifying turtle of Gessho-ji Temple.

START Take the Lake Line bus from JR Matsue Station to stop no. 15, Gesshoji-mae. Matsue is 313km (194 miles) northwest of Kyoto.

❶ Gessho-ji Temple (月照寺). Built in 1664 as the family temple and burial ground of the Matsudaira Clan, who once ruled the area, Gessho-ji's beautiful gardens and eerie cemetery ground remain well preserved today. There is an interesting story about the sixth lord's grave, which is decorated with the statue of an enormous tortoise. According to legend, the turtle came to life one night, descending upon the city and eating several residents—think *Gamera*. A Gessho-ji monk intervened and convinced it to return to the graveyard, where a massive stone column was used to weigh the beast down so it wouldn't terrorize the city again. ⏱ 30 min. Sotonakabara-cho. ☎ 0852/21-6056. ¥500 adults, ¥300 high-school students, ¥150 junior-high students and kids. Daily 8:30am–5:30pm (Nov–Mar until 5pm). Bus: Lake Line bus stop n 15, Gesshoji-mae.

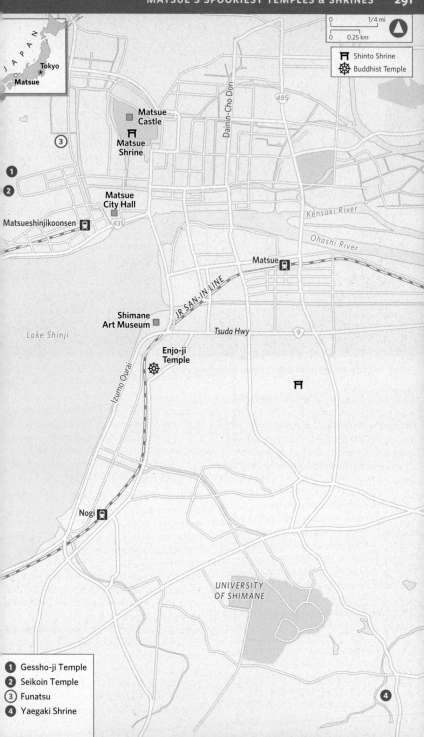

JAPAN

Tokyo

Matsue

0   1/4 mi
0   0.25 km

⛩ Shinto Shrine
卍 Buddhist Temple

Matsue Castle

Matsue Shrine

Dainin-Cho Dori

485

Matsue City Hall

Matsueshinjikoonsen

431

Kansaki River

Ohashi River

Matsue

JR SAN-IN LINE

Lake Shinji

Shimane Art Museum

Tsuda Hwy

9

Enjo-ji Temple

Izumo Ourai

Nogi

UNIVERSITY OF SHIMANE

1 Gessho-ji Temple
2 Seikoin Temple
3 Funatsu
4 Yaegaki Shrine

> *An elegant banner welcomes lovers to Yaegaki Shrine.*

2 Seikoin Temple (清光院)**.** An otherwise unassuming spot that is famed for a supposedly true incident that took place in the Edo Era, some 200 years ago: It seems a geisha, already betrothed to another, spurned the advances of a young samurai here. Their disagreement escalated, and she fled to Seikoin for refuge. Quickly catching up, her would-be suitor unsheathed his sword and cut her down as she ran; she took three steps before collapsing on the temple's stone staircase. No matter how hard the monks scrubbed, her bloody footprints remained—even to this day—and some say that her ghostly singing can be heard issuing from the stairs at night. ⏱ 30 min. 194 Sotonakabara-cho. ☎ 0852/21-2912. Free. Daily 9am–5pm. Bus: Lake Line bus stop no. 15, Gesshoji-mae.

---

③   🍜 **Funatsu** (ふなつ)**.** This little restaurant, located right outside of Gessho-ji and Seikoin temples, is a great place to take a break. The must-try dish here is the local specialty, *warigo* soba, which consists of three mini-bowls of soba stacked up atop one another. Variations include tempura *warigo* soba and *chidori warigo* soba (with chicken). 117–6 Sotonakaharacho. ☎ 0852/22-2361. Noodles from ¥900. Lunch & dinner daily. Bus: Lake Line bus stop no. 15, Gesshoji-mae.

4 Yaegaki Shrine (八重垣神社)**.** As described in the 8th-century text *Nihon Shoki*, Lord Susano, brother of the Sun Goddess, and Princess Inata married here in celebration of Susano defeating an eight-headed dragon that had been terrorizing the area. Princess Inata used the pond behind Yaegaki Shrine as a mirror as she made her preparations. Today, visitors place a ¥5 coin atop special paper (sold at the shrine shop) and float it on the pond; the distance it travels and time it takes to sink reveal one's future in love and marriage. What, you don't think that's as scary as a carnivorous turtle or a treacherous samurai? Depends on your fate! ⏱ 30 min. 227 Sakusacho. ☎ 0852/21-1148. Free. Daily 9am–5pm. Bus: city bus 63 from Matsue Station to Yaegaki Jinja.

Lafcadio Hearn

Matsue's most famous resident wasn't Japanese at all—his name was Lafcadio Hearn, or Koizumi Yakumo, the name he adopted after becoming a naturalized Japanese citizen. Hearn had quite a nontraditional upbringing: He was born in Greece in 1850, raised in Dublin, and sent to the United States at the age of 19. He worked as a journalist in Cincinnati, specializing in gruesome portrayals of local crime and murder scenes; later he moved to New Orleans as a freelance writer, where the stories he sold to popular magazines helped mold the now-popular image of the city as an exotic blend of American and Caribbean influences. But inexorably drawn to the different and otherworldly, he jumped at the chance to travel to Japan as a newspaper correspondent in 1890.

Quickly falling out with his editor, Hearn learned of a teaching position in Matsue, where he fell in love with Koizumi Setsuko, the beautiful daughter of a local samurai family. As it happened, Koizumi happened to be something of a walking encyclopedia of local oral traditions. In spite of the language barrier between them, she patiently explained and re-enacted famous historical episodes, ghost stories, and tales of terror for Hearn, who put them down in writing for the first time in English or any other language. Compiled into a series of books over the next 14 years, these stories would define his reputation both in Japan and abroad.

Although he spent only 15 months in Matsue, it was the first Japanese city in which he lived, and it is safe to say he took a great deal of inspiration from its inhabitants and environs. Hearn's writings coincided with a huge surge of foreign interest in Japan in the late 19th century, and his down-to-earth tales gave the Western world one of its first true glimpses into the Japanese psyche. Though Hearn died in 1904, his retellings of classic Japanese stories have a timeless feel, and you'll appreciate Matsue—and the rest of Japan—all the more if you read some before making a visit. We heartily recommend *Glimpses of Unfamiliar Japan,* which features several episodes set in Matsue; *In Ghostly Japan;* and our personal favorite, *Kwaidan: Stories and Studies of Strange Things,* which was made into a very scary movie, *Kwaidan,* in 1964. Many of Hearn's books are in the public domain and available for free download online, as well as in Japanese bookstores that carry English-language books.

GHOSTS &
GOBLINS

In Japan, scary stories aren't just for
Halloween—they're part of the fabric of daily life

BY MATT ALT & HIROKO YODA

N TIMES OF OLD—up until not so very long ago—the people of Japan believed that their lands were inhabited by all sorts of supernatural creepy-crawlies. Chief among them were the *yokai*, monsters that are essentially superstitions with personalities, and *yurei*, the souls of dead humans who remain bound to the mortal world for whatever reason. They re Japan's bogeymen, and while their tradition is a long one, they're far from history here.

Yokai

here are literally housands of different species" of *yokai*. ere's a sampling of a ew to get you started.

ENGU

hese humanoid reatures sport angel-ke wings, but they're nown as tricksters nd superb martial rtists. Masks of the ng-nosed *tengu* are ommon throughout apan.

ANUKI

anuki are raccoon ogs based on real-life nimals; they're capable f shape-shifting to play icks on humans and re known for their gi-nt testicles, which they an fashion into all sorts f tools and disguises.

KITSUNE
Kitsune, or foxes, were once believed to possess supernatural powers, namely the ability to shape-shift into the form of a hu-man, the better to trick unsuspecting victims.

KAPPA
These river-dwelling creatures are like frog men with tortoiseshell backs. The depressions atop their heads are filled with water. If it spills, they're power-less. They love two things in life: attacking unwary swimmers, and eating cucumbers.

Yurei

Arguably the scarier of the two, Japan's ghosts tend to be angry. Here are some of the most famous from Japanese literature and legend.

▲ OKIKU-SAN
Also known as the "Plate-Counting Ghost," she was brutally killed and tossed in a well by her samurai employer for breaking one of a set of priceless antique plates. Ever after, her voice counted spookily from deep within the well.

OIWA-SAN
Star of the kabuki play *Yotsuya Kaidan*. Poisoned by her philandering samurai husband, she came back from the grave to wreak havoc upon him and everyone he knew. She's considered such a potent force that any kabuki, TV, or film production of *Yotsuya Kaidan* gets a pre-emptive exorcism at the Tamiya Oiwa Shrine in Yotsuya, Tokyo.

TAIRA NO MASAKADO
This samurai lost his head in battle—which was brought across the country to Tokyo, where it remains today. His grave sits atop some of the city's most expensive real estate. Legend has it anyone who attempts to move it will be cursed.

Ghost Season

In the West, ghosts and ghouls are associated with Halloween. But Japan's supernatural season is the summer, particularly the doldrums of August. According to one theory, there's a simple reason for that: Before air-conditioning, getting together and swapping spooky stories was a great way to get a shiver. Not coincidentally, August is also associated with another tradition: Obon, when the souls of departed family members are said to drop by the house to check on their loved ones. During mid- to late-August, neighborhoods have Obon festivals in which locals sing and dance around a raised stage, while peddlers sell finger foods. During the summer months, listen for the distinctive drumming of these innumerable parties.

Matsue

Matsue is a relatively small city of less than 200,000 residents that lies on the northern coast of Western Honshu. It's off the beaten track for most foreign tourists, who tend to hug the southern coast, where Okayama and Hiroshima are located. Particularly in the summer months, Matsue is a beloved destination for many Japanese, and its castle and gardens are popular sights for domestic travelers. But the city is also quite open to international tourists. In fact, many of its attractions offer discounts to visitors who show foreign passports—give it a try when paying for entry.

> The almost-dainty Meimei-an Teahouse.

START Lake Line bus from JR Matsue Station to stop no. 10, Koizumi Yakumo Kinenkan-mae. Matsue is 313km (194 miles) northwest of Kyoto.

① Lafcadio Hearn Memorial Museum and Residence (小泉八雲記念館). This museum is packed with memorabilia related to Matsue's most famous literary figure and chronicler of all things spooky, including manuscripts, photographs, even smoking pipes. His former residence, right next door to the museum, retains the garden Hearn wrote about in his book *Glimpses of Unfamiliar Japan*. For more information about Hearn, see p. 293. ⏱ 1 hr. 322 Okudani-cho. ☎ 0852/21-2147. ¥300 adults, ¥150 kids. Daily 8:30am–5pm (Apr–Sept until 6:30pm). Bus: Lake Line bus stop no. 10, Koizum Yakumo Kinenkan-mae.

② Buke Yashiki (武家屋敷). *Buke yashiki* literally means "warrior family manor," and true to its name, this one belonged to a family of retainers of the warlord who once occupied Matsue Castle. It is a rare opportunity to see exactly how samurai lived in the Edo Period (early

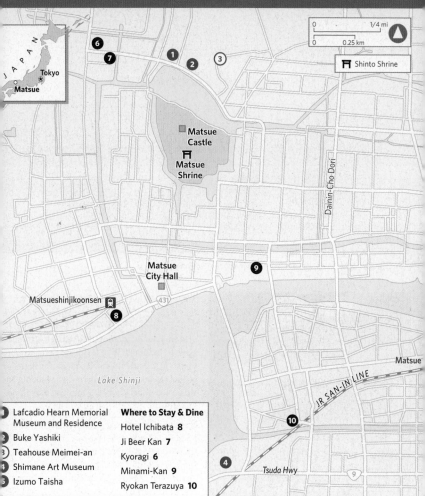

1/4 mi
0.25 km

🛉 Shinto Shrine

Matsue Castle

Matsue Shrine

Dainin-Cho Dori

Matsue City Hall

Matsueshinjikoonsen

Matsue

JR SAN-IN LINE

Lake Shinji

Tsuda Hwy

1 Lafcadio Hearn Memorial Museum and Residence
2 Buke Yashiki
3 Teahouse Meimei-an
4 Shimane Art Museum
5 Izumo Taisha

Where to Stay & Dine
Hotel Ichibata **8**
Ji Beer Kan **7**
Kyoragi **6**
Minami-Kan **9**
Ryokan Terazuya **10**

8th to mid-19th centuries). It isn't as opulent s some of the manors that can be found in arger cities and so doesn't take long to go hrough—a half-hour, absolute tops—but is efinitely worth a visit. ⊙ 20 min. 305 Kitahori-no. ☎ 0852/22-2243. ¥300 adults, ¥150 kids. aily 8:30am–5pm (Apr–Sept until 6:30pm). us: Lake Line bus stop no. 10, Koizumi Yakumo inenkan-mae.

♨ **Teahouse Meimei-an** (明々庵茶室). Built in 1799 by the seventh of the Matsudaira warlords who once ruled Matsue, this elegant little structure is a perfect example of austere Japa-

nese teahouse design. Note the thickly thatched roof and low entryway (designed to prevent visitors from bringing swords inside). Although you can't actually drink inside the teahouse, an adjacent shop sells bitter green tea and sweets for an additional ¥400. ⊙ 30 min. 278 Kitahori-cho. ☎ 0852/21-9863. ¥400 adults, ¥300 students, free for kids. No credit cards. Daily 9am–5pm (last tea served 4:15pm). Bus: Lake Line bus stop no. 9, Shiomi Nawate.

④ **Shimane Art Museum** (島根県立美術館). This modern museum focuses on the works of local artists, with a smattering of pieces from

> *Sunset over Lake Shinji, as seen from the Shimane Art Museum.*

> *The oversized* **shimenawa** *rope is meant to ward off evil spirits at Izumo Taisha.*

Tip: If you don't feel like taking the bus, it's only a 15-minute walk to Matsue Station. ⏱ 1 hr. 1–5 Sodeshi-cho. ☎ 0852/55-4700. www1. pref.shimane.lg.jp/contents/sam/en/ex/index. html. ¥300 adults, free for kids; special exhibitions ¥1,000 adults, ¥600 college and high-school students, ¥300 junior-high students and kids. Wed–Mon 10am–6:30pm. Bus: Lake Line bus stop no. 27, Kenritsu Bijitsukan.

⑤ Izumo Taisha (出雲大社)**.** Located roughly an hour outside of Matsue by train (take the train from Matsue to Izumoshi Station, and then the Izumo Taisha bus), Izumo is revered as the land of the gods in Shinto, and this is one of the largest, oldest, and most important shrines in all of Japan. It is dedicated to Okuninushi-no-mikoto, the Shinto deity of farming, health, marriage, and happiness. Nobody is quite sure when Izumo Taisha was first constructed, but it is mentioned in historical records dating back to 950, when it was described as being the tallest building in Japan. (The temple shop features a scale reconstruction of what the original is believed to have looked like: a 45m/148-ft.-high tower accessed by a massive staircase.) As you might expect, the temple has been rebuilt many times over the last thousand years, and the main hall is closed until May of 2013 for extensive renovations. ⏱ 2 hr. 195 Kizuki Higashi, Taisha-cho, Izumo-shi. ☎ 0853/53-3100. Free.

foreign masters such as Monet and Rodin. Although it isn't very large as art museums go, it has a nice rooftop terrace and a free outdoor sculpture garden. Its location right on the shore of Lake Shinji makes it the perfect place to end a day in Matsue with a sunset stroll.

Where to Stay & Dine in Matsue

★ Hotel Ichibata（ホテル一畑）
Although the rooms are small and showing their age, you cannot beat the lake views from the Japanese-style and twin rooms. Other pluses include indoor and outdoor hot-spring public baths and a nearby jogging path along the lakeside. 30 Chidori-cho. ☎ 0852/22-0188. www.ichibata.co.jp/hotel. 142 rooms. Doubles from ¥17,100, Japanese-style rooms from ¥23,400. AE, DC, MC, V. Bus: Shinjiko Onsen Station.

★★ Ji Beer Kan（地ビール館）*PUB*
This pub serves up three types of beer—pilsner, pale ale, and herb-infused ale—alongside noodle dishes and Mongolian-style grilled meats (or "Genghis Khan" in Japanese vernacular). Although you can order a la carte, many diners opt for the ¥2,500 all-you-can-eat special. For true party animals, an additional ¥1,500 for women and ¥2,500 for men gets you all you can drink for 90 minutes as well. 509-1 Kuroda-cho. ☎ 0852/55-8877. All-you-can-eat ¥2,500. AE, MC, V. Lunch & dinner daily. Bus: Lake Line bus stop no. 11, Horikawa Yuransen Noribo.

★★ Kyoragi（京らぎ）*ORGANIC JAPANESE*
This modern seafood restaurant specializes in dishes based on original Izumo recipes, using organic meats and vegetables whenever possible. There are pictures of some of the set meals offered on the Japanese-language menu. 512-5 Kuroda-cho. ☎ 0852/25-2233. Set lunches from ¥1,260, set dinners from ¥2,625. DC, MC, V. Lunch & dinner Tues–Sun. Bus: Lake Line bus stop no. 11, Horikawa Yuransen Noribo.

★★ Minami-Kan（皆美館）
This is Japanese tradition at its most luxurious. Although extensively renovated with modern amenities (including one Western-style room), the beautiful *ryokan* (traditional inn) on the shores of Lake Shinji dates back to 1888. Several rooms have sinks and toilets, but not showers; you'll use the (gender-segregated) bathing area instead. The Minami-Kan's restaurant is famed for its skill with *taimeshi* (steamed fish and rice), the

> *Kyoragi restaurant is a haven for seafood lovers.*

local delicacy. 14 Suetsugu Honmachi. ☎ 0852/21-5131. www.minami-g.co.jp/minamikan. 15 rooms. Rooms ¥23,250–¥30,180 per person. Rates include 2 meals. AE, DC, MC, V. Train: Matsue Station.

★★ Ryokan Terazuya（旅館寺津屋）
Terazuya offers good value for your money, but it also offers something money can't buy: true hospitality. This Japanese inn has been in business since 1893, owned by the Terazu family, who has shown so much kindness to foreigners that many consider their stay here a highlight of their trip. While nothing special on the outside, it is spotless and colorful inside, and the Terazus treat guests like family. 60-3 Tenjinmachi. ☎ 0852/21-3480. www.mable.ne.jp/~terazuya/english. 9 rooms. Rooms from ¥5,000 per person with breakfast, ¥7,000 per person with breakfast & dinner. No credit cards. Train: Matsue Station.

Okayama & Kurashiki

Although the city of Okayama is a major transit hub for the region, it is a window into Japan's traditional side. It is home to Korakuen, widely considered one of Japan's most beautiful gardens, and you'll definitely want to make time for a trip to nearby Kurashiki, home of the Bikan Historical Quarter.

> *The bridges of Korakuen garden.*

START Take the Okayama streetcar to the Shiroshita stop. Okayama is 212km (132 miles) west of Kyoto.

❶ **Korakuen** (後楽園). This centuries-old traditional garden is Okayama's star attraction. Originally created as a retreat for samurai, now anyone can enjoy its floral charms. ⏱ 2 hr. 1-5 Korakuen. ☎ 086/272-1148. ¥350 adults, ¥140 kids, free for seniors. Daily Apr–Sept 7:30am–6pm; Oct–Mar 8am–5pm. Streetcar: Shiroshita.

❷ **Okayama Prefectural Products Center** (晴れの国おかやま館). *Bizen* pottery (unglazed pottery with a history stretching back 1,000 years), *igusa* (rush-grass mats), wooden trays, bamboo ware, papier-mâché toys, sake, and more local treats are all for sale here. ⏱ 30 min. 1-1-22 Omotecho. ☎ 086/234-2270. Wed–Mon 10am–7pm. Streetcar: Shiroshita.

❸ **Okayama Castle** (岡山城). Okayama Castle is popularly known as "Crow Castle" for its black facade, a rarity among Japanese castles. (It was intended to contrast with Himeji's "White

1. Korakuen
2. Okayama Prefectural Products Center
3. Okayama Castle
4. Kurashiki
5. Miyake Shoten
6. Inujima Island

Where to Stay & Dine

Comfort Hotel **11**
Hotel Okura Okayama **13**
Kuriya Sen **9**
Matsunoki Ryokan **7**

Matsunoki-Tei **8**
Ryokan Kurashiki **10**
Shikisai **12**

Train
Tram

Okayama

Nishigawaryokudoen
Okayamaekimae　　Yanagawa　　Momotaro Dori
　　　　　　　　　　　　Shiroshita

Shiyakusho-suji

Yubinkyokumae　　Kencho Dori
　　　　　　　　Kencho Dori

Tamachi

Shinsaidaidaijichosuji　　Saidaijicho　　Kobashi
　　　　　　　　　　　　　　　　Chunagon

Daiunjimae

J A P A N
Tokyo ★
Okayama

1/4 mi
0.25 km

Higashichuocho

Heron Castle"; p. 289). Although this is a replica that was built in 1966, it was built using the original blueprints, making it more realistic than many other reconstructions. ⏲ 1 hr. 2-3-1 Marunouchi. ☎ 086/225-2096. ¥300 adults, ¥120 kids. Daily 9am–5pm. Streetcar: Shiroshita.

④ **Kurashiki** (倉敷美観地区)**.** This suburb of Okayama, just minutes away from the station by train, is widely considered to be one of Japan's most picturesque neighborhoods. Its **Bikan Historical Quarter** is filled with antique storehouses that have been lovingly restored and renovated into a variety of museums and shops. Also worth a stop are the **Rural Toy Museum** and **Ohara Museum of Art**. See p. 285, ③.

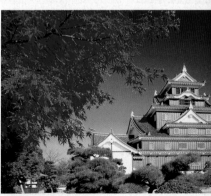

> Okayama Castle, also known as "Crow Castle."

> *A resident of the Bikan Historical Quarter on an errand.*

⑤ 🍵 **Miyake Shoten** (三宅商店). This neighborhood cafe located on the edge of the Bikan Historical Quarter serves light lunches (including curry), but the real reason to come are its Japanese-style parfaits and desserts. The menu is filled with photos, making it easy to pick out what you'd like. 3–11 Honmachi, Kurashiki. ☎ 086/426-4600. Entrees from ¥850, set meals (includes entree, coffee, and mini-dessert) ¥1,100. No credit cards. Lunch daily. Train: Kurashiki Station.

⑥ **Inujima Island** (犬島)**.** Although it isn't easy to get to, this island turned art installation is an interesting detour for fans of modern art and architecture. It is home to two museums: the **Inushima Art Project,** a series of galleries; and the **Seirensho,** a renovated refinery complex that utilizes existing structures and natural terrain so as to minimize the art facility's impact on the environment. The fastest way to get there is to take the JR Ako Line from Okayama Station (20 min.), disembark at Saidaiji Station, and take a taxi to Hoden Port (30 min.), then take the ferry to Inujima (10 min.). Inujima is open year-round but is best as a day trip in the summer, when the local beaches open for swimming. Make sure to dress for the weather, as most of the installations are exposed to the elements. ⏱ 3 hr. Inushima Art Project and Seirensho: 327–5 Inujima, Higashi-ku, Okayama. ☎ 086/947-1112. www.benesse-artsite.jp/en/inujima. ¥1,000. Wed–Sun 10am–4pm (open Mon–Tues if a national holiday but then closed Wed). Ferry:

Momotaro

You can't truly experience Okayama without knowing the tale of Momotaro, the "Peach Boy." Tradition holds that this quintessential Japanese fairy tale actually took place here. It goes like this: An elderly, childless couple finds a giant peach floating down the river near their home; when they cut it open, they are shocked to find a baby inside, whom they adopt and name Momotaro, or "Peach Boy." Growing far faster than normal into a powerful young man, Momotaro heads off to Oni-ga-shima, or "Demon Island," to take on an army of monsters who have been terrifying Japan. Aided in his quest by a monkey, fox, and pheasant, Momotaro and his pals take on the demons in an epic battle, returning safely to a hero's welcome back home.

There is a statue of Momotaro right outside of Okayama Station, and the city's main street is named Momotaro Odori ("Momotaro Boulevard") in his honor. The millet dumplings Momotaro and his comrades ate along the way, *kibidango*, are considered a local delicacy and are widely available throughout the city and region.

> *A mind-bending installation by architect Hiroshi Sambuichi at the Inushima Art Project.*

Where to Stay & Dine Around Okayama

> *Food artists at work: Kuriya Sen.*

★ **Comfort Hotel** (コンフォートホテル岡山) OKAYAMA
This no-frills business hotel has a great location for sightseeing: across from the Shiroshita streetcar stop and halfway between Okayama Station and the castle, a 15-minute walk from each. Spotlessly clean and opened in 2005, it offers small but modern, mostly double rooms (a rarity in Japan). 1-1-13 Marunouchi. ☎ 086/801-9411. www.comfortinn.com. 208 units. Doubles from ¥12,000. Rates include breakfast. AE, DC, MC, V. Streetcar: Shiroshita.

★★ **Hotel Okura Okayama** (ホテルオークラ岡山)
OKAYAMA A relative of the famed Hotel Okura in Tokyo, this Western-style hotel has been a local favorite since it opened in 1973. In spite of its age, it is clean and comfortable, with larger-than-average rooms. The only real drawback is its location; it's a bit far from the station. However, there are free shuttle buses from the Higashiyama streetcar stop—the last stop from Okayama Station (in the mornings and evenings every 30 min. 7:30–9am and 6–9:30pm). 4-1-16 Kadota Honmachi. ☎ 086/273-7311. www.okura.com. 175 units. Doubles from ¥22,000. AE, DC, MC, V. Streetcar: Higashiyama.

★★ **Kuriya Sen** OKAYAMA *KAISEKI*
Although expensive, this *kaiseki* (multicourse set menu) restaurant is absolutely worth it both for sweeping views of the city (it's on the 20th floor of the ANA Hotel, right across from Okayama Station's west exit) and for its steaks. It's one of the most upscale restaurants in the city; reservations are recommended. 15-1 Ekimotomachi. ☎ 086/898-2284 Entrees from ¥4,100. AE, DC, MC, V. Lunch & dinner daily. Train: Okayama Station.

★★ **Matsunoki Ryokan** (まつのき旅館) OKAYAMA
This family-owned inn welcomes foreigners. Although it offers rooms with and without bathrooms in a cluster of three buildings, foreigners are automatically given rooms in the

> Tranquility awaits at Ryokan Kurashiki.

newer, main building, all with bathrooms at a price normally given to bathroomless units.) Foreigners are only assigned rooms in the older buildings if accommodations in the main building are full.) Spotless rooms are mostly Japanese style. The *ryokan*'s restaurant, Matsunoki-Tei (see below), is worth visiting even if you aren't staying here. 19-1 Ekimotomachi. ☎ 086/253-4111. www.matunoki.com. 58 units. Doubles from ¥8,400. Breakfast ¥600 extra, dinner ¥1,300 extra. V (5% extra if paying by credit card). Train: Okayama Station.

★★★ Matsunoki-Tei (まつのき亭) OKAYAMA SHABU-SHABU
Run by the family who owns the Matsunoki Ryokan (see above), this is a luxurious, traditional sort of experience. Diners sit in private tatami-floored rooms while they eat either *kaiseki* (set-course meals) or *shabu-shabu* (thinly sliced beef and pork simmered in broth). (The *shabu-shabu* is all you can eat with a 2-hour time limit.) If you plan to eat dinner here, be aware that reservations are required by noon for evening meals. 20-1 Ekimotomachi. ☎ 086/253-5410. Kaiseki from ¥3,700, all-you-can-eat shabu-shabu ¥3,400. No credit cards. Lunch & dinner daily. Train: Okayama Station.

★★★ Ryokan Kurashiki (旅館倉敷) KURASHIKI
If you want to stay in Kurashiki rather than Okayama, this is an unforgettable experience:

It's located right in the middle of Kurashiki's Bikan Historical Quarter (p. 285, ③). Consisting of an old mansion and three converted rice-and-sugar warehouses each more than 250 years old, all interconnected in a little compound, there's no other *ryokan* in Japan quite like this one. With only five rooms, it fills quickly, so make reservations in advance. 4-1 Honmachi. ☎ 086/422-0730. www.ryokan-kurashiki.jp. 5 units. Rooms ¥28,000–¥48,000 per person. Rates include 2 meals. AE, DC, MC, V. Train: Kurashiki Station.

★★ Shikisai (色彩) OKAYAMA JAPANESE
A must-try for those interested in sampling Okayama's regional cuisine. In particular, Shikisai is known for its exquisite handling of *barazushi,* a casserole of sorts that consists of locally caught seafood (which varies by season) set atop a bed of rice mixed with wild mountain vegetables, shredded ginger, and cooked egg. In the colder months, Shikisai also serves *nabe* (hot pots). Although the menu is entirely Japanese, don't be afraid to be adventurous and order what you see others eating. The restaurant's location right outside of Korakuen's (p. 300, ③) entrance gate makes it a convenient lunch stop. 1-5 Korakuen-gaien. ☎ 086/273-3221. Entrees from ¥1,260. No credit cards. Lunch daily. Streetcar: Shiroshita.

Hiroshima

Even those unfamiliar with Japan know the name—and unfortunate history—of this city, site of the world's first atomic bombing. Given that the average photograph of Hiroshima in school textbooks shows smoldering piles of rubble, many are surprised to find that it pretty much resembles any major Japanese city today. Americans in particular occasionally express apprehension about visiting the city, but no need to worry: Its residents are as welcoming and accommodating of foreign visitors as anywhere else in Japan. The city's wide boulevards and extensive streetcar network give it a very different feel than other similarly sized Japanese cities.

> *The Genbaku (A-Bomb) Dome.*

START Take the no. 2 or no. 6 streetcar to the Genbaku Domu Mae stop. Hiroshima is 360km (224 miles) west of Kyoto.

❶ Hiroshima Peace Memorial Park (広島平和記念公園)**.** Dedicated to the city's legacy of surviving the atomic bombing, the enduring symbol of Hiroshima is the Hiroshima Peace Memorial Park. Built near the epicenter of the explosion, in what was once the city's downtown commercial and residential district, it contains many key sights and facilities that are worth visiting. See p. 309.

SITE GUIDE PAGE 309

② 🍴 **No no Budoh** (野の葡萄)**.** This popular buffet restaurant in the Pacela shopping complex specializes in healthy, organic foods, with some 50 choices that change daily but always include choices of Chinese and Japanese dishes, from noodles and fried vegetables to soups and salads. It gets crowded at lunch—try to eat early or late to avoid the crush. Motomachi CRED Complex, 7th floor of Pacela, 78-6 Motomachi. ☎ 082/502-3340. Buffet lunch ¥1,575, buffet dinner ¥1,890. AE, DC, MC, V. Lunch & dinner daily. Streetcar 1, 2, or 6 to Kamiya-cho.

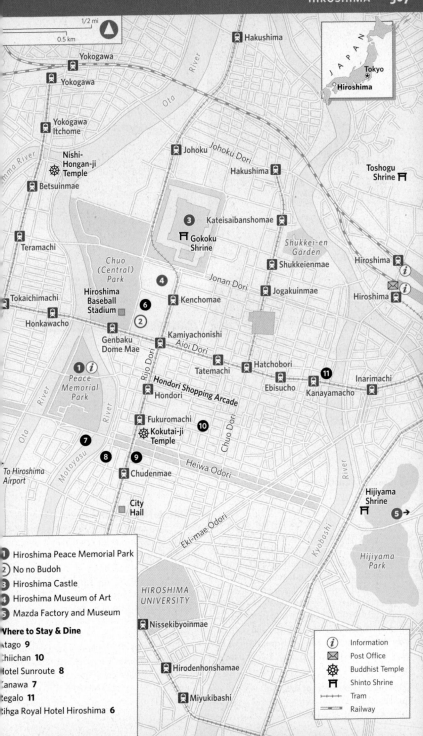

🚈 Hakushima

JAPAN
Tokyo ★
Hiroshima ○

🚈 Yokogawa
🚈 Yokogawa
🚈 Yokogawa Itchome

Nishi-
Hongan-ji
Temple ☸
🚈 Betsuinmae

🚈 Johoku
Johoku Dori
🚈 Hakushima
Toshogu
Shrine ⛩

⊝ **3** Kateisaibanshomae 🚈
🚈 Gokoku
Shrine ⛩

Shukkei-en
Garden

🚈 Teramachi

Chuo
(Central)
Park

🚈 Shukkeienmae

🚈 Tokaichimachi

Hiroshima
Baseball
Stadium ⊝ **4** Kenchomae 🚈
Jonan Dori
🚈 Jogakuinmae

Hiroshima 🚈
ⓘ
✉ ⓘ
Hiroshima 🚈

🚈 Honkawacho
⊝ **6**
②

Kamiyachonishi 🚈
Aioi Dori

Genbaku
Dome Mae 🚈
Rijo Dori

Tatemachi 🚈
🚈 Hatchobori
⊝ **11** Inarimachi
🚈

🚈 **1** ⓘ
Peace
Memorial
Park

Hondori Shopping Arcade
🚈 Hondori

Ebisucho
🚈 Kanayamacho

River

🚈 Fukuromachi
☸ Kokutai-ji
Temple
⊝ **10**

Chuo Dori

⊝ **7**
⊝ **8**
⊝ **9**

🚈 Chudenmae
Heiwa Odori

Hijiyama
Shrine ⛩
5 →

Motoyasu

City
Hall ⊝
To Hiroshima
Airport

Kyobashi River

Hijiyama
Park

Eki-mae Odori

1 Hiroshima Peace Memorial Park

2 No no Budoh

3 Hiroshima Castle

4 Hiroshima Museum of Art

5 Mazda Factory and Museum

Where to Stay & Dine
Atago **9**
Chiichan **10**
Hotel Sunroute **8**
Kanawa **7**
Regalo **11**
Rihga Royal Hotel Hiroshima **6**

HIROSHIMA
UNIVERSITY

🚈 Nissekibyoinmae

🚈 Hirodenhonshamae

🚈 Miyukibashi

ⓘ Information
✉ Post Office
☸ Buddhist Temple
⛩ Shinto Shrine
⊢⊢⊢ Tram
═══ Railway

> *Hiroshima Castle.*

> *Mechanical curiosities at the Mazda Museum.*

❸ **Hiroshima Castle** (広島城). Completed in 1591 but destroyed in the atomic blast, Hiroshima Castle was reconstructed in 1958. Its five-story wooden *donjon* is a faithful reproduction of the original keep, but the main reason to come here is the very good museum housed in the castle's modern interior, which has excellent English-language explanations of castles and their role in Japanese history. The castle is just a 15-minute walk north from the Peace Park. 🕐 30 min. 21-1 Motomachi, Naka-ku. ☎ 082/221-7512. ¥360 adults, ¥180 kids. Daily 9am–6pm (Dec–Feb until 5pm weekdays, 6pm weekends). Streetcar: 1, 2, or 6 to Kamiya-cho.

❹ **Hiroshima Museum of Art.** This wonderful little museum just a stone's throw from the castle is half filled with a spectacular collection of works by Western masters such as Van Gogh, Matisse, and Renoir. The other half consists of Japanese artists working in the Western style. 🕐 45 min. 3-2 Motomachi, Naka-ku. ☎ 082/223-2530. www.hiroshima-museum.jp. ¥1,000 adults, ¥500 college and high-school students, ¥200 junior-high and elementary students. Daily 9am–5pm. Streetcar 1, 2, or 6 to Kamiya-cho.

❺ **Mazda Factory and Museum.** Even if you aren't a car fanatic, this is an interesting diversion. Mazda was founded in Hiroshima in 1920, and this tour covers both a quick view of a working assembly line and a visit to a museum with mint-condition specimens of vintage Mazda cars and bikes. They offer 90-minute English tours at 10am on weekdays, but space is limited and you must call at least a day (and preferably even earlier) in advance to reserve a spot. You can also reserve a spot online. 🕐 1½ hr. 3-1 Shinchi, Fuchu-cho. ☎ 082/252-5050. www.mazda.com/mazdaspirit/museum/guide.html. Free. Tours Mon–Fri at 10am. Train: Mukainada Station.

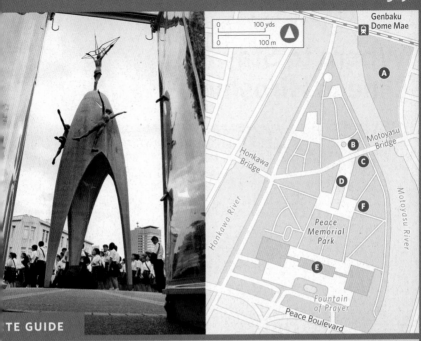

TE GUIDE

1 Hiroshima Peace Memorial Park

r the majority of World War II, Allied rces left Hiroshima unscathed, the better gauge the impact of a new weapon then development. On the morning of August 1945, the B-29 Superfortress *Enola Gay* omber dropped an atomic device code- amed "Little Boy" over the city. Although a gitimate military target—Hiroshima housed e Japanese Second Army Headquarters— vilians outnumbered soldiers six to one, and e blast killed man, woman, and child alike discriminately. This park commemorates e event through a series of sights and onuments. The first thing you'll see off the reetcar is the Ⓐ **Genbaku Dome (A-Bomb ome),** one of the few structures left standing the blast and a UNESCO World Heritage te. The skeletal ruins of the former Industrial romotion Hall have been left virtually ntouched as a visual reminder of the death d destruction caused by the bomb. The Ⓑ **hildren's Peace Monument** (pictured above) dedicated to the memory of the many

children who lost their lives in the blast. This statue depicts a girl with outstretched arms; rising above her is a crane, a symbol of happiness and longevity in Japan. The Ⓒ **Rest House** is another building that survived the fateful day; today it houses a branch of the Hiroshima Tourist Office. The Ⓓ **Peace Flame** will continue to burn until all atomic weapons are vanquished. The park is also home to the Ⓔ **Hiroshima Peace Memorial Museum** and the Ⓕ **Hiroshima National Peace Memorial Hall.** The former is of particular interest. It is split into East and West buildings. The East offers a surprisingly nuanced view of the events leading up to the bombing, including the city's role in Japan's military infrastruc- ture. The West focuses on the suffering caused by the bomb itself. ⏱ 3 hr. Nakajima- cho. ☎ 082/228-0815. www.pcf.city.hiroshima. jp. Free. Daily sunrise–sunset. Memorial Mu- seum: 1-2 Nakajima-cho. ☎ 082/242-7798. ¥50. Daily Mar–Nov 8:30am–6pm; Dec–Feb 8:30am– 5pm. Streetcar: 2 or 6 to Genbaku Domu-mae.

Where to Stay & Dine in Hiroshima

> *Float on: Kanawa is oyster dining at its best.*

★★ **Atago** *TEPPANYAKI*
This steak restaurant, on the ground floor of an office building on Heiwa Odori ("Peace Street") just east of Rijo Dori, is good and convenient if you're visiting the Peace Memorial Museum just across the river. It's strikingly modern with its marble tables and geometric lines, and chefs prepare steak or seafood before your eyes. Reservations recommended. 7–20 Nakamachi. ☎ 082/241-9129. Entrees from ¥8,000. AE, DC, MC, V. Lunch & dinner Tues–Sun. Streetcar: 1 to Fukuromachi.

★★ **Hotel Sunroute**
The rooms at this moderately priced hotel are of the standard no-frills "business hotel" variety, with only basic amenities; try to get one with a view of the park and river. (The hotel is very close to the museums in Hiroshima Peace Memorial Park.) The pair of decent restaurants here (one Italian, one Japanese) can be a boon for times when you're too tired to hit the town again after sightseeing. 3-3-1 Otemachi, Naka-ku. ☎ 082/249-3600. www.sunroute.jp. 284 units. Doubles ¥15,750–¥26,250. AE, DC, MC, V. Streetcar: 1 Chuden-mae.

★★ **Kanawa** *SEAFOOD*
There are 10,000 rafts cultivating oysters in Hiroshima Bay, with a yearly output of 30,000 tons of shelled oysters. Needless to say, oysters are a Hiroshima specialty, and this houseboat, moored east of Peace Memorial Park on the Motoyasu River at the Heiwa Odori Bridge, is one of the best places to enjoy them. Although winter is the optimal time for fresh oysters, the owner has his own oyster rafts and can harvest them in summer too, as well as freeze his best stock in January so he'

The lobby of the Hotel Sunroute.

ole to serve excellent oysters year-round.
his floating restaurant has been here more
an 45 years. Reservations recommended.
n the Motoyasu River, at Heiwa-Ohashi Bridge.
☎ 082/241-7416. Entrees from ¥5,500. AE, DC,
MC, V. Lunch & dinner Mon–Sat; dinner only Sun
holidays. Streetcar: 1 to Chuden-mae.

★ Regalo

very reasonably priced hotel with an excel-
nt location. Make sure to request a room
acing the river; those that don't face another
uilding, which isn't much fun. An open-air
verside cafe across the street, run by the ho-
el, is a popular destination even for those who
ren't staying there. 9–2 Hashimoto-cho, Naka-
u. ☎ 082/224-6300. www.regalo-h.com/
iroshima. 63 units. Doubles ¥9,500–¥10,000.
ates include breakfast. AE, DC, MC, V. Street-
ar: 1, 2, or 6 to Kanayama-cho.

★ Rihga Royal Hotel Hiroshima

his is the city's largest hotel, conveniently lo-
ated right between Hiroshima Castle and the
eace Park. It is also connected to a shopping
omplex and department store. The rooms are
arge and luxuriously furnished—but you pay
or the privilege. 6–78 Motomachi, Naka-ku.
☎ 082/502-1121. www.rihga.com. 490 units.
oubles ¥23,100–¥35,805. AE, DC, MC, V.
treetcar: 1, 2, or 6 to Kamiya-cho.

Hiroshima-Style *Okonomiyaki*

Mention "Hiroshima" to many Japanese
and the first think that will come to mind is
the legendary Hiroshima-style *okonomiyaki*. A savory batter mixed with seafood and
meat, pan-fried into thick circular cakes,
and smothered in a sweet sauce, *okonomiyaki* is available throughout Japan. It originated in Osaka (p. 208), but Hiroshima has
its own take on the dish in which crepe-thin
pancakes are laid atop a bed of deep-fried
yakisoba noodles. It may sound like a carb
overload, but you owe it to yourself to try it
if you're in the area. For novices, we recommend **Okonomi-mura,** a building that is
home to 25 different specialists in the dish.
They're all good, but we recommend **Chiichan,** on the second floor, 5–3 Shintenchi (
☎ 082/249-8102; www.okonomimura.jp);
entrees run from ¥735.

Shimonoseki

Perched at the southwestern tip of Honshu, with a clear view of Kyushu across the waters of the Kanmon Strait, this otherwise unassuming little city has sat at the crossroads of Japanese culture for more than a millennium. Today it is famed largely as Japan's biggest purveyor of fugu, the poison pufferfish, and its fugu cuisine is considered the best in the nation. (See below for some recommendations for places to sample this regional specialty.) Shimonoseki has a reliable bus system, but if you don't mind a little exercise, most destinations are clustered along Route 9, within walking distance of the train station.

> A fugu pufferfish at the Kaiyokan Aquarium.

START Take the bus to Akama-Jingu Mae. Shimonoseki is 554km (344 miles) west of Kyoto.

1 ★ **Akama Jingu**（赤間神宮）. This shrine is dedicated to the soul of child-emperor Antoku, who perished beneath the waves of Kanmon Strait during the epic Battle of Dan-no-Ura in 1185, when the Genji clan wrested control of the country from the Heike clan. Originally constructed just after the battle and rebuilt many times over the centuries (most recently in 1958), it houses the graves of the Heike clan, who were wiped out to a man in the confrontation. Note its staircase, which extends across the road and into the sea, the better for the souls of the Heike to make their way to the shrine from their watery graves.

When you visit, make sure to drop by the statue of Mimi-nashi Hoichi ("Hoichi the Earless") just to the left of the shrine proper. He is the subject of a famous story by Lafcadio Hearn (p. 293), in which Hoichi, a blind lute player, found himself forced to play concerts

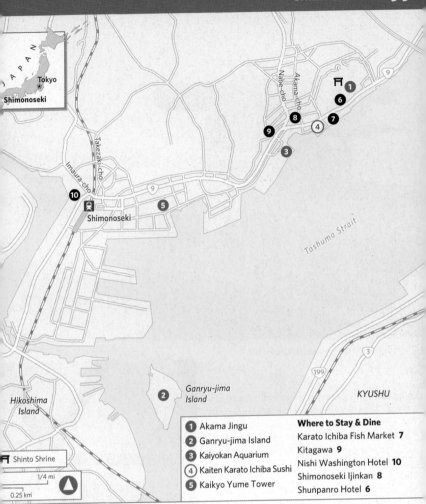

Shinto Shrine

1/4 mi
0.25 km

① Akama Jingu	**Where to Stay & Dine**
② Ganryu-jima Island	Karato Ichiba Fish Market **7**
③ Kaiyokan Aquarium	Kitagawa **9**
④ Kaiten Karato Ichiba Sushi	Nishi Washington Hotel **10**
⑤ Kaikyo Yume Tower	Shimonoseki Ijinkan **8**
	Shunpanro Hotel **6**

...r the ghosts of the Heike clan nightly. The ...elpful abbot of the local temple painted Hoi-...hi's body with Buddhist sutras in a ploy to ...nder him invisible to the ghosts, but forgot ...oor Hoichi's ears, which were ripped off by the ...ngry spirits. ⏲ 1 hr. 4-1 Amidaiji-cho. ☎ 0832/ ...-4138. www.tiki.ne.jp/~akama-jingu. Free. Daily ...nrise–sunset. Bus: Akama-Jingu Mae.

...★ **Ganryu-jima Island** (巌流島). The site of a ...med duel between two wandering swords-...en in 1612 is a short ferry hop from down-...wn Shimonoseki's Kanmon Wharf. See ...288.

③ ★★★ [kids] **Kaiyokan Aquarium** (しものせき水族 館海響館). One of Japan's better aquariums, this state-of-the-art facility boasts some high-tech displays, including large transparent tubes that cross through the waters of several of its tanks. As you might expect in Japan's home of fugu cuisine, there are more pufferfish on display here than at any other aquarium in the world. There is also a large penguin and sea-bird colony and regular dolphin shows. ⏲ 2½ hr. 6-1 Arcaport. ☎ 083/228-1100. www. kaikyokan.com/english. ¥2,000 adults, ¥700 junior-high students and younger. Daily 9:30am–5:30pm. Bus: Kaiyokan.

> *The guns of Mimosusogawa Park.*

④ 🍣 **Kaiten Karato Ichiba Sushi** (回転から
と市場寿司). This conveyor-belt sushi restaurant on the second floor of the Karato
Ichiba Fish Market (see below) is within
walking distance of Kaiyokan Aquarium,
making it a convenient stop for lunch.
5–50 Karatomachi. ☎ 083/233-2611.
www.kaitenkaratoichibazusi.com. Sushi
plates ¥105–¥525. No credit cards. Lunch
& dinner daily. Closes irregularly; check
website for up-to-date information. Train:
Shimonoseki Station.

❺ ★ **Kaikyo Yume Tower** (海峡ゆめタワー). On
clear days, the observation deck offers unparalleled views of the strait and surrounding
area. (Incidentally, the city of Kokura, right
across the water, was the original target for
the "Fat Man" atomic bomb, but poor visibility
on that day diverted the bombers to Nagasaki instead.) ⏱ 30 min. 3-3-1 Buzenda-cho.
☎ 083/231-5600. www.kaikyomesse.jp. ¥600
adults, ¥300 kids. Daily 9:30am–9pm. Train:
Shimonoseki Station.

> *A view from Kaikyo Yume Tower.*

Where to Stay & Dine in Shimonoseki

Karato Ichiba Fish Market (唐戸市場) *SEAFOOD*
Although this is a wholesale fish market, it also features a variety of vendors that sell prepared sushi, fugu, and other seafood fresh off the boat. It's most fun to visit early in the morning, when the sellers have their freshest wares on display, but it stays open for lunch as well. There are several sit-down restaurants on the second floor, though many prefer to grab some takeout from the vendors and picnic on the riverside boardwalk right outside. 5–50 Karatomachi. ☎ 083/231-0001. www.karatoichiba.com. Entrees ¥00–¥1,000. No credit cards. Breakfast & lunch daily. Bus: Karato.

★ Kitagawa (ふく所 喜多川) *SEAFOOD*
In business since 1871, this classy establishment is many locals' go-to place for seafood. Their most expensive fugu sashimi platters, which feature the slices of fish arranged into the shapes of flying cranes, are as beautiful to behold as they are delicious to eat. For the less adventurous, there are plenty of non-fugu dishes on the menu as well. 7–11 Nabe-cho. ☎ 083/32-3212. www.fuku-kitagawa.com. Lunch entrees from ¥3,150, dinner entrees from ¥5,250. AE, DC, V. Lunch & dinner daily. Bus: Karato.

Nishi Washington Hotel (西ワシントンホテル)
The reasonably priced, no-frills Western-style hotel has courteous staff and clean, larger-than-average rooms. Right across from Shimonoseki station, it earns points for convenience as well. 1–4–1 Yamatomachi. ☎ 083/261-410. http://shimonoseki.washington.jp. 239 units. Doubles from ¥10,000. AE, DC, MC, V. Train: Shimonoseki Station.

Shimonoseki Ijinkan (下関異人館) *COFFEE SHOP*
Located in Shimonoseki's old British consulate, this is a fun diversion for teatime. There isn't much in the way of food, but they claim to be the "top café au lait servers in all of Japan." Order one and a tuxedoed waiter will pour your beverage with a flourish. 4–11 Karatomachi. ☎ 083/222-262. Drinks from ¥1,000. No credit cards. Breakfast, lunch & dinner Tues–Sun. Bus: Karato.

★★★ Shunpanro Hotel (春帆楼)
Hands down Shimonoseki's top accommodations, this is a historic place: the Treaty of Shimonoseki, which ended the first Sino-Japanese War, was signed here in 1865. (A small museum dedicated to the subject is on the hotel grounds.) Shunpanro is a hybrid hotel-*ryokan;* most rooms are Japanese-style, but the VIP room features both a tatami-mat floor and a separate Western-style bedroom. The Shunpanro is most well known for is its fugu cuisine, served in elaborate courses in guests' rooms. If you have the money to splurge, it doesn't get any better than this. 4–2 Amida-dera. ☎ 083/223-7181. www.shunpanro.com. 9 units. Doubles ¥26,000 per person with breakfast & kaiseki dinner, ¥35,700 per person with breakfast & fugu dinner. AE, DC, MC, V. Bus: Akama-Jingu Mae.

Fugu

Hype and hyperbole surrounds fugu cuisine (or *fuku,* as Shimonoseki locals call it), which is prepared from the skin and meat of a species of pufferfish called *torafugu.* The internal organs of *torafugu,* also known as blowfish or globefish, are undeniably toxic, but a special training program and license are required for any establishment that serves it; in modern times, cases of poisonings at restaurants are all but unknown. In the past decade or so, some 50 people in Japan have died of fugu poisoning, usually because they tried preparing it at home.

Fugu is usually served in courses that consist of a sashimi plate, a marinated mix of meat and skin, and battered and fried chunks of fugu meat. In winter months, hot pots and *hire-zake*—hot rice wine with a dried fugu fin floating in it—are popular accompaniments. Overexcited diners sometimes report tingling lips and fingers after consuming fugu, ostensibly from traces of the poison, but most experts generally dismiss the effect as wishful thinking.

Western Honshu Fast Facts

> Hiroshima's Heiwa Odori Boulevard.

Arriving & Getting Around

BY PLANE Most travelers come through **Hiroshima Airport** (☎ 0848/86-8151; www.hij.airport.jp), which is serviced by Japan Airlines and All Nippon Airways. Limousine buses connect the airport with Hiroshima Station's north exit (48 min.; ¥1,300 one-way). Flights from Tokyo to **Okayama Airport** (☎ 086/294-5201; www.okayama-airport.org) take about 1 hour and 15 minutes (¥27,100). An airport limousine bus runs to Okayama Station (30 min.; ¥680). **BY TRAIN Hiroshima** is about 6 hours from Tokyo by Shinkansen bullet train, 3 hours from Kyoto, and 1⅓ hours from Kyushu (¥17,540). The easiest way to reach **Matsue** is from Okayama via a JR Limited Express train (2½ hr.; ¥4,850). **Okayama** is a major stop on the Shinkansen bullet train from Tokyo (4 hr.; ¥15,850), from Kyoto (1¼ hr.; ¥6,820), and Hiroshima (50 min.; ¥5,350). **BY BUS** Buses depart from Tokyo Station every night at 8 and 9pm, both reaching **Hiroshima Station** at 8am the next morning (¥11,600 one-way). From Osaka, buses depart six times a day (5 hr.; ¥5,000). Buses depart from Tokyo's Shibuya Station (in front of Mark City) nightly at 8pm, arriving at **Matsue Station** at 6:35am (¥11,550 one-way). Buses depart nightly from Shinjuku Station's west exit in Tokyo, arriving at **Okayama Station** the next morning (¥9,800 one-way). From Tokyo Station, JR buses depart from the south exit at 9:20pm and arrive in Okayama at 7:15am (¥10,000). **BY BOAT** You can reach **Hiroshima** by high-speed boat from Matsuyama on Shikoku in 70 min. (¥6,300), but slower ferries are cheaper (2½ hr.; ¥2,900) and provide better views of the Seto Inland Sea.

ATMs

In contrast to those abroad, many ATMs only operate during banking hours. ATMs are also very hard to find outside of major cities, so plan accordingly. Most post offices (see below) have ATM facilities, although hours are limited. For 24-hour access, your best bet are the ATMs in **7-Eleven** convenience stores which accept Visa, Plus, American Express, JCB, Union Pay, or Diner's Club International cards for cash withdrawals. (They recently stopped accepting MasterCard, Maestro, and Cirrus cards.) **Citibank** and **Shinsei Bank** ATMs accept foreign bank cards as well.

Doctors & Hospitals

Consult with your hotel for information about nearby clinics or hospitals. **Hiroshima University Hospital** (☎ 082/257-5555; www.hiroshima-u.ac.jp/en/hosp) is at Kasumi 1-2-3, Minami-ku.

Emergencies

The all-around emergency number in Japan is ☎ **119.**

Internet Access

Most business hotels (but few traditional-style *onsen* or *ryokan*) offer Internet access as a perk to customers, and Internet cafes are common (though most do not allow customers to hook up their own laptops, requiring them to use the facility's machines instead).

Pharmacies

Drugstores, called *yakkyoku* (薬局) are ubiquitous in Japan, but they are not 24-hour operations. Your best bet is to ask your hotel concierge for the closest location. Note that you must first visit a doctor in Japan before

Trolleys are the classic way to commute in Hiroshima.

reign prescriptions can be filled, so it's
so best to bring an ample supply of any
rescription medication with you.

olice

 reach the police, dial ☎ **110.** You can also
op by the nearest *koban* (police substation)
r assistance.

ost Office

/estern Honshu's post offices are generally
en from 9am to 5pm, Monday through
iday. **HIROSHIMA:** Hiroshima East Post
ffice, south exit of Hiroshima Station, 2–62
atsubara-cho. **MATSUE:** Matsue Central
ost Office, north exit of Matsue Station,
8 Asahi-Cho. **OKAYAMA:** Okayama Station
ost Office, east exit of Okayama Station,
-3–1 Ekimae-cho, Kita-ku. **SHIMONOSEKI:**
himonoseki Post Office, west exit of
himonoseki Station, 2-12-12 Takezaki-Cho.

Safety

Western Honshu is extremely safe, but take
the normal common-sense precautions for
personal safety and valuables that you would
anywhere else.

Visitor Information

HIROSHIMA Peace Memorial Park Rest House
(☎ 082/247-6738; daily Apr–Sept 9:30am–
6pm, Oct–Mar 8:30am–5pm). **MATSUE**
Matsue International Tourist Information,
north exit of Matsue Station (☎ 0852/21-
4034; daily 9am–6pm). **OKAYAMA** Okayama
International Center, 5 minutes from west
exit of central gate, 2–2–1 Hokancho, Kita-Ku
(☎ 086/256-2914; Mon–Sat 9am–5pm).
SHIMONOSEKI Shimonoseki City Tourism
Promotion Division, 1–1 Nabe-cho
(☎ 0832/31-1350; www.city.shimonoseki.
yamaguchi.jp/seisaku/kokusai/gaikoku;
Mon–Fri 9am–5pm).

Favorite Moments

The island of Shikoku has been considered a far-flung destination for centuries. In times of old, the only way to reach it was by boat, but thanks to a series of bridges built in the 1980s and 1990s connecting Shikoku to Okayama, Hiroshima, and Kobe, it's no longer as far off the beaten track as it used to be. This is a place of spiritual, culinary, and natural delights.

> PREVIOUS PAGE No, you aren't on Gilligan's Island—it's only the rope bridge at Takamatsu's Shikoku Mura Village. THIS PAGE Udon noodles: Shikoku's gift to the culinary world.

❶ **Working those leg muscles at Konpira Shrine.** Tromping up this holy spot's legendary 1,368 stairs is a centuries-old tradition for those visiting Takamatsu. See p. 324, ❹.

❷ **Listening to the click-clack of *geta* sandals in Dogo Onsen.** Visitors dressed in traditional *yukata* robes and wearing wooden *geta* (clogs) are a common sight in this wonderfully relaxing "spa quarter" of Matsuyama City. If you visit any one hot spring in all of Japan, make it the spectacular **Dogo Onsen Honkan** public bathhouse. See p. 332, ❸.

❸ **Slurping some *sanuki udon*.** Udon noodles are believed to have spread throughout Japan via the city of Takamatsu, and there's no better place to try them than here. The thick white wheat noodles are the quintessential Takamatsu dish. See p. 331.

❹ **Watching the pilgrims go by.** The Shikoku Henro, or 88 Temple Pilgrimage route, is completed entirely on foot—a journey that takes two months. Pilgrims dressed in distinctive traditional white clothing are a common sight in Shikoku. You'll see them at any of the temples along the route, such as **Ishite-ji Temple.** See p. 332, ❷.

❺ **Cycling the Shimanami Kaido.** This beautiful highway connects Shikoku to the main island of Honshu by hopscotching along a series of islands in the Seto Inland Sea. In the warmer months it's a great way to see the countryside and tour some of Shikoku's lesser-known sights. See p. 325.

❻ **Wandering the gardens of Ritsurin Koen Park.** A picture-perfect example of a Japanese garden, Ritsurin is a must-see in Takamatsu even if you don't have a green thumb yourself. Divided into northern and southern gardens, its fiercely twisted pine trees and exquisite landscaping are hallmarks. See p. 336, ❷.

❼ **Time-traveling through Shikoku Mura.** This collection of antique homes and buildings, gathered from precarious locations across Shikoku and brought here for preservation, is like a window back in time—right in the middle of downtown Takamatsu. See p. 339, ❹.

❽ **Gazing into the whirlpools of Naruto.** The swirling waters of the Seto Inland Sea are famed for their ferocious riptides and whirlpools. The largest and most famous of these is the Naruto, visible at certain times of day right off the coast of Tokushima. See p. 342, ❶.

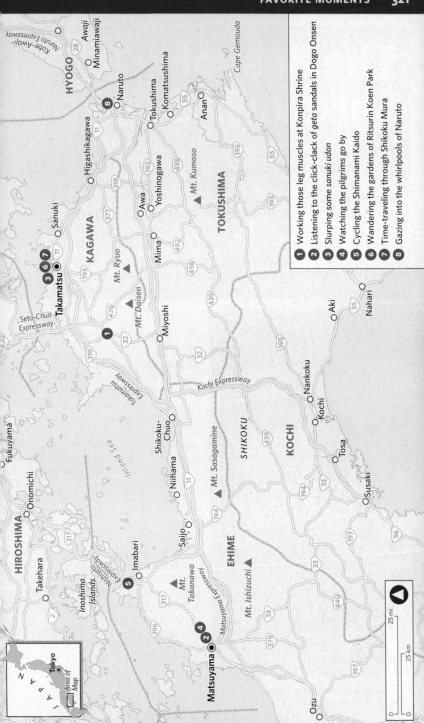

1 Working those leg muscles at Konpira Shrine
2 Listening to the click-clack of *geta* sandals in Dogo Onsen
3 Slurping some *sanuki udon*
4 Watching the pilgrims go by
5 Cycling the Shimanami Kaido
6 Wandering the gardens of Ritsurin Koen Park
7 Time-traveling through Shikoku Mura
8 Gazing into the whirlpools of Naruto

The Best of Shikoku in 3 Days

Few casual travelers make the journey to Shikoku, the smallest of the four main islands of the Japanese archipelago, which is shame, as stunning sights both man-made and natural abound in this corner of the country. It's perhaps most famous for its 88 sacred Buddhist temples: Many Japanese try to make a pilgrimage to all of them once in their lifetime, as a tribute to the great priest Kobo Daishi, who was born on Shikoku in 774 and who founded the Shingon sect of Buddhism. It takes 2 months to make the circuit on foot, the traditional way; these days, however, many opt for organized tours by bus, which take about 2 weeks. You will undoubtedly see many pilgrims as you travel through Shikoku; they're dressed in white clothing, with traditional cone-shaped woven hats.

> The imposing fortifications of Matsuyama Castle have stood for close to 4 centuries.

START Take the train to Matsuyama Station. Matsuyama is 394km (245 miles) southwest of Kyoto.

❶ **Matsuyama.** Your trip begins in Matsuyama, a favorite setting for the works of artists such as famed novelist Natsume Soseki (p. 334) and the home of **Matsuyama Castle.** Unlike many other castles in Japan, Matsuyama's isn't a replica. Completed in 1627 and renovated in the mid 19th century, it is one of the oldest surviving examples of its kind. A small museum inside houses relics from former inhabitants, including swords, armor, and scrolls.

There are several ways to reach the castle from the city. Those in the mood for a little exercise can hike through the surrounding park up to the entrance (a fairly easy 20-min. walk uphill). Otherwise, a chairlift and cable car (¥1,000 round-trip for adults, ¥400 for kids) are available from the nearby train station.

Nearby **Ishite-ji Temple,** the 51st of Shikoku's 88 sacred temples, is a good example of the sorts of places that the devout visit on their pilgrimages to the island. The beautiful main gate, Niomon, was built in 1318, which sounds old until you realize the temple itself was established in 728. The temple's main hall, which features floor-to-ceiling paintings of Buddhist deities, is a recognized Tangible Cultural Property, as is the compound's

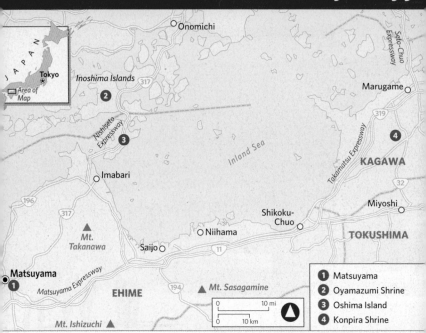

three-story pagoda. But perhaps most important for visitors is a tunnel containing statues representing the 88 temples of Shikoku; praying to each in turn is considered a shortcut to walking the entire pilgrimage route.

Dogo Onsen Honkan is the star attraction of the city, and the reason many Japanese plan visits to Shikoku in the first place. The oldest *onsen* (traditional spa) in Japan—3,000 years old, according to some accounts—it is a picture-perfect example of the Japanese hot-spring aesthetic. (In fact, it was the model for the supernatural spa in the Oscar-winning studio Ghibli anime film *Spirited Away*.)

Easily the most famous *onsen* in Japan, the Honkan is the crown jewel of an entire hot-spring resort district brimming with hotels and *ryokan* (traditional inns). But no matter where you stay, a visit to the Honkan is absolutely not to be missed. While you can't spend the night here, you can soak in its communal (gender-segregated) baths. We highly recommend paying the separate fee for a communal (¥800) or private (¥1,200–¥1,500) room to relax in after you bathe. It is also well worth the extra ¥250 to peek into the Yushinden, special rooms built especially for visits from the emperor and his retinue. See p. 332, ❸.

From Matsuyama Station, take the JR Limited Express Yosan Line to Imabari Station (37 min.). From Imabari Station, take the Seto-naikai Kotsu bus bound for Omishima (40 min.). Disembark at the Oyamazumi Jinja-mae stop.

❷ **Oyamazumi Shrine.** Located on the island of Omishima, Oyamazumi is a beautiful Shinto shrine. But the real reason to visit is its treasure museum. For centuries, top military leaders prayed for victory in battle here. When they achieved it, they returned to offer tokens of gratitude such as helmets, armor, and swords. Today, the shrine's museum houses some 80% of the country's designated national treasures, including items once owned by some of Japan's most famous warriors. ⏲ 2 hr. 327 Miyaura, Omishima-cho, Imabari-shi, Ehime-ken. ☎ 897/82-0032. ¥1,000. Daily 8:30am–5pm (last entry 4:30pm). Bus: Oyamazumi Jinja-mae.

Travel Tip

For hotels and restaurants in Matsuyama, see p. 334.

> *The majestic entrance to the Oyamazumi Shrine hints at the treasures within.*

From Oyamazumi Jinja-mae stop, take the Setonaikai Kotsu bus bound for Imabari Station. Change buses at the Yoshiumi Shisho Mae stop to a Setonaikai Kotsu bus bound for Tomoura (18 min.). Disembark at the Murakami Suigun Hakubutsukan stop.

❸ **Oshima Island.** A former Buddhist retreat, this small island is now home to the kids **Murakami Suigun Hakubutsukan (Naval Museum),** a repository of info on the pirate naval forces that stalked the straits 500 years ago during Japan's Era of Warring States. Activities include the chance to try on kimono and armor, and the museum's observation deck offers spectacular views of the inland sea.

Shikoku's waters are famed for whirlpools. The largest and most famous are found in the city of Naruto, near Tokushima (see below), but many others exist as well, such as those off of Oshima. On weekends, a local tour operator set up across from the naval museum offers 30-minute kids **Tide Rides** that skirt a whirlpool and give great views of the rugged coastline. Murakami: ◷ 1 hr. 1293-2 Miyakubo,

Miyakubo-cho, Imabari. ☎ 0897/74-1065. ¥200. Tues–Sun 9am–5pm (Wed–Sun if Mon was a holiday). Tide Rides: 1293-2 Miyakubo, Miyakubo-Cho, Imabari. ☎ 0897/86-3323. ¥1,000. Tues–Sun 9am–4pm (Wed–Sun if Mon was a holiday). Bus: Setonaikai Kotsu Line to Hakubutsukan.

Take a Kotsu bus bound for Imabari. From Imabari Station, take the JR Limited Express Yosan Line and return to Matsuyama Station. From Matsuyama Station, take the JR Express Shiokaze to Tadotsu Station. At Tadotsu, switch to the JR Dosan Line and board an express for Kotohira Station (2¾ hr.).

❹ **Konpira Shrine.** Located roughly an hour from Takamatsu by train, this shrine's official name is **Kotohiragu (Kotohira Shrine).** Konpira, as locals affectionately call it, is dedicated to seafarers and is one of the nation's oldest and most famous Shinto shrines. The innermost shrine of the complex sits atop 1,368 stairs, so proper footwear is a must. Porters are on call to ferry visitors up the first

> Who needs a StairMaster when you have the 1,368
> stairs of Konpira Shrine?

Shikoku by Bike

Oyamazumi Shrine sits just off the Shimanami Kaido, a scenic highway that bridges
the islands between Shikoku and the main
island of Honshu. A separate cycling path
that parallels the road makes it a breeze to
traverse on bike, and Oyamazumi is a fun
day trip from Matsuyama even for novice
cyclists. The best part is that you can bail
out at any time, returning the bikes along
the way and taking a bus back. Here's how
the system works:

Rental bikes are available all along the
Shimanami Kaido, but the easiest spot to
start is a hotel called **Sunrise Itoyama,**
2-8-1 Sunabacho, Imabari (☎ 0898/41-
3196; www.sunrise-itoyama.jp). To get
there take the express from Matsuyama
Station to Imabari Station (40 min.). There
are regular buses from Imabari to Sunrise
Itoyama, or you can switch to the local train
line and ride one stop to Hashihama Station, a 20-minute walk from Sunrise Itoyama. Bikes are ¥500 a day plus a ¥1,000
deposit that you forfeit if you decide to
return the bike to one of the drop-off sites
along the way rather than bringing it back.
Oyamazumi Shrine is roughly 2½ hours
(one-way) from Sunrise Itoyama, which
might sound like a lot of cycling, but the
trip goes by in the blink of an eye. You still
have to pay bridge tolls even on bikes, and
don't forget to ask for a bus schedule when
you set out on your journey, in case you get
tired along the way.

365 steps of the way via a touristy but fun pa-
lanquin for ¥5,300 one-way or ¥6,800 round-
trip. Restaurant stalls, souvenir stands, and
other attractions line the staircase, so take
your time; most famous is a old kabuki theater
called the **Konpira Grand Playhouse.** Built in
1865, it is a beautiful example of its kind and
open for tours on days when kabuki isn't being
performed. See p. 339, **⑤**. Playhouse: 241 Otsu,
Kotohira-cho. ☎ 0877/73-3846. ¥500 adults,
¥300 junior-high and high-school students,
¥200 elementary students and younger. Daily
9am-5pm. Train: Kotohira Station.

HOLY HOUSES

Japan is home to uncountable Shinto shrines and
Buddhist temples—here's how to tell them apart.

BY MELINDA JOE

SHRINES DEDICATED TO THE GODS OF JAPAN'S NATIVE RELIGION OF SHINTO, and temples for the adopted religion of Buddhism, dot Japanese cities and the countryside. Newcomers often have a difficult time telling them apart, and with good reason, for the religions have co-existed for centuries and continue to influence one another in Japan. That said, there are specific features—and ways of showing respect—that are unique to each. The following is a (very!) brief guide to what kind of holy spot you're looking at, and what to do once you get inside.

Shinto Shrines

Shinto shrines come in all shapes and sizes, from tiny altars to large buildings.

TORII
These distinctively shaped gates mark the entrances and exits of shrine compounds where the profane meets the sacred. While there are exceptions, they tend to be associated with shrines rather than temples.

KOMAINU
These "heavenly dogs" are gargoyle-like statues found inside shrine grounds. Many shrines feature *inari* (fox-gods) instead of *komainu* dogs. Generally, one is posed with its mouth open, and the other closed.

HAIDEN
The shrine proper. The general method of praying in the *haiden* is to make an offering of a coin, ring the bell, bow twice, clap twice, make your wish or prayer, then bow again. (There are regional variations, but this is the most generally accepted method.)

WASHING TROUGH
Before proceeding to the *haiden*, it is customary to wash one's hands and mouth with the water from these troughs. Ladle the water so it splashes outside the trough, not inside, when washing with it.

Buddhist Temples

Buddhist temples tend to be larger affairs than Shinto shrines.

GATE
In contrast to the *torii* of a shrine, the gates of Buddhist temples can be buildings in their own right. Larger ones are used to store holy texts, and are often flanked by statues of the deity Nio.

INCENSE BURNER
These large vats contain sticks of burning incense left as offerings. It is customary to "bathe" in the smoke before entering.

MAIN HALL
This is where services are conducted. Visitors pay their respects from outside the main hall. In cases where visitors are allowed inside, always remove your shoes before entering. To show your respects, simply bow your head before the offering box.

PAGODA
Based on the Indian *stupa*, these elaborately tiered buildings are common sights on the grounds of larger temples.

GARDENS
The arrangement of the trees and gardens within temple compounds is an elaborately circumscribed affair. The raked stone gardens associated with Japanese landscaping are mainly found in Buddhist temples.

The Best of Shikoku in 1 Week

Even a week isn't enough to truly take in all of this island's sights, but it definitely gives you a little extra time to explore. This extension of the 3-day tour takes you to parks and museums in several of Shikoku's most-famous cities—and lets you eat your fill of a certain famed noodle dish, too.

> *The gardens of Shikoku Mura Village.*

START From Kotohira Station, take the JR Express Sunspot to Takamatsu Station (45 min.). Takamatsu is 232km (144 miles) southwest of Kyoto.

❶ Takamatsu. A port town that has flourished for centuries, Takamatsu is perhaps best known among average Japanese as the home of *sanuki udon* noodles (see p. 331 for more about enjoying this signature dish). But it also happens to be home to several world-class shrines and gardens. (In fact, this city boasts more bonsai nurseries than anywhere else in the country.)

Quintessentially Japanese, **Ritsurin Koen Park** is one of the most beautiful examples of its kind in Japan. The landscaping is carefully designed so that viewers get a new perspective of arranged stones, trees, and the mountain backdrop with every turn of the path that runs through it. In addition to the natural scenery, the park also contains a tea house, a folk-art museum, and a market selling a wide variety of local products and traditional crafts, so it is a great way to while away a morning or afternoon.

Shikoku Mura Village, a replica of an old village, is an open-air folk museum with an interesting twist: The buildings themselves *aren't* replicas. The traditional homes, storehouses, and other structures were rescued and relocated here from their original sites across Shikoku. Nestled in a forest area, the picturesque collection contains thatched-roof homes, cottages, a tea-ceremony house, and a traditional vine-suspension bridge from the Iya Valley area. It's amusing to wonder what the original, long-since-departed inhabitants would make of their humble dwellings being tourist attractions now. See p. 339, ❹.

From Takamatsu Station, take the JR Express Uzushio from Takamatsu to Tokushima City (1¼ hr.).

Travel Tip

For hotels and restaurants in Takamatsu, see p. 340. For hotels and restaurants in Tokushima, see p. 344.

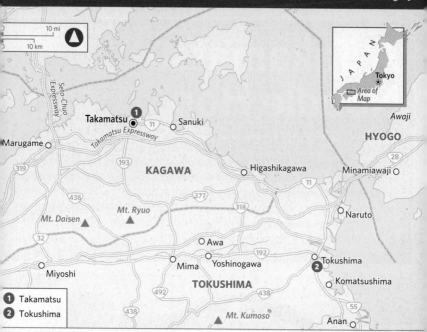

1 Takamatsu
2 Tokushima

2 Tokushima. Somewhat off the beaten path, this is generally the place where people begin rather than end their visits to Shikoku. The city's biggest claim to fame is the Awa-Odori festival, a 400-year-old tradition that takes place every August 12 to 15 on the city's streets. (*Tip:* While it's fun to watch the festival and even more fun to participate in it, hotels fill up quickly with celebrants visiting from around Japan, so make plans well in advance if you plan to visit during this time.) But even if your schedule doesn't let you experience the actual event, you can get the next best thing at the **Awa-Odori Kaikan Hall,** which is filled with exhibits, videos, studios, and semi-regular exhibitions by local dancers. The Awa-

Odori Kaikan Hall is also a convenient jumping-off (or is that "jumping up"?) point for the **Mount Bizan Ropeway.** This cable car leaves from the fifth floor of Awa-Odori Kaikan and traverses up the mountainside. Named for the Japanese word for "eyebrow," which Bizan is said to resemble, the peak offers stunning 360-degree panoramas of the surrounding area; the views of the city and surrounding islands are particularly beautiful at night (though you'll have to hike down yourself, as the cable car stops running well before dark). See p. 342. Mount Bizan Ropeway: 2-20 Shinmachi Hashi. ☎ 088/611-1611. ¥600 one-way, ¥1,000 round-trip. Daily 9am–5:30pm. Bus: Awa-Odori Kaikan Mae.

Getting the Spins

Tokushima happens to be fairly close to one of Shikoku's most famous sights: the **whirlpools of Naruto** (p. 342, **1**), located off the coastline of the neighboring city of the same name. While it's definitely worth a trip if you're interested in natural phenomena, you'll need to budget 3 to 4 hours round-trip and time it carefully: The fiercely spiraling waters,

which can reach some 15m (49 ft.) wide and 2m (6½ ft.) deep, are only visible at certain times of day between high and low tides. You can gaze at the whirlpools from on high along the Naruto suspension bridge (which charges a ¥500 fee for pedestrians), but the most fun way to see them is via the **Uzushio Line ferry** that departs from Kameura Port.

A Takamatsu Noodle Hop

Takamatsu claims to be the first to have introduced *udon* noodles to Japan, courtesy of a Buddhist scholar who brought the original recipe for the thick wheat-flour pasta back from China in the 13th century. Today the ubiquitous *sanuki udon* (讃岐うどん) noodle soup is a regional superstar, and this tour samples our favorite purveyors in Takamatsu. We've picked a handful of well-regarded shops in the Ritsurin Koen area (p. 336, ❷) to minimize your travel time, but you will see *sanuki udon* shops all over the city (and the region, for that matter).

> Sanuki udon: *the classic Shikoku snack.*

START Take the train to JR Ritsurin Koen Kitaguchi Station. Takamatsu is 232km (144 miles) southwest of Kyoto.

❶ **Sakaeda** (さか枝). Renowned for the flavor of its broth, Sakaeda uses five types of *katsuo* (skipjack tuna) bullion. Locals prize it as a quick and reasonably-priced lunch. 5-2-23 Bancho. ☎ 087/834-6291. www.sakaedaudon. jp. Breakfast & lunch Mon–Sat. No credit cards. Train: JR Ritsurin Koen Kitaguchi Station.

❷ **Matsushita Seimenjo** (松下製麺所). The homey little "Matsushita Noodle Factory" has been serving Takamatsu *sanuki udon* for 40 years. They're also open a bit later than other places. 2-2 Nakano-cho. ☎ 087-831-6279. No credit cards. Breakfast & lunch Mon–Sat. Train: JR Ritsurin Koen Kitaguchi Station.

❸ **Chikusei** (竹清). Known for the quality of both their noodles and their tempura toppings, this is another local favorite—but only open 4 days a week. 2-23 Kameoka-cho. ☎ 087/834-7296. No credit cards. Lunch Mon–Tues & Fri–Sat. Train: JR Ritsurin Koen Kitaguchi Station.

Travel Tip

For more restaurants in Takamatsu, see p. 341.

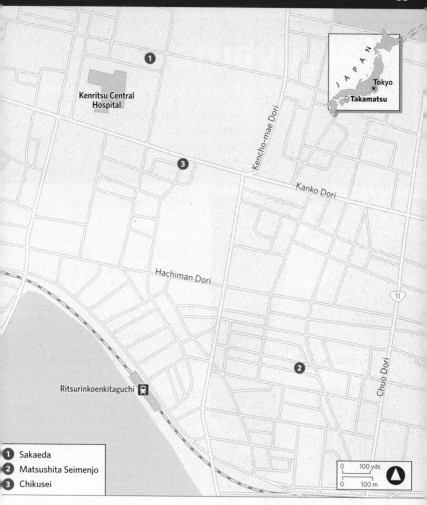

1 Sakaeda
2 Matsushita Seimenjo
3 Chikusei

Enjoying *Sanuki Udon*

Whatever its origins, over the centuries *sanuki udon* has evolved into a distinctively Japanese dish that has become virtually synonymous with Takamatsu. (Though the *udon* in Takamatsu tends to be thicker and chewier than that served in other parts of Japan.) It's a simple affair that's easy to make yet difficult to master—perhaps you could think of it as the area's culinary equivalent of pizza. *Sanuki udon* is served in small portions for around ¥150 a helping, either in a hot broth or cold alongside a dipping broth. You accentuate this basic dish with deep-fried tempura toppings (¥80 or so each) that you choose yourself. When you're done, feel free to order *kae-dama* (additional helpings of noodles), or hop from shop to shop to taste and compare. Most are family-run operations that are only open for lunch (or for as long as the noodles last), and the vast majority only accept payment in cash.

Matsuyama

The capital of Shikoku's Ehime Prefecture, Matsuyama is the largest city on the island. But "large" is a relative term, and Matsuyama has a comfortably provincial feel that contrasts pleasingly with the frenzy of Japan's major cities. The site of one of Japan's most beautifully preserved castles and its most distinguished spa, Matsuyama is a great place to get away from it all in a truly Japanese fashion.

> Stones inscribed with prayers and wishes from visitors to Ishite-ji Temple.

START Take the train to Okaido Station. Matsuyama is 394km (245 miles) southwest of Kyoto.

① Matsuyama Castle (松山城). This mountaintop castle in the center of Matsuyama has stood watch over the city for close to 400 years.

Although extensively renovated over the centuries, it retains much of its original structure. Besides offering stunning views of the surrounding area, it's worth a visit for its collection of antique weapons and ephemera once owned by the castle's lords. Strategically located, like most castles, on high ground, it's accessible via a fairly easy 20-minute hike uphill or via a chairlift and cable car from nearby Kencho-mae or Shinome-guchi train stations. ⏱ 2 hr. 1 Marunouchi Matsuyama. ☎ 089/921-4873. ¥500 adults, ¥150 kids. Daily 9am–5pm (Dec–Jan until 4:30pm Aug until 5:30pm). Train: Okaido Station.

② Ishite-ji Temple (石手寺). Matsuyama sits along the Shikoku Henro, or 88 Temple Pilgrimage route, first said to have been traversed in the 9th century. Traditionally, it is completed entirely on foot—a journey that takes 2 months. (Most modern pilgrims opt to shorten the duration by using cars or buses.) Ishite-ji is the 51st of the 88; its main hall features huge straw sandles that, when touched, provide health to those with foot or leg ailments. Good news for those who can't make the full 2-month pilgrimage: A tunnel contains statues representing the 88 temples, and pausing at each is considered a convenient shortcut to the actual route. ⏱ 1 hr. 2-9-21 Ishite. ☎ 089/977-0870. Free. Daily 24 hr. Train: Dogo Onsen Station.

③ ★★★ Dogo Onsen Honkan (道後温泉本館). This spa is Matsuyama's star attraction, and the reason many Japanese people plan visits to the city. Virtually unchanged for centuries, it is a picture-perfect example of the Japanese hot-spring aesthetic. ⏱ 3 hr. 5–6 Yunomachi, Dogo. ☎ 089/921-5141. ¥400 adults, ¥150 kids 11 and under. Daily 6am–10pm. Train: Dogo Onsen Station.

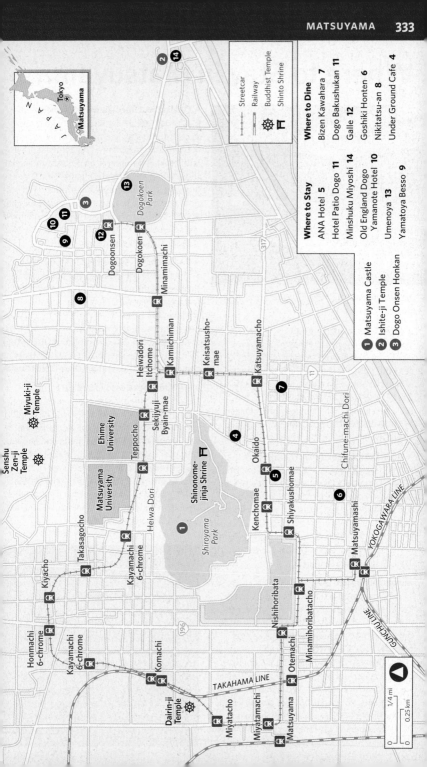

Tokyo
Matsuyama
JAPAN

Streetcar
Railway
Buddhist Temple
Shinto Shrine

Where to Dine
Bizen Kawahara **7**
Dogo Bakushukan **11**
Galle **12**
Goshiki Honten **6**
Nikitatsu-an **8**
Under Ground Cafe **4**

Where to Stay
ANA Hotel **5**
Hotel Patio Dogo **11**
Minshuku Miyoshi **14**
Old England Dogo
Yamanote Hotel **10**
Umenoya **13**
Yamatoya Besso **9**

Matsuyama Castle **1**
Ishite-ji Temple **2**
Dogo Onsen Honkan **3**

Dogokoen Park

Dogoonsen
Dogokoen
Minamimachi

Miyuki-ji Temple
Senshu Zen-ji Temple

Heiwadori Itchome
Kamiichiman
Keisatsusho-mae
Katsuyamacho

Sekijyuji Byain-mae
Teppocho
Ehime University
Matsuyama University

Shinonome-jinja Shrine
Shiroyama Park

Okaido
Kenchomae
Shiyakushomae
Matsuyamashi

Chifune-machi Dori

YOKOGAWARA LINE

Takasagocho
Kiyacho
Kayamachi 6-chome
Heiwa Dori

Honmachi 6-chome
Kayamachi 6-chome
Komachi

Nishihoribata
Minamihoribatacho
Otemachi

TAKAHAMA LINE
GUNCHULINE

Dairin-ji Temple
Miyatacho
Miyatamachi
Matsuyama

1/4 mi
0.25 km

Where to Stay in Matsuyama

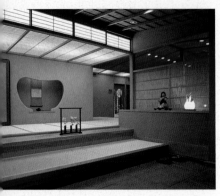

> *Yamatoya Besso's classically Japanese elegance.*

★ ANA Hotel (松山全日空ホテル)

This Western-style hotel has a very convenient central location: Streetcars to Dogo Onsen stop right out front. For a little extra flair, request a room with a view of Matsuyama Castle. 3-2-1 Ichiban-cho. ☎ 089/933-5511. 327 units. www.ichotelsgroup.com. Doubles ¥17,000–¥32,000. AE, DC, MC, V. Streetcar: Dogo Onsen.

★ Hotel Patio Dogo (ホテル パティオ・ドウゴ)

Located right across the street from the Dogo Onsen spa area, this reasonably priced Western-style hotel is perfect for those who want to experience Dogo Onsen but would rather sleep in a bed than on a futon. 20-12 Yunomachi. ☎ 089/941-4128. www.patio-dogo.co.jp. 101 units. Doubles ¥11,025–¥12,600. AE, DC, MC, V. Train: Dogo Onsen Station.

Minshuku Miyoshi (民宿みよし)

This tiny inn is on a side street near Ishite-ji Temple (call ahead to have a clerk meet you at the Dogo Onsen streetcar stop). The tatami rooms, with straw mats, shoji screens, and platform beds, are spare—even rustic—but clean; the staff doesn't speak much English but foreigners are definitely welcome. Perfect for budget travelers. 3-7-23 Ishite. ☎ 089/977-2581. 6 units. Rooms ¥4,000 per person without meals, ¥5,000 per person with breakfast, ¥7,350 per person with breakfast and dinner. No credit cards. Train: Dogo Onsen Station.

★ Old England Dogo Yamanote Hotel (オールドイングランド道後山の手ホテル)

Although most people opt to stay in a traditional inn when in Dogo, this European-style hotel decorated with antique furniture is an upscale choice for those who prefer Western amenities. It does, however, have Japanese-style indoor and outdoor communal baths. 1-13 Dogosagidani-cho. ☎ 089/998-2111. www.dogo-yamanote.com. 70 units. Doubles ¥12,900–¥36,000. AE, DC, MC, V. Train: Dogo Onsen Station.

★★★ Umenoya (旅亭うめ乃や)

An intimate and secluded experience right in the heart of the city, this tiny Japanese-style inn features a beautiful inner garden and stylishly traditional rooms. Unlike at many inns, you can pay extra for a room with its own (Western-style) bathroom. 2-8-9 Kami-ichi. ☎ 089/941-2570. 10 units. Doubles ¥23,250–¥29,250 per person. AE, DC, MC, V. Train: Dogo Onsen Station.

★★★ Yamatoya Besso (大和屋別荘)

For a truly authentic spa experience, you can't beat this 140-year-old inn, housed in a building that looks like something from a movie set. The rates include breakfasts and dinners, the latter of which are exquisite *kaiseki* (multicourse) affairs to rival those served in the best restaurants. 2-27 Dogo Sagidani-cho. ☎ 089/931-7771. http://yamatoyabesso.com. 19 units. Doubles from ¥46,350 per person. AE, DC, MC, V. Train: Dogo Onsen Station.

Required Reading

On a literary note, Matsuyama is the setting for novelist Natsume Soseki's 1906 novel *Botchan,* which is based on the author's experiences teaching in the city. It is required reading for all Japanese schoolchildren. Many local souvenir shops and attractions cater to fans of the book, and if you watch carefully, you might catch a glimpse of a Botchan steam engine plying the city's streetcar lines. (Those interested can find a translation of the novel, now in the public domain, online at http://en.wikisource.org/wiki/Botchan.)

Where to Dine in Matsuyama

Why not have a beer or three at Dogo Bakushukan?

★ Bizen Kawahara (美膳 かわはら) SEAFOOD

This upscale eatery specializes in elaborate courses based on local fish, *ise-ebi* (spiny lobster), and *watarigani* (blue crab), all of it served in a variety of styles. 1-2-7 Niban-cho. ☎ 089-931-5963. Lunch entrees from ¥1,500, dinner entrees from ¥5,000. MC, V. Lunch & dinner Tues–Sun (open all week in Dec). Train: Matsuyamacho Station.

Dogo Bakushukan (道後麦酒館) PUB

Dogo Bakushukan means "Dogo Beer Hall," and it's exactly what the name implies: an *izakaya* (pub) specializing in the locally made brew. It's conveniently located right across the street from the Dogo Onsen area, making it a popular stop to cool off with a frosty one after a hot soak. 20-13 Yunomachi. ☎ 089/945-866. www.dogobeer.co.jp. Beer ¥470, small plates from ¥650. AE, DC, MC, V. Lunch & dinner daily. Train: Dogo Onsen Station.

Galle CAFE

Though Galle is more of a sit-down coffee shop than an actual restaurant, they do serve cakes and light meals here as well. But this is the place to go when you need a local caffeine fix. 12-1 Yunomoto. ☎ 089/921-8676. Set meals ¥500–¥800. No credit cards. Breakfast & lunch Tues–Sun. Train: Dogo Onsen Station.

★★ Goshiki Honten (郷土料理 五志喜) JAPANESE

One of the oldest establishments in Matsuyama—its roots extend back some 375 years!—this is your one-stop shop for experiencing local cuisine. Best known for their colorful *somen* noodles (stretched wheat noodles served cold), they also serve *shabu-shabu* (hot-pot dishes) and a wide variety of regional dishes, including tempuras and grilled vegetables and meats. 3-5-4 Sanban-cho. ☎ 089/933-3838. Lunch entrees from ¥1,000, dinner entrees from ¥3,000. AE, V. Lunch & dinner daily. Train: Okaido Station.

★★★ Nikitatsu-an (にきたつ庵) JAPANESE

A cozy yet sophisticated Japanese restaurant run by the local brewery. The seafood is excellent (the sashimi in particular is great), but then again, so are the *wagyu* (Japanese beef) dishes. It also boasts a very well-stocked rice-wine cellar filled with local brands. 3-18 Kitamachi. ☎ 089/924-6617. Lunch entrees from ¥1,000, dinner entrees from ¥2,500. AE, DC, MC, V. Lunch & dinner Tues–Sun (drinks only 2–5pm). Train: Dogo Onsen Station.

★ Under Ground Cafe MEXICAN

For those times when you hanker for a hunk of cheese, this is the place. More about stylish atmosphere than authenticity (its trademark is a giant Union Jack flag), this is Matsuyama's one and only Mexican-style restaurant. It's also open very late. 3-6-6 Okaido. ☎ 089/998-7710. Lunch entrees from ¥1,000, dinner entrees from ¥2,000. No credit cards. Lunch, dinner & late-night daily. Train: Okaido Station.

Takamatsu

Located on the northeast coast of Shikoku, surrounded by beautiful views of the Seto Inland Sea and the Sanuki mountain range, Takamatsu has long been considered one of the "gateways" to the island. Although Takamatsu is considered a "castle town," its castle is actually a recent reconstruction and nowhere near as impressive as that of Matsuyama's. Takamatsu is far better known for its green thumb: Many of Japan's bonsai nurseries are located here, as is a garden park considered one of the nation's best.

> *The bridges of Ritsurin Koen Park.*

START Take the train to Takamatsu Chikko Station. Takamatsu is 232km (144 miles) southwest of Kyoto.

① Tamamo Park (**Takamatsu Castle;** 玉藻公園). This pleasant park is ringed with the beautiful stone ramparts of the former Takamatsu Castle. The castle itself is a reconstruction (and a recent one at that, with work ongoing as of the writing of this book). It was dismantled in the 19th century; in recent decades locals organized a rebuilding effort. The lack of any solid reference material as to what the castle originally looked like has slowed progress, though.

Takamatsu Castle is one of the few castles in Japan that was built on the seaside rather than atop a mountain or on a plain. Matsuyama-shi Tamomocho. ☎ 087/851-1521. Daily sunrise-sunset. ¥200 adults; ¥100 children. Train: Takamatsu Chikko Station.

② Ritsurin Koen Park (栗林公園). Once, this was a private retreat for the exclusive use of the Matsudaira clan, who ruled the Sanuki region for more than 2 centuries until the Meiji Restoration of 1868. Fortunately, you don't have to be a samurai aristocrat to enjoy this superb example of a Japanese garden today. Work

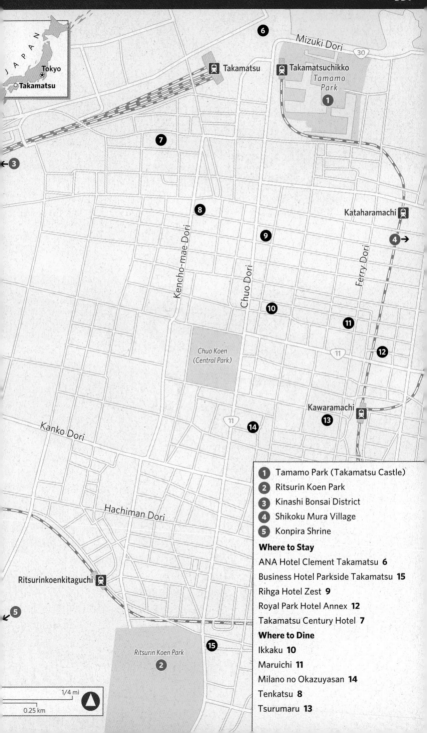

Mizuki Dori

30

Takamatsu

Takamatsuchikko

Tamamo Park

1

7

3

8

Kencho-mae Dori

Kataharamachi

9

4

Chuo Dori

Ferry Dori

10

11

12

Chuo Koen (Central Park)

11

Kawaramachi

13

Kanko Dori

11

14

Hachiman Dori

Ritsurinkoenkitaguchi

1 Tamamo Park (Takamatsu Castle)

2 Ritsurin Koen Park

3 Kinashi Bonsai District

4 Shikoku Mura Village

5 Konpira Shrine

Where to Stay

ANA Hotel Clement Takamatsu 6

Business Hotel Parkside Takamatsu 15

Rihga Hotel Zest 9

Royal Park Hotel Annex 12

Takamatsu Century Hotel 7

Where to Dine

Ikkaku 10

Maruichi 11

Milano no Okazuyasan 14

Tenkatsu 8

Tsurumaru 13

Ritsurin Koen Park

2

5

15

JAPAN

Tokyo

Takamatsu

1/4 mi

0.25 km

> *Nature, sculpted by the human hand: Ritsurin Koen.*

Sanuki

In times of old, Takamatsu and its surrounding area were known as Sanuki. The appellation remains today in the form of *sanuki udon*, a noodle dish that locals claim is the precursor to all *udon* recipes throughout Japan. If you're visiting the city, you absolutely owe it to yourself to try this distinctive, fun-to-eat local cuisine, a sort of "build-it-yourself" dish consisting of tempura set atop a bowl of hot or cold noodles. For a quick guide to several of the city's most well known *sanuki udon* restaurants, see p. 330.

egan on the garden in 1642; it wasn't completed for more than a hundred years, giving ou some sense of the sheer amount of attention and effort devoted to its construction. s koi-filled ponds, lovely arching bridges, nd beautiful mountain backdrop make it one f the most-popular attractions in the city. nglish-speaking guides are often on duty to rovide free tours to those who want them. 2½ hr. 1-20-16 Ritsurin-cho. ☎ 087/833-7411. ww.pref.kagawa.jp/ritsurin. ¥400 adults, ¥170 ds. Daily sunrise–sunset. Train: Ritsurin Koen tation.

Kinashi Bonsai District (鬼無　盆栽の里)**.** The harming suburb of Kinashi, located just two tops from Takamatsu Station, is the center of e city's bonsai culture. Some 80 nurseries e located here; many are clustered on "Bonai Street," just a few minutes north of Kinashi tation. The vast majority welcome windowhoppers, so feel free to look around. The th, 15th, and 20th of every month are public uction days, when serious cultivators bid on e best specimens. A good place to start is

> *Shikoku Mura's structures were all rescued from other parts of the island.*

Nakanishi Chinshoen nursery. Nakanishi: 8-2 Kinashi-cho. ☎ 087/882-0526. Daily 9am–5pm. Train: Kinashi Station.

④ **Shikoku Mura Village.** This open-air folk museum boasts more than 30 Edo-era houses and assorted structures. It's picturesquely located on the wooded slope of Yashima Hill, on the northeastern edge of town. ⏱ 2 hr. 91 Yashima-naka-machi. ☎ 087/843-3111. ¥800 adults; ¥500 high-school students; ¥300 children. Daily 8:30am–6pm (Nov–Mar to 5:30pm). Streetcar: Kotoden Yashima Station.

⑤ **Konpira Shrine** (金刀比羅宮)**.** Located roughly an hour from Takamatsu by train, Konpira is one of the nation's oldest and most famous Shinto shrines. 892 Kotohira-cho. ☎ 0877/75-2121. Free. Daily sunrise to sunset. Train: Kotohira Station.

Where to Stay in Takamatsu

> *The convenient Takamatsu Century Hotel.*

★★★ **ANA Hotel Clement Takamatsu** (全日空ホテルクレメント高松) Centrally located and so sleek it almost feels out of place, this unique-looking, well-appointed, and nautical-themed hotel is certainly the most luxurious Western-style facility in the city. The higher floors offer excellent views. 1-1 Hamano-cho. ☎ 087/811-1111. www.ichotelsgroup.com. 300 units. Doubles from ¥20,790. AE, DC, MC, V. Train: Takamatsu Station.

★ **Business Hotel Parkside Takamatsu** (ビジネスホテルパークサイド高松) It's just your average business hotel, but you can't beat the location: right across from the famed Ritsurin gardens (p. 336, ②). The top floors have clear views of the gardens; unfortunately, the nonsmoking rooms are limited to the lower floors, so you'll have to put up with the scent of tobacco for the best views. 1-3-1 Ritsurin-cho. ☎ 087/837-5555. 116 units. Doubles from ¥7,950. AE, DC, MC, V. Train: Ritsurin Koen Station.

★★ **Rihga Hotel Zest** (リーガホテルゼスト高松) Offering a wide variety of price ranges for all sorts of travelers, this centrally located hotel has two annexes. The cheaper rooms are in the main building, more expensive rooms in the annex. The rooftop beer garden, open in the summer months, is a favorite hangout for locals and visitors alike. 9-1 Furujinmachi. ☎ 087/822-3555. www.rihga.com/kagawa. 122 units. Doubles from ¥15,015. No credit cards. Train: Takamatsu Station.

★ **Royal Park Hotel Annex** (ロイヤルパークホテル) fairly standard, no-frills, Japanese-style business hotel, the Royal Park is located right in the center of Takamatsu's nightlife district. Although clean and well-maintained, the lower floors (which mainly house single rooms) can be a little loud at night. 11-1 Fukudamachi. ☎ 087/823-1111. 117 units. Doubles from ¥13,860. AE, DC, MC, V. Train: Kawaramachi Station.

★ **Takamatsu Century Hotel** (高松センチュリーホテル) This business hotel has pleasant staff, a laid-back atmosphere, and clean rooms. What it lacks in frills it makes up for in location (just a 5-minute walk from Takamatsu Station) and cost. 1-4-19 Nishimachi. ☎ 087/851-0558 www.takamatsu-century.com/en. 70 units. Doubles from ¥9,240. AE, DC, MC, V. Train: Takamatsu Station.

Where to Dine in Takamatsu

Tenkatsu's terrifically tempting tempura.

kaku (一鶴高松店) *JAPANESE*

Takamatsu institution since 1952, Ikkaku specializes in chicken dishes, particularly *onetsuki-dori* (roasted chicken on the bone), nd *tori-meshi* (a flavorful steamed rice dish). ~1 Kajiyamachi. ☎ 087-823-3711. www.ikkaku. o.jp. Entrees from ¥450. No credit cards. Lunch dinner daily. Train: Kawaramachi Station.

aruichi (まるいち焼鳥居酒屋) *PUB*

ne of the few *izakaya* pubs that accepts cred- cards and has staff that speak a modicum English, Maruichi is a great place to unwind ith a few beers and yakitori chicken skewers ter a long day of tromping through the city. It n be a little tough to find: Take the west exit Kawaramachi Station, cross the street, and ok for the sign with a red circle in an alley- ay on your right. 1-4-13 Tokiwa-cho. ☎ 087/ 1-7623. Entrees from ¥550. AE, DC, MC, V. nner & late-night Mon-Sat. Train: Kawarama- i Station.

Milano no Okazuyasan (ミラノのおかず屋さん)

ALIAN Italian restaurants of dubious prov- ance abound in Japan, but this one is a cut ove the rest. Featuring handmade pastas d pizzas, the set lunch menus include all- u-can-eat salad and fresh-baked bread. It's

the place to go when you're craving a little fettuccine Alfredo and a glass of wine. 11-14 Kamei-cho. ☎ 087/837-1782. www.okazuyasan. info. Entrees ¥840-¥1,280. MC, V. Lunch & dinner daily. Train: Kawaramachi Station.

Tenkatsu (天勝 本店) *JAPANESE*

This reliable purveyor of Japanese cuisine specializes in tempura, sushi, and *kaiseki* (mul- ticourse) cuisine. The restaurant's plastic food displays are a boon for the language-impaired. While it has both standard and tatami-mat seating, the counter is a lot of fun, too, as it faces a large tank from which fresh fish are netted and prepared to order. 7-8 Hyogomachi. ☎ 087/821-5380. Lunch entrees from ¥840, dinner entrees from ¥1,050. AE, DC, MC, V. Lunch & dinner daily. Train: Takamatsu Station.

Tsurumaru (鶴丸) *NOODLES*

A Takamatsu standard. Renowned for their curried *udon* noodles, Tsurumaru also serves a wide variety of variations on the dish, includ- ing the regional favorite, *sanuki udon*. Open un- til 4am, it turns into a bustling nightspot many evenings. 9-34 Furubaba-cho. ☎ 087/821-3780. www.turumaru.jp. Noodles from ¥800. No cred- it cards. Lunch, dinner & late-night Mon-Sat. Train: Kawaramachi Station.

Tokushima

In the late 19th century, this was a bustling port city that ranked as one of the 10 largest in Japan. Today it remains a major regional transport hub, but with only slightly more than a quarter of a million residents, it retains a small-town feel in comparison to the nation's major cities.

> *Cable cars are the fastest, most scenic way up Mount Bizan.*

START From Tokushima take the bus to Naruto Koen. Tokushima and Naruto are about 180km (112 miles) southwest of Kyoto.

❶ Naruto Whirlpools (鳴門の渦潮). This is the first thing most Japanese associate with Tokushima, although it is actually located in the neighboring city of Naruto, a roughly 1-hour bus ride away. The strait between Naruto and Awaji Island funnels massive amounts of water between the Pacific and the Seto Inland Sea, creating fiercely spiraling vortexes that can reach some 15m (49 ft.) wide and 2m (6½ ft.) deep.

The whirlpools are only visible at certain times of day between high and low tides, so you will need to time your visit carefully; the **Uzushio Line ferry** website posts monthly charts in Japanese. You might want to try this as a separate day trip.

To get there from Tokushima, take a Tokushima Line bus from the bus terminal in front of JR Tokushima train station bound for Naruto Koen (鳴門公園); buses generally depart hourly on the hour between 9am and 5pm, and take a little more than an hour to reach Naruto. Be aware that the last bus from Naruto Park for Tokushima Station departs at 4:30pm (times subject to change). Ferry: Kameura Port, inside Naruto Park. ☎ 088/687-0101. www.uzusio.com. ¥1,530 adults, ¥770 elementary students and younger. Daily 9am-4:20pm. Bus: Naruto Koen.

❷ Awa-Odori Kaikan Hall (阿波おどり会館). If you're lucky enough to be visiting between August 12 and 15, the Awa-Odori festival—a 400-year dance tradition—is a blast to watch and even more fun to join in. Hotels fill up quickly with celebrants visiting from around Japan, so make plans well in advance—several months at least—if you plan to visit during this time. Even if your schedule doesn't let you experience the actual event, you can get the next best thing at the Awa-Odori Kaikan Hall, which is filled with exhibits, videos, studios, and semi-regular exhibitions by local dancers. 2-20 Shinmachi Hashi. ☎ 088/611-1611. ¥300. Daily 9am-5pm. Bus: Awa-Odori Kaikan Mae.

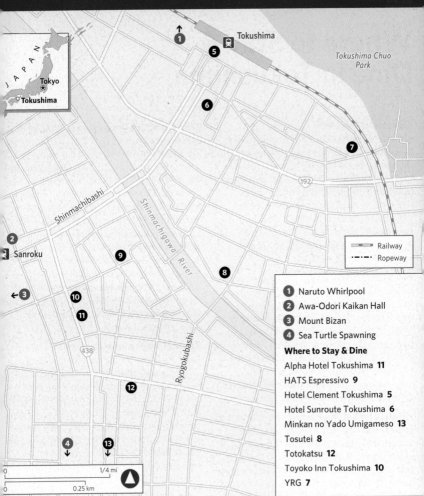

Tokushima

Tokushima Chuo Park

Railway
Ropeway

1. Naruto Whirlpool
2. Awa-Odori Kaikan Hall
3. Mount Bizan
4. Sea Turtle Spawning
Where to Stay & Dine
Alpha Hotel Tokushima 11
HATS Espressivo 9
Hotel Clement Tokushima 5
Hotel Sunroute Tokushima 6
Minkan no Yado Umigameso 13
Tosutei 8
Totokatsu 12
Toyoko Inn Tokushima 10
YRG 7

❸ **Mount Bizan** (眉山ロープウェイ). A tram leaves from the fifth floor of Awa-Odori Kaikan (see above) and traverses this mountainside, Tokushima's major peak. The mountain is a great way to get a good view of the surrounding area; the views of the city and surrounding islands are particularly beautiful at night though you'll have to walk down, as the tram tops running after dark). 2-20 Shinmachi Hashi. ☎ 088/611-1611. ¥300. Daily 9am-5pm. Bus: Awa-Odori Kaikan Mae.

❹ **Sea Turtle Spawning** (日和佐ウミガメの産卵). The town of Hiwasa in Minami City, an hour south of Tokushima by train, is one of the few places where endangered sea turtles can lay their eggs on natural beaches in Japan. The egg-laying season runs May through August; visitors are free to walk the local shoreline searching for turtles, but the beaches are placed strictly off-limits from 7pm to 4am to give the weary turtles the quiet they require. From mid-August through late September, Hiwasa also stages occasional releases of baby turtles raised in hatcheries into the ocean. To reach Hiwasa, take a Mugi Line Express from Tokushima Station to Hiwasa Station. Like the Naruta Whirlpool, this trip might be easier done as a day excursion.

Where to Stay & Dine in Tokushima

Alpha Hotel Tokushima (アルファホテル徳島)
HIGASHI DAIKUMACHI This straightforward business hotel has some very convenient amenities: Its on-site coin laundry can be a lifesaver (the reception desk sells detergent for ¥50 a pop), and it also rents bicycles to guests. Popular for its convenience and reasonable prices, it can fill up quickly. 2–11 Higashidaikumachi. ☎ 088/655-6006. 84 units. Doubles from ¥9,800. AE, DC, MC, V. Bus: Yamashiromachi.

HATS Espressivo HIGASHI SHINMACHI *CAFE*
When you're craving Western-style cuisine, this trendy cafe is a good bet. It specializes in pizzas, pastas, and the homegrown "Tokushima burger," which is slathered in a tangy teriyaki-mayo combination. Their coffee drinks are excellent as well. 1–16–15 Higashi Shinmachi. ☎ 088/635-4698. www.hats-espressivo.com. Entrees ¥700–¥980. No credit cards. Lunch & dinner daily. Bus: Shinmachi.

★ Hotel Clement Tokushima (ホテルクレメント徳島)
TOKUSHIMA If you're looking for a more upscale experience in the city, this is it. In addition to well-appointed rooms, the hotel contains numerous restaurants, including one on the 18th floor with excellent views of the city. 1–61 Nishi, Terashima-honcho. ☎ 088/656-3111. http://www.hotelclement.co.jp. 250 units. Doubles from ¥20,790. AE, DC, MC, V. Train: Tokushima Station.

Hotel Sunroute Tokushima (ホテルサンルート徳島)
TOKUSHIMA Located right outside JR Tokushima Station, the Sunroute's shared (but, of course, gender-segregated) *onsen* and sauna makes it a popular stop. It also has several on-site restaurants, handy for times when you don't want to go out on the town. 1–5–1 Motomachi. ☎ 088-653-8111. www.sunroute-tokushima.com. 177 units. Doubles from ¥12,600. AE, DC, MC, V. Train: Tokushima Station.

Minkan no Yado Umigameso (民間の宿うみがめ荘) HIWASA
For those who plan to take a day trip to see sea turtles spawning (p. 343, ④), overnighting in Hiwasa is an option. This hotel, whose name translates as "sea turtle inn," caters to turtle fans with detailed information about conditions, and offers volunteer guides for local tours. It also has a public bath with wonderful views of the ocean. The rooms are all Japanese style, and rates vary depending on season. 370–4 Hiwasa-Ura, Minami, Kaifu-gun. ☎ 0884/77-1166. www.umigamesou.com. 34 units. Rooms ¥6,600–¥8,700 per person. Rates include breakfast & dinner. No credit cards. Train: Hiwasa Station.

Tosutei (鳥巣亭) SHINMACHIKAWA PARK *PUB FARE* An *izakaya*-style restaurant a quick 7-minute walk from Tokushima Station, Tosute specializes in tapas-style small dishes of locally-sourced poultry, much of it grilled with a "secret sauce." Their ¥680 *oyako-don* (chicken and fried egg on rice) lunch special is a neighborhood favorite. 2–18 Ryogoku-Honcho. ☎ 088/652-1773. Small plates from ¥577. No credit cards. Lunch & dinner Mon–Sat. Train: Tokushima Station.

★★ Totokatsu (徳島魚問屋とゝ喝) KONYAMACHI
SEAFOOD This upscale restaurant specializes in exquisitely prepared traditional Japanese seafood cuisine based almost entirely on locally-caught ingredients. The signature dish, *taimeshi*, consists of grilled red snapper caught in nearby Naruto Strait on a bed of rice. Perhaps the best way to enjoy Totokatsu's cuisine, however, is by ordering a set menu, which contains of 10 smaller dishes. Reservations recommended. 13–1 Konyamachi. ☎ 088/625-0110. www.uma-e.net/tokushima/home/totokatu. Entrees from ¥5,250. AE, DC, MC, V. Dinner Mon–Sat. Train: Tokushima Station.

Totokatsu's dishes are all based on locally sourced ingredients, like crab.

Toyoko Inn Tokushima (東横イン徳島) HIGASHI
DAIKUMACHI Toyoko is nondescript but clean,
and conveniently located right next to the
Mount Bizan tram (see p. 343, ❸). It's part
of the Toyoko Inn chain of business hotels,
so you can expect solid, no-frills service. 2-7
Higashidaikumachi. ☎ 088/626-1045. www.
toyoko-inn.com/e_hotel/00116/index.html. 139
rooms. Doubles ¥7,800. AE, DC, MC, V. Train:
Tokushima Station.

YRG TERASHIMA HONCHO HIGASHI *CAFE*
This hip little cafe specializes in healthy and
organic foods, with constantly changing daily
specials, and boasts a wider-than-usual selection of teas. More of a lunch place and coffee
shop than a dinner destination, it turns into a
bar in the evening hours. YRG offers wireless
internet access. 1-33-4 Terashima Honcho
Higashi. ☎ 088/656-7889. http://yrgcafe.digi2.
Entrees from ¥700. No credit cards. Lunch
& dinner Sun–Wed; lunch, dinner & late-night
Fri–Sat. Train: Tokushima Station.

> *A Japanese-style room at Minkan no Yado
Umigameso.*

Shikoku Fast Facts

Arriving & Getting Around

BY PLANE The fastest way to get to Shikoku from Tokyo is by plane, to Matsuyama Airport (MYJ), Takamatsu Airport (TAK), or Tokushima Awa-Odori Airport (TKS). Flights connect **Matsuyama** with Tokyo, Osaka, Nagoya, Fukuoka, Sapporo, Kumamoto, Kagoshima, and Okinawa. The flight from Tokyo takes 1 hour and 25 minutes. Buses connect the airport to downtown in 30 minutes for ¥400. Japan Airlines (JAL) flies from Tokyo's Haneda Airport to **Takamatsu** in 1 hour and 15 minutes. There is also air service from Osaka, Sapporo, Nagoya, and Fukuoka. An airport bus delivers passengers downtown in about 45 minutes for ¥740. BY TRAIN It is possible to get from Tokyo to Shikoku via bullet and express trains, though it is quite time-consuming. To get to **Matsuyama** from Tokyo, take the JR Shinkansen Nozomi to Okayama and then JR Express *Shiokaze* (roughly 7 hr). To get to **Takamatsu,** take the JR Shinkansen Nozomi from Tokyo to Okayama and then the JR Express Marine Liner (roughly 4½ hr). To get to **Tokushima,** take the JR Shinkansen Nozomi from Tokyo to Shin-Kobe Station. Switch to Awa Express Bus Kobe bound for Tokushima (roughly 4½ hr). BY BUS Buses to **Matsuyama** depart nightly from Tokyo Station at 8:20pm and from Shinjuku Station at 7:10pm, arriving at Matsuyama Station the next day at 8:36am and at Matsuyama Shieke (City Station) at 7:10am. One-way fares for either are ¥12,000. A JR bus (☎ 03/3516-1950) departs Tokyo Station nightly at 8:50pm and then picks up passengers at Shinjuku Station at 9:30pm, reaching **Takamatsu** at 7:33am the next day. The one-way fare is ¥10,000. BY BOAT **Matsuyama** is linked by ferry to various ports on Honshu and Kyushu islands, including Kobe (overnight trip time: 9 hr.), Osaka (overnight: 9½ hr.), Oita (near Beppu; 3½ hr.), and Hiroshima (70 min. by hydrofoil). The fare to Matsuyama is ¥6,300 from Osaka or Hiroshima and ¥3,200 from Beppu. Boats dock at Matsuyama Port (Matsuyama Kanko Ko), where buses transport passengers to Matsuyama Station in about 20 minutes for ¥450.

ATMs

In contrast to those abroad, many ATMs only operate during banking hours. ATMs are also very hard to find outside of major cities, so plan accordingly. Most post offices (see below) have ATM facilities, although hours are limited. For 24-hour access, your best bets are the ATMs in **7-Eleven** convenience stores which accept Visa, Plus, American Express, JCB, Union Pay, or Diner's Club International cards for cash withdrawals. (They recently stopped accepting MasterCard or any card on the Maestro network.) **Citibank** and **Shinsei Bank** ATMs accept foreign bank cards as well.

Doctors & Hospitals

For the nearest doctor or dentist, consult your hotel concierge. In addition, the following municipal hospitals offer medical services. MATSUYAMA **Ehime Prefectural Central Hospital** (愛媛県立中央病院) is at 83 Kasukamachi (☎ 089/947-1111; http://pref.ehime.jp) and is open 8:30am to 11pm daily. TAKAMATSU **Takamatsu City Health Center** (高松市保健センター) at 1-9-12 Sakuramachi (☎ 087/839-2363) and is open 8:30am to 5pm Monday to Friday. TOKUSHIMA There is a constantly updated list of English-speaking hospitals in Tokushima on the TOPIA website: **www.topia.ne.jp**.

Emergencies

The national emergency numbers are ☎ **110** for police and ☎ **119** for ambulance and fire.

Internet Access

Most business hotels (but few traditional-style *onsen* or *ryokan*) offer Internet access as a perk to customers, and Internet cafes are common (though most do not allow customers to hook up their own laptops, requiring them to use the facility's machines instead).

Pharmacies

Drugstores, called *yakkyoku* (薬局) are found readily in Japan. Ask your hotel for a recommendation for the closest location. Remember

The ferry to Matsuyama.

ou cannot have a foreign prescription filled
thout first visiting a doctor in Japan.

olice

o reach the police, dial ☎ **110.** You can also
op by the nearest *koban* (police substation)
r assistance.

ost Office

ATSUYAMA **Matsuyama Central Post Of-
ce** is at 3-5-6 Sanbancho (☎ 089/941-0810;
on–Fri 9am–9pm, Sat–Sun and holidays
m–7pm). TAKAMATSU **Takamatsu Central
ost Office** is at 1-15 Uchimachi (☎ 087/851-
709; Mon–Fri 9am–9pm, Sat–Sun and
lidays 9am–7pm). TOKUSHIMA **Tokushima
entral Post Office** is at 1-2 Yaoyamachi
☎ 088/622-2741; Mon–Fri 9am–9pm, Sat–
n and holidays 9am–7pm).

afety
iikoku is extremely safe, but take the nor-
al common-sense precautions for personal

safety and valuables that you would anywhere
else.

Visitor Information
MATSUYAMA The **Matsuyama Convention and
Visitors Bureau,** 3–2–46 Okaido (☎ 089/935-
7511), which offers limited services (mainly in
the form of English-language tourist brochures), is located in the Matsuyama Castle
chairlift and cable car station. TAKAMATSU The
Takamatsu City Information Plaza, 1–16 Hamano-cho
(☎ 087/851-2009), located right next to JR
Takamatsu Station, offers service in Japanese,
English, Chinese, and Korean. TOKUSHIMA The
**Tokushima Prefecture International Ex-
change Association (TOPIA),** 1-61 Honamchi
Nishi (☎ 088/656-3303; www.topia.ne.jp),
located on the sixth floor of the Clement Plaza
building (which also houses the train station),
offers a variety of local information and free
Internet access.

9
Kyushu

Favorite Moments

The island of Kyushu offers a real taste of Japanese southern comfort. Its mild climate is home to some of Japan's most well-known hot springs and national parks. Historians believe that Japan's earliest inhabitants lived on Kyushu before gradually pushing northward; many consider it a cradle of Japanese civilization. Whatever its origins, it's hard to imagine anywhere else on earth where you can experience samurai castles, Buddhist temples, active volcanoes, and rocket launches all in one place.

> PREVIOUS PAGE *Just another day underwater at the Kagoshima City Aquarium.* THIS PAGE *Mount Sakurajima dominates the Kagoshima skyline.*

1 **Getting a preview of the afterlife in Fukuoka's Tocho-ji Temple.** This temple—also home to the country's third-largest Buddha sculpture—features a room filled with portrayals of the torments awaiting doomed souls in the underworld, complete with a dark tunnel to escape for "rebirth." See p. 378, **1**.

2 **Visiting ground zero in Nagasaki.** Regardless of how you feel about the use of the atomic bomb to end World War II, seeing the effects of its devastation on this harbor city is a sobering—and some would say necessary—experience. See p. 372, **1**.

3 **Imagining life as a wealthy foreign trader in 1800s Nagasaki.** The well-preserved mansions of the Glover, Alt, and Ringer families in Glover Garden provide a glimpse of life for foreigners of a bygone age. See p. 375, **5**.

4 **Watching a rocket launch from the Tanegashima Space Center.** They only happen a few times a year, but there's nothing more thrilling than watching a spacecraft soar into orbit from this tropical paradise. See p. 369, **7**.

5 **Soaking tired fingers and feet in the free public hot springs of Unzen-Amakusa.** For an added treat, time a visit for April, when the azaleas are in full bloom. See p. 356, **1**.

6 **Dreaming of warlord ambitions as you tour Kumamoto Castle.** The gloriously gilt Honmaru Goten palace inside is a historical and aesthetic treat. See p. 357, **2**.

7 **Browsing for damascene boxes and other souvenirs in the Display Hall of Kumamoto Products.** Even if you're only window-shopping, seeing the beautifully handcrafted products on sale here is like visiting a museum. See p. 358.

1. Getting a preview of the afterlife in Fukuoka's Tocho-ji Temple
2. Visiting ground zero in Nagasaki
3. Imagining life as a wealthy foreign trader in 1800s Nagasaki
4. Watching a rocket launch from the Tanegashima Space Center
5. Soaking tired fingers and feet in the free public hot springs of Unzen-Amakusa
6. Dreaming of warlord ambitions as you tour Kumamoto Castle
7. Browsing for damascene boxes and other souvenirs in the Display Hall of Kumamoto Products
8. Getting up close and personal with a live volcano
9. Knocking back Kyushu's signature beverage in a local watering hole
10. Visiting some thousand-year-old friends on Yakushima Island
11. Taking a trip to a ghost city just off the coast of Nagasaki Harbor

8 Getting up close and personal with a live volcano. Few cities can boast a view like the one of Kagoshima's Mount Sakurajima, an active composite volcano. While you can't climb it, seeing Sakurajima from the base is a sight to behold. See p. 391, 2.

9 Knocking back Kyushu's signature beverage in a local watering hole. Now popular throughout Japan, the distilled liquor known as *shochu* got its start here in Kagoshima—and many Japanese feel the best brands can only be sampled here. Take a distillery tour and find out for yourself. See p. 360, 1.

10 Visiting some thousand-year-old friends on Yakushima island. Accessible by plane or ferry from Kagoshima, tiny Yakushima island is Japan's wettest—and is covered with groves of ancient giant cedar trees. This is an outdoor adventure without parallel in Japan. See p. 364, 1.

11 Taking a trip to a ghost city just off the coast of Nagasaki Harbor. Gunkanjima (aka Hashima island) was once a mining operation and the most densely populated plot of land on Earth. Now abandoned, its high-rises and buildings are slowly crumbling into the earth. It's an eerie sight to behold. See p. 375.

The Best of Kyushu in 3 Days

Kyushu is a long haul from Tokyo, so 3 days gives you just enough time to hit some of the island's most famous destinations. Fukuoka is the island's largest city, home to abundant regional culture—and famed as the location of Mongol ruler Kublai Khan's failed 13th-century invasion. And Nagasaki, of course, was the site of the second atomic bombing of Japan. It's also home to one of Japan's most beloved southern cuisines: the noodle dish known as *champon*.

> *"Oni-gawara"—gargoyle-like roof tiles—are a common feature of temples like Tocho-ji.*

START Take the train to Hakata Station. Fukuoka is 642km (399 miles) west of Kyoto.

1 Fukuoka. Although one of Japan's largest cities, Fukuoka is also considered one of its most livable, both by locals and by the many expats of various nationalities who have chosen to make their home here. While the city is host to many interesting shrines and museums, such as those listed below, it is perhaps most well known for its shopping and entertainment districts. Put these aside for now, though; your first stop should be **Tocho-ji Temple,** probably best known for its giant Buddha carving—at 10m (33 ft.) tall, the third-largest in Japan. But this temple's defining feature is its portrayal of the travails awaiting tormented

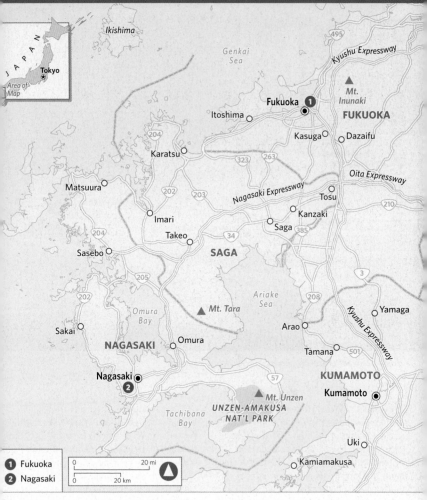

ouls in the afterlife. Housed in a small room eside the Buddha are paintings of unfortunates uffering the burnings and boilings of hell; after iewing them, you are guided through a pitch-ark hallway in a symbolic "rebirth."

The **Hakata Machiya Folk Museum** cel-brates the history and cultural heritage of lakata, the old merchants' town, concentrat-ng primarily on the Meiji and Taisho eras. occupies three buildings filled to the brim vith items used in everyday life, as well as ioramas depicting festivals, everyday street cenes, and a home typical of a Hakata mer-hant family. A must-see for those interested n local Kyushu culture.

Kushida Shrine is Fukuoka's oldest shrine. Site of the Yamakasa Festival, it has long been the shrine for merchants praying for good health and prosperity. It also houses the towering floats that are paraded through the streets during the festival every year.

Finally, the **Fukuoka Asian Art Museum** is devoted to contemporary and modern art from around Asia. From folk pop art to politi-cal art, the permanent exhibition presents the cutting edge of art from the region. ⏱ 1 day. See p. 378.

From Hakata Station, take the JR Express Kamome to Nagasaki Station (120 min.).

> *Ground Zero at Nagasaki is marked with a park and memorial.*

❷ Nagasaki. Nagasaki may not have a castle, a famous landscaped garden, or hot-spring spas; its charms are subtler than that. But many residents and visitors consider this city one of the country's most beautiful. And thanks to a long history in centuries past as Japan's sole window to the foreign world, traditionally it has been one of Japan's most cosmopolitan cities, with a unique blend of outside cultures interwoven into its history, architecture, food, and festivals. Of course, today Nagasaki is best known as the second city to be destroyed by an atomic bomb. On August 9, 1945, 3 days after the atomic bombing of Hiroshima, American forces dropped codename "Fat Man" over the city. The epicenter of the blast is located in the ★★★ **Nagasaki Peace Park,** as is the **Nagasaki Atomic Bomb Museum.** The museum is by no means pleasant, but something every concerned individual should see.

Nagasaki also has a long and complex history and relationship with Christianity. When the ban on Christianity was lifted with the Meiji Restoration in the mid-19th century, the faithful (who had been practicing in secret for 2 centuries) built **Urakami Tenshudo Church** (浦上天主堂) with their own hands. The neighborhood of Urakami was Ground Zero for the atomic blast; this is a faithful reconstruction of the original Tenshudo cathedral.

In 1597, the year after Christianity was officially banned, 26 male Christians (20 Japanese and 6 foreigners) were arrested in Kyoto and Osaka, marched 30 days through the snow to Nagasaki, and crucified at **Nishizaka Hill** as examples of what would happen to offenders. (In 1862, the Twenty-Six martyrs were sainted by the pope.) Today, the Monument to the Twenty-Six Martyrs marks the spot, as well as the remains of other Japanese martyrs returned to Nagasaki in 1995 after more than 380 years of interment in Macau.

★★ **Mount Inasa** offers the best panoramic view of Nagasaki. It is accessible via cable car which is just 7 minutes from Nagasaki Station.

We recommend you arrive before sunset on your first day in Nagasaki and stay for the zillion twinkling lights. Make ★★ **Glover Garden** your first stop on your second day in Nagasaki. This collection of 19th-century mansions in downtown Nagasaki is proof positive that interest in Japan isn't a recent phenomenon. Once occupied by wealthy foreign traders, the homes were designed by European architects but were built by local craftsmen, making them a fascinating hybrid of foreign and Japanese styles. In addition to the **Glover Mansion** itself, the adjacent **Alt House** and **Ringer House** contain a wide variety of vintage ephemera.

When the Tokugawa shogunate adopted a national policy of isolation in the 1630s, the tiny island of ★★★ **Dejima** became Japan's sole window to the foreign world. Today it's home to a tourist quarter of shops and restaurants.

The **Nagasaki Museum of History and Culture** (長崎歴史文化博物館) is a fun way to gain an understanding of Nagasaki's unique and important role in Japan's exchange of culture, trade, and ideas with the outside world. With the help of English explanations and a free audio guide, you'll learn about the introduction of Western languages, medicine, astronomy, and other sciences via Nagasaki's contact with the Dutch; Japan's cultural exchanges with China and Korea; Christianity in Japan; and Nagasaki's role as a trading port.

Suwa Shrine (諏訪神社) was built to promote Shintoism at a time when the feudal government was trying to stamp out Christianity. Today, with a good location on top of a hill (atop a 277-step staircase) with views over the city, the shrine symbolizes better than anything else the spiritual heart of the Japanese community. The shrine is perhaps best known as the site of the Okunchi Festival, held every year from October 7 to 9. ◷ 2 days. See p. 553. Urakami Tenshudo: 1–79 Moto-Oumachi. ☎ 095/844-1777. www1.odn.ne.jp/uracathe. Free. Daily 8:30am–7pm. Closed third Tues of the month. Streetcar: Matsuyama. Nagasaki Museum of History and Culture: 1-1-1 Tateyama. ☎ 095/818-8366. www.nmhc.jp. ¥600 adults, ¥400 high-school students, ¥300 kids. Daily 8:30am–7pm. Closed third Tues of the month. Streetcar: 3 to Sakuramachi (5 min.). Suwa Shrine: 18–15 Kami-Nishiyamamachi. ☎ 095/824-0445. Free. Daily 24 hr. Streetcar: Suwa Jinja-mae.

> *The tranquil environs of the Nagasaki Peace Park.*

The Best of Kyushu in 1 Week

One week gives you more time to push further into Kyushu, exploring its spas, castles, and wildlife. If your schedule accommodates it, we highly recommend visiting one of its outlying islands, such as tropical Tanegashima or the verdant paradise Yakushima, both of which can be easily accessed from the city of Kagoshima. (See "The Southern Islands" on p. 364 for more information about them.)

> *Suizen-ji Gardens: 80 years in the making.*

START From Nagasaki's Ken-Ei Bus Terminal, take the bus to Unzen (100 min.). Unzen Spa is 800km (497 miles) west of Kyoto.

❶ Unzen Spa (雲仙温泉)**.** Unzen consists of just a few streets with hotels and *ryokan* (traditional inns) spread along them, but it is a welcome relief if you've spent your first 3 hectic days rushing Fukuoka and Nagasaki and catching buses and trains. It's also home to **Unzen-Amakusa Park,** one of the nation's first

national parks. Its hiking paths wind into the tree-covered hills, and dense clouds of steam arise from vents and fumaroles. For visitors, the best result of all that volcanic activity is the abundance of hot springs.

This hot-spring hangout is just barely close enough to make in a day trip from Nagasaki, but the spas make a great stop for those who want to overnight. They're so dedicated to thermal relaxation here that there are even

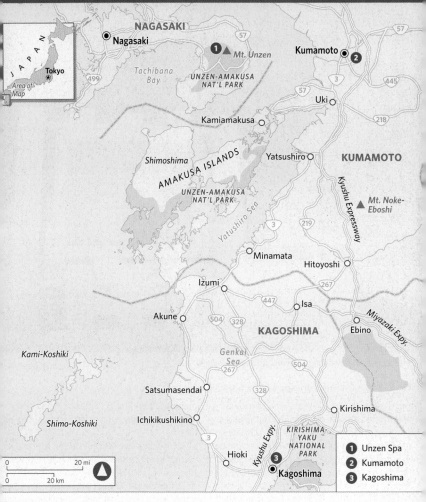

inger and foot spas on the main street, where
ou can soak the appropriate appendages in
outdoor baths for free. The best times of year
are late April to June, when Unzen's famous
azalea bushes are in glorious bloom, and late
October and early November, when the maple
leaves turn brilliant reds

Jigoku (**"The Hells";** 地獄) may not sound
like a great place to spend a holiday, but the
bubbling, steaming show of geothermal activity makes this spot Unzen's number-one
attraction.

From Unzen, take a bus for Shimabara Port
(40 min.). Board the Ocean Arrow Ferry to
Kumamoto Port (30 min.). From Kumamoto
Port, board the bus for Kumamoto Station
(20 min.).

2 Kumamoto. Kumamoto was once one
of Japan's most important "castle towns."
Known for its greenery and backdrop of scenic
Mount Aso, today it's a progressive city with
abundant greenery and a variety of interesting
cultural attractions. But it flourished under
the lordship of the samurai warrior Kato
Kiyomasa, who greatly expanded its titular
castle after Tokugawa Ieyasu came to power
in 1601. A restored and renovated version
of ★★ **Kumamoto Castle** still stands guard
over the city today. Ground broke on the
castle's most famous incarnation in 1601 and

> *Unzen-Amakusa was one of Japan's first national parks.*

took 7 years to build. A massive affair, it was constructed atop strategic high ground and featured 2 main towers, 49 turrets, 29 gates, and 18 two-story gatehouses. The main castle keep, which burned down during an 1877 rebellion, was rebuilt in the 1960s, but many of the compound's other structures are original. Particularly of interest is the reconstruction of the Honmaru Goten Palace, with its beautiful gilt interior.

Located a 10-minute walk north of Kumamoto Castle, the 300-year-old ★ **Hosokawa Mansion** was built by a subsidiary member of the Hosokawa samurai clan, Lord Gyobu, and was enlarged in the 1800s.

Laid out in the 1630s by Hosokawa Tadatoshi as a retreat for tea ceremonies and as the grounds of a nearby temple, ★ **Suizen-ji Garden** took about 80 years to complete. The garden wraps itself around a cold spring–fed lake (considered particularly good for making tea). But the place is especially interesting for its design that incorporates famous scenes in miniature from the 53 stages of the ancient **Tokaido Highway,** which connected Kyoto and Tokyo.

Because it's free (except during special exhibitions) and centrally located in downtown Kumamoto, consider taking a jaunt through the ★ **Contemporary Art Museum.** This forerunner in contemporary art, which showcases works by talents both local and regional, treats art as an experience rather than something to be viewed passively by the viewer.

The ★ **Display Hall of Kumamoto Products** (熊本県物産館) is a fun way to wind up your day in Kumamoto. One of Kumamoto's most famous products is its Higo Inlay, or damascene, in which gold, silver, and copper are inlaid on an iron plate to form patterns of flowers, bamboo, and other designs. Originally used to adorn sword guards and armor, damascene today is used on such accessories as paperweights, jewelry, and tie clasps. The Display Hall is a great place to buy—or just browse—this beautiful craftwork. See p. 384. Display all: ⏱ 30 min. NTT Bldg., 3-1 Sakuramachi. 096/324-4930. Daily 10am–6:30pm. Free. reetcar: Kumamotojo-mae.

om Kumamoto Station, take the Mizuho nikansen train to Kagoshima-Chuo Station 5 min.), then transfer to the Kagoshima ne to Kagoshima Station (4 min.).

Kagoshima. The capital of Kagoshima Pre-cture, this is a city of palm trees, flowering ushes, wide avenues, and, like the weather, eople who are warm, mild-tempered, and asygoing. The city spreads along Kinko Bay d boasts one of the most unusual bay vistas the world: ★★ **Mount Sakurajima,** an ac-ve volcano whose last major eruption was in 14. You can't climb it, though—the caldera ill regularly belches forth ash and smoke. nce an island, now connected to the main-nd via the solidified lava of a 1904 eruption, akurajima is Kagoshima's defining feature. agnificent from far away and impressive if u're near the top, it can be visited by ferry, eparting from the Sakurajima Ferry Terminal. he terminal is about an 8-minute walk from owntown Kagoshima or the Shiyakusho-mae reetcar stop, or a 2-minute walk from the agoshima Suizokukan-mae/Sakurajima-anbashi City View bus stop. Ferries run 24 ours, departing every 10 to 15 minutes during e day and about once an hour through the ght. The 15-minute trip to Sakurajima costs 150 for adults, ¥80 for kids.

The ★ kids **Kagoshima City Aquarium,** also nown as Io World, concentrates on sea life om waters surrounding Kagoshima Prefec-re. The largest tank is home to stingrays, uefin tuna, Japanese anchovy, a whale shark, nd other creatures from the Kuroshio (Black urrent), which flows from the East China Sea ast Kagoshima to the Pacific Ocean.

★★ **Sengan-en,** however, is Kagoshima's ost widely visited attraction. The grounds f a countryside villa, it's a garden laid out ore than 300 years ago by the Shimadzu an, incorporating Sakurajima and Kinko Bay to its design scheme in a principle known as orrowed landscape." The **Shoko Shuseikan useum,** located next to the garden, was built the mid-1850s as Japan's first industrial ctory. It houses items relating to the almost 00-year history of the Shimadzu clan.

> *A tiny resident of the Kagoshima City Aquarium.*

The ★ kids **Kagoshima Prefectural Museum of Culture Reimeikan** occupies the former site of Tsurumaru Castle (only the stone ramparts and moat of the castle remain). It offers an overview of Japanese history in general and Kagoshima Prefecture in particular. See p. 390.

Spending the Night in Unzen Spa

Despite its name, the **Kyushu Hotel,** 320 Obamacho, Unzen-shi (☎ 0957/73-3234; www.kyushuhtl.co.jp), built in 1917, is a lovely, old-style *ryokan* in an updated building with a view of a traditional garden from its luxurious lobby. While this is a great place to spend the night, it's also an ideal stop-off for day-trippers as well: daily packages, starting at ¥2,000, get you lunch and access to the hotel's legendary spas. For those who don't want to bathe with others, you can reserve the private family bath, also with outdoor bath, for ¥2,100 for 40 minutes. For guests, pluses include a gracious and accommodating staff (the third-generation owners speak English) and fusion cuisine that blends Western and Japanese styles. Rooms run from ¥14,000 per person including breakfast and dinner. For Kumamoto and Kagoshima hotels, see p. 388 and p. 394.

A *Shochu* Bar Hop

When it comes to government and business, Japan's capital city may be Tokyo. But when it comes to the distilled spirit known as *shochu*, the island of Kyushu—and the city of Kagoshima in particular—reigns supreme. There are somewhere between 2,000 and 3,000 distilleries in Kagoshima prefecture alone, which should give you a sense of this drink's popularity here. Bars serving *Satsuma-shochu* (see below) are a dime a dozen in Kagoshima— you'll even see them on the bullet train platforms. But to make your hunt easier, we've rounded up a handful of our favorites to get you started. Bottoms up—or *kanpai*, as the Japanese say!

> *A plethora of choices at Shochu-an Takezo.*

START Take the Kagoshima streetcar to the Taniyama stop. Kagoshima is 908km (564 miles) southwest of Kyoto.

❶ Galleria Hombo (薩摩郷中蔵)**.** There's no better way to start a *shochu* tour of Kagoshima than with an actual distillery, one of the few actually open to the public. Although the tour is entirely in Japanese, it's fun to see the delightfully low-tech style of the production process—and sample its results. The one caveat: It's by appointment only; you need to fill out a request form on the website no later than 48 hours ahead of your visit. ⏱ 1 hr. 3-27 Nannei, Kagoshima. www.hombo.co.jp/factory/hombo. html. Free. Daily 9am-4pm. Streetcar: Taniyam

❷ Shochu-an Takezo (焼酎庵 武三)**.** Located inside the Hotel Gasthof, this is one of a select few pubs that features a (limited) English menu. Offering a wide variety of grilled foods served tapas style and 100 varieties of *shochu*, it's absolutely worth a visit even if you aren't staying in the hotel itself. For heartier

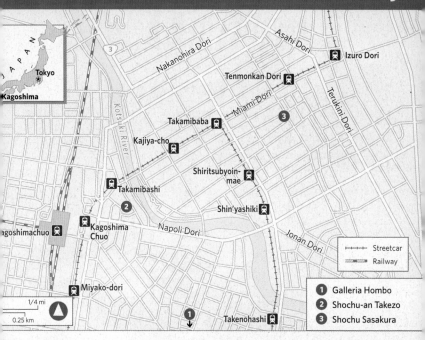

ous, ¥3,675 a person gets you a set of seven menu items plus 2 hours of all you can drink beer and *shochu*. 7-1-1F, Chuo-cho, Kagoshima. 099/255-8035. Set menu ¥3,675. AE, MC, V. Mon-Sat 6pm-midnight. Streetcar: Kagoshima-chuo Station.

Shochu Sasakura (酒々蔵). This place has more than 400 types of *shochu* on hand. Don't expect an English menu, but do expect a warm reception. We love their ¥2,000-per-person *omakase* set menu of local dishes; ¥1,500 more per person gets you all you can drink. Open late. 9-17-1F Yamanokuchi-cho, Kagoshima. ☎ 099/224-1356. www4.synapse.ne.jp/sasakura-k. Shochu from ¥400. No credit cards. Daily 6:30pm-3am (till 2am Sun). Closed 3rd Sun of the month. Streetcar: Tenmonkan Dori.

Behind the Drink

Unlike sake, which is brewed in a process similar to beer, *shochu* is a distilled spirit. First concocted in Kagoshima back in the Muromachi Period (1333-1573), it quickly spread throughout Japan. Although sales declined after World War II, when it was pooh-poohed as a working man's drink, *shochu* has made a resurgence and is popular with all sorts of people today. You can think of it as Japan's bourbon (though the appearance and taste are much closer to that of vodka).

Similar to vodka, *shochu* can be distilled from all sorts of ingredients that contain sugars, including rice, wheat, and barley. But most prized for their flavor and fragrance are potato-based *imo-jochu*, which are known as *Satsuma-shochu* in Kagoshima. By law limited to 45% alcohol by volume, the vast majority clock in at 20% to 30%. There are two main types: *honkaku*, or single-distilled *shochu*, and *korui*, which is distilled multiple times for a smoother taste. Most Japanese drink *honkaku shochu* on the rocks or cut with water, while using *korui* as a mixer for fruity cocktails (the ubiquitous *chu-hai* and "sours" found on nearly every bar menu in Japan). But Kagoshima's preferred method is the *oyu-wari*—*honkaku shochu* mixed with hot water. Typically it is ordered by brand name, followed by the style. (And if you can't decipher the names on the menu, feel free to point at the page—or a bottle!)

DOWN THE HATCH

Izakaya pubs are the way Japan unwinds

BY MATT ALT & HIROKO YODA

IZAKAYA ARE THE WAY MANY JAPANESE SPEND A NIGHT OUT ON THE TOWN.
Hybrid restaurant-drinking establishments that are more akin to British or Irish pubs
than bars, they specialize in serving up all sorts of finger foods along with the booze. The
tiny dishes aren't just a way to avoid drinking on an empty stomach; they're also a great
entree to a wide variety of Japanese foods and beverages that can be difficult to find
outside of Japan. The boisterous, lively atmosphere of *izakaya* makes it easy to make new
friends and acquaintances at the next table over—especially after a beer or three.

Drinking at *Izakaya*

Visits to an *izakaya* inevitably begin with a *"toriaezu no biiru,"* the first beer of the evening. After washing down your first few plates of food with a cold one, you can continue with the suds or switch to something a little more local. Sake is almost always on hand, but *izakaya* regulars are particularly fond of *shochu*, a distilled spirit made from potatoes, rice, or other ingredients (p. 361). In addition to being served on the rocks, it is often consumed in sweet "sours," which consist of *shochu* mixed with various juices, or *"chu-hi,"* which use unsweetened mixers such as soda water or oolong tea. Old-school "highballs" of whiskey and soda water are popular as well.

SHIOYAKI

Grilled fish, usually served whole, with meat on the bone. A variety of fish are served this way, often changing based on the season. Although delicious, *shioyaki* is only recommended for those comfortable enough with chopsticks to navigate through all the little bones. Fish served as *shioyaki* include *sanma* (saury), *hokke* (arabesque greenling), and *ika* (squid).

EDAMAME

Boiled soybeans, served in the pod, often lightly salted. A classic sort of thing to nosh with beer, particularly in the summer.

EIHIRE

Stingray fin dried to a jerky-like consistency and served with mayonnaise.

TSUKEMONO

Pickled vegetables—cucumbers, eggplant, baby onions, and other vegetables—are commonly used for *tsukemono*. Often served with a side of spicy mustard.

KARA-AGE

Fried chicken. Usually served boneless, and often with a wedge of lemon and side of mayonnaise.

Food for Thought

YAKITORI

The de rigeur *izakaya* dish, yakitori consist of skewers of chicken meat and other parts of the bird. *Moriawase*, or chef's choice, are the most common and contain a variety of organ meats. Less adventurous eaters should stick to basics like *negima* (chicken meat and scallions), *tsukune* (ground chicken meat dumplings), or plain old *momo* (breast meat). Diners typically have a choice of *shio* (salt) or *tare* (sweet) sauces.

OTOSHI

Nearly every *izakaya* has a table charge that includes the first dish of the night: the *otoshi*. Usually served up in a small bowl and consisting of only a mouthful or two of food, it often takes the form of marinated seafood or vegetables. (For this reason table charges are also called *otoshi-dai*.)

The Southern Islands

The southernmost of Japan's four major islands, Kyushu stretches from merely warm in the north to subtropical in the south. Nowhere is this climactic shift more evident than on the tiny offshoot islands of Yakushima and Tanegashima. While you're better off going to Okinawa if you're looking to be pampered in an all-out resort-style experience, these islands are a fascinating diversion for adventurous travelers, both from historical and natural standpoints. Yakushima is a natural paradise covered in a lush rainforest teeming with unique wildlife that is perfect for more active types. Tanegashima is home to Japan's spaceflight center and features beautiful white-sand beaches; many Japanese see it as a more reasonably priced alternative to visiting resorts in Okinawa. Take 3 days for this tour.

> The otherworldly atmosphere of Yakushima's ancient forests is unlike anywhere else on Earth.

START From the mainland, take a jetfoil (see below) from Kagoshima Port to Yakushima's Miyanoura Port. Yakushima is more than 1,000km (621 miles) southwest of Kyoto.

❶ Yakushima Environmental Culture Village Center. Covered in rainforests, Yakushima is a primeval wonderland geared toward self-starting types such as hikers and adventure travelers. It is home to unique species such as the *yakushika* deer and the *yakuzaru* macaque, among many others, but is most famed for its cryptomeria cedar groves. As you might expect for a place so lush with greenery, this is one of Japan's single wettest islands; locals joke it rains 35 days a month here. Expect precipitation and dress accordingly, because the trails can be quite slick and muddy even in the sunniest weather. The JNTO offers an excellent overview of the island at www.jnto.go.jp/eng/location/rtg/pdf/pg-708.pdf.

Your first stop on Yakushima should be the Environmental Culture Village Center,

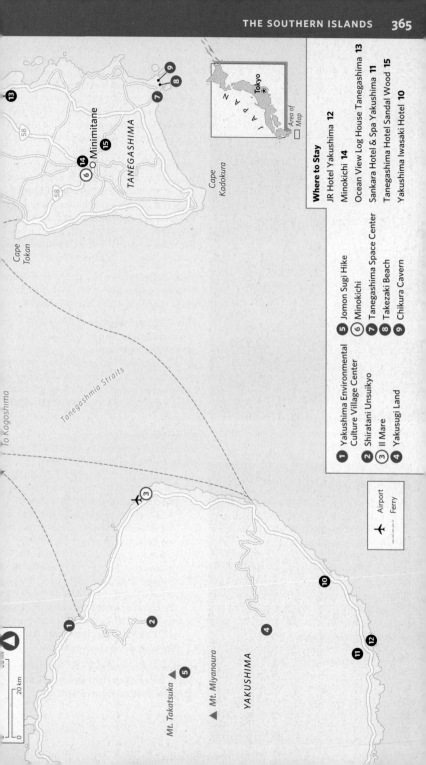

Minimitane

TANEGASHIMA

Cape Kadokura

Cape Tokan

Area of Map

JAPAN

Tokyo

Where to Stay

JR Hotel Yakushima 12
Minokichi 14
Ocean View Log House Tanegashima 13
Sankara Hotel & Spa Yakushima 11
Tanegashima Hotel Sandal Wood 15
Yakushima Iwasaki Hotel 10

1 Yakushima Environmental Culture Village Center
2 Shiratani Unsuikyo
3 Il Mare
4 Yakusugi Land
5 Jomon Sugi Hike
6 Minokichi
7 Tanegashima Space Center
8 Takezaki Beach
9 Chikura Cavern

✈ Airport
--- Ferry

Tanegashima Straits

To Kagoshima

YAKUSHIMA

Mt. Takatsuka
Mt. Miyanoura

20 km

> Roots from the Stewartia tree spread uninhibited in Shiratani Unsuikyo.

By Air and By Sea

Access to the islands of Yakushima and Tanegashima has never been easier, with regular flights and ferries servicing each. **Flights** from Kagoshima to Yakushima are operated five times daily by JAC (☎ 0120/51-1283; www.jac.co.jp), a commuter airline subsidiary of JAL. As of this writing, tickets are ¥13,900 one-way.

The fastest **ferry** is the **"Rocket" Jetfoil** service (☎ 099/233-1011; www.cosmoline.jp), which offers both direct service to Yakushima and stopovers in Tanegashima. Departing from the port of Kagoshima three times daily, the journey takes about 2 hours and costs ¥6,500 one-way. The **"Toppy" Jetfoil** (☎ 099/223-4251; www.toppy.jp) is another option. Travel time and prices are the same as the "Rocket," with staggered launch times.

especially if you plan on doing the Jomon Sug hike the next day (p. 367, ❺), as you will nee to purchase advance bus tickets here. (The center is a 10-minute walk up the hill from the port.) The facility's main claim to fame is an IMAX-style documentary about the island's natural charms, screened eight times daily. It also serves as a tourist information desk for visitors. For those who want information or reservations without having to pay an admission fee, try the nearby **Yakushima Tourist Center** (☎ 099/742-0091; www.yksm.com). ⏱ 30 min. 823-1 Miyanoura, Yakushim-cho. ☎ 0997/42-2900. ¥500 adults, ¥350 junior-high and high-school students, ¥250 kids. Tues-Sun 9am–5pm. Bus: Miyanoura Port.

Drive about 1km (⅔ mile) southeast on Rte. 77, then make a right on Rte. 594, and then a left to stay on 594 for 10km (6¼ miles).

❷ ★★ **Shiratani Unsuikyo** (白谷雲水峡). This mossy valley was the direct inspiration for the setting of director Hayao Miyazaki's 1997 animated feature *Princess Mononoke*. A series of well-marked hiking paths, ranging from 1 to 5 hours in length, snake through the area. ⏱ 1 hr. ¥300. Bus: Miyanoura Port to Shiratani Unsukyo.

Return the 10km (6¼ miles) north on Rte. 594 to Rte. 77, then make a right on 77 and take it for another 10km (6¼ miles).

③ 🍴 **Il Mare.** While we generally prefer steering visitors toward local cuisine, we'll make an exception for this cozy little Italian restaurant, close to Yakushima Airport. The owners rely heavily on local ingredients, including herbs harvested from their own garden right outside. Their local "black pork" dishes are particularly good. 815-92 Oseda, Yakushima-cho. ☎ 0997/43-5666. www.ilmare3.jp. Set lunches with drink from ¥2,000. No credit cards. Lunch & dinner Fri-Wed. Bus: Yakushima Airport.

Head southeast on Rte. 77 for 10km (6¼ miles), then make a right on Rte. 592 and take it for another 15km (9⅓ miles).

Yakusugi Land, home to ghostly landscapes.

★★★ **Yakusugi Land** (ヤクスギランド). For those who don't want (or simply don't have time) to make the 10-hour roundtrip to see the Jomon Sugi (see below), this nature park is the next best thing. It features trails geared toward all ability levels, ranging from 30-minute loops to ½- to 3-hour hikes, to see a variety of *yakusugi* trees. ⏱ 1 hr. Anbo, Yakushima-cho. ☎ 0997/46-2221. ¥300. Daily 9am–5pm. Bus: Miyanoura port to Yakusugi Land.

Return on Rte. 77 to the port, then make a left on Rte. 594, and then another left at the fork to stay on 594 for 11km (6¾ miles).

★★★ **Jomon Sugi Hike** (縄文杉登山). Although Yakushima island was a major source of lumber for centuries and much of its forest is post-logging "second generation" growth, several groves of ancient cryptomeria—called *yakusugi*—remain, inhabited by giant trees a

thousand years old or more. The Jomon Sugi is the oldest tree of them all, towering some 25m (82 ft.) and estimated to be more than 2,000 years old. Getting to the Jomon Sugi is serious

Travel Tip

Although this 3-day itinerary connects Yakushima and Tanegashima islands into a single tour via air and ferry, those with more limited schedules can choose one island or the other and still have a great time. If you're focused, both are also do-able as day trips from Kagoshima. And the islands are accessible via flights from Tokyo and Osaka as well. Be aware that bus service, especially on Tanegashima, is sporadic; renting a car is the easiest way to get around the islands. Rental cars are available at island ports and airports.

> *Takezaki Beach, a little piece of paradise.*

business and an all-day affair: It's a 5-hour one-way hike through steep terrain and across (occasionally terrifying) suspension bridges.

You will need to overnight on the island to visit the Jomon Sugi for several reasons: For one, it's recommended you begin the hike no later than 6am. For another, during peak seasons—late April, early May, and the mid-summer months—you will need to purchase the bus ticket to the trailhead at least 24 hours in advance via one of the island's tourist info centers (such as the Yakushima Environmental Culture Village Center, p. 364, ❶). Although the trails are very well marked and maps are provided, you can hire a guide at the trailhead if you are uncertain of your abilities. An extremely rewarding hike for those who put in the effort, this is one of the main reasons people visit Yakushima. Don't forget to bring a boxed bento lunch. (Most hotels will prepare them for you on request.) ⊕ 8 hr. Bus: Miyanoura Port to Arakawa Dam Trailhead (1 hr.).

Return on Rte. 594 to the port. From Miyanoura Port, take the ferry to Tanegashima's Nishiomote Harbor. Rent a car and take Rte. 58 40km (25 miles) south to Minamitane.

⑥ 🍴 **Minokichi** (美の吉). Owned and operated by the same folks who run the nearby Hotel Sandal Wood (p. 371), this combo business hotel and eatery has been serving up local favorites such as sashimi, ramen, and pork cutlets for close to 50 years. Makes an excellent brunch on the long drive to or from the Space Center (see below). Think of this as the island equivalent of a diner. 2264-4 Nakanokami, Tanegashima-cho. ☎ 0997/26-0033. Ramen from ¥600. Lunch & dinner daily. No credit cards.

Take Rte. 586 east at Minamitane-chyo Kaminaka intersection and follow it 1.6km (1 mile) to the Space Center.

7 ★★ kids **Tanegashima Space Center** (種子 島). The name of the otherwise unassuming little subtropical island of Tanegashima is well known to every Japanese citizen for two reasons: First, it is where firearms first entered Japan via Portuguese explorers in 1543. (To this day, the island's name is synonymous with flintlock and harquebus rifles.) Second, the Tanegashima Space Center is famed as the center of Japan's space program—rockets and satellites are assembled here, launched into orbit, and subsequently tracked after launch. The Space Center's **Space Museum** features a life-sized mockup of the Kibo module, Japan's contribution to the International Space Station. There is also a movie theater that screens documentaries about Japanese rocket launches. For those looking for something more in-depth, you can call ahead to arrange a guided tour of the rocket assembly facility and Range Control Center. The facility (and a 3km/1.75-mile radius around it) is closed on days of rocket launches, which happen sporadically throughout the year; consult the website for information about schedules and observation points. ⏱ 3 hr. Mazu, Kukinaga, Minamitane-cho. ☎ 0997/26-2111. www.jaxa.jp/index_e.html. Free. Tues–Sun 9:30am–5pm. Bus: Tanegashima Space Center.

Takezaki and Hamada beaches are just off the coast of the Space Center.

8 ★★ **Takezaki Beach** (竹崎海岸). Blessed with beautiful beaches and oceans, Tanegashima is popular with scuba divers, surfers, and sunbathers alike. And after the long drive to the Space Museum, you'll undoubtedly be in the mood to cool off. This beach is a great place for snorkeling and just lying around. It also has changing rooms and a spigot for hosing yourself off. Kukinaga, Minamitane-cho. Free. Bus: Tanegashima Space Center.

9 ★ kids **Chikura Cavern** (千座の岩屋). **Hamada Beach** is wonderful for swimming, sunbathing, and snorkeling, but the real star is this large cavern abutting the beach, carved out of the cliffside by millennia of wave action. The cavern becomes accessible at low tide and can be easily explored on foot. (It's quite large and open, with no danger of getting lost inside.) Minamitane-cho. Free. Bus: Tanegashima Space Center.

> *Chikura Cavern: Where else can you go caving and sunbathing at the same time?*

ATMs

Be aware that ATMs are few and far between on Yakushima and Tanegashima, as are establishments that accept credit cards. It's a good idea to estimate your costs and try to bring enough cash to cover them ahead of time. (This is a good idea for nearly anywhere in the Japanese countryside, but particularly so on small islands such as these.)

Where to Stay on the Southern Islands

> *The soaring lobby of the Yakushima Iwasaki Hotel.*

★★ JR Hotel Yakushima YAKUSHIMA
This hotel is dramatically situated atop a bluff overlooking the ocean. Rooms are spacious and clean, and the hotel is one of the few on the island with its own natural *onsen* (hot-spring spa). (Nonguests are welcome to drop by for a soak for a fee.) Views from the ocean-facing rooms and the outdoor spas are gorgeous. 136–2 Onoaida, Yakushima-cho. ☎ 0997/47-2011. www.jrhotelgroup.com/eng/hotel/eng154.htm. 46 units. Doubles from ¥15,000. Bus: Onoaida.

Minokichi TANEGASHIMA
This bare-bones but clean business hotel is often booked solid during rocket launches because of its proximity to the Space Center. Although the hotel and neighborhood are nothing special, they're clean and quiet, and you can't beat the prices. It also features free wireless Internet access, a rarity on an island like this. The attached restaurant has been serving up local favorites for close to a half-century. (The owner-proprietor does double duty as an organic vegetable farmer.) 2264–4 Nakanokami, Tanegashima-cho. ☎ 0997/26-0033. 35 units. Rooms from ¥6,825 per person. Rates include breakfast & dinner. No credit cards. Bus: Tanegashima Space Center.

★ Ocean View Log House Tanegashima
TANEGASHIMA   Fully equipped with bathrooms, kitchens, and bedrooms, these log cabins arranged on a bluff overlooking the sea are more like apartments than hotel rooms. Although a little rustic, the rooms are clean,

The luxe pool at Sankara Hotel.

e atmosphere is fun, and the separated na-
re of the accommodations ensures privacy.
ices (for two) range from ¥6,300 for a tiny
tudio" cabin to ¥11,000 for a more luxuriously
ppointed one, making this a very reasonably
iced place to stay. If there's any downside,
s that meals aren't provided. (But hey, that's
hat the kitchen is for.) 140 Anjo, Nishinoomote.
0120/25-1077. www.uminoyado.com. 6 units.
oubles from ¥6,300. No credit cards. Car or taxi:
0 min. from Tanegashima Airport.

★★ Sankara Hotel & Spa Yakushima

AKUSHIMA The closest thing to a resort on
e island, this brand-new luxury hotel spe-
alizes in pampering guests, with day spas
d masseuses on hand. Most rooms are in
martly appointed stand-alone villas sur-
unded by trees and overlooking the ocean.
he hotel's restaurant offers Japanese-French
sion cuisine and is one of the island's best.
's become a popular stop even for people
t staying at the hotel.) 553 Haginoue, Mu-
o, Yakushima-cho. ☎ 0997/47-3488. www.
nkarahotel-spa.com/en. 29 units. Villas from
40,000. AE, MC, V, D. Car or taxi: 30 min. from
iyanoura Port.

Tanegashima Hotel Sandal Wood

ANEGASHIMA Located just 7 minutes by car
om the Space Center, this is a cozy yet stylish
little locally run establishment. Perks like free
access to washing machines and wireless Internet are a rarity among island hotels. We highly
recommend paying extra for the very well done
Japanese-style meals (served in a dining room,
not in-room). 525 Nakanoue, Minamitane-cho.
☎ 0997/26-0015. www.hotel-sandalwood.com. 9
units. Doubles from ¥6,000 without meals; doubles from ¥6,500 with breakfast; doubles from
¥8,400 with breakfast & dinner. No credit cards.
Car or taxi: 30 min. from Tanegashima Airport.

★ Yakushima Iwasaki Hotel YAKUSHIMA

Although showing its age, this is still a clean
and comfortable place to stay, and the lobby,
with its floor-to-ceiling windows, is quite
breathtaking. Popular with domestic tourists,
the restaurant (which serves up excellent local
seafood cuisine alongside amazing views) can
fill up quickly, so make sure to make reservations even if you're staying here. But perhaps
most useful (especially for those not inclined
to hoof it on the Jomon Sugi hike; p. 367, ⑤) is
that daily half- and full-day island bus tours
depart from here. Reservations are required;
contact the concierge directly at ☎ 0997/46-
2221. 1306 Onoaida Yakushima-cho. ☎ 0997/
47-3888. http://yakushima.iwasakihotels.com/
en. Doubles from ¥22,000. AE, MC, V, D. Bus:
Yakushima Iwasaki Hotel.

Nagasaki

Nagasaki, capital of Nagasaki Prefecture and located on the northwest coast of Kyushu, opened its harbor to European vessels in 1571 and became a port of call for Portuguese and Dutch ships. Chinese merchants soon followed and set up their own community. Along with traders came Francis Xavier and other Christian missionaries, primarily from Portugal and Spain, who found many converts among the local Japanese. During Japan's more than 200 years of isolation, only Nagasaki was allowed to conduct trade with outsiders and thus served as the nation's window to the rest of the world. Even today, Japanese come to Nagasaki for a dose of the city's intermingled cultures. All the city's major attractions are connected to its diversified, and sometimes tragic, past.

> The Alt House, one of the mansions you can tour at Glover Gardens.

START Take the Nagasaki streetcar no. 1 or 3 to the Hamaguchimachi stop. Nagasaki is 780km (485 miles) southwest of Kyoto.

1 ★★★ **Nagasaki Peace Park** (平和公園)**.** On August 9, 1945, at 11:02am, American forces dropped an atomic bomb over Nagasaki, 3 days after the one dropped on Hiroshima (p. 306). The bomb, which exploded 480m (1,575 ft.) aboveground, destroyed about a third of the city, killed an estimated 74,000 people, and injured 75,000 more. Today, the museum, memorials, and statues of Nagasaki Peace Park, located north of Nagasaki Station, serve as a reminder of that day of destruction. Nagasaki's citizens are among the most vigorous peace activists in the world; a peace demonstration is held in the park every year on the anniversary of the bombing, along with a declaration for peace by the city mayor.

By far the most important thing to see in the park is the **Nagasaki Atomic Bomb Museum.** It illustrates events leading up to the bombing, the devastation afterward, Nagasaki's postwar restoration, the history of nuclear weapons, and the subsequent peace movement.

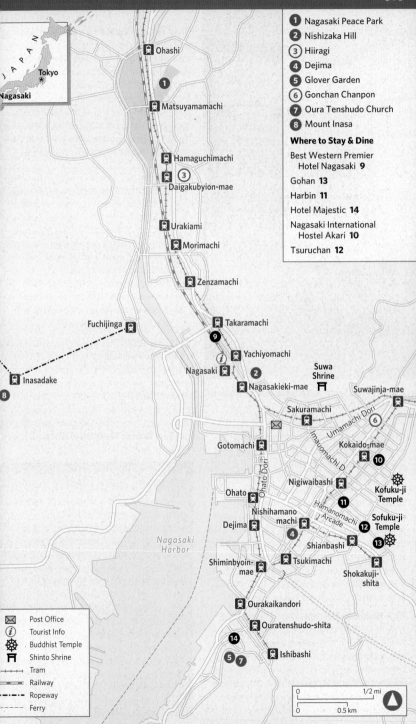

JAPAN

Tokyo

Nagasaki

1. Nagasaki Peace Park
2. Nishizaka Hill
3. Hiiragi
4. Dejima
5. Glover Garden
6. Gonchan Chanpon
7. Oura Tenshudo Church
8. Mount Inasa

Where to Stay & Dine

Best Western Premier
  Hotel Nagasaki 9

Gohan 13

Harbin 11

Hotel Majestic 14

Nagasaki International
  Hostel Akari 10

Tsuruchan 12

Ohashi

Matsuyamamachi

Hamaguchimachi

Daigakubyion-mae

Urakiami

Morimachi

Zenzamachi

Fuchijinga

Inasadake

Takaramachi

Yachiyomachi

Nagasaki

Nagasakieki-mae

Suwa
Shrine

Suwajinja-mae

Sakuramachi

Umamachi Dori

Kokaido-mae

Gotomachi

Imauomachi.D.

Ohato Dori

Nigiwaibashi

Kofuku-ji
Temple

Ohato

Nishihamano
machi

Dejima

Hamanomachi
Arcade

Sofuku-ji
Temple

Shianbashi

Shiminbyoin-
mae

Tsukimachi

Shokakuji-
shita

Nagasaki
Harbor

Ourakaikandori

Ouratenshudo-shita

Ishibashi

Post Office
Tourist Info
Buddhist Temple
Shinto Shrine
Tram
Railway
Ropeway
Ferry

0   1/2 mi
0   0.5 km

> *Teatime on Dejima, where foreigners were seques-tered until the mid-1800s.*

Objects, photos, and artifacts graphically depict the bomb's devastation, including an iconic wristwatch with its hands frozen at 11:02. While many of the displays are positively gut-wrenching, this is a must-see for any visitor to the city. One caveat: If you've already seen the far more comprehensive Peace Memorial Museum in Hiroshima (p. 309, ❶), this one will be largely repetitive. ⏱1½ hr. 7-8 Hiranomachi. ☎ 095/844-1231. www1.city.nagasaki.nagasaki.jp/peace. ¥200 adults, ¥100 kids. Daily 8:30am–5:30pm (May–Aug until 6:30pm). Train: Matsuyamamachi. Streetcar: Hamaguchimachi.

❷ ★ **Nishizaka Hill** (西坂)**.** About a 4-minute walk north of Nagasaki Station up a steep slope is this hill, home to the **Monument to the Twenty-Six Martyrs** (日本二十六聖人殉教地)**,** honoring Christian martyrs from the era when the religion was banned (p. 354, ❷). Immediately striking is that three of them look very young; indeed, the youngest was only 12. Behind the relief is the

small **Twenty-Six Martyrs Museum,** housing artifacts relating to the history of Christianity Japan. The religion was practiced secretly by the faithful throughout Japan's isolation policy surviving more than 200 years underground without the benefits of a church or clergy. ⏱4 min. 7-8 Nishizakimachi. ☎ 095/822-6000. www.26martyrs.com. ¥250 adults, ¥150 junior-high and high-school students, ¥100 kids. Daily 9am–5pm. Streetcar: Oura-Tenshudoshita.

③ 🍵 **Hiiragi.** This otherwise unassuming little coffee shop happens to serve up a really excellent *omuraisu*—an omelet wrapped around rice, with a demi-glace topping. The atmosphere is pure neighborhood hangout, with elderly locals sitting side by side with younger students. (It's located near a college campus.) 8-1 Hamaguchimachi. ☎ 095/846-9345. Set lunches from ¥1,000. No credit cards. Lunc & dinner Sun–Thurs; lunch only Fri–Sat. Streetcar: Hamaguchimachi.

❹ **Dejima** (出島)**.** Dejima was for centuries the only spot where foreigners (mainly Dutch and Chinese traders) were permitted to interact with Japan. Once an island, the surrounding straits were filled up in 1904, and today the area is home to a tourist quarter of shops, restaurants, and reconstructions, including the excellent **Dejima Museum of History.** It gives

Nagasaki by Streetcar

Streetcars have been hauling passengers in Nagasaki since 1915 and have changed little in the ensuing years; they're still the easiest—and most charming—way to get around. Four lines run through the heart of the city, with stops written in English. Because streetcars have their own lanes of traffic here, during rush hour they're usually the fastest vehicles on the road. It costs a mere ¥120 (half-price for kids) to ride one no matter how far you go; pay at the front when you get off. You are allowed to transfer to another line only at **Tsukima-chi Station** (ask the driver for a *nori-tsugi*, or transfer, when you disembark from the first streetcar); otherwise, you must pay each time you disembark.

etailed account of the historical development
f the island and what life was like for the for-
gners who lived here. Incidentally, long-term
lans call to re-excavate the land around Dejima
nd return it to its former island state. ⏱ 30 min.
-1 Dejimamachi. ☎ 095/829-1194. Tues–Sun
am–5pm. Free. Streetcar: Dejima.

★ **Glover Garden** (グラバー園). After Japan
pened its doors to the rest of the world and
stablished Nagasaki as one of a handful
f international ports, the city emerged as
ne of the most progressive in the country,
ith many foreign residents. A number of
Vestern-style houses were built during the
Meiji Period (1868–1912), many of them on a
ill overlooking Nagasaki and the harbor. Most
amous is **Glover Mansion,** Japan's oldest
Vestern-style house, built on the grounds of
e Glover Garden in 1863 and romanticized
s the home of Madame Butterfly, the ficti-
ous, tragic heroine of Puccini's opera. Also
n the site are the **Ringer House** and the **Alt
ouse,** each of which were once owned by
ealthy foreign traders—and which have
nce been turned into a public park. ⏱ 1 hr.
-1 Minami Yamatemachi. ☎ 095/822-8223.
ww.glover-garden.jp. ¥600 adults, ¥300 high-
chool students, ¥180 kids. Daily 8am–6pm (to
:30pm late Apr to early May and mid-July to
id-Oct). Streetcar: Oura Tenshudoshita.

🍜 **Gonchan Chanpon** (ごんちゃん). No
visit to Nagasaki would be complete
without a taste of *champon*. It's a
Chinese-inspired noodle dish, usually
served in soup with meat, seafood, and
vegetables—and Gonchan serves up
some of the best. 40 Imahakatamachi.
☎ 095/822-4170. *Champon* from ¥700.
No credit cards. Lunch & dinner Mon–Sat;
lunch only Sun. Streetcar: Kokaidomae.

★ **Oura Tenshudo Church** (浦上天主堂).
onstructed in 1864 to honor the 26 Chris-
an martyrs crucified when Japan banned
e religion in 1597 (p. 354, ❷), this is the
ngle oldest church in Japan. Designated
National Treasure, the building features
eautiful stained-glass windows and other
atures. This makes a good side trip from
lover Garden (see above). ⏱ 30 min. 5-3
inami-Yamate. www1.bbiq.jp/oourahp. Daily

Gunkanjima

For an offbeat side trip, book a tour of this
"ghost city" located on an island 15km (9
miles) away from Nagasaki. For decades
★ **Gunkanjima,** literally "Battleship Island,"
was home to a city of 5,000 coal miners,
making the tiny (500m/1,640-ft long)
place one of the most densely populated
on Earth. Completely abandoned in 1974,
the entire city is slowly sliding into decay,
giving the place an eerie, apocalyptic feel.
(Visitors are not allowed to enter the city
itself due to safety concerns and must
remain behind fences on the periphery.) A
3-hour chaperoned tour (Japanese only;
¥4,300) of the island departs from the
Nagasaki Port Ferry Terminal, 17–3 Motofu-
namachi (☎ 095/822-5002), twice daily at
9am and 1:10pm. Counter 7 sells same-day
tickets, but advance booking is recommended for weekends and holidays.

8am–6pm. ¥300 adults, ¥250 junior-high and
high-school students, ¥200 kids. Streetcar:
Oura-Tenshudoshita.

❽ ★★ **Mount Inasa** (稲佐山). The Nagasaki
Ropeway delivers you to the top of Mount
Inasa—and to the best panoramic view of
Nagasaki—in only 5 minutes. There's a hillside
observation deck; we recommend you arrive
just before sunset and stay to watch the city
come alive at night. ⏱ 2 hr. 364-1 Insasamachi.
☎ 095/861-6321. www.nagasaki-ropeway.
jp. ¥1,200 adults, ¥900 junior-high and high-
school students, ¥600 kids. Daily 9am–10pm.
Bus: 3 or 4 from Nagasaki Ekimae Station to
Ropeway-mae.

Where to Stay & Dine in Nagasaki

★★★ Best Western Premier Hotel Nagasaki

One of Nagasaki's finest, the Best Western's marbled lobby, decorated with large Oriental vases, has a distinct Asian flair. Rooms, which combine colonial-style decor with Chinese accents, offer the usual comforts, with one floor reserved for women only and offering amenities geared toward female travelers. Rooms on the 14th Sky Floor, with so-called Hollywood twins (two singles pushed together) or double beds, have the best views; otherwise, visit the 15th-floor buffet restaurant or bar for panoramic vistas. 2-26 Takaramachi. ☎ 095/821-1111. www. bestwestern.co.jp/nagasaki. 183 units. Doubles from ¥22,526. Rates include breakfast. AE, DC, MC, V. Train: Nagasaki Station. Streetcar: Takaramachi.

★★ Gohan (御飯) JAPANESE

Although it can be hard to find (walk one block down Sofukuji Dori toward the temple and take the first left), dining at Gohan is an experience in and of itself. English-speaking owner-chef Tsunehiro Yoshimura is a musician, so you'll hear interesting music as you sample creative, original meals. The interior of the restaurant is authentically old; salvaged beams and pieces from five different houses were given new lives here. The handwritten menu changes daily, but the set dinner more than satisfies. Included may be sashimi, new potato with sesame seed, whole snapper, crayfish, tofu, soup, and rice. 2-32 Aburayamachi. ☎ 095/825-3600. Set dinners from ¥3,150. AE, MC, V. Lunch & dinner Mon–Sat. Streetcar: Shokakujishita.

★★ Harbin (ハルビン) FRENCH/RUSSIAN

Established in 1959, Harbin is a Nagasaki tradition. Its owner was born in Manchuria and named his restaurant after Harbin, a town close to his birthplace that was once an international city of Russian, Chinese, and Japanese residents. His family-run restaurant serves a unique blend of French and Russian cuisine. The coulibiac (traditional Russian salmon pie), when available, is perhaps the best thing on the menu. It's located in the Kanko Dori covered shopping arcade (which bisects Hamanomachi). 4-13 Yorozuyamachi. ☎ 095/824-6650. Set meals from ¥3,675. No credit cards. Lunch & dinner daily. Closed every other Wed. Streetcar: Kanko Dori.

★ Hotel Majestic

A small, charming, quiet hotel located near Glover Garden (p. 375, ❺). The beautifully appointed rooms are decorated in one of several themes; the country-living theme, for example, sports wooden floors, light-oak furnishings, and claw-foot bathtubs. All rooms have small balconies and larger-than-average bathrooms. The views are terrible, but don't let that turn you away—the small size means no tour groups and an all-around more intimate experience. One big caveat: This otherwise classy place unfortunately allows smoking in all rooms, so if you are sensitive, you may want to book elsewhere. 2-28 Minami Yamatemachi. ☎ 095/827-7777. 23 units. Doubles from ¥31,185. AE, DC, MC, V. Streetcar Oura-Tenshudoshita.

★ Nagasaki International Hostel Akari

With the best prices in central Nagasaki, this is a family-owned, nonsmoking establishment While the vibe is definitely more "hostel" than "hotel"—in addition to private rooms, it has dorm-style bunks for backpackers—the super-friendly, English-speaking owners are a huge plus. They offer their own guide map, a rooftop hangout, and even free "Short Walks with Nagasaki Locals," daily guided walks led by natives. Rooms (doubles, twins, and triples have tatami-mat floors but are outfitted with Western beds. 2-2 Kojiyamachi. ☎ 095/801-7900. www.nagasaki-hostel.com. 11 units, 9 with bathroom. Doubles from ¥5,900. Streetca Kokaido-mae.

★★ Tsuruchan (ツル茶ん) TURKISH/JAPANESE

This little establishment is, hands down,

A noodle maker in Nagasaki's Chinatown.

...he best place to experience the uniquely ...agasaki dish of *toruko raisu* (Turkish rice), ... cultural mash-up consisting of a fried pork ...utlet sitting atop spaghetti sitting atop ...ry-curried rice. Tsuruchan, which opened ... 1925, originated the dish and remains a ...avorite for carb-hungry locals and visitors even today. In addition to the basics, they offer many variations on the dish; one of our favorites is the *teki-toruko,* which substitutes beef stroganoff for the pork cutlet. **2–47 Aburayamachi. ☎ 095/824-2679. Turkish rice ¥980. No credit cards. Breakfast, lunch & dinner daily. Streetcar: Shianmachi.**

Fukuoka

With a population of 1.41 million, Fukuoka is Kyushu's

largest city and serves as a major international and domestic gateway to the island.
During Japan's feudal days, Fukuoka was divided into two distinct towns separated
by the Nakagawa River. Fukuoka was where the samurai lived; merchants lived
across the river in Hakata, the commercial center of the area. Both cities were
joined in 1889. Today, Fukuoka is a modern, internationally oriented commercial
and business center with a highly developed port and coastal area.

> A doll on display in the Hakata Machiya Folk Museum.

START Take the train to Gion Station. Fukuok
is 642km (399 miles) west of Kyoto.

❶ Tocho-ji Temple（東長寺）. This modern reconstruction of a temple originally establishe
by Kobo Daishi in the 9th century may not
look like much—but it houses Japan's largest
seated wooden Buddha, measuring 10m (33
ft.) tall. Also particularly interesting is the trip
through the "Hells of Buddhism," which you
embark upon by entering the small room to
the left of the Buddha. After viewing colored
reliefs of unfortunate souls burning in hell, be
ing boiled alive, and suffering other tortures,
enter the darkened, twisting passageway and
walk through it guided by a rail, whereupon
you'll reach the end—enlightenment! It's
fun for older kids. ⏱ 1 hr. 2–4 Gokushomachi.
☎ 092/291-4459. Free. Daily 9am–5pm. Train:
Gion Station.

❷ Hakata Machiya Folk Museum（博多町家ふるさ
と館）. This folk museum occupies three buildings, two of which are Meiji Era replicas; the
third is an authentic 150-year-old weaver's
house. On display are items used in everyday
life, as well as dioramas depicting festivals,
everyday street scenes, and a home typical
of a Hakata merchant family. A telephone
allows you to listen to *Hakata-ben,* the local
dialect, which is quite difficult even for native Japanese speakers to understand. You
can also watch artisans at work on Hakata's
most famous wares, including the highly refined Hakata dolls, tops, wooden containers,
and *Hakata-ori* cloth, used for obi sashes and
famous for loincloths worn by sumo wrestlers. Be sure to see the 22-minute film of the

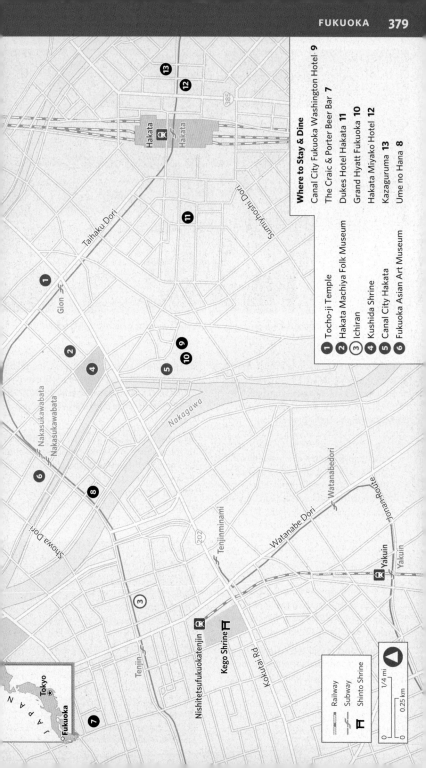

> *Elaborate parade floats, like this one on display at Kushida Shrine, play a key role in Fukuoka festivals.*

Yamakasa Festival, Fukuoka's most famous festival, featuring races of men carrying enormous floats. ⏱1 hr. 6–10 Reisenmachi. ☎092/281-7761. www.hakatamachiya.com. ¥200. Daily 10am–6pm. Train: Gion Station.

③ 🍜 **Ichiran** (一蘭). This is Fukuoka's most well-known ramen chain, famed for its *tonkotsu* (pork broth). Diners purchase tickets from a vending machine and hand them to the staff, whereupon they are given a questionnaire about details such as how firmly you want your noodles cooked. Don't be intimidated! Simply circle the middle choices down the line— *kihon* (standard). This is ramen at its heaviest and heartiest. Inside Canal City, 1-2-1 Sumiyoshi, Hakata-ku. ☎092/262-0433. www.ichiran.co.jp/index.html. Ramen from ¥690. No credit cards. Lunch daily. Bus: Canal City Hakata-mae.

④ **Kushida Shrine** (櫛田神社). Fukuoka's oldest shrine has long been a holy place for merchants praying for good health and prosperity. But the most interesting thing here is the towering parade float on view (except in June when it is being rebuilt), used in the Yamakasa Festival held in mid-July. It's decorated with

dolls made by Hakata doll makers. Incredibly, the elaborate floats are made anew every year. ⏱30 min. 1 Kamikawabatamachi. ☎092/291-2951. Free. Grounds open daily 24 hr. Train: Gion Station.

⑤ **Canal City Hakata.** Located just outside of Kushida Shrine in Hakata, this massive "entertainment city" is home to 250 shops, a movie theater complex, and dozens of restaurants, ranging from Chinese, Italian, and Japanese t fast food and bar snacks. Shoppers can while away an afternoon—rain or shine—under the

Birth of the Kamikaze

Fukuoka lies closer to Seoul, Korea, than to Tokyo; in fact, it was a window to continental Asian culture for centuries. But that same closeness worked against Fukuoka in the 13th century, when Kublai Khan selected the city as the best place to invade Japan. The largest attack came in 1281, but a typhoon blew in and sank the entire Mongol fleet. Japanese called this gift from heaven *kamikaze*, or "divine wind," a word that took on a far different meaning during World War II, when it was applied to suicide squadrons that attacked Allied forces.

Canal City Hakata is one of the city's premiere shopping areas.

overed shopping arcade. ⊕ 1 hr. 1–2 Sumiyoshi, akata-ku. www.canalcity.co.jp/eg/index.html. ree. Daily 10am–9pm (restaurants open until pm). Bus: Canal City Hakata-mae.

Fukuoka Asian Art Museum (福岡アジア美術館). his large collection is devoted to contempo-ary and modern art from around Asia. From olk pop art to political art, the permanent xhibition presents the cutting edge of art om the Philippines, Indonesia, Malaysia,

Singapore, Thailand, China, Mongolia, Korea, India, and other Asian countries, with chang-ing displays culled from the museum's own collection. It's very much worth the hour you'll spend here. ⊕ 1 hr. 3-1 Shimo-Kawabatamachi. ☎ 092/263-1100. http://faam.city.fukuoka.lg.jp. ¥200 adults, ¥150 college and high-school stu-dents, free for junior-high students and younger. Thurs–Tues 10am–8pm. Subway: Nakasu-Kawa-bata Station. Bus: Kawabatamachi.

Take Me Out to the Ballgame

If you're in town March through Septem-ber, consider seeing the **Fukuoka Softbank Hawks** baseball team play one of its 70-some home games in Fukuoka Yahoo! Japan Dome (☎ 092/847-1006), the first retractable-roof stadium in Japan. Tickets start at ¥1,500 for an unreserved seat in the outfield and are available at major convenience stores or at the box office. Watching the spectators can actually be as much fun as watching the game, with their coordinated cheering, flag waving, trumpet blowing, and more. Oddly enough, the roof is kept closed (in case it rains and so that players aren't distracted by their shadows), but when the Hawks win, they open the roof and celebrate with fireworks. And this being Japan, the dome is part of a larger **Hawks Town** complex (www. hawkstown.com) with a hotel, restaurants, and other amusements. To reach Hawks Town, take the subway to the Tojinmachi stop; it's about a 15-minute walk from there. Or take bus no. 39 or 306 from gate 5 of the Kotsu Bus Center in front of Hakata Station to the Fukuoka Dome-mae. On game days, there are also special shuttle buses departing from the bus centers in Tenjin and Kotsu Cen-ter near Hakata Station.

Where to Stay & Dine in Fukuoka

> *Style and minimalist elegance at the Grand Hyatt Fukuoka.*

Canal City Fukuoka Washington Hotel
Though part of a nationwide business-hotel chain, this branch has more style: It's located inside Canal City Hakata, Fukuoka's number-one shopping and entertainment complex. The cheapest singles face the Grand Hyatt above the Canal City complex, while higher-priced larger singles and all twins and triples have views outward toward the city. The downside: Its location makes it popular; you'll find the lobby crowded at check-in and checkout times. 1-2-20 Sumiyoshi, Hakata-ku. ☎ 092/282-8800. www.wh-rsv.com/english. 423 units. Doubles from ¥15,000. AE, DC, MC, V. Train: Hakata Station. Bus: Canal City Hakata-mae.

The Craic & Porter Beer Bar *PUB*
Normally we aren't big fans of expat hangouts, but we'll make an exception for this warm and welcoming pub. Founded by a New Yorker, it's centrally located in the Tenjin area downtown and carries a wide variety of craft beers and whiskeys. In fact, it's more of a bar than a restaurant, but they do carry a selection of finger and bar foods as well. 2F Kusano Building, 3-5-16 Tenjin, Chuo-ku. ☎ 090/4514-9516 Draft beers from ¥900. No credit cards. Dinner & late night daily. Train: Nishitetsu Fukuoka Tenjin Station.

★ Dukes Hotel Hakata
Flower boxes, plants, and evergreens outside the entrance hint that this is no ordinary hotel. Indeed, it's a reasonably priced hotel with class, with a small but very civilized lobby that exudes charm and invites you to linger among its Chinese vases, palm trees, antiques, and classical music. Most of the rooms are singles, with only nine twins and nine doubles—and they're all tiny but comfy, with a simple decor that suggests an English-style countryside manor. In the world of cloned business hotels this establishment, a short walk from Hakata Station in the direction of Canal City, is a welcome relief. While it is farther from the station

an some other choices, it's still in the heart
f the city. 2-3-9 Hakataeki-mae, Hakata-ku.
092/472-1800. www.dukes-hotel.com. 153
nits. Doubles from ¥12,600. AE, DC, MC, V.
rain: Hakata Station (west exit).

★★ Grand Hyatt Fukuoka

ukuoka's top hotel commands a grand setting
the innovative Canal City Hakata, with easy
edestrian access to the city's main sights.
s black-marbled lobby has a curved facade
at overlooks the shopping complex, but for
uests who desire solitude, the hotel also has
private roof garden. Service throughout the
otel is superb—along the order of "Your wish
our command." Small but stylish rooms
rovide views of the private garden or the river
nd its night scenes. Besides all the luxury, a
tay here is fun, with Canal City's many shops
nd restaurants right outside the door. 1-2-82
umiyoshi, Hakata-ku. ☎ 092/282-1234. www.
ukuoka.grand.hyatt.com. 370 units. Doubles
om ¥34,000. AE, DC, MC, V. Train: Hakata
tation.

Hakata Miyako Hotel

ear Hakata Station's east (Shinkansen)
xit, this attractive property with the famous
Miyako name offers a convenient connection
Fukuoka Airport (just 5 min. via subway)
nd is close to shops and restaurants. The
pacious rooms have floor-to-ceiling windows
at let in plenty of light, though city views are
ot spectacular. The one disadvantage: Tour-
t sights are on the west side of the station,
o you have to go through the station con-
ourse to reach them. 2-1-1 Hakataeki-higashi,
akata-ku. ☎ 092/441-3111. www.miyakohotels.
e.jp/hakata/english. 266 units. Doubles from
21,945. AE, DC, MC, V. Train: Hakata Station.

Kazaguruma (かざぐるま) *PUB*

his lively *izakaya* (traditional pub) in a relo-
ated 200-year-old farmhouse accented with
eavy wooden beams specializes in locally
rewed *shochu* (p. 360). It offers a fish of the
ay (because the description is in Japanese
nly, you might try asking a neighboring diner

for help with translations; this is a friendly
place), yakitori, sashimi, and other local favorites. Or order one of the set meals (though
you must make a reservation the day before to
do this). 1-13-1 Hakata-eki Higashi. ☎ 092/481-
3456. Entrees ¥420–¥1,000. AE, DC, MC, V.
Lunch, dinner & late night Mon–Fri; dinner & late
night Sat. Train: Hakata Station.

★ Ume no Hana (梅の花) *VEGETARIAN*

Located along the Naka River on Nakasu Island, this restful and low-key chain is known
for its appetizing low-calorie, light vegetarian
cuisine. It offers a variety of meals centered on
tofu and vegetables, though some set meals
may include fish and seafood. It's simply
decorated in that sparse yet elegant Japanese
way, with seating at low tables with leg wells.
There's a branch nearby in the ACROS building, 1-1-1 Tenjin (☎ 0120/20-9022). Hakata
Excel Tokyu Hotel, 2nd floor, 4-6-7 Nakasu.
☎ 092/262-3777. Set lunches from ¥1,400, set
dinners from ¥3,100. AE, MC, V. Lunch & dinner
daily. Subway: Nakasu-Kawabata Station. Bus:
Higashi-Nakasu.

Eats on the Street

The outdoor ★★★ *yatai,* or street-side
food stalls along the Nakagawa River
are *the* Fukuoka way to enjoy a late-night
snack. The highest concentration of these
stalls can be found right outside of Canal
City Hakata; the Tenjin area (Tenjin Station) is another hotspot. The majority
specialize in ramen, though others serve
up classics like *oden,* yakitori, tempura, and
other simple fare. They're open daily from
about 6pm to 2am but get quite crowded
later at night, as revelers stop here before
or after a spin through the Nakasu entertainment district. Simply choose a stall and
sit down, and you'll be served a steaming
bowl of ramen—the average price is around
¥700. If you don't see prices posted, don't
hesitate to ask, "*Ikura?*" ("How much?").
Most do not accept credit cards.

Kumamoto

Located roughly halfway down Kyushu's western side,
Kumamoto is mainly known for its castle, silhouetted against the beautiful
backdrop of Mount Aso, and its landscaped garden, both with origins stretching
from the first half of the 17th century. Once one of Japan's most important castle
towns, Kumamoto today is the progressive capital of Kumamoto Prefecture,
with a population of some 750,000. But it retains a small-town atmosphere,
which is precisely what attracts many people to the city.

> Kumamoto's historic castle still watches over the city today.

START Take the streetcar from Kumamoto
Station to Kumamotojo-mae or Shiyakusho-
mae stop. Kumamoto is 735km (457 miles)
southwest of Kyoto.

❶ ★★ **Kumamoto Castle** (熊本城). This is the
city's star attraction. The walls are particularly
impressive examples of what are known as
musha-gaeshi, literally "warrior-stoppers"—
steeply curved and crowned with an overhang
to keep footsoldiers, samurai, and other
intruders (such as ninja) at bay. Much of
the castle was destroyed in 1877 during the
Seinan Rebellion led by Saigo Takamori, a

samurai who was unhappy with the new policies of the Meiji government, which rescinded
ancient samurai rights. Takamori and his men
holed up here for 53 days before government
reinforcements finally arrived and quelled the
rebellion. When the smoke cleared, most of
the castle lay in smoldering ruins. The castle
was reconstructed in 1960 of ferroconcrete,
and although it's not nearly as massive as
before, it's still quite impressive (director Kurosawa Akira used it for his epic drama *Ran*).
The interior houses a museum with armor and
swords from the Edo Era, and rifles and other

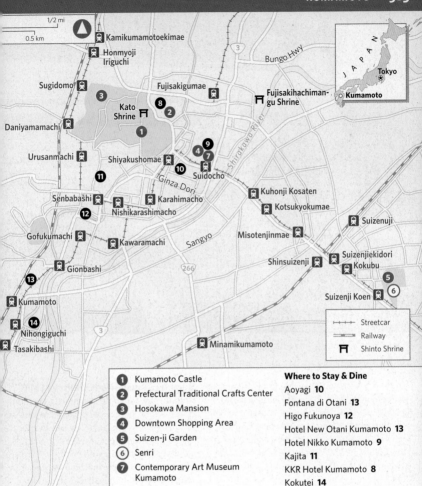

1 Kumamoto Castle
2 Prefectural Traditional Crafts Center
3 Hosokawa Mansion
4 Downtown Shopping Area
5 Suizen-ji Garden
6 Senri
7 Contemporary Art Museum Kumamoto

Where to Stay & Dine

Aoyagi **10**
Fontana di Otani **13**
Higo Fukunoya **12**
Hotel New Otani Kumamoto **13**
Hotel Nikko Kumamoto **9**
Kajita **11**
KKR Hotel Kumamoto **8**
Kokutei **14**

Streetcar
Railway
Shinto Shrine

rtifacts from the Seinan Rebellion. Beside the astle is a replica of Honmaru Goten Palace, a 7th-century palace that was destroyed in the einan Rebellion but has been painstakingly econstructed using traditional methods. ⏰1 ☆. 1–1 Honmaru. ☎ 096/352-5900. ¥500 adults, 200 kids; combination ticket for Hosokawa Mansion (see below) and Kumamoto Castle ¥640 adults, ¥240 kids. Daily Apr–Oct 8:30am– :30pm; Nov–Mar 8:30am–4:30pm. Streetcar: umamotojo-mae or Shiyakusho-mae.

2 Prefectural Traditional Crafts Center
(熊本県伝統工芸館). This showroom near Kumamoto Castle offers a wide selection of tradi-
ional crafts from throughout the prefecture,

including Yamaga paper lanterns, Amakusa pearls, bambooware, ceramics, woodworks, toys, musical instruments, and more. ⏰ 45 min. 3-35 Chibajyomachi. ☎ 096/324-4930. http://cyber.pref.kumamoto.jp/kougei. Free. Tues–Sun 9am–5pm. Streetcar: Skiyakusho-mae.

3 ★ **Hosokawa Mansion** (細川家). A 10-min-
ute walk north of Kumamoto Castle, this 300-year-old samurai mansion was built by a subsidiary member of the Hosokawa clan, Lord Gyobu, and was enlarged in the 1800s. Fifteen-minute guided tours (some even available in English) take visitors through 24 rooms, including the lord's study and reception room, teahouse, kitchen, and servants'

> Torii *gates lead the way into Suizen-ji Garden.*

quarters, where you'll see Edo Era furnishings and personal items. ⏱ 1 hr. 3-1 Furukyomachi. ☎ 096/352-6522. ¥300 adults, ¥100 kids; combination ticket for Hosokawa Mansion and Kumamoto Castle (see above) ¥640 adults, ¥240 kids. Daily Apr–Oct 8:30am–5:30pm; Nov–Mar 8:30am–4:30pm. Bus: Kumamoto Castle Loop, stop 7.

❹ **Downtown Shopping Area.** Kumamoto is known for its shopping districts, which center on three covered shopping streets called **Shimotori, Kamitori,** and **Sunroad Shinshigai.** They are home to many department stores, shops, hotels, bars, pachinko parlors, and restaurants and are a fun way to spend a morning or afternoon, browsing or just people-watching. The downtown district is also home to the **Kumamoto Kotsu Center,** from which all buses in the city depart. ⏱ 1 hr.

❺ ★ **Suizen-ji Garden** (水前寺公園)**.** This 17th-century garden is another iconic Kumamoto attraction. Its design incorporates famous scenes in miniature from the 53 stages of the ancient **Tokaido Highway,** which connected Kyoto and Tokyo. (The 53 stages were also immortalized in Hiroshige's famous woodblock prints.) Most recognizable are cone-shaped Mount Fuji and Lake Biwa; near the garden's entrance is Nihon Bashi ("Bridge of Japan"), Edo's starting point on the Tokaido Highway. The park is admittedly rather small and many have a hard time figuring out the different stages, but that's part of the charm. ⏱ 1 hr. 8-1 Suizen-ji Koen. ☎ 096/383-0074. ¥400 adults, ¥200 kids. Daily Mar–Nov 7:30am–6pm; Dec–Feb 8:30am–5pm. Streetcar: Suizen-ji-Koen-mae.

Kumamoto by Streetcar

Getting around Kumamoto via its distinctive streetcars is easy because there are only two lines. Streetcar no. 2 is most convenient for tourists; the only one departing from Kumamoto Station, it passes through downtown and near Kumamoto Castle (stop: Kumamotojo-mae) before going onward to Suizen-ji Garden (stop: Suizen-ji-Koen-mae). Tram fare is a flat rate of ¥150; pay when you get off.

🍴 ★★ **Senri.** There's no better way to sample Kumamoto's local dishes than at this restaurant right in Suizen-ji Garden. For lunch, you can choose main dishes such as eel, river fish, or tempura, served with side dishes of vegetable, soup, rice, and tea. Or order the *kyodo-ryori* (local specialty) course, which could include fried lotus, *basashi* (horsemeat sashimi), and *dengaku* (tofu coated with bean paste and grilled on a fire). In the evening, only *kaiseki*—an elaborate multi-course meal—is available and it must be ordered at least one day in advance. Reservations recommended. 8-1 Suizen-ji Koen. ☎ 096/381-1415. Set lunches from ¥2,100. No credit cards. Lunch & dinner daily. Streetcar: Suizen-ji-Koen-mae.

7 ★ **Contemporary Art Museum Kumamoto** (熊本市現代美術館)**.** In addition to special exhibits, this museum showcases works by local talent Ide Nobumichi and features commissioned installations by Kusama Yayoi (look for her *Infinity Mirrored Room*) and Miyajima Tatsuo (the pillar of flashing diodes). It seems more like a community center than a museum, with a children's play corner and a Ping-Pong table designed by Ishii Hiroshi that responds digitally to the ball. There's a free jam session

> *The Infinity Mirrored Room at the Contemporary Art Museum.*

the second and fourth Friday of every month at 6:30pm, as well as nightly piano music from 7 to 7:30pm. ⏱ 1 hr. 2-3 Kamitori-cho. ☎ 096/278-7500. www.camk.or.jp. Free, except for some special exhibits. Wed–Mon 10am–8pm (last entry at 7:30pm). Streetcar: Toricho-suji.

Riding the Rapids

If you've had enough of shrines, castles, and gardens, consider shooting the **Kumagawa Rapids.** Compared to wild rivers in the United States the Kumagawa is pretty tame; people do the trip not so much for the thrill of the ride but for the scenery and for the camaraderie afforded by sitting on tatami in a traditional wooden boat steered by boatmen fore and aft. Given the travel time (1½ hr. each way, plus 2 hr. or so for the ride itself) consider this an all-day activity.

The **Kumagawa Kudari Kabushiki Company,** Shimoshinmachi 333-1, Hitoyoshi City (☎ 0966/22-5555), offers two different 90-minute routes in its wooden boats. The Seiryu Course ("Calm Course") covers 8km (5 miles) of a gentle stretch of the river beginning in Hitoyoshi and ending in Watari. It's offered year-round; December through

February, the boats have *kotatsu* (small, quilt-covered tables with heaters). The cost is ¥2,835 for adults and ¥1,890 for kids; winter trips with *kotatsu* cost ¥3,675 and ¥2,835, respectively. The Kyuryu Course ("Rapids Course") covers 10km (6¼ miles), beginning downriver in Watari and ending in Kyusendo, and is more exciting and requires more skillful maneuvering. It's offered April through October and costs ¥3,675 for adults and ¥2,100 for kids. During rainy season (mid-June to mid-July), this trip is sometimes canceled due to swollen rivers or high winds. You can reach Hitoyoshi City by bus from the Kumamoto Kotsu Center in about 1½ hours, with fares costing ¥2,300 one-way. There are also six trains a day from Kumamoto Station to Hitoyoshi Station; the express train takes 1½ hours and costs ¥1,774.

Where to Stay & Dine in Kumamoto

> *Kokutei's been serving up ramen for more than half a century.*

★ **Aoyagi** (青柳) *JAPANESE*

Everyone in Kumamoto knows this restaurant, located in the downtown area just off the Shimotori covered shopping arcade. The modern building offers seating on tatami, at the counter, or at low tables with leg wells. There are photos outside the front door and in the menu showing dishes of *basashi,* eel, *kamameshi* (rice casseroles), and other local specialties. A tasty vegetarian set meal for ¥2,000 includes *dengaku* and *renkon* (lotus root boiled, stuffed, and then deep-fried), while three types of set dinners for ¥5,250 include all the local favorites. Set lunches center on *kamameshi* and sushi, such as the Ladies' Sushi Set for ¥1,600. 1-2-10 Shimotori. ☎ 096/353-0311. Set lunches ¥1,000–¥3,150, set dinners ¥1,580–¥5,250. AE, MC, V. Lunch & dinner daily. Streetcar: Toricho-suji.

Fontana di Otani *ITALIAN/CONTINENTAL*

For dining near Kumamoto Station, this casual restaurant in one of Kumamoto's most well-known hotels is a good bet. Its menu features lighter fare such as spaghetti, curry, and sandwiches, available all day, as well as a very reasonably priced set lunch (served until 2pm) that includes a trip through a salad bar. The set dinner (available 5–9pm) offers a choice of main dish, such as sea bream and clams in a Marsala sauce, along with side dishes. Hotel New Otani Kumamoto, 1-13-1 Kasuga. ☎ 096/326-1111. Entrees ¥1,260–¥1,680, set lunches ¥1,300–¥1,500, set dinners ¥3,000. AE, DC, MC, V. Lunch & dinner daily. Train: Kumamoto Station.

★ **Higo Fukunoya** (肥後 福のや) *ORGANIC/JAPANESE* Although its location is not convenient o either Kagoshima Station or downtown (it es on the streetcar route between them), eople who like healthy, organic meals go out f their way to dine at this restaurant, simply ecorated with rough wooden floors, contemporary Japanese background music, and ables overlooking a canal. It's located at the ack of a complex of Edo Era buildings, which lso contain an organic health-food store and hops selling natural, environmentally friendly roducts. For lunch there's a vegetarian set unch, two bento box choices, and a *kaiseki* meal, while dinner features three *kaiseki* menus. Reservations required for dinner. 15 Nakatojimachi. ☎ 096/323-1552. Set lunches ¥1,260–¥3,150, set dinners ¥3,150–¥7,350. AE, MC, V. Lunch & dinner Thurs–Tues. Streetcar: Gofukumachi.

★★ Hotel New Otani Kumamoto

A convenient location next to the station, the respected New Otani name, a perceptive taff, a unique design, and reasonable rates re reasons to stay here. Rooms are comfortble, with queen-size beds in both single and ouble rooms, and come with little extras like ndividual reading lights with dimmer switches, windows with blinds to block light and ouble-paned glass to block noise, massage howerheads, and bathroom phones. 1-13-1 Kasuga. ☎ 096/326-1111. www.newotani.co.jp. 30 units. Doubles from ¥20,790. AE, DC, MC, V. Train: Kumamoto Station.

★★★ Hotel Nikko Kumamoto

n the same building as the Contemporary Art Museum Kumamoto (p. 387, ❼) and djoining a shopping complex in the heart of downtown, this 14-story hotel with upbeat modern decor is the most luxurious in Kumamoto. Large, comfortable rooms, with views of either Kumamoto Castle or Mount Aso in the distance, offer sitting areas, closets that light up as soon as you open them, focused bedside reading lights so your partner can sleep, blackout curtains for total darkness, and excellent nsulation from traffic noise. Singles sport double-size beds, doubles have queen-size beds, and twins have large bathrooms with separate tub/shower/toilet areas. 2-1 Kamitoori-cho. ☎ 096/211-1111. www.nikko-kumamoto. co.jp. 191 units. Doubles from ¥31,185. AE, DC, MC, V. Streetcar: Toricho-suji.

Kajita (民宿梶田)

Stuffed birds, a mongoose, and a cobra greet you at this funky and friendly family-run *minshuku* (budget bed-and-breakfast); a stay here certainly won't be your cookie-cutter hotel experience. It has a central location, just a 10-minute walk to the castle grounds and a 2-minute walk to the streetcar that will take you onward to Suizen-ji Garden. Tatami rooms (traditional Japanese rooms with mats on the floor, almost devoid of furniture) are simple but clean. No promises, but if you call ahead, there's a good chance you'll be picked up at the station. 1-2-7 Shinmachi. ☎ 096/353-1546. http://1st.geocities.jp/higoshiro. 10 units, none with bathroom. Doubles ¥7,200; with breakfast ¥700 extra, with dinner ¥2,000 extra. AE, MC, V. Bus: 1 from Kumamoto Station to Shinmachi.

★ KKR Hotel Kumamoto

Located north of Kumamoto Castle across the street, this trendy hotel buzzes with activity as a popular wedding and banquet venue (weekdays are quieter and also cheaper). The best reason to stay here is its up-close view of the castle, with the absolute best views provided by twin and triple rooms above the hotel's rooftop garden (visible also from the hotel's Japanese restaurant). Unfortunately, none of the hotel's 11 single rooms have castle views (solo travelers can stay in a castle-view twin for ¥10,000), and there are no double rooms. 3-31 Chibajomachi. ☎ 096/355-0121. 54 units. Twins from ¥16,000. AE, DC, MC, V. Streetcar: Shyakusho-mae.

Kokutei (黒亭) *NOODLES*

Located in a simple black-and-white building, this famous ramen restaurant has been serving homemade noodles since 1959. Popular with locals from office workers to grandmothers, it can get quite crowded (avoid the lunch rush). Prices depend on the number of pork slices you choose to eat with your ramen or whether you add an egg or vegetables. Don't eat noodles? Ask for *me iranai* and you'll be served a steaming bowl of soup. 1-2-29 Nihongi. ☎ 096/352-1648. Noodles ¥590–¥820. No credit cards. Breakfast, lunch & dinner daily. Closed first and third Thursday of every month. Train: Kumamoto Station.

Kagoshima

The capital of Kagoshima Prefecture, population 600,000, spreads along Kinko Bay and boasts one of the most unusual bay vistas in the world: Sakurajima, an active volcano, rising from the waters. But it's also a city of rich history: Because of its relative isolation at the southern tip of Japan, far away from the capitals of Kyoto and Tokyo, Kagoshima has developed an independent spirit through the centuries that has fostered a number of great men and accomplishments. Foremost is the Shimadzu clan (also spelled Shimazu), a remarkable family that for 29 generations (almost 700 years) ruled over Kagoshima and its vicinity before the Meiji Restoration in 1868. Much of Japan's early contact with the outside world—first with China and then with the Western world—was via Kagoshima. And Japan's first contact with Christianity occurred in Kagoshima when St. Francis Xavier landed here in 1549.

> A shrine on Mount Sakurajima, across the water from Kagoshima.

START Take the streetcar to Suizokukan-guchi stop. Kagoshima is 908km (564 miles) southwest of Kyoto.

① ★ kids **Kagoshima City Aquarium** (いおワールド かごしま水族館). The Japanese love a good aquarium, and so do we. This is one of the country's better ones. In addition to a massive tank featuring some equally massive animals, such as whale sharks, highlights include the world's only display of deep-sea tube worms, a 3-D movie of the surrounding seas, the world's largest eel, and a children's touch pool.

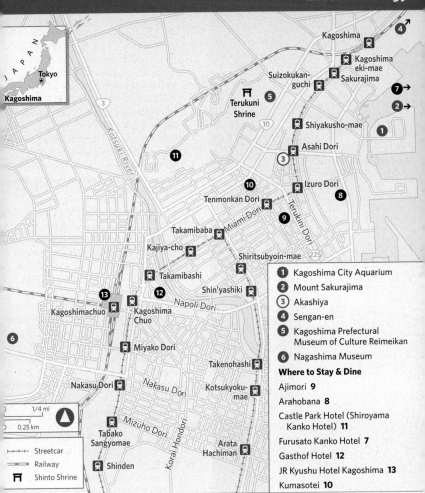

1. Kagoshima City Aquarium
2. Mount Sakurajima
3. Akashiya
4. Sengan-en
5. Kagoshima Prefectural Museum of Culture Reimeikan
6. Nagashima Museum

Where to Stay & Dine

Ajimori **9**
Arahobana **8**
Castle Park Hotel (Shiroyama Kanko Hotel) **11**
Furusato Kanko Hotel **7**
Gasthof Hotel **12**
JR Kyushu Hotel Kagoshima **13**
Kumasotei **10**

Dolphins, which have access to open waters, are used only for educational shows (conducted in Japanese only). ⏱ 1½ hr. 1 Honkoshinmachi. ☎ 099/226-2233. ¥1,500 adults, ¥750, junior-high and high-school students, ¥350 kids. Daily 9:30am–6pm. Closed first week in Dec. Streetcar: Suizokukan-guchi.

② ★★ **Mount Sakurajima** (桜島)**.** With ties to Naples, Italy, as its sister city, Kagoshima bills itself the "Naples of the Orient." That's perhaps stretching things a bit, but Kagoshima is balmy most of the year and even has its own Mount Vesuvius: Mount Sakurajima. This active volcano has erupted 30 times through recorded history. It continues to puff steam

into the sky and occasionally even covers the city with fine soot and ash. Sakurajima means "Cherry Blossom Island," but isn't officially an island anymore—a 1914 eruption connected it to the far side of the bay. That said, the only way to get there from Kagoshima is a 15-minute **ferry** ride. You can't actually climb the caldera for safety reasons, but it's still a fascinating place to visit, with massive lava flows and other natural attractions, not to mention some great hot springs. During summer vacation (July 21–Aug), there are also nightly fireworks displays over the bay in front of Sakurajima (with a huge one held the end of Aug). When you get there, make the **Sakurajima Visitor Center** your first stop, for

③ 🍴 **Akashiya** (明石屋). Kagoshima's most famous sweet treat (the one all Japanese tourists must buy before returning home) is *karukan,* a delicious spongy white cake made from rice with Chinese and Korean origins. And this little shop is the most famous maker of *karukan* today. While it isn't exactly a restaurant, you owe it to yourself to drop by and sample some of these unique—and tasty—desserts. 4-16 Kinseicho. ☎ 099/226-0431. Cakes from ¥189. Daily 9am-7pm. Streetcar: Asahi Dori.

④ ★★ **Sengan-en** (仙巌園). This is Kagoshima's most widely visited attraction. It's a garden on the grounds of a countryside villa laid out more than 300 years ago by the Shimadzu clan, incorporating Mount Sakurajima and Kinko Bay into its design scheme in a principle known as "borrowed landscape." There's a lovely grove of bamboo, a waterfall located a 30-minute walk up a nature trail with good views over the bay, and the requisite pond. It remains Japan's only garden with its original *kyokusui* (poem-composing garden) still intact. A must after visiting the garden is the **Shoko Shuseikan Museum**, which was built in the mid-1850s as Japan's first industrial factory. It houses items relating to the almost 700-year history of the Shimadzu clan, including family heirlooms ranging from lacquerware to tea-ceremony objects. ⏱ 1 hr. 9700-1 Yoshinocho. ☎ 099/247-1551. ¥1,000 adults, ¥500 kids (includes admission to Shoko Shuseikan Museum). Daily 8:30am-5:30pm (until 5:20pm in winter). Bus: Sengan-en-mae.

⑤ ★ kids **Kagoshima Prefectural Museum of Culture Reimeikan** (鹿児島県立歴史資料センター黎明館). This museum occupies the former site of **Tsurumaru Castle,** which today consists only of stone ramparts and a moat. It offers an overview of Japanese history focusing on Kagoshima Prefecture in particular. Upon entering the museum, you'll walk over a glass floor above a map of Kagoshima Prefecture (much of it is islands). The museum then traces the history of the people of Kagoshima over the last 30,000 years, through the rise of the Shimadzu clan in the 11th century and Kagoshima's preeminence as a pottery center after Korean potters were brought here in the

> *A stingray swims with friends at the Kagoshima City Aquarium.*

maps and information about local attractions such as hiking trails. Ferry: Sakurajima Ferry Terminal, 4-1 Honshinkomachi. ☎ 099/223-7271. www.sakurajima-ferry.jp. Ticket window 7am-7pm daily (ferries run 24 hr.). ¥150 adults, ¥80 elementary students. Train: Kagoshimaeki-mae or Suizokukanguchi stations. Visitor Center: 1722-29 Sakurajimayokoyamacho. ☎ 099/293-3111. Tues-Sun 9am-5pm. Train: Kagoshimaeki-mae or Suizokukan-guchi stations.

The moat at Tsurumaru Castle park is filled with lotus plants.

te 1500s. Kids will enjoy the hands-on learn-
g room with old-fashioned toys and samurai
utfits that can be tried on. ⏱ 45 min. 7-2
hiroyama-cho. ☎ 099/222-5100. ¥300 adults,
190 college and high-school students, ¥120
ds. Tues–Sun 9am–5pm; closed 25th of each
onth unless it falls on Sat or Sun. Streetcar:
hiyakusho-mae.

● ★★ **Nagashima Museum** (長島美術館). Al-
ough inconveniently located, this is a very
orthwhile private museum on a hill high atop
the city with great views of Sakurajima and
Kagoshima. While its focus is mostly works by
such Kagoshima artists as Kuroda Seiki, it also
contains some art by well-known Western
artists. But most impressive is an outstanding
collection of mainly 19th-century white Satsuma pottery. The museum's French restaurant, **Camellia** (lunch only) has great views of
the city. ⏱ 30 min. 3-42-18 Take. ☎ 099/250-
5400. ¥1,000 adults, ¥800 college and high-
school students, ¥400 kids. Daily 9am–5pm.
Taxi: 7 min. from Kagoshima Chuo Station.

Where to Stay & Dine in Kagoshima

> Kumasotei is your one-stop shop for local delicacies.

★ **Ajimori** (黒豚料理あぢもり) *JAPANESE*
This 30-year-old establishment specializes in pork from small black pigs, which the locals claim is more tender and succulent than regular pork. The restaurant is divided into two parts: The upper floors, with both table seating and private tatami rooms, serve *Satsuma-kuroshabu*, a Kagoshima take on black-pork *shabu-shabu;* the first floor is a casual dining room specializing in *tonkatsu,* breaded black-pork cutlet. If you order the *kuroshabu,* you'll eat it just like the more common beef *shabu-shabu,* cooking it yourself at your table by dipping it into a boiling broth and then in raw egg or sauce. Portions are generous, but if you wish, you can also order *tonkatsu* as a side dish. Otherwise, go to the first floor for perhaps the lightest, best-tasting *tonkatsu* you'll ever have. 13–21 Sennichi-cho. ☎ 099/224-7634. Tonkatsu set lunches from ¥680, shabu-shabu set dinners from ¥4,200. AE, DC, MC, V (but only for meals costing more than ¥10,000). Lunch & dinner Thurs–Tues. Streetcar: Tenmonkan Dori.

★★★ **Arahobana** (新穂花) *PACIFIC RIM/JAPANES*
Amami-Oshima, a tropical isle in Kagoshima Prefecture 380km (236 miles) south of Kagoshima City, has its own distinct local cuisin and culture. You can learn about some of that island culture here, where there's live music and dancing in the evening; the Amami musicians and waiters will even teach you their dance. The healthy cuisine, utilizing guava, mango, sugar cane, and spices and featuring dishes like free-range chicken and sweet potato, has a unique flavor very different from Japanese cuisine. It's just a stone's throw from the aquarium. Dolphin Port 2F, 5–4 Honko-Shinmachi. ☎ 099/219-8670. Set lunches from ¥1,580, set dinners ¥1,480–¥4,200. AE, MC, V Lunch & dinner daily. Streetcar: Izuro Dori.

★★ **Castle Park Hotel (Shiroyama Kanko Hotel**
Kagoshima's foremost hotel sits 106m (348 ft.) high atop the wood-covered Shiroyama Hill and commands the best views of the city below and Sakurajima across the bay. Opened more than 40 years ago, it offers updated, comfortable rooms, the most recommended (and more expensive) of which face the volcano and city. Other pluses include hot-spring (including open-air) baths with views of Kinko Bay, a free English-language movie shown nightly on a screen off the lobby, and good restaurants that take advantage of the hotel's views and gardenlike setting. 41-1 Shinshoin-cho. ☎ 099/224-2211. www.shiroyama-g.co.jp. 365 units. Doubles ¥22,000–¥49,000. AE, DC, MC, V. Taxi: 12 min. from Kagoshima Chuo Station. Free shuttle bus: 12 min. from Kagoshima Chuo Station. Bus: City View Bus to Shiroyama.

★★ **Furusato Kanko Hotel**
Although this *ryokan* on Sakurajima is inconvenient for sightseeing, it's great for relaxation. It boasts open-air, hot-spring baths set amid rocks right beside the sea, an indoor 25m (82-ft.) lap pool heated with hot springs, and indoor hot-spring baths overlooking the sea. Rooms are all Japanese-style, most with balconies overlooking great sea views. Some even boast

iews from their bathrooms, while the very est (and most expensive) have private terraces with outdoor hot-spring baths. Breakfast features *kamameshi* (rice casseroles) made with hot-spring water; dinner consists mainly of seafood, *tonkotsu* (slowly stewed pork), and other local specialties. Movies (sometimes English-language) are shown nightly in a small theater. Where else can you claim to have slept next to an active volcano? This is a great getaway. 1076 urusato-cho. ☎ 099/221-3111. info@furukan. o.jp. 42 units. Doubles ¥14,150–¥22,150 per erson including breakfast & dinner. AE, DC, MC, '. Ferry: Sakurajima.

Gasthof Hotel

After traveling to Europe, the owner of this inexpensive, 40-year-old hotel decided to re-create the coziness of a German bed-and-breakfast with a cafe in the lobby, antiques in the hallway, and rooms that vary in decor, furniture, and bedspreads, including four-poster

Specialties of Kagoshima

While in Kagoshima, be sure to try its local dishes, known as *Satsuma-ryori* (Satsuma was the original name of the Kagoshima area). This style of cooking supposedly has its origins in food cooked on battlefields centuries ago; if that's the case, it certainly has improved greatly since then. Popular Satsuma specialties include *Satsuma-age* (ground fish mixed with tofu and sake and then deep-fried), *tonkotsu* (black pork that has been boiled for several hours in miso, *shochu*, and brown sugar—absolutely delicious), *sakezushi* (a rice dish flavored with sake and mixed with vegetables and seafood), and *Satsuma-jiru* (miso soup with chicken and locally grown vegetables including Sakurajima radishes). The local fish is *kibinago*, which belongs to the herring family and can be caught in the waters around Kagoshima; a silver color with brown stripes, it's often eaten raw and arranged on a dish to resemble a chrysanthemum.

beds in some. Although it falls a little short, the Gasthof has a lot more character than a regular business hotel and is convenient to Kagoshima Chuo Station. If you are lucky, the owner may even take you on a personal tour of his private Asian art museum, overflowing with priceless treasures from pottery to Buddha statues. Another plus are the Japanese restaurant and two *izakaya* (Japanese pubs) in the same building. 7-1 Chuo-cho. ☎ 099/252-1401. info@gasthof.jp. 48 units. Doubles from ¥8,925. Breakfast ¥525 extra. AE, DC, MC, V. Train: Kagoshima Chuo Station.

JR Kyushu Hotel Kagoshima

Convenient to Kagoshima Chuo Station (you can enter it right from the station), this business hotel offers clean, mostly single rooms, devoid of character but equipped with the basics, including larger than usual desks. A new annex opened in spring of 2010 adds 273 higher-priced rooms (from ¥7,300 for a single and ¥12,800 for a double). The biggest plus besides convenience: Japan Rail Pass holders receive a 10% discount. 1-1-2 Take. ☎ 099/213-8000. www.jrhotelgroup.com. 375 units. Doubles from ¥12,800. AE, DC, MC, V. Train: Kagoshima Chuo Station.

★★ Kumasotei (熊襲亭) *JAPANESE*

Located in the city center, this restaurant specializes in local Satsuma dishes but carries them one step further by featuring them as part of *kaiseki* set meals. It reminds us more of a private home or *ryokan* because dining is in individual tatami rooms. If there isn't a crowd, you'll probably have your own private room; otherwise, you'll share. The main menu is in Japanese, but there's a smaller English-language menu with photos of the various set meals, which may include such local dishes as *Satsuma-age, tonkotsu, Satsuma-jiru, kibinago,* or *sakezushi,* as well as *shabu-shabu.* 6-10 Higashi Sengoku-cho. ☎ 099/222-6356. Set dinners from ¥3,360. AE, DC, MC, V. Lunch & dinner daily. Streetcar: Tenmonkan Dori.

Kyushu Fast Facts

> *Kumamoto's streetcars are a fun and nostalgic way to get around town.*

Arriving & Getting Around

BY PLANE This is by far the fastest way to reach Kyushu from Tokyo, either through Fukuoka Airport (FUK), Nagasaki Airport (NGS), Kumamoto Airport (KMJ), or Kagoshima Airport (KOJ), all of which are serviced by the major Japanese lines. **BY TRAIN** It is possible to travel to Kyushu from Tokyo by bullet train. The nearest destination is Fukuoka, last stop on the Nozomi Shinkansen from Tokyo, which takes roughly 5 hours. (Japan Rail Pass users cannot use the Nozomi and will have to take the Hikari Shinkansen, changing trains in Osaka or Okayama; total travel, not including transfer time, is 6 hr.)

ATMs

In contrast to those abroad, many ATMs only operate during banking hours. ATMs are also very hard to find outside of major cities, so plan accordingly. Most post offices (see below) have ATM facilities, although hours are limited. For 24-hour access, your best bets are the ATMs in **7-Eleven** convenience stores, which accept Visa, Plus, American Express,

CB, Union Pay, or Diner's Club International ards for cash withdrawals. (They recently topped accepting MasterCard, Maestro, nd Cirrus cards.) **Citibank** and **Shinsei Bank** TMs accept foreign bank cards as well.

octors & Hospitals
he general level of healthcare availability in apan is high. FUKUOKA The **International linic Tojinmachi** is at 1–4–6 Jigyo, Chuo-ku ☎ 092/717-1000). NAGASAKI **Amamoto Internal Medical Clinic** is at 7-1 Manzaimachi ☎ 095-823-8575). KUMAMOTO **Honda Clinic** is at 3–4–18 Honmachi, Yatsushiro-shi ☎ 0965/33-5508). KAGOSHIMA **Imamura linic** is at 1-13 Yasui-cho (☎ 099/222-5758).

mergencies
he all-around emergency number in Japan is : **119.** The all-around police number is ☎ **110.**

nternet Access
Most business hotels (but few traditional-tyle *onsen* or *ryokan*) offer Internet access as perk to customers, and Internet cafes are ommon (though most do not allow customers to hook up their own laptops, requiring hem to use the facility's machines instead).

harmacies
rugstores, called *yakkyoku* (薬局) are ubiqitous in Japan, but they are not 24-hour perations. Your best bet is to ask your hotel oncierge for the closest location. Note that ou must first visit a doctor in Japan before oreign prescriptions can be filled, so it's also est to bring an ample supply of any prescription medication with you.

olice
o reach the police, dial ☎ **110.** You can also top by the nearest *koban* (police substation) r assistance.

ost Office
entral post offices are generally open Monay to Friday 9am to 7pm, Saturday 9am to pm, and Sunday 9am to 12:30pm. Their TMs are generally available Monday to riday 7am to 11pm, Saturday 9am to 9pm, nd Sunday 9am to 7pm. Branches will have horter hours. FUKUOKA **Hakata Post Office**

> *A Sakurajima ferry.*

is located at 8-1 Hakata Eki Chuogai (Hakata Station; ☎ 092/713-2455). NAGASAKI NAGASAKI CENTRAL POST OFFICE IS AT 1–1 EBISUMACHI (☎ 095/822-9580). KUMAMOTO **Kumamoto Central Post Office** is at 2-1-1 Shinmachi (☎ 096/352-1870). KAGOSHIMA **Kagoshima Central Post Office** is at 1-2 Chuomachi (☎ 099/252-4188).

Safety
Kyushu is extremely safe, but take the normal common-sense precautions for personal safety and valuables that you would anywhere else.

Visitor Information
FUKUOKA **Fukuoka Tourist Information Office** is inside Hakata Station near the east gate (☎ 092/431-3003; www.yokanavi.com/eg; daily 8am–7pm). NAGASAKI **Nagasaki City Tourist Information Office** is located just outside the main ticket gates of Nagasaki Station (☎ 095/823-3631; www.at-nagasaki.jp/foreign/english; daily 8am–8pm daily). KUMAMOTO **Kumamoto Tourist Office** is inside Kumamoto Station by the ticket gate (☎ 096/352-3743; daily 8:30am–7pm). KAGOSHIMA **Kagoshima Prefectural Visitors Bureau** is in the Sangyo Kaikan Building, 9–1 Meizan-cho (☎ 099/223-5771; www.kagoshima-kankou.com/for; Mon–Fri 8:30am–5:15pm). Take the streetcar to Asahi Dori.

Favorite Moments

No region was hit harder by the earthquake and tsunami that struck Japan on March 11, 2011, than Tohoku, and a large swath of countryside along the coastline was rendered uninhabitable by the nuclear meltdown that occurred in the Fukushima Nuclear Power facility several days later. In spite of this, its naturally resilient residents have taken great strides to return to their daily lives. With the exception of Sendai, the following tours mainly lead through mountain areas that were not directly affected by the quake or flooding. Although you may have some reservations about traveling here, it's important to remember that every dollar you spend in Tohoku goes a long way toward helping locals recover, and that none of these itineraries are considered unsafe or off-limits. Plus you'll be rewarded with spectacular mountain scenery, national parks, and hot springs in abundance.

> *PREVIOUS PAGE Nyuto Onsen's spas are tucked deep in the forest. THIS PAGE A sightseeing boat plies the tranquil waters of Lake Tazawa, one of Japan's highest and deepest.*

① **Taking in the splendor of Chuson-ji's Konjikido pavilion.** One of Japan's most elaborately decorated traditional structures, this gilt mausoleum in Hiraizumi is close to a thousand years old. Painstakingly restored in the 1960s, it contains the mummies of several of Japan's most famous warriors. See p. 405, **②**.

② **Browsing the Asaichi Dori market.** Downtown Sendai's market is open all day long, and will give you a sense of the sorts of things locals buy for their daily meals. It's also a great place to sample some regional delicacies. See p. 418, **②**.

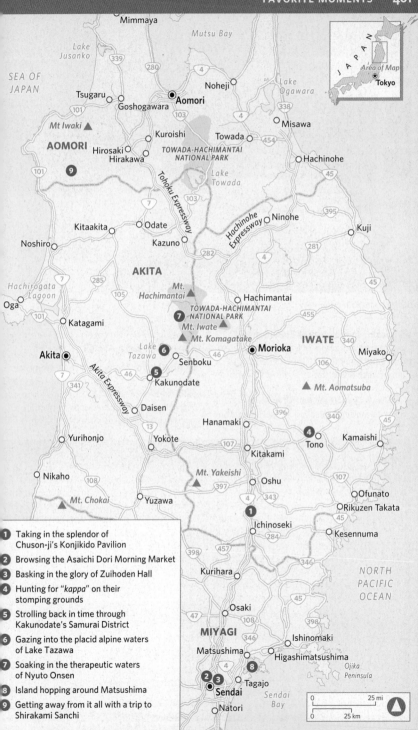

1 Taking in the splendor of Chuson-ji's Konjikido Pavilion

2 Browsing the Asaichi Dori Morning Market

3 Basking in the glory of Zuihoden Hall

4 Hunting for "*kappa*" on their stomping grounds

5 Strolling back in time through Kakunodate's Samurai District

6 Gazing into the placid alpine waters of Lake Tazawa

7 Soaking in the therapeutic waters of Nyuto Onsen

8 Island hopping around Matsushima

9 Getting away from it all with a trip to Shirakami Sanchi

> *Visitors purifying themselves before entering Chuson-ji Temple.*

❸ Basking in the glory of Zuihoden Hall.
This stunning example of traditional funereal architecture, created in the 17th century to memorialize one of Japan's greatest warlords and local legend Daté Masamune, is a feast for the eyes and a fascinating window into the age of samurai. It's also a great steppingstone to seeing the remains of his castle in nearby Aobajo Park. See p. 418, ❹.

❹ Hunting for "kappa" on their stomping grounds. Famed throughout Japan as a cradle of folklore stories, the city of Tono is a great place to learn about the *kappa*. They're the amphibious creatures once believed to haunt

Volunteering in Tohoku

The 2011 tsunami destroyed vast sections of the Tohoku coastline, and while recovery efforts began almost as soon as the waters receded, a great amount of work remains. Even if you don't speak any Japanese, several travel agencies and relief organizations have begun running volunteer tours to some of the hardest-hit areas. The sites are all well outside of the 80km (50-mile) restricted radius around the reactors specified by the U.S. government for visitors to Japan (and the 20km/12.4-mile zone recommended by the Japanese government).

These tours are all about helping locals, so you need to approach them with more flexibility than you might a tourist trip. You will almost definitely share your (often rustic) accommodations with other volunteers, and be willing to accept the tasks assigned to you. These range from physical labor, such as cleaning up debris, to helping serve food to other workers and refugees. These trips tend to be less regularly scheduled than the usual tours, and may require a bit more effort on your part to set up. Here are a few organizations to get you started. Check the websites for the most up to date information and pricing.

HIS "Destination Japan"
www.destination-japan.com

Japan Experience
www.japan-experience.com

Habitat for Humanity Japan
www.habitatjp.org

Peace Boat Japan
http://peaceboat.jp/relief/volunteer

The deep, serene forest around Nyuto Onsen.

...vers and lakes throughout Japan—and that ...ve *kappa maki* sushi its name. See p. 422.

Strolling back in time through Kakunodate's ...amurai District. Seven samurai mansions built ...uring the Edo Period remain in this corner of ...akunodate. The district retains its feudal atmo- ...phere to an amazing degree, thanks to its wide ...reets flanked by weeping cherry trees and ...rk wooden fences. A must-see for fans of ...aditional architecture. See p. 428, ❶.

Gazing into the placid alpine waters of ...ke Tazawa. At 423m (1,388 ft.) deep, this is ...ite a drink of water. In the summer months, ...e transparent waters of Japan's deepest ...ke make for great swimming; in the cooler ...asons, you can rent a bike and take a spin ...ound the lake for some truly beautiful views. ...e p. 410.

Soaking in the therapeutic waters of ...yuto Onsen. This incredibly out-of-the-way

spot is popular among those in the know for a reason: This is Japanese spa bathing at its most traditional—the experience of soaking in the waters here hasn't changed much for the last few centuries. See p. 432.

❽ **Island hopping around Matsushima.** This stretch of coastline, a short distance from Sendai, is considered one of the most scenic in Japan. Legend has it that haiku poet Matsuo Basho was so enchanted he could only exclaim, "Matsushima, ah! A-ah, Matsushima, ah! Matsushima, ah!" See p. 419.

❾ **Getting away from it all with a trip to Shirakami Sanchi.** One of Japan's best-protected natural habitats—the interior is off-limits to outsiders in order to protect the fragile ecosystem—the fringes of this park offer up some of Japan's most beautiful natural sights, such as Anmon Falls. See p. 411, ❹.

The Best of Tohoku in 3 Days

Three days is just enough to get the briefest taste of the charms Tohoku has to offer. This itinerary makes the most of it by touring several of the region's most famed temples and ending in Tono, considered a cradle of Japanese folklore. If you're traveling by train, you can also begin in Hiraizumi, then go to Sendai, and finally end in Tono. Although Hiraizumi is closer to Tono geographically, the need to rely on local train lines means that travel time is almost the same as from more distant Sendai, which covers much of the distance by bullet train.

> A statue of poet Matsuo Basho, who passed through Hiraizumi centuries ago.

START From Tokyo Station, take the JR Tohoku Shinkansen Yamabiko to Sendai Station (129 min.).

① Sendai. One of Tohoku's most popular tourist destinations, Sendai is the region's largest city and the capital of Miyagi prefecture. It was the former stomping grounds of a *daimyo* (warlord) named Daté Masamue, whose shadow still looms over the city in the form of various castles, shrines, and mausoleums—but Sendai also features a host of modern-day attractions such as museums, zoos, and a large marketplace.

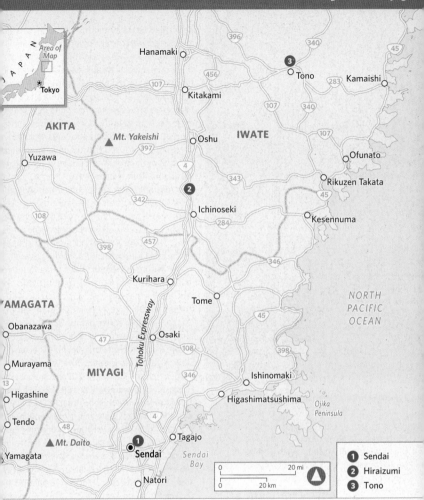

... saichi Dori ("Morning Market Avenue") is open all day long, despite its name. Popular with Japanese tourists, the avenue's 70 stalls and shops feature a wide variety of local and regional foods and products.

★★ **Zuihoden Hall,** an opulent mausoleum for Daté Masamune, was constructed in 1637. It features bold colors and designs similar to that of Nikko's Toshogu shrine (p. 127, ...), albeit on a smaller scale. Although the main building is a reconstruction (the original burned down during World War II), the grounds are a stunning example of the "funerary architecture" used for Japanese warlords.

Finally, ★ **Aobajo Koen** (青葉城址) is a thickly forested park that's home to the remnants of Aobajo Castle itself and a famed statue of Daté Masamue. It's also a hop, skip, and a jump from your last stop, the **Sendai City Museum.** See p. 419, ⑤.

From Sendai Station, take the JR Tohoku Shinkansen Yamabiko to Ichinoseki Station. At Ichinoseki Station, switch to local JR Tohoku Main Line bound for Morioka. Ride two stops to Hiraizumi Station (49 min.).

❷ **Hiraizumi.** Centuries ago, this city rivaled Kyoto for sheer sophistication. Today, all that

> *Jozenji Dori, in downtown Sendai.*

remains of its glory days are a handful of temples that are very much worth visiting: It's not for nothing that UNESCO officially recognized the area as a World Heritage Site in 2011. There are three ways to explore them: Hardier souls can hoof it; the temples are about a 40-minute walk from the station. There is also a loop bus that runs between the station and the sights several times an hour. And if the weather is nice, you can rent bicycles from a shop in Hiraizumi Station (¥500 for 2 hr. or ¥1,000 for a full day), open 9am to 4pm daily April through November (closed if raining). The sights are few enough and close enough together that ambitious travelers can try to do them in a day, heading to Kakunodate to spend the night.

Start with the stunning approach via a path curving through massive cedars, which adds to the atmosphere of ★★★ **Chuson-ji Temple** (中尊寺), an ancient temple complex that dates back nearly a millennium. The grounds, which are dotted with dozens of smaller temples and a museum, are fascinating enough. But the crown jewel is **Konjikido,** a stunning gold mausoleum for the once all-powerful Fujiwara clan's leaders. It now stands within a larger protective structure to protect its delicate gilt exterior. Access to the complex is free, but there is a separate charge for entering the Treasure Hall museum and Konjikido pavilion. Located right in front of Chuson-ji Temple, the **Hiraizumi Rest House** (平泉レストハウス) tourist information center serves up surprisingly good food. Of the two on-site restaurants, we prefer **Gen,** whose set lunches of ever-changing local goodies are well worth the price. As an added bonus, there are a variety of souvenir shops and a small museum in the building as well.

★★ **Motsu-ji Temple** (毛越寺) was founded in 850; at its peak in the 12th century this was reputedly a massive religious complex with dozens of buildings, even larger than that of Chuson-ji. But a series of fires shortly thereafter reduced it to ashes. Today only a 1989 reconstruction of the original main hall and Ozumi-ga-ike, an original Pure Land Buddhist garden, remain. Chuson-ji: 202 Koromonoseki, Hiraizumi-cho, Iwate-ken. ☎ 0191/46-2211. Free; Treasure Hall and Konjikido ticket ¥800. Daily Apr–mid-Nov 8am–5pm; mid-Nov–Mar 8:30am–4:30pm. Train: Hiraizumi Station. Hiraizumi Rest House: 10-7 Aza Sakashita, Hiraizumi, Hiraizumi-cho. ☎ 0191/46-2011. www.kpc.co.jp/hirarest/. Set lunches ¥1,800. No credit cards. Lunch daily. Train: Hiraizumi Station. Motsu-ji Temple: 58 Osawa, Hiraizumi, Iwate. ☎ 0191/46-2331. www.motsuji.or.jp/english. ¥500 adults, ¥300 high-school students, ¥100 junior-high students and younger. Daily Nov 5–Apr 4 8:30am–4:30pm; Apr 5–Nov 4 8:30am–5pm. Train: Hiraizumi Station.

From Hiraizumi Station, return to Ichinoseki Station. Take the JR Tohoku Shinkansen Yamabiko to Shin-Hanamaki Station. Switch to JR Kamaishi Line bound for Kamaishi. Disembark at Tono (90 min.).

❸ **Tono.** Tono is famed throughout Japan for its folk tales, which were first compiled in a book called *Tono Monogatari (Legends of Tono)* by the writer Kunio Yanagita at the turn of the 20th century. The otherwise unassuming countryside town is the supposed home

Kappa, kappa *everywhere in Tono.*

f the *kappa*, a *yokai* (monster) once believed
o dwell in local streams, ponds, and rivers.
oughly child-sized, the bipedal creatures
port tortoiseshell backs, froglike skin, and
ndentations atop their head filled with water;
hould it spill while they're on land, they lose
ll of their power. Or so the saying goes. You
ight not be able to spot an actual *kappa*
hese days, but there are plenty of places
round town to help you learn more about the
egendary creatures.

The **Tono Municipal Museum** is one such
lace, a fun little facility that focuses on local
raditions and handicrafts. One of our favorite
hings about the museum is the theater, which
creens animated documentaries about local
olk tales. It's right outside the station and quick
o go through, so make this your first stop.

The next stop, ★ **Tono Folk Village,** is a col-
ection of traditional Tohoku-style dwellings

so realistic that it is often used as a backdrop
for television shows and films. It is home to
six *magariya* (traditional *L*-shaped farmhouses
unique to the Tohoku region) that were relocated here from around Tono.

A short walk from Denshoen (p. 424, ❹),
the humble little shrine of **Joken-ji Temple**
isn't particularly thrilling in and of itself. But
it's located right next to ★ **Kappa Pool,** a
babbling brook that is said to be home to the
kappa—those mischievous monsters from
Japanese folklore. Don't be surprised if you
happen across little kids trying to catch one
with makeshift fishing rods made out of cucumbers on the end of a string.

Your final stop is difficult to get to without
a car: ★★ **Gohyakurakan.** This holy site deep
in the woods is filled with hundreds of stones
carved into Buddhist effigies by a monk honoring those who died in a famine. See p. 422.

The Best of Tohoku in 1 Week

One week gives you the advantage of being able to push deeper into Tohoku, exploring areas that most tourists don't ever get to see. You'll notice that the distances between stops grow longer in this tour, but trust us, it's worth it—from ancient samurai houses to hidden hot springs, traditional festivals to the natural splendors of national parks, this is Tohoku at its finest.

> *Although Kakunodate Castle is long gone, exquisite replicas of parts of it adorn the site.*

START From Tono Station, take the JR Kamaishi Line to Shin-Hanamaki Station (50 min.). At Shin-Hanamaki, switch to the JRTohoku Shinkansen Yamabiko bound for Morioka (90 min.). At Morioka, switch to the JR Komachi Shinkansen bound for Kakunodate Station (80 min.).

1 Kakunodate. Although the castle is long gone, Kakunodate's original layout remains remarkably intact, and includes one of the country's best-preserved samurai districts. It is also a great jumping-off point for exploring Towada-Hachimantai Park, which is perfect for more active travelers.

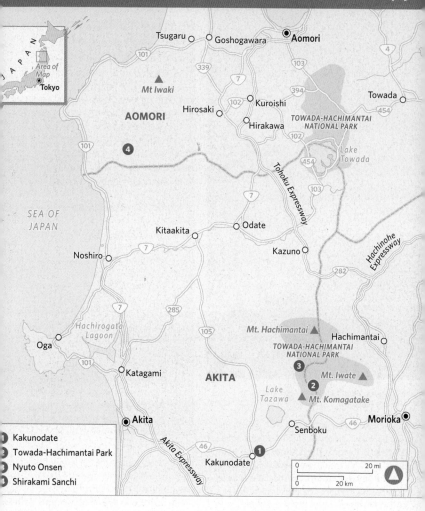

f Kakunodate's 80-some samurai mansions
ilt during the Edo Period, only 7 remain. Still,
e **Samurai District** retains its feudal atmo-
here to an amazing degree, thanks to wide
reets flanked by weeping cherry trees and
rk wooden fences. (These fences and tradi-
nal entry gates are employed even today to
nceal more modern homes, giving a clean,
isp line of vision throughout the district. It's
strong contrast to the jumble of most Japa-
se cities, and even to the merchant district
at's just a short walk away.) Chief among
e mansions is the **Aoyagi Samurai Manor,**
ich shows how the upper crust lived in
mes of old.

Kakunodate has also been famous for its
cherry-bark crafts since the Edo Period. You
can observe this painstaking craft by watching
artisans at work in **Kakunodatemachi Denshokan.** See p. 428.

From Kakunodate station, take the JR
Shinkansen Komachi (15 min.) or the JR
Tazawako Line train (20 min.) to Tazawako
Station. Then take the bus to Tazawakohan
bus stop (20 min.).

② **Towada-Hachimantai Park** (十和田八幡平国
立公園). Towada-Hachimantai National Park,
spreading 86,000 hectares (213,000 acres)
through north-central Tohoku and shared by

> *Spring is Japan's excuse to revel under the cherry blossoms.*

Spending the Night Around Shirakami Sanchi

If you're going to visit Shirakami Sanchi, your best bet for accommodations is the city of Hirosaki. The unpretentious, unassuming little **Blossom Hotel Hirosaki** (ブロッサムホテル弘前), 7-3 Ekimae-cho (☎ 0172/32-4151; http://blossom.el2.jp), located just a stone's throw from Hirosaki Station, is known for the quality of its breakfasts, which are included in the price and cooked up in seasonal menus based on local ingredients in both Japanese and Western versions. For single travelers looking to save money, they also offer an "eco plan" with no breakfast and no in-room amenities (such as toothbrushes) for just ¥5,000 a night. Doubles run from ¥12,000.

If you're hungry, **Tsunezushi** (常寿し) sushi bar, 9-2 Shinkaji-machi (¥0172/33-1837), is a local favorite. In addition to the normal nigiri and maki sushi, the specialty is giant-sized "ohmaki" rolls (¥2,415 standard, ¥2,940 deluxe) that are jam-packed with local seafood delicacies—sort of like an entire meal in a roll. They also have a rudimentary English menu with pictures, though daily and regional specialties are only displayed in Japanese on the boards on the wall. Entrees from ¥1,260.

three prefectures, is blessed with mountain ranges, lakes, streams, and hot-spring spas. It's geared towards the outdoor enthusiast, offering hiking in summer and skiing in winter.

Lake Tazawa (田沢湖), the most easily accessible part of the park, is a cool drink of water during the warmer months. Just 20km (12 miles) in circumference, it's Japan's deepest lake (a whopping 423m/1,388 ft.), and popular for its small swimming beach a couple minutes' walk from Tazawakokohan bus stop. Outside the swimming season—mid-July through August—you'll find nary a soul there. You can rent bicycles here for ¥400 for the first hour and ¥300 for every additional hour; mountain bikes run ¥600 per hour. It takes about 2 hours to ride around the lake; unfortunately, you have to share the road with vehicular traffic, but because this is a popular cycling route, motorists know to keep a lookout. Except for one small stretch, the road is mostly flat and is pleasantly wooded and relatively unspoiled; circle the lake

counterclockwise in the left lane, which puts you on the inside track closer to the lake. From May through September, you can also take a 40-minute tour of the lake by boat (¥1,170; fou launches a day.)

The casual restaurant ★ **Orae** is located beside Lake Tazawa, a 15-minute walk counterclockwise from the bus stop or a short bike ride. It's a great place to stop for lunch, due in no small part to its on-site Tazawako microbrewery (the German Dunkel beer is very good) and views of the lake from both its glass-enclosed dining room and outdoor terrace. Tazawako Tourist Information Center: Tazawako Station. ☎ 0187/43-2111. www.city.semboku.akita.jp. Daily 8:30am–6:30pm. Orae: 37-5 Haruyama, Tazawako. ☎ 0187/58-0608. Entrees from ¥800. No credit cards. Lunch & dinner daily. Bus: Tawazakohan.

eturn to Tazawakohan bus stop and board a
s bound for Nyuto Onsen (30 min.).

Nyuto Onsen. This out-of-the-way loca-
on doesn't show up on many tourist guides.
nat's precisely why you should make it a
oint to go here. There is quite possibly no
ore quintessential Japanese hot-spring town
an Nyuto Onsen. You won't find any slick
sort-style hotels here; in fact, many of the
aths are housed in ramshackle buildings that
ok ready to fall down. But this is precisely
e charm, because the experience of soaking
the waters here hasn't changed much for
e last few centuries. It's also a great step-
ngstone to local hiking trails and ski areas.
ee p. 432.

om Nyuto Onsen Village, board any bus
ound for Tazawako Station. From Tazawako,
oard the JR Shinkansen Komachi train for
kita Station. At Akita Station, switch to the JR
hinkansen Express Komachi for Hirosaki (3¾
r.). From Hirosaki Station, take the Konan bus
Tsugaru Mountain Pass (see below).

Shirakami Sanchi (白神山地). If you plant
our flag here, you'll have bragging rights for
aving seen some of the most remote wilder-
ess and beautiful scenery Japan has to offer.
verlapping Akita and Aomori prefectures
nd extending westward to the Sea of Japan,
hirakami Sanchi is centered on a protected
orest area that cannot be entered without
permit, but the borders feature extensive
iking trails and overlooks. But the best thing
, its closest point is just a 45-minute drive
om the city of Hirosaki, making it accessible
ven to those who aren't experienced hikers.
visit to Shirakami Sanchi can easily be done
s a day trip, but there is a combination camp-
round and a series of rental cottages on-site
alled Aqua Green Village Anmon.

   While Shirakami Sanchi is filled with fasci-
ating sights—including **Tanashiro Swamp,**
he **Nihon Canyon,** and the **Juniko Lakes**
rea—if you're making a day trip, we recom-
nend aiming for **Anmon Falls.** Located on the
vest side of the park, the Anmon Falls trail
eads up a valley and past three beautiful wa-
erfalls, the highest of which plummets more
han 40m (131 ft.) into a gorge. Budget at least
hours for the round trip.

> *One of Shirakami Sanchi's Anmon waterfalls.*

Getting to Shirakami Sanchi

The west side of Shirakami Sanchi is only
accessible by bus; the east can be reached
by train (2½ hr. one-way) or via rental car.
A rental car is highly recommended to give
you the freedom to move around the park
as you please. (From Hirosaki Station, take
Route 101 east to Route 317; some sections
unpaved.) From June 19 to November 3, the
Konan Bus Line (http://konanbus.com/
sirakami/sirakami.html) operates a daily
Shirakami Line direct bus that departs Hirosaki's bus terminal at 8:50 and 9:50am, returning from the Tsugaru Mountain Pass stop
at 1:20pm. The cost is ¥2,400 round-trip.

Exploring Lake Towada

If you visited the city of Kakunodate (p. 428), you may have taken a day trip to Towada-Hachimantai National Park (p. 409, ❷). But many feel the park's most beautiful aspect lies farther north, on the border between Aomori and Akita prefectures. Lake Towada (Towadako in Japanese) is widely considered Towada-Hachimantai's top scenic gem. It's certainly one of Japan's least spoiled lakes, with only two small villages on its perimeter and encircled by wooded cliffs and mountains. Its remoteness has saved it from the worst of Japan's runaway infrastructure development efforts—but this also makes it difficult to work into an itinerary that covers the other highlights of the area, which is why we're treating this very worthy destination separately here.

> *From above, Lake Towada's volcanic origins become more apparent.*

START From Tokyo Station, take the JR Tohoku Shinkansen Yamabiko Line to Hachinohe Station, then switch to a JR bus to the Yasumiya stop (140 min.).

❶ ★ **Lake Towada** (**Towadako;** 十和田湖)**.** This double caldera was formed some 20,000 years ago by a volcanic eruption. Today the lake's 44km (27 miles) of undulating coastli

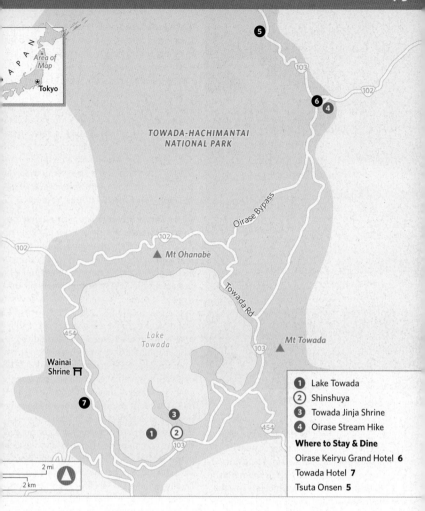

Legend:
1. Lake Towada
2. Shinshuya
3. Towada Jinja Shrine
4. Oirase Stream Hike

Where to Stay & Dine
Oirase Keiryu Grand Hotel **6**
Towada Hotel **7**
Tsuta Onsen **5**

arked by capes, inlets, cliffs, and trees that ut on a spectacular autumn show make it he of Towada-Hachimantai National Park's ajor draws. The best way to see Towada is ooard excursion boats that cruise the waters. wo cruises are available: a 50-minute cruise at travels between Yasumiya and Nenoku- i (available only from Apr to early Nov), d a 45-minute cruise that begins and ends Yasumiya (available year-round). Many sitors take the boat to Nenokuchi (Oirase ream trail head), send their luggage onward . 567), and begin hiking. ⏱ 50 min. Towada- i, Aomori-ken/Kosakamachi, Kazuno-gun,

Akita-ken. ☎ 0176/75-2425. Cruise: www. toutetsu.co.jp/jikoku/yuuransen.html. ¥1,400 adults, ¥700 kids (¥500 extra if you wish to sit in the top lounge). Cruises run daily 8am–5:20pm; check website for specific times. Bus: Yasumiya.

② 🍴 **Shinshuya** (信州屋)**.** This restaurant is located on the second floor above a souvenir shop beside the lake. It has an English-language menu, views of Lake Towada, and a convenient location near the path to Towada Jinja Shrine (see below). *Inaniwa udon* (noodles with

> The banks of the Oirase Stream.

❸ Towada Jinja Shrine (十和田神社). Towada Jinja is surrounded by giant cedars and boasts marvelous woodcarvings of animals. But it's most remembered for a curious custom: Visitors to the shrine buy a fortune, put money or rice inside, twist it into the shape of a missile and then hike 20 minutes up the steep flight of wooden steps beside the shrine to a scenic spot. (The last part of the hike is down metal ladders—only for the adventurous on a rainy day.) At the top of the climb, you throw your missile into the lake. If it sinks, your wish will come true. ⏱ 25 min. 486 Yasumiya. ☎ 0176/75-2508. Free. Open 24 hr. Bus: Yasumiya.

❹ ★★ Oirase Stream Hike. Hiking along the Oirase Stream is the major draw for a trip to Lake Towada. A clear-running, gurgling stream that runs 67km (42 miles) on its way from the lake to the Pacific Ocean, it's at its picture-perfect best in **Oirase Gorge,** where hikers are treated to some 13 waterfalls, rapids coursing over moss-covered boulders, and a dense wood of ferns, Japanese beech, oaks, and other broad-leaved trees—particularly stunning in autumn. A trail runs beside the stream from Nenokuchi on the lakeshore 14km (8⅔ miles) to Yakeyama. Most hikers, however, go only as far as Ishigedo, hiking the 9km (5⅔ miles) in about 2 hours. (There are kilometer markers along the path in English.) The hike upstream (toward Nenokuchi) is considered the most picturesque, as it affords a full view of the cascading rapids. There are nine bus stops on the road beside Oirase Stream, including Nenokuchi, Ishigedo, and Yakeyama. Because buses run only once an hour or so, you might consider taking a bus first and then hiking back. ⏱ 2 hr. Free. Bus: Nenokuchi, Ishigedo, or Yakeyama.

mountain vegetables), *kiritampo nabe* (a one-pot stew consisting of newly harvested rice pounded into a paste and then charcoal grilled before simmering in chicken broth with vegetables), Towada beefsteaks, and fish are just some of the local specialties. Once you've decided on your meal, purchase tickets at the counter. 16–11 Yasumiya. ☎ 0176/75-3131. Entrees from ¥1,000. No credit cards. Lunch daily. Bus: Towadako.

Travel Tip

As with most out-of-the-way spots in Japan, restaurants are few and far between around Lake Towada. Breakfasts and dinners will be provided by your hotel. On the Oirase Gorge trail, a small snack bar at Ishigedo sells ramen noodles, tempura soba, ice cream, and drinks

Getting to Lake Towada

As Lake Towada does not lie anywhere near a train station, your final journey to the lake must be by **car** or **bus** to Yasumiya, a small village on Lake Towada with a tourist office and a few accommodations. This is where you'll be staying. The bus winds through scenic, mountainous terrain (which means you might want to pack some Dramamine if you get motion sickness).

Where to Stay & Dine Around Lake Towada

Oirase Keiryu Grand Hotel (奥入瀬渓流ホテル)

OIRASE The main reason for staying in this large, rather ordinary hotel is its location on Oirase Stream, making it an easy base for walking the trail. Buses that traverse the Oirase stop here, including those that travel to or from Aomori and Hachinohe stations, but the hotel also offers its own free shuttle bus approximately three times a day from Hachinohe Station. The hotel is divided into two sections: the older, rustic Daiichi Wing with 105 rooms, and the newer Daini Wing with 85 (more expensive) rooms. We prefer the Daini with its lobby overlooking the stream and maple trees and its hard-to-overlook giant fireplace sculpture by eccentric Okamoto Taro. It offers both Japanese tatami rooms (with straw mats on the floor, shoji screens, and traditional furnishings) and twin rooms, about half with views of Oirase Stream. Public hot-spring baths also take advantage of river views. Meals are served communally in a dining room. 231 Aza Tochikubo, Oaza Okuse, Towada-shi, Aomori. ☎ 0176/74-2121. 190 units. Doubles from ¥13,380 per person. Rates include meals. AE, DC, MC, V. Bus: Yakeyama.

★★ Towada Hotel (十和田ホテル) YASUMIYA

This imposing, elegant hotel, secluded on a wooded hill overlooking the lake (and practical only if you have your own car), is our top choice for a splurge on Lake Towada. It was built in 1938 using huge cedar logs in a mix of western-lodge-meets-Japanese-temple style, with a modern addition built years later. Although all rooms face the lake, best are the elegant Japanese rooms, all in the older part of the hotel, with great views. Western-style rooms, though spacious and beautifully designed, do not have as good a view; be sure to ask for a room on the top floor and be sure, too, to wander over to the older wing for a look at its beautiful wood details in the old lobby (crafted by shrine and temple carpenters). Public baths have lakeside views and outdoor tubs. Meals, served in a communal dining room with a mix of Japanese and Western dishes, are substantial. Western-style breakfasts are available. Kosakamachi, Towadako Nishi-kohan, Akita. ☎ 0176/75-1122. 50 units, 42 with bathroom, 8 with toilet only. Doubles from ¥15,750 per person. Rates include 2 meals. AE, DC, MC, V. Bus: Yasumiya (pickup service available from bus terminal).

★★ Tsuta Onsen (蔦温泉) TSUTA ONSEN

This classic north-country inn dates to 1909 and is one of Tohoku's most famous *ryokan* (traditional inn). *Tsuta* means "ivy" in Japanese, a theme carried out not only in pillars, transoms, and other architectural details but also in the dense, surrounding beech forest. Rooms in the oldest wooden structure (built in 1918) and an annex (built in 1960), both up a long flight of stairs, have beautiful wood-carved details and good views but are without bathrooms (they're also cheaper). The west wing 1988 addition, with gleaming wood floors salvaged from an old *ryokan*, has an elevator and the convenience of toilets, but its rooms lack the character of the older rooms. For those who don't like sleeping on futons, three units offer tatami areas, beds, and bathrooms. The hot-spring baths are new but preserve traditional bathhouse architecture, with high ceilings and cypress walls. Breakfast is served in a dining room, while dinner is served your room. Although not on the Oirase Stream and not as conveniently located as the Oirase Keiryu Grand Hotel, the Tsuta is one of a kind and is served by the same JR bus that travels between Aomori and Lake Towada (it's about a 15-minute bus ride to Yakeyama). It also has its own 1-hour hiking trail to a nearby lake. Okuse, Aza Tsutanoyu, Towada-shi, Aomori. ☎ 0176/74-2311. www.thuta.co.jp. 50 units, 4 with bathroom, 20 with toilet only. From ¥10,650 per person. Rates include 2 meals. AE, DC, MC, V. Bus: Tsuta Onsen.

Sendai

Although small in comparison to sprawling megalopolises like Tokyo or Osaka, with just over a million residents, Sendai is the largest city in Tohoku and the capital of Miyagi Prefecture. Its downtown area is compact, and with most attractions on the west side of the station, easy to traverse on foot. In the early 17th century, the city and environs were the domain of a powerful *daimyo* (warlord) named Daté Masamune, whose influence can still be felt over the city today in the form of various statues, shrines, and the ruins of his clan's castle.

> *Ichibancho Arcade is one of Sendai's largest shopping areas.*

START Take the train to Sendai Station. Sendai is 365km (227 miles) north of Tokyo.

1 AER Building. Although it recently lost the title of tallest building in Sendai to the nearby Sendai Trust Tower, the AER's observation deck remains a great way to take in the entire city at a glance. It's located just a few minute walk from the station; feel free to time your visit for the morning or evening, depending o what sort of view you're after. ⊕ 20 min. 1-3-1 Chuo, Aoba-ku. ☎ 022/723-8000. Free. Daily 10:30am–8pm. Train: Sendai Station.

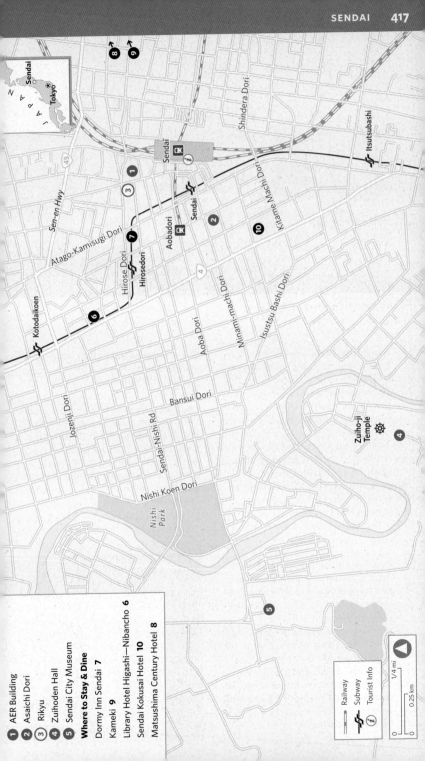

1 AER Building
2 Asaichi Dori
3 Rikyu
4 Zuihoden Hall
5 Sendai City Museum

Where to Stay & Dine
Dormy Inn Sendai **7**
Kameki **9**
Library Hotel Higashi—Nibancho **6**
Sendai Kokusai Hotel **10**
Matsushima Century Hotel **8**

Sendai

Tokyo

JAPAN

45

Sen-en Hwy

Sendai

Sendai

Aobadori

Atago-Kamisugi Dori

Hirose Dori

Hirosedori

Kotodaikoen

Shindera Dori

Itsutsubashi

Kitamie Machi Dori

Minami-machi Dori

Isutsu Bashi Dori

Aoba Dori

Bansui Dori

Jozenji Dori

Sendai-Nishi Rd

Nishi Koen Dori

Nishi
Park

Zuiho-ji
Temple

Railway
Subway
Tourist Info

0   0.25 km
0   1/4 mi

> *Sendai from afar.*

② ★ **Asaichi Dori** (朝市). Also known as "Sendai's kitchen," this shopping street is open all day long. Popular with Japanese tourists, its 70 stalls and shops feature a wide variety of local and regional foods and products. While the emphasis is on produce and such—meaning there isn't a lot of souvenir shopping to be done—it is a great window into Japanese culinary culture. The nearby **Ichibancho Arcade,** located just north of the morning market, is a similar series of covered shopping streets that represent one of the largest shopping complexes in Tohoku. The shops range from "everything ¥100" budget stores to high-end boutiques.

③ 🍽 **Rikyu** (牛たん炭焼 利久). This local chain focuses on one of Sendai's specialties: *gyutan* (beef tongue). We're fans of the *gyutan-don teishoku,* a set meal that includes beef tongue on rice with a side of oxtail soup and pickles. In addition to the Rikyu listed below, which is near the AER Building (see above), there's another location on the third floor of the Sendai Station building as well. 1-6-1 Chuo, Aoba-ku. ☎ 022/266-5077. Lunch & dinner daily. *Gyutan-don teishoku* ¥1,365. MC, V. Train: Sendai Station.

④ ★★ **Zuihoden Hall** (瑞鳳殿). Although it isn't quite as over-the-top as Nikko's Toshogu shrine (p. 127, **②**), which was built in honor of the shogun Tokugawa Ieyasu, this opulent mausoleum for Daté Masamune is another standout, with bold colors and designs set against a sylvan backdrop. Although the main building is a reconstruction (the original burned down during World War II), the grounds are a stunning example of the "funeral architecture" used for Japanese warlords. The "campus" consists of five main structure the Honden (main hall), the Haiden (prayer hall), the Karamon (gate), the Gokusho (hall

The Star Festival

Sendai is famous for its elaborate Tanabata Matsuri, also known as the Star Festival, held annually from August 6 to 8. On the evening of August 5, there are traditional dances and other events held in Kotodai Park. In addition, the entire Ichibancho Arcade (see above) is decorated in colorful, festive streamers handcrafted from *washi* paper. Be aware that hotels fill up very quickly during the festival; if you plan to be in the area during this time, book well in advance. For more information, see p. 552.

r offerings), and the Nehanmon (gate). ⏱ 2
r. 23-2 Otamayashita, Aoba-ku. ☎ 022/262-
250. www.zuihoden.com. Feb 1–Nov 30 daily
am–4:30pm; Dec 1–Jan 31 daily 9am–4pm.
550 adults, ¥400 high-school students,
200 junior-high students and younger. Bus:
)tamayahashi.

) Sendai City Museum (仙台市博物館). This mu-
eum traces the city's roots back to the Stone
ge, but the main focus is unsurprisingly on

the Daté clan; Masamune's famed suit of
armor is here, as are other artifacts from the
clan's glory days. A smattering of other rotating collections of art and artifacts from around
the world are on display as well. ⏱ 1 hr. 26
Kawauchi. ☎ 022/225-2557. www.city.sendai.
jp/kyouiku/museum/english. Tues–Sun 9am–
4:15pm. ¥400 adults, ¥200 high-school students and younger. Bus: Hakubutsukan-Kokusai
Center Mae.

A Side Trip to Matsushima

If you have time to spend another night in
Sendai, or even as an alternate itinerary to
the Sendai tour, we highly recommend taking
a side trip to the city of Matsushima, located
to the north of Sendai. Matsushima means
"pine-clad islands"—and that's exactly what
the area is. More than 260 pine-covered
islets and islands dot Matsushima Bay; the
complex terrain actually acted as a natural
buffer during the 2011 tsunami, sparing the
area from the extensive damage that occurred
elsewhere. This is considered one of the most
beautiful views in Japan, and the best way to
see it is by boat.

Make your first stop the tourist information center at Sendai Station, open daily from
8am, to pick up a free map of the Matsushima
area and ferry timetables. Take the local JR
Senseki Line to Hon-Shiogama Station (20

min.). From Hon-Shiogama, take a right out of
the station, cross the street, turn right at the
first red light (crossing under the tracks), and
continue straight on to the pier. Tickets for the
hour-long ferry to Matsushima Kaigan Pier
cost ¥1,400 for adults and ¥1,260 for kids;
the boats leave every half-hour from 9am to
3:30pm (until 3pm Dec–Mar). Try to ignore
the unfortunately located power station that
mars the early part of the cruise; the rest is
fairly uninterrupted nature. Note the oyster
rafts as you pass through the bay: The shellfish are a local delicacy. There are a variety of
temples and sights within walking distance of
the Matsushima Kaigan Pier, making this a full
and fun day trip. You can also overnight here;
see "Where to Stay & Dine in Sendai," p. 420,
for a hotel suggestion.

Where to Stay & Dine in Sendai

> *The Library Hotel's stately lounge area.*

Dormy Inn Sendai (ドーミーイン仙台) SENDAI
For those on a budget, it's hard to beat the convenience and price of this no-frills business hotel. Rooms are tiny but clean, and the staff is helpful. While the Spartan decor and cramped bathrooms are nothing to write home about, there's free Wi-Fi in rooms and a communal (gender-segregated) Japanese-style bath on the top floor. 2-10-17 Chuo, Aoba-ku. ☎ 022/715-7077. 148 units. Doubles from ¥12,074. Breakfast ¥1,100 extra per person. AE, DC, MC, V. Train: Sendai Station.

★★ Kameki (亀喜寿司) SENDAI SUSHI
Widely considered to be one of the finest sushi restaurants in all of Japan, Kameki is a local institution. Sendai is known for the quality of its seafood, and the chefs here pride themselves on only using local ingredients

to prepare exquisite *nigiri, maki,* and sashimi plates that look and taste like nothing you've had before. On the downside, it's a 30-minute subway ride from downtown—but well worth the trip. It's located close to the pier for the ferry to Matsushima, making it easy to combine with a visit to the area (p. 419). For those on a budget, aim for lunch rather than dinner. 6-12 Shintomi-cho. ☎ 022/362-2055. www.kamekisushi.jp. Sushi assortment from ¥3,000, omakase from ¥5,250. No credit cards. Lunch & dinner Tues-Sun. Train: Honshiogama Station.

★★ Library Hotel Higashi—Nibancho (ライブラリーホテル東二番丁) SENDAI So named for its library of books that guests can borrow, this centrally located boutique hotel offers clean, modern elegance within a stone's throw of Sendai Station. More than half of the rooms

fancy Western-style steakhouse on the 30th floor offers excellent views of the city (and prices to match). 4–6–1 Chuo, Aoba-ku. ☎ 022/268-1111. www.tobu-skh.co.jp/english. 234 units. Doubles from ¥12,000 per person. AE, DC, MC, V. Train: Sendai Station.

★ **Matsushima Century Hotel**（松島センチュリーホテル）MATSUSHIMA If you choose to stay in Matsushima rather than Sendai, this gleaming white hotel, near Fukuurajima island, is a nice choice and popular with families. The Japanese-style rooms and combination rooms (with both tatami area and beds) face the bay, and both types have balconies. Otherwise, if you're on a budget, the cheapest Western-style rooms, though sunny and cheerful, are small with unit baths, face inland, and have no balconies. Public baths have views of the bay. Meals are served in a restaurant; breakfast is an all-you-can-eat buffet. The hotel is a 5-minute walk east of the pier, or you can call for a pickup from the station. 8 Aza Senzui, Matsushima-cho. ☎ 022/354-4111. www.centuryhotel.co.jp. 135 units. From ¥12,600 per person; ¥3,000 extra Sat and nights before a holiday. AE, DC, MC, V. Bus: Loop Line bus to Century Hotel.

 An elegant course from a traditional kaiseki meal.

re nonsmoking, a rarity in Japan. All rooms offer free Wi-Fi. The free coffee in the lobby (from 2pm through midnight) is also a nice touch. There is a second Library Hotel, the **Ekimae,** right in front of Sendai Station. 2-15-0 Honcho, Aoba-ku. ☎ 022/221-7666. www.libraryhotel.jp. 230 units. Doubles from ¥11,000 per person; only ¥2,000 per kid (elementary student and younger) staying with adults. Breakfast buffet ¥1,000 extra. AE, DC, MC, V. Train: Kotodaikoen Station.

★ **Sendai Kokusai Hotel**（仙台国際ホテル）SENDAI Although the rooms are on the small side considering the price, the Kokusai—something of a hybrid between a business and luxury hotel—offers excellent service and is in a convenient location within walking distance of JR Sendai Station. Although the rooms are Western-style, the breakfasts (included in the price) are Japanese. French, Japanese, and Chinese restaurants are on the premises; a

Sendai and the Tsunami

Sendai, by virtue of its seaside location close to the epicenter of Japan's 2011 earthquake, was rocked especially hard by the ensuing tsunami, which swept away cars and flooded buildings along the coastline. At press time, the restaurants and hotels listed here were open for business, but the economic aftermath of the earthquake and tsunami is likely to be long-lasting, causing problems with suppliers, for example. Call your hotel or restaurant before visiting to confirm prices and hours, as they may change. And remember, Sendai is still safe to visit—and better yet, your tourist dollars will help in the recovery effort.

Tono

This otherwise unassuming little countryside town is

famed throughout Japan as a repository of domestic folklore. It's particularly well known for its legends involving the mythological creatures known as *kappa*. Although it doesn't have the large-scale tourist attractions of bigger cities, what it does have is a taste of life in the countryside long before cars, computers, and the trappings of modern society came along.

> *Rice dries after the harvest in a Tono field.*

START Take the train to Tono Station. Tono is 554km (344 miles) north of Tokyo.

① ★ kids **Tono Municipal Museum** (遠野市立博物館). Located just outside of Tono Station, this is a fun little facility that focuses on local traditions and handicrafts. One of our favorite things about the museum is the theater, which screens animated documentaries about local folk tales (all in Japanese, but simple enough to understand visually). ⏱ 30 min. 3-9 Higasidate-cho. ☎ 0198/62-2340. ¥310 adults, ¥210 high-school students, ¥150 junior-high students and younger; ¥520 combo ticket including entrance to Tono Folk Village. Daily 9am–5pm. Closed last day of every month and Mon Nov–Mar. Train: Tono Station.

② ★ kids **Tono Folk Village** (遠野ふるさと村). The most recent of several replica villages in Tono, the Folk Village is so realistic that it is often used as a backdrop for television shows and films. It is home to six *magariya* (traditional *L*-shaped farmhouses unique to the Tohoku region; see "Where to Stay & Dine," p. 425) that were relocated here from around Tono. Regular programs at the village involve re-enactments of traditional farming methods and tools. The on-site restaurant is a great way to taste some local cuisine. ⏱ 1½ hr. 5-89-1 Kamitsukimoushi, Tsukimoushi-cho.

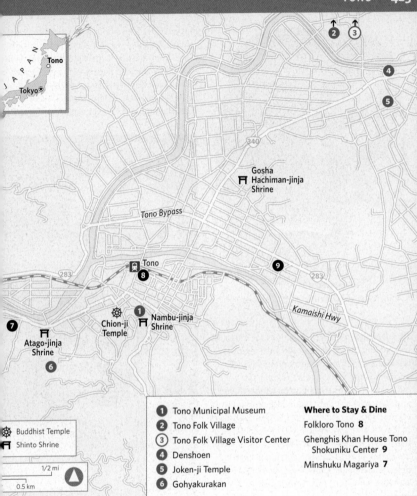

JAPAN

Tono
Tokyo

Gosha
Hachiman-jinja
Shrine

Tono Bypass

Tono

8

9

283

Kamaishi Hwy

7
Atago-jinja
Shrine

6

Chion-ji
Temple

Nambu-jinja
Shrine **1**

⚘ Buddhist Temple

⛩ Shinto Shrine

1/2 mi

0.5 km

1 Tono Municipal Museum
2 Tono Folk Village
3 Tono Folk Village Visitor Center
4 Denshoen
5 Joken-ji Temple
6 Gohyakurakan

Where to Stay & Dine

Folkloro Tono **8**

Ghenghis Khan House Tono
　Shokuniku Center **9**

Minshuku Magariya **7**

: 0198/64-2300. www.tono-furusato.jp. ¥500
dults, ¥310 high-school students and younger;
520 combo ticket including entrance to Tono

Getting Around Tono

We highly recommend either using taxis or
renting a car here, as bus service is quite
spotty, but there's another option as well. If
you're the sort who doesn't mind getting a
little exercise, renting a bike is a fun way to
get around the various sights. Rent them at
the Tono Tourism Association (☎ 0198/62-
1333), which is open from 8am to 5pm between April 1 and October 15, and 8:30am
to 5pm from October 16 through March.

Municipal Museum. Daily 9am–5pm (last entry
4pm). Bus: Tono Furusato Mura.

③ 　🍴 **Tono Folk Village Visitor Center.** Not
only is the Tono Folk Village well worth a
visit, but the restaurant in its visitor center is an excellent way to acquaint yourself with local Tono cuisine. Our personal
favorite set meal is the *sansai teishoku*
(¥1,260), which features locally picked
wild vegetables served as tempura, atop
tofu, and in a broth. 5-89-1 Kamitsukimoushi, Tsukimoushi-cho. ☎ 0198/64-2300.
www.tono-furusato.jp. *Sansai teishoku*
¥1,260. No credit cards. Lunch daily. Bus:
Tono Furusato Mura.

> A traditional mask on display at Denshoen.

④ ★ Denshoen (伝承園). This outdoor museum will get you better acquainted with regional folklore and culture: In addition to several relocated *magariya*, it hosts regular storytelling events (in a charmingly thick local dialect impenetrable to many Japanese) and re-creations by locals, such as how to farm or how to make silk and handicrafts. ⏱ 1 hr. 6-5-1 Tsuchibuchi, Tsuchibuchi-cho. ☎ 0198/62-8655. www.densyoen.jp. ¥310 adults, ¥210 junior-high students and younger. Daily Apr-Dec 9am-4:30pm; Jan-Mar 9am-4pm. Bus: Senzokukawa.

⑤ ★ Joken-ji Temple (常堅寺、カッパ淵). Across the street from Denshoen, this humble little temple isn't particularly thrilling visually, but it does happen to be located right next to **Kappabuchi**, a brook said to be home to the *kappa*—those mischievous monsters from Japanese folklore (p. 424). Don't be surprised if you happen across little kids (and even an adult or two) trying to catch one with makeshift fishing rods made out of cucumbers tied to the end of a string. ⏱ 20 min. 7-50 Tsuchibuchi, Tsuchibuchi-cho. Free. Daily 8:30am-4:30pm. Bus: Senzokukawa.

⑥ ★★ Gohyakurakan (五百羅漢). This holy spot deep in the forest is filled with 500 mossy stones carved into Buddhist effigies by a monk in the 1760s. They honor the victims of a local famine. A serene yet somewhat eerie sort of place, many strange supernatural phenomena have been reported here over the years, such a hearing voices or visitors becoming temporarily frozen in place. ⏱ 1 hr. Nissato, Ayaori-cho. Free. Daily sunrise–sunset. Bus: Tono Eigyosho.

Meet the *Kappa*

Kappa are a type of *yokai*—the Japanese term for mythological folklore creatures. Roughly the size of a child, *kappa* are amphibious humanoids once believed to dwell in bodies of freshwater throughout Japan. Their characteristics include slimy, frog-like skin; tortoiseshell backs; and dishlike indentations atop their head that remain filled with water even when they are on land. Should the dishes spill for any reason, they're powerless. Hobbies include challenging passersby to sumo wrestling matches and giving swimmers impromptu colonoscopies with their webbed fingers. They also happen to love cucumbers—which is why cucumber roll sushi is called *kappa maki*. If you'd like to try your luck finding one, you can purchase a *kappa*-catching license at any of the town museums' gift shops.

Where to Stay & Dine in Tono

The Folkloro Tono hotel is conveniently located right above the train station.

Folkloro Tono (フォルクローロ遠野)

Located right atop Tono Station and run by Japan Railways, this is about as convenient as it gets. It's also a standard Western-style hotel, useful for those who may be a little nervous at diving headfirst into super-traditional places like the Minshuku Magariya (see below). In spite of its location near the station, this is a quiet sort of place (particularly if you get a room facing away from the tracks) with surprisingly large rooms by Japanese standards. 5–7 Shinkokucho. ☎ 0198/62-0700. www.folkloro.jp/tohno. 16 units. Doubles from ¥12,600; ¥1,050 discount for stays longer than 2 days. Rates include breakfast. AE, DC, MC, V. Train: Tono Station.

Ghenghis Khan House Tono Shokuniku Center

MONGOLIAN Located about 3km (1¾ miles) from the station, this is a great choice for

Staying in a *Magariya*

Tono is known as one of the few places in Japan where *magariya*, or traditional northern-style *L*-shaped farmhouses, survive. Several are on display at local museums, and if you're feeling adventurous, you can even try spending the night in one.

carnivores. It specializes in serving up cutlets of sheep that you cook yourself tableside. Other meats such as beef and pork are available as well. Everything is locally sourced from Iwate Prefecture's many farms, so the quality is excellent. 20-13-1 Shiraiwa, Matsusaki-cho. ☎ 0198/62-2242. www.tononamaram.com. Set lunches from ¥780; entrees from ¥1,250. No credit cards. Train: Tono Station.

★★★ Minshuku Magariya (民宿曲り屋)

It doesn't get any more traditional than this. Opened in 1970 inside a century-plus-old *magariya* farmhouse and run by descendents of the original owner, it is filled with antiques and brimming local charm and hospitality. Elaborate meals prepared in a local style are served to the group at a sunken hearth. All rooms are tatami, without bathrooms; guests share the same baths and toilet facilities. The common area is heated by a roaring fire, so if you're sensitive to smoke, you may find the air in the rooms a little cloying, but this is an only-in-Tohoku experience that is not to be missed. Be aware that they do not allow kids 15 and under to stay here. 30-58-3 Niisato, Ayaori-cho. ☎ 0198/62-4564. www.tonotv.com/members/magariya. ¥8,580 per person (¥10,500 per person Dec 30–Jan 5), including 2 meals. No credit cards. Train: Tono Station.

A HOME FOR ALL SEASONS

Traditional Japanese architecture serves a variety of need

BY MELINDA JOE

BASED ON ZEN BUDDHIST DESIGN, JAPANESE HOMES SINCE THE EDO PERIOD
have been elegant, minimalist spaces that could be easily adjusted according to the season as well as the family's needs. Stately *magariya* (farmhouses) and stylishly functional *machiya* (town houses) exemplify this economy and simplicity of traditional Japanese architecture. Although these traditional homes are quickly disappearing from cities and the countryside, a number of preserved *machiya* can still be found in and around Kyoto, while beautifully restored examples of *magariya* can be seen on display at open-air architecture museums outside of central Tokyo and Osaka.

The Architecture

Japanese farmhouses are typically vast, cavernous structures, topped with a thick thatched roof hand-woven from reeds. Most have the following elements.

DOMA Through the entranceway is a tamped-earth-floored vestibule called the *doma,* which functions as a workspace as well as the kitchen.

▲ IRORI At the center of the house is the *irori,* a hearth built into the floor, where the family gathers for meals and to warm themselves in the cooler months.

SHOJI These sliding doors can be opened, closed, or removed to alter the configuration of the rooms, allowing breezes to circulate in summer and shutting out the cold in winter.

HIROMA The *doma* is separated from the raised *hiroma,* or main living space, by a low beam called the *agari-kamachi* (stepping-up sill); upon entry, shoes are always removed.

The Sustainability

As author of *Just Enough: Lessons in Living Green from Traditional Japan* (2009) Azby Brown notes, *magariya* and *machiya* were remarkably sustainable. They were constructed almost exclusively from natural materials. The wood, bamboo, and *tatami* used were easily repaired and recycled; old wall plaster could be crushed and returned to the soil. Moreover, the people of the Edo era devised clever ways of using materials efficiently, such as bundling fallen twigs into strong beams, or growing "green curtains" to provide both shade and vegetables.

The Community

hough *machiya* share ome architectural fea-ures (such as a *doma,* aised-platform living paces, and sliding oors) with *magariya,* ey differ greatly in ayout. Edo-era cities ere densely packed reas, and street-front roperty was at a remium. *Machiya* ere necessarily nar-ow and long (6m/20 . wide but up to 0m/66 ft. deep), with ne or more stories, nd doubled as retail paces and homes. The ont of the *machiya* ould serve as the

shop, while the rest would be the office and living area. They often contained small courtyard gardens called *tsuboniwa.*

The tightly organized rows of *machiya* that formed neighborhoods helped create a strong sense of community. Separated by only a small alley, the proximity encouraged interaction and communication, and the courtyard areas were usually shared. And often, the town houses were actually tenement complexes.

Kakunodate

Although the castle is long gone, Kakunodate's castle-town architectural layout remains remarkably intact, with one of the country's best-preserved (though small) samurai districts. It's also famous for its cherry trees, not only in the samurai district but also along the banks of the Hinokinai River, and for its crafts produced from local cherry bark. Yet Kakunodate is an unpretentious village, with only a few of the souvenir and tourist shops that plague other picturesque towns.

> *Kakunodate's stately boulevards teem with samurai manors.*

START Take the train to Kakunodate Station. Kakunodate is 587km (365 miles) north of Tokyo.

❶ **Samurai District** (武家屋敷通り)**.** Of Kakunodate's 80-some samurai mansions built during the Edo Period, only 7 remain. Still, the district retains its feudal atmosphere to an amazing degree, thanks to its wide streets flanked by weeping cherry trees and dark wooden fences. These fences and traditional entry gates are employed even today to conceal more modern homes, giving a clean, crisp line of vision throughout the district. It's a strong contrast to the jumble of most Japanese cities and even to the merchant district that's just a short walk away.

If you're walking from the station, you'll pass several samurai houses in the district that are free and open to the public (though admittance inside is restricted), including the **Odano Samurai House** to the right, the **Kawarada Samurai House** next door, the **Matsumoto Samurai House** across the street (where you can usually see craftsmen at work) and the city-owned **Iwahashi Samurai House** on the right.

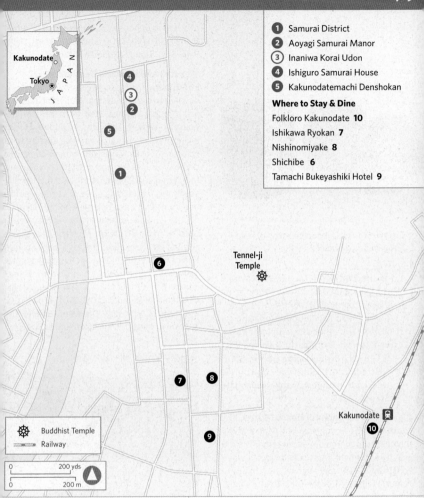

1. Samurai District
2. Aoyagi Samurai Manor
3. Inaniwa Korai Udon
4. Ishiguro Samurai House
5. Kakunodatemachi Denshokan

Where to Stay & Dine

Folkloro Kakunodate 10
Ishikawa Ryokan 7
Nishinomiyake 8
Shichibe 6
Tamachi Bukeyashiki Hotel 9

Kakunodate

Tennel-ji Temple

Buddhist Temple
Railway

0   200 yds
0   200 m

2 ★★★ **Aoyagi Samurai Manor** (角館歴史村青柳
家). Of all the houses in Kakunodate's Samurai
District, this is definitely the one to see. An
impressive entry gate serves as testimony to
the Aoyagi family's high samurai status. This
is more than a mere manor, however, as it's
actually a compound of several traditional
buildings spread throughout an unkempt
garden, each filled with a wealth of eclectic
treasures from the 17th to 20th centuries,
collected through the ages by the Aoyagi family and well documented in English. As you
wander through the buildings, you'll see samurai armor, rifles, swords, dolls, kimono, sake
cups, *ukiyo-e* (woodblock prints), scrolls and
screens, Meiji Era uniforms and medals, farm
tools, antique phonographs, and cameras.
Other buildings hold shops, a teahouse, and a
restaurant. ⏱ 1 hr. 3 Uramachi, Kakunodatecho. ☎ 0187/54-3257. www.samuraiworld.com.
¥500 adults, ¥300 junior-high and high-school
students, ¥200 kids. Daily 9am–5pm (until 4pm
in winter). Train: Kakunodate Station.

> *Cherrywood-lacquered containers are one of Kakunodate's specialties.*

③ 🍜 **Inaniwa Korai Udon** (稲庭古来堂青柳家店)**.** This simple dining room inside the Aoyagi Samurai Manor offers noodle dishes, including tempura soba and *inaniwa udon* (noodles with mountain vegetables). 3 Uramachi, Kakunodatecho. ☎ 0187/52-8015. *Inaniwa udon* ¥960. No credit cards. Lunch daily (but only on weekends in winter). Train: Kakunodate Station.

④ ★★ **Ishiguro Samurai House** (石黒家)**.** In contrast to the Aoyagi Samurai Manor, this thatched-roof home next door remains almost exactly as it might have looked when it was constructed 200 years ago by the Ishiguro samurai family. After the Meiji Restoration, the family became landlords and collected rice as rent. Today, English-speaking, 12th-generation Ishiguro Naotsugi continues to live here; he has opened five simple but elegant rooms to the public in the main house. Family heirlooms, including samurai gear, winter *geta* (fur-lined or spiked sandals), scales for weighing rice, and old maps of Kakunodate, are on display in

a former warehouse. 🕐 30 min. Omotemachi. ☎ 0187/55-1496. ¥300 adults, ¥150 kids. Daily 9am–5pm. Train: Kakunodate Station.

❺ ★ **Kakunodatemachi Denshokan** (角館 伝承館)**.** This specialty shop and museum devoted to birch craftsmanship is located just a couple minutes' walk from the samurai houses on Bukeyashiki Dori. In addition to seeing how strips of cherry bark are applied to tea canisters, boxes, vases, and other goods in live demonstrations by local craftsmen, you can tour a museum devoted to the craft. The museum also features displays of samurai outfits and items that once belonged to the Kakunodate feudal lord, as well as everyday items used by common people such as straw raincoat and geta ice skates. There's a large collection of wonderful photos of days long past as well. And of course, you can also browse for cherry-bark products in its large shop. 🕐 1 hr. Omotemachi Shimocho 10-1. ☎ 0187/54-1700. ¥300 adults, ¥150 kids. Daily 9am–5pm (until 4:30pm in winter). Train: Kakunodate Station.

Seeing the Cherry Blossoms

Kakunodate is at its most glorious (and crowded) in late April, when its hundreds of cherry trees are in full bloom. The most popular viewing spot is along the Hinokinai River, where two rows of some 400 cherry trees form a shimmering tunnel of blossoms for 2km (1¼ miles). They were planted in 1933 to commemorate the birth of the present emperor, Akihito.

Kakunodate or Semboku?

Technically speaking, Kakunodate merged with the town of Tazawako and another village to form a new administrative city called Semboku in 2005, but for clarity's sake, we refer to Kakunodate and Tazawako by their historic and popular names.

Where to Stay & Dine in Kakunodate

Folkloro Kakunodate (フォルクローロ角館)
Little English is spoken at this JR-affiliated hotel, but its location next to Kakunodate Station and its simple but clean, modern, and inexpensive Western-style rooms make it a logical choice for a 1-night stopover, especially if you have a Japan Rail Pass, which gives a 10% discount. Only two types of rooms are available: 11 twins and 15 deluxe twin family rooms that sleep up to four. Note, however, that the family rooms, with twin beds and two sleeper sofas, seem cramped for four but are roomy for two. Nakasuga-sawa 14. ☎ 0187/53-3070. 26 units. Doubles from ¥12,600. Rates include breakfast buffet. AE, DC, MC, V. Train: Kakunodate Station.

Ishikawa Ryokan (石川旅館)
One of Kakunodate's oldest *ryokan,* open since the Edo Period and now in its fifth generation of innkeepers, Ishikawa now occupies a dated building constructed in 1920. Although corridors suggest the ordinary, the Japanese-style rooms are simple but with nice wood details. And the elderly owners are every bit as self-effacing and hospitable to guests as their ancestors must have been to traveling samurai and other high officials. Though they don't speak English, they make your stay here a real treat. Meals, should you opt for them, are served in your room. Iwasemachi 32. ☎ 0187/54-2030. 11 units. Doubles from ¥6,500 per person without meals; ¥13,500 per person with 2 meals. No credit cards. Train: Kakunodate Station.

Nishinomiyake (西宮家) *JAPANESE*
This pleasant and inexpensive restaurant is located in the family compound of the Nishinomiya clan, a samurai family that later became merchants and built the main house and five warehouses that are on display today. The restaurant is in a warehouse dating from 1919 and offers a limited menu of fried seafood, noodles, beef hash with rice, hamburger steak, *ebi* (shrimp) fry, and other dishes. Best, perhaps, is to order one of the bento lunch boxes. After your meal, be sure to wander through

the other warehouses, including a small museum housing family treasures and a crafts shop. Tamachi Kami-cho 11-1. ☎ 0187/52-2438. Bento from ¥1,500–¥2,000. No credit cards. Lunch daily. Train: Kakunodate Station.

★ **Shichibe** (しちべえ) *JAPANESE*
Take your shoes off at the entrance and then head for one of the tables with chairs or tatami seating with leg wells towards the back, where you'll have a view of a small garden. Traditionally decorated with white walls, wood crossbeams, and shoji, Shichibe serves most of Kakunodate's local specialties, including *inaniwa udon, oyakodon,* and *kiritampo nabe* (a stew consisting of newly harvested rice pounded into a paste and then charcoal grilled before simmering in chicken broth with vegetables), along with *tonkatsu* and a tofu set meal. The menu is only in Japanese, but there are pictures. Yokomachi 15. ☎ 0187/54-3295. Entrees ¥1,200–¥2,000, set lunch ¥900, set dinners ¥1,600–¥3,000. No credit cards. Lunch & dinner Mon–Sat, lunch Sun. Train: Kakunodate Station.

★★ **Tamachi Bukeyashiki Hotel** (田町武家屋敷ホテル) This delightful hotel is deceiving—it looks as though it has been here since the Edo Period, with its whitewashed walls, open wooden beams, and rustic ambience, but it was built in 1999. It combines tradition with modern comfort: The gleaming wood floors, contemporary Japanese art, and Japanese- and Western-style rooms exude class, from sensuously curving paper lampshades to ceramic tissue holders. Breakfast (Western breakfast is available) is served in a restaurant with dark-wood tables overlooking a garden. This small, intimate establishment is a perfect choice for experiencing Kakunodate's relaxed, small-town charm. Tamachi Shimocho 23. ☎ 0187/52-1700. 12 units. Doubles from ¥17,850 per person with 2 meals; from ¥12,600 with breakfast only. AE, DC, MC, V. Train: Kakunodate Station.

A Side Trip to Lake Tazawa and Nyuto Onsen

Nyuto Onsen-Go Village (乳頭温泉郷) doesn't have much in the way of traditional tourist attractions. But what it lacks in glitz it makes up for in spades with tradition and atmosphere. Often used as a backdrop for movies, television dramas, and documentaries, it's located in a cozy mountain valley. The "village" consists of a handful of spartan little inns (with adjacent all-natural hot springs) located over several kilometers, all within an easy hike or bike ride of each other. Relaxing in their milky therapeutic waters, mingling with other visitors from around Japan, and sampling the local cuisine are the reasons people come to out of the way "secret spas" such as this. While Nyuto Onsen (*onsen* means "spa") isn't as inaccessible as it once was, it is about as far off the beaten path as you can get with public transportation. While the area is stunningly beautiful in the winter, we recommend visiting during the warmer months if it is your first time here. This is both because it's generally easier to get around and because the rooms can get quite cold at night, which is typical for rustic Japanese inns but can be a shock to those used to central heating or warmer climes. Nyuto Onsen is recommended for those who already have familiarized themselves with how to use hot springs at other, more tourist-focused sorts of places. (There's also a handy guide to *onsen* etiquette on p. 538.) Some of the outdoor baths are mixed gender; feel free to wrap an extra towel around yourself if you're shy. (But never, ever wear a bathing suit or underwear into the springs.) As with a lot of out-of-the-way places such as this, there isn't much in the way of restaurants. Meals are generally served up by the inn at which you're staying. While breakfasts and dinners are included, lunches are charged separately, giving you an opportunity to get out and try the cuisine of neighboring inns. A handful of inns allow guests to cook for themselves, making them appealing for budget travelers who want to bring in their own food, but we recommend spending the extra for the meals prepared by the inns themselves, which are often excellent examples of regional rural cuisine. In addition to the inns listed below, the waters of **Oogama Onsen** (☎ 0187/46-2438), **Magoroku Onsen** (☎ 0187/46-2224), and **Kuroyu Onsen** (☎ 0187/46-2214) are all worth dropping by if you're in the mood for daytime "spa hopping."

★★★ **Tsurunoyu Onsen** (鶴の湯)**,** Kokuyurin 50 (☎ 0187/46-2139; www.tsurunoyu.com) is by far the best place to stay in Nyuto Onsen, if not in all of Tohoku. Contrary to what you might think, however, it's not refined or elegant; it's not even expensive. Rather, nestled in a wooded valley more than 2.5km (1½ miles) off the already isolated main Nyuto Onsen road, this is about as remote as you can get in Japan. And with its thatched-roof row house of tiny tatami rooms lit by oil lamps, complemented by the sound of rushing water and steam rising from the outdoor baths, it seems positively ancient.

Tsurunoyu opened as an *onsen* 350 years ago; its oldest building—the thatched row house of connected rooms with blackened walls—is 100 years old. Your dinner will be cooked on your *irori* (open-hearth fireplace); breakfast is served in a tatami dining hall, with all the guests dressed in *yukata* (cotton kimono). Additions that ramble along the hillside were constructed over the years, along a rushing stream that serenades you to sleep. If you're on a budget, however, you can stay in the self-cooking wing, which offers simple tatami rooms and allows you to cook your own meals in a communal kitchen. Outdoor sulfurous baths are separated for men and women, but there is one mixed bath where you can wrap a towel around you. Unfortunately, day-trippers spoil some of the fun of staying here (baths are open to the public daily 10am–3pm for ¥500). Evenings, however, are magical. Rooms run from ¥9,600 per person including two meals, or from ¥2,780 per person in the self-cooking wing, plus ¥200 for kitchen use and ¥735 futon charge.

★★ **Taenoyu** (妙の湯)**,** Komagatake 2-1 (☎ 0187/46-2740; http://taenoyu.com/web-english.html) is a relative newcomer in Nyuto Onsen (it opened in 1952). This inn merges old-fashioned comfort (updated tatami rooms, polished wood floors, antiques) with classy elegance, making it a good choice for those who find the Tsurunoyu too rustic. Located on the main road, across from a river, it offers both indoor and outdoor baths, including a private family outdoor bath available for free for 1 hour and a mixed-sex bath. (Shy females can wrap a towel around them, but men are supposed to bathe in the buff.) Meals, which include Akita Prefecture specialties and edible wild plants gathered from around the hotel, are served communally in a tatami room with a view of the river or in a cozy lounge with tables, antiques, and a fireplace. Best are rooms with a view of the river. Rooms run from ¥11,000 per person including two meals.

To get to Nyuto Onsen from Kakunodate Station, take the Komachi bullet train one stop to Tazawako Station (15 min.). At Tazawako Station, board an Ugokotsu Bus bound for Nyuto Onsen (45 min.).

Tohoku Fast Facts

> If you're not hiking, biking can be a great way to see the Oirase Gorge area.

Arriving & Getting Around

BY PLANE Northern Tohoku's major airports are in Aomori (AOJ) and Akita (AXT). Japan Airlines flies from Tokyo's Haneda Airport to both. **BY TRAIN** Train is by far the easiest way to get to Tohoku if traveling from Tokyo. The Tohoku Shinkansen bullet train connects Tokyo to Shin-Aomori at the tip of Honshu, with hourly departures daily. Hayate (Tokyo-Shin Aomori) and Yamabiko (Tokyo-Sendai) are the lines you'll be most likely using. **BY CAR** Bus service to Tohoku is infrequent or nonexistent, so a rental car may be a great convenience or even a necessity. In addition to car-rental gencies at both Aomori and Akita airports, ere are **JR Eki Rent-A-Car** offices at train ations throughout Japan, including Aomori, orioka, Kakunodate, and Tazawako stations, hich offer 20% discounts for train fares ooked in conjunction with car rentals. You'll so find **Toyota Rent-A-Car** (www.toyotaren-car.net) offices virtually everywhere.

TMs

contrast to those abroad, many ATMs only perate during banking hours. ATMs are also ry hard to find outside of major cities, so an accordingly. Most post offices (see be-w) have ATM facilities, although hours are nited. For 24-hour access, your best bets e the ATMs in **7-Eleven** convenience stores, hich accept Visa, Plus, American Express, CB, Union Pay, or Diner's Club International rds for cash withdrawals. (They recently opped accepting MasterCard, Maestro, nd Cirrus cards.) **Citibank** and **Shinsei Bank** TMs accept foreign bank cards as well.

octors & Hospitals

he general level of healthcare availability in pan is high. If you need to consult a physi-an, you should always first ask your hotel oncierge for a nearby recommendation, as e facilities below may only have limited Eng-sh capabilities and are generally only open uring business hours. The U.S. Embassy's ebsite carries an up-to-date list of foreign-iendly doctors throughout Japan: http://kyo.usembassy.gov/e/acs/tacs-7119.html. ENDAI **Hokubu Kyukan Shinryojo** is at 1–1–2 sutsumimachi, 2nd floor (☎ 022/301-6611). ONO **Tono Byoin** is at 14–74 Shiraiwa, Matsu-ki-cho (☎ 0198/62-2222; www.tono-hospi-l.com). KAKUNODATE **Kakunodate General ospital** is at 18 Ueno, Kakunodatemachi ☎ 0187/54-2111).

mergencies

he all-around emergency number in Japan is **119.** The all-around police number is ☎ **110.**

ternet Access

ost business hotels (but few traditional-yle *onsen* or *ryokan*) offer Internet access as perk to customers, and Internet cafes are ommon (though most do not allow custom-s to hook up their own laptops, requiring em to use the facility's machines instead).

Pharmacies

Drugstores, called *yakkyoku* (薬局) are ubiq-uitous in Japan, but they are not 24-hour operations. Your best bet is to ask your hotel concierge for the closest location. Note that you must first visit a doctor in Japan before foreign prescriptions can be filled, so it's also best to bring an ample supply of any prescrip-tion medication with you.

Police

To reach the police, dial ☎ **110.** You can also stop by the nearest *koban* (police substation) for assistance.

Post Office

Central post offices are generally open Mon-day to Friday 9am to 7pm, Saturday 9am to 5pm, and Sunday 9am to 12:30pm. Their ATMs are generally available Monday to Fri 7am to 11pm, Saturday 9am to 9pm, and Sun-day 9am to 7pm. Branches will have shorter hours, as specified below. SENDAI **Sendai Central Post Office** is at 1–7 Kitamemachi, Aoba-ku (☎ 022/267-8035). TONO **Tono Post Office** is at 6–10 Chuo Dori (☎ 0198/62-2830; ATM Mon–Fri 8:45am–7pm, Sat–Sun 9am–5pm). KAKUNODATE **Kakunodate Post Office** is at 21–1 Omachi (☎ 0187/54-1400).

Safety

Tohoku is extremely safe, but take the normal common-sense precautions for personal safe-ty and valuables that you would anywhere else.

Visitor Information

SENDAI **Sendai City Information Office** is at Sendai Station, 2nd floor (☎ 022/222-4069; www.stcb.or.jp/eng/tbic.html; daily 8:30am–8pm). KAKUNODATE **Kakunodate Tourist Information Center** is just outside Kakuno-date Station on the right, housed in a replica of a traditional warehouse (☎ 0187/52-1170; http://kakunodate-kanko.jp/language/en/kanko.html; Mon–Fri 9:30am–4:30pm, Sat–Sun 9am–5pm). LAKE TAZAWA **Folake Tourist Information Office** is inside Tazawako Station (☎ 0187/43-2111; daily 8:30am–6:30pm). MATSUSHIMA **Matsushima Tourist Associa-tion Office** is immediately outside Matsu-shima Kaigan Station on the right side (☎ 022/354-2263; Mon–Fri 9:30am–4:30pm, Sat–Sun 9am–5pm).

11
Hokkaido

Favorite Moments

America's frontier was the Wild West; Japan's was Hokkaido.
The northernmost of Japan's four main islands, Hokkaido has a striking range of landscapes different from that of any other place in Japan, coupled with vast tracts of nearly unspoiled wilderness. Yet despite all the island has to offer, Hokkaido remains virtually undiscovered by foreign tourists. Part of this is because of the sheer distances involved in traversing the island; as you will see in the following tours, it can take hours to drive or train between its far-flung towns and cities. But when it comes to exploring Hokkaido, the journey between the destinations is half the fun. The seafood here is some of the best in the country—crab and salmon in particular—and where else in Japan could you hope to run into wild foxes, bears, and even the occasional harbor seal over the course of a day?

> PREVIOUS PAGE *Stairway to heaven? No, just a Furanodake hiking trail.* THIS PAGE *Relaxing in Sapporo's Odori Park.*

① **Perusing some of Japan's freshest seafood in Hakodate's morning market.** The sights, sounds, and scents of the city's morning market are a treat for the senses. It's also great for some fresh-off-the-boat sashimi. See p. 452, ②.

② **Browsing for glassware and other souvenirs in Hakodate's historic warehouse district.** The boutiques in Hakodate's brick buildings and warehouses are a great way to spend an afternoon in the city. See p. 441, ①.

③ **Taking a trip to Hell.** The steaming, bubbling cauldrons of sulfur found throughout Jigokudani ("Hell Valley") in Shikotsu-Toya

National Park are an otherworldly natural wonder to behold. See p. 441, ②.

④ **Relaxing year-round in Sapporo's Odori Park.** In the summer months, this ribbon of trees and greenery that cuts right through the heart of the city is a great place for a picnic lunch. And at the peak of winter, it's home to the incredible ice sculptures of the legendary Sapporo Snow Festival. See p. 460, ③.

⑤ **Stopping to smell the flowers in Furano.** Furano's seemingly endless fields of lavender and other flowers have grown into one of Hokkaido's must-see destinations, especially for photographers. See p. 466, ④.

⑥ **Cruising the coastline of the Shiretoko Peninsula.** A stretch of wilderness so unspoiled it was declared a UNESCO World Heritage Site in 2005, the Shiretoko Peninsula is the (literal) polar opposite of Japan's crowded and high-tech cities, and a boat cruise is the best to see it. See p. 473, ③.

⑦ **Breaking out of Abashiri Prison.** This notorious gulag, located in what was once frozen northern wastelands, was Japan's answer to Alcatraz. See p. 447, ⑤.

⑧ **Taking some quality time with the harbor seals of Utoro.** In the depths of winter, ice floes jam the harbors of Hokkaido's northernmost cities. Utoro offers a variety of whale- and seal-watching expeditions out into the frozen expanse. See p. 450, ②.

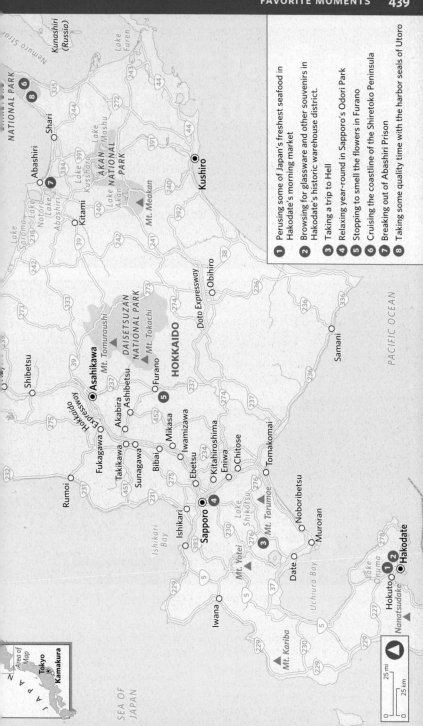

1 Perusing some of Japan's freshest seafood in Hakodate's morning market

2 Browsing for glassware and other souvenirs in Hakodate's historic warehouse district.

3 Taking a trip to Hell

4 Relaxing year-round in Sapporo's Odori Park

5 Stopping to smell the flowers in Furano

6 Cruising the coastline of the Shiretoko Peninsula

7 Breaking out of Abashiri Prison

8 Taking some quality time with the harbor seals of Utoro

The Best of Hokkaido in 3 Days

No tour of Hokkaido would be complete without a stop in Hakodate, the "gateway to Hokkaido." Hakodate makes a great stopover because it has both nighttime and early morning attractions, which you can do in whatever order you like depending on your travel plans. (For convenience's sake we've listed the morning attractions first.) For those who want to linger, strolling through the quaint historic districts of renovated warehouses (now housing restaurants and shops), old Western-style homes, churches, and former government buildings will make you wonder if you're really in Japan.

> *Meijikan is just one of many buildings that will make you think you've left Japan behind.*

START Take the train to Hakodate Station. Hakodate is 832km (517 miles) north of Tokyo.

1 Hakodate. Founded during the Japan's feudal era in the 15th century, Hakodate was one of Japan's first ports opened to international trade following the Meiji Restoration. With its clanking streetcars, sloping streets lined with historic buildings, and port, it retains the atmosphere of a provincial outpost even today.

The **morning market** is housed in a series of warehouses just a minute's walk south of Hakodate Station. Local seafood vendors put

1 Hakodate
2 Noboribetsu Onsen
3 Poroto Kotan
4 Sapporo

eir freshest wares on sale to the public every
orning starting at 5am (6am in the winter
onths). You'll find all sorts of foods for sale,
t the undisputed stars of the show are
okkaido's culinary delicacy: crabs. Many of
e 300 vendors offer free samples, and there
e also a variety of mom-and-pop restaurants
lling seafood fresh from the marketplace.
though it's open until the afternoon, things
eak at around 7:30 in the morning, so try to
t here early for the best experience.

Meijikan, an imposing brick building lo-
ted just down the street from the morning
arket, was built in 1911 as Hakodate's central
ost office. Today, the heavily renovated
ructure serves as home to boutiques carry-
g two distinct local specialties: glassware
nd music boxes. Several of the studios of-
r hands-on sand-etching and music-box
orkshops for children, but the instruction is
tirely in Japanese.

In the late afternoon, head for **Mount Ha-
odate.** Few vacationing Japanese spend the
ght in the city without taking the cable car
the top of this long-dormant volcanic cone.
sing 330m (1,083 ft.), Mount Hakodate is
aditionally ascended in the evening for a
unning view of the city and harbor at night;

from the peak, the lights of Hakodate shimmer
and glitter like jewels on black velvet. ⊙ 1 day.
Market: 9–19 Wakamatsu-cho. ☎ 0138/22-7981.
Free. Daily 5am–3pm. Train: Hakodate Station.
Meijikan: 11–17 Toyokawa-cho. ☎ 0138/27-7070.
Free. Daily 9am–7pm. Streetcar: Jujigai. Mount
Hakodate cable car: 19–7 Motomachi. ☎ 0138/
23-3105. ¥1,160 adults, ¥590 kids. Daily May–
Oct 10am–10pm; Nov–Apr 10am–9pm. Street-
car: Jujigai.

Take the JR Special Express Super Hokuto
from Hakodate Station to Noboribetsu Station
(2 hr.). From Noboribetsu Station, take a bus to
Noboribetsu Onsen (15 min.).

2 **Noboribetsu Onsen.** Famous for the variety of its hot-water springs ever since the
first public bathhouse opened here in 1858,
Noboribetsu Onsen is the most popular of
Hokkaido's many spa towns. It boasts 11 different types of hot water, each with a different
mineral content, and gushes 10,000 tons of it
a day. Make sure to stop by the **Noboribetsu
Tourist Association** (p. 477) on Noboribetsu
Onsen's main street, just a minute's walk
north of the bus depot, for a copy of the very
useful pamphlet *A Guide to Walking Trails in
Noboribetsu Onsen.*

> The steaming cauldrons of "Hell Valley."

One of the charms of Noboribetsu Onsen is its location inside **Shikotsu-Toya National Park.** The 99,000-hectare (245,000-acre) nature preserve encompasses lakes, volcanoes, and other spectacular scenery. Perhaps the park's most famous sight is ★ **Jigokudani ("Hell Valley").** Not to be confused with the monkey-filled Jigokudani in Nagano prefecture (p. 149), this volcanic crater 446m (1,463 ft.) in diameter has a huge depression full of bubbling, boiling water and rock formations of orange and brown. A concrete footpath that runs along the crater leads to lookouts over volcanic ponds and vistas. ⏰ Half-day. Shikotsu-Toya: ☎ 0143/84-3311. Free. Daily sunrise–sunset. Bus: Noboribetsu Bus Terminal.

From JR Noboribetsu Station, JR Shiraoi Station is 13 min. by JR Special Express train o 25 min. by local train.

❸ ★★ **Poroto Kotan.** Nestled on the shores o Lake Poroto in the neighboring town of Shirao Poroto Kotan ("Big Lake Village" in Ainu, the indigenous language) is a mock village of native houses made entirely from wood and reeds; a native plant garden; a dance area; probably the most important **Ainu museum** anywhere; and a research center dedicated to preserving Ainu culture. If you're lucky, your visit will coincide with two annual festivals: one in the spring to pray for life's necessities; the other in the fall to give thanks for the harvests (call for festival dates). Although the village isn't large—it can be toured in about a hour—it's an important stop for those wishin to learn about Ainu culture and the indigenou people who have little left of what was once a rich heritage. ⏰ 1 hr. 2-3-4 Wakakusa-cho, Shiraoi-cho. ☎ 0144/82-3914. www.ainu-museum.or.jp. ¥750 adults, ¥550 high-school students, ¥450 junior-high students, ¥300 kids. Daily 8:45am–5pm. Closed 1 week for New Year's. Train: JR Shiraoi Station.

Take the JR Special Express Super Hokuto from Noboribetsu Station to Sapporo Station (65 min.).

❹ **Sapporo.** The capital of Hokkaido Prefecture, Sapporo has a population of 1.9 million residents, making it the largest city north of Tokyo (and the fifth largest in Japan). It was introduced to the world when the 1972 Winte Olympics were held here, and its many fine s slopes continue to attract winter vacationers as does the Snow Festival, held every Februa (p. 550). In JR Sapporo Station, the excellent **Hokkaido-Sapporo Tourist Information Cen ter** (p. 477), located opposite the west ticket gate, offers a wealth of information not only on Sapporo but all of Hokkaido, making it a must-stop for travelers to other destinations on the island.

The oldest structure in the city is the **Cloc Tower (Tokeidai),** an otherwise unassuming Western-style wooden building built in 1878 as a study hall for the Sapporo Agricultural College (now Hokkaido University). The large clock at the top was made in Boston and was installed in 1881. In summer, it attracts

A recreation of an Ainu ceremony at Poroto Kotan. Note the distinctive style of dress, very different from traditional Japanese.

...ock-crazed tourists even at night; they hang ...ound the outside gates just to listen to the ...ock strike the hour. While the clock's worth ...ook-see if you're in the area, the little mu-...um inside is eminently skippable.

Located nearby, the 13-hectare (32-acre) **...okkaido University Botanical Gardens** ...ntain more than 4,000 varieties of plants ...thered from all over Hokkaido, arranged in ...arshland, herb, alpine, and other gardens. ...e grounds are also home to Japan's oldest **...tural science museum,** founded in 1882 to ...cument the wildlife of Hokkaido and housed ...a turn-of-the-20th-century, Western-style ...ilding. And don't miss the one-room **Ainu ...useum,** which displays a small but fascinat-...g array of Ainu artifacts.

What better way to cap off a trip to the city ...an with the **Sapporo Beer Factory**? Housed ...an iconic brick building, it has been convert-...d into a museum devoted to the city's most ...mous beverage. Admission is free, but the ...er, alas, isn't; it's served in a tasting lounge ...the first floor in flights of three seasonal ...riations for ¥400. A museum visit is a great ...peritif" for the full-service Sapporo Bier ...arten right next door (p. 463). ⏲1 day. Clock ...wer: N1 W2, Chuo-ku, ☎011/231-0838. www. ...keidai.co.jp. ¥200 (museum). Daily 8:45am–...0pm (museum). Train: Odori Station. Botani-...l Gardens: N3 W8, Chuo-ku, ☎011/221-0066.

> *For refreshing times, make it "Sapporo Time" at the Sapporo Beer Factory.*

Grounds ¥400 adults, ¥280 junior-high students and younger; greenhouse only ¥110. Grounds May–Nov daily 9am–3:30pm; green-houses and museums daily 9am–3:30pm. Train: Sapporo Station. Beer Factory: N7 E9, Higashi-ku. ☎011/731-4368. Free. Daily 9am–5:30pm. Train: Sapporo Station.

The Best of Hokkaido in 1 Week

Big adventure awaits in Hokkaido's heart. While many have visited the easier-to-access cities of Hakodate and Sapporo, few can boast of having penetrated Hokkaido's lush interior and to its farthest reaches, where bears roam and ice floes drift in wintertime. That's what makes dedicating an entire week to exploring Japan's "final frontier" so much fun. Think of it as your opportunity to break some new ground in an otherwise well-explored country.

> *Akanko's foothills and trails are a great way to get away from it all.*

START From JR Sapporo Station, take the JR Super Express Kamui to Asahikawa Station (80 min.). To reach the zoo (see below), take the no. 5 Asahikawa Denki Kido bus bound for Asahiyama Zoo (bus stop is right across the street from Asahikawa Station; 40 min.). Asahikawa is more than 1,200km (746 miles) north of Tokyo.

1 Asahikawa. Hokkaido's second-largest city, Asahikawa is also famed for being the site of Japan's lowest-ever recorded temperature of –42°F (–41°C). (Don't worry; it was set in 1902 and hasn't been matched in the more than a century since.) Although Asahikawa is known for its skiing, during the warmer months its main attraction is ★★★ kids **Asahiyama Zoo.** This first-rate zoological park is one of Japan's most popular. It's a progressive

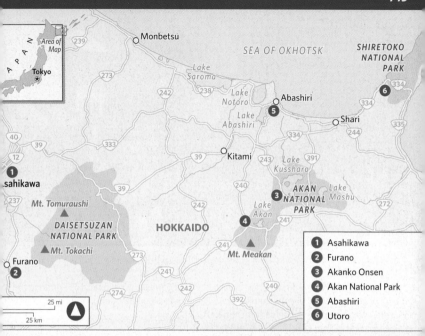

rt of place with interactive exhibits and
bitats tailored to the animals. In addition
the usual tigers, orangutans, and such, the
al enclosure features giant acrylic tubes for
e animals to swim through, and the penguin
cility features a massive transparent tunnel
at lets visitors see the birds "fly" through the
ater. From December through mid-March,
11am and 2:30pm daily, the zoo's penguins
e marched out of their enclosure and down
snow-covered walkway—a great chance
r an up-close-and-personal encounter
ithout walls or glass. Although the zoo isn't
articularly large in terms of square footage,
e sheer density and quality of the displays
ill take you a solid 2 or so hours to work your
ay through. Zoo: Higashi Asahikawa-cho,
aranuma. ☎ 0166/36-1104. ¥800. May–Oct
30am–5:15pm; Nov–Apr 10:30am–3:30pm.
ain: Asahikawa Station.

eturn to Asahikawa Station. Take the JR
rano Line to Furano Station (60 min.).

Furano. Nicknamed the "Belly Button"
r its location in the center of Hokkaido,
is city has both fields of flowers in the
mmer months and excellent skiing in the
inter. From late June through early August,

> *Farm Tomita's flowers are a sight to behold come springtime.*

> *Asahiyama Zoo's distinctive enclosures let sea animals "mingle" with visitors.*

photographers flock here to shoot the area's rolling hills ablaze with lavender and other flowers, often seeming to stretch from horizon to horizon. **Farm Tomita** is the single most famous spot for viewing them. The flower season, which runs from late June through early August, attracts photographers and flower aficionados from all over Japan, so make sure to book early. It's such a big deal that Japan Railways even opens a dedicated train station, called Lavender Farm Station, right next to the farm during peak season. Can't make it there in time to catch the flowers? Don't worry. There's a greenhouse for enjoying lavender out of season as well. See p. 464.

From JR Furano Station, take the JR Nemuro Honsen to Shintoku Station. Switch to the JR Special Express Super Oozora for Kushiro Station (4K hr.). At Kushiro Station, board an Akan Bus for Akanko (2 hr.). Tip: The bus between Kushiro and Akanko is not covered by rail passes.

❸ **Akanko Onsen.** This small hot-spring resort on the edge of Lake Akan is surrounded by stunning views. It's a great base for active vacations, ranging from fishing to hiking to exploring nearby Akan National Park (see below) and Kushiro Marshland National Park (p. 470, ❹), famous for its red-crested cranes. But after nearly a solid day of travel from Furano, you're probably going to want to check in to one of the city's numerous spas and soak your

tired bones in anticipation of exploring the park the next day. See p. 468.

Take the Akan Panorama Bus from Lake Aka to Bihoro Station (5 hr.). Departures at 8am or 9:25am (season depending).

❹ **Akan National Park.** The rich habitat of thi natural wonderland features volcanic mountains, dense forests of subarctic primeval tree and three caldera lakes, including Lake Akan. If you're not renting a car, the best way to see Akan National Park's most important natural wonders is aboard a sightseeing bus. The Aka Panorama bus departs Lake Akan daily February to early October, making stops at several scenic spots along the way, including Mashu and Kussharo lakes. **Mashu,** a crater lake that is considered one of Japan's most beautiful lakes, was called "lake of the devil" by the Ain because no water flows either into it or out of it. Surely Mashu is one of Japan's least-spoile lakes: Because of the steep, 200m-high (656 ft.) rock walls ringing it, the lake has remained inaccessible to humans (the bus stops at an observation platform high above the water). **Kussharo** is one of Japan's largest mountain lakes, but what makes it particularly interesting is its hot-spring waters right on the beach, in summer, you can see people digging holes sit in the hot springs. The bus also stops at the foot of **Mount Iou,** with its sulfurous caldrons and at **Bihoro Pass** (a scenic overlook) before reaching Bihoro Station north of the park.

ke the JR Sekihoku Honsen Line to Abashiri ation (30 min.).

Abashiri. The name of this distant outpost the Japanese frontier once struck terror into e hearts of criminals, for it was the site of Ja-n's first high-security penal facility. Now con-rted into the **Abashiri Prison Museum,** it was mething like Japan's answer to Alcatraz. The pposedly unescapable prison was founded in 90, when 1,200 prisoners and 173 wardens ere sent to the city of Abashiri for the pur-ses of constructing Hokkaido's first central ghway. Actually more of a gulag than a correc-nal facility, Abashiri Prison housed political iminals in the late 19th through the early 20th ntury before being transformed into a (semi-) odern correctional institution in the postwar a. In 1984, it was closed down, the prisoners oved to a new facility across the river, and e old prison reopened as this museum. Filled ith artifacts dedicated to its decades of use a penal colony, its displays are occasionally a tle lighthearted for our tastes, but it remains fascinating window into a grim period in okkaido's history. It's a 30-minute walk from e station, so consider taking a taxi (around 1300 one way). Museum: 1-1 Yobito, Abashiri. 0152/45-2411. www.kangoku.jp/world. ¥1,050

adults, ¥750 college students, ¥520 high-school students and younger. Daily Apr–Oct 8am–6pm; Nov–Mar 9am–5pm. Train: Abashiri Station.

Rent a car at Abashiri Station and drive Route 334 (Shiretoko National Highway) to Utoro (2 hr.).

6 Utoro. Hands down the farthest-flung destination in the pages of this book, Utoro is a tiny port town located on the Shiretoko Peninsula, a slim spur of land projecting into the Sea of Okhotsk. Marked by massive stone formations and soaring cliffs, the town serves as the unofficial gateway to **Shiretoko National Park,** which was registered as a UNESCO World Heritage Site in 2005 and features some of Japan's last pristine wilderness. The park is home to a variety of wild animals including brown bears, deer, fox, *tanuki* (rac-coon dogs), salmon, and in the winter months, harbor seals and the occasional killer whale. Hikers can easily spend a half-day exploring the trails connecting the **Five Lakes of Shire-toko** (p. 472, **1**); meanwhile, the best way to catch sight of some of the park's biggest waterfalls and other natural formations is via a half- or full-day **Shiretoko Peninsula Cruise** (p. 473, **3**).

Lake Mashu at dusk. It's considered one of Japan's most picturesque lakes.

Arctic Adventure

Although most associate winter sports in Hokkaido with skiing, snowboarding, and snowmobiling, the northernmost reaches of the island offer a chance to interact with exotic arctic environments and creatures. The arctic season is as harsh as it is beautiful, and generally speaking visitors must arrange tours with one of the local operators to explore the Sea of Okhotsk's ice floes and snowdrift-filled forests. Rest assured that these professionally run tours are wholly geared towards safety and fun; you don't need to be an experienced arctic explorer to participate, and some don't even require much in the way of physical exertion.

> *Rental drysuits are the style of choice for hiking on ice floes.*

START Overnight bus service runs from Sapporo's Chuo Bus Terminal to Utoro Bus Terminal (7 hr.). Train service also runs from Sapporo Station to Abashiri Station on the Okhotsk Line (5½ hr.); transfer at Abashiri to the Semmo Line to Shiretokoshari Station (50 min.). The coastal route from Abashiri to Shiretokoshari is incredibly scenic. Buses then run from Shiretokoshari Station to Utoro Bus Terminal. Utoro is almost 1,500km (932 miles) north of Tokyo.

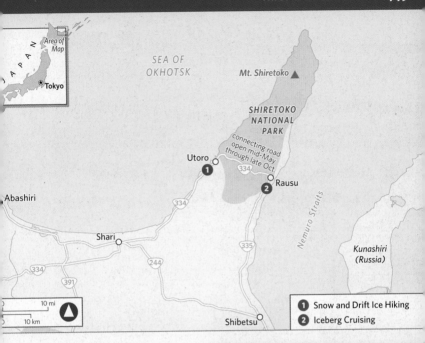

1 Snow and Drift Ice Hiking
2 Iceberg Cruising

1 ★★★ kids Snow and Drift Ice Hiking. Snowshoeing is a unique way to experience the frozen expanse of Utoro's coastline and forests. These all-day expeditions are arranged through **Gojira Iwa Kanko** in downtown Utoro. For the morning leg, hikers are provided with snowshoes and led on a 2km (1.2-mile) guided tour to Furepe Falls, which in the summer months erupts from a cliff face directly into the sea but will be frozen solid during the winter season. (Although snowshoes are provided, customers should arrive attired in proper cold-weather gear, such as the sort worn for skiing or snowboarding.) After lunch (provided by a downtown seafood restaurant), participants are shuttled to the trailhead for a drift-ice hike. For this portion of the journey, you'll be provided with a dry suit of the same sort normally worn by scuba divers, allowing you to tromp through deep snow and slush without actually getting cold or wet. The highlight of the tour is your chance to jump into the shallows and paddle around the floes yourself—thanks to the dry suit, you'll be nice and toasty, and if you get lucky, you might even catch a glimpse of the elusive sea creature known as the clione (p. 451). While all of this might sound rather extreme, everything

> *Ice floes almost totally obscure the Sea of Okhotsk.*

> *Deep winter in Hokkaido: "Iceberg season" generally lasts from February to March.*

is about safety first and the trip is fun for all ages and experience levels. For those who don't have an entire day to spare, Gojira Iwa Kanko also offers standalone drift-ice hikes in the morning, afternoon, and evening. Reservations are required to ensure space and dry suit availability. Season varies based on actual ice conditions. Gojira Iwa Kanko: 51 Utoro Higashi, Shari-Cho. ☎ 0152/24-3060. www.kamuiwakka jp/driftice. Shiretoko Mankitsu Plan (full-day snow and ice hike) ¥9,000 adults, ¥5,000 elementary students and younger. No credit cards Season runs from end of Jan through end of Mar Bus: Utoro Bus Terminal.

❷ ★ **Iceberg Cruising.** Specially outfitted boats from **Ryuhyo Cruising** ferry passengers through the frozen waters of the Sea of Okhotsk to see the sights of the Shiretoko Peninsula. There are three main tours: a photography trip for serious shutterbugs with single-lens reflex cameras and telephoto lenses; a bird-watching trip; and a sightseeing cruise for more casual tourists. The first two last some 3 to 4 hours, while the kids **sightseeing cruise** clocks in at under 2. This is the best way to see whales, seals lounging on ice floes, and a variety of large birds such as eagles.

Travel Tip

While arctic tour operators will rent out any special gear needed for their excursions, coming prepared with warm clothes, boots, hats, and other common-sense cold-weather gear is a must. Don't hesitate to contact any of the operators directly for more information about current conditions and suggested gear, and be aware that ever-changing weather conditions may result in delays or cancellations.

Arctic Climate Change

Locals of the northernmost reaches of Hokkaido claim that they experience not four but five seasons: spring, summer, fall, winter, and iceberg season, which generally lasts from February to March. In decades past, virtually Hokkaido's entire northeastern coast facing the Sea of Okhotsk froze over; environmental changes have largely reduced the extent of the spread to the tip of the Shiretoko Peninsula. In fact, Utoro (p. 472) is now one of the southernmost points in the northern hemisphere where sea ice begins to form. At the height of winter, massive ice floes fill the harbor, accompanied by seasonal wildlife including owls, eagles, and large marine mammals such as seals and even the occasional killer whale. Formerly considered remote and snowbound, in today's era of growing environmental awareness, Utoro has reinvented itself as a center of ecotourism.

Angels of the Sea

The unassuming, fingernail-sized sea animals known as **clione** are one of Hokkaido's star attractions; you'll see all sorts of souvenirs based on the tiny creatures while visiting the island. Although they live in northern oceans throughout the world, they have a cultlike following in Japan, where they've been dubbed "sea angels" for their shape and the way they "fly" though the water with a pair of winglike fins. They may be little more than sacs of jelly, but their transparent bodies, small size, and graceful movements do seem to give them more charm than your average sea slug. Normally found only in deep, frigid water, they rise into the shallows during the coldest months of the year. If you're lucky, you may encounter one while taking a dip at the end of a drift-ice hike. For those less fortunate (or who simply don't feel like venturing into icy waters), several of Utoro's hotels, including the Shiretoko Grand Hotel Kitakobushi (p. 475), have mini-aquariums of clione.

Mid-March offers the highest chance for animal spotting.)

The only trick is, the cruises only leave from the city of Rausu, which is located on the opposite coast of the Shiretoko Peninsula and has thicker ice than that of Utoro. Although Rausu is only a 30-minute drive in the summer months, from November through early May the direct road through the mountains is closed down, making it a 2-hour haul. You'll have to overnight in Rausu if you want to catch the photo and bird tours, which depart at 5am and 9am. (The sightseeing one departs at 9am and 1pm, so you could theoretically make the drive over from Utoro for the afternoon sailing.) One option is the rustic but clean **Rausu Dai-Ichi Hotel,** 1 Yunosawacho, Rausu-cho ☎ 0153/87-2259; ¥8,550 per person including two meals). Ryuhyo Cruising: 74 Kaigan-cho, Rausu-cho. ☎ 0153/89-2036. http://kamuiwakka.jp/ryuhyocruising. Reservations required. Photo tour ¥10,000; bird tour ¥7,000; sightseeing tour ¥4,000 adults, ¥2,000 elementary school and younger. No credit cards. Season runs from end of Feb to early Apr. Bus: Rausu.

Hakodate

Hokkaido's third-largest city, with a population of 285,000,
Hakodate is about as far as you may care to get in a day if you arrive in Hokkaido from Tokyo by train. But we highly recommend taking a plane there to save time—it's a charming bayside city. At night, the city lights spread to the sea, which in turn is illuminated by lights of numerous squid-fishing boats. It's also an excellent introduction to Hokkaido's distinctive city planning and architecture, which often looks more Western than it does Japanese—particularly so in the historic district of Motomachi.

> *The European-style architecture of the Motomachi district is one of Hakodate's trademark attractions.*

START **Take the streetcar from Hakodate Eki-mae (adjacent to Hakodate Station) to Jujigai or Suehiro-cho stops. Hakodate is 832km (517 miles) north of Tokyo.**

1 Blue Moon Bay Cruise. This double-decker cruiser ferries passengers around Hakodate Port by day and out to the Tsugaru Strait for a beautiful view of Hakodate by night. The rides (which last 40–60 min.) depart hourly from a pier next to the red-brick warehouses (p. 454, **4**). Check the website for the most up-to-date schedule information. ⏱ 1 hr. 14–17 Suehiro-cho. ☎ 0138/26-6161. www.hakodate-factory.com/bluemoon. Day cruise ¥1,600

adults, ¥800 kids; night cruise ¥2,500 adults, ¥1,250 kids. Apr–May & Sept 10:30am–6pm; Jun–Aug 10:30am–6:30pm; Oct 10:30am–5pm. Streetcar: Jujigai or Suehiro-cho.

2 Morning Market. A must-do is a visit to Hakodate's morning market, which is spread out just south of the train station. Walk around and look at the variety of foods for sale, especially the hairy crabs for which Hokkaido is famous. You can make an unusual breakfast of fruit, raw sea urchin, or grilled crab from the stalls here. ⏱ 20 min. Daily 5am–noon. Train: JR Hakodate Station.

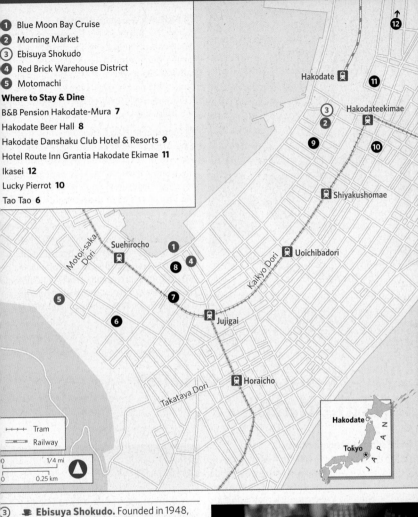

1. Blue Moon Bay Cruise
2. Morning Market
3. Ebisuya Shokudo
4. Red Brick Warehouse District
5. Motomachi

Where to Stay & Dine

B&B Pension Hakodate-Mura **7**
Hakodate Beer Hall **8**
Hakodate Danshaku Club Hotel & Resorts **9**
Hotel Route Inn Grantia Hakodate Ekimae **11**
Ikasei **12**
Lucky Pierrot **10**
Tao Tao **6**

3 🍽 **Ebisuya Shokudo.** Founded in 1948, this is the oldest restaurant in Hakodate's morning market, and its sashimi and *donburi* (rice bowl) dishes are the stuff of legend. Delicacies like *ikura* (salmon roe) and *uni* (sea urchin) are as fresh as you'll ever taste them, and the homey atmosphere is a fun touch. Even if you're only in the mood for a snack, their mini-sized *donburi* bowls, which start at only ¥1,000, are a great way to get a taste of the local seafood. 9-16 Wakamatsu-cho. ☎ 0138/23-1602. www8. ncv.ne.jp/~evisuya. Entrees from ¥1,000. No credit cards. Breakfast & lunch daily. Train: JR Hakodate Station.

> Glassware is a Hakodate specialty.

> *Fresh fish is always on the menu at the Hakodate Morning Market.*

4 **Red Brick Warehouse District.** These handsome brick storehouses, arrayed along a boardwalk running alongside the bay, are no longer used for their intended purpose but rather house a variety of shops and restaurants. ⏱ 45 min. 14–12 Suehiro-cho. ☎ 0138/23-0350. Free. Daily 9:30am–7pm. Streetcar: Jujig or Suehiro-cho.

5 **Motomachi.** Hakodate's historic district is a picturesque neighborhood of steep slopes and turn-of-the-20th-century Western-style clapboard homes, consulates, churches, and other buildings; most impressive include the **Old Branch Office of the Hokkaido Government,** which also happens to contain a Touris Information Center, and the colonial-style **Old Public Hall,** which lets visitors dress in antiqu formalwear for portraits in a period setting. ⏱ 1 hr. Old Branch Office: 12–18 Motomachi. ☎ 0138/27-3333. Old Public Hall: 11–13 Motoma chi. ☎ 0138/22-1001. ¥300. Daily 9am–7pm (until 5pm in winter). Streetcar: Suehiro-cho.

Where to Stay & Dine in Hakodate

B&B Pension Hakodate-Mura
An immaculate, mostly Western-style hotel decorated with whitewashed walls, wood furniture, and fresh and dried flowers. In addition to spotless Western-style rooms with wood floors, there are three tatami rooms with straw mats, shoji screens, and platform beds. The only catch are the rules, similar to a youth hostel's (check-in at 3pm, checkout at 10am, and the door locks at 11pm), but you can't beat the location: near the waterfront warehouse district and Motomachi, and only a 15-minute walk from Hakodate Station. 16–12 Suehiro-cho. ☎ 0138/22-8105. www.bb-hakodatemura.com. 16 units, 1 with bathroom. Doubles ¥10,540–¥12,960. Western breakfast ¥800 extra. AE, MC, V. Streetcar: Jujigai.

Hakodate Beer Hall *EUROPEAN-ASIAN FUSION*
Located conveniently in the heart of the old warehouse district, this is a great spot to drop

> *Hakodate's legendary Lucky Pierrot burger.*

y for a glass of locally brewed beer at the nd of the day. Though the emphasis is on the uds, the surprisingly eclectic menu offers verything from sausage to sushi, all of it well one. 14–12 Suehirocho. ☎ 0138/27-1010. www. kumaiyo.com. Entrees from ¥720. AE, DC, MC, . Lunch & dinner daily. Streetcar: Suehirocho.

★ kids Hakodate Danshaku Club Hotel & esorts

With a convenient location near akodate Station and the morning market, is locally owned hotel is named after a Hok-aido potato. Standard rooms would qualify as uites elsewhere, with one or two bedrooms sleeping up to four persons) that can be osed off from the living area by shoji-like oors, as well as fully stocked kitchens, bal-onies facing Mount Hakodate, and spacious athrooms complete with generous tubs and vindows also providing views. 22–10 Otema-hi. ☎ 0138/21-1111. www.danshaku-club.com. 2 units. Doubles from ¥38,000. AE, DC, MC, V. rain: JR Hakodate Station.

Hotel Route Inn Grantia Hakodate Ekimae

espite a no-flair atmosphere and small ooms, this hotel rises above the ordinary with convenient location near the station, reason-ble prices, good views (reserve a room above he fourth floor for the best harbor views; the op floor is nonsmoking), and large hot-spring aths on the 13th floor. 21–3 Wakamatsu-cho. ☎ 0138/21-4100. www.route-inn.co.jp. 286 nits. Doubles from ¥12,500. AE, DC, MC, V. rain: JR Hakodate Station.

kasei SEAFOOD

you're in the mood for some tentacles, this estaurant is the place to go to sample one of lakodate's famed delicacies: squid. Mainly erved as *ika-sashi* (sashimi), but also grilled, oiled, stuffed, or fried, Ikasei is your one-stop hop for squid cuisine. Although the menus re entirely in Japanese, many of the dishes are hown as photographs, letting you point and hoose even if you don't speak the language.)ther types of fish are on the menu as well, as is nice selection of regional sake. 2–14 Motoma-hi. ☎ 0138/54-1919. Ika-sashi ¥1,200. V, MC. inner Tues–Sun. Streetcar: Chuo Byoin Mae.

ucky Pierrot BURGERS

his legendary local chain serves up burgers vith a Japanese twist—some 16 different va-eties, in fact, from standard beef to "Chinese

> *Local beers on parade at the Hakodate Beer Hall.*

chicken," squid, scallop, shrimp, lamb, and even (for better or worse) a whale burger. There are franchises all over the city, but the easiest to find is right in front of the station. 17–12 Waka-matsu-cho. ☎ 0138/26-8801. www.luckypierrot. jp. Entrees from ¥350. No credit cards. Lunch & dinner daily. Train: JR Hakodate Station.

Tao Tao ASIAN FUSION

This eclectic cafe in a bright yellow building in the Motomachi District offers interesting Asian food, including *obachahan* (Manila-style pork fried rice), tacos with rice, and pad Thai (rice noodles Thai-style). The tofu salad is very good, with lots of greens and a spicy dressing. There's an outdoor patio out back, open in summer. 15–19 Motomachi. ☎ 0138/22-0002. Entrees from ¥800. No credit cards. Dinner Tues–Fri; lunch & dinner Sat–Sun and holidays. Streetcar: Suehiro-cho.

Squid Dancing

Every year from August 1 to 6, the city hosts the **Hakodate Port Festival.** Launched in 1935 to boost public morale after a major fire, it's been going strong ever since. Highlights include fireworks and a nightly parade in which residents and visitors throng the streets to perform the *ika odori*—the "squid dance"—named after the local seafood delicacy. Anyone and anyone is welcome to join in the parade as it winds through the city's streets. If you plan to visit at this time, make sure to place reservations well in advance.

Noboribetsu

Located right inside Hokkaido's Shikotsu-Toya National

Park, the town of Noboribetsu is renowned for its seasonal beauty. It is an impressive sight in spring, when 2,000 cherry trees lining the road into the *onsen* (hot springs resort) are in full bloom. And in autumn, the leaves of its thousands of Japanese maples turn beautiful shades of crimson. Noboribetsu also happens to be a great springboard to getting acquainted with the culture of the Ainu, the native inhabitants of Japan's northernmost island. As in most spa towns, the food is generally included with your accommodations. While you will find scattered restaurants and coffee shops and such here and there, they are nothing to write home about.

> *A view from the footpath over Lake Mashu, Shikotsu-Toya National Park.*

START Take the bus from Noboribetsu Onsen or JR Noboribetsu Station to Jidai Mura. Noboribetsu is about 1,000km (621 miles) north of Tokyo.

① ★ kids **Noboribetsu Date Jidai Mura.** A visit to this reproduction of a Feudal-era village is the closest you can get to taking a time machine back to the last days of the Edo Period.

Shops, restaurants, theaters, the downtown, and a samurai district are built as they were of yore, staffed by people dressed in period clothing. See ninja warriors fighting in a trick mansion or outdoor theater, local merchants hawking their wares, Edo Era tenements with life-size models, and courtesans performing in this Disney-esque re-creation of how Japan might have looked when the shogun reigned.

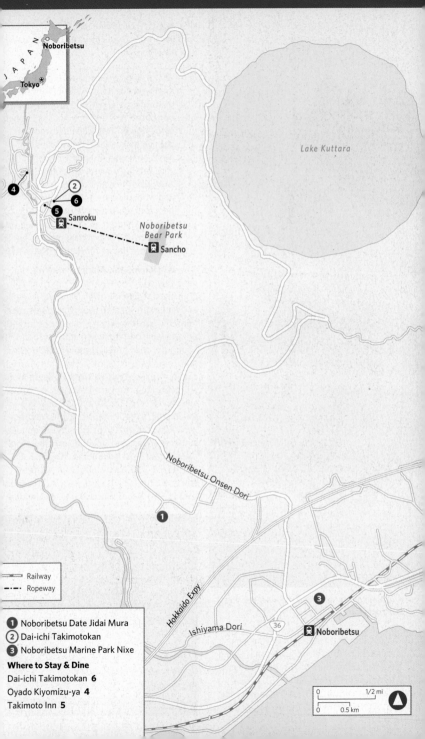

Lake Kuttara

Sanroku

Noboribetsu
Bear Park

Sancho

Noboribetsu Onsen Dori

Railway
Ropeway

Hokkaido Expy

Ishiyama Dori 36

Noboribetsu

JAPAN

Noboribetsu

Tokyo

1 Noboribetsu Date Jidai Mura
2 Dai-ichi Takimotokan
3 Noboribetsu Marine Park Nixe
Where to Stay & Dine
Dai-ichi Takimotokan 6
Oyado Kiyomizu-ya 4
Takimoto Inn 5

0   1/2 mi
0   0.5 km

> *A resident of the Noboribetsu Marine Park Nixe steps out for a bit.*

Although shows are in Japanese (the ninja shows are probably the only ones that would interest children), the various attractions are fun for the entire family. ⏱ 3 hr. 53-1 Naka-Noboribetsu-cho. ☎ 0143/83-3311. www.edo-trip.jp. ¥2,900 adults, ¥2,100 seniors, ¥1,500 kids. Apr–Oct daily 9am–5pm; Nov–Mar Thurs–Tues 9am–4pm. (Last entry 1 hr. before closing. Bus: Jidai Mura.

② 🛁 **Dai-ichi Takimotokan.** Even if you aren't staying here, you should make a point of dropping by this storied hotel, one of the very first bathhouses to open in the region. Today its huge, modern bathing halls offer some 30 tubs and pools containing a variety of waters with varying mineral concentrations. Although the baths are separate for men and women, there's an indoor swimming pool for families with a slide and play area for children, so be sure to bring your swimsuit. It's also a great place to get a bite to eat before moving on. See p. 459.

❸ ★ 👶 **Noboribetsu Marine Park Nixe.** It's definitely on the touristy side, but small children love this combination Danish theme park and aquarium, located near Noboribetsu Station. (If you're traveling with luggage, lockers are available both here and at the station.) The aquarium, one of the largest in northern Japan, is in Castle Nixe, modeled after a Danish castle. You'll see sharks, moray eels, salmon, sturgeon, king crab, giant octopus, and other sea creatures. More attractions include a touch pool, a reptile house, dolphin and sea-lion shows, a penguin parade, the ubiquitous souvenir shops, and a handful of little kiddie rides. ⏱ 2 hr. 1-22 Noboribetsu Higashimachi. ☎ 0143/83-3800. www.nixe.co.jp. ¥2,400 adults, ¥1,200 kids. Daily 9am–5pm. Closed 5 days in early Dec. Train: Noboribetsu Station.

About the Ainu

Noboribetsu's neighboring town of Shiraoi was settled by the Ainu people many centuries before Japanese began emigrating to Hokkaido. Not much is known about the origins of the Ainu people—it isn't even clear whether they're Asian or Caucasian, but they are of different racial stock than the Japanese. Years of forced assimilation and intermarriage with Japanese means there are few if any "pure" Ainu anymore, but an estimated 23,000 people of Ainu descent still live in Hokkaido, some of whom earn their living from tourism.

Where to Stay & Dine in Noboribetsu

★ Dai-ichi Takimotokan (登別温泉 第一滝本館) This is Noboribetsu's best-known *ryokan* (traditional inn), thanks to its long history (opened in 1858) and its gigantic public baths. That very fame, however, means it is often filled with noisy tour groups. The most compelling reasons to stay here are its location near Jigokudani (p. 442) and its famous hot-spring baths, which hotel guests are entitled to use free anytime, night or day. Guests staying in the East and West buildings or Western-style rooms dine in a buffet restaurant offering Japanese, Chinese, and Western food (or can pay more for a traditional Japanese meal), while those staying in tatami rooms in the South and Main building can opt for a Japanese dinner served in their rooms. 55 Noboribetsu Onsenmachi. ☎ 0143/84-3322. www.takimotokan. co.jp. 399 units. Rooms from ¥13,275 per person. Rates include 2 meals. AE, DC, MC, V. Bus: Noboribetsu.

★★ Oyado Kiyomizu-ya (御やど清水屋) This *ryokan* is beside a roaring river, the sounds of which will sing you to sleep as you snuggle against fur-lined futons and down covers. But it's the delicious seasonal *kaiseki* (traditional multicourse meals) that assure the *ryokan* many repeat guests; the parade of beautifully prepared dishes includes local specialties. Service is impeccable, and the owner Mr. Iwai speaks excellent English; he can answer your questions regarding Noboribetsu and the area. If you're looking for a place far from tour groups, souvenir shops, and impersonal service, you'll be happy here. The staff will pick you up at the station if you ask in advance. 173 Noboribetsu Onsenmachi. ☎ 0143/84-2145. www.kiyomizuya.co.jp. 43 units. Doubles from ¥21,150 per person. Rates include meals. AE, DC, MC, V. Bus: Noboribetsu.

Takimoto Inn (滝本イン) If you prefer a hotel with beds to a *ryokan* with futons, this quiet and moderately priced inn has the additional advantage of allowing guests to use Dai-chi Takimotokan's famous

> *The massive entry to Dai-ichi Takimotokan's spa.*

baths across the street for free, 24 hours a day. All rooms are twins (but can be used as singles or triples) and Spartan, with metal doors that clang shut with the finality of a prison, and miniscule bathrooms. There's no view, but windows do open. Buffet meals offer a mix of Japanese and Western food, and there's a shuttle to the airport. 76 Noboribetsu Onsenmachi. ☎ 0143/84-2205. Fax 0143/84-2645. www.takimotoinn.co.jp. 47 units. Rooms from ¥7,350 per person; Sat ¥1,200 extra. Rates include 2 meals. AE, DC, V. Bus: Noboribetsu.

Sapporo

Sapporo is one of Japan's newest cities. About 140 years ago, it was nothing more than a scattering of huts belonging to Ainu and Japanese families. With the dawning of the Meiji Period, however, the government decided to colonize the island. The area of Sapporo (the name comes from the Ainu word meaning "big, dry river") was chosen as the new capital site, and construction began in 1871.

> *The Sapporo TV Tower lights up the night sky.*

START Take the train to Odori Station. Sapporo is 1,130km (702 miles) north of Tokyo.

1 Pole Town and Aurora Town. This pair of linked underground shopping arcades is filled with numerous shops and boutiques. They also connect to some of the city's bigger department stores and other buildings, making this a fun way to spend a morning in the colder seasons. S1 W4, Chuo-ku. ☎ 011/251-4912. Daily 10am–8pm. Train: Odori Station.

2 🍜 Ramen Yokocho. Sapporo is famed for creating "miso ramen"—a widely popular version of the dish using a miso-based rather than soy sauce–based broth. And there is no better place to sample it than Ramen Yokocho alley. Located just 1 short block east of the Susukino Station, this is a strip of hole-in-the-wall joints that focus on Sapporo specialties. In addition to miso ramen, don't miss "corn-butter ramen," a bowl of noodles with a healthy dollop of butter on top. It doesn't matter which shop you choose—you can't go wrong, so just look for an empty seat. W3 S5, Chuo-ku. Ramen from ¥500. No credit cards. Lunch & dinner daily. Train: Odori Station.

3 Odori Park. This is the large, tree-lined boulevard that extends from east to west right through the heart of Sapporo. It's fun to stroll through any time, and it hosts a variety of events and festivals throughout the year. The ★★★ kids **Sapporo Snow Festival** is the quintessential city event, held annually in early February on Odori Park Promenade. Begun in

JAPAN

Sapporo

Tokyo

HOKKAIDO UNIVERSITY

Buddhist Temple
Shinto Shrine
Tourist Info
Railway
Streetcar
Subway

Soen

JR HAKODATE LINE

NANBOKU LINE

TOHO LINE

Kita-Junijo

JR Sapporo

Sogo Dept. Store

Sapporo

Tokyu Dept. Store

Kita Gojo

Eki-mae Dori/West 4th St.

Botanical Gardens

Governor's Residence

Kita Ichijo

City Hall

Odori

Odori

Bus Center Mae

Odori

Nishi-Yon-Chome

TOZAI LINE

Nishi-Juitchome

Nishi-Hatchome

Nishi-hatchome

Nishi-Jugo-Chome

Chuo-Kuyakusha-Mae

Tanuki Koji

Susukino

To Chitose Airport

Sosei-Shogakko-Mae

Susukino

Hosuisusukino

CHUO-KU

Higashi-Honganji Temple

Higashi-Honganji-Mae

Nakajima Koen

Minami Kujo

Ishiyama Dori

Chuo-Hokenjo-Mae

Nakajima Park

Toyohira

Nakajima-Koen-Dori

Baseball Stadium

Minami Juyojo

Gokoku Shrine

Minami Juyojo

1 Pole Town and Aurora Town
2 Ramen Yokocho
3 Odori Park
4 Sapporo Bankei Ski Area

Where to Stay & Dine

Hotel Monterey Edelhof **8**
JR Tower Hotel Nikko Sapporo **6**
Kani Fukumura Kami **10**
Mikuni Sapporo **7**
Nakamuraya Ryokan **9**
Sapporo Bier Garten **5**

1950 to add a bit of spice and life to the cold winter days, the weeklong Snow Festival now features some 240 snow and ice sculptures of everything from famous architecture to anime characters, and attractions such as ice slides and houses. One snow structure may require as much as 300 truckloads of snow, the majority of it brought in from the surrounding mountains. The snow and ice carvings are done with so much attention to detail that it seems a crime they're doomed to melt. The festival is one of Hokkaido's major tourist draws, with more than 2 million locals and tourists thronging the downtown area every year—so if you plan to visit during this time, make sure to book accommodations far in advance. For up to date information about the dates and attractions of the festival, check the official website at www.snowfes.com/english.

The ★ **Sapporo Summer Festival** occupies the other end of the temperature spectrum.

Odori Park hosts numerous beer gardens from late July to mid-August, open every day from noon. Various Japanese beer companies set up their own booths and tables under the trees, while vendors put up stalls selling fried noodles, corn on the cob, and other goodies. In the evenings, live bands serenade the beer drinkers under the stars. Check the city's online sightseeing guide for the annual dates and times. www.welcome.city.sapporo.jp/english.

④ ★ Sapporo Bankei Ski Area. Just 20 minutes from downtown Sapporo (a taxi from the station will cost roughly ¥3,000) is this mountain, popular for after-work and night skiing. (It stays open to 10pm.) And for those looking for a little exercise during the summer months, Bankei's slopes are open to hikers as well. 410 Bankei, Chuo-ku. ☎ 011/641-0071. www.bankei.co.jp. Season: Dec–Apr. Train: Sapporo Station.

Where to Stay & Dine in Sapporo

> *Heaven for crab lovers: Kani Fukumura Kami.*

★★ Hotel Monterey Edelhof

Although opened in 2000, this elegant hotel embraces the architectural exuberance of early 1900s Vienna, with lots of marble, stained-glass windows, Art Deco embellishments, and Otto Wagner–inspired designs.

The elevators have old-fashioned floor dials, classical music plays in public spaces, and function rooms carry such names as Belvedere. The guest rooms are small but smartly decorated with Art Deco motifs. The hotel spa is a huge (though pricey) plus. N2 W1, Chuo-ku. ☎ 011/242-7111. www.hotelmonterey.co.jp/eng. 181 units. Doubles ¥32,340–¥43,890. AE, DC, MC, V. Train: Sapporo Station.

★★★ JR Tower Hotel Nikko Sapporo

Elegance and convenience—not to mention top-class restaurants, a deluxe spa offering everything from reflexology to indoor/outdoor hot-spring baths, and spectacular views from all rooms—make this the best place to stay in Sapporo. Located 23 stories directly above Sapporo Station, it offers rooms with high-end amenities such as embroidered towels (to dispense with the guessing game of which towel belongs to whom). Of course, you pay for the luxury. JR Rail Pass holders get a 10% discount on rates. W2 N5, Chuo-ku. ☎ 011/251-2222. www.jrhotels.co.jp/tower/english. 350 units. Doubles ¥26,000–¥44,000. AE, DC, MC, V. Train: Sapporo Station.

★ Kani Fukumura Kami *SEAFOOD*

Hokkaido is famed for its seafood, and in particular its multitude of crab varieties, and this is the best place in the city to sample them. It's located right in the heart of Hokkaido's nightlife district of Susukino. The crab tempura and crab salad are great ways to start off the evening, but don't miss the crab *shabu-shabu*, in which diners cook strips of raw crab meat in a fragrant, steaming broth at their table. W4 S5, Susukino. ☎ 011/513-6778. www.kanitei.com. Shabu-shabu courses from ¥4,980 per person. AE, DC, MC, V. Dinner daily. Subway: Suskino.

★ Mikuni Sapporo *FRENCH*

Mikuni Kiyomi has a reputation as the Japanese authority on French food. Hokkaido-born and the proprietor-chef of several restaurants in Tokyo and elsewhere, Mikuni has brought his expertise home to triumphant reviews. Located on the ninth floor of Stellar Place in Sapporo Station in a setting that is less than stellar (and accessed by an elevator that is hard to find), the restaurant overcomes its disappointing decor with great cuisine, available only as set meals. Reservations strongly suggested. Stellar Place 9F, W2 N5. ☎ 011/251-0392. Set dinners from ¥8,000. AE, DC, MC, V. Lunch & dinner daily. Train: Sapporo Station.

★ Nakamuraya Ryokan (中村屋旅館)

If you want to stay in a comfortable Japanese Inn rather than a hotel, this is a good choice. First opened more than 110 years ago but now occupying a nondescript 50-year-old building, it offers pleasant tatami rooms, some with a sitting area near the window. The hallways, with eaves and slatted wooden doors to each room, are a nice touch. Rooms have their own tubs, but you might want to take advantage of the public baths here. If you order dinner, it

> *Drinking straight from the source at the Sapporo Bier Garten.*

will be served *ryokan*-style in your room by kimono-clad women. To receive the low rates listed below, you must book in advance and mention the Japanese Inn Group. N3 W7, Chuo-ku. ☎ 011/241-2111. www.nakamura-ya.com. 26 units. Doubles from ¥13,650. AE, MC, V. Train: Sapporo Station.

★ Sapporo Bier Garten *MONGOLIAN*

No trip to Sapporo would be complete without sampling the beer that takes its name from the city! The food here is served in the style of Mongolian barbecue (which is generally called Jingisukan—"Ghenghis Khan"—in Japanese); you cook it yourself on a hot skillet at your table. The best deal in the house is the appropriately named King Viking, which for ¥3,670 gives you as much Jingisukan and draft beer as you can consume in 100 minutes. N7 E9, Higashi-ku. ☎ 011/742-1531. www.sapporo-bier-garten.jp. All you can eat (not including alcohol) from ¥2,620. AE, DC, MC, V. Lunch & dinner daily. Bus: Sapporo Biiruen.

Navigating Sapporo

Central Sapporo is easy to cover on foot: Unlike notoriously difficult-to-navigate Tokyo, the streets here are laid out in an easy to understand grid. "N1 W4," for example, the address for the Sapporo Grand Hotel, means it's located in the first block north of Odori and 4 blocks west of West 1st Street. Even better, street signs in Sapporo are in English.

Furano

Famed for its rolling hills covered in lavender fields, Furano is also well known for its local cuisine, including cheese and wine. Located in the geographic center of the island, locals affectionately refer to Furano as Hokkaido's "Belly Button." In fact, every July, residents dress up in belly-revealing costumes and parade through the streets in the Hokkai Heso Matsuri ("Belly Button Festival"). Surrounded by mountains and forests, Furano is the perfect destination for active travelers interested in hiking, skiing, and other outdoor sports. If you aren't into outdoor activities, make sure to time your trip to coincide with flower season (the end of June through the beginning of August) to see the fields at Farm Tomita.

> Early spring on a Furanodake trail.

START From Furano Station, take the train to Kami-Furano Station, and then continue on by bus to Tokachi Onsen. Furano is more than 1,200km (746 miles) north of Tokyo.

❶ ★★ Furanodake. One of Hokkaido's least-developed areas, Furanodake (Mount Furano) is great for scenery and nature watching. Located in beautiful Daisetsuzan National Park and very popular with campers, it can also be tackled as a **day hike.** The trailhead is located about an hour from downtown Furano, but is

well worth the effort it takes to get there. From Furano Station, ride to Kami-Furano Station (14 min.), then board a bus bound for Tokachi Onsen (50 min.). Disembark at the final bus stop. The ascent will take about 3 hours, and the descent 2½, so consider this an all-day activity. For the most up-to-date trail information, stop by the **Furano Biei International Tourism Centre,** located right next to Furano Station (p. 477). They can recommend a variety of outdoor operators who offer guided hikes in the summer and snowshoe tours in the winter.

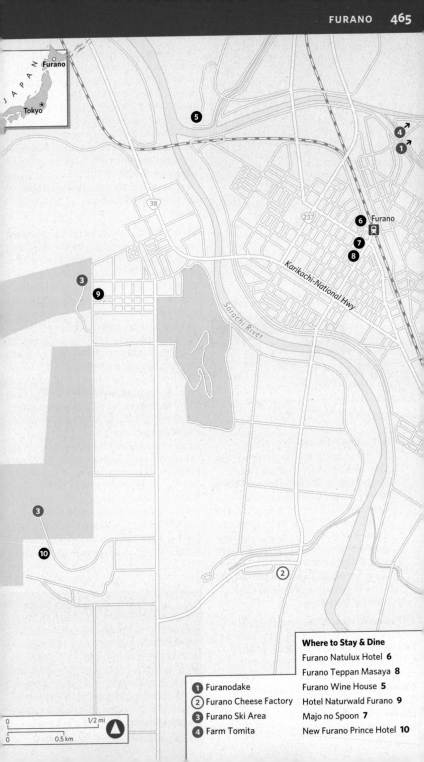

JAPAN

Furano

Tokyo

38

237 Furano

Karikachi-National Hwy

Sorachi River

Where to Stay & Dine

Furano Natulux Hotel **6**

Furano Teppan Masaya **8**

Furano Wine House **5**

Hotel Naturwald Furano **9**

Majo no Spoon **7**

New Furano Prince Hotel **10**

1 Furanodake

2 Furano Cheese Factory

3 Furano Ski Area

4 Farm Tomita

0   1/2 mi
0   0.5 km

> *Ride alongside champions at Furano Ski Area.*

② 🍴 **Furano Cheese Factory.** Although it's located a little ways out of town, just down the street from the New Furano Prince Hotel (p. 467), the **Furano Cheese Factory** is a fun diversion—you can sample fresh cheeses atop a pizza baked in a brick oven in the factory's pizza restaurant, or purchase a variety of local cheeses as souvenirs in the factory's gift shop. Nakagoku. ☎ 0167/23-1156. www. furano-cheese.jp. Cheeses ¥360–¥4,360. No credit cards. Lunch & dinner daily. Train: Furano Station.

❸ **Furano Ski Area.** While the majority of tourists choose to visit Furano in the summer months for flower viewing, hiking, and wine tasting, come winter the city turns into one of Japan's top ski destinations. The **Furano Ski Area** is known throughout Japan for its abundant snowfall—some 8m (26 ft.) of powder every season. With 23 runs geared to all ability levels, it's popular among everyone

from families to pros, and has played host to numerous major events, such as the World Snowboarding Cup, held every February. The ski area is divided into two interlinked areas called Furano Zone and Kitanomine Zone, with lift passes covering access to gondolas, chairlifts, and cable cars in both. The hotels of Furano offer easy access to the area; some even offer regular shuttle buses to the lifts. Nakagoryo. ☎ 0167/22-1111. www.snowfurano. com/resort.htm. Daily late Nov–early May 8:30am–9pm. Adult lift pass: ¥4,200. Train: Furano.

❹ **Farm Tomita.** This is Furano's single most famous spot for lavender viewing. While that might sound less than thrilling, in person the sheer amount of flowers on display is breathtaking. Although the Tomita family began farming this land in 1903, they didn't turn to flower cultivation until the early 1950s, mainly focusing on the production of lavender extracts and essences. The farm has grown into such an attraction that Japan Railways even opens a dedicated train station, called Lavender Farm Station, right next to the fields during the peak tourist season of June through October. In addition to gazing over endless plains of flowers against a backdrop of snow-capped mountain peaks, you can munch on light meals and lavender-flavored ice cream in the farm's cafe. In the winter months, the Tomitas operate a greenhouse so visitors can enjoy the lavender out of season as well. ⏱ 1 hr. Hokusei, Nakafurano-cho, Sorachi-gun. ☎ 0167/39-3939. www.farm-tomita.co.jp/en. Free. Daily June–Aug 8:30am–5:30pm; May & Sept 8:30am–5pm Feb–Apr & Oct–Nov 9am–4:30pm; Dec 9:30am–4:30pm. Train: Lavender Batake-eki Station.

Travel Tip

While Furano has a public bus system, stops and timetables are far more limited than those of urban centers. For those not renting a car, in the warmer months the downtown area is easily explored on foot, and a variety of operators located in front of the station rent bicycles by the day. In colder seasons, hotel shuttle buses and taxis are the easiest ways to get around.

Where to Stay & Dine in Furano

★★ **Furano Natulux Hotel** Surprisingly chic for a countryside hotel, this is one of Furano's newest and certainly hippest accommodations. Although some of the smaller rooms are a little cramped, they are spotless and modern. The hotel's restaurant, which serves up a variety of foods from curries to fondues to elegant set menus dinner sets, is above par as well. Located just a minute's walk from Furano station, the hotel runs free shuttle buses to the ski slopes during the winter season. 1–35 Asahicho. ☎ 0167/22-1777. www.natulux.com. 8 units. Doubles from ¥18,900. AE, DC, MC, V. Train: Furano Station.

Furano Teppan Masaya *TEPPANYAKI*
In the mood for meat? This very reasonably priced and homey little restaurant is your place. For some extra fun, try to grab a seat at the counter so you can watch the chefs cook up your meal on a huge iron griddle that stretches across the room. In addition to solid performers like chicken, steaks, and spareribs, the *okonomiyaki* (savory pancakes) are excellent as well. 11–15 Hinodemachi. ☎ 0167/23-4464. www.furanomasaya.com. Entrees from ¥880. No credit cards. Lunch & dinner Wed–Mon. Train: Furano Station.

Furano Wine House *CONTINENTAL*
Run by the Furano Winery, this upscale restaurant features pizzas, fondues, pastas, and steaks accompanied by (of course!) locally made wine. It's a bit of a hike from the station, so you might want to consider taking a taxi. Shimizuyama. ☎ 0167/23-4155. Entrees from ¥1,000. V. Daily 11am–8pm. Train: Furano Station.

Hotel Naturwald Furano
Although truthfully starting to look a little run down inside, the Naturwald's proximity to the slopes makes it a popular choice for many skiers. Most of the rooms are Western-style twins—as in many Japanese hotels, there aren't any queen- or king-sized beds at all—but there are also a handful of Japanese-style rooms (with shared bathrooms). It's a bit of a hike from the station—consider taking a taxi or city bus. 14–46 Kitanomine-cho. ☎ 0167/

> *The accompaniment of choice to a pizza at the Furano Wine House.*

22-1211. www.naturwald-furano.com. 264 units. Twins from ¥10,500 per person. AE, DC, MC, V. Train: Furano Station.

★★ **Majo no Spoon** *CURRY*
The name means the "witches spoon," and there is a sort of magic to this local favorite's cooking. Only the freshest potatoes and other locally grown vegetables are used to make the curries here. Curry is an old standby of tourist traps throughout Japan, but Majo no Spoon's sense of play and experimentation (as can be seen in menu items like squid-ink cheese curry) carry it head and shoulders above the rest. 12–29 Hinodemachi. ☎ 0167/23-4701. Entrees from ¥850. No credit cards. Lunch & dinner daily (Closed Wed Oct–Apr). Train: Furano Station.

★ **New Furano Prince Hotel**
Described in hotel literature as being "reminiscent of a space station" (a comparison, quite frankly, we don't exactly get), this offers clean if somewhat small rooms surrounded by magnificent views of the Furano countryside. Abundant on-site amenities include a large convenience store, a large garden, and several restaurants. It's well situated for skiers, with regular shuttles to the slopes, and even has an on-site ski school. Nakagoryo. ☎ 0167/22-1111. www.princehotels.com/en/newfurano. 112 units. Doubles from ¥12,000. AE, DC, MC, V. Train: Furano Station.

Akanko Onsen

Akanko Onsen is located within Akan National Park

The area's volcanic mountains, dense forests of subarctic primeval trees, and three caldera lakes are stunning even by Hokkaido standards. Akanko Onsen itself is a tiny hot-spring resort on the edge of Lake Akan, home to some 2,000 residents. It makes a good base for active vacationers and the perfect springboard to explore both Akan National Park and nearby Kushiro Marshland National Park, famous for its red-crested cranes. While hiking trails abound, those less inclined to hoof it can reserve a spot on one of the tour buses that shuttle visitors to the park's natural wonders. Like most *onsen* (spa) towns, there is little in the way of standalone restaurants other than souvenir stands offering lunches on the side. Meals are generally included with your lodging.

> *Leaving Japan without leaving Japan: the sign to Ainu Kotan Village.*

START Take the bus from Kushiro (about 4 hr. from Sapporo by train) to Akanko BC. Akanko Onsen is 900km (559 miles) northeast of Tokyo.

1 ★★ **Ainu Kotan Village** (アイヌコタン). This is actually a street lined with souvenir shops (selling mostly woodcarvings), but it leads to a thatched-roof lodge, where you can see Ainu performing traditional dances and playing bamboo mouth harps. The productions here tend to be less blatantly touristy than those in other areas, so this is highly recommended even if you've already been to other Ainu villages such as Poroto Kotan (p. 442, **3**). Thirty-minute shows are performed five times a day in summer (including evenings), less frequently in winter. 2-6-20 Akanko Onsen, Akan-cho, Kushiro-shi. ☎ 0154/67-2727. www.lake-akan.com/en/ainu/index.html. Performances ¥1,000 adults ¥500 kids. Bus: Akanko BC.

Lake Akan

JAPAN

Akanko

Tokyo

Shotoku-ji
Temple

1 Ainu Kotan Village
2 Poronno
3 Marimo Discovery Cruise
4 Kushiro Marshland National Park

Where to Stay & Dine

Hotel Akankoso **7**
Onsen Minshuku Kiri **6**
Yuku-no-Sato Tsuruga **5**

0   200 yds
0   200 m

Poronno (民芸喫茶ポロンノ). For a different kind of lunch, while in the Ainu Kotan
Village look for a souvenir shop called
Mingei Kissa with a sign reading HAND-
MADE FOLKCRAFT AND AINU TRADITIONAL
FOOD. In the back you'll find two tables, a
counter, and funky decor and music. The
menu lists *rataskepu,* a cold vegetable
dish with beans, corn, and pumpkin;
pochimo, a fried potato cake (a bit hard);
Ainu curry with venison and local vegetables; pumpkin cakes; and drinks such
as *shikerebe* (bark tea). They also serve
teishoku (set meals), such as rice with red
beans and venison soup. Ainu Kotan Village, 2-6-20 Akanko Onsen, Akan-cho,
Kushiro-shi. ☎ 0154/67-2159. Entrees
from ¥1,000. No credit cards. Lunch &
dinner daily. Bus: Akanko BC.

3 ★ kids **Marimo Discovery Cruise** (マリモ展示観
察センター遊覧船). This cruise of Lake Akan run
by Akan Kanko Kisen provides a close-up view
of the mountains, islands, and shoreline, all
stunningly beautiful. But the real attraction
is Lake Akan's extraordinarily rare spherical
green algae, a spongelike ball of duckweed
called *marimo.* Found in only a few places in

> Keep an eye peeled for marimo *on the Lake Akan
cruise.*

> *The inspiration for the logo of Japan Air Lines: Tancho-Tsuru Koen's red-crested crane.*

the world, *marimo* is formed when many separate and stringy pieces of algae at the bottom of the 43m-deep (141-ft.) lake roll around and eventually come together to form a ball. It takes 150 to 200 years for *marimo* to grow to the size of a baseball; some in Lake Akan are as much as 29cm (11 in.) in diameter—meaning they are very old indeed. The cruises last about 90 minutes start to finish, including a stopover at the Marimo Observation Center on the lake's Chuurui Island. 1-5-20 Akanko Onsen, Akancho, Kushiro-shi. ☎ 0154/67-2514.

Winter or Summer?

The Akanko Onsen area is geared toward self-starting, outdoors-focused travelers. Although we prefer visiting during the warmer months for hiking and canoeing, in winter Akanko (Lake Akan) freezes over and becomes a wonderland for winter sports such as cross-country skiing, ice skiing, and ice fishing (gear for all of which is rented by a wide variety of local businesses).

www.akankisen.com. ¥1,850 adults, ¥960 kids. Hourly cruises daily May–Sept 6am–9pm; Sept–Oct 20 6am–3pm; Oct 21–Nov 20 6:30am–3pm Bus: Akanko BC.

❹ ★★ **Kushiro Marshland National Park** (釧路湿原国立公園). Kushiro Shitsugen is Japan's largest marshland. If you don't have a car, the best way to see the marshlands and catch a glimpse of the cranes in their natural habitat is via sightseeing bus. Tours are conducted in Japanese only, but they traverse the marshland and make stops at several observatories and **Tancho-Tsuru Koen** (the red-crested crane reserve). The bus tours last roughly 5 hours, so this is an all-day activity. For the most up-to-date information, contact the Kushiro Tourism Association at ☎ 0154/31-1993 or www.kushiro-kankou.or.jp/english. Bus tours: Akan Bus Company. ☎ 0154/37-2221. ¥2,870 adults, ¥1,330 kids. Buses depart 8:25am and 2pm daily May–Oct. Train: Kushiro Station.

Where to Stay & Dine in Akanko

Dining the Ainu way at the Ainu Kotan Porono restaurant.

otel Akankoso

lthough it lacks the personal touches of
maller accommodations such as *ryokan*, this
a solid and reasonably priced hotel right on
e shores of Lake Akan. In addition to a series
very nice shared indoor and outdoor baths,
oups of two to four can pay extra to rent
private bath as well. Nine of the rooms
ave sunken *irori* hearths, with meals served
-room. 1–5–10 Akanko Onsen, Akancho,
ushiro-shi. ☎ 0154/67-2231. www.akanko.
om. 97 units. Rooms ¥5,000–¥14,000. Bus:
kanko BC.

nsen Minshuku Kiri (温泉民宿桐)

ocated above a souvenir shop on the main
reet (look for a wooden free-standing sign
ith black lettering on white), these tiny,
mple accommodations include Japanese-
yle rooms and a shared cypress hot-spring
ath. It's nobody's idea of luxury, but it's
ean, quiet, and you can't beat the price.
-3–26 Akanko Onsen, Akancho, Kushiro-shi.
0154/67-2755. 7 units. Rooms from ¥3,500

per person. Breakfast ¥500 extra. AE, MC, V.
Bus: Akanko BC.

★★★ Yuku-no-Sato Tsuruga

Cranes are the main motif throughout, but
what makes this hotel a standout are its beautiful and fantasy-provoking hot-spring baths.
One is designed as a village, spread on several
levels and including a cavelike room and an
outdoor bath beautifully landscaped with
stones and pines overlooking the lake. The
rest of the hotel, with natural woods throughout and well-appointed guest rooms, does not
disappoint. Most rooms are Japanese-style,
the best (and most expensive) of which have
lakeside views, large bathrooms (some with
open-air tubs), bar areas for entertaining, and
seating around an indoor hearth. If you call
ahead, they will send a shuttle bus to pick
you up from Kushiro Station. 4–6–10 Akanko
Onsen, Akancho, Kushiro-shi. ☎ 0154/67-2531.
www.tsuruga-g.com. 233 units. Rooms ¥19,950–
¥39,375 per person. Rates include 2 meals. AE,
DC, MC, V. Bus: Akanko BC.

Utoro

Quite possibly the single most remote destination in this book, Utoro is located adjacent to the Shiretoko National Park, a stretch of wilderness so pristine that it was declared a UNESCO World Heritage Site in 2005. A port town, Utoro is an isolated and distinctive sort of place, marked by massive stone formations (such as the 60m/197-ft. behemoth known as Oronko Rock, which sits in its harbor). The shorelines teem with salmon and other fish; the forests that surround the town are home to a huge amount of wildlife. (In fact, hikers are recommended to wear "bear bells" when venturing out onto the trails.) In the warmer months, Utoro is a wonderful destination for nature-watching cruises and hiking. But its main claim to fame is that it is one of the southernmost points in the northern hemisphere where sea ice begins to form. At the height of winter, massive ice floes fill the harbor, accompanied by harbor seals and a variety of other seasonal wildlife such as eagles and the occasional killer whale.

> The only way to see some of Shiretoko National Park's waterfalls is by boat.

START Overnight bus service runs from Sapporo's Chuo Bus Terminal to Utoro Bus Terminal (7 hr.). Train service also runs from Sapporo Station to Abashiri Station on the Okhotsk Line (5½ hr.); transfer at Abashiri to the Semmo Line to Shiretokosha Station (50 min.). The coastal route from Abashiri to Shiretokoshari is incredibly scenic. Shari buses (see below) then run from Shiretokoshari Station to Utoro Bus Termina Utoro is almost 1,500km (932 miles) north of Tokyo.

① ★★★ **Shiretoko Goko (Five Lakes of Shireto ko;** 知床五湖**).** The Five Lakes of Shiretoko National Park are linked by narrow trails that can be traversed in part (for as little as a 15-min. excursion) or in their entirety (which takes roughly 2 hr.). In addition to the hiking trail, a boardwalk offers beautiful views of the surrounding mountains and coastline. The lakes are one of Shiretoko's prime attractions and can get extremely crowded on weekends—if you are looking for a quiet experience, try to arrive as early in the morning as possible. If bears have been sighted in the area, rangers may temporarily close down the trail connecting lakes 3 and 5. ⏱ 2 hr. 531 Azaiwaubetsu, Shari-cho. ☎ 0152/24-2114. www.shiretoko. or.jp. Free entry; parking ¥410. Daily 7:30am-6pm. Bus: Utoro Bus Terminal.

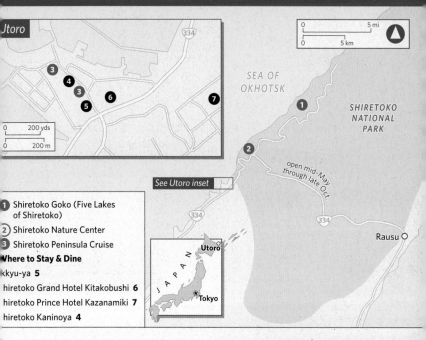

Utoro

🔊 **Shiretoko Nature Center** (知床自然センター). This combination nature center and souvenir shop is located just outside of the Five Lakes area. It features a variety of materials explaining local flora and fauna and an IMAX-style theater with multiple daily screenings of a 20-minute documentary about Shiretoko National Park (¥500 adults, ¥200 junior-high students and younger). The center's coffee shop offers a variety of local snacks, including the ubiquitous, ultramarine-hued, beerlike Okhotsk Blue beverage popular throughout the region. We also recommend the Ezo-deer venison curry plate for a taste of the same animals you'll see wandering around the grounds. A 2km (1.2-mile) loop trail behind the center leads to an overlook for **Furepe Falls,** which cascade straight from a cliff face into the sea. 531 Azaiwaubet-su, Shari-cho. ☎ 0152/24-2114. www. shiretoko.or.jp. Snacks from ¥630. No credit cards. Lunch & dinner daily. Bus: Utoro Bus Terminal.

⭐⭐ **Shiretoko Peninsula Cruise** (知床半島観光船). The best way to see the

> *Interesting tidbits abound in the Shiretoko Nature Center.*

farthest reaches of the peninsula is via boat, which ply the waters from June through early October. While you can't disembark, you will get spectacular views of the coastline and its inhabitants: massive rock formations, water-falls, and (depending on the season) seals,

> *Cruises are the best way to see the far reaches of the Shiretoko Peninsula, which are off limits to foot and vehicle traffic.*

bears, eagles, and other otherwise hard-to-spot animals. There are two types of cruisers: large vessels capable of hauling up to 400 passengers at a time, and smaller boats that offer a more intimate experience. You need to reserve a spot on the boats no later than the day before setting sail; if you are staying in Utoro, your hotel should be able to assist with reservations. **Shiretoko Kankosen** (Shiretoko Tour Boats) operates the larger cruisers. They offer two tours: a 3-hour 45-minute cruise from Utoro Port all the way up to Cape

Shiretoko at the very tip of the peninsula, and a shorter 90-minute cruise to Mount Iouzan, about halfway up the peninsula.

An alternative is **Gojira Iwa Kanko** (Godzilla Rock Tours). Named after a formation in the harbor that supposedly resembles the giant monster (a stretch, if you ask us), the smaller size of this scrappy little company's vessels allows them to approach sights more closely than the cruise liners. They offer a variety of courses, but their *higuma* (brown bear) cruise is our favorite. Even if the weather seems fine, launches can be cancelled due to conditions up along the coast, so it's a good idea to have a backup plan just in case your tour doesn't make it out. ⏱ 4 hr. Shiretoko Kankosen: 107 Utoro Higashi, Shari-cho. ☎ 0152/24-2127. www.ms-aurora.com/shiretoko/en. Shiretoko Cape Line: ¥6,500 adults, ¥3,250 kids elementary school and younger. June–Sept. Mount Iouzan Line: ¥3,100 adults, ¥1,550 elementary students and younger. Apr–Oct. Gojira Iwa Kanko: 51 Utoro Higashi, Shari-Cho. ☎ 0152/24-3060. Cape Shiretoko cruise: ¥8,000 adults, ¥4,000 elementary students and younger. Higuma-watching cruise: ¥5,000 adults, ¥2,500 elementary students and younger. Bus: Utoro Bus Terminal.

Travel Tip

While Utoro has a public bus system, the schedule is far more limited than you might find in larger towns. For this reason, we highly recommend either renting a car or pre-arranging a tour of the sights via chartered tour bus. For example, the tours run by **Shari Bus** (www.sharibus.co.jp), which operate between June 1 and September 30, are 4-hour courses that include stops at the Five Lakes and the Nature Center (see below). The price is ¥4,000 per person and reservations are required.

Where to Stay & Dine in Utoro

★ Ikkyu-ya (一休屋) *SEAFOOD*

onsidered by many visitors to be the finest afood restaurant in town, this tiny establishent serves up some of the freshest sushi and shimi in the city. It also carries a variety of cal delicacies such as smoked venison and ckled *ainu negi*, a wild plant with a garlicky ste. The *donburi* (rice bowls) are excellent, d there's even a nod to non-fish eaters with veral *katsu* (fried pork cutlet) dishes. 13 toro Higashi, Shari-cho. ☎ 0152/24-2557. Set nches from ¥850. No credit cards. Lunch daily. s: Utoro Bus Terminal.

★★ kids Shiretoko Grand Hotel Kitakobushi

ands down the best hotel in Utoro, the Grand es up to its name with spacious rooms, a ooftop public bath with incredible views, and variety of on-site amenities such as a local avel agency and regular presentations about cal attractions. (The lobby even has a refrig-ated display so visitors can see sea ice dur-g the summer.) But perhaps most impres-ve is its daily gourmet dinner buffet, which is ght-years beyond the usual halfhearted hotel re and worth trying even if you aren't staying ere. 172 Utoro Higashi, Shari-cho. ☎ 0152/24-021. www.shiretoko.co.jp/english. 179 units. oubles ¥10,500–¥35,700. AE, DC, MC, V. Bus: toro Bus Terminal.

Shiretoko Prince Hotel Kazanamiki

lthough the rooms are definitely starting to how their age (aim for the New South Wing ather than the South Wing or West Wing), his is still a clean, comfortable, and unfail-ngly friendly place to stay. New South Wing ooms are large with twin beds and tatami lcoves; dinners are served either buffet style a large dining hall or (for an additional fee) your room, multicourse style. It's a bit of a ike from the bus terminal; they offer a regu-ar shuttle bus, but times are irregular and ou should confirm with the hotel. 192 Utoro agawa, Shari-cho. ☎ 0152/24-2104. www. hiretoko-kazanamiki.com/english/index.html. 78 units. Doubles from ¥12,000. AE, DC, MC, . Bus: Utoro Bus Terminal.

> The salmon is not to be missed in Utoro. A donburi *from Shiretoko Kaninoya.*

★ Shiretoko Kaninoya (知床かに乃家) *SUSHI*

The first floor of this charming restaurant is dominated by a conveyor-belt sushi bar; feel free to belly up and order directly from the chef even if it isn't in operation. Their *donburi* (rice bowls) are excellent as well; if you're feeling extravagant, splurge on the excellent Shiretoko Uni Chirashi Don (¥3,500), which features sea urchin, salmon roe, crab, and a variety of local sashimi. 78 Utoro Higashi, Shari-cho. www.kaninoya.jp. ☎ 0152/24-2671. Set meals from ¥1,575. No credit cards. Lunch & dinner daily. Bus: Utoro Bus Terminal.

Hokkaido Fast Facts

> *A streetcar runs through it: Hakodate's European-esque Motomachi district.*

Arriving & Getting Around

BY PLANE The fastest way to reach Hokkaido is via air from Tokyo's Haneda Airport. Flights to **Sapporo**'s New Chitose Airport take about 1½ hours. Although traditional airfare to Sapporo from Tokyo costs ¥30,700, budget airline **Air Do** (☎ 0120/057-333) offers tickets from Tokyo for ¥24,700 or less. For other destinations, Japan Airlines (JAL) flies from Tokyo to **Hakodate** and from Tokyo to **Kushiro**. JAL also flies from Osaka to Sapporo. All airfares go up by about ¥2,000 in peak season, but there are discounts for advance purchase and the off season. Better yet, buy domestic tickets from JAL or ANA in conjunction with international flights to Japan, which must be purchased outside Japan. **BY TRAIN** The only city easily accessible by a 1-day train ride from Tokyo is **Hakodate.** Take the **Tohoku Shinkansen bullet train** from Ueno or Tokyo Station in Tokyo to Hachinohe in Tohoku, followed by the limited express Hakucho train from Hachinohe all the way to Hakodate on Hokkaido. The fastest expresses get to Hakodate in about 6 hours; expect 7 to 8 on others. **BY BUS** In addition to regular bus lines, **sightseeing buses** link the national parks and major attractions. Although they're more expensive than trains and regular buses, and although commentaries are in Japanese only, they offer unparalleled views of the countryside and usually stop at scenic wonders, albeit sometimes only long enough for the obligatory photo. Keep in mind that bus schedules fluctuate with the seasons and can be infrequent; some lines don't run during snowy winter months. **BY CAR** Because distances are long and traffic is rather light, Hokkaido is one of the few places in Japan where driving your own car is actually recommended. However, it's economical only if there are several of you. Rates for a 1-day rental of a compact car in July or August with unlimited mileage and insurance begin at ¥8,920 per day, with each additional day costing ¥7,770; rates run about ¥2,000 cheaper the rest of the year. Car-rental agencies are found throughout Hokkaido, often near train stations as well as at Chitose Airport outside Sapporo and at Kushiro Airport in Kushiro.

TMs

contrast to those abroad, many ATMs only erate during banking hours. ATMs are also ry hard to find outside of major cities, so an accordingly. Most post offices (see below) have ATM facilities, although hours are imited. For 24-hour access, your best bets re the ATMs in **7-Eleven** convenience stores, hich accept Visa, Plus, American Express, B, Union Pay, or Diner's Club International rds for cash withdrawals. (They recently opped accepting MasterCard, Maestro, d Cirrus cards.) **Citibank** and **Shinsei Bank** TMs accept foreign bank cards as well. **SAP- RO Sapporo Central Post Office,** N6 E1 011/748-2380), has a ATMs for interna- nal credit cards (Mon–Fri 7am–11pm, Sat am–9pm, Sun and holidays 9am–7pm).

octors & Hospitals

he general level of healthcare availability in pan is high. For non-emergencies, consult ur hotel for a recommendation as to the osest health or dental clinic.

mergencies

he national emergency numbers are ☎ **110** r police and ☎ **119** for ambulance and fire.

ternet Access

ost business hotels (but few traditional on- n or ryokan) offer Internet access as a perk customers, and Internet cafes are common hough most do not allow customers to hook o their own laptops, requiring them to use e facility's machines instead).

harmacies

rugstores, called yakkyoku (薬局) are ubiq- itous in Japan, but they are not 24-hour perations. Your best bet is to ask your hotel oncierge for the closest location. Note that ou must first visit a doctor in Japan before reign prescriptions can be filled, so it's also est to bring an ample supply of any prescrip- on medication with you.

olice

o reach the police, dial ☎ **110.** You can also op by the nearest koban (police substation) r assistance.

Post Offices

Hokkaido's post offices are generally open from 9am to 5pm, Monday through Friday. SAPPORO **Sapporo Central Post Office,** N6 E1 (☎ 011/ 748-2380), has a 24-hour window for stamps and mail.

Safety

Hokkaido is extremely safe, but take the normal common-sense precautions for personal safety and valuables that you would anywhere else.

Visitor Information

AKANKO **Akanko Onsen's Tourist Association** (☎ 0154/67-2254; daily 9am–6pm) is located just a couple minutes' walk from the Akanko Onsen bus terminal, in the direction of the lake and on the main street through town. FURANO In the winter months, the **Furano Biei International Tourism Centre** (☎ 0167/22-5777; daily 9am–7pm) is located on the ground floor of the Kitanomine gondola terminal of the Furano Ski Area. In the summer months, their website is at www.furano.ne.jp/furabi/english. HAKODATE The **Hakodate Tourist Office** (☎ 0138/23-5440; daily 9am–7pm, to 5pm Nov–Mar) is inside the station to your left as you exit the wicket. It has an excellent English-language map and brochure of Hakodate and can help with accommodations. Check www. hakodate-kankou.com for more information. NOBORIBETSU The **Noboribetsu Tourist Association** (☎ 0143/84-3311; daily 9am–6pm) is on Noboribetsu Onsen's main street, just a minute's walk north of the bus depot (continue up the hill; it will be on your left side with a clock above the door). SAPPORO The excellent **Hokkaido-Sapporo Tourist Information Center** (☎ 011/213-5088; daily 8:30am–8pm), located opposite the west ticket gate of JR Sapporo Station, offers a wealth of information not only on Sapporo but all of Hokkaido. UTORO The **Shiretoko Nature Center** (☎ 0152/ 24-2114; Apr 20–Oct 20 9am– 5:40pm, Oct 21–Apr 19 9am–4pm; p. 473, ❷), located a 20-minute bus or car ride from downtown, serves as the local information center. Some English-language information and advice is available.

Favorite Moments

Okinawa Prefecture, an archipelago of 160 islands between Kyushu and Taiwan, seems like its own country. Maybe that's because once upon a time, it was its own kingdom—the Ryukyu Kingdom—with its own language, cuisine, and culture. Even native Japanese speakers are flummoxed by the accents; the cooking is a mixture of Chinese and Japanese influences; and the distinctive red-tile roofs and *shisa* gargoyles of traditional Okinawan homes are different from those anywhere else in Japan. Even today, well over a century since its incorporation into Japan, Okinawa often feels like a completely different country—making it the perfect escape.

❶ **Getting a taste of tropical royalty at Shuri Castle Park.** This beautiful example of a 14th-century Ryukyu Kingdom temple may be a reconstruction, but that doesn't make it any less impressive. If you're visiting Okinawa Island, this should be one of your first stops. See p. 492, ❷.

❷ **Seeing a natural "house of the holy."** Okinawa Island's most sacred spot—so sacred, in fact, that men were prohibited entry until modern times—the natural shrine of **Seifa Utaki** was the first stop for a newly crowned king in times of old. Even today, its distinctive triangular stone formation feels like a portal to another world. See p. 494, ❸.

❸ **Communing with sea life at Churaumi Aquarium.** Easily the top aquarium in all of Japan, the massive seawater tank here is home to giant whale sharks and other animals you'd normally be hard-pressed to see without scuba gear. See p. 485, ❷.

❹ **Sipping *awamori* in an Okinawan bar.** No trip to Okinawa would be complete without a taste of the islands' favorite alcoholic beverage: *awamori*. While you can find it in establishments all over Okinawa, Naha's Bar Dick serves it up with a literal twist in a variety of cocktails. See p. 495.

❺ **Floating above Kabira Bay.** The gleaming, emerald waters of Kabira Bay are a tropical dream, but strong currents

> *PREVIOUS PAGE Mangroves are a hallmark of the Okinawan ecosystem, particularly on Iriomote Island. THIS PAGE Whale sharks, like this one at Churaumi Aquarium, are huge but harmless vegetarians.*

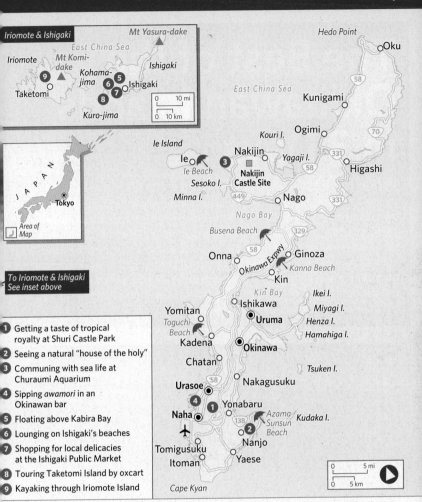

1. Getting a taste of tropical royalty at Shuri Castle Park
2. Seeing a natural "house of the holy"
3. Communing with sea life at Churaumi Aquarium
4. Sipping *awamori* in an Okinawan bar
5. Floating above Kabira Bay
6. Lounging on Ishigaki's beaches
7. Shopping for local delicacies at the Ishigaki Public Market
8. Touring Taketomi Island by oxcart
9. Kayaking through Iriomote Island

...ean you can't swim there. A glass-bottomed ...oat is a fun way to peek beneath the waves. ...ee p. 497, 4.

Lounging on Ishigaki's beaches. On an island ...overed with great beaches, isolated Yonehara ...s one of the best. This is a great place to spend ...few hours—or lay around all day long. See ... 496, 3.

Shopping for local delicacies at the Ish-gaki Public Market. What better way to take ... taste of island life than from the food stalls at ...his public marketplace? It's a treat for all the ...enses—and a great place for souvenirs to boot. ...ee p. 496, 1.

8 Touring Taketomi Island by oxcart. Taketomi Island is like a little time capsule of traditional Okinawan life. We can't think of any better way to see it than on a leisurely water buffalo–drawn cart ride—set to the strains of the tour guide's singing and strumming. See p. 500, 1.

9 Kayaking through Iriomote Island. If you have the time to spare, you absolutely will not regret taking one of these tours deep into one of Japan's most mysterious islands. Iriomote Island's primeval interior is like Jurassic Park, minus the dinosaurs. See p. 501, 2.

The Best of the Okinawan Islands in 3 Days

While the vast majority of travelers to Okinawa content themselves with loafing on the archipelago's numerous beaches—not that there's anything wrong with that!—the main island is filled with attractions such as castles and aquariums that make a multiday visit more than worth the while even if you never even dip a toe in the water. You might be surprised at the distances between some of the attractions though; to maximize your time, renting a car is highly recommended. (That being said, the island's public transportation system is extremely reliable as well.) Your first day will be spent mostly in and around the capital city of Naha.

> *Visitors explore the ancient shrine that is Seifa Utaki.*

START Take the Naha monorail to Omoromachi Station. Okinawa is about 2,000km (1,243 miles) south of Tokyo (3 hr. by air) or 1,600km (994 miles) south of Kyoto.

❶ Naha. Although Okinawa Island is undoubtedly the most developed and crowded of the islands, not to mention dotted with numerous American military bases, its ease of access makes it a popular getaway. Having come all this way, chances are you won't want to stay in urban Naha, the capital of Okinawa Island, but the city and its suburbs are home to a series of cultural attractions that are more than worth a visit.

Mt Yasura-dake

Ishigaki

East China Sea

3 Ishigaki

Kuro-jima

0 ___ 10 mi
0 ___ 10 km

Hedo Point

Oku

58

East China Sea

Kunigami

Ogimi

70

Kouri I.

Nakijin

le Island

le

le Beach

2 **Nakijin Castle Site**

Yagaji I.

331

58

Higashi

Sesoko I.

Motobu

Minna I.

449

Nago

Nago Bay

331

329

Busena Beach

58

Ginoza

Onna

Okinawa Expwy

Kanna Beach

Kin

Yaka Beach

Ishikawa

Kin Bay

Ikei I.

Yomitan

58

Uruma

Miyagi I.

Toguchi Beach

Teruma Beach

Henza I.

Kadena

Hamahiga I.

Okinawa

Chatan

Kitanakagusuku

Tsuken I.

0 ___ 5 mi
0 ___ 5 km

Ginowan

329

Tomari Port

58

Nakagusuku

Urasoe

Naha Port

Nishihara

Naha

Yonaburu

Azama Sunsun Beach

Kudaka I.

1

J A P A N

Tokyo

Nanjo

138

Tomigusuku

Yaese

Itoman

Cape Kyan

Area of Map

To Ishigaki
See inset above

1 Naha
2 Ocean Expo Park (Kaiyohaku Kinen Koen)
3 Ishigaki Island

> At the Okinawa Prefectural Museum: not all masks are meant to scare.

Make the ★★ **Okinawa Prefectural Museum & Art Museum** (p. 492, ❶), two museums under one roof, your first stop in Naha. While the art museum is interesting for its changing exhibits of contemporary art, including works by artists with a connection to Okinawa, the prefectural museum is a must. You'll learn about Okinawa's history, culture, and natural history—and therefore gain a better understanding for what you'll see elsewhere.

Naha's top attraction, ★★★ **Shuri Castle Park** (p. 492, ❷), was first constructed between the 13th and 14th centuries and became the epicenter of the Ryukyu Kingdom for about 500 years, until the establishment of Okinawa Prefecture in 1897. Serving as both a residence for the king and an administrative and religious center, it shows architectural influences from both China and Japan but is uniquely Ryukyuan in style.

If you need to make a pit stop, the quaint restaurant **Ashibiuna,** 2-13 Tounokura Shuri (☎ 098/884-0035), occupies a wooden house with a red-tiled roof—a reconstructed home of a high-ranking official of the Ryukyu Kingdom. Its English lunch menu offers set meals of all the local favorites, including *tebichi,* Okinawa noodles, and *goya champuru.*

For centuries off-limits to males—even the king had to dress in women's clothing to gain entrance—the sacred shrine of ★★ **Seifa Utaki** (p. 494, ❸) is now open to the public. Its numerous altars, arranged around a massive triangular rock formation, are a designated UNESCO World Heritage Site. ⏱ 1 day.

From Naha Bus Terminal, take express bus no. 111 to Nago Bus Terminal (1¾ hr.); transfer to bus no. 65, 66, or 70 (55 min.).

SITE GUIDE PAGE 485

❷ **Ocean Expo Park (Kaiyohaku Kinen Koen;** 海洋博公園**).** This compound of museums, aquariums, and otherwise, contains some of Okinawa Island's best attractions—both for education and for relaxation. If you're planning to spend more than a day on the island, make a point of coming here. For more information, visit http://oki-park.jp/en. See p. 485, ❷.

❸ **Ishigaki Island.** Ishigaki Island is the second largest in what is known as the Yaeyama Islands, a series of nine islands that constitute Japan's southwestern-most landmasses. If you only have 3 days on the Okinawan Islands you should end up here, since this is home to Okinawa's best beaches. But before you hit the sand, start in **Ishigaki City.** This surprisingly urbanized area is home to the ferry dock and a seemingly endless array of touristy shops, bars, and restaurants. The **Ayapani Mall** is a covered shopping arcade home to the **Ishigaki Public Market,** which is a great place to stock up on local foods and souvenirs. Just outside of the Ayapani Mall, **Uechi Jersey Bokujo Soft Cream Outlet** (上地ジャージー牧場ソフトクリーム販売店), 281-2 Okawa (☎ 090/9571-6760), specializes in yogurt and soft-serve ice cream handmade from the milk of Jersey cows raised on a local farm. Although there's only one flavor—vanilla—this is quite possibly the freshest soft-serve cone you'll ever have.

Of course, the main reason to visit Ishigaki is its pristine beaches; off-the-beaten-path **Yonehara Beach** is one of its best. See p. 496.

Travel Tip

Okinawa's climate extends from subtropical to tropical. The rainy season begins in early May and continues through June, while September and October are typhoon season. The prime tourist seasons are spring (Mar–Apr), summer (Jul–Aug), and winter (Nov–Dec). Our favorite time to visit is just after the Golden Week holiday in early May, when crowds have subsided and the rainy season hasn't quite kicked off in earnest.

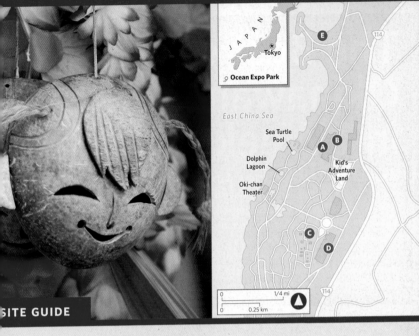

2 Ocean Expo Park

Created for the 1975 International Ocean Expo, this sprawling park is located quite a haul from downtown Naha (closer to the city of Naga). The complex covers some 3km (1¾ miles) along the northwest coast of Okinawa—big enough that shuttle buses (¥200 for 1-day pass) operate between the various facilities. It's divided into the Flowers and Greenery Zone (home to an arboretum), the History and Culture Zone, and the Ocean Zone.

Your first stop should be the **A** ★★★ **Okinawa Churaumi Aquarium (美ら海水族館),** in our opinion Japan's single best aquarium. Highlights include whale sharks and manta rays in the world's second-largest aquarium enclosure, dolphin shows, American manatees, and a close look at the colorful tropical fish that call the surrounding waters home. Located on the fourth floor of the Churaumi Aquarium, the buffet-style **B** **Restaurant Inoh** is a great way to refuel while in the Expo Park. It carries a wide variety of Okinawan dishes, such as *soki* soba (pork spare ribs in noodle soup).

The **C** **Native Okinawan Village and Omoro Arboretum** features more than a dozen sites modeled after a village from the Ryukyu Kingdom Period, including thatch-roofed houses and storehouses, grand homes where the manor lord and priestess lived, and an *utaki* (sacred forest). Follow this with a visit to the **D** **Oceanic Culture Museum,** which displays items relating to oceanic people from Asia through the South Pacific (like masks, pictured above, or the Yap islanders' stone currency).

E kids **Emerald Beach** is a large stretch of public shoreline located within a lagoon. It's covered with gleaming white coral sand, outfitted with jellyfish nets, and has lifeguards on duty, making this the perfect place to splash for those who don't want to worry about accidental encounters with denizens of the sea. ⏱1 day. Aquarium: ☎ 098/48-3740. www.oki-churaumi. jp/en. ¥1,800 adults, ¥1,200 high-school students, ¥600 junior-high and elementary students, free for 6 and under. Daily Mar-Sept 8:30am-8pm; Oct-Feb 8:30-6:30pm. Restaurant: Buffet ¥1,260 adults, ¥750 elementary students, ¥500 kids, ¥1,000 seniors. AE, DC, DISC, MC, V. Daily 9am-5:30pm (Mar-Sept until 7pm). Museum: ☎ 098/48-2741. ¥170 adults, ¥50 kids. Daily May-Aug 8:30am-7pm; Sept-Apr 8:30am-5:30pm. Bus: Nago Bus Terminal.

The Best of the Okinawan Islands in 1 Week

Your first 3 days on the Okinawan Islands should be spent on Okinawa and Ishigaki. If you have a week here, continue on to Taketomi, Iriomote, and Yabu islands. Sitting amid the East China Sea, these are some of the most remote islands in the Japanese archipelago. There is no better place to get a taste for just how different the local culture is from that on the mainland. From quaint villages that seem like they haven't changed in centuries to tropical mangroves that feel like they haven't changed in millennia, this is some of the most interesting travel Japan has to offer.

> A shisa *gargyole stands guard on a traditional red-roofed Taketomi home.*

START From Ishigaki Port, take the jet ferry to Taketomi Island (10 min.). Taketomi is about 2,000km (1,243 miles) south of Tokyo (3 hr. by air).

1 kids **Taketomi Island.** Taketomi is a little time capsule of just 300 full-time residents who have dedicated themselves to preserving Okinawan architecture and culture. Located just 10 minutes by ferry from Ishigaki Island,

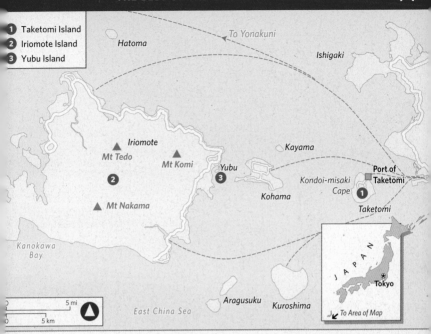

1 Taketomi Island
2 Iriomote Island
3 Yubu Island

To Yonaguni
Hatoma
Ishigaki
Iriomote
Mt Tedo
Mt Komi
Kayama
Yubu
Port of Taketomi
Kondoi-misaki Cape
Kohama
Taketomi
Mt Nakama
Kanokawa Bay
JAPAN
Tokyo
To Area of Map
5 mi
5 km
East China Sea
Aragusuku
Kuroshima

his is a great place to get acquainted with ow Okinawans once lived in times of old. ake time to simply explore the streets of the sland's single village, admiring the distinctive ed clay roofs and *shisa* gargoyles adorning he homes. Plus **Nagomi-no-to Tower,** in the middle of the village, offers great views of the sland and surrounding waters. **Water buffalo art tours** are another fun way to explore the area, especially for smaller kids. Although the our guides only speak Japanese, the sounds of the *sanshin* (Japanese lutes) they play are a wonderful accompaniment to the sights.

But for all the things to do, the real emphasis here is on relaxation. Make sure to bring your swimming trunks and a snorkel—Taketomi's beaches are a little slice of heaven, their waters populated by all sorts of beautiful tropical fish and other animals. Our favorite is secluded **Kaji Beach,** otherwise known as **Star Sand Beach,** which is covered not in sand but the discarded shells from countless tiny crustaceans. Somewhat more crowded **Kondoi Beach,** just down the road, offers pay showers and changing facilities.

At the end of it all, there is absolutely no better way to cool off on a hot Taketomi afternoon than by going to **Parlor Painushima,** 417 Aza-Taketomi (☎ 0980/85-2505). This snack bar–like establishment specializes in *kakigori,* Japanese shaved-ice desserts. (The mango *kakigori,* which features a dollop of vanilla ice cream and a generous helping of mango chunks, is our favorite.) They also serve up an assortment of soft-serve ice creams, cakes, tropical juices, and ice-cream floats.

Meet the *Shisa*

These ubiquitous little monsters, once made as simple home decorations from leftover construction materials, have been elevated to folk art and are a de-facto mascot for the islands of Okinawa. Essentially playing the same role as a gargoyle in Western architecture, they are generally placed in pairs on rooftops or entrances as good-luck charms. Note that one always has its mouth open to scare away evil spirits, while the other has its mouth closed to keep good ones in. You will find *shisa* all over the Okinawan Islands, but Taketomi is an excellent place to see them in what could be called their "native habitat" atop traditional homes.

> *You may not be able to tell, but Hoshizuna no Hama's sand is shaped like stars.*

The vast majority of visitors make Taketomi a day trip from Ishigaki, but if you really want to get away from it all, you can stay at one of the island's handful of tiny hotels and hostels. ⏱ 1 day. See p. 500.

From Ishigaki Port, take the jet ferry to Iriomote Island (45 min.).

2 Iriomote Island. This large, almost primeval tropical island is only accessible via ferry from Ishigaki Island, making it one of the most remote destinations in the pages of this book. If you don't have time for an overnight stay, we highly recommend a guided tour. There are two ports on opposite sides of the island: Uehara (northern) and Ohara (southern). Make sure you pick the right one for your tour or travel plans.

Hirata Tourism Company, 2 Misaki-cho in Ishigaki City (☎ 0980/82-6711; www.hirata-group.co.jp/english), offers several guided tours in English into Iriomote's remote wilderness that involve hiking and boat trips. The Sangara Falls Tour, for example, available year-round, includes a 30-minute kayak ride along a river beside a mangrove forest, followed by a hike over rough terrain to a waterfall, where you have the chance to swim and eat a boxed lunch before heading back. Departing at Ishigaki at 8:40am and returning at 4:10pm, it costs ¥14,500 for adults and ¥1,100 for kids, including the ferry and lunch.

Ox-drawn cart is pretty much the only way to travel to Yubu Island.

Although tours provide a closeup view f Iriomote's wilderness, you might want to tay another day or two to enjoy the island's eaches and other destinations at your own ace. **Hoshizuna no Hama (Star Sand Beach)** ocated north of Uehara Port, is famed for its oral and star-shaped sand. Aim for low tide or the best views, and make sure to keep an ye peeled for venomous sea life (p. 491).

There may be better places to stay on the sland than **Pension Hoshinosuna**, 289-1 Jehara, Taketomi-cho (☎ 0980/85-6448), erched on a bluff overlooking Hoshizuna no Hama, but the restaurant of this pension is a reat place to stop by for a quick bite to eat. he menu is basic but satisfying—*soki* soba, urgers, curry rice, and the like—and the iews of the beach and ocean below can't be eat. ⏱ 1 day. See p. 503.

rom Mihara Village, on the eastern side of riomote Island, cross to Yubu Island by oxcart.

❸ **Yubu Island.** Surrounded by water so shallow it's accessible exclusively by water buffalo carts, this tiny island is home to a botanical garden and small zoo of domestic animals. See p. 502, ❸.

Gastronomic Okinawa

Okinawan cuisine is big on pork, including *tebichi* (pigs' feet, simmered for hours in soy sauce and sake to make them soft and glutinous) and *rafute* (pork belly simmered in fish broth), as well as *awamori* liquor (a wonderfully sharp-tasting spirit that is like a low-proof vodka). Other favorites include Okinawa soba noodles, made with white flour instead of the mainland's usual buckwheat; and dishes made with *goya* (bitter melon), like stir-fried *goya champuru* containing tofu, pork, egg, and other ingredients. *Champuru* means "to mix together" in Okinawan dialect, with the ultimate example being taco rice, an adaptation of Mexican tacos (introduced by Americans stationed here) served with rice instead of tortillas.

Okinawa Under the Sea

Even old hands agree: Okinawa is one of the best diving spots in the world, with warm surface temperatures, crystal-clear waters, and coral reefs teeming with marine life. Typhoon season from September to November is dicey, weather-wise, but Okinawa offers diving year-round (though the Pacific waters require wet suits). Plan dive trips well in advance; if you don't speak Japanese or aren't familiar with Japanese-style diving, we highly recommend using one of the dive operators listed below.

> Getting to know some of Okinawa's residents on a dive.

START Take the train to Naha Airport Station. Okinawa is about 2,000km (1,243 miles) south of Tokyo (3 hr. by air).

1 Okinawa Island. While there are a variety of dive sites around Okinawa Island, the majority are clustered around the Kerama Islands, a small archipelago roughly 30km (19 miles) southwest of the city of Naha. Several dive operations service this area; they're located in Chatan, just outside of Kadena Air Base.

Dive Okinawa, which is run by a pair of American divers, has seven shops, including one in Naha. This full-service operation offers dives and training courses of all levels. They can assist with local accommodations as well.

Reef Encounters International, run by a U.S. military veteran, caters to both Japanese and English speakers. This full-service dive operation offers dive training of all levels, from basic certification up through technical diving, and can arrange dive tours of other islands as well, including Ishigaki and Iriomote. They can assist with local accommodations as well. Dive Okinawa: 2-3-13 Minatomachi. ☎ 0120/10-2743. Snorkeling trips from ¥7,350. Reef Encounters: 1–273 Miyagi. ☎ 098/936-8539. www.reefencounters. org. Beach diving or snorkeling from ¥9,800.

2 Ishigaki Island. Ishigaki's main claim to fame is the Ishizaki "manta scramble," an area just off the coast of Kabira Bay that is famed for its high number of manta rays. These massive—3 to 4m (10–12 ft.) wide—animals, which filter-feed plankton out of the water, are incredibly graceful swimmers.

Umicoza Diving School mainly services Japanese divers, but (as of late 2010) have Canadian staff who can work with English, French, and Spanish speakers. This full-service shop arranges trips to the manta scramble and other sites for the novice and expert alike. 827-15 Kabira, Ishigaki. ☎ 0980/88-2434. www. umicoza.com/english. Two-tank boat dives from ¥12,600 (includes lunch).

3 Iriomote Island. This tiny island has virgin coral in the south, and all the sealife that comes along with it. Unfortunately, dive operators based on the island don't speak English, so use one of the operators above to charter a dive for you.

1. Okinawa Island
2. Ishigaki Island
3. Iriomote Island

Dangerous Natives

Okinawa's undersea inhabitants are its major attraction for snorkelers and divers alike, but be aware that several are actually quite dangerous. Regardless of what water activity you're pursuing, the safest bet is to look and never touch. The following can be found in waters both deep and shallow.

Box Jellyfish

These translucent jellyfish tend to have a somewhat squared bell in comparison to other jellyfish. Their sting is incredibly painful and can be fatal if an allergic reaction is triggered. *Treatment:* Apply vinegar, remove tentacles (use towel or gloves), and contact emergency services.

Blue-Ringed Octopus

These tiny, palm-sized octopi with a pretty pattern of bright blue circles look like something out of a Pokemon cartoon, but they possess an incredibly powerful toxin. *Treatment:* Apply pressure and contact emergency services immediately.

Sea Krait

Sea snakes with a distinctive black-and-white pattern. Although their venom is, drop for drop, more toxic than that of a cobra, they are extremely docile and do not bite unless provoked. *Treatment:* In the very unlikely event of a bite, contact emergency services immediately.

Lionfish

These beautiful fish known for their distinctive fins and striped pattern are often kept in aquariums. Their back spines, which are used for defense, end in sharpened quills that can deliver a powerful sting. *Treatment:* Soak affected area in hot water, and contact a doctor immediately.

Fire Coral

Generally mustard-yellow in color, this common coral is actually a relative of jellyfish and stings if touched or even brushed against. *Treatment:* Apply vinegar (or, in a pinch, urine) and consult a doctor, as the sting can break out in a secondary rash.

Okinawa Island

Okinawa's capital, Naha, is the perfect stepping stone to the island's numerous cultural sites. But this is also a subtropical paradise, so opportunities for leisure abound: shopping and dining in downtown Naha, sunning and swimming on the island's many white sandy beaches, and snorkeling and scuba diving among the island's surrounding coral reefs. While rental cars are the easiest way to get around, Naha also has an excellent public transportation system. The Yui Rail monorail covers most of the attractions downtown, and bus service extends to the farthest reaches of the island.

> *The sellers at Makishi Public Market are experts on local ingredients and cuisine.*

START Take the Naha monorail to Omoromachi Station. Okinawa is about 2,000km (1,243 miles) south of Tokyo (3 hr. by air) or 1,600km (994 miles) south of Kyoto.

① ★★ kids **Okinawa Prefectural Museum & Art Museum.** Here you'll learn about the formation of the Ryukyu archipelago; the rise and fall of the mighty Ryukyu Kingdom with its extensive trade routes to China, Japan, and Southeast Asia; the Battle of Okinawa and subsequent U.S. occupation; and Okinawan folklore, crafts, and culture. A discovery room for children is equipped with traditional toys, clothing, musical instruments, and more. Be sure to ask for the free audio guides to both museums. ⏱ 1 hr. 3-1-1 Omoromachi, Naha. ☎ 098/941-8200. www.museums.pref. okinawa.jp. Prefectural Museum: ¥400 adults,

¥250 college and high-school students, ¥150 kids. Art Museum: ¥300 adults, ¥200 college and high-school students, ¥100 kids (special exhibits cost more). Daily 9am–6pm (Fri–Sat until 8pm). Monorail: Omoromachi Station.

② ★★★ **Shuri Castle Park** (首里城). This castle served as both a residence for the king and an administrative and religious center. It shows architectural influences from both China and Japan but is uniquely Ryukyuan in style. Unfortunately, the original structure was destroyed in the Battle of Okinawa, but as a reflection of the site's importance, this partial re-creation was built. Lots of information and pamphlets in English explain the significance of what you're seeing. Absolutely do not miss one of the 40-minute traditional court dances (performed on Wed, Fri–Sun, and holidays

Southern Okinawa

Tomari Port
Naha Port
Nahakuko
Ashimine
Naha
Furujima
Shuri
Nishihara
Yonabaru
Haebaru
Onoyamakoen
Nanjo
Tomigusuku
Yaese
Itoman
Tomigusuku Rd
Nashiro Bypass
Cape Kyan
Azama Sunsun Beach

0 — 2 mi
0 — 2 km

Monorail
(not all stations mapped)

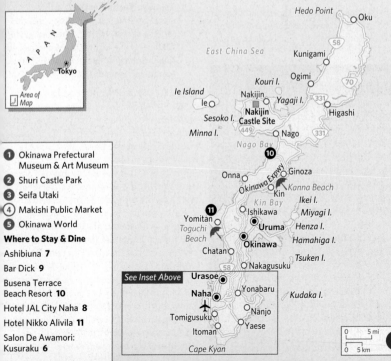

JAPAN
Tokyo
Area of Map

Hedo Point
Oku
East China Sea
Kunigami
Ogimi
Kouri I.
Ie Island
Ie
Nakijin
Yagaji I.
Nakijin Castle Site
Higashi
Sesoko I.
Minna I.
Nago
Nago Bay
Onna
Ginoza
Okinawa Expwy
Kin
Kanna Beach
Kin Bay
Ikei I.
Ishikawa
Miyagi I.
Yomitan
Toguchi Beach
Uruma
Henza I.
Chatan
Okinawa
Hamahiga I.
Tsuken I.
Nakagusuku
See Inset Above
Urasoe
Naha
Yonabaru
Kudaka I.
Tomigusuku
Nanjo
Itoman
Yaese
Cape Kyan

0 — 5 mi
0 — 5 km

1 Okinawa Prefectural Museum & Art Museum

2 Shuri Castle Park

3 Seifa Utaki

4 Makishi Public Market

5 Okinawa World

Where to Stay & Dine

Ashibiuna **7**

Bar Dick **9**

Busena Terrace Beach Resort **10**

Hotel JAL City Naha **8**

Hotel Nikko Alivila **11**

Salon De Awamori: Kusuraku **6**

> *Walk the line between stalactite and stalagmite at Gyokusendo Cave.*

at 11am, 2pm, and 4pm). ⏱ 1 hr. 1–2 Kinjocho, Shuri, Naha. ☎ 098/886-2020. http://oki-park. jp/shurijo-park/english. ¥800 adults, ¥600 high-school students, ¥300 kids. Daily July–Sept 8:30am–8:30pm; Apr–June and Oct–Nov 8:30am–7:30pm; Dec–Mar 8:30am–6:30pm. Monorail: Shurijo Station (15-min. walk). Bus: 8 to Shurijo-mae.

❸ ★ Seifa Utaki (斎場御嶽). The area around the UNESCO World Heritage Shinto shrine of Seifa Utaki today consists mainly of caves and outcroppings—the original buildings were all destroyed. But the natural stone altars here, arranged around a massive triangular rock formation, are nonetheless striking. For centuries they were strictly off-limits to men, but today anyone can enter—disguise not necessary. The easiest way to visit Seifa Utaki is by car, but buses run there as well (roughly 60 min.) Seifa Utaki is also within striking distance of several public beaches, such as **Azama Sansan Beach,** that are far less crowded than those closer to downtown. ⏱ 1 hr. 254 Sayahabaru, Aza Kudeken, Chinen Village. ☎ 098/ 948-1149. ¥200 adults, ¥100 kids. Daily 9am–6pm. Bus: 38 from Naha Bus Terminal to Seifu Utaki Iriguchi. For Azama Sansan Beach, disembark at the Azama Sansan Beach stop.

Trouble in Paradise

Okinawa Island was annexed by Japan in 1868 and used as a virtual "human shield" to protect the central islands of Japan during World War II. Today nearly 20% of the island is covered with American military bases. Many protests have been lodged against the U.S. presence: In 2010, protests erupted again over Marine Corps Air Station Futenma's proximity to an elementary school; months of extensive negotiations resulted in an extremely unpopular decision to relocate it to another part of the island. (Residents had wanted it off the island completely.) Okinawans are good at separating people from politics, so if you're American, you don't have to worry about suffering a negative reception, but you should be aware that relations between the U.S. and Okinawans can be strained at times.

④ 🍴 ★ Makishi Public Market (牧志公設市場). Located just a few minutes' walk south of Kokusai Dori via the covered Heiwa Dori shopping arcade, the Makishi Market features food items unique to Okinawa, including pigs' face, feet, and stomach! Another 7-minute walk farther south on Heiwa Dori will bring you to **Tsuboya Yachimun Dori,** with its 20-some ceramic-art workshops and galleries—definitely worth the stroll. 2-10-1 Matsuo, Naha. Daily 10am–9pm (closed fourth Sunday of every month and other Sundays irregularly). Monorail: Makishi.

❺ ★★ kids Okinawa World (おきなわワールド 文化王国・玉泉洞). Okinawa's largest theme park promotes the region's history, culture, and natural sciences. The variety of attractions include **Gyokusendo Cave,** which you can walk through in about 30 minutes along an 890m (2,920 ft.) walkway suspended above water and filled with impressive stalagmite and stalactite formations. There's also a museum devoted to the *habu*, Okinawa's indigenous poisonous snake; an orchard of 450 tropical fruit trees; an outdoor plaza for performances of the local Eisa dance; and workshops for potters, glassblowers, weavers, and other artisans housed in restored century-old Okinawan homes. ⏱ 2 hr. 1336 Maekawa, Tamagusuku, Nanjo. ☎ 098/949-7421. Pass for all attractions ¥1,600 adults, ¥600 kids. Daily Apr–Oct 9am–6:30pm; Nov–Mar 9am–6pm. Bus: 54 or 83 to Gyokusendo-mae.

Where to Stay & Dine on Okinawa Island

★★★ **Ashibiuna** (あしびうなぁ) NAHA OKINAWAN
you're feeling up to the challenge of navi-
ating without English menus, this beautiful
restaurant is an amazing introduction to
kinawan dishes. Appetizers such as *mozuku*
(vinegared seaweed), *shima rakkyo* (pickled
wild onions), and *tofuyo* (pungent fermented
ofu) are great, as are the hot pots: *buta shabu-
habu* (pork), *sakana chiri nabe* (fish), and *tori-
abe* (chicken). 2-13 Shurito-no-kuracho, Naha.
☎ 098/884-0035. www.ryoji-family.co.jp/
shibiuna/una_top_page.html. Hot pots from
¥3,000 per person. AE, DC, MC, V. Lunch & diner daily. Monorail: Shuri.

★★ **Bar Dick** (バーディック) NAHA PUB This re-
ned, low-key bar features first-class bartend-
rs and a great selection of spirits from around
he world, but it's best known for pioneering
he use of *awamori* in cocktails. A classy way
to end an evening in Naha. 1-1-4 Makishi,
Naha. ☎ 098/861-8283. Small plates ¥800. AE,
DC, MC, V. Dinner & late night daily. Monorail:
Miebashi.

★★ kids **Busena Terrace Beach Resort** (ザ・ブセ
ナテラス) NAGO Located on the northern tip of
Okinawa Island, this resort has an elegant yet
tropical atmosphere. Busena Beach and Busena Marine Park are just a short walk or free
shuttle ride away. The resort offers a range of
activities, from a kids' club to sunset cruising
and fishing, along with rentals for sea kayaks,
and windsurfing. The restaurants here take
advantage of the beautiful views, making this a
good choice for a romantic retreat. 1808 Kise,
Nago City. ☎ 098/51-1333. www.terrace.co.jp.
410 units. Doubles from ¥42,735. AE, DC, MC,
V. Shuttle Bus: Naha Airport Limousine (☎ 098/
869-3301) from Naha Airport.

Hotel JAL City Naha (ホテル シティ那覇) NAHA
Honestly, it seems a shame to come all this
way just to spend the night in the middle of
downtown Naha, but this is a good choice if
you're in transit to another island or prefer this
hotel's location right on Kokusai Dori. Rooms
are small but stylish, with good views out over

> *A sumptuous spread at Ashibiuna restaurant.*

the city from the higher floors. 1-3-70 Makishi,
Naha. ☎ 098/866-2580. www.naha.jalcity.co.jp.
304 units. Doubles from ¥18,480. AE, DC, MC,
V. Monorail: Makishi.

★★ **Hotel Nikko Alivila** (ホテル日航アリビラ) NAGO
This large resort hotel with a vaguely Spanish-
colonial design theme does a bustling business in beachside weddings. The isolated
location makes it ideal for those who want a
little peace and quiet, but those looking for
bustling nightlife would probably do better
elsewhere. The recently renovated rooms
are spacious and clean. 600 Gima, Yomitan
Village, Nakagami District. ☎ 098/982-9111.
www.alivila.co.jp/en. 396 units. Doubles from
¥37,800 per person. AE, DC, MC, V. Shuttle
Bus: Naha Airport Limousine (☎ 098/869-3301)
from Naha Airport.

★ **Salon De Awamori: Kusuraku** (古酒楽) NAHA
PUB Although more of a bar than a restaurant
per se, this is a favorite hangout of locals that
stocks more than 200 types of local *awamori*
liquor. The food selection tends toward light
meals and snacks, but you can't beat the
beautiful fifth-floor open-deck view of the city.
2-4-35 Mekaru, Naha. Awamori from ¥600,
small plates from ¥800. AE, DC, MC, V. Dinner &
late night Mon–Sat. Monorail: Furujima.

Ishigaki Island

The Yaeyama archipelago, closer to Taiwan than to Okinawa Island, is a chain of 19 islands, most of them small. Ishigaki Island, with 80% of the Yaeyama Islands' population, serves as the area's gateway and administrative center. It is an excellent stepping-stone to more remote, off-the-beaten-path locales.

> *Beautiful Yaeyama palms dot the Yonehara coastline.*

START From Ishigaki Airport, take a taxi downtown (to the ferry terminal area). Ishigaki is about 2,000km (1,243 miles) south of Tokyo (3 hr. by plane).

1 Ayapani Mall & Ishigaki Public Market (あやぱにモール). This pair of covered shopping arcades, located just a few minutes' walk from the port, are fun places to browse for local foods and knickknacks. It's also home to the Ishigaki Public Market, whose third floor is a "dance market" in which locals perform a variety of island dances for customers daily (except Fri) at 5:30pm; admission to see the dances is ¥1,000 per person. ⏱ 1 hr. 208 Okawa. ☎ 0980/84-3477. Daily 8am–9pm; closed 1st and 4th Monday of every month. Bus: Azuma Bus Terminal.

2 kids Yaeyama Culture Park (石垣やいま村). This low-key but surprisingly fun outdoor museum shines a spotlight on native architecture and culture, with regular re-enactments and demonstrations of traditional arts and crafts. There is also a nice mangrove area, allowing visitors to see crabs, mudskippers, and other small animals in their natural habitat. Somewhat inexplicably, as they aren't a native species, there's also a squirrel monkey enclosure. The on-site restaurant is quite good as well, serving up a variety of Okinawan soba dishes. ⏱ 1 hr. 967-1 Moto-nagura. ☎ 0980/82-8798. www.minzokuen.com. ¥840 adults, ¥420 kids. Daily 9am–5pm. Bus: Meizo Anbaru.

3 kids Yonehara Beach (米原ビーチ). Ishigaki Island's main claims to fame are its pristine beaches and emerald seas. Yonehara is one

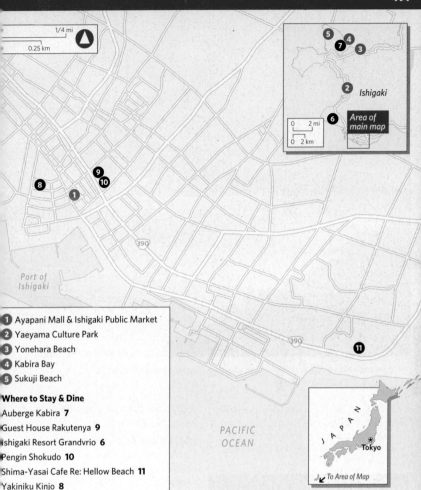

1 Ayapani Mall & Ishigaki Public Market

2 Yaeyama Culture Park

3 Yonehara Beach

4 Kabira Bay

5 Sukuji Beach

Where to Stay & Dine

Auberge Kabira **7**

Guest House Rakutenya **9**

Ishigaki Resort Grandvrio **6**

Pengin Shokudo **10**

Shima-Yasai Cafe Re: Hellow Beach **11**

Yakiniku Kinjo **8**

f our favorite spots for surf 'n' sun. Just off
oute 97, it's located on the exact opposite
de of the island from Ishigaki port. This
ee, large beach is popular with families. It
so features a grove of Yaeyama Palm Trees,
hich are found only on these islands. Yo-
ehara can fill up in the peak season, but it's
n absolutely beautiful stretch of ocean with
reef just offshore, making it popular with
wimmers and snorkelers. It also features a
ay) camping area with toilet and shower
cilities. Don't forget to obey posted signs,
articularly those describing daily conditions,
s currents can be strong at times. **Bus:** Yone-
ara Palm Grove.

4 kids **Kabira Bay** (川平湾). Though it's a favorite sightseeing and scuba-diving spot, much
of the shoreline of Kabira Bay is actually off-
limits for swimming for safety and economic
reasons—it has strong currents, and also happens to be one of Japan's two main cultivation

Island Temps

The Yaeyama island chain has a tropical rainforest climate that is significantly
warmer and wetter than subtropical Okinawa Island. Even at the height of winter in
January and February, temperatures rarely
drop below 70°F (2°C).

> *The emerald waters of Kabira Bay are one of Ishigaki's prime pearl-cultivating areas.*

areas for black pearls. In addition to lounging on the beach, glass-bottom boat tours are a fun (if touristy) way to see what's beneath those emerald blue waters. 934 Aza-Kabira.

Spirit of the Islands

Something like Okinawa's version of bourbon, *awamori* is a transparent liquor made the traditional way—water, Thai rice, and black *koji*-yeast cultures, hand-mixed and fermented in large open vats. Available throughout Okinawa, *awamori* and *kusu* (a stronger, aged version) are the islanders' alcoholic drink of choice, straight up or on the rocks. While you can find it anywhere in Okinawa, Ishigaki Island is a particularly fortuitous place to try *awamori*, as two of our favorite distilleries, Yaesen and Seifuku, are located here. **Seifuku**, 149-3 Arakawa (☎ 0980/82-3166; free; Mon-Sat 9am–6pm), even has a little museum showing how the stuff is made.

☎ 0980/88-2335. Daily 9am–5pm. ¥1,000 adults. Bus: Kabira.

⑤ kids **Sukuji Beach** (底地ビーチ)**.** The seclude and free Sukuji Beach is one of our favorite beaches on the island, thanks to its long, sandy shoreline. Located opposite Kabira Bay it is extremely shallow, with lots of shade tree and even a jellyfish net during jellyfish seasor From Route 207, follow signs for Club Med and then the Ishigaki Seaside Hotel. Bus: Seamen's Club.

Getting Around

We highly recommend renting a car to get around on Ishigaki Island, particularly if you aren't staying downtown. If you do choose to use buses instead, make sure to purchase a 5-day Michikusa Free Pass (¥2,000) at the Azuma Bus Terminal near the port. It covers all island bus lines and pays for itself with a single ride as far as Kabira.

Where to Stay & Dine on Ishigaki Island

Auberge Kabira (オーベルジュ川平)
Although the rooms here are tiny and lack balconies, they're clean and quiet, and you absolutely cannot beat the views of Kabira Bay from the rooftop observation deck. Auberge is near several beaches, and offers free bike rentals. The French-fusion restaurant is worth a visit even if you aren't staying here. Local bus and taxi service can be irregular, so this is better suited for those renting cars. 934–4 Kabira. ☎ 0980/88-2229. www.nikikabira.com. units. Doubles from ¥23,100. AE, DC, MC, V. Bus: Kabira Bus Terminal (on the Kabira Resort bus line from the Ishigaki Bus Terminal).

Guest House Rakutenya (民宿楽天屋)
This homey *minshuku* (Japanese-style farmhouse B&B) is located just a 6-minute walk from the Outer Islands Ferry Terminal. It occupies two buildings, one of which is a rare, two-story wooden dwelling and the other a typical Okinawan home with a red-tile roof. Both are filled with quirky collectibles and antiques. Two of the rooms have twin beds, while the rest are tatami rooms (covered by tatami mats on the floor) with futons. 291 Okawa. ☎ 0980/83-8713. www3.og.or.jp/~erm8p3gi/english/english.html. 10 units. Rooms from ¥3,000 per person; ¥500 extra per person in peak season. No credit cards. Bus: Ishigaki Bus Terminal.

Ishigaki Resort Grandvrio (石垣リゾートグランヴィオホテル) This stylish resort hotel has spacious Western-style rooms, stunning views of the ocean, and luxury facilities. In addition to three on-site restaurants (a steakhouse, a traditional Okinawan eatery, and a buffet-style cafeteria), there are indoor and outdoor pools, an *onsen*-style hot-spring bath, and a day spa. 2481–1 Tonakura Arakawa. ☎ 0980/88-0030. www.route-inn.co.jp/gv/ishigaki/index.html. 200 units. Doubles from ¥29,400–¥50,400. AE, DC, MC, V. Bus: Grandvrio.

kids Pengin Shokudo (辺銀食堂) *NOODLES*
This spot is well known among locals and visitors alike for its fun approach to noodle dishes.

> *Yakiniku Kinjo's Ishigaki beef is some of the island's best.*

The rainbow-colored *shima gyoza* dumplings are a must-try, and their "*jya-jya*" soba with *ra-yu* (chili-infused sesame oil topping) is to die for. 199–1 Okawa. ☎ 0980/82-8777. Noodles from ¥780. No credit cards. Lunch & dinner Mon–Sat. Bus: Ishigaki Bus Terminal.

★★ **Shima-Yasai Cafe Re: Hellow Beach** (島野菜 カフェ リハロウ ビーチ) *OKINAWAN FUSION*
This bright, airy little cafe with an odd name serves up dishes made from local ingredients alongside great views of the bay. Okinawan favorites such as *chanpuru* (made with Spam and tofu) and pork spareribs are here, as are localized versions of foreign foods, such as Hawaiian *loco moco*. 192-2 Maezato. ☎ 0980/87-0865. www.rehellow.com. Entrees from ¥780. No credit cards. Lunch & dinner Wed–Mon. Bus: Ishigaki Bus Terminal.

★★ **kids Yakiniku Kinjo** (焼肉金城) *STEAKHOUSE*
This homey little local chain restaurant specializes in Ishigaki beef sourced from the owner's personal ranch. It's served raw, either as steaks or in bite-sized chunks, that you grill yourself over tabletop braziers, Korean barbeque-style. The first day of every month they offer half-price set dinners. 11–1 Misakicho. ☎ 0980/83-7000. Steaks from ¥850. MC, V. Lunch & dinner daily. Bus: Ishigaki Bus Terminal.

Taketomi & Iriomote Islands

Accessible exclusively via high-speed jet-ferry from Ishigaki Island, these are two of the most remote locales in this book. Taketomi is a living museum of Okinawan life and culture; Iriomote is a sparsely inhabited natural getaway covered in primeval forests and mangroves.

> Oxcart drivers typically serenade riders with local songs on the way to Yubu Island.

START Take the ferry from Ishigaki's terminal to Taketomi Island. Taketomi is about 2,000km (1,243 miles) south of Tokyo.

1 Taketomi Island. While most people choose to visit Taketomi as a day trip, it can be fun to stay in one of the island's several homey little inns as well. During the daylight hours, the main form of recreation is exploring the streets of Taketomi's Ryukyu village, either by foot, by rental cycle, or via a **water buffalo cart tour** (水牛車観光). These 30-minute loops are accompanied by a guide who both explains

the sights and strums Okinawan songs on his *sanshin*—though in Japanese.

When you're done with the oxcart tour, stop by **Nagomi-no-to Tower** (なごみの塔) for excellent views of the village and surrounding waters; from its perch, you can see that the island is a completely flat oval amidst emeral seas.

But the real attraction is the beaches, whic feature reefs far less disturbed than those of Okinawa Island or even Ishigaki. **Kaji Beach** (カイジ浜) is our favorite, but **Kondoi Beach's** (コンドイビーチ) changing facilities are a nice

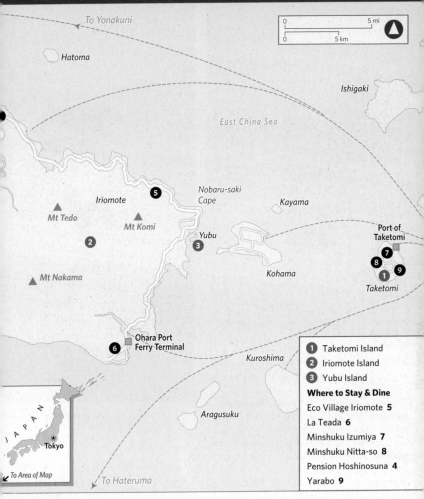

To Yonakuni

Hatoma

Ishigaki

East China Sea

Iriomote

Mt Tedo

Mt Komi

Nobaru-saki
Cape

Kayama

Yubu

Port of
Taketomi

Mt Nakama

Kohama

Taketomi

Ohara Port
Ferry Terminal

Kuroshima

JAPAN

Tokyo

↙ To Area of Map

To Hateruma

Aragusuku

1. Taketomi Island
2. Iriomote Island
3. Yubu Island

Where to Stay & Dine

Eco Village Iriomote 5
La Teada 6
Minshuku Izumiya 7
Minshuku Nitta-so 8
Pension Hoshinosuna 4
Yarabo 9

us, particularly for day-trippers. The best
ay to get around the island is via rental
cles, which are available on the main street
ading in from the port. The rental shops
e clustered together; feel free to rent from
aichever you like. **Nitta Kanko** (which also
ns the water buffalo tours) rents cycles and
ers a free bus service from the port. Nitta
anko: ◷ 30 min. 97 Aza-Taketomi, Taketomi-
o. ☎ 0980/85-2103. www.ishigaki.com/nit-
/index.htm. ¥1,200 adults, ¥600 elementary
udents and younger. Daily 8:30am–5:30pm.
rt: Taketomi.

ke the ferry to Ishigaki Ferry Terminal.
itch to the jetfoil bound for Iriomote Island.

2 Iriomote Island. Iriomote is the largest and
most famous of Yaeyama's islands, a rather
mysterious sort of place sometimes called the
"Galapagos of Okinawa" for its unique animal life. (It isn't the farthest of the Yaeyama
islands, but it is the best for communing with
nature.) Covered with dense subtropical forests and edged with mangroves, Iriomote is
geared towards active visitors who explore by
kayak and on foot. There are two main ways to
enjoy the island: either with a guided tour that
can be done as a day trip, or by renting a car
and navigating the sights yourself, for which
at least one overnight stay is recommended.
There are two ports on opposite sides of the

> *Iriomote's Hoshizuna no Hama comes alive at low tide.*

island: Uehara (northern) and Ohara (southern). Make sure you pick the right one for your travel plans.

Iriomote's best-known beach, **Hoshizuna no Hama (Star Sand Beach; 星砂の浜),** is named for the starlike sand formed from the shells of innumerable tiny crustaceans. **Pension Hoshinosuna,** a pension-restaurant on the beach (p. 503), offers cold showers and rents snorkeling equipment for ¥1,050 for 3 hours, plus a ¥1,000 deposit.

The only way to reach the interior of Iriomote Island is by boat, and the only way to get on a boat is via an **Urauchi or Nakama River guided kayak tour.** Generally running 4 to 5 hours and including hiking as well as kayaking, this is an all-day activity. These trips are easily doable even for novice kayakers, but they do require a certain amount of physical effort (not to mention willingness to get wet). But the rewards are tropical waterfalls and other sights you simply can't see from the coastal tours—or anywhere else in Japan, for that matter. The easiest way to arrange a kayak tour is through your hotel, which will also assist with arrangements for getting you to the

> *The sun always seems to be out on Iriomote Islan*

launch. One of the few services that offers English tour information is **Mansaku.** Mansaku: ⏱ 5 hr. ☎ 0980/85-6222. www.cosmos.ne.jp/mansaku/index-m.html. Day tours from ¥10,500 per person (includes lunch). Port: Uehara (call for pickup).

3 kids **Yubu Island** (由布島). This sliver of land off the coast of Iriomote Island is separated water so shallow it can be walked, but most choose to use the water buffalo cart service instead. The island itself has been converted into a large **botanical garden** and is home to an impressive array of tropical flora. A variet of native and imported animals are on displa as well. Botanical Garden: ⏱ 2 hr. 689 Aza-Komi, Taketomi-cho. ☎ 0980/85-5470. ¥1,30 adults, ¥650 elementary students and younge Daily 9:15am–4:15pm. Port: Ohara.

Where to Stay & Dine on Taketomi & Iriomote

Pension Hoshinosuna overlooks Star Sand Beach.

Eco Village Iriomote IRIOMOTE ISLAND This cozy little "eco-village" specializes in assisting people who stay here in arranging diving, kayaking, and hiking tours of Iriomote. Rooms are bright and airy; on-site amenities include a private beach, pool, and restaurant. 280–36 Takana. ☎ 0980/85-5115. www. eco-village.jp. 15 units. Doubles from ¥12,000. Rates include breakfast. AE, MC, V. Port: Uehara or Ohara.

La Teada (ラ・ティーダ西表) IRIOMOTE ISLAND Consisting of a campus of little bungalows facing a central courtyard, this almost feels like staying at someone's house rather than a hotel. The rooms are spacious and clean. The restaurant offers an interesting mix of Italian and Okinawan dishes. 508–205 Aza-Haemi. ☎ 0980/85-5555. www.lateada.co.jp. 24 units. Doubles from ¥12,000 per person. AE, DC, MC, V. Port: Uehara (after booking ferry tickets from Ishigaki, phone ahead for a pickup from Uehara).

Travel Tip

The vast majority of restaurants on Iriomote are incorporated into hotels. If you spend the night on the island, expect dinners and breakfasts to be included as part of your stay.

kids **Minshuku Izumiya** (民宿泉屋) TAKETOMI ISLAND Like all of the accommodations on the island, this is a loose, low-key, family-run operation more hostel than hotel (though you'll get your own room, of course!). It's a good family-friendly choice. 377 Taketomi. ☎ 0980/ 85-2250. 5 units. Rooms from ¥5,250 per person per night. Rates include breakfast & dinner. No credit cards. Port: Taketomi (call ahead for free shuttle bus).

Minshuku Nitta-so (民宿新田荘) TAKETOMI ISLAND Run by the same family who operates the water buffalo tours (p. 500, ❶), this is a clean but no-frills sort of place. 347 Taketomi. ☎ 0980/85-2201. www.ishigaki.com/nitta/ fnittaso.htm. 9 units. Rooms from ¥5,000 per person. Rates include breakfast & dinner. No credit cards. Port: Taketomi (call ahead for free shuttle bus).

★ **Pension Hoshinosuna** (ペンション星の砂) IRIOMOTE ISLAND On a hill above the famous Hoshizuna no Hama beach, with its pretty islet-studded bay and sand shaped like stars, this pension is popular for its dive shop, rental snorkeling equipment, and Okinawan restaurant with outdoor terrace facing the sea. It has Western- and Japanese-style rooms with dreamy views of the ocean. A great, inexpensive getaway. 289–1 Uehara. ☎ 0980/85-6448. hoshizuna@lime.ocn.ne.jp. 10 units. Doubles from ¥7,500 per person. Rates include 2 meals. AE, MC, V. Port: Uehara (pickup available).

Yarabo TAKETOMI ISLAND NOODLES This little shack of a restaurant is one of our favorite places to take a break on the island. The specialty here is soba, specifically *soki* soba, which is soba with a pork-rib topping. If you're feeling adventurous, try the *goya* juice—made from (extremely!) bitter melon, it is an only-in-Okinawa flavor experience. 107 Asa-Taketomi. ☎ 0980/85-2268. Entrees from ¥800. No credit cards. Lunch daily. Port: Taketomi.

The Okinawan Islands Fast Facts

> Naha airport's monorail whisks passengers from terminal to terminal.

Arriving & Getting Around

BY PLANE Generally, by plane is the only way to reach the islands of Okinawa. Okinawa Island is serviced by **Naha Airport.** Ishigaki Island is serviced by **Ishigaki Airport;** while there are a few direct flights, generally you can make a connection at Okinawa Island's Naha Airport. **BY FERRY** Taketomi Island and Iriomote Island are accessibly exclusively via ferry from Ishigaki Island.

ATMs

In contrast to those abroad, many ATMs only operate during banking hours. ATMs are also very hard to find outside of major cities, so plan accordingly. Most post offices (see below) have ATM facilities, although hours are limited. For 24-hour access, your best bets are the ATMs in **7-Eleven** convenience stores which accept Visa, Plus, American Express, JCB, Union Pay, or Diner's Club International cards for cash withdrawals. (They recently stopped accepting MasterCard, Maestro, and Cirrus cards.) **Citibank** and **Shinsei Bank** ATMs accept foreign bank cards as well.

Doctors & Hospitals

The general level of healthcare availability in Japan is high. For medical or dental attention visit the nearest hospital. **OKINAWA ISLAND** **Naha City Hospital** is located at 2–31–1 Furujima (☎ 098/884-5111). **ISHIGAKI ISLAND** **Yaeyama Hospital** is located at 732 Ogawa (☎ 0980/83-2525; Japanese only). **TAKETOMI & IRIOMOTE ISLANDS** Contact your hotel operator.

The high-speed ferry to Ishigaki.

Emergencies

The all-around emergency number in Japan is ☎ **119.** The all-around police number is ☎ **110.**

Internet Access

Most business hotels—but few *onsen* (spa resorts) or *ryokan* (traditional inns)—offer internet access as a perk to customers, and internet cafes are common (though most do not allow customers to hook up their own laptops, requiring them to use the facility's machines instead).

Pharmacies

Drugstores, called *yakkyoku* (薬局) are ubiquitous in Japan, but they are not 24-hour operations. Your best bet is to ask your hotel concierge for the closest location. Note that you must first visit a doctor in Japan before foreign prescriptions can be filled, so it's also best to bring an ample supply of any prescription medication with you.

Police

To reach the police, dial ☎ **110.** You can also stop by the nearest *koban* (police substation) for assistance.

Post Office

OKINAWA ISLAND **Naha Central Post Office** is located at 50 Tsubogawa (Mon–Fri 8:45am–7pm; Sat–Sun 9am–5pm). ISHIGAKI ISLAND **Yaeyama Main Post Office** is located at 112 Ogawa, Ishigaki City (Mon–Fri 8:45am–7pm; Sat–Sun 9am–5pm). TAKETOMI ISLAND **Taketomi Post Office** is located at 500 Taketomi (Mon–Fri 8:45am–7pm; Sat 9am–5pm; closed Sun). IRIOMOTE ISLAND **Iriomote Post Office** is located at 201-117 Haemi, Ohara Port (Mon–Fri 8:45am–7pm; Sat 9am–5pm; closed Sun).

Safety

Okinawa's islands are extremely safe, but take the normal common-sense precautions for personal safety and valuables that you would anywhere else.

Visitor Information

OKINAWA ISLAND In addition to Visitor Information Centers in the domestic and international terminals of the airport, you'll find the **Naha Tourism Information Center** on Okiei Street, just off Kokusai Dori, at 2-1-4 Makishi (☎ 098/868-4887; www.naha-navi.or.jp; Mon–Fri 8:30am–8pm; Sat–Sun 10am–8pm). ISHIGAKI, TAKETOMI & IRIOMOTE ISLANDS The **Tourist Information Office** is at 14 Misaki-cho, Ishigaki (☎ 0980/82-1243; http://guythegeek.com/cir/?page_id=255; Mon–Fri 8:30am–4:30pm).

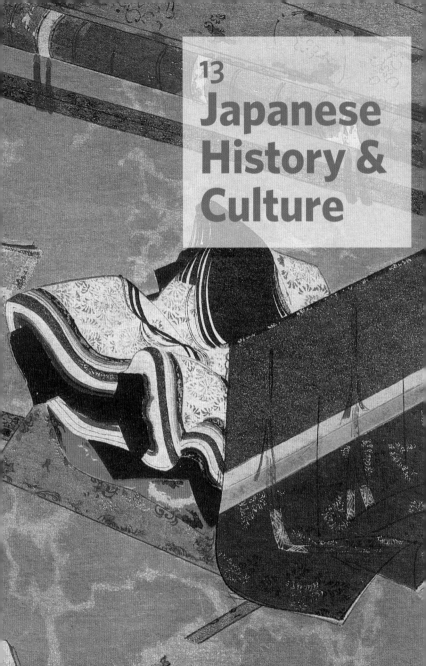

A Brief History of Japan

> **PREVIOUS PAGE** A dramatic rendering of Murasaki Shikibu composing The Tale of Genji. **THIS PAGE** A Meiji Era scroll depicting Izanami and Izanagi creating Japan.

Japan often presents a puzzle to outsiders. Superficially, at least, it seems we all know Japan—or at least its products.

Kids everywhere play with Japanese toys and watch Japanese *anime*. Teens pore over Japanese manga comic books while booting up their Japanese video game systems. Meanwhile their parents drive Japanese cars, while their Japanese televisions and computers hum with news about Japanese trade, scientific discoveries, and fashions. Sushi, tempura, and soba noodles are served up in Japanese restaurants around the globe.

Yet go a little deeper and you realize there's something more to Japan than Pocket Monsters, Priuses, and PCs. Nestled among sparkling skyscrapers (and even occasionally atop them) can be found tiny Shinto shrines. Traditionally clad Buddhist monks conduct religious ceremonies at their temples as they have for centuries. Cultural arts abound: the intricacies of *shodo* (Japanese calligraphy), the studied performances of geisha entertainers, the punctilious tea ceremony, the soothing harmony of bonsai and flower arrangement. Modern or ancient? Substance or style? Perhaps none has summed the disconnect up as succinctly as playwright Oscar Wilde, who wryly commented that "the whole of Japan is a pure invention. There are no such people. They are simply a mode of style, an exquisite fancy of art."

While we can assure you that Japan and its people most definitely exist, there's no question that there's more to this nation than meets the eye. An intricate blend of East and West, its cities may look Westernized—often disappointingly so—but, beyond first impressions, there's very little about the Land of the Rising Sun that could lull you into thinking you're anywhere else in the world. Discovering it is like peeling an onion—you uncover one layer only to discover more layers underneath. No matter how long you stay in Japan, you never stop learning something new about it—and to us, that constant cycle of discovery is one of the most fascinating aspects of being here, as a visitor or a resident.

In any case, with a population of about 127 million; a history stretching back thousands of years; the world's longest-reigning monarchy; and unique forms of culture, art, food, etiquette, and religion, Japan merits more than this short chapter can deliver. We urge you to delve deeper by seeking out our recommendations in "Japanese Pop Culture," later in this chapter

Prehistory

Ask a geologist about the origins of Japan and you'll hear about the powerful volcanic forces that shaped and pulled the islands from the Asian

The UNESCO Horyu-ji Temple in Nara.

mainland some 15 million years ago. But according to mythology, they're the product of a pair of gods named Izanagi and Izanami, who churned the empty waters of the sea with a sacred halberd. Pulling it forth, the resulting water droplets fell back to the ocean and coalesced into the islands of Japan.

Izanagi's daughter of sorts, the sun goddess Amaterasu, sent one of her descendants down to the island of Kyushu to unify the people of Japan. Unification, however, was not realized until a few generations later when Jimmu, the great-grandson of the goddess's emissary, succeeded

in bringing all of the country under his rule. Jimmu became emperor in 660 B.C. (the date is mythical), reigning until his death at the age of 126 (also, of course, mythical), thus establishing the line from which all of Japan's emperors are said to derive. However legendary the origin of this imperial dynasty, it is acknowledged as the longest reigning such family in the world.

Getting back to the world of science, archaeologists know that the territory of Japan was occupied as early as 35,000 B.C. From about 10,000 B.C. to 400 B.C., hunter-gatherers, called Jomon,

thrived in small communities primarily in central Honshu; they're best known for their hand-formed pottery decorated with cord patterns. The Jomon Period was followed by the Yayoi Period, which was marked by metalworking, the pottery wheel, and the mastering of irrigated rice cultivation. The Yayoi Period lasted until about A.D. 300, ruled from an imperial court established in what is now Nara Prefecture. This is the time when Japan first began turning cultural feelers toward its great neighbor to the west, China.

This is also when Japan's long-held animistic beliefs

> *The Great Buddha of Nara.*

Asuka Period (538 A.D.–710)

In the 6th century, **Buddhism**, which originated in India, came to Japan via China and Korea, followed by the importation of Chinese cultural and scholarly knowledge—including art, architecture, and the use of Chinese written characters. In 604, the prince regent, Shotoku, greatly influenced by the teachings of Buddhism and Confucianism, drafted a document calling for political reforms and a constitutional government. By 607, he was sending Japanese scholars to China to study Buddhism, and he started building Buddhist temples. The most famous is **Horyu-ji Temple** near Nara. For this, he is still a beloved figure today. (As a side note, Shotoku is also famed for introducing Japan to the arts of espionage, creating a spy network known as the *shinobi*—predecessors of the ninja of the Feudal Era.)

began formalizing into the religion known as Shinto. Shintoism is marked by the veneration of the natural world and its wonders—the sun and sky, mountains, trees, waterfalls, rivers and seas, fire, and just about anything that allowed the Japanese to make their livings from the earth—as *kami* (gods). Polytheistic in the truest sense of the word, Shintoism supposes innumerable *kami* of all shapes, sizes, and powers dwelling in the heavens, earth, and underworld. (In the decades leading up to World War II, the emperor was ensconced at the top of this divine hierarchy, but none save very few diehard fundamentalists believe

this today.) While there are ordained Shinto priests, there are no scriptures or holy texts associated with Shintoism. Along with Buddhism, which would be imported from China in the 6th century, Shintoism remains a subtle yet definite force in Japanese life. Very generally speaking, Japanese tend to rely on Shinto for life-related events such as births and marriages, while turning to Buddhism for death-related events such as funerals and memorial ceremonies—though the division is not a hard and fast one. (For example, Christian-styled weddings are quite popular as well.)

Nara Period (710–794)

Before the 700s, the site of Japan's capital changed every time a new emperor came to the throne. In 710, however, a permanent capital was established at Nara. Although it remained the capital for just 74 years, seven successive emperors ruled from here. The period was graced with the expansion of Buddhism and flourishing temple construction throughout the country. Buddhism also inspired the arts, including Buddhist sculpture, metal casting, painting, and lacquerware. Simultaneously, Shintoism was codified as a national religion at this time, in an effort to bolster the legitimacy of the emperor. Yet in a classic

A woodblock print of the brutal Battle of Dan-No-Ura, off the coast of Shimonoseki.

xample of how comfortable apanese were and are with ompeting religious ideas, his is also the period in which mperor Shomu, the most evout Buddhist of the Nara mperors, ordered the cast-ng of a huge bronze statue f Buddha to be erected in Jara. Known as the **Daibutsu** p. 223, ❹), it remains Nara's iggest attraction today.

Heian Period (794-1192)

n 794, the capital moved to Heian-kyo (present-day Kyoto). Following the example f cities in China, Kyoto was aid out in a grid pattern with road roads and canals. Heian-kyo means "capital of peace and tranquility," and the Heian Period was a glorious time for aristocratic families, an era of luxury and prosperity during which court fe reached new artistic heights. Chinese characters were blended with a new apanese writing system, allowing for the first time the lowering of Japanese iterature and poetry. The life

of the times was captured in the works of two women: Sei Shonagon, who wrote a collection of impressions of her life at court known as *The Pillow Book;* and Murasaki Shikibu, who wrote what many scholars consider the world's first true novel, *The Tale of Genji.*

Because the nobles were so completely engrossed in their luxurious lifestyles, however, they failed to notice the growth of military clans in the provinces. The two most powerful warrior clans were the Taira (also called Heike) and the Minamoto (also called Genji), whose fierce civil wars tore the nation apart until a young warrior, Minamoto Yoritomo, established supremacy in the epic battle of Dan-no-Ura, just off the coast of the city of Shimonoseki in Western Honshu. The graves of the vanquished Heike—and some say, their ghosts—can be found in Shimonoseki's **Akama Jingu** (p. 312, ❶).

> *Early samurai armor on display at the Tokyo National Museum.*

Kamakura Period (1192-1333)

Consolidating his pow-er, Minamoto Yoritomo, now shogun of all Japan, isolated the emperor and the aristoc-racy by moving the capital to a remote seaside village named Kamakura. In becom-ing the nation's first shogun, or military dictator, Minamoto Yoritomo laid the groundwork for 700 years of military

> *The tranquil stone garden of Ryoan-ji temple.*

governments—in which the power of the country passed from the aristocratic court into the hands of the warrior class—until the imperial court was restored in 1868.

The Kamakura Period is perhaps best known for the ascendancy of the warrior caste, or **samurai.** Ruled by a rigid honor code, samurai were bound in loyalty to their feudal lord, and they became the only caste allowed to carry swords. They were expected to give up their lives for their lord without hesitation, and if they failed in their duty, they could regain their honor only by committing ritualistic suicide, or *seppuku.* Spurning the soft life led by court nobles, samurai embraced a Spartan lifestyle. When **Zen Buddhism,** with its tenets of mental and physical discipline, was introduced into Japan from China in the 1190s, it appealed greatly to the samurai. Weapons and armor achieved new heights in artistry. Over the subsequent centuries, these ideas would be codified and popularized as Bushido, a code of conduct translated as the "Way of the Warrior."

In 1274, Mongolian forces under Kublai Khan made an unsuccessful attempt to invade Japan. They returned in 1281 with a larger fleet, but a typhoon destroyed it. Regarding the cyclone as a gift from the gods, Japanese called it *kamikaze,* meaning "divine wind," which took on a different significance at the end of World War II when Japanese pilots flew suicide missions in an attempt to turn the tide of war.

Muromachi & Azuchi-Momoyama Periods (1336–1603) After the eventual fall of the Kamakura shogunate, a new feudal government was re-established at Muromachi in Kyoto. The next 200 years, however, were marred by bloody civil wars as *daimyo* (feudal warlords) staked out their fiefdoms. Similar to the barons of Europe, the *daimyo* owned tracts of land, had complete rule over the people who lived on them, and had an army of retainers, the samurai, who fought their enemies. This period of civil war is called Sengoku-Jidai, or **Era of the Warring States.** More than a few non-Japanese bear at least a passing familiarity with this era of Japanese history, as it is the setting for many samurai films, such as Akira Kurosawa's *Yojimbo, Seven Samurai, Kagemusha,* and *Ran.* It also marks the ascendance of what would later be known as "ninja," assassins that would variously pledge and freelance their services to warlords as soldiers for hire and espionage operatives.

Yet these centuries of strife also saw a blossoming of art and culture. Kyoto witnessed the construction of the extravagant golden and silver pavilions **Kinkaku-ji** (p. 250, ❸) and **Ginkaku-ji** (p. 202, ❶), as well as the artistic arrangement of **Ryoan-ji** temple's famous rock garden (p. 250, ❹). Noh drama, the tea ceremony, flower arranging, and landscape gardening became the passions of the upper class.

In the second half of the 16th century, a brilliant military strategist by the name of Oda Nobunaga almost succeeded in ending the civil wars. This was due in large part to his shrewd use of firearms, introduced to Japan by the Portuguese in 1543 but largely disdained by tradition-minded warlords. Upon Oda's assassination by one of his own retainers, one of his best generals, Toyotomi Hideyoshi took up the campaign, built magnificent Osaka Castle, and crushed rebellion to unify Japan. Oda and Toyotomi's successive rules are known as the Azuchi-Momoyama period, after the names of their castles.

Edo Period (1603–1867)

Upon Toyotomi's death in 1598, the legendary Tokugawa Ieyasu seized power. He was a statesman so shrewd and skillful in eliminating enemies that his heirs would continue to rule Japan for the next 250 years. After defeating his greatest rival in the famous battle of Sekigahara, Tokugawa set up a shogunate government in 1603 in Edo (present-day Tokyo), leaving the emperor intact but virtually powerless in Kyoto. In 1615, the Tokugawa government assured its supremacy by getting rid of Toyotomi's descendants in a fierce battle at Osaka Castle that destroyed the castle and annihilated the Toyotomi clan.

Meanwhile, European influence in Japan was spreading. The first contact with the Western world had occurred in 1543, when Portuguese merchants (bearing firearms) arrived, followed shortly thereafter by Christian missionaries. St. Francis Xavier landed in Kyushu in 1549, remaining for 2 years and converting thousands of Japanese; by 1580, there were perhaps as many as 150,000 Japanese Christians. Although Japan's rulers at first welcomed foreigners and trade (three Kyushu *daimyo* even went so far as to send emissaries to Rome, where they were received by the pope), they gradually became alarmed by the Christian missionary influence. Hearing of the Catholic Church's power in Rome and fearing the expansionist policies of European nations, Toyotomi banned Christianity in the late 1500s. In 1597, 26 Japanese and European Christians were crucified in Nagasaki (p. 374, ❷).

The Tokugawa shogunate intensified the campaign against Christians in 1639 when it closed all ports to foreign trade. Adopting a policy of **total isolation,** the shogunate forbade foreigners from landing in Japan and Japanese from leaving; even Japanese who had been living abroad in overseas trading posts were never allowed to return. The only exception was in Nagasaki, home to a colony of tightly controlled Chinese merchants and a handful of Dutch confined to a tiny island trading post called Dejima.

Yet even though the Tokugawa government took

> *Change on the horizon: Perry's "Black Ships" arrive.*

> *Japan surrenders aboard the USS* Missouri.

such extreme measures to ensure its supremacy, by the middle of the 19th century it was clear that the feudal system was outdated and economic power had shifted into the hands of the merchants. Many samurai families were impoverished, and discontent with the shogunate became widespread.

In 1853, American Commodore Matthew C. Perry sailed to Japan, seeking to gain trading rights. He left unsuccessful, but returning a year later, he forced the shogun to sign an agreement despite the disapproval of the emperor, thus ending Japan's 2 centuries of isolation. In 1867, powerful families toppled the Tokugawa regime and restored the emperor as ruler, thus bringing the Feudal Era to a close.

Meiji Period Through World War II (1868–1945)
In 1868, Emperor Meiji moved his imperial government from Kyoto to Edo, renamed it Tokyo ("Eastern Capital"), and designated it the official national capital. During the next few decades, known as the **Meiji Restoration,** Japan rapidly progressed from a feudal agricultural society of samurai and peasants to an industrial nation. The samurai were stripped of their power and no longer allowed to carry swords, thus ending a privileged way of life begun almost 700 years earlier in Kamakura. A prime minister and a cabinet were appointed, a constitution was drafted, and a parliament (called the Diet) was elected. With the enthusiastic support of Emperor Meiji, the latest in Western technological know-how was imported, including railway and postal systems—and specialists and advisers.

Meanwhile, Japan made incursions into neighboring lands. In 1894 to 1895, it fought and won a war against China; in 1904 to 1905, it attacked and defeated Russia; and in 1910, it annexed Korea. After militarists gained control of the government in the 1930s, these expansionist policies continued; Manchuria was seized, and Japan went to war with China again in 1937. On the other side of the world, as **World War II** flared in Europe, Japan formed a military alliance (the Axis) with Germany and Italy and attacked French Indochina.

After several years of tense diplomatic confrontations between Japan and America, Japanese extremists decided to attack Pearl Harbor in the hope that by striking first they could prevent U.S. mobilization. On December 7, 1941, Japan bombed Pearl Harbor, drawing the United States into World War II. Although Japan went on to conquer Hong Kong, Singapore, Burma, Malaysia, the Philippines, the Dutch East Indies, and Guam, the tide eventually turned, and American bombers reduced every major Japanese city to rubble with the exception of historic Kyoto. On August 6, 1945, the United States dropped the world's first atomic bomb over Hiroshima, followed on August 9 by a second over Nagasaki. Japan submitted to unconditional surrender on August 14, with Emperor Hirohito's radio broadcast telling his people the time had come for "enduring the unendurable and suffering what is insufferable." American and other **Allied occupation** forces arrived and remained until 1952. For the first time in history, Japan had admitted defeat by a foreign power; the country had never before been invaded or occupied by a foreign nation.

Modern Japan
(1946–PRESENT)

The experience of World War II had a profound effect on the Japanese people, yet they emerged from their defeat and began to rebuild. In 1946, under the guidance of the Allied military authority headed by U.S. General Douglas MacArthur, they adopted a democratic constitution renouncing war and the use of force to settle international disputes and divesting the emperor of divinity, giving power to the people instead. A parliamentary system of government was set up, and 1947 witnessed the first general elections for the National Diet, the government's legislative body. After its founding in 1955, the **Liberal Democratic Party (LDP)** remained the undisputed majority party for decades, giving Japan the kind of political stability it needed to grow economically and compete in world markets.

To the younger generation, the occupation was less a painful burden to be suffered than an opportunity to remake their country, with American encouragement, into a modern, peace-loving, and democratic state. A special relationship developed between Japanese and their American occupiers. In the early 1950s, as the Cold War between the United States and the Communist world erupted in hostilities in Korea, that relationship grew into a firm alliance, strengthened by a security treaty. In 1952, the occupation ended, and Japan joined the United Nations as an independent country.

> *Miniaturized radios and televisions signaled Japan's drive to modernize in the postwar era.*

Avoiding involvement in foreign conflicts, Japanese concentrated on economic recovery. Through a series of policies favoring domestic industries and shielding Japan from foreign competition, they achieved **rapid economic growth.** In 1964, Tokyo hosted the Summer Olympic Games, showing the world that the nation had transformed itself into a formidable industrialized power. Incomes doubled during the 1960s, and a 1967 government study found that 90% of Japanese considered themselves middle class. By the 1980s, Japan was by far the richest industrialized nation in Asia and the envy of its neighbors, who strove to emulate Japan's success. Sony was a household word around the globe; books flooded the international market touting the economic secrets of Japan, Inc. In 1989, Emperor Hirohito died of cancer at age 87, bringing the 63-year **Showa Era** to an end and ushering in the **Heisei Period** under Akihito, the 125th emperor, who proclaimed a new "Era of Peace" (Heisei).

In the early 1990s, shadows of financial doubt began to spread over the Land of the Rising Sun, with alarming reports of bad bank loans, inflated stock prices, and overextended corporate investment abroad. In 1992, financial crisis hit Japan, bursting the economic bubble and plunging the country into its worst **recession** since World War II. The Nikkei (the Japanese version of the American Dow) fell a gut-churning 63% from its 1989 peak, and, over the next decade, bankruptcies reached an all-time high and unemployment climbed to a level not seen since World War II. Meanwhile, the LDP, which had held power uninterruptedly for nearly 4 decades, suffered a huge loss of public confidence after its top officials were accused of participating in a series of political and financial scandals.

> *Floor traders on the Tokyo Stock Exchange.*

Public confidence was further eroded in 1995, first by a major earthquake in Kobe that killed more than 6,000 people (proving that Japan's cities were not as safe as the government had maintained), and then by an attack by an obscure religious sect that released the deadly nerve gas sarin on Tokyo's subway system during rush hour, killing 12 people and sickening thousands. But the worst blow came in 2001, when a knife-wielding man stormed into an elementary school in Osaka Prefecture, fatally stabbing 8 children and wounding 15 others. For many Japanese, it seemed that the very core of their society had begun to crumble.

In April 2001, after yet another prime minister resigned due to scandal, Koizumi Junichiro took the political helm. Although a member of the LPD, the long-haired, 59-year-old Koizumi had been considered something of a maverick, battling against the established power brokers of the LPD and vowing to overturn the LPD's pork-barrel politics by slashing public spending on bridges, dams, and roads; forcing Japanese banks to write off bad loans; and dismantling regulations that protected large sectors of the economy. His cries for reform, coupled by media attention that gave him the revered status of a rock star, won Koizumi more voter support than any prime minister since the bubble economy of the 1980s.

Japan Today

In contrast to the champagne-and-caviar excesses of the 1980s bubble economy, where only designer goods would do and expense accounts seeme[d] unlimited, today's Japan is a far more reasonable sort of place. While decades of reces[s]sion have yet to dampen the spirits of citizens, it has made them far more open to bargains. There are deals across the country only for foreigners, including regional rail passes and plane tickets.

Which sounds great, but there's (of course) a major catch: the strong yen. This makes everything roughly 10[%] to 20% more expensive than it was during most of the first decade of the 2000s, when the exchange rate hovered between roughly ¥100 and

Honda's ASIMO robot symbolized Japan's manufacturing prowess in the late 1990s.

110 to the U.S. dollar. *Endaka,* s the Japanese call a strong en, is a boon for locals but a eal pain in the neck for those isiting from abroad.

Japan also continues to face social problem of a sort it's ever had to confront before: declining birth rate coupled ith one of the most rapidly ging populations in the world. bout 22% of its population 65 and older; by 2055, that umber is expected to double. Meanwhile, Japan's ratio of hildren aged 14 and younger believed to the lowest in he world, accounting for nly 13.5% of the population. his will undoubtedly lead to shortage of labor, severely training the country's esources for tax revenues, ensions, and health care. (As side note, the recent surge development of humanoid obots, such as Honda's vorld-famous ASIMO, is

directly linked to the problem, as Japanese struggle to come up with technological solutions to caring for the elderly population without relaxing their notoriously strict immigration laws.)

That's not the only bad news to hit Japan recently. In March 2011, a 9.0-magnitude earthquake struck off the eastern coast of Tohoku, sending a tsunami reaching as high as 40m (131 ft.) surging toward the coastline, wiping away everything in its path. It was the most powerful earthquake in Japan's history and one of the strongest ever recorded; it shifted the Earth on its axis by 10 to 25cm (4–10 in.) and moved the island of Honshu 2.4m (8 ft.) east. While the earthquake caused massive damage to buildings throughout Honshu, it was its effect on the power plants of Fukushima that will have

the most long-lasting effects. Fukushima Daichi Power Plant experienced a meltdown, and the Japanese government evacuated a 20km (12-mile) area around it. All told, more than 20,000 people died as a result of the tsunami (though none from radiation so far), more than 4,000 are still missing, and the damage totals in the hundreds of billions of U.S. dollars. But as always, Japan and its resilient citizens soldier on. Rebuilding efforts have restored most of the country to normal; while the immediate surroundings of the power plant will likely be uninhabitable for decades, and hundreds of thousands have been displaced from their homes in northern Honshu, Tohoku is generally regarded as safe. For more information on the earthquake, see p. 26. For information on volunteering in Tohoku, see p. 402.

A Timeline of Japanese History

35,000–250 B.C.

35,000–30,000 B.C. Very first humans occupy the Japanese islands.

12,000 B.C. The **Jomon Era** begins—Japan's first true civilization, wit rudimentary agriculture and distinctive pottery (see left).

400 B.C. The **Yayoi Era** begins. Bronze and iron implements first appear. Rice farming techniques spread throughout the country.

250 B.C. The **Kofun Era** marks the rise of an organized military and political system. Leaders were buried in elaborate keyhole-shaped tumulus mounds called *kofun*.

500–1400 A.D.

538–710 A.D. The **Asuka Era:** A true centralized city-state, with codified laws, emerges. Buddhism first imported to Japan.

710–93 The **Nara Era:** Japan's first permanent capital established in the city of Nara. Buddhism continues to gain great popularity, thanks in large part to the efforts of Prince Shotoku (574–622; see left).

794 The rise of the aristocracy ushers in a period of great artistic achievement, **Heian Era.**

800 The Japanese syllabaries of *hiragama* and *katakana* are invented.

1000 *The Tale of Genji,* the world's first modern novel, is penned by Murasaki Shikibu.

1185 The Minamoto clan puts an end to the Taira clan at the naval battle of Dam-no-Ura, ushering in the rise of a military state.

1191 Zen Buddhism first introduced to Japan.

1192 Minamoto Yoritomo becomes Japan's first shogun, moving the capital to Kamakura. **Kamakura Era** begins.

1274–81 Mongols attempt two invasions of Japan but are sunk by a typhoon the Japanese came to call the *kamikaze* (divine wind).

1338 **Muromachi Era** begins. Capital moved back to Kyoto.

1400–1600

1467 Gradual weakening of central authority leads to warlords in provinces throughout Japan battling for supremacy. The **Era of Warring States** begins, ushering in more than a century of civil war.

1481 Ninja forces manage to kill the shogun during a guerilla engagement at the Battle of Magari, ushering in a time of clandestine warfare.

1543 Shipwrecked Portuguese introduce firearms to Japan via Tanegashima island.

1549 St. Francis Xavier lands in Kyushu, introducing Christianity to Japan and converting thousands of Japanese to the religion (see left).

1560 Warlord Takeda Shingen orders creation of Japan's first flush toile

600–1945

1600 Battle of Sekigahara seals Tokugawa Ieyasu's claim as ruler, effectively unifying Japan for the very first time.

1603 **Edo Era** begins, ushering in 250 years of isolation. A great flourishing of traditional arts (such as woodblock printing; see left) follows.

1707 Mount Fuji's last recorded eruption. (Keep those fingers crossed.)

1853 U.S. Commodore Matthew Perry, leading a fleet of heavily armed steam-powered gunboats, opens Japanese ports. An already weak Tokugawa Shogunate collapses shortly thereafter.

1868 The **Meiji Era** begins as the emperor is restored to power for the first time in centuries. One of his first official acts is to change the name of Edo to Tokyo ("Eastern Capital").

1894–95 Japan defeats China in the First Sino-Japanese War, fought over which nation would control the Korean peninsula (see left).

1904–05 Japan defeats Russia in the Russo-Japanese War.

1941 Japanese forces bomb Hawaii's Pearl Harbor, stirring a reluctant America to enter World War II and ushering in the war in the Pacific.

1945 Nuclear weapons dropped on the cities of Hiroshima and Nagasaki result in Japan's unconditional surrender to American forces; U.S. occupation lasts until 1952.

POST–WORLD WAR II

1957 First Japanese car sold in the U.S.: the Toyota Crown.

1950s–70s In a phenomenon that would come to be called "Japan's postwar economic miracle," a confluence of massive amounts of U.S. investment and protectionist Japanese trade policies lead to record economic growth.

1979 Sony's Walkman portable audiocassette player debuts.

1980s Japan's **"Bubble Era."** Officially lasting from 1986 to 1991, this marked a period of unprecedented economic success, resulting in major trade frictions with the United States. The Nintendo Entertainment System debuts in Japan (see left).

1995 The Aum doomsday cult launches a sarin-gas attack on the Tokyo subway system. In the same year, the Kobe area is heavily damaged by what is known as the Great Hanshin Earthquake.

2004 Japan sends support troops to Iraq, the first time going to a war zone since 1945.

2009 Exports fall to lowest level ever recorded; no Japanese companies make the top-10 list of largest corporations worldwide.

2011 Most powerful earthquake in Japan's history hits eastern seaboard, triggering tsunamis of up to 40m (131 ft.).

Religion in Japan

> A traditional Japanese graveyard. Graveyards are always found in temples, never shrines.

The main religions in Japan are Shintoism and Buddhism, and many Japanese consider themselves believers in both. Most Japanese, for example, will marry in a Shinto ceremony, but when they die, they'll have a Buddhist funeral. A native religion of Japan, **Shintoism** is the worship of ancestors and national heroes, as well as of all natural things, both animate and inanimate. These natural things are thought to embody gods and can be anyone or anything—mountains, trees, the moon, stars, rivers, seas, fires, rocks, and animals. Shintoism also embraces much of Confucianism, which entered Japan in the 5th century and stressed the importance of family and loyalty. There are no scriptures in Shintoism, nor any ordained code of morals or ethics.

The place of worship in Shintoism is called a *jinja*, or **shrine.** The most obvious sign of a shrine is its *torii*, an entrance gate, usually of wood, consisting of two tall poles topped with either one or two crossbeams. Another feature common to shrines is a water trough with communal cups, where the Japanese will wash their hands and sometimes rinse out their mouths. Purification and cleanliness are important in Shintoism because they show respect to the gods. At the shrine, worshipers will throw a few coins into a money box, clap their hands twice to get the gods' attention, and then bow their heads and pray for whatever they wish—good health, protection, the safe delivery of a child, or a prosperous year.

Founded in India in the 6th to 5th centuries B.C., **Buddhism** came to Japan in the 6th century A.D. via China and Korea, bringing with it the concept of eternal life. By the end of the 6th century, Buddhism had gained such popularity that the prince regent Shotoku, one of Japan's most remarkable historical figures, declared Buddhism the state religion and based many of his governmental policies on its tenets. Another important Buddhist leader to emerge was a priest called Kukai, known posthumously as Kobo Daishi. After studying Buddhism in China in the early 800s, he returned and built temples throughout Japan, including the famous 88 temples on Shikoku Island and those on Mount Koya, which continue to attract millions of pilgrims today.

Of the various Buddhist sects in Japan today, Zen Buddhism is probably the best known in the West. Considered the most Japanese form of Buddhism, Zen is the practice of meditation and a strictly disciplined lifestyle to rid yourself of desire so that you can achieve enlightenment. There are no rites in Zen Buddhism, no dogmas, no theological conceptions of divinity. You do not analyze rationally, but rather know things intuitively. The strict and simple lifestyle of Zen appealed greatly to Japan's samurai warrior class, and many of Japan's arts, including the tea ceremony, arose from the practice of Zen. Whereas Shintoists have shrines, Buddhists have **temples,** called *otera*. Instead of *torii*, temples will often have an entrance gate with a raised doorsill and heavy doors. Temples may also have a cemetery on their grounds (which Shinto shrines never have) as well as a pagoda.

Japanese Traditional Arts

Puppeteers prepare a Bunraku puppet for its moment onstage.

Theater

KABUKI Probably Japan's best-known traditional theater art, Kabuki is also one of the country's most popular forms of entertainment. Visit a performance and it's easy to see why. The plays are dramatic, the costumes are gorgeous, the stage settings are often fantastic, and the themes are universal—love, revenge, and the conflict between duty and personal feelings. Probably one of the reasons Kabuki remains popular even today is that it was developed centuries ago as a form of entertainment for the common people. Back in the 1800s, before the advent of movies, a hit Kabuki play would be the talk of the town, its actors treated almost like royalty. Many of Japan's most famous stories and characters have their roots in Kabuki productions.

Kabuki has changed little in the past 100-some years. One of its most interesting aspects is that all roles—even those depicting women—are portrayed by men. Altogether there are more than 300 Kabuki plays, nearly all written before the 20th century. Kabuki stages almost always revolve and have an aisle that extends from the stage to the back of the spectator theater. Actors stamp their feet and strike poses; occasionally, a "professional caller" in the audience may shout out an actor's name during a key scene. (Don't try this yourself, as only longtime fans know the protocol for these seemingly spontaneous but carefully timed reactions.) You may notice black-clad stagehands, called *kuroko*, scurrying about helping the actors with props; they're supposed to be ignored. Kabuki isn't about realism. It's pure, unadulterated theatricality, and that is precisely what makes it so much fun.

Of course, you won't be able to understand what's being said if you don't speak Japanese—and maybe not even then: Because much of Kabuki drama dates from the 18th century, even native speakers sometimes have difficulty understanding the language. But it doesn't matter, though some theaters have English-language programs and earphones that describe the plots in minute detail. The best place to enjoy Kabuki is Tokyo, where performances are held throughout much of the year. Its famed Kabuki-za theater in the Ginza closed for renovations in 2009, and is scheduled to re-open in 2013.

NOH Whereas Kabuki developed as a form of entertainment for the masses, Noh was a much more traditional and aristocratic form of theater. Most of Japan's shogun were patrons of Noh; during the Edo Period, it became the exclusive entertainment of the samurai class. In contrast to Kabuki's extroverted liveliness, Noh is very calculated, slow, and restrained. The oldest form of theater in Japan, it has changed very little in the past 600 years, making it the oldest theater art in the world. The language is so archaic that Japanese cannot understand it at all, which explains in part why Noh does not have the popularity that Kabuki does.

As in Kabuki, all Noh performers are men, with the principal characters consisting mostly of ghosts or spirits, who illuminate foibles of human nature or tragic-heroic events. Performers often wear masks. Spoken parts are chanted by a chorus of about eight; music is provided by a

Noh orchestra that consists of several drums and a flute.

Because the action is slow, watching an entire evening can be a little tedious unless you are particularly interested in Noh dance and music. In addition, most Noh plays do not have English translations. You may want to drop in for just a short while. In between Noh plays, short comic re-liefs, called *kyogen,* usually make fun of life in the 1600s, depicting the lives of lazy husbands, conniving servants, and other characters with universal appeal.

BUNRAKU Bunraku is tradition-al Japanese puppet theater. But contrary to what you might expect, Bunraku is for adults, and themes center on love and revenge, sacrifice and suicide. Many dramas now adapted for Kabuki were first written for the Bunraku stage.

Popular in Japan since the 17th century—at times even more popular than Kabuki—Bunraku is fascinating to watch because the puppeteers are right onstage with their pup-pets. Dressed in black, they're wonderfully skilled in making the puppets seem like living beings. Usually, there are three puppeteers for each puppet, which is about three-quarters human size: One puppeteer is responsible for movement of the puppet's head, as well as for the expression on its face, and for the movement of the right arm and hand; another puppeteer operates the puppet's left arm and hand; while the third moves

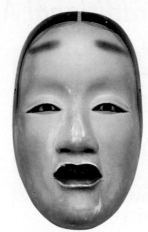

> A stereotypical Noh mask.

the legs. Although at first the puppeteers are somewhat distracting, after a while you forget they're there as the puppets assume personali-ties of their own. The narrator, who tells the story and speaks the various parts, is an impor-tant figure in the drama. The narrator is accompanied by a traditional three-stringed Japanese instrument called a *shamisen.* By all means, try to see Bunraku. The most famous presentations are at the Osaka Bunraku Theater, but there are performances in Tokyo and other major cities as well.

Tea Ceremony
Tea was brought to Japan from China more than 1,000 years ago. It first became popular among Buddhist priests as a means of staying awake dur-ing long hours of meditation; gradually, its use filtered down among the upper classes, and in the 16th century, the tea ceremony was perfected by a

merchant named Sen no Riky Using the principles of Zen and the spiritual discipline of the samurai, the tea ceremon became a highly stylized ritual with detailed rules on how tea should be prepared, served, and drunk. The simplicity of movement and tranquility of setting are meant to free the mind from the banality of everyday life and to allow the spirit to enjoy peace. In a way it is a form of spiritual therapy

The tea ceremony, *cha-no yu,* is still practiced in Japan today and is regarded as a form of disciplinary training for mental composure and f etiquette and manners. Mas tering the ceremony can take years; that may seem like a long time, but the study of th tea ceremony includes relate subjects, including the crafts manship of tea vessels and implements, the design and construction of the teahouse the landscaping of gardens, and literature related to the tea ceremony.

Several of Japan's more famous landscape gardens have teahouses on their grounds where you can sit on tatami, drink the frothy green tea (called *matcha*), ea sweets (meant to counterac the bitter taste of the tea), and contemplate the view. Teahouses are traditionally quite small and have room fo five or fewer people. There's one entrance for the host and another for guests, so small that guests must craw through it to enter. In the center of the room is a small

> *The mossy tranquility of a Kyoto temple garden.*

azier for the teapot along with utensils needed for the making of tea—tea bowl, tea addy, bamboo whisk, and amboo spoon. After hot water is added to powdered tea the bowl and beaten with he whisk, the bowl is passed om guest to guest. Tea etiquette requires that guests ompliment the host on the xcellent flavor of the tea nd on the beauty of the tea mplements, which of course hange with the seasons and re often valuable art objects.

loral & Landscape Arts

KEBANA Whereas a Westrner is likely to put a bunch f flowers into a vase and be one with it, Japanese consid-r the arrangement of flowers n art in itself. Most young irls have at least some train-ng in flower arranging, known s ikebana. First popularized mong aristocrats during the eian Period (794–1192) and preading to the common eople in the 14th to 16th centuries, traditional ikebana, in s simplest form, is supposed o represent heaven, man, nd earth; it's considered a ruly Japanese art without utside influences. As important as the arrangement itself, s the vase chosen to display t. Department store galleries ometimes have ikebana ex-ibitions, as do shrines; oth-rwise, check with the local ourist office.

ARDENS Nothing is left to hance in a Japanese land-cape garden: The shapes of ills and trees, the placement of rocks and waterfalls—everything is skillfully arranged in a faithful reproduction of nature. To Westerners, it may seem a bit strange to arrange nature to look like nature, but to Japanese, even nature can be improved upon to make it more pleasing through the best possible use of limited space. Japanese are masters at this, as a visit to any of their famous gardens will testify.

In fact, Japanese have been sculpting gardens for more than 1,000 years. At first, the gardens were designed for walking and boating, with ponds, artificial islands, and pavilions. As with almost everything else in Japanese life, however, Zen Buddhism exerted an influence, making gardens simpler and attempting to create the illusion of boundless space within a small area. To the Buddhist, a garden was not for merriment but for contemplation—an uncluttered and simple landscape on which to rest the eyes. Japanese gardens often use the principle of "borrowed landscape"—that is, the incorporation of surrounding mountains and landscape into the overall design and impact of the garden.

Basically, there are three styles of Japanese gardens. One style, called *tsukiyama*, uses ponds, hills, and streams to depict nature in miniature. Another style, known as the *karesansui*, uses stones and raked sand in place of water and is often seen at Zen Buddhist temples; it was developed during the Muromachi Period as a representation of Zen spiritualism. The third style, called *chaniwa*, emerged with the tea ceremony and is built around a teahouse with an eye toward simplicity and tranquility; such a garden will often feature stone lanterns, a stone basin filled with water, or water flowing through a bamboo pipe.

Famous gardens in Japan include Kenrokuen Park in Kanazawa, Korakuen Park in Okayama, Ritsurin Park in Takamatsu, and the grounds of the Adachi Museum. Kyoto alone has about 50 gardens, including the famous Zen rock gardens at **Daitoku-ji** (p. 251, **7**) and **Ryoan-ji** (p. 250, **4**) temples, the gardens at both **Kinkaku-ji** (p. 250, **3**) and **Ginkaku-ji** (p. 202, **1**), and those at Heian Jingu Shrine in Kyoto and **Nijojo** (p. 248, **2**).

Sumo: Japan's Stereotypical Sport

Japan boasts dozens of traditional martial arts and sports, but perhaps none attracts as much attention from foreigners as that of sumo. And while it's easy to laugh at the concept of fat men body-slamming one another, make no bones about it: This is a serious sport, and getting to the highest echelons requires serious discipline and training. This form of wrestling began perhaps as long as 1,500 years ago and was immensely popular by the 6th century. Often taller than 1.8m (6 ft.) and weighing well over 136kg (300 lb.), sumo wrestlers follow a rigorous training period, which usually begins when they're in their teens. They eat special foods (mainly *chanko nabe*, a protein-rich chicken-and-fish stew) and take naps after meals to pack on the weight. Young wrestlers usually live together in dormitories at their training schools, called "sumo stables."

From 2009 to 2011, a series of scandals rocked the sumo world, with the death of a young trainee by hazing, allegations of organized crime involvement, and illegal gambling by wrestlers. In spite of it all, the sport still remains very popular. The best wrestlers are revered as national heroes, much as baseball or basketball players are in the United States.

A sumo match takes place on a sandy-floored ring less than 4.5m (15 ft.) in diameter. Wrestlers dress much as they did during the Edo Period—their hair in a traditional topknot, an ornamental belt/loincloth around their huge girths. Before each bout, the two contestants scatter salt in the ring to purify it from the last bout's loss; they also squat and then raise each leg, stamping it into the ground to crush, symbolically, any evil spirits. They then squat down and face each other, glaring to psych each other out. Once they rush each other, each wrestler's object is to either eject his opponent from the ring or cause him to touch the ground with any part of his body other than his feet. This is accomplished by shoving, slapping, tripping, throwing, and even carrying the opponent, but punching with a closed fist and kicking are not allowed. Altogether, there are 48 holds and throws, and sumo fans know all of them. Most bouts are very short, lasting only 30 seconds or so. The highest-ranking players are called *yokozuna,* or grand champions. Nowadays foreign-born sumo wrestlers are common, though their numbers are restricted by the Japan Sumo Association. Most hail from Mongolia, though a few are from Europe and the Americas as well. In 1993, a Hawaiian named Akebono was promoted to the highest rank, the first non-Japanese ever to be so honored.

There are six 15-day sumo tournaments in Japan every year: Three are held in Tokyo (Jan, May, and Sept); the others are held in Osaka (Mar), Nagoya (July), and Fukuoka (Nov). Each wrestler in the tournament faces a new opponent every day; the winner of the tournament is the wrestler who maintains the best overall record. Sumo matches are held in Tokyo at the **Kokugikan,** 1-3-28 Yokoami, Sumida-ku (☎ 03/3622-1100; www.sumo. or.jp). Matches are held in January, May, and September for 15 consecutive days, beginning at around 9:30am and lasting until 6pm; the top wrestlers compete after 3:30pm. The best seats are ringside box seats, but they're snapped up by companies or the friends and families of sumo wrestlers. Usually available are balcony seats, which can be purchased at Ticket Pia and JTB travel agencies. You can also purchase tickets directly at the Kokugikan ticket office beginning at 9am every morning of the tournament. Prices range from about ¥2,100 for an unreserved seat (sold only on the day of the event at the stadium, with about 400 seats available) to ¥8,200 for a good reserved seat. If you can't make it to a match, watching on TV is almost as good. Tournaments in Tokyo, as well as those that take place annually in Osaka, Nagoya, and Fukuoka, are broadcast on the NHK channel from 4 to 6pm daily during matches.

Japanese Pop Culture

For decades, Japan was renowned as an economic powerhouse thanks to its manufacturing industry, which churned out cars and consumer electronics that made their way around the globe. While these still remain popular, the vast majority of Japan's factories have migrated abroad to China and Southeast Asia. But today, Japan is still wowing the world with another, more ethereal type of domestic export: its pop culture. From anime (animation) and manga (comic books) to toys, video games, and fashion, Japan consistently manages to score an astonishing level of "mindshare" around the world for such a tiny country. Icons such as Godzilla, Super Mario, Hello Kitty, the Transformers (which originated here), and the Pocket Monsters are virtually synonymous with Japan around the world today.

Ukiyo-e, Anime & Manga

Japanese pop creations are powered by tradition. Japan has a long history of illustrated storytelling. The word manga, which transliterates to something like "whimsical pictures," has been in use since at least the late 18th century, when it was applied to picture books illustrated with woodblock prints. These prints were later honed into a mass-produced art form called ukiyo-e, or "pictures of the floating world," with gloriously full-color prints portraying everything from

> Cartoon characters such as this one represent one of Japan's top exports today.

landscapes and scenes of everyday life to Kabuki actors and heroes and monsters from folklore; there were even a fair share of pornographic prints. When ukiyo-e first came to light abroad in the late 19th century—accidentally, since the Japanese had been crumpling them up as packing material for ceramics, which they considered far more worthy artistic products—the prints inspired European art luminaries such as Vincent van Gogh and Henri de Toulouse-Lautrec. By the late 1800s, Europe and America were in the grips of a phenomenon known as Japonisme: a craze for all things Japanese, driven by an interest in popular culture.

If this sounds suspiciously familiar, it's because a very similar sort of thing is happening today. While Japan has long since shifted from woodblocks to modern forms of printing and broadcasting,

> *Godzilla's archenemy Mechagodzilla.*

many woodblock prints seem like long-lost relatives of the comic books on shelves today, with similar themes, approaches, and styles. The postwar era gave rise to a generation of artists who honed Japan's illustration techniques into cutting-edge manga and *anime*. Sponsored by Japanese toy companies, who produced intricate merchandise based on their characters, Japanese comic-book artists and animators launched television series and films that rose to world popularity in the 1980s and 1990s. These in turn inspired a variety of American film-makers, who incorporated *anime* style—and even *anime* segments—into their works, including the Wachowski brothers' *The Matrix* and Quentin Tarantino's *Kill Bill*. Today, Japan's pop culture is a huge draw for visitors, particularly younger ones who

grew up watching Japanese *anime* and playing Japanese video games.

But all is not quiet on the pop-cultural front. The animation industry, once a seeming endless fount of creativity, is today suffering from a variety of maladies. One is a reluctance to embrace computer animation techniques so successful abroad; while this is slowly changing, many studios still rely on hand illustration rather than 3-D computer graphics. (Of course, that's also part of *anime*'s charm.) But more of an issue are shockingly low salaries that preclude many animators from making a living wage; in fact, a 2006 government report made it clear that a third of the industry toiled below the poverty line. Low budgets and wages have resulted in a "brain drain" of talent going to other industries and massive outsourcing abroad, contributing to a marked decline in the number and quality of animated productions coming out of the country. An archaic production system that deprives most animation studios of revenue from royalties and lack of unions are partly to blame, but perhaps it's just part of the cycle of things. One can easily imagine woodblock print artists throwing up their hands at the dawn of the 20th century, when their techniques fell by the wayside in favor of lithography and other modern printing processes.

Yet all is far from lost. As it has proved again and again,

> *The films of Studio Ghibli are family favorites the world ove...*

Japan is nothing if not a rebound king. The *anime* and manga industries may have lost some of their energy in th... early part of the 21st century... but they are rapidly being replaced by cutting-edge vide... games. Japanese-made vide... games dominated arcades in... the 1980s and continued to enjoy unprecedented succe... throughout the 1990s. (It's a rare individual under the age of 40 who can't hum at least the first few bars to the Supe... Mario Brothers theme.) Whi... foreign game companies are... giving the Japanese a run for their money abroad, Japanes... made games reign supreme in their home country. But there's no question that whil... Japan's pop culture industrie... may not exactly dominate th... world in the way they once d... the creativity that drove then... remains. What will come nex... Perhaps you'll get an inkling when you visit the country.

JAPANESE *ANIME*-INDUSTRY LUMINARIES You can't talk about *anime* or manga without talking about the people who made it famous. Here's a (very) short list of some of the people who made Japan's pop culture so popular throughout the world.

Osamu Tezuka (1928–89). Often described as the God of Comics in Japan, he single-handedly launched Japan's *anime* industry in the 1960s and created some of Japan's most popular characters, including Astro Boy. Heavily inspired by Walt Disney, his style formed the basis for the wide-eyed "*anime*" look so associated with Japanese animation today.

Shotaro Ishimori (1938–98). Tezuka's friend and rival, Ishimori was a manga illustrator whose characters rose to prominence as the subject of animated and live-action television shows. He's perhaps best known for creating the Gorangers ("Five Rangers"), the first show in a series that would years later morph into the Power Rangers.

Hayao Miyazaki (b. 1941). Co-founder of Studio Ghibli and director of some of Japan's most lavishly designed animated features, including *Nausicaa of the Valley of Wind, My Neighbor Totoro, Princess Mononoke,* and *Spirited Away,* many of which feature quiet (and not-so-quiet) counter-cultural and conservation-oriented themes. Disney's acquisition of the foreign rights to Ghibli's works was seen as a major validation for the *anime* industry.

Yoshiyuki Tomino (b. 1941). Determined to create animated fare that appealed to an older demographic, Tomino shook the *anime* world with his 1979 series *Mobile Suit Gundam.* Although it featured giant robots, it took the form of an epic narrative highlighting the horrors of war, making it wildly popular among a teen and young adult audience. Gundam is virtually synonymous with giant Japanese robots to this day.

Go Nagai (b. 1945). Nagai's 1972 animated series *Mazinger Z* (eventually aired as *Tranzor Z* in the United States) kicked off a fad for giant robots that has barely subsided in the decades since. His later, edgier works got him into hot water with Japanese school PTA associations, leading to stricter regulation of animated content for kids.

Mamoru Oshii (b. 1951). This talented director had helmed numerous local classics in the 1980s, but rose to international prominence with the worldwide success of his animated film *Ghost in the Shell,* based on a comic book by Shirow Masamune. The creators of the mind-bending cyberpunk drama *The Matrix* cited it as a direct influence.

Katsuhiro Otomo (b. 1954). Rose to international fandom with his apocalyptic 1989 sci-fi epic *Akira.* Darker and grittier than nearly any *anime* before it, the comic book and animated film wowed foreign audiences, who began to realize that *anime* and manga weren't just for kids.

Satoshi Kon (1963–2010). Satoshi's gentle yet wildly imaginative works pushed the envelope of the *anime* medium, tackling such heady topics as homelessness, obsession, and reality itself. *Tokyo Godfathers, Paprika,* and *Paranoia Agent* are his signature works. His untimely death at the age of 46 from cancer was a major blow to the industry.

► *A classic scene from Katushiro Otomo's Akira. 821A*

Japan in Print

HISTORY The definitive work of Japan's history through the ages is *Japan: The Story of a Nation* by Edwin O. Reischauer, a former U.S. ambassador to Japan. *Everyday Life in Traditional Japan,* by Charles J. Dunn, details the daily lives of samurai, farmers, craftsmen, merchants, courtiers, and outcasts during the Edo Period. Lafcadio Hearn (p. 293), a prolific writer about things Japanese, describes life in Japan around the turn of the 20th century in *Writings from Japan, Glimpses of Unfamiliar Japan,* and *Kwaidan: Stories and Studies of Strange Things.*

CULTURE Although somewhat dated, the classic text on Japanese culture is Ruth Benedict's brilliant *The Chrysanthemum and the Sword: Patterns of Japanese Culture,* first published in the 1940s. But for a more recent take,

try *Japan: A Reinterpretation,* by former *International Herald Tribune* Tokyo bureau chief Patrick Smith, who gives a spirited reinterpretation of Japan's economic miracle and demise. Alex Kerr's *Dogs and Demons: Tales from the Dark Side of Modern Japan* is a scathing (and controversial) indictment of a country he loves but believes was ruined by corrupt bureaucracy. Jake Adelstein, a former Tokyo crime reporter, writes of his personal descent into the underworld in *Tokyo Vice: An American Reporter on the Police Beat in Japan.*

POP CULTURE Frederik Schodt's *Manga! Manga! The World of Japanese Comics* is the single best primer to the art form, though it was first published in the 1980s and so misses covering more recent developments in the industry. Roland Kelts's *Japanamerica:*

How Japanese Pop Culture Has Invaded the U.S. explores how the two nations inspire each other through comics, films, and books. Patrick Macias's *Japanese Schoolgirl Inferno: Tokyo Teen Fashion Subculture Handbook* is a handy field guide to the history of female fashion and subculture. Meanwhile, the trilogy of *Yokai Attack! The Japanese Monster Survival Guide; Ninja Attack! True Tales of Samurai, Assassins, and Outlaws;* and *Hello Please! Very Helpful Super Kawaii Characters from Japan,* co-authored by two of the authors of this book, are fun illustrated guides to Japanese pop cultural traditions.

FICTION The world's first major novel was written by a Japanese woman, Murasaki Shikibu, whose classic, *The Tale of Genji,* dating from the 11th century, describes the aristocratic life of Prince Genji. Be aware that it can be a bit of a sink-or-swim experience for those not versed the Japanese culture, but it is a fascinating window into daily goings-on almost a millennium ago.

Tokyo bookstores have entire sections dedicated to English translations of Japan best-known modern and contemporary authors, including Mishima Yukio, Natsume Soseki, Abe Kobo, Tanizaki Junichiro, and Nobel Prize winners Kawabata Yasunari and Oe Kenzaburo. An overview of Japanese classical literature from the earliest times t the mid-19th century is provided in *Anthology of Japanese Literature, From the Earliest Era to the Mid-Nineteenth Century* edited by Donald Keene.

> Novelist Murakami Haruki.

Lost in Translation: *Tokyo as seen through the eyes of foreigners.*

 kewise, *The Showa Anthol-
gy: Modern Japanese Short
ories,* edited by Van C. Ges-
l and Tomone Matsumoto,
vers works by Abe Kobo,
ishima Yukio, Kawabata
asunari, Oe Kenzaburo, and
hers, written between 1929
d 1984. *Modern Japanese
ories: An Anthology,* edited
Ivan Morris, introduces
ort stories by some of
pan's top modern writers,
cluding Mori Ogai, Tanizaki
nichiro, Kawabata Yasunari,
d Mishima Yukio.

For novels, you might read
ishima's *Confessions of a
ask,* a touching and at times
rrowing look into the life of
young man struggling with
s sexuality; or *The Sound of
aves,* about young love in a
panese fishing village. Oth-
famous works by Japanese
thors include Nobel Prize
nner Kawabata Yasunari's
ow Country,* translated by
ward G. Seidensticker.

Oe Kenzaburo gained in-
ternational recognition when
he became the second Japanese to win the Nobel Prize in
Literature in 1994. One of his
best-known novels is *Nip the
Buds, Shoot the Kids,* a disturb-
ing tale of a group of reform-
school boys in the waning
days of World War II. But his
best-known work remains
A Personal Matter, which is
about a man in search of
himself after the birth of a son
with a severe disability.

Favorite writers of Japan's
baby-boom generation
include Murakami Haruki,
whose writings run the gamut
from nonfiction to love stories
to the supernatural. Some of
his best include *A Wild Sheep
Chase; Hard-Boiled Wonderland and the End of the World;
The Wind-Up Bird Chronicle;
South of the Border, West of the
Sun; Kafka on the Shore;* and
Norwegian Wood, a coming-
of-age story set during the

1969 student movement in
Japan that was turned into a
2010 movie of the same name.

Japan on Film

The classic samurai film is
probably Akira Kurosawa's
The Seven Samurai (1954),
remade into the western *The
Magnificent Seven* (1960).
Other films by what some
consider to be Japan's
greatest filmmaker include
Rashomon (1951), about a
murder and a rape and that
raises as many questions as it
answers about human nature;
Kagemusha (1980), about
warlords battling for control
at the end of feudal Japan;
and *Ran* (1985), an epic
drama set in 16th-century
Japan and based on Shake-
speare's *King Lear.* For a look
at Japan's mountain people in
the 1880s, nothing can beat
Kinoshita Keisuke's *Ballad
of Narayama* (1958), with its
unsentimental portrait of an
elderly woman who goes off

FATHERS OF THE MODERN NOVEL

They brought new style to Japanese literature

BY MELINDA JOE

	REQUIRED READING	CLAIM TO FAME	CAREER
KAWABATA YASUNARI (1899–1972)	*Snow Country, Thousand Cranes, The Sound of the Mountain.*	Subtle, lyrical prose that combines classical aesthetics based on Zen principles with modern themes. Was the first Japanese author awarded the Nobel Prize for literature in 1968.	Started the literary journal *Bungei Jidai* to promote a new artistic movement influenced by Cubism, Expressionism, and Dada. He also worked as a journalist for the *Mainichi Daily News*.
ENDO SHUSAKU (1923–96)	*Silence, The Sea and Poison, Deep River.* 	A spare, deeply reflective style infused with images of alienation and sometimes shocking violence.	Japan's most highly acclaimed Catholic writer. Crafted novels with overtly Christian themes that explore the culture clash between East and West, morality, and the question of identity.
MISHIMA YUKIO (1925–70)	*Confessions of a Mask, The Sailor Who Fell from Grace with the Sea, The Temple of the Golden Pavilion.*	One of Japan's most famous and controversial authors, thanks to transgressive novels such as *Confessions of a Mask,* a fictionalized memoir partly describing the life of a young homosexual.	Considered for the Nobel Prize, but in 197 nationalistic views spurred him to stage a coup d'etat to restore power to the emperor. The attempt failed miserably. Mishima later committed *seppuku*, or ritual suicide.
OE KENZABURO (b. 1935)	*A Personal Matter, The Silent Cry, The Changeling.* 	The semi-autobiographical novel *A Personal Matter,* which describes a father's dilemma when his son is born with brain damage.	Won the Nobel Prize for literature in 1994. Influenced by French and American writers such as Sartre and Twain, Oe's novels deal with social and philosophical issues of existentialism and nonconformism.
MURAKAMI HARUKI (b. 1949)	*Hard-Boiled Wonderland, Norwegian Wood, The Wind-Up Bird Chronicle.* 	An emotionally detached style and postmodern worldview that deals with themes of alienation and loneliness.	Heavily influenced by Western culture, he left Japan to travel in Europe and the U.S. He has been criticized by the Japanese literary establishment over negative portrayals of Japanese history.

HE OPENING OF JAPAN'S BORDERS during the Meiji Period (1868–1912) witnessed a ourishing of new Japanese literary styles influenced by writers and intellectual movements rom overseas. Native postwar authors pushed the envelope even further, using a diverse ange of literary conventions to illustrate the conundrum of Japanese identity in a rapidly hanging modern world. Today, these 20th-century Japanese novelists have achieved an nprecedented level of international acclaim—they've received Nobel Prizes and have been ranslated into dozens of languages. The five below are truly the fathers of the genre.

ERSONAL LIFE	SPECIAL PLACE	LITTLE-KNOWN FACT	QUINTESSENTIAL QUOTE
rphaned and raised y his grandparents, ho then died when e was a teenager. He truggled with poor ealth and depression roughout his life. our years after winning the Nobel Prize, ommitted suicide.	The hot-spring resort town of Echigo-Yuzawa, in Niigata prefecture, which was made famous by his novel *Snow Country*.	Often writing tales of longing and unfulfilled desire, Kawabata was a hopeless romantic but was tragically unlucky in love.	"The single flower contains more brightness than a hundred flowers."
Vas bitterly conflicted bout his faith, comparing his relationship o Catholicism to an arranged marriage." inally reconciled Western Christianity nd Japanese thinking fter researching the life f Christ in Palestine.	Nagasaki (p. 372), the city most closely associated with the West, and the site where Portuguese missionaries first landed in Japan. The Endo Museum there houses his books and manuscripts, along with other artifacts.	Catholic groups successfully lobbied to prevent him from receiving the Nobel Prize for literature.	"Christianity, to be effective in Japan, must change."
Obsessed with physical beauty, he was an nternational dandy in is youth and worked s a model and actor. Despite marrying and athering two children, e was rumored to ave had several same-ex relationships.	The noir-esque cluster of bars in Tokyo's Shinjuku ward called Golden Gai, frequented by Mishima and other leading artists and intellectuals in the '50s and '60s.	He was born Kimitaka Hiraoka but changed his name to keep his publications secret from his father, who had disapproved of his writing.	"If we value so highly the dignity of life, how can we not also value the dignity of death? No death may be called futile."
he birth of his first son, likari, marked a turning oint in his career. Born vith a mental disability, likari appears as a haracter in Oe's books. everal of his novels iscuss the relationship etween disabled and ondisabled people.	The mountain village of Ose, where he was born, on the island of Shikoku. His grandmother maintained a Taoist shrine there, and in one of his later books, he attempts to retell the mythological history of the village.	Oe started writing novels as a college student because he had trouble sleeping. He enjoys drinking but says that he doesn't go to bars because he gets into fights—usually over politics—after a few whiskies.	"I'm an anarchist who loves democracy."
Vhile studying drama t Waseda University n Tokyo, he met his vife, Yoko Takahashi, nd the two married in 971. A self-professed oner, Murakami confesses that married life asn't been easy.	The Tokyo suburb of Kokobunji, where Murakami and his wife ran a jazz club for 7 years called Peter the Cat, named after their pet. Much of the action in his novel *Norwegian Wood* also takes place here.	An avid marathon runner and triathlete, Murakami didn't take up running until he was 33 years old, after years of smoking.	"Pain is inevitable. Suffering is optional."

> Rashomon *and other Kurosawa classics single-handedly changed the world's perception of Japanese film.*

into the snowy countryside to die, as was the custom of her people.

Director Oshima Nagisa created a stir in the film world with *In the Realm of the Senses* (1976), a story of obsessive love so graphic and erotic it remains censored in Japan. Juzo Itami, a famous Japanese director who purportedly leapt to his death in Tokyo in 1997 (the circumstances are mysterious), is remembered for his humorous satires on Japanese life, including *Tampopo* (1985), about sex and food and a Japanese woman who achieves success with a noodle shop; *The Funeral* (1984), which takes a comic look at death in Japan, including the surviving family's helplessness when it comes to arranging the complex rituals of the Buddhist ceremony; and *A Taxing Woman* (1987), about a female tax auditor.

Love and Pop (1998), by director Anno Hideaki, best known for *anime* films, is a low-budget film based on a novel by Murakami Ryu about "compensated dating," in which teenage girls are paid to go out with older businessmen. Another film dealing with this phenomenon rarely covered in the Western press is Harada Masato's *Bounce Ko Gals* (1998), which presents a shocking but heartfelt story of sexual exploitation and loss of innocence.

A commentary on Japan's economic woes on a personal level is *Tokyo Sonata* (2008), directed Kurosawa Kiyoshi, about a father who loses his job but is too ashamed to tell his family and thus pretends he's going to work every day. *Departures* (2008) is Takita Yojiro's moving Academy Award–winning film (for best foreign film) about a musician who takes a job preparing corpses and eventually comes to see it as a deeply rewarding profession. Probably the most

internationally well-known film shot in Tokyo in recent years is Sophia Coppola's *Lost in Translation* (2003), in which two lost characters take solace in each other's company as they drift through an incomprehensible—and at times hilarious—Tokyo, while *The Harimaya Bridge* (2009), by Aaron Woolfolk, is a moving story about a man whose hatred for the Japanese (his father died in a Japanese POW camp) slowly dissolves when he travels to Kochi to pick up his dead son's belongings. One of Japan's most famous animated films is Miyazaki Hayao's *Spirited Away* (2001), about a young girl who must call upon her inner strength to save herself and her family. *Norwegian Wood*, based on Murakami Haruki's novel and directed by Tran Anh Hung, was nominated for a Golden Lion at the Venice Film Festival in 2010.

Japanese Cuisine

A tasteful (and tasty) tempura arrangement from Kyoto's Yoshikawa.

> Loading up on toppings for sanuki udon, a Shikoku specialty.

Altogether, there are more than a dozen different and distinct types of Japanese cuisine, plus countless regional specialties. In fact, a big part of traveling around the country is sampling the *meibutsu*—local specialties—that each region has to offer. A good deal of what you eat may be completely new to you as well as completely unidentifiable. Sometimes, particularly with elaborately prepared *kaiseki* meals (see below), even natives have a hard time knowing what they're eating, so varied and so wide is the range of available edibles.

The Japanese cultural ideal is to be open-minded to tasting everything at least once. This is particularly important when being treated to a meal by someone else. That said, if you have dietary or religious restrictions on what you can eat, don't hesitate to let people know. The Japanese are

nothing if not accommodating hosts and will generally bend over backward to make sure you're having a pleasant time. The only rule is simply to enjoy, and enjoyment begins even before you raise your chopsticks to your mouth.

To the Japanese, **presentation** of food is as important as the food itself, and dishes are designed to appeal not only to the palate but also to the eye. In contrast to the American way of piling as much food as possible onto a single plate, the Japanese use lots of small plates, each arranged artfully with bite-size morsels of food. After you've seen what can be done with maple leaves, flowers, bits of bamboo, and even pebbles to enhance the appearance of food, your relationship with what you eat may change forever. If there's such a thing as designer cuisine, Japan is its home.

Types of Cuisine

KAISEKI *Kaiseki* isn't a specific dish but rather a complete meal. It is the epitome of delicately and exquisitely arranged food, the ultimate in Japanese aesthetic appeal. A *kaiseki* meal is usually a lengthy affair with various seasonally chosen dishes appearing in set order. These multicourse extravaganzas don't come cheaply, though, and can cost ¥25,000 or more per person. The better *ryokan* (traditional inns) serve *kaiseki*, a reason for their high cost. *Kaiseki* itself is expensive because much time and skill are involved in preparing each of the many dishes, with the ingredients cooked to preserve natural flavors. Even the plates are chosen with great care.

NOODLES There are many different kinds of noodles, and it seems like almost every region of Japan has its own special style or kind—some are

> Okonomiyaki, *Osaka's savory pancakes.*

> *Maguro (tuna) sushi, a perennial favorite.*

eaten plain, some in combination with other foods such as shrimp tempura, some served hot, some served cold. **Soba,** made from unbleached buckwheat flour and enjoyed for its nutty flavor and high nutritional value, is eaten hot (*kake soba*) or cold (*zaru soba*). *Udon* is a thick white wheat noodle originally from Osaka; it's usually served hot. **Ramen** actually hails from China, but the noodles are a longtime Japanese favorite as well. Be forewarned: In Japan, slurping noodles is considered proper etiquette.

OKONIMIYAKI Okonimiyaki originated in Osaka after World War II and literally means "as you like it"; it's often referred to as Japanese pizza (which is kind of a stretch). The standard *okonomiyaki* is a savory pancake cooked with meat or shellfish, shredded cabbage, and vegetables, topped with mayonnaise and Worcestershire sauce. The simple ingredients

make it very reasonably priced. At some places the cook makes it for you, but at others it's do-it-yourself, which can be quite fun if you're with a group. (Feel free to ask for help if you need a quick lesson; it's an easy thing to pick up.) Hiroshima-style *okonomiyaki* is served atop a bed of *yakisoba* (fried ramen-like noodles).

SUSHI & SASHIMI It's estimated that the average Japanese eats 38kg (84 lb.) of seafood a year—that's six times the average American consumption. Although this seafood may be served in any number of ways from grilled to boiled, a great deal of it is eaten raw.

Sashimi is simply raw seafood, usually served as an appetizer and eaten alone (that

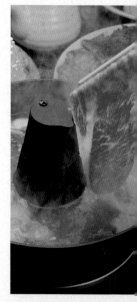

> *Shabu-shabu, or hot-pot cook*

> A donburi (bowl) style of sukiyaki, served atop rice.

> A variety of vegetables and seafood done up tempura style, or deep-fried.

s, without rice). If you've never eaten it, a good choice to start out with is *maguro,* or lean tuna, which doesn't taste fishy at all and is so delicate in texture that it almost melts in your mouth. The way to eat sashimi is to first put a dot of wasabi (pungent green horse-radish) onto each morsel and then dip it in soy sauce using your chopsticks. (Unlike abroad, Japanese tend not to premix the wasabi with the soy sauce.)

Sushi, which is raw fish with vinegared rice, comes in many varieties. The best known is *nigiri-zushi:* raw fish, seafood, or vegetables placed on top of vinegared rice with just a touch of wasabi. It's also dipped in soy sauce. Use chopsticks or your fingers to eat sushi; remember you're supposed to eat each piece in one bite—quite a mouthful,

but about the only way to keep it from falling apart. To keep a piece of sushi from crumbling, turn it upside down and only dip the topping, not the rice.

By the way, the least expensive sushi is *chirashi,* which is a selection of fish, seafood, and omelet chunks atop a shallow bowl of sushi rice. Because you get more rice, those of you with bigger appetites may want to order *chirashi.* Another way to enjoy sushi without spending a fortune is at a *kaiten* sushi shop, in which plates of sushi circulate on a conveyor belt on the counter—customers reach for the dishes they want and pay for the number of dishes they take.

SHABU-SHABU Shabu-shabu is prepared at your table and consists of thinly sliced beef

cooked in a broth with vegetables in a kind of Japanese fondue. (It's named for the swishing sound the beef supposedly makes when cooking.) Using their chopsticks, diners submerge pieces of meat in the watery broth until they're cooked. This usually takes only a few seconds. Vegetables are left in longer to swim around until fished out. There are generally two kinds dipping sauce: a tangy *ponzu* (citrus-based) one and a thicker sesame-based one. (As a side note, it's always "shabu-shabu" and never just "shabu." The latter is street slang for methamphetamine, so watch what you tell people you're looking for.)

SUKIYAKI This is among Japan's best-known beef dishes and is often served to foreigners who are leery of more

> *Yakitori: finger food for bars throughout Japan.*

> *Most types of Japanese cuisine pair well with lager.*

traditional foods. Like fondue, it's cooked at the table. It consists of thinly sliced beef cooked in a sweet broth of soy sauce, stock, and sake along with scallions, spinach, mushrooms, tofu, bamboo shoots, and other vegetables. All diners serve themselves from the simmering pot and then dip their morsels into their own bowl of raw egg. You can skip the raw egg if you want, but it adds to the taste and also cools the food down enough so that it doesn't burn.

SHOJIN-RYORI The ultimate vegan meal, created centuries ago to serve the needs of Zen Buddhist priests and pilgrims. Dishes may include *yudofu* (simmered tofu) and an array of local vegetables; at its

most elaborate it's somewhat like *kaiseki* (see above), but entirely vegan. Even if you're a devoted carnivore, these are usually very filling and satisfying meals. Kyoto is the best place to experience this type of cuisine.

TEMPURA Today a well-known Japanese food, tempura was actually introduced by the Portuguese in the 16th century. It consists of seafood and vegetables coated in a batter of egg, water, and wheat flour and then deep-fried; it's served piping hot. To eat it, dip it in a sauce of soy, fish stock, *daikon* (radish), and grated ginger; in some restaurants, only some salt, powdered green tea, or a lemon wedge is provided

as an accompaniment. Kyoto is known for the quality of its tempura, but it can be found throughout the country.

YAKITORI This is chunks of chicken or chicken parts basted in a sweet soy sauce and grilled over a charcoal fire on thin skewers. *Yakitori-ya*, places that specialize in yakitori (often identifiable by a red paper lantern outside the front door), are technically not restaurants but drinking establishments; they usually don't open until 5 or 6pm. Most *yakitori-ya* are popular with workers as inexpensive places to drink, eat, and be merry. The cheapest way to dine on yakitori is to order a *moriawase* ("chef's selection") set course, which will often include various parts of the chicken including the skin, heart, and liver. If this isn't entirely to your taste, you may wish to order a la carte, which is more expensive but gets you exactly what you want.

Japanese Etiquette

Don't worry about the details of etiquette too much; a good attitude is the most important thing.

Much of Japan's system of etiquette and manners stems from its feudal days, when the social hierarchy dictated how a person spoke, sat, bowed, ate, walked, and lived. In times of old, failure to comply with the rules of the social hierarchy would bring social stigma at best and severe punishment—even death—at worst.

Of course, nowadays it's quite different. You don't have to worry about your head, but as a sensitive traveler should try to familiarize yourself with the basics of Japanese social etiquette. As a foreigner, you can get away with a lot; Japanese give foreigners great leeway for not knowing the ins and outs of their culture. But there is at least one "cardinal sin" that is easy to avoid. **Never wear your shoes inside a private home or a temple.** (A tatami mat is a good sign you should be taking your shoes off.) Generally, guests are provided with little slippers to wear around

inside. They're often far too small for foreign feet, but do your best to shuffle around with them on.

But shoes are the easy part; social niceties are harder to get a read on. That said, the Japanese are very appreciative of foreigners who take the time to learn about their country and are quite patient in helping you. If you're perceived as making even a cursory effort in this regard, you will find your way through nearly any situation. If you do happen to commit a faux pas, a smile, apology, and keeping an open mind about whatever caused it will go a long way toward fixing things.

Most forms of behavior and etiquette in Japan developed to allow relationships to be as frictionless as possible, particularly in a public context. This is perhaps best illustrated by the recent buzzword "KY," an acronym for the Japanese words **kuuki wo yomenai** and meaning literally

"one who can't read the air." Japanese culture places a great emphasis on reading nonverbal cues and judging the content and context of situations without needing to be explicitly told. Someone who is "KY"—who can't put themselves in their listener's shoes and anticipate what is going on—is seen as something of a social lummox in Japan.

Another aspect of Japanese behavior that sometimes causes difficulty for foreigners, especially in business negotiations, is the **reluctance of Japanese to say no when they mean no.** As such, you need to be attentive to keywords that indicate negativity. "It's difficult" is a classic way for a Japanese to try and let you down lightly without explicitly saying "no." If you hear this kind of thing in response to a request, accept it as a "no" and drop it or compromise. Complaining, showing impatience, or getting angry will do nothing to serve your cause; Japan is not an emotionally demonstrative culture, especially so with regard to negativity. But don't mistake this for lack of emotion. Whenever someone does give in to a request or does you a favor, make sure to show proper gratitude with profuse thanks. Trust us, it will be deeply appreciated—and remembered.

Do not be surprised or insulted if you aren't invited to the home of a friend; Japanese homes, particularly

> *After a long day, nothing beats a soak in a Japanese bath.*

those in crowded cities, often have very little room for entertaining guests. This is precisely why the cities are home to so many restaurants, coffee shops, and bars. If you are invited to a Japanese home, you should know that it's both a rarity and an honor. If you're invited to a home, **don't show up empty-handed.** Bring a small gift such as candy, fruit, flowers, or perhaps a souvenir from your hometown. Alcohol is also appreciated. And if someone does extend you a favor, be sure to thank him again the next time you see him—even if it's a year later.

Bowing

Whether business or personal, the main form of greeting in Japan is the bow rather than the handshake. Although at first glance it may seem simple enough, the bow—together with its implications—is actually quite complicated. The depth of the bow and the number of seconds devoted to performing it, as well as the total number of bows, depend on who you are, to whom you're bowing, and how they're bowing back. That said, no Japanese person expects a foreigner, particularly a tourist, to understand the ins and outs of proper bowing. In fact, many Japanese won't even expect a foreign person to bow, though an attempt will always be welcomed.

In addition to bowing in greeting, Japanese also bow upon departing and to express gratitude. The proper form for a bow is to bend from the waist with a straight back and to keep your arms at your sides if you're a man or clasped in front of you if you're a woman, but if you're a foreigner or among friends, a simple nod of the head is often enough.

Don't be surprised to see Japanese bowing to their speaker even when using the telephone; the bows are so intertwined with the use of polite speech that even foreigners find themselves doing it from time to time.

Business Card Etiquette

You're almost a nonentity in Japan if you don't have a business card, called a **meishi.** No matter their age or level, every professional carries *meishi* to give out during introductions. Even if you're only visiting as a tourist, they can be a great way to start a conversation. And if you're trying to conduct business in Japan, you simply won't be taken seriously if you don't have a business card.

Needless to say, there's a proper way to present a *meishi*. Turn it so that the other person can read it (that is, upside-down to you) and present it with both hands and a slight bow. If you are of equal status, you exchange *meishi* simultaneously; otherwise, the lower person on the totem pole presents the *meishi* first and delivers it underneath the card being received, to show deference. Afterward, don't simply put the *meishi* away. It's customary to leave it out on the tabletop during discussions. And when you're done, refrain from stuffing it into your wallet; sitting on someone else's *meishi* is seen as rude. If you plan to meet a wide variety of people, invest in a standalone business card holder or wallet.

Bathrooms & Bathing

As you might expect, a great deal of Japanese etiquette deals with using the toilet and bath facilities. First of all, toilets and baths are generally separated; bathrooms in Japan are literal rooms for baths.

If you need to relieve yourself, ask for the *toire*—pronounced *toy*-ray—and not the bathroom. In Japanese homes, inns, and restaurants of the sort where guests remove their shoes, you'll notice a pair of slippers—again plastic or rubber—sitting right inside the restroom door. Step out of the slippers you're wearing and into the bathroom slippers, and wear them the entire time you're in the restroom. When you're finished,

The first rule of the bath is wash and rinse before getting in the tub.

change back into the hallway slippers. If you forget this last changeover, you'll regret it—nothing is as embarrassing as walking into a room wearing toilet slippers!

Perhaps no other aspect of Japanese culture is as perplexing to first-time visitors as bathing. But don't let that scare you: Japanese baths are delightful. You'll find them at japanese-style inns, at *onsen* (hot-spring spas), and at *sento* (neighborhood baths); not everyone has his or her own bath in Japan. Sometimes they're elaborate affairs with indoor and outdoor tubs, and sometimes they're nothing more than a tiny tub. Public baths have long been regarded as social centers for Japanese—friends and coworkers will visit hot-spring resorts together; neighbors exchange gossip at the neighborhood bath. Sadly, neighborhood baths have been in great decline over the past decades, as the vast majority of Japanese have their own private baths.

Hot-spring spas, however, remain hugely popular.

Whether large or small, the procedure at all Japanese baths is the same. The most important rule to keep in mind is simple and inviolable: **never, ever wash with soap inside a communal Japanese bathtub. Soap and rinse yourself thoroughly before getting in.**

After completely disrobing in the changing room and putting your clothes in either a locker or a basket, hold a washcloth (provided free or available for sale at the bathhouse) in front of you so that it covers your vital parts and walk into the bathing area. There you'll find plastic basins and stools (sometimes they're still made of wood), and faucets along the wall. Sit on the stool in front of a faucet and repeatedly fill your basin with water (or use the hand-held faucet if available), splashing water all over you. If there's no hot water from the faucet, it's acceptable to dip your basin into the hot bath, but your

washcloth should never touch the tub water. Rinsing yourself thoroughly is not only proper *onsen* manners; it also acclimatizes your body to the bath's hot temperature so you don't suffer a heart attack. While some Japanese just throw a bit of water over themselves, others soap down completely—and we mean completely—and then rinse away all traces of soap before getting into the tub. At any rate, only when you feel squeaky-clean should you enter the tub.

Your first attempt at a Japanese bath may be painful—simply too scalding for comfort. It helps if you ease in gently and then sit perfectly still. You'll notice all tension and muscle stiffness ebbing away, a decidedly relaxing way to end the day. At an *onsen*, where hot-spring waters are considered curative, Japanese will bathe both at night and again in the morning, often making several trips between the faucet and the tubs and being careful not to rinse off the curative waters when they're done.

Note: Because tattoos in Japan have long been associated with *yakuza* (the Japanese mafia), the vast majority of public baths do not admit people with tattoos. If your tattoo is small and discreet, you may not have as much of a problem, but be prepared for the possibility that you may be asked to leave. Those with full-body or "sleeve" tattoos will almost always be refused service. Tattoos for purely decorative purposes are a very recent trend in Japan, and the association between the underworld and tattoos remains quite strong.

The Japanese Language

> *Japanese is a mixture of local and imported syllabaries.*

Without a doubt, no aspect of traveling in Japan gives visitors more pause than the language barrier. Japanese is (somewhat hyperbolically, we feel) renowned as one of the world's most difficult languages to learn, and suddenly you find yourself transported to a crowded land of 127 million people where you can neither speak nor read the language. To make matters worse, many Japanese cannot speak English. And outside big cities and major tourist sites, menus, signs at train stations, and shop names are often in Japanese only. Even within them, the lack of systematic addresses can make getting around an exercise in

detective work.

However, millions of foreign visitors before you who didn't speak a word of Japanese have traveled throughout Japan on their own with great success. Much of the anxiety travelers experience elsewhere is eliminated in Japan because the country is safe and the vast majority of people are kind and helpful to foreigners. Partially because of its perceived extreme difficulty, the Japanese have zero expectations of foreigners being able to speak their language, so your requests for help will nearly always be accommodated (if not always answered). In addition, the country has done

a mammoth job during the past decade updating street signs, subway directions, and addresses in Roman letters, especially in major cities such as Tokyo, Osaka, Kyoto, and other destinations popular with tourists. There are local **tourist information offices,** called *kanko annaijo,* in almost all cities and towns, usually at train stations. While not all staff speak English, they can provide maps, point out directions, and help with hotel reservations.

In addition, the **Japan National Tourist Organization (JNTO)** does a super job publishing helpful brochures, leaflets, and maps, including a nifty booklet called ***The***

Because Japanese only has one consonent for both r and l sounds, the two letters are often confused on English signage—hilarity may ensue.

Tourist's Language Handbook. It contains sentences in English and their Japanese equivalents for almost every activity, from asking directions, to shopping, to ordering in a restaurant, to staying in a Japanese inn. Pick up a copy at a Tourist Information Center in Tokyo or at Narita or Kansai airports, or download it from www.jnto.go.jp/eng/touristhandbook/eng.pdf. For basic linguistic help, a glossary and pronunciation guide follows in "The Savvy Traveler" chapter (p. 548). And for more in-depth coverage, there are many language books geared toward travelers, including *Japanese for Travelers* by Scott Rutherford, with useful phrases and travel tips.

You should never hesitate if you feel the need to ask directions of strangers in Japan, but you should use your common sense. Younger people may be more willing (or simply have more time) to help than businessmen rushing to a meeting or elderly folks who may not leave their section of town much. Having "visual aids" such as a sketched map or the name of your destination written out may help (for this reason we've included Japanese *kanji*—letters—for many establishments that might otherwise be hard to locate by their English names), as will a pen and paper. Many Japanese read and write English far better than they speak it; those who can't understand a word you say may still have a surprising grasp of syntax and English grammar. It also doesn't hurt to be armed with a small pocket English-Japanese dictionary, though you probably won't need it for asking directions. As a side note, many cultural guidebooks describe situations where the Japanese would rather give incorrect directions rather than admitting they don't know the way. We have never, ever encountered this sort of thing ourselves, and suspect it's more due to linguistic issues than cultural ones.

Another excellent source of directional info are the *koban* (police boxes) stationed throughout the city. While the police will be more than happy to help—providing directions is part of their job—they will probably not speak much English, particularly outside of city centers. They are specialists of their districts and can pinpoint exactly where you want to go if you have the address, written in Japanese, with you. And you can always call the **Tourist Information Center** (☎ 03/3201-3331) to help with translation. But most of all, don't panic. Japan is an extremely safe country, and getting lost is often part of the fun of getting around. This is particularly true in major cities, which teem with far more shops, restaurants, attractions, and quiet little moments than can be shoehorned into any single guidebook.

14

The Best Special Interest Trips

> *PREVIOUS PAGE The view from the Hakone cable car can't be beat. THIS PAGE Anime-inspired fashion dolls on display in Akihabara.*

Anime & Pop Culture Tours

Pop Japan Travel offers custom and group tours centered on *otaku* (Japanese animation– and manga-related) experiences, such as the Tokyo Anime Fair and ninja/samurai themes. 1487 W. 178th St., Ste. 300, Gardena, CA 90248 U.S. ☎ 310/817-8010, ext. 111. www.popjapan travel.com.

Barrier-Free Tours

In a country not known for accessibility, **JTB USA** can arrange tours for travelers with disabilities. 156 W. 56th St., 3rd floor, New York, NY 10019 U.S. ☎ 800/235-3523. www.jtbusa.com.

Culinary Tours

Sake-World.com offers a 5-day Sake Brewery Tour hosted by sake expert John Gauntner. It is a hands-on, intensive educational experience involving both lectures and visits to top breweries in Kyoto, Osaka, Kobe, and other areas. 1–4–4 Jomyoji, Kamakura-shi, Kanagawa-ken 248-0003 Japan. ☎ 0467/23-6895. www.sake-world.com.

Cultural Tours

Very generally speaking, if your primary interest lies with traditional pursuits such as *ikebana* (Japanese flower arranging), the tea ceremony, or the like, Tokyo and Kyoto are your best bets for finding English-language instruction.

Sunrise Tours offers the chance to experience the tea ceremony on 2- or 3-hour tours in both Tokyo and Kyoto, along with other cultural pursuits such as making sushi or writing calligraphy. 2–3–11 Higashishinagawa, Shinagawa-ku, Tokyo 140-8604 Japan. ☎ 03/5796-5454. www.jtb-sunrisetours.jp.

Destination Japan offers a bonsai tour that centers on a major bonsai festival and stops at a variety of gardens and nurseries. 420 E. 3rd St., Ste. 608, Los Angeles, CA 90013 U.S. ☎ 877/447-8721. www.destination-japan.com.

The **Women's Association of Kyoto** doesn't arrange travel, but offers a wide variety of classes on the tea ceremony, flower arranging, origami, Japanese calligraphy, Japanese cooking, and other cultural activities in the Kyoto area. 761 Tenshucho, Takakura Dori, Nijo-agaru, Nakagyo-ku, Kyoto 604-0812 Japan. ☎ 075/212-9993. www.wakjapan.com.

Guided Tours

If you've picked up this guide, chances are you aren't the sort who wants a structured tour with a group leader. But if you do want a little guidance, the following are good places to start.

Artisans of Leisure provides luxury tours with private guides that are tailored to your interests. It offers a concierge-type service that can take care of logistics for those who want guidance but don't like group tours. 18 E. 16th St., Ste. 301, New York, NY 10003 U.S. ☎ 800/214-8144. www.artisansofleisure.com.

General Tours offers tour packages to major tourist destinations in Japan. 53 Summer St., Keene, NH 03431 U.S. ☎ 800/221-2216. www.generaltours.com.

JTB USA offers a variety of guided tours both general and specialized. 156 W. 56th St., 3rd floor, New York, NY 10019 U.S. ☎ 800/235-3523. www.jtbusa.com.

Origami cranes in the Hiroshima Peace Park.

> *Hitting the slopes at Mount Naeba, just a few hours from Tokyo.*

Outdoor Activities

Skiing

enerally, the ski season in Japan runs from ecember through March.

Deep Powder Tours, located in Australia nd Hokkaido, boasts 16 years of experience rranging ski and snowboard tours throughout apan. 189-16 Aza Yamada, Kutchan-cho, Abu-a-gun, Hokkaido 044-0081 Japan. ☎ 0136/21-327. www.deeppowdertours.com.

Ski Japan Holidays works with local tour perators to arrange trips to Hokkaido, Na-ano, Niigata, and Tohoku: 6660 Hokujo Kitaa-umigun, Hakuba, Nagano 399-9301 Japan. 0261/72-6663. www.japanspecialists.com.

Japan Ski Experience, based in the United ingdom, offers custom-tailored packages r ski enthusiasts. They offer flight-inclusive ackages from the U.K. and Japan-based ar-angement for visitors from other starting oints. ☎ 020/8099-9034 in the U.K. http://panskiexperience.com.

Scuba

/hile dive operators abound in Japan, only a w offer English-language support. For ad-tional information about diving in Okinawa, e p. 490.

Goodwill Guides

You can meet locals and learn about destinations at the same time through **Goodwill Guides,** a national organization of volunteers (mostly retirees, housewives, and students) who donate their time to guide you around their city free of charge (you pay their travel expenses, admission fees to sights, and meals). There are Goodwill Guides in cities throughout Japan, including Fukuoka, Kumamoto, Beppu, Kagoshima, Takamatsu, Matsuyama, Hiroshima, Himeji, Kurashiki, Matsue, Kobe, Osaka, Kyoto, Nara, Kanazawa, Matsumoto, Nagoya, Tokyo, Yokohama, Kamakura, Hakone, Nikko, and Matsushima. Reservations for a guide must be made in advance—usually a week or more. For information, including contact information, ask for the pamphlet *Goodwill Guide Groups of Japan Welcome You* at Tourist Information Centers in Tokyo or Narita and Kansai international airports; or go to JNTO's website at **www.jnto.go.jp,** and click "Essential Info" (under "Arrange Your Travel"), and then "Guide Services."

> *The Shimanami Cycling Road is a great way to see Shikoku.*

Mar Scuba is Tokyo's oldest foreign-run dive operation. It arranges instruction and dive tours and sells equipment as well. Higashi Nakano 3–15–9, Nakano-ku, Tokyo 164-0003 Japan. ☎ 090/3851-3901. www.marscuba.com.

  Discovery Divers Tokyo, founded and run by an American diver, arranges instruction, tours, and equipment throughout Japan for divers beginning to expert level. 6-25-26 Asamizodai, Sagamihara, Kanagawa 228-0828 Japan. ☎ 080/5707-3260. www.discoverydiverstokyo.com.

  Reef Encounters is a full-service, fully bilingual dive operation based in Okinawa. It offers instruction, tours, and equipment sales. 1–493 Miyagi, Chatan-cho, Okinawa 904-0113 Japan. ☎ 098/995-9414. www.reefencounters.org.

Cycling

Founded by an avid Japanese cyclist, **Oka Tours** is a small operation that specializes in arranging tours for non-Japanese visitors. 2-24-5 Kichijoji-higashi-cho, Musashino, Tokyo 180-0002 Japan. ☎ 0422/26-6644. www.okatours.com.

  Bike Tours Japan specializes in arranging privately guided and supported or self-guided cycling trips in Hokkaido. 2-14 Kitanomine cho, Furanoshi, Hokkaido 076-0034 Japan. ☎ 0167/22-5655. www.biketoursjapan.com.

  Run by an expat who lives in Kyushu, **Japan Bike and Hike** is a solo operation that arrange cycling tours throughout Kyushu. 135-116 Tsukahara Yufuin, Oita 879-5101 Japan. ☎ 0977/85-5410. www.japanbikenhike.com.

Hiking

Quest Japan specializes in guided "walking holidays" throughout Japan, organized by effort level and geared to all levels of walker/hiker. 408-1-1 Ichiban Cho, Chiyoda-ku, Tokyo 1020-0082 Japan. ☎ 03/5226-1169. www.questjapan.co.jp.

  Run by a trio of expats, **Walk Japan** bills itself as the "pioneer of off-the-beaten-track walking tours in Japan." It offers both backcountry trekking and urban walking tours. 529–1 Matamizu Ota Kitsuki 879-0941 Japan. www.walkjapan.com.

Mountain Travel Sobek is a California-based travel company that offers a variety active itineraries around the world. Their mperial Trail tour focuses on the Kiso Valley ea and includes Kyoto. 1266 66th St., Ste. 4, meryville, CA 94608 U.S. ☎ 510/594-6000. ww.mtsobek.com.

urfing

yphoon Surf Tours is a New Zealand–based mpany that specializes in surf tours cen-red on southern Japan. But it offers a mix surfing and land-based touring. Instruction fered as well. ☎ 64/7-825-8087 in New Zea-nd. www.typhoonsurftours.com.

hotography Tours

he South Africa–based **C4 Safaris** offers a -week winter tour of Hokkaido's top photo nooting spots. 34 Bel Monte, Maiana St., Pre-ria 00814 South Africa. ☎ 012/993-1946 in outh Africa. www.c4safaris.co.uk.

olunteering Tours

or information about volunteering in and round earthquake-ravaged Tohoku and Hon-nu, see p. 403.

> *The rope bridge at Shikoku Mura, made with ancient techniques.*

The Home-Visit System

Recognizing the difficulty foreigners may face in meeting Japanese people, a half-dozen or so cities offer a **Home Visit**, allowing overseas visitors the chance to visit an English-speaking Japanese family in their home for a few hours. Not only does such an encounter bring you in direct contact with Japanese, it also offers a glimpse into their lifestyle. You can even request that a family member share your occupation, though such requests are, of course, sometimes impossible to fulfill.

The program doesn't cost anything, but it does take some advance preparation. You must make arrangements in advance—this varies and can range from one day to two weeks in advance—by calling or applying in person at the local administrative authority or private organization (which is sometimes the local tourist office) that handles the city's home-visit program. After contacting a local family, the office will inform you of the family and the time of the visit.

Most visits take place for a few hours in the evening (dinner is not served). You should bring a small gift such as flowers, fruit, or a small souvenir from your hometown. Before your visit, you may be asked to appear in person at the application office to obtain detailed directions; or the office may call with the directions. Note that application offices may be closed on weekends and holidays.

Cities participating in the Home-Visit System include **Nagoya** (☎ 052/581-5689), **Kyoto** (☎ 075/752-3511), **Osaka** (☎ 06/6345-2189), **Kobe** (☎ 078/303-1010), **Kurashiki** (☎ 086/475-0543), **Hiroshima** (☎ 082/247-9715), **Fukuoka** (☎ 092/733-2220), and **Kumamoto** (☎ 096/359-2121). For more information, contact local tourist information offices.

For more information about the program in general, including restrictions and requirements, see the official website at www.homestay-in-japan.com/eng.

15
The Savvy Traveler

> The ever-changing skyline is one of Tokyo's charms. This view is from Asakusa.

Before You Go

Japan National Tourism Organization (JNTO) Overseas Offices

IN THE UNITED STATES

11 W. 42nd St., 19th floor, New York, NY 10036 (☎ 212/757-5640). Little Tokyo Plaza, 340 E. 2nd St., Ste. 302, Los Angeles, CA 90012 (☎ 213/623-1952).

IN CANADA

481 University Ave., Ste. 306, Toronto, ON M5G 2P1 (☎ 416/366-7140).

IN THE UNITED KINGDOM

12–13 Nicholas Lane, 5th floor, London EC4N 7BN (☎ 020/7398-5670).

Best Times to Go

The best seasons to visit Japan are **autumn** (Oct–Nov) and **spring** (Apr–May), when the temperatures are pleasant and the natural scenery is at its most beautiful. Summer, which begins in June, is the least desirable time to go. In addition to the fickle rainy season, which lasts from about mid-June to mid-July, the weather turns unbearably hot and uncomfortably humid throughout the country in late July and August.

Reservations can be extremely difficult to come by at certain times of the year: Oshogatsu (New Year holiday), from the end of December to January 4; Golden Week, from April 29 to May 5; and Obon in mid-August. If you plan to visit during those times (the weekends before and after these holidays are also likely to be crowded), book accommodations and make other arrangements as far in advance as possible.

Another busy time is during the school summer vacation, from around July 19 or 20 through August. It's best to reserve train seats and book accommodations ahead of time.

Festivals & Special Events

JANUARY

New Year's Day. The most important national holiday in Japan. Because this is a time when Japanese are with their families and because virtually all businesses, restaurants, museums, and shops close down, it's not a particularly rewarding time of the year for foreign visitors. Best bets are shrines and temples, where Japanese come in their best kimono or dress to pray for good health and happiness in the coming year. Jan 1.

Coming-of-Age Day. This honors young people who have reached the age of 20, whe they can vote, drink alcohol, and assume oth responsibilities. On this day, they visit shrine throughout the country to pray for their futu with many women dressed in kimono. In To-kyo, the most popular shrine is Mei-ji Shrine 2nd Mon in Jan.

Toh-shiya, Kyoto. This traditional Japanese archery contest is held in the back corridor o Japan's longest wooden structure, Sanjusan-gendo Hall. Sun closest to Jan 15.

Yamayaki, Nara. As evening approaches, Wakakusayama Hill is set ablaze and fire-works are displayed. The celebration marks a time more than 1,000 years ago when a dis-pute over the boundary of two major temple in Nara was settled peacefully. 4th Sun in Jan

FEBRUARY

Oyster Festival, Matsushima. The city is fame for the quality of its shellfish, and this is the time they're considered to be at their best. Oysters are given out free at booths set up a the seaside park along the bay. 1st Sun in Feb

Setsubun. This bean-throwing festival isn't a specific event—it's an activity you'll see happening at temples throughout Japan ever winter. According to the lunar calendar, this the last day of winter; people throng to tem-ples to participate in the traditional ceremor of throwing beans to drive away imaginary devils, shouting, *"Oni wa soto! Fuku wa uchi!"* ("Demons out! Good luck in!"). Feb 3 or 4.

Sapporo Snow Festival, Odori Park, Sappor Locals turn mountains of snow into exquisite sculptures; competitors come from around the world. With all of the effort and attentio to detail, it seems a crime they're doomed to melt in the end. More than 2 million people visit annually, so if you're planning to go, ma reservations well in advance. Early Feb.

Sedo Matsuri, Matsuri. More a rite than a festival, the Sedo Matsuri is a beloved folk tr dition. It's based on a local New Year's custo in which men dress up in costumes resembli monsters called Namahage. Tromping throu the snow, they pound on doors looking for misbehaving children to punish. The public festival, held a month later, takes a slightly d ferent form: After a sacred Shinto dance cal Chinkamayu no Mai, locals in Namahage co tume parade down the mountain with torch

VERAGE DAILY TEMPERATURE & MONTHLY RAINFALL IN TOKYO

	JAN	FEB	MAR	APR	MAY	JUNE	JULY	AUG	SEPT	OCT	NOV	DEC
MP °F	41	45	50	61	70	72	79	81	75	68	57	48
MP °C	5	7	10	16	21	22	26	27	24	20	14	9
AINFALL (IN.)	1.9	2.6	4.0	5.0	5.6	7.0	5.1	5.9	7.0	6.1	3.3	1.8

alled *sedo* in Japanese), then perform a ance to the accompaniment of drums. **2nd eekend of Feb.**

ARCH

kyo International Anime Fair, Tokyo Big ght, Odaiba. One of the world's largest Japa- ese animation events (www.tokyoanime.jp) aws more than 100 production companies, V and film agencies, toy and game software ompanies, publishers, and other *anime*-relat- d companies. **Usually last weekend in Mar.**

Cherry Blossom Viewing. The cherry- ossom season is a big deal in Japan. It starts warm southern Kyushu in mid-March, hits okyo in late March or early April, and reaches okkaido in early May. The blossoms them- elves last only a few days, symbolizing to apanese the fragile nature of beauty and of e itself. While they are in bloom, it is a tradi- on to picnic beneath them in what are called *anami,* or flower-watching parties. Parks fill ith celebrants who drink and carouse till the ee hours as the petals rain down. In Tokyo, okashira Park is one of the most famous ots; other cities have their own favorite aces to gather. **Mar–Apr.**

PRIL

anamara Matsuri, Kanayama Shrine, Kawa- aki. This festival extols the joys of sex and rtility (and more recently, raises awareness out AIDS), featuring a parade of giant phal- ses, some carried by transvestites. You'll efinitely get some unusual photographs here. t **Sun in Apr.**

Hana Matsuri. Ceremonies honoring uddha's birthday are held at all Buddhist mples. **Apr 8.**

Kamakura Matsuri, Tsurugaoka Hachiman- u Shrine, Kamakura. This festival honors eroes from the past, including Minamoto oritomo, who made Kamakura his shogu- ate capital back in 1192. Highlights include horseback archery (truly spectacular to watch), a parade of portable shrines, and sa- cred dances. **2nd to 3rd Sun of Apr.**

Takayama Spring Festival, Takayama. Sup- posedly dating from the 15th century, this festival is one of Japan's grandest with a dozen huge, gorgeous floats that are wheeled through the village streets. **Apr 14–15.**

Golden Week. A major holiday period throughout Japan, when many Japanese of- fices and businesses close down and families go on vacation. It's a crowded time to travel; reservations are a must. **Apr 29–May 5.**

MAY

Children's Day. National holiday honoring all children, especially boys. The most common sight throughout Japan is colorful streamers of carp—which symbolize perseverance and strength—flying from poles. **May 5.**

Kanda Festival, Kanda Myojin Shrine, Tokyo. This festival, which commemorates Tokugawa Ieyasu's famous victory at Sekiga- hara in 1600, began during the Feudal Period as the only time townspeople could enter the shogun's castle and parade before him. Today this major Tokyo festival features a parade of dozens of portable shrines carried through the district, plus geisha dances and a tea ceremony. **Odd-numbered years, Sat and Sun closest to May 15.**

Aoi Matsuri, Shimogamo and Kamigamo Shrines, Kyoto. This is one of Kyoto's biggest events, a colorful parade with 500 participants wearing ancient costumes to commemorate the days when the imperial procession visited the city's shrines. **May 15.**

Kobe Matsuri, Kobe. This relatively new festival celebrates Kobe's international past with fireworks at Kobe Port, street markets, and a parade on Flower Road with participants wearing native costumes. **Mid-May.**

Shunki Reitaisai, Nikko. Commemorating the day in 1617 when Tokugawa Ieyasu's remains were brought to his mausoleum in Nikko, this festival re-creates that drama with more than 1,000 armor-clad people escorting three palanquins through the streets. May 17–18.

Sanja Matsuri, Asakusa Shrine, Tokyo. Tokyo's most celebrated festival features about 100 portable shrines carried through the district on the shoulders of men and women in traditional garb. 3rd Sun and preceding Fri and Sat of May.

JUNE

Hyakumangoku Matsuri, Kanazawa. Celebrating Kanazawa's production of 1 million *goku* of rice (1 goku is about 150kg/330 lb.), this extravaganza features folk songs and traditional dancing in the streets, illuminated paper lanterns floating downriver, public tea ceremonies, geisha performances, and—the highlight—a parade that winds through the city in reenactment of Lord Maeda Toshiie's triumphant arrival in Kanazawa on June 14, 1583, with lion dances, ladder-top acrobatics by firemen, and a torch-lit outdoor Noh performance. Jun 8–14.

Sanno Festival, Hie Shrine, Tokyo. This Edo Period festival, one of Tokyo's largest, features the usual portable shrines, transported through the busy streets of the Akasaka District. Jun 10–16.

Ukai, Nagara River, Gifu; and Kiso River, Inuyama. Visitors board small wooden boats after dark to watch cormorants dive into the water to catch *ayu,* a kind of trout. **Generally end of May to Oct.**

JULY

Tanabata Matsuri (Star Festival). According to myth, the two stars Vega and Altair, representing a weaver and a shepherd, are allowed to meet once a year on this day. If the skies are cloudy, however, the celestial pair cannot meet and must wait another year. Celebrations differ from town to town, but in addition to parades and food/souvenir stalls, look for bamboo branches with colorful strips of paper bearing children's wishes. Jul 7.

Yamakasa, Fukuoka. Just before the crack of dawn, seven teams dressed in loincloths and *happi* coats (short, colorful, kimonolike jackets) race through town, bearing 1-ton floats on their shoulders. In addition, elaborately decorated, 9m-tall (30-ft.) floats designed by Hakata doll masters are on display throughout town. Jul 15.

Gion Matsuri, Kyoto. One of the most famous festivals in Japan, this dates back to the 9th century, when the head priest at Yasaka Shrine organized a procession to ask the gods' assistance to eradicate a plague ravaging the city. Although celebrations continue throughout the month, the highlight is on the 17th, when more than 30 spectacular wheeled floats wind their way through the city streets to the accompaniment of music and dances. Many visitors plan their trip to Japan around this event. Jul 16–17.

Obon Festival. This festival commemorates the dead who, according to Buddhist belief, revisit the world during this period. Many Japanese return to their hometowns for religious rites, especially if a family member has died recently. Mid-Jul or mid-Aug, depending on the region.

Tenjin Matsuri, Temmangu Shrine, Osaka. One of Japan's biggest festivals, this dates from the 10th century when the people of Osaka visited Temmangu Shrine to pray for protection against diseases prevalent during the long, hot summer. They would take pieces of paper cut in the form of human beings and while the Shinto priest said prayers, would rub the paper over themselves in ritual cleansing. Afterward, the pieces of paper were taken by boat to the mouth of the river and disposed of. Today, events are reenacted with a procession of more than 100 sacred boats making their way downriver, followed by a fireworks display. There's also a parade of some 3,000 people in traditional costume. Jul 24–25.

Hanabi Taikai, Tokyo. This is Tokyo's largest summer celebration, and everyone sits on blankets along the banks of the Sumida River near Asakusa to see the show, a fireworks competition. Last Sat of Jul.

Fuji Rock Festival, Naeba Ski Resort, Niigata. Japan's biggest outdoor rock 'n' roll festival, with an impressive lineup of international acts in a beautiful mountain setting. Last weekend in Jul.

AUGUST

Oshiro Matsuri, Himeji. This celebration is

mous for its Noh dramas lit by bonfire and rformed on a special stage on the Himeji astle grounds, as well as a procession from e castle to the city center with participants essed as feudal lords and ladies in tradional costume. **First Fri and Sat of Aug.**

Neputa Matsuri, Hirosaki. With roots tending back to at least the 18th century nd undoubtedly even earlier), it's similar in ncept to the Aomori Nebuta Matsuri (see low): Large parade floats made out of paper a bamboo frame are pulled through the reets by local children as visitors watch and nce along. **Aug 1-7.**

Nebuta Matsuri, Aomori. Large, dramatic ree-dimensional renditions of everything m everyday objects (such as toilets) to warrs, dragons, and anime characters are paded through the city streets. There's a great al of corporate sponsorship—it's sort of like e Macy's Thanksgiving Day Parade of Tooku—but it still feels authentically Japanese, ith most floats featuring historical themes d tens upon thousands of spectators flockg to see and participate. (Anyone can join in d *haneru,* or dance, though they need to be earing a proper dancing costume to do so.) e Aomori Nebuta is an evening affair, with ults needed to control the much larger and ore elaborate floats. It's also a party, with a ardi Gras–like atmosphere (and lots and lots drinking). **Aug 2-7.**

Akita Kanto Matsuri, Kanto Odori, Akita. is is a festival of lanterns. Not just any nterns, though—these are suspended on ant bamboo frameworks that are expertly alanced on the chests of the performers, ho parade through town with the massive ntraptions held aloft. As darkness falls, the ght of these enormous lantern frames is a ght to behold; the largest weigh more than 0kg (110 lb.) and extend 12m (39 ft.) in the r. The festival's roots extend back to the id-18th century, when it began as a way to ckon an abundant rice harvest. **Aug 3-6.**

Peace Ceremony, Peace Memorial Park, roshima. This ceremony is held annually in emory of those who died in the atomic bomb ast of August 6, 1945. In the evening, thouands of lit lanterns are set adrift on the Ota ver in a plea for world peace. A similar cernony is held on August 9 in Nagasaki. **Aug 6.**

Tanabata Matsuri, Sendai. *Tanabata,* or "star festivals," are held throughout Japan, usually on July 7 (see above); Sendai's Tanabata Matsuri, the largest and most famous, is held in August, however, in keeping with an old lunar-based calendar. The entire city explodes with color as beautiful paper decorations, symbols of prosperity and wishes for a happy and healthy year, are hung throughout the streets. They take the form of everything from basic paper strips to origami cranes and kimono to giant streamers. A fireworks show and concerts make this a great family event. **Aug 6-8.**

Awa-Odori, Tokushima. Awa-Odori festivals are held throughout Japan, but they all originate in Tokushima, where the festival has been a tradition for 4 centuries. In mid-August, thousands throng the city streets to perform a dance and parade. The female dancers in particular are striking, with folded sedge hats and a distinctive dance step. Spectators are encouraged to join in at certain parts; in fact, the lyrics to the traditional song are "A fool dances and a fool watches; if both are fools, all might as well dance!" **Aug 12-15.**

Toronagashi and Fireworks Display, Matsushima. A fireworks display is followed by the setting adrift on the bay of about 5,000 small boats with lanterns, which are meant to console the souls of the dead; another 3,000 lanterns are lit on islets in the bay. **Evening of Aug 15.**

SEPTEMBER

Yabusame, Tsurugaoka Hachimangu Shrine, Kamakura. Archery performed on horseback recalls the days of the samurai. **Sept 16.**

OCTOBER

Okunchi Festival, Suwa Shrine, Nagasaki. This 370-year-old festival, one of Kyushu's best, illustrates the influence of Nagasaki's Chinese population through the centuries. Highlights include a parade of floats and dragon dances. **Oct 7-9.**

Marimo Matsuri, Lake Akan, Hokkaido. This festival is put on by the native Ainu population to celebrate *marimo* (a spherical weed found in Lake Akan) and includes a pine-torch parade and fireworks. **Early Oct.**

Nagoya Festival, Nagoya. Nagoya's biggest event commemorates three of its heroes—Tokugawa Ieyasu, Toyotomi Hideyoshi, and Oda Nobunaga—in a parade that goes from City Hall to Sakae and includes nine floats with mechanical puppets, marching bands, and a traditional orchestra. **2nd weekend in Oct.**

Naha Tug of War, Naha, Okinawa. Anyone can join in this tug of war with the world's largest rope (186m/619 ft.), once held to welcome Chinese ambassadors. **2nd Sun in Oct.**

Nikko Toshogu Shrine Festival, Nikko. A parade of warriors in early-17th-century dress are accompanied by spear carriers, gunmen, flag bearers, Shinto priests, pages, court musicians, and dancers as they escort a sacred portable shrine. **Oct 17.**

Jidai Matsuri (Festival of the Ages), Kyoto. Another of Kyoto's grand festivals, this one began in 1894 to commemorate the founding of the city in 794. It features a procession of more than 2,000 people in ancient costumes representing different epochs of Kyoto's 1,200-year history, who march from the Imperial Palace to Heian Jingu Shrine. **Oct 22.**

NOVEMBER

Ohara Matsuri, Kagoshima. About 15,000 people parade through the town in cotton *yukata,* dancing to the tune of local folk songs. This event attracts several hundred thousand spectators each year. **Nov 2–3.**

Shichi-go-san (Children's Shrine-Visiting Day). Shichi-go-san literally means "seven-five-three" and refers to children of these ages who are dressed in their kimono best and taken to shrines by their elders to express thanks and pray for their future. **Nov 15.**

DECEMBER

Gishi-sai, Sengaku-ji Station, Tokyo. This memorial service honors 47 *ronin* (masterless samurai) who avenged their master's death by killing his rival and parading his head around; for their act, all were ordered to commit suicide. Forty-seven men dressed as the *ronin* travel to Sengaku-ji Temple with a replica of the head, which is placed on their master's grave. **Dec 14.**

New Year's Eve. At midnight, many temples ring huge bells 108 times to signal the end of the old year and the beginning of the new. Families visit temples and shrines throughout Japan to pray for the coming year. **Dec 31.**

Weather

Most of Japan's islands lie in a temperate seasonal wind zone similar to that of the East Coast of the United States, which means there are fo distinct seasons, but the temperatures vary widely from region to region. Japanese are ver proud of their seasons and place much more emphasis on them than people do in the West Kimono, dishes and bowls used for *kaiseki* (ela orate multicourse meals), and even Noh plays change with the season. Certain foods are eate during certain times of the year, such as eel in summer and fugu (blowfish) in winter.

During the **summer** rainy season from mid June to mid-July (there's no rainy season in Hokkaido), umbrellas are imperative. After th rain stops in August, average temperatures range from highs of 78°F (26°C) in Hokkaidc to well over 86°F (30°C) in Tokyo, with up tc 80% humidity. Throughout the summer, the humidity is a killer.

Autumn, lasting through November, is on of the best times to visit Japan. The days are pleasant and slightly cool (around 68°F/ 20°C), and the changing red and scarlet of leaves contrast brilliantly with the deep blue skies. There are many chrysanthemum show in Japan at this time, popular maple-viewing spots, and many autumn festivals. Bring a warm jacket for the chilly nights.

Winter, lasting from December to March, i marked by snow in much of Japan, especially the mountain ranges where the skiing is super Many tourists also flock to hot-spring resorts during this time. The climate is cold (with high temperatures of around 46°F, or 8°C, in Kyotc and generally dry, and on the Pacific coast the skies are often blue. Northern Japan's weathe in Tohoku and Hokkaido, can be quite severe (with highs around 33°F, or 1°C, in Sapporo), while southern Japan, especially Kyushu and Okinawa (around 66°F/ 19°C), enjoys general mild, warm weather.

Spring arrives with a magnificent fanfare of plum and cherry blossoms in March and April, an exquisite time when all of Japan is ablaze in whites and pinks. The cherry-blossom season starts in southern Kyushu in mid-March and reaches Hokkaido in early May. It can still get quite chilly, especially in the evenings, so brinç sweater or jacket. Temperatures range from 75°F (24°C) in Okinawa to 57°F (14°C) in Sapporo.

Useful Websites

Check individual sections for relevant websites. Other useful sites include the Japan **National Tourism Organization (JNTO),** the largest English-language information service (www.jnto.go.jp); the **Japan Ministry of Foreign Affairs** (www.mofa.go.jp), which provides information on visas, scholarships, and embassy/consulate locations; and the **Jorudan Route Finder** (www.jorudan.co.jp/english/norikae), a great resource when looking for the best train and subway routes in and between cities. In Tokyo, **Tokyo Sights** (www.tokyotojp.com) lists hours, admission fees, phone numbers, and other info on Tokyo's major sights. **Bento.com** (www.bento.com) is one of the most useful bilingual Japanese food resources and guides to restaurant and bars in Tokyo.

JTB's **JapaniCan** (www.japanican.com) offers special discounts on travel and lodging packages to various destinations in Japan. **Rakuten Travel** (www.travel.rakuten.co.jp/en) is Japan's largest reservations company for budget and moderate-priced accommodations. Also recommended are the members of **Welcome Inns** (www.itcj.jp), operated in cooperation with the Japan National Tourism Organization (JNTO) and International Tourism Center of Japan (ITCJ).

Cellphones (Mobiles)

Unfortunately, Japan uses a cell-phone system that is incompatible with GSM, the system used most everywhere else in the world. You can, however, use your own mobile phone number in Japan by bringing your own SIM card from home and inserting it into a handset rented from Softbank Global Rental or NTT DoCoMo. It only works, however, if your home service provider has a roaming agreement with Softbank or NTT. For more information, contact your mobile phone company, **NTT DoCoMo** (http://roaming.nttdocomo.co.jp), or **Softbank Global Rental** (www.softbank-rental.jp), where you can also find out about rental costs and rental locations and make online reservations. Another option is to bring your own mobile phone and rent a SIM card from Softbank.

Otherwise, if you want to have a telephone number before arriving in Japan, consider renting a phone before leaving home. North Americans can rent one from **InTouch USA** (☎ 800/872-7626; www.intouchglobal.com) or **Roadpost** (☎ 888/290-1606; www.roadpost.com).

You can also rent a phone when you arrive at Tokyo's Narita Airport. Lots of companies maintain counters at both terminals, including NTT DoCoMo and Softbank Global Rental (see above), as well as **G-Call** (www.g-call.com/e), **Telecom Square** (www.telecomsquare.co.jp/en), and **PuPuRu** (www.pupuru.com/en), which have the extra convenience of easy pickup and drop-off and offer online reservations. Most rentals start at ¥525 per day, though bargains are often offered online or onsite. Charges for domestic and international calls vary, but incoming calls are usually free.

Getting There

Japan has three international airports. Outside Tokyo is **Narita International Airport (NRT),** where you'll want to land if your main business is in the capital, the surrounding region, or at points north or east such as Hokkaido.

Another international airport, **Kansai International Airport (KIX)** outside Osaka, is convenient if your destination is Osaka, Kobe, Nara, Kyoto, or western or southern Japan; it is also convenient for domestic air travel within Japan, since most domestic flights out of Tokyo depart from Haneda Airport, necessitating an airport transfer if you arrive at Narita International Airport.

As of October 2010, the new international terminal at **Haneda Airport (HND),** located in central Tokyo, offers service to and from 17 cities in Asia, Europe, and North America.

In between Narita and Kansai airports, outside Nagoya, is the **Central Japan International Airport (NGO),** nicknamed Centrair, which offers the advantage of slick airport facilities (including hot-spring baths) and easy access to Nagoya, the Shinkansen bullet train, the Japan Alps, and beyond.

Getting Around

Japan has an extensive public transport system, the most convenient segment of which is the nation's excellent rail service. You can also travel by plane (good for long-distance hauls but expensive unless you plan ahead), bus (the cheapest mode of travel), ferry, and car.

By Train

The most efficient way to travel around most of Japan is by train. Whether you're being whisked through the countryside aboard the famous Shinkansen bullet train or are winding your way up a wooded mountainside in a two-car electric streetcar, trains in Japan are punctual, comfortable, dependable, safe, and clean. All trains except local commuters have washrooms, toilets, and drinking water. Bullet trains even have telephones and carts selling food and drinks. And because train stations are usually located in the heart of the city next to the city bus terminal or a subway station, arriving in a city by train is usually the most convenient method. Furthermore, most train stations in Japan's major cities and resort areas have tourist offices. The staff may not speak English, but the office usually has maps or brochures in English and can point you in the direction of your hotel. Train stations also often have a counter where hotel reservations can be made free of charge. Most of Japan's trains are run by the six companies (such as JR East and JR Kyushu) that make up the **Japan Railways (JR) Group,** which operates as many as 27,800 trains daily, including more than 500 Shinkansen bullet trains.

SHINKANSEN (BULLET TRAIN)

The Shinkansen is probably Japan's best-known train. With a front car that resembles a space rocket, the Shinkansen hurtles along at a maximum speed of 300kmph (186 mph) through the countryside on its own special tracks.

There are six basic Shinkansen routes in Japan, plus some offshoots. The most widely used line for tourists is the **Tokaido Shinkansen,** which runs from Tokyo and Shinagawa stations west to such cities as Nagoya, Kyoto, and Osaka. The **Sanyo Shinkansen** extends westward from Osaka through Kobe, Himeji, Okayama, and Hiroshima, before reaching its final destination in Hakata/Fukuoka on the island of Kyushu. Only **Nozomi Super Express** trains, the fastest and most frequent trains, cover the entire 1,175km (730 miles) between Tokyo and Hakata; the Nozomi runs on the Tokaido and Sanyo Shinkansen lines. Since the Nozomi is not covered by the Japan Rail Pass, most travelers must transfer in Osaka or Okayama if they're traveling the entire line. Trains run so frequently—as often as four times an hour during peak times, not includin[g] the Nozomi—that it's almost like catching the local subway.

The **Tohoku Shinkansen** line runs north from Tokyo and Ueno stations to Sendai, Morioka, Kakunodate, and Hachinohe, and, mos[t] recently, Aomori (some trains require reserva[-]tions), with branches extending to Shinjo and Akita. The **Joetsu Shinkansen** connects Toky[o] and Ueno stations with Niigata on the Japan Sea coast, while the **Nagano Shinkansen,** completed in time for the 1998 Winter Olympics, connects Tokyo and Ueno stations with Nagano in the Japan Alps. The newest line is the **Kyushu Shinkansen,** which currently runs between Shin-Yatsuhiro and Kagoshima but will extend all the way from Kagoshima to Hakata by 2011.

Shinkansen running along these lines usually offer two kinds of service—trains that stop only at major cities (like the Nozomi on the Tokaido-Sanyo Line) and trains that make more stops and are therefore slightly slower. If your destination is a smaller city on the Shinkansen line, make sure the train you take stops there. As a plus, each stop is announced in English through a loudspeaker and a digital signboard in each car.

REGULAR SERVICE

In addition to bullet trains, there are also two types of long-distance trains that operate on regular tracks. The **Tokkyu (Limited Express trains, or LEX),** branch off the Shinkansen system and are the fastest after the bullet trains, often traveling scenic routes, while the **Kyuko (Express trains)** are slightly slower and make more stops. Slower still are **Shin-Kaisoku (Rapid Express trains)** and the even slower **Kaisoku (Rapid trains).** To serve the everyday needs of Japan's commuting population, **Futsu (local trains)** stop at all stations.

For long distances, say, between Tokyo and Sapporo, JR operates **Shindai-sha (overnight sleeper trains),** which offer compartments and berths.

There are also privately owned lines that operate from major cities to tourist destinations. **Kintetsu (Kinki Nippon Railway)** lines, for example, are useful for traveling in the Kansai area and to the Ise Shima Peninsula, while **Odakyu** serves Hakone.

FORMATION

he **Jorudan Route Finder** website (www.
udan.co.jp/english/access.html) is one of
e most convenient ways to check train
hedules and calculate fares in English. If
u've missed a connection, it is immensely
lpful for finding out when the next (or, more
portantly, last) train will leave.

For more detailed information on destina-
ns, discount tickets, fares, timetables,
d maps, visit the **JR East** website at www.
ast.co.jp/e. You can also call the JR East
oline in Tokyo for information in English
: 050/2016-1603) daily from 10am to 6pm;
 reservations are accepted by phone, but
u can inquire about time schedules, fares,
ation of reservation offices, lost-and-found
ices, and more.

In Japan, stop by the Tourist Information
nter in downtown Tokyo or at the interna-
nal airports in Narita or Osaka for the invalu-
le *Railway Timetable*, published in English
d providing train schedules for the Shinkan-
n and limited-express JR lines. To be on the
fe side, stop by the train information desk or
e tourist information desk as soon as you
ive at a new destination to check on train
hedules onward to your next destination.

AIN DISTANCES/TRAVELING TIME

cause Japan is an island nation, many
ople erroneously believe that the traveling
ne between destinations is of little concern.
e country is much longer than most people
agine. Its four main islands, measured
om the northeast to the southwest, cover
ughly the distance from Maine to Florida.
addition, transportation can be slow in
ountainous regions, especially if you're on a
cal train.

AIN FARES & RESERVATIONS

ains are expensive in Japan; ticket prices are
sed on the type of train (Shinkansen bullet
ains are the most expensive), the distance
aveled, whether your seat is reserved, and
e season, with slightly higher prices during
ak season (Golden Week, July 21–Aug 31,
ec 25–Jan 10, and Mar 21–Apr 5). Children
ges 6–11) pay half-fare, while up to two
ildren 5 and younger travel for free if they
 not require a separate seat. Unless stated
herwise, prices in this guide are for adults

for *nonreserved* seats on the fastest train available during regular season.

No matter which train you ride, be sure to
hang onto your ticket—you'll be required to
give it up at the end of your trip as you exit
through the gate.

SEAT RESERVATIONS

You can reserve seats for the Shinkansen,
as well as for Limited Express and Express
trains (but not for slower Rapid or local trains,
which are on a first-come, first-served basis)
at any major Japan Railways station in Japan. Reserved seats cost slightly more than
unreserved seats (¥510 for the Shinkansen).
The larger stations have a special reservation
counter called **Midori-no Madoguchi (Reservation Ticket Office)** or **View Plaza (Travel
Service Center),** easily recognizable by their
green signs with RESERVATION TICKETS written
on them. If you're at a JR station with no special reservation office, you can reserve your
seats at one of the regular ticket windows.
You can also purchase and reserve seats at
several travel agents, including the giant **Japan Travel Bureau (JTB),** which has offices
all over Japan. It's a good idea to reserve your
seats for your entire trip through Japan as
soon as you know your itinerary, especially if
you'll be traveling during peak times; however,
you can only reserve 1 month in advance. If it's
not peak season, you'll probably be okay using a more flexible approach to traveling—all
trains also have nonreserved cars that fill up
on a first-come, first-seated basis. In some
cases, traveling with a nonreserved seat ticket
can be more comfortable: You may be able to
have an entire row to yourself, an uncommon
circumstance for reserved seat ticket holders.
You can also reserve seats on the day of travel
up to departure time. If you want to sit in the
nonsmoking car of the Shinkansen bullet train,
ask for the *kinensha,* though nowadays most
trains are completely smoke-free.

TIPS FOR SAVING MONEY

If your ticket is for travel covering more than
100km (62 miles), you can make as many
stopovers en route as you wish as long as you
complete your trip within the period of the
ticket's validity. Tickets for 100 to 200km
(62–124 miles) are valid for 2 days, with 1 day
added for each additional 200km (124 miles).

Note, too, that stopovers are granted only for trips that are not between major urban areas, such as Tokyo, Osaka, Nagoya, Kyoto, Kobe, Hiroshima, Kitakyushu, Fukuoka, Sendai, or Sapporo. In addition, stopovers are not permitted when traveling by express and limited express. Ask about stopovers when purchasing your ticket.

You can also save money by purchasing a round-trip ticket for long distances. A round-trip ticket by train on distances exceeding 600km (373 miles) one-way costs 20% less than two one-way tickets.

There are also regional tickets good for sightseeing. The **Hakone Free Pass,** for example (p. 121), offered by Odakyu railways (www.odakyu.jp/english), includes round-trip transportation from Tokyo and unlimited travel in Hakone for a specific number of days. The **Hokkaido Furii Pasu** (www.jrhokkaido. co.jp), valid for 7 days of JR train and bus travel in Hokkaido, costs ¥25,500, though some restrictions apply; note that this pass is only worth buying if you are traveling rather long distances.

If you don't qualify for a Japan Rail Pass (see below), the **Seishun 18** (Seishun Juhachi Kippu) is a 5-day rail pass for ¥11,500, good for travel anywhere in Japan so long as you use JR local and Rapid trains (no Shinkansen, Limited Express, or Express trains). It's a good bet for day excursions in the countryside, albeit very slow ones. You can use it on 5 consecutive days or on any 5 days within a limited time period. It's available, however, only 3 times a year, during school holiday seasons; check at the ticket office for exact information. There are also special passes for seniors (**Full Moon Pass,** valid for married couples with a total age of 88) and for two or three women over age 30 traveling as a group (**Nice Midi Pass**). For more information, inquire at the JR ticket offices or check online at www.jreast. co.jp/e/pass. If you qualify, the Japan Rail Pass, however, is more economical than these alternatives.

JAPAN RAIL PASS

The **Japan Rail Pass** is without a doubt the most convenient and most economical way to travel around Japan. With the rail pass, you don't have to worry about buying individual tickets, and you can reserve your seats on all JR trains for free. The rail pass entitles you to unlimited travel on all JR train lines including the Shinkansen (except, regrettably, the Nozomi Super Express), as well as on most JR buses and the JR ferry to Miyajima. Another advantage to a rail pass is that it offers a 10% discount or more off room rates at more than 50 JR Hotel Group hotels, including the Hotel Granvia in Kyoto, Okayama, and Hiroshima; the Crowne Plaza Metropolitan in Tokyo; and Hotel Kurashiki, Nara Hotel, JR Kyushu Hotel Fukuoka, JR Kyushu Hotel Kumamoto, JR Kyushu Hotel Nagasaki, ANA Hotel Clement Takamatsu, and many more. A Japan Rail Pass booklet, which comes with your purchase of a rail pass, lists member hotels (or go to www. jrhotelgroup.com).

There are several types of rail passes available; make your decision based on your length of stay in Japan and the cities you intend to visit. You might even find it best to combine several passes to cover your travels in Japan, such as a 1-week standard pass for longer journeys, say, to Kyushu, plus a regional pass just for Kyushu. Information on passes is available online at www.japanrailpass.net.

If you wish to travel throughout Japan, your best bet is to purchase the **standard Japan Rail Pass.** It's available for ordinary coach class and for the first-class Green Car and is available for travel lasting 1, 2, or 3 weeks. Rates for the ordinary pass (as of Jan 2010) are ¥28,300 for 7 days, ¥45,100) for 14 days and ¥57,700 for 21 days. Rates for the Green Car are ¥37,800, ¥61,200, and ¥79,600 respectively. Children (ages 6–11) pay half-fare. Generally, standard-class seats are perfectly comfortable, making first-class seats somewhat unnecessary. However, during peak travel times (New Year's, Golden Week, and the Obon season in mid-Aug), you may find it easier to reserve a seat in the first-class Green Car, which you can get by paying a surcharge in addition to showing your ordinary pass.

The standard Japan Rail Pass is available only to foreigners visiting Japan as tourists and *can only be purchased outside Japan.* It's available from most travel agents (chances are your travel agent sells them), including **Kintetsu International** (☎ 800/422-3481; www.kintetsu.com) and **JTB USA** (☎ 800/

35-3523; www.jtbusa.com). If you're flying **pan Airlines** (JAL; ☎ 800/525-3663; www..jal.com/en) or **All Nippon Airways** (ANA; 800/235-9262; www.anaskyweb.com), u can also purchase a rail pass from them.

Upon purchasing your pass, you'll be issued voucher (called an exchange order), which u'll then exchange for the pass itself after u arrive in Japan. Note that once you pur-ase your exchange order, you must ex-ange it in Japan for the pass itself within 3 onths of the date of issue of the exchange der. When obtaining your actual pass, you ust then specify the date you wish to start ing the pass within a 1-month period.

You can exchange your Japan Rail Pass oucher at more than 40 JR stations that have pan Rail Pass exchange offices; you simply esent your passport and specify the date u wish to begin using the pass. Most offices e open daily from 10am to 6 or 7pm, some en longer.

At both **Narita Airport** (daily 6:30am–45pm) and **Kansai International Airport** aily 5:30am–11pm), you can pick up Japan il Passes at either the Travel Service Center the Ticket Office. Other Travel Service Cen-rs or Ticket Offices, all located in JR train ations, include those at Tokyo (daily 30am–10:45pm), Ueno, Shinjuku, Ikebukuro, d Shibuya stations in Tokyo; Kyoto Station; in-Osaka and Osaka stations; and Hiro-ima, Sapporo, Nagoya, Okayama, Taka-atsu, Matsuyama, Hakata, Nagasaki, Kuma-oto, Miyazaki, and Kagoshima Chuo sta-ons. Stations and their open hours are listed a pamphlet you'll receive with your voucher.

GIONAL PASSES

addition to the standard Japan Rail Pass ove, there are regional rail passes available r ordinary coach class that are convenient r travel in eastern or western Honshu, yushu, or Hokkaido. These passes can be rchased before arriving in Japan from the me vendors that sell the standard pass. *They n also be purchased inside Japan,* usually only ithin the area covered by the pass but also at arita Airport for some passes. These region-passes are available *only to foreign visitors* d require that you present your passport to rify your status as a "temporary visitor"; you

may also be asked to show your plane ticket. Only one pass per region per visit to Japan is allowed.

If you're arriving by plane at the Kansai Airport outside Osaka and intend to remain in western Honshu, you may wish to opt for one of two different **JR West Passes** (www.westjr.co.jp/english), available at Kansai Airport, Osaka JR Station, and other locations. The **Kansai Area Pass,** which can be used for trav-el between Osaka, Kyoto, Kobe, Nara, Himeji, and other destinations in the Kansai area, is available as a 1-day pass for ¥2,000, a 2-day pass for ¥4,000, a 3-day pass for ¥5,000, or a 4-day pass for ¥6,000. Travel is restricted to JR Rapid and local trains, as well as unre-served seating in Limited Express trains that operate only between Kansai Airport, Shin-Osaka, and Kyoto (that is, Shinkansen are not included in the pass). Children pay half-price for all passes.

The other JR West Pass available is the **Sanyo Area Pass,** which covers a larger area, allows travel via Shinkansen (including the superfast Nozomi) and JR local trains from Osaka as far as Hakata (in the city of Fukuoka on Kyushu), and includes Hiroshima, Okaya-ma, Kurashiki, Himeji, and Kobe. It's available for 4 days for ¥20,000 and for 8 days for ¥30,000. Though not as popular as western Honshu, eastern Honshu also offers its own **JR East Pass** (www.jreast.co.jp/e), which includes travel from Tokyo to parts of the Ja-pan Alps and throughout the Tohoku District, including Sendai, Kakunodate, and Aomori via Shinkansen and local JR lines. Passes for travel in ordinary coach cars are available for 5 days for ¥20,000 and 10 days for ¥32,000; a 4-day flexible pass (which is valid for any 4 consecutive or nonconsecutive days within a month) costs ¥20,000. Green Car passes are also available. Passes are available at Narita Airport and JR stations in Tokyo, including Tokyo, Shinagawa, and Shinjuku.

If your travels are limited to the island of Kyushu, consider the **JR Kyushu Rail Pass** (www.jrkyushu.co.jp), valid for 3 days for ¥13,000 and for 5 days for ¥16,000 and avail-able for purchase at Hakata, Nagasaki, Kuma-moto, Kagoshima Chuo, Miyazaki, and Beppu JR stations. Likewise, there's a **Hokkaido Rail Pass** (www.jrhokkaido.co.jp) valid for 3 days of travel for ¥14,000 or 5 days for ¥18,000, sold at Narita Airport and Hakodate and Sapporo JR stations.

By Plane

Because it takes the better part of a day and night to travel by train from Tokyo down to southern Kyushu or up to northern Hokkaido, you may find it faster—not to mention cheaper if you buy your ticket in advance—to fly at least one stretch of your journey in Japan. You may, for example, fly internationally into Osaka and then onward to Fukuoka on Kyushu, from where you can take a leisurely 2 weeks to travel by train through Kyushu and Honshu before returning to Osaka. Flying short distances is not advised simply because the time spent getting to and from airports is longer than the time spent traveling by Shinkansen.

Almost all domestic flights from Tokyo leave from the much more conveniently located **Haneda Airport.** If you're already in Tokyo, you can easily reach Haneda Airport via Airport Limousine Bus, monorail from Hamamatsucho Station on the Yamanote Line, or the Keikyu Line from Shinagawa. If you're arriving on an international flight at Narita Airport, therefore, make sure you know whether a connection to a domestic flight is at Narita or requires a transfer to Haneda Airport via the Airport Limousine Bus.

Two major domestic airlines are **Japan Airlines** (JAL; ☎ 0120/25-5971 toll-free in Japan; www.ar.jal.com/en) and **All Nippon Airways** (ANA; ☎ 0120/029-222 toll-free in Japan; www.anaskyweb.com). Regular fares with these two companies are generally the same no matter which airline you fly domestically. However, fares change often, with the most expensive fares charged for peak season including New Year's, Golden Week, and summer vacation. But bargains do exist. Some flights early in the day or late at night may be cheaper than flights during peak time; you can also save by purchasing tickets 7 days in advance and even more by purchasing them 21 days in advance (ask carriers for details). Round-trip tickets provide a slight discount.

Otherwise, there are small, regional airlines that generally offer fares that are cheaper than the standard full fare charged by JAL or ANA. These include **Skymark** (☎ 03/3433-7670 in

Tokyo, or 092/736-3131 in Fukuoka), operating out of Fukuoka on the island of Kyushu; **Skynet Asia Airways** (☎ 03/5733-5859 in Tokyo), connecting Nagasaki, Kumamoto, Kagoshima, and Miyazaki on Kyushu with Tokyo and **Air Do** (☎ 0120/0570-333 toll-free), out of Sapporo on the island of Hokkaido.

Although it's subject to change, the regular fare for a one-way flight aboard JAL from Tokyo to Kagoshima, for example, which takes 1 hour and 45 minutes, is ¥35,700 during the regular season, though discounts may be available for advance purchases of certain flights. Skynet Asia Airway's regular fare is ¥28,500. For comparison, a train ticket between the two cities is ¥26,980 one-way for trip that takes 9 hours, not including transfer Tickets can be purchased directly through th airline or at a travel agent such as Japan Trav Bureau (JTB), which has offices virtually everywhere in Japan.

SAVING MONEY ON AIRFARES

Purchasing domestic tickets in advance in connection with your international flight is by far the most economical way to go. JAL's **oneworld Yokoso/Visit Japan Fare** ticket, purchased in conjunction with a flight to Japan with JAL or one of its oneworld partners (such as American Airlines) and sold only outside Japan, provides discount fares of ¥10,000 (as of April 2011) per flight for domestic travel to 42 cities in Japan served by JAL and its two subsidiaries, JAL Express and Japan Trans-Ocean Air.

Visitors flying other airlines into Japan can take advantage of JAL's **Welcome to Japan Fare,** which provides discounts on JAL's domestic flights regardless of which international airline is used to reach Japan. Also sold only outside Japan, it costs ¥13,650 per flight, with a minimum of two flights required (www.jal.co.jp/yokosojapan). ANA offers a similar program, with its **Star Alliance Japan Airpass** ticket costing ¥11,000 per flight if yo fly ANA or one of its Star Alliance partners such as United Airlines, and its **Visit Japan Fare** for ¥13,000 per ticket if you don't. Note that there are blackout dates for all these fares, mostly in mid-March, during summer vacation (mid-July through Aug), and New Year's, and that fares above exclude airport

xes and insurance. You should first purchase
ur international ticket and then contact JAL
ANA to purchase and book your Japan do-
estic tickets.

Bus

uses often go where trains don't and thus
ay be the only way for you to get to the more
mote areas of Japan, such as Shirakawago in
e Japan Alps. In Hokkaido, Tohoku, Kyushu,
d other places, buses are used extensively.

Some intercity buses require you to make
servations or purchase your ticket in advance
the ticket counter at the bus terminal. For
hers (especially local buses), when you board
bus you'll generally find a ticket machine by
e entry door. Take a ticket, which is number-
ded with a digital board displayed at the front
the bus. The board shows the various fares,
hich increase with the distance traveled. You
y your fare when you get off. On most buses
ithin the Tokyo city center, however, you will
eed to pay when you get on.

In addition to serving the remote areas
the country, long-distance buses (called
okyori basu) also operate between major
ties in Japan and offer the cheapest mode
transportation. Although Japan Railways
perates almost a dozen bus routes eligible
r JR Rail Pass coverage, the majority of
uses are run by private companies. Some
ng-distance buses travel during the night
d offer reclining seats and toilets, thus sav-
g passengers the price of a night's lodging.
r example, special buses depart from Tokyo
ation's Yaesu south side every night for Kyo-
(¥8,180), Osaka (¥8,610), and Hiroshima
11,600), arriving at those cities' main train
ations the next morning. Night buses also
epart from Shinjuku Station's new south exit
from the Shinjuku Highway Bus Terminal (a
min. walk from Shinjuku Station's west exit)
ound for Kyoto, Nagoya, Okayama, and be-
ond. Night buses also travel from these cities
reverse back to Tokyo. Slight discounts are
ven for round-trip travel completed within
to 10 days, depending on the city. There are
so day buses traveling between Tokyo and
yoto or Osaka for ¥6,000. Long-distance
us tickets can be purchased at View Plazas
major JR stations (for JR buses), at travel
encies such as JTB, or at bus terminals.

By Car

With the exception, perhaps, of Izu Peninsula,
the Tohoku region, Hokkaido, and parts of
Central Honshu, driving is not recommended
for visitors wishing to tour Japan. Driving
is British style (on the left side of the road),
which may be hard for those not used to it;
traffic can be horrendous; and driving isn't as
economical as you might imagine. Not only is
gas expensive, but all of Japan's expressways
charge high tolls: The one-way toll from Tokyo
to Kyoto is almost the same price as a ticket
to Kyoto on the Shinkansen. And whereas the
Shinkansen takes only 3 hours to get to Kyoto,
driving can take about 8 hours. In addition,
you may encounter few signs in English in
remote areas. Driving in cities is even worse:
Many roads don't have sidewalks so you have
to dodge people, bicycles, and telephone
poles. Free parking is hard to find, and garages
are expensive.

There are approximately a dozen major car-
rental companies in Tokyo alone, with branch
offices throughout the city and at the Narita
Airport, including **Nippon Rent-A-Car Service**
(☎ 03/3485-7196 for the English Service
Desk), **Toyota Rent-A-Car** (☎ 03/5954-8008
in Tokyo, or 0070/8000-10000 toll-free),
Nissan Rent-A-Car (☎ 0120/00-4123), and
Avis (☎ 03/6436-6404); these companies
also have branches throughout Japan. In almost every city with a JR train station, there is
also a **JR Eki Rent-A-Car** office (www.ekiren.
co.jp), offering 20% discounts on train fares
booked in conjunction with car rentals; you
can reserve these cars at any JR Travel Service
Center (located in train stations) anywhere in
Japan. Rates vary, but the average cost for 24
hours with unlimited mileage averages about
¥12,070 for a subcompact including insurance but not gas; in some tourist areas, such
as Hokkaido, rates are more expensive in peak
season.

If you do intend to drive in Japan, you'll
need either an international or a Japanese
driving license. Remember, cars are driven on
the left side of the road, and signs on all major
highways are written in both Japanese and
English. It is against the law to drink alcohol
and drive, and you must wear seat belts at all
times. Be sure to purchase a bilingual map,
as back roads often have names of towns

written in Japanese only. Recommended is the **Shobunsha Road Atlas Japan,** available in bookstores that sell English-language books; it also contains maps of major cities, including Tokyo, Sapporo, Hiroshima, and others. **Note:** These days, rental cars in Japan come equipped with GPS navigation systems. Enter the address or phone number of your destination to calculate the route.

BREAKDOWNS/ASSISTANCE

The **Japan Automobile Federation (JAF)** maintains emergency telephone boxes along Japan's major arteries to assist drivers whose cars have broken down or drivers who need help. Calls from these telephones are free and will connect you to JAF's operation center.

By Ferry

Because Japan is an island nation, an extensive ferry network links the string of islands. Although travel by ferry takes longer, it's also cheaper and can be a pleasant, relaxing experience. For example, you can take a ferry from Osaka to Beppu (on Kyushu), with fares starting at ¥9,000 for the 11-hour trip. Contact the Tourist Information Center for more details concerning ferries, prices, schedules, and telephone numbers of the various ferry companies.

Tips on Accommodations

When to Book

Although you can travel throughout Japan without making reservations beforehand, it's essential to book in advance if you're traveling during peak travel seasons and is recommended at other times. (See "When to Go," earlier in this chapter for peak travel times.) It is inadvisable to show up to a *ryokan* or *minshuku* (see "Types of Accommodations," below) without a reservation. Most of these traditional places are small and often booked in advance. If you arrive in a town without reservations, most local tourist offices can help find you a room. When making reservations at Japanese-style accommodations and small business hotels, it's usually best if the call is conducted in Japanese or by fax or e-mail if available, as written English is always easier for most Japanese to understand. First-class hotels, however, always have English-speaking staff.

Types of Accommodations

Accommodations available in Japan range from Japanese-style inns to large Western-style hotels, in all price categories. Note that a 5% consumption tax is included in all hotel rates, including those given in this book. Furthermore, upper-end hotels and some moderately priced hotels also add a 10% to 15% service charge to their published rates, while expensive *ryokan* will add a 10% to 20% service charge. No service charge is levied at business hotels, pensions, and *minshuku* (accommodations in a private home).

RYOKAN

The word *ryokan* refers to a category of traditional Japanese inns. Usually, *ryokan* are small, only one or two stories high, contain about 10 to 30 rooms, and are made of wood with a tile roof. Rooms are fitted with tatami floorings and are almost void of furniture except for a low table in the middle of the room with floor cushions. Instead of a Western-style bed, you'll sleep on traditional futon, which are laid out by maids every evening and folded up and stored in large closets during the day. A stay a *ryokan* might cost anywhere from ¥7,000 to ¥150,000 or more (per person, per night) and includes one or two beautiful Japanese meals often served in your room. This is a highly recommended experience, at least for 1 night.

For more information on *ryokan* in Japan, pick up the *Japan Ryokan Guide* at one of the Tourist Information Centers in Japan, which lists some 1,300 members of the **Japan Ryokan Association** (☎ 03/3231-5310; www.ryokan.or.jp). Another useful resource is **Japanese Guest Houses** (www.japaneseguesthouses.com).

INNS

If you want the experience of staying in a Japanese-style room but cannot afford the extravagance of a *ryokan,* you might consider staying in one of the participating members of the **Japanese Inn Group** (www.japanese-inngroup.com), an organization of more than 80 Japanese-style inns and hotels throughout Japan offering inexpensive lodging and catering largely to foreigners.

MINSHUKU

Technically, a *minshuku* is inexpensive Japanese-style lodging in a private home. Usually cated in tourist areas, rural settings, or small wns, *minshuku* can range from charming atched farmhouses and rickety old wooden ildings to modern concrete structures. Most not offer personal services and also do not pply a towel or *yukata* (cotton kimono), nor they have rooms with a private bathroom. ere is, however, a public bathroom, and eals, included in the rates, are served in a mmunal dining room.

The average per-person cost for 1 night in *minshuku,* including two meals, is generally 7,000 to ¥9,000 with two meals. Reserva- ons for *minshuku* should be made directly ith the establishment. Or, contact the **Min- uku Network Japan** (☎ 0120/07-6556; ww.minshuku.jp).

OKUMIN-SHUKUSHA

atering largely to Japanese school groups nd families, government-supported *koku- in-shukusha* lodging facilities offer basic, apanese-style rooms at an average daily rate about ¥8,000 to ¥9,000 per person, in- uding two meals. Because they're usually full uring the summer, peak seasons, holidays, nd weekends, reservations are a must and an be made directly at the facility or through travel agency.

HOKUBO

hukubo are lodgings in a Buddhist temple, milar to inexpensive *ryokan,* except they're ttached to temples and serve vegetarian od. Prices at *shukubo* generally range from bout ¥7,000 to ¥15,000 per person, includ- g two meals.

OTELS

Hotels vary widely in price, service, and facili- es provided. The most expensive (and luxuri- us) hotels in Japan are in Tokyo and Osaka, vhere you'll pay at least ¥32,000 for a double r twin room in a first-class hotel and ¥16,000 o ¥32,000 for the same in a mid-priced hotel. Outside the major cities, rooms for two people ange from about ¥20,000 to ¥30,000 for irst-class hotels and ¥10,000 to ¥20,000 for mid-priced hotels. Check out the 400 some members of the **Japan Hotel Association** isted in the brochure *Hotels in Japan* available rom the Tourist Information Centers in Japan r online at www.j-hotel.or.jp.

BUSINESS HOTELS

Catering traditionally to traveling Japanese businessmen, a business hotel is a no-frills establishment with tiny, sparsely furnished rooms, most of them singles but usually with some twin and maybe double rooms also available. Most business hotels have non-smoking rooms, but a few still do not. The advantages of staying in business hotels are price (starting as low as ¥6,000 or ¥7,000 for a single) and location (usually near major train and subway stations). Check-in is usually not until 3 or 4pm, and checkout is usually at 10am; you can leave your bags at the front desk.

PENSIONS

Pensions are like *minshuku,* except that ac-commodations are Western-style with beds instead of futons, and the two meals served are usually Western. Often managed by a young couple or a young staff, they cater to young Japanese and are most often located in ski resorts and in the countryside. The average cost is ¥8,000 per person per night, including two meals.

HOSTELS

There are some 350 youth hostels in Japan, most of them privately run and operating in locations ranging from temples to concrete blocks. There's no age limit (though children younger than 4 may not be accepted), and although most of them require a youth hostel membership card, they let foreigners stay without one at no extra charge or for ¥600 extra per night (after 6 nights you automati-cally become a YH member). Youth hostels are reasonable, averaging about ¥3,000 per day without meals, and can be reserved in advance. However, there are usually quite a few restrictions, such as a 9 or 10pm curfew, a lights-out policy shortly thereafter, an early breakfast time, and closed times through the day, generally from about 10am to 3pm.

If you plan on staying almost exclusively in hostels, pick up a pamphlet called **Youth Hos-tel Map of Japan** (www.jyh.or.jp), available at the Tourist Information Centers.

CAPSULE HOTELS

Capsule hotels (p. 98), which became popu-lar in the early 1980s, are used primarily by

Japanese businessmen who have spent an evening out drinking and missed the last train home—costing about ¥4,000 per person, a capsule hotel is sometimes cheaper than a taxi to the suburbs. Units are small—no larger than a coffin and consisting of a bed, a private TV, an alarm clock, and a radio—and are usually stacked two deep in rows down a corridor; the only thing separating you from your probably inebriated neighbor is a curtain. Most do not accept women, but those that do have separate facilities.

LOVE HOTELS

Usually found close to entertainment districts and along major highways, love hotels (p. 101) do not provide sexual services themselves; rather, they offer rooms for rent by the hour to couples. You'll know that you've wandered into a love-hotel district when you notice hourly rates posted near the front door, though gaudy structures shaped like ocean liners or castles are also a dead giveaway. During the day, you can stay for a 2- or 3-hour "rest" for an average of ¥4,000, but overnight stays vary greatly in price.

Fast Facts

ATMs

Post offices throughout Japan are convenient for their ATMs, which accept international bank cards operating on the PLUS and Cirrus systems, as well as MasterCard and Visa. In addition, 7-Eleven convenience stores, with many locations throughout the country, accept most foreign-issued cards (though not MasterCard or the Cirrus network), so getting cash is rarely a problem these days.

Business Hours

Government offices and private companies are generally open Monday through Friday 9am to 5pm. Banks are open Monday through Friday 9am to 3pm (but usually will not exchange money until 10:30 or 11am, after that day's currency exchange rates come in). Neighborhood post offices are open Monday through Friday 9am to 5pm. Major post offices, however (usually located near major train stations), have longer hours and may be open weekends as well. (Some central post offices, such as those in Tokyo and Osaka, are open 24 hr. for mail.)

Department stores are open from about 10am to 8pm; they sometimes close irregularly (but always the same day of the week). Smaller stores are generally open from 10am to 8pm, closed 1 day a week. Convenience stores such as 7-Eleven are open 24 hours.

Keep in mind that museums, gardens, and attractions stop selling admission tickets at least 30 minutes before the actual closing time. Similarly, restaurants take their last orders at least 30 minutes before the posted closing time (even earlier for *kaiseki* restaurants). Most museums are closed on Mondays.

Credit Cards

Japan is still very much a cash society. With the exception of large hotels, department stores, and some restaurants, many establishments do not accept travelers' checks or even credit cards. Although credit-card use is becoming more common, you should always carry adequate cash with you. ATMs at post offices and 7-Eleven convenience stores throughout the country accept most foreign-issued bank cards, so getting cash is rarely a problem these days. (However, 7-Eleven no longer accepts MasterCard or the Cirrus network.) Thanks to Japan's low crime rate, you can carry a significant amount of money on your person without worrying too much about safety, but you should exercise the same caution you would elsewhere.

Customs

If you're 20 or older, you can bring duty-free into Japan up to 400 non-Japanese cigarettes; three bottles (760cc/26 oz. each) of alcohol; and 59cc (2 oz.) of perfume. You can also bring in goods for personal use that were purchased abroad whose total market value is less than ¥200,000.

Directions

Japan is easy to navigate between major cities, but street addresses can be tricky to work out, especially in the electric rabbit warrens of

kyo. Detailed—and frequently bilingual—
aps are posted outside of train stations,
it's a good idea to consult them before
ading out. If you're lost, you can ask for
rections at the *koban* (police boxes) located
ross the country. If you're meeting up with
ends, it's best to carry a cell phone that will
ork in Japan.

octors & Hospitals

ffices of the Japan National Tourism As-
ciation (JNTO; www.jnto.go.jp) have lists of
glish-speaking doctors and hospitals that
fer service in English. You can also contact
e **International Association for Medical
ssistance to Travellers** (☎ 716/754-4883,
416/652-0137 in Canada; www.iamat.org),
organization that lists many local English-
eaking doctors and also posts the latest
velopments in global outbreaks. Hospitals
d clinics in Japan will usually ask you to pay
front, and you can apply for reimbursement
om your health-insurance provider.

riving

you plan to drive for part of your trip, don't
ave home without your international driver's
ense. Recommended is the **Shobunsha Road
tlas Japan,** available in bookstores that sell
glish-language books; it also contains maps
major cities, including Tokyo, Sapporo, Hi-
shima, and others. These days, rental cars
Japan come equipped with GPS navigation
stems. Enter the address or phone number
your destination to calculate the route.

rugstores

rugstores, called *yakkyoku,* are found readily
Japan. Note, however, that you cannot have
foreign prescription filled in Japan without
st consulting a doctor in Japan, so it's best
bring an adequate supply of important
edicines with you. No drugstores in Japan
ay open 24 hours.

ectricity

he electricity throughout Japan is 100 volts
C, but there are two different cycles in use.
ading hotels in Tokyo often have two out-
ts, one for 120 volts and one for 220 volts;
most all have hair dryers in the rooms. You
an use many American appliances in Japan
ecause the American standard is 120 volts
d 60 cycles, but they may run a little slowly.

Note, too, that the flat, two-legged prongs
used in Japan are the same size and fit as in
North America, but three-pronged appliances
are not accepted.

Embassies & Consulates

Most embassies are located in Tokyo. There
are, however, U.S., British, and Australian consulates in Osaka. For the location of other consulates, inquire at the respective embassies.

U.S. EMBASSY 1-10-5 Akasaka, Minato-ku,
near Toranomon Station, Tokyo (☎ 03/3224-
5000; http://japan.usembassy.gov; consular
section Mon–Fri 8:30am–noon and Mon,
Tues, Thurs, and Fri 2–4pm; phone inquiries
Mon–Fri 8:30am–1pm and 2–5:30pm). **CANA-
DIAN EMBASSY** 7-3-38 Akasaka, Minato-ku,
near Aoyama-Itchome Station, Tokyo (☎ 03/
5412-6200; www.international.gc.ca/mis-
sions/japan-japon/menu-eng.asp; consular
section Mon–Fri 9:30–11:30am; embassy
Mon–Fri 9am–12:30pm and 1:30–5:30pm).
BRITISH EMBASSY 1 Ichibancho, Chiyoda-ku,
near Hanzomon Station, Tokyo (☎ 03/5211-
1100; http://ukinjapan.fco.gov.uk/en; Mon–Fri
9am–12:30pm and 2–5:30pm; consulate inquiries Mon–Fri 9:15am–2:15pm). **IRISH EMBASSY**
Ireland House, 2-10-7 Kojimachi, Chiyoda-ku,
near Hanzomon Station, exit 3, Tokyo (☎ 03/
3263-0695; www.irishembassy.jp; Mon–Fri
10am–12:30pm and 2–4pm). **AUSTRALIAN
EMBASSY** 2-1-14 Mita, Minato-ku, near Azabu-
Juban Station, exit 2, Tokyo (☎ 03/5232-
4111; www.australia.or.jp; consular section
Mon–Fri 9am–5:30pm; embassy Mon–Fri
9am–12:30pm and 1:30–5pm). **NEW ZEALAND
EMBASSY** 20-40 Kamiyama-cho, Shibuya-ku,
a 15-min. walk from Shibuya Station, Tokyo
(☎ 03/3467-2271; www.nzembassy.com/
japan; Mon–Fri 9am–5:30pm; call for consular
hours).

Emergencies

The national emergency numbers are ☎ **110**
for police and ☎ **119** for ambulance and fire.
You do not need to insert money into public
telephones to call these numbers. However, if
using a green public telephone, you must push
a red button before dialing. If calling from a
gray public telephone or one that accepts only
prepaid cards, simply lift the receiver and dial.
Be sure to speak slowly and precisely.

Entry Requirements

For most tourists, including those from the United States, Canada, Australia, New Zealand, and the United Kingdom, the only document necessary to enter Japan is a passport. Since November 2007, all foreigners arriving in Japan are fingerprinted and photographed to prevent terrorists from entering Japan.

Family Travel

Japan is a great destination for families. You don't have to worry about safety, and there always seems to be an amusement park, aquarium, or game center wherever you travel in Japan. Still, plan your itinerary with care. To avoid crowds, visit tourist sights on weekdays. Never travel on city transportation during rush hour or on trains during popular public holidays. Children 6 to 11 years old are generally charged half-price for everything from temple admission to train tickets, while children under 6 are often admitted free. Many upper-range hotels in major cities like Tokyo and Osaka provide babysitting services, although they are prohibitively expensive. Note that outside of major cities, though, there are few English-speaking child-care facilities.

Gay & Lesbian Travelers

While there are many gay and lesbian establishments in Tokyo and Osaka, the gay community in Japan is not a vocal one, and in any case, local information in English is hard to come by. A useful website for gay club listings is www.utopia-asia.com/tipsjapn.htm, where you can also order the **Utopia Guide to Japan,** which covers the gay and lesbian scene in 27 cities in Japan.

Internet Access

With the exception of some budget hotels, virtually all hotels in Japan's major cities provide Internet access in their guest rooms. While most provide high-speed LAN cable connections, more are going Wi-Fi (wireless fidelity). If you want to connect via your own laptop, make sure that it's Japanese current-compatible.

Many hotels in Japan, especially medium-range and business hotels, have computers in their lobbies, either coin-operated (usually ¥100 for 10 minutes) or for free. Otherwise, Internet cafes can be found in most cities, though they're often nonexistent in small towns.

Language

English is widely understood in major hotels, restaurants, and shops, but you shouldn't assume that it's possible to use English everywhere, particularly in rural areas. As when traveling to any foreign country, learning a few words in the native language will, along with a smile, go a long way in bridging the communication gaps. Japanese people are very welcoming and will go out of their way to help you if they can. Be sure to pick up the free *Tourist Language Handbook,* at the Tourist Information Center.

Legal Aid

Contact your embassy if you find yourself in legal trouble. The **Legal Counselling Center,** 1–4 Yotsuya, Shinjuku (☎ 03/5367-5280; www.horitsu-sodan.jp), is operated by three bar associations and provides legal counseling with English interpreters Monday to Friday from 1 to 4pm.

Liquor Laws

The legal drinking age is 20. Beer, wine, and spirits are readily available in grocery stores, some convenience stores, and liquor stores. Many bars, especially in nightlife districts in major cities, are open until dawn. If you intend to drive in Japan, you are not allowed even one drink.

Lost Property

Be sure to notify all your credit card companies the minute you discover your wallet has been lost or stolen, and file a report at the nearest police precinct. Your credit-card company or insurer may require a police report number or record of the loss. Most credit card companies have an emergency toll-free number to call if your card is lost or stolen; they may be able to wire you a cash advance immediately or deliver an emergency credit card in a day or two. **Visa**'s emergency number in Japan is ☎ 00531/11-15555. **American Express** cardholders can call ☎ 03/3220-6220 and for traveler's checks it's ☎ 0120/779-656. **MasterCard** holders should call ☎ 00531/11-3886 in Japan. If you need emergency cash over the weekend when all banks are closed, you can have money wired to you via **Western Union** (☎ 800/325-6000; www.westernunion.com).

Luggage & Lockers

Because storage space on Shinkansen bullet trains is limited, travel with the smallest bag you can get away with. Coin-operated lockers are located at all major train stations as well as most subway stations, but most lockers are generally not large enough to store huge pieces of luggage. Lockers generally cost ¥300 to ¥900 depending on the size, and many require exact change. Some major stations also have check-in rooms for luggage, though these tend to be rare. If your bag becomes too much to handle, you can have it sent ahead via *takkyu-bin,* a wonderful and efficient luggage/parcel forwarding service available at upper-range hotels and all convenience stores in Japan. At Narita and Kansai international airports, delivery service counters will send luggage to your hotel the next day (or vice versa) for about ¥2,000 per bag for bags up to 20kg (44 lb).

Mail

If your hotel cannot mail letters for you, ask the concierge for the location of the nearest post office, recognizable by the red logo of a capital T with a horizontal line over it. Mailboxes are bright orange-red. It costs ¥110 to airmail letters weighing up to 25 grams and ¥70 to mail postcards to North America and Europe. Domestic mail costs ¥80 for letters weighing up to 25 grams, and ¥50 for postcards.

Although all post offices are open Monday through Friday from 9am to 5pm, international post offices (often located close to the central train station) have longer hours, often until 7pm or later on weekdays and with open hours also on weekends (in Tokyo and Osaka, counters are open 24 hr.). If your hotel does not have a shipping service, it is only at these larger post offices that you can mail packages abroad. For more information, check the website www.post.japanpost.jp.

Measurements

Before the metric system came into use in Japan, the country had its own standards for measuring length and weight. One of these old standards is still common: Rooms are still measured by the number of tatami straw mats that will fit in them. A six-tatami room, for example, is the size of six tatami mats, with a tatami roughly 1m (3⅓ ft.) wide and 2m (6½ ft.) long.

Money & Costs

Narita, Kansai, and Nagoya international airports all have exchange counters for all incoming international flights that offer better exchange rates than what you'd get abroad, as well as ATMs.

All banks in Japan displaying an AUTHORIZED FOREIGN EXCHANGE sign can exchange currency and traveler's checks, with exchange rates usually displayed at the appropriate foreign-exchange counter. Banks are generally open Monday through Friday from 9am to 3pm, though business hours for exchanging foreign currency usually don't begin until 10:30 or 11am (be prepared for a long wait; you'll be asked to sit down as your order is processed). More convenient—and quicker—are **Travelex** (www.travelex.com) foreign-exchange kiosks, with locations in several cities in Japan, including Tokyo, Kyoto, Nagoya, Osaka, and Sapporo.

Japan has the reputation of being one of the most expensive countries in the world. While it's certainly true that transportation and lodging can be costly, you don't have to spend a fortune on basics like food and drink. Generally speaking, the cost of traveling in Japan is comparable to that of countries in Europe and North America. Taking advantage of discount travel passes for tourists (p. 558), booking hotel rooms at off-peak rates (p. 562), and avoiding taxis—which start at ¥710 for 2km (1¼ miles)—will help you conserve your yen. Set lunches in Japan offer excellent value and are a little-known secret. Even top-end restaurants have great deals at lunchtime (some have weekday "business lunch" prix-fixe menus for around ¥2,700), but most moderate eateries have lunch specials starting around ¥1,000. Picking up *onigiri* (rice balls) and bento (lunch boxes, available at convenience and specialty stores as well as train stations) for lunch on the go is another way to reduce costs while traveling between destinations.

Newspapers & Magazines

Three English-language newspapers are published daily in Japan: *The Japan Times* and *The Daily Yomiuri* (both with weekly supplements from the *Los Angeles Times, Washington Post,* and London's *Times*), as well as the *International*

Herald Tribune/Asahi Shimbun. Hotels and major bookstores carry the international editions of such newsmagazines as *Time* and *Newsweek.* You can also read *The Japan Times* online at www.japantimes.co.jp.

Police

The national emergency number for police is ☎ **110.**

Restrooms

If you need a restroom, your best bets are at train and subway stations, big hotels, department stores, and fast-food restaurants. Use of restrooms is free in Japan, and though most public facilities supply toilet paper, it's a good idea to carry a packet of tissues. Though more common recently, many public restrooms don't have soap or paper towels, so you may wish to bring your own hand towel.

In parks and some restaurants, especially in rural areas, don't be surprised if you go into some restrooms and find men's urinals and private stalls in the same room. Women are supposed to walk right past the urinals without noticing them.

Many toilets in Japan, especially those at train stations, are Japanese-style toilets: They're holes in the ground over which you squat facing the end that has a raised hood. Men stand and aim for the hole. Although Japanese lavatories may seem uncomfortable at first, they're actually not so bad once you get used to them. (There's usually a metal bar to hold on to.)

Across Japan, many restrooms feature **Washlets,** combination toilet/bidets with heated toilet seats, buttons and knobs directing sprays of water of various intensities to various body parts, and even lids that raise when you open the stall. However, instructions are usually in Japanese only.

Senior Travel

More and more attractions are offering free admission or discounts to seniors over 65 or 70 (be sure to have your passport handy). However, discounts may not be posted, so be sure to ask. Seniors also receive discounts on domestic plane fares. Older visitors to Japan should be aware that there are many stairs to navigate in metropolitan areas, particularly in subway and train stations and even on pedestrian overpasses.

Smoking

You must be 20 years old to smoke in Japan. Smoking is banned in most public areas, including train and subway stations and office buildings. In many cities, there are also nonsmoking ordinances that ban smoking on sidewalks but allow it in marked areas, usually near train stations. Many restaurants nowadays have nonsmoking sections, though bars do not. Most hotels have designated nonsmoking floors, except for some business hotels and Japanese-style inns. If you want to sit in the nonsmoking car of long-distance trains, such as the Kintetsu Nara Tokkyu (Limited Express) train, ask for the *kinensha* (though some lines are completely smoke-free). During peak times, be sure to reserve a seat in the nonsmoking car in advance.

Student Travel

Students sometimes receive discounts at museums, though occasionally discounts are available only to students enrolled in Japanese schools. Bring along an **International Student Identity Card (ISIC)** together with your university student ID and show them both at ticket windows. For information on the ISIC card and where and how to obtain one, check the website www.isic.org.

Taxes

A 5% consumption tax is imposed on goods and services in Japan, including hotel rates and restaurant meals. Although hotels and restaurants are required to include the tax in their published rates, a few have yet to comply (especially on English-language menus). In Tokyo, hotels also levy a separate accommodations tax of ¥100 per person per night on rooms costing ¥10,000 to ¥14,999; rates ¥15,000 and up are taxed at ¥200 per night per person. Some hotels include the local tax in their published rack rates, others do not. In hot-spring resort areas, a ¥150 *onsen* tax is added for every night of your stay.

In addition to these taxes, a 10% to 15% service charge will be added to your bill in lieu of tipping at most of the fancier restaurants and at moderately priced and upper-end hotels and *ryokan,* or Japanese-style inns. Business hotels, *minshuku,* youth hostels, and inexpensive restaurants do not impose a service charge.

As for shopping, a 5% consumption tax is also included in the price of most goods. (Some the smaller vendors are not required to levy x.) Travelers from abroad, however, are eligible for an exemption on goods taken out of the country, although only the larger department stores and specialty shops seem equipped to deal with the procedures (many shops have begun posting DUTY-FREE signs at the cash register). In any case, most department stores grant a refund on the consumption tax only when the total amount of purchases for the day exceeds ¥10,000. You can obtain a refund immediately by having a sales clerk fill out a list of your purchases and then presenting the list to the tax-exemption counter of the department store; you will need to show your passport. Note that no refunds for consumption tax are given for food, drinks, tobacco, cosmetics, film, or batteries.

Time Zone

Japan is 9 hours ahead of Greenwich Mean Time, 14 hours ahead of New York, 15 hours ahead of Chicago, and 17 hours ahead of Los Angeles. Since Japan does not go on daylight saving time, subtract 1 hour from the above times in the summer when calling from countries that have daylight saving time such as the United States.

Because Japan is on the other side of the International Date Line, you lose a day when traveling from the United States to Asia. (If you depart the United States on Tues, you'll arrive on Wed.) Returning to North America, however, you gain a day, which means that you arrive on the same day you left.

Tipping

One of the delights of being in Japan is that there's no tipping—not even to waitresses, taxi drivers, or bellhops. Instead, you'll have a 10% to 15% service charge added to your bill at higher-priced accommodations and restaurants.

Travelers with Disabilities

Although Japan does not rank as highly as many other countries in terms of facilities for travelers with disabilities, things have improved in the last few years. Many new buildings are equipped with ramps, and several train stations in Tokyo have been renovated to include elevators and escalators.

Most major train and subway stations now have elevators, but they can be difficult to locate. Otherwise, smaller stations, especially in rural areas, may be accessible only by stairs or escalators, though in recent years some have been equipped with powered seat lifts. If you require assistance, speak with a station attendant when you enter the station.

For information on traveling with a wheelchair, including limited information on a handful of sights and hotels offering facilities for travelers with disabilities, visit the **Accessible Japan** website at www.tesco-premium.co.jp/aj.

When it comes to facilities for the blind, Japan has a very advanced system. At subway stations and on many major sidewalks in large cities, raised dots and lines on the ground guide blind people at intersections and to subway platforms. In some cities, streetlights chime a theme when the signal turns green east-west, and chime another for north-south.

Water

The water is safe to drink anywhere in Japan, and bottled water is also readily available.

Vaccines

No vaccines are required for Japan.

Visas

Ninety-day temporary visitor visas are granted to citizens of the U.S., Australia, and New Zealand. Three-month visas are issued to citizens of Canada, France, Singapore, and several other countries (check with your embassy); while citizens of the U.K., Austria, Germany, Ireland, Mexico, and Switzerland can apply for visa extensions of up to 3 months (a 6-month stay in total).

Useful Phrases & Words

Pronunciation

When pronouncing the following vocabulary, keep in mind that there's very little stress on individual syllables. (Pronunciation of Japanese is often compared to that of Italian.) Here's an approximation of some of the sounds of Japanese:

a	as in *father*
aa	held slightly longer than *a*
e	as in *pen*
i	as in *pick*
ii	held slightly longer than *i*
o	as in *oh*
oo	held slightly longer than *o*
u	as in *boo*
uu	held slightly longer than *u*
g	as in *gift* at the beginning of words; like *ng* in *sing* in the middle or at the end of words

Vowel sounds are almost always short unless they are doubled, in which case you hold the vowel a bit longer. *Okashi,* for example, means "a sweet," whereas *okashii* means "strange." As you can see, even slight mispronunciation of a word can result in confusion or hilarity. Similarly, double consonants are given more emphasis than only one consonant by itself.

Getting Around/Street Smarts

ENGLISH	JAPANESE
yes	hai
no	iie
good morning	ohayo gozaimasu
hello/good afternoon	konnichiwa
good evening	konbanwa
goodnight (when saying goodbye)	oyasumi nasai
How are you?	Ogenki desu ka?
I'm fine	genki desu
nice to meet you	hajimemashite
goodbye	sayonara
see you later	dewa mata
excuse me/pardon me	sumimasen
I'm sorry	gomen nasai
please (when offering something)	doozo
please (when requesting something)	kudasai
thank you (formal)	(domo) arigato (gozaimasu)
thanks (informal)	Domo
no, thank you	iie, kekko desu
you're welcome	doo itashimashite
Cheers!	Kanpai!

m American	Amerikajin desu
m Canadian	Kanadajin desu
y name is . . .	. . . to mooshimasu
What's your name?	Onamae wa?
orry, I don't speak Japanese	sumimasen, nihongo ga dekimasen
o you speak English?	Eigo ga dekimasu ka?
o you understand?	Wakarimasu ka?
understand	wakarimasu
don't understand	wakarimasen
ust a minute, please	chotto matte kudasai
lease speak slowly	yukkuri hanashite kudasai
lease say that again	moo ichido itte kudasai
Where is (the restroom)?	(Toire) wa doko desu ka?
When is (the departure)?	(Shuppatsu) wa itsu desu ka?
What is this?	Kore wan an desu ka?
like this	kore ga suki desu

mergencies

NGLISH	JAPANESE
lease help me	tasukete kudasai
all a doctor	isha o yonde kudasai
all the police	keisatsu o yonde kudasai
m lost	michi ni mayoimashita
olice	keisatsu
olice box	koban
ospital	byooin
mbassy	taishikan

Transport & Travel Words

NGLISH	JAPANESE
rain station	eki
irport	kuukoo
ubway	chikatestsu
us	basu
axi	takushii
irplane	hikooki
erry	ferii
rain	densha
ullet train	Shinkansen
imited Express train	Tokkyu
xpress train	Kyukoo
apid train	Kaisoku
ocal train (stops at every station)	kakueki teisha
latform	hoomu

destination	ikisaki
passport	pasupooto
I'd like to go to (Kyoto)	(Kyoto) ni ikitai no desu
How much is the fare to (Kyoto)?	(Kyoto) made ikura desu ka?
I'd like a reserved seat/nonreserved seat	Shiteiseki/jiyuuseki o kudasai.
I'd like a seat in the nonsmoking car	Kinensha no shiteiseki o kudasai.
one-way ticket	katamichi-kippu
round-trip ticket	oofuku-kippu
I'd like to buy one ticket	Kippu ichimai o kaitain desu ga.
I'd like to buy two tickets	Kippu nimai o kaitain desu ga.
Does this (train, etc.) go to (Osaka)?	Kore wa (Osaka) ni ikimasu ka?
Where should I transfer?	Norikae wa doko desu ka?

Directions

ENGLISH	JAPANESE
exit	deguchi
entrance	iriguchi
north	kita
south	minami
east	higashi
west	nishi
left	hidari
right	migi
straight ahead	massugu
Where is the train station?	Eki wa doko desu ka?
Is it far?	Tooi desu ka?
Is it near?	Chikai desu ka?
Can I walk there?	Aruite ikemasu ka?
street	dori/michi
tourist information office	kankoo annai jo
I'd like a map, please	chizu o kudasai

Shopping & Services

ENGLISH	JAPANESE
post office	yuubin-kyoku
I'd like to buy a stamp	kitte o kaitai no desu ga
I'd like to send this to (America)	(Amerika) e okuritai no desu ga
bank	ginkoo
drugstore/pharmacy	yakkyoku
convenience store	konbini
department store	depaato
What time do you open?	Nan ji ni akimasuka?
What time do you close?	Nan ji ni shimarimasuka?
How much is it?	Ikura desu ka?

Do you accept credit cards?	Kurejitto kaado ga dekimasu ka?
big	okii
small	chisai
cheap	yasui
expensive	takai

Lodging

ENGLISH	JAPANESE
hotel	hoteru
Japanese-style inn	ryokan
family-style inn	minshuku
youth hostel	yuusu hosuteru
Do you have a room available?	Akibeya ga arimasu ka?
How much is it per night?	Ippaku de ikura desu ka?
Does that include meals?	Shokuji wa tsuite imasu ka?
I'd like a single/double/twin room	shinguru/daberu/tsuin no heya o kudasai
Does it have a private toilet?	Heya ni wa toire ga tsuite imasu ka?
I'd like a private bathroom	basu toire tsuki no heya o kudasai
tax	zeikin
key	kagi
hot-spring spa	onsen
outdoor hot-spring bath	rotenburo
bath	ofuro
public bath	sentoo

Dining Terms & Phrases

ENGLISH	JAPANESE
restaurant	resutoran
dining hall	shokudo
coffee shop	kissaten
Japanese pub	izakaya
I'd like to make a reservation	go-yoyaku onegaishimasu
Please show me the menu	menyuu o misete kudasai
What do you recommend?	Nani ga osusume desu ka?
I'm a vegetarian	bejitarian desu
I can't eat meat	oniku ga taberaremasen
fish	sakana
chicken	toriniku
beef	gyuuniku
pork	butaniku
I'm allergic to (crab)	(kani) no arerugii desu
nuts	nattsu/kinomi
milk	gyuunyuu/miryku

shellfish	kai
I'd like a fork/spoon/knife	fooku/supuun/naifu o kudasai
Japanese green tea	ocha
black tea	koocha
coffee	koohii
water	omizu
beer	biiru
sake	nihonshu
wine	wain
salt	shio
pepper	koshoo
May I have some more (water)?	(Omizu) moo sukoshi onegaishimasu
I'd like to pay the bill	Okanjoo onegaishimasu
This is delicious	Oishii desu
Thank you for the meal	Gochisoo sama deshita

Numbers

ENGLISH	JAPANESE
1	ichi
2	ni
3	san
4	shi/yon
5	go
6	roku
7	nana
8	hachi
9	kyuu
10	juu
11	juuichi
12	juuni
13	juusan
14	juuyon
20	nijuu
30	sanjuu
40	yonjuu
100	hyaku
1,000	sen
2,000	nisen
10,000	ichiman
20,000	niman

Days of the Week

ENGLISH	JAPANESE
Sunday	Nichiyoobi
Monday	Getsuyoobi
Tuesday	Kayoobi
Wednesday	Suiyoobi
Thursday	Mokuyoobi
Friday	Kinyoobi
Saturday	Doyoobi

Months of the Year

ENGLISH	JAPANESE
January	Ichi-gatsu
February	Ni-gatsu
March	San-gatsu
April	Shi-gatsu
May	Go-gatsu
June	Roku-gatsu
July	Shichi-gatsu
August	Hachi-gatsu
September	Ku-gatsu
October	Juu-gatsu
November	Juuichi-gatsu
December	Juuni-gatsu

Index

Accommodations

hoto Credits

ver Photo Credits: Front cover (l to r): © Hiro Komae; © Deco Images II/Alamy Images; © RichVintage/ :tta Collection/iStock Photo. Back cover (t and b): © Norihiro Haruta; © Marco Garcia. Cover flap to b): © Image Asset Management Ltd./SuperStock; © Damon Coulter; © Ei Katsumata/Alamy; Nobuyuki Masaki/Associated Press. Inside front cover (clockwise from tr): © Norihiro Haruta; Marco Garcia; © Hiro Komae; © JTB Photo/SuperStock; © Marco Garcia; © Marco Garcia; © Hiro ›mae; © Marco Garcia; © Norihiro Haruta; © Jérémie Souteyrat. **Interior Photo Credits:** Alain apel; p234; Alamy: AF archive/Alamy: 526(r), 529, 530(tl); © amana images inc./Alamy: p156, 301, p364; © Aqua Image/Alamy: pp478-79; © Arcaid Images/Alamy: p295(tc); © The Art Archive/ amy: pp506-07, p513; © The Art Gallery Collection/Alamy: p295(r); © Asia Images Group Pte Ltd/ amy: p363(tr); © Tibor Bognar/Alamy: p419; © Yaacov Dagan/Alamy: p35; © Terry Donnelly/Alamy: 327(2nd from tr); © Oscar Elias/Alamy: p530(2nd from bl); © FantasticJapan/Alamy: pp18-19; © Ilya ـnkin/Alamy: p300; © Hackenberg-Photo-Cologne/Alamy: p347; © Peter Horree/Alamy: p518(c); INTERFOTO/Alamy: p528, p530(bl); © Rich Iwasaki/Alamy: p292; © Japan Stock Photography/ amy: p289; © Japanese Temples/Alamy: p327(br); © JTB Photo Communications, Inc./Alamy: 67, p172, p327(tr), p430(b), p474, p505; © Ei Katsumata/Alamy: p263, p327(tl and 3rd from); © David Kleyn/Alamy: pp426-27; © John Lander/Alamy: p295(l), p363(br); © Guillem Lopez/ amy: p517; © Yannick Luthy/Alamy: p358, p427(b); © Iain Masterton/Alamy: p vi(t), p223(r), p525; Oleksiy Maksymenko/Alamy: p166(b); © Moviestore collection Ltd/Alamy: p532; © Paris Pierce/ lamy: p139; © Photo Japan/Alamy: p293; © Photos 12/Alamy: p527; © searagen/Alamy: p327(bl); Skye Hohmann Japan Images/Alamy: p327(3rd from tl); © StockbrokerXtra/Alamy: p363(bl); © Jeremy ـtton-Hibbert/Alamy: p27; © Ulana Switucha/Alamy: pp362-63(tl); © Travel Pictures/Alamy: p326; Glen Turvey/Alamy: p137; © V&A Images/Alamy: pp138-39, p511(t); © Chris Willson/Alamy: p284, 327(2nd from tl), p486, p502(r), p504; © Romain Alary: p130, p375, p534(tr); ANA Hotel: p271; AP ıages: AP Photo: p514; AP Photo/Katsumi Kasahara: p516; AP Photo/Nobuyuki Masaki: p530(cl); Rex ـatures via AP Images: p26(t); Izanami and Izanagi Creating the Japanese Islands, Meiji era, Japan, c.1885 anging scroll: ink & colour on silk), Eitaku, Kobayashi/Museum of Fine Arts, Boston, Massachusetts, ـSA/William Sturgis Bigelow Collection/The Bridgeman Art Library: p508; St. Francis Xavier (1506-51) ıd his entourage, detail of the right-hand section of a folding screen depicting the arrival of the Portuguese Japan, Kano School (lacquer), Japanese School (16th century)/Musee Guimet, Paris, France/The idgeman Art Library: p518(b); Jomon figurine (earthenware), Japanese School/Musee Guimet, Paris, ـance/Giraudon/The Bridgeman Art Library: p518(t); Cerulean Tower Tokyu Hotel: p95; Claska: p98; ـai-ichi Takimotokan: p459; Folkloro Tono: p425; © Marco Garcia: pii(c), piii(b), piii(c), piv(t), p3, p4, p8, 7, p23, p24, p25(b), p28, p30, p31, p36, p37, p38, p39, p41, p52, p56, p58, p59, p64, p66(t and b), p67, ٢0, p71(t), p72, p74, p75, p76, p78, p79, p82, p83(t and b), p84, p85(l and r), p91(l), p101(b), p107, p141, ۱68, p182, p184(r), p196, p198, p200, p202, p204, p206, p213, p216, p217, p219, p220, p222, p223(l), 224, p225(l), p227, p230, p233, p235, p236, pp238-39, p240, p242, p243, p244, p246, p247, p248, 250(l and r), p251, p252, p254, p255, p257, p260, p262, p264, p265, p266, p272, p277, pp278-79, p285, 286, p288, p295(bc), p302, p306(t), p308(l), p311(r), p312, p314(t and b), p317, pp348-49, p350, p352, 356, p359, p360, p378, p380, p381, p384, p386, p392, p393, p397, p421, p510, p511(b), p512, p520, 523, p526(l), p533(l), p535(r), p536(l), p538, p544, pp548-49; Getty: Bloomberg via Getty Images: 26(b); Keystone/Getty Images: p515; Sankei Archive/Getty Images: p530(2nd from tl); Grand Hyatt ـkuoka: p382; © Norihiro Haruta: p iii(t), p iv(b); p10, p32, p86, p87, p90, p93, p102, p103, p106, p109, ۱32, pp142-43, p144, p149, p162, p164, p165, p178, p180, p184(l), p369, p387, p390, p394, pp398-99,